PRACTICAL COUNSELLING
AND HELPING SKILLS

PRACTICAL COUNSELLING AND HELPING SKILLS

Text and Exercises for the Lifeskills Counselling Model

Fourth edition

Richard Nelson-Jones

SAGE Publications

London • Thousand Oaks • New Delhi

© Richard Nelson-Jones 1997, 2004

First published 1997
Reprinted 1997, 2000, 2003 (twice)

SAGE Publications Ltd
6 Bonhill Street
London EC2A 4PU

SAGE Publications Inc.
2455 Teller Road
Thousand Oaks, California 91320

SAGE Publications India Pvt Ltd
B-42, Panchsheel Enclave
Post Box 4109
New Delhi 100 017

British Library Cataloguing in Publication data

A catalogue record for this book is available from the British Library

ISBN 1-4129-0052-2

Library of Congress Control Number available

Typeset by York House Typographic Ltd., London
Printed and bound in Great Britain by Athenaeum Press Ltd., Gateshead

CONTENTS

PART TWO
STAGE 1: DEVELOP THE RELATIONSHIP AND CLARIFY PROBLEM(S)

PART THREE
STAGE 2: ASSESS AND RESTATE PROBLEM(S) IN SKILLS TERMS

List of Exercises

Preface

Welcome to *Practical Counselling and Helping Skills: Text and Exercises for Using the Lifeskills Counselling Model*. The following are answers to some questions you may have about the book.

WHAT IS THIS BOOK'S PURPOSE?

This is a practical 'how to' counselling and helping skills textbook. In this book I present the component skills for DASIE, a systematic five-stage model for assisting clients to develop specific lifeskills to change how they feel, think and act. The book's main focus is on counselling individuals. It is intended primarily as a text for counselling skills classes led by skilled trainers. I have designed the book for both introductory and more advanced training purposes. For example, the book pays great attention to skills of offering good counselling relationships and clarifying problems. In addition, the book presents more advanced assessment skills and a large repertoire of counselling interventions.

FOR WHOM IS THIS BOOK INTENDED?

I intend the book for the following audiences.

- Lecturers teaching practical classes in counselling skills in colleges, universities, adult education centres and voluntary settings.

- Students in educational settings who are training for the helping services: for instance, as counsellors, psychologists, nurses, health care workers, social workers, youth workers, community workers, welfare advisers, personnel officers, career advisers, human relations consultants, pastoral care workers and teachers.

- Students developing counselling and helping skills in voluntary agencies: for instance, church-related agencies and agencies focusing on special populations, such as the mentally ill, the bereaved, gay people, and those in crisis.

- Students undergoing supervision as part of continuing training and development.

- Helping service professionals and voluntary agency counsellors for skills development and reference purposes.

WHAT ARE THIS BOOK'S CONTENTS?

Part One of the book consists of four introductory chapters. Chapter 1 asks who counsellors are and what counselling is. Chapter 2 reviews lifeskills counselling's theoretical framework and Chapter 3 overviews lifeskills counselling's five-stage DASIE model of practice. Chapter 4 looks at what students and counsellors bring to their counselling work. The next five parts of the book systematically present the lifeskills counselling model's five stages. Chapters 5, 6 and 7 focus on the component skills of stage 1: develop the relationship and clarify problem(s). Chapters 8, 9 and 10 present skills for stage 2: assess and restate problem(s) in skills terms. Chapters 11 and 12 describe skills for stage 3: state goals and plan interventions. The next five chapters present skills for stage 4: intervene to develop lifeskills. Chapter 13 describes central training skills for delivering interventions. Chapters 14 and 15 review interventions focused on thinking skills. Chapters 16 and 17 review interventions focused on action skills and feelings, respectively. Chapters 18 and 19 present skills for stage 5: emphasize take away of lifeskills. Part Seven of the book, Chapter 20, looks ahead to how you can monitor and develop your counselling skills.

WHAT FEATURES DOES THIS BOOK POSSESS?

- *Based on lifeskills counselling theory.* This book is based upon my lifeskills counselling integrative approach, which I regard as using cognitive-behaviourism to implement humanistic-existential values.

- *Updated five-stage model of practice.* Most students learning counselling skills find that it helps to structure their interviewing round a model of the counselling process. This book presents the latest version of my five-stage DASIE model, incorporating changes in the light of further use. The DASIE model focuses not only on problems, but on the problematic skills clients possess that sustain their problems and leave them vulnerable to future problems.

- *Emphasis on good counselling relationships.* Counsellors require the ability to offer supportive and caring human relationships as well as assessment and intervention skills. Good counselling relationships provide the context for using technical skills.

- *Comprehensiveness.* I offer a comprehensive coverage of the skills you require for effective counselling and helping.

- *Recency.* The book incorporates the latest theoretical, research and practitioner literature about counselling and helping.

- *Practical exercises.* The book includes 87 practical exercises to help you develop your knowledge and skills. You can complete these exercises on your own, with a partner, or in a group.

- *Practical examples.* The book contains numerous case studies and vignettes as well as some counselling interview excerpts.

- *Anglo-Australian emphasis.* Unlike most counselling and helping texts, which are American, this book draws on British and Australian demographic data, books, articles and research findings.

- *User-friendly format.* Each chapter follows the same user-friendly format: chapter questions, text, chapter highlights and exercises.

- *Readability.* I have endeavoured to write the book in clear, simple English.

ACKNOWLEDGEMENTS

The lifeskills counselling approach owes much to others' work. For example, the emphasis on the counselling relationship and the importance of understanding clients on their own terms shows the influence of Carl Rogers's person-centred therapy. The emphasis on thinking skills reflects the work of Aaron Beck, Albert Ellis, Arnold Lazarus and Donald Meichenbaum, among others. The emphasis on action skills represents the influence of the behaviourists. The emphasis on personal responsibility and choice has origins in the work of Viktor Frankl, William Glasser, Abraham Maslow, Rollo May, Hobart Mowrer, Irvin Yalom and the theologian Paul Tillich. In addition, Harry Stack Sullivan, Gerard Egan and Robert Carkhuff are forerunners in presenting stage models of counselling sessions and the counselling process. I express appreciation to all these writers and to the many others mentioned in this book's Bibliography.

I also thank the following people who assisted in bringing this book to life: Naomi Roth, my editor for the past decade or so, for her constant faith in my work and willingness to allow me freedom to be different. In addition, I appreciate the contribution of the manuscript editing, production and design staff at Cassell for their work in adding quality to this book's presentation.

A FINAL WORD

I hope that *Practical Counselling and Helping Skills: Text and Exercises for Using the Lifeskills Counselling Model* challenges you to think somewhat differently about how you help and live. In addition, I hope this book offers you an integrative theoretical framework and model of practice with which to develop your potential for effective and humane counselling.

PART ONE

Introduction

Chapter 1 examines who counsellors are and what counselling is. In addition, the chapter introduces lifeskills counselling. Chapter 2 reviews lifeskills counselling's theoretical framework and Chapter 3 overviews its five-stage DASIE model of practice. Chapter 4 reviews what students and counsellors bring to their counselling work.

PART ONE

ONE
Introduction

Give a man a fish and you feed him for a day, teach a man to fish and you feed him for a lifetime.

Chinese proverb

CHAPTER QUESTIONS

- *Who are counsellors and helpers?*

- *What is counselling?*

- *What is lifeskills counselling?*

- *What are lifeskills counsellors?*

INTRODUCTION

Below are concerns that people might wish to share with another.

'I'm feeling depressed and lonely.'

'I've lost my job and feel very scared.'

'I find it difficult to make my mind up about my career.'

'I'm having difficulty coming to terms with being physically disabled.'

'Now that I've had a heart attack, I must learn to live more sensibly.'

'I feel stressed out all the time.'

'I wish I knew how to make and hold friends.'

'I wish I were better at controlling my temper.'

'We haven't had sex for the past six months.'

'Our marriage seems to be heading towards the rocks.'

'I carry my parents round in my head all the time, even though I've left home.'

'I get very tense over exams and under-perform.'

'I find it difficult to say "no" to people.'

'My life seems meaningless.'

Four main categories of other people might be available to help with such concerns.

- *Counselling and helping professionals.* Persons specializing in helping others with their problems and paid to do so. Such people include counsellors, psychologists, psychiatrists and social workers.

- *Voluntary counsellors and helpers.* People trained in counselling and helping skills who work on a voluntary basis in settings such as Relate, youth counselling services, church-related agencies and numerous other voluntary agencies.

- *Those using counselling and helping skills as part of their jobs.* Here the main focus of the job may be nursing, teaching, preaching, supervising, managing, providing services such as finance, law, recreation or funerals, trade union work and so on. These jobs require people to use counselling and helping skills some of the time if they are to be maximally effective.

- *Informal counsellors and helpers.* All of us have the opportunity to assist others, be it in the role of partner, parent, relative, friend or work colleague.

COUNSELLING AND HELPING

A word is needed about my use of terms in this book. Possibly in relation to the above fourfold classification of people who offer help, the word 'counsellor' refers more to counselling professionals and voluntary counsellors, whereas the word 'helper' refers more to those using counselling and helping skills as part of their jobs and to informal helpers. Some would even query this distinction and view counselling and helping as synonymous (Murgatroyd, 1985). Often the word *helper* is used as a short-hand term to describe the above categories of counsellors and helpers. Egan's *The Skilled Helper* (1994) is a prime example of such usage. Helpers help by using helping skills.

Throughout this book, I use the term *counsellor* to refer to both counsellors and helpers. Counsellors counsel by using counselling skills. I have been guided in this choice by three considerations. First, the term helper is insufficiently specific to the population I wish to define. Anyone who provides a service – whether a shopkeeper, electrician or plumber – could be regarded as a helper. However, such people are much less likely to be regarded as counsellors. Second, the word helper has connotations of placing recipients of help in dependent positions. The helper may be doing things *to* or *for* the person being helped rather than *with* him or her. Third, the world helper obscures the idea of self-help that I wish to emphasize. The purpose of counselling and helping is to help people to become their own best helpers. Thus both givers and recipients of help become helpers – so why use the term helper for only one of the two categories? Throughout the book I use the term *client* for the recipient of counselling and helping.

WHAT IS COUNSELLING?

The term 'counselling' is used in a number of ways. One dimension, already discussed, is the *people who counsel*. Other dimensions for defining counselling include viewing it: as a *relationship*; as a *repertoire of interventions*; as a *psychological process*; and in terms of its *goals*, *clienteles* and *relationship to psychotherapy*. I discuss each in turn.

Counselling as a relationship

Virtually all counsellors agree that a good counselling relationship is necessary to be effective with clients. Some counsellors regard the counselling relationship as not only necessary, but sufficient for constructive changes to occur in clients (Rogers, 1957). One way to define counselling involves stipulating central qualities of good counselling relationships. Suffice it for now to say that these counsellor offered qualities, sometimes called the 'core conditions', are empathic understanding, respect for clients' potentials to lead their own lives and congruence or genuineness. Terms like 'active listening' and 'rewarding listening' are other ways of expressing the central skills of the basic helping relationship. Those viewing counselling predominantly as a helping relationship tend to be adherents of the theory and practice of person-centred counselling (Rogers, 1961; Raskin and Rogers, 1995).

Counselling as a repertoire of interventions

Most counsellors would regard the counselling relationship as neither sufficient nor sufficiently expeditious for constructive client changes to occur. Consequently, they require a set of interventions in addition to the counselling relationship. Alternative terms for interventions are counselling methods or helping strategies. Counsellors who have a repertoire of interventions need to address the questions of which interventions to use, with which clients, when and with what probability of success. Counsellors' repertoires of interventions reflect their theoretical orientations: for instance, psychoanalytic counsellors use psychoanalytic interventions, rational emotive behaviour counsellors use rational emotive behaviour interventions and Gestalt counsellors use Gestalt interventions. Some counsellors are eclectic and use interventions derived from a variety of theoretical positions. Corsini goes even further and writes: 'I have come to believe that what counts in psychotherapy is who does it and how and to whom it is done: the whohowwhom factor' (Corsini, 1995, p. 11). He suggests that counsellor personality and counsellor–client match are also important, along with specific interventions.

Counselling as a psychological process

In this book the word counselling is used as a shorthand version of the term psychological counselling. Whether viewed either as a relationship characterized by the core conditions or as a repertoire of interventions derived from different theoretical positions, counselling is a psychological process. Reasons for the fundamental association between psychology and counselling include the following. First, the *goals* of counselling have a mind component in them. In varying degrees, all counselling approaches focus on altering how people feel, think and act so that they may live their lives more effectively. Second, the *process* of counselling is psychological. Counselling is not static, but involves movement between and within the minds of both counsellors and clients. In addition, much of the process of counselling transpires within clients' minds between sessions and when clients help themselves after counselling ends. Third, the underlying *theories* from which counselling goals and interventions are derived are psychological (Nelson-Jones, 1995). Many of the leading counselling theorists have been psychologists: Rogers and Ellis are important examples. Most of the other leading theorists have been psychiatrists: for instance, Beck and Berne. Fourth, psychological *research* contributes both to creating counselling theories and to evaluating counselling processes and outcomes.

Goals for counselling

Counsellors may have different goals with different clients: for instance, assisting them to heal past emotional deprivations, manage current problems, handle transitions, make decisions, manage crises and develop specific lifeskills. Sometimes goals for counselling are divided between remedial goals and growth or developmental goals. The dividing line between remedying weaknesses and developing strengths is unclear. Moreover, attaining both remedial and developmental goals can serve preventive functions.

Though much counselling is remedial, its main focus is on the developmental tasks of the vast majority of ordinary people rather than on the needs of the more severely disturbed minority. This developmental emphasis is echoed by van Hesteren and Ivey (1990, p. 524), who write: '*Counselling and development* is first and foremost concerned with positive human change. This positive change may occur in negotiating the developmental tasks we face in daily life or in dealing with issues of severe developmental disturbance.'

Developmental tasks are tasks which people face at various stages of their lifespan: for instance, becoming independent, finding a partner, raising children and adjusting to old age. Attaining developmental tasks involves both containing negative qualities and fostering positive qualities. Counselling's major focus is on psychological wellness or on positive mental health (Jahoda, 1958). Maslow's description of the characteristics of self-actualizing people represents an attempt to state goals positively in developmental rather than remedial terms (Maslow, 1970). His self-actualizing characteristics include creativity, autonomy, social interest and problem-centredness.

Whatever the theoretical position, counselling goals emphasize increasing clients' personal responsibility for creating and making their lives. Clients need to make choices that enable them to feel, think and act effectively. They require the capacity to experience and express feelings, think rationally and take effective actions to attain their goals. Counsellors tend to be most effective when they enable clients to help themselves when counselling ends. Thus the ultimate goal of counselling is self-helping, so that clients become their own best counsellors.

Counselling and psychotherapy

Attempts to differentiate between counselling and psychotherapy are never wholly successful. Both counselling and psychotherapy represent diverse rather than uniform knowledge and activities. It is more accurate to think of counselling approaches and psychological therapies. Both claim to be based on 'informed and planful application of techniques derived from established psychological principles' (Meltzoff and Kornreich, 1970, p. 6). Attempts to distinguish counselling and psychotherapy include the following: psychotherapy focuses on personality change of some sort while counselling focuses on helping people to use existing resources for coping with life better (Tyler, 1961); they are the same qualitatively, but differ only quantitively, in that therapists listen more and engage in less informing, advising and explaining than counsellors (Corsini, 1995); and psychotherapy deals with more severe disturbance and is a more medical term than counselling. Both counselling and psychotherapy use the same theoretical models and 'stress the need to value the client as a person, to listen sympathetically and to hear what is communicated, and to foster the capacity for self-help and responsibility' (BPS Division of Clinical Psychology, 1979, p. 6).

Many psychologists, such as Truax and Carkhuff (1967), Corey (1991) and Patterson (1974, 1986), use the terms counselling and psychotherapy interchangeably. Patterson concludes that there are no essential differences upon which agreement can be found. I agree that there is considerable overlap between counselling and psychotherapy. Nevertheless, throughout this book I use the terms counselling and counsellor in preference to therapy and therapist. This is partly for the sake of consistency and partly because I regard counselling as a less elite term than therapy.

WHAT IS LIFESKILLS COUNSELLING?

Lifeskills counselling is a people-centred approach for assisting clients to develop self-helping skills. This approach spurns psychological jargon in favour of a simple, direct educational framework. Geared to the needs of the vast majority of ordinary people, lifeskills counselling assumes that all people have acquired and sustain lifeskills strengths and deficits. Following are four key concepts of this approach.

1. Most problems brought to counsellors reflect clients' learning histories.

2. Though external factors contribute, clients sustain problems by possessing deficits or weaknesses in how they think and how they act (in their thinking skills and in their action skills).

3. Counsellors are most effective when, within good counselling relationships, they train clients in relevant thinking and action skills.

4. The ultimate goal of lifeskills counselling is self-helping, whereby clients maintain and develop thinking skills and action skills strengths, not just to cope with present problems, but to prevent and handle future problems.

Lifeskills counselling is based on a psychological education theoretical framework. The word education has a double derivation from its Latin origins. Education is derived from the verb *educare*, 'to nurture, rear'. However, the verb *educare* is a variant of the verb *educere*, 'to lead out' (Jones, 1990). Lifeskills counselling's psychological education theoretical framework encompasses both meanings of the word education. On the one hand, the framework acknowledges the importance of nurturing and facilitation. On the other hand, the framework stresses the need for training to lead out people to develop better lifeskills. Another way of viewing lifeskills counselling's psychological education theoretical framework is to say that it takes a developmental approach to conceptualizing and working with clients' problems and potentials. In Chapters 2 and 3 I overview the theory and practice of lifeskills counselling.

Problems and potentials

Lifeskills counselling not only focuses on helping people to cope with their problems, it also focuses on freeing their potentials. Lifeskills counselling is people-centred in that it focuses on the range of skills or competencies that all people require for their survival, maintenance and enhancement. It is an egalitarian approach that assumes that everyone, regardless of age, sex, race, colour or creed, has the 'potential for growth and the right to personal maximization of competence' (Albee, 1984, p. 230). Problems for which people require adaptive feelings, thoughts and actions to maximize their potentials can occur at all ages of the lifespan and in all areas of life (Egan and Cowan, 1979; Erikson, 1963; Havighurst, 1972; Kohlberg and Gilligan, 1971; Masterpasqua, 1989; Perry, 1970; Sugarman, 1986).

The kinds of problems and potentials for which lifeskills counselling is appropriate range from basic thinking and action skills for all ages of the lifespan to developmental competencies that are more life-stage specific: for example, learning intimacy and sexual relating skills for late adolescents and coping with ageing and dying skills for the elderly. Lifeskills counselling can focus on problems and potentials in all areas of life: couple relationships, sex, parenting, occupational choice, work, study and exam taking, leisure and health. Furthermore, lifeskills counsellors work with many symptoms often more indicative of dis-ease than illness, including depression, acute and chronic anxiety, phobias, delinquent behaviour, substance abuse and aggression.

THE LIFESKILLS COUNSELLOR
What lifeskills counsellors are

Lifeskills counsellors hold humanistic values either within or outside of religious frameworks (Kelly, 1995). These values include respect for each individual, acknowledgement of human fallibility, belief in human educability, belief in the human potential for reason and social living and a sincere desire for a better world. Lifeskills counsellors subscribe to the psychological education theoretical framework overviewed in the next chapter. This theoretical framework integrates elements of existential-humanistic and cognitive-behavioural psychology.

Lifeskills counsellors are practitioner-researchers who constantly make, implement and evaluate hypotheses about helping clients to change. At least four sources of knowledge enlighten their counselling. First, they attend to theoretical knowledge. The lifeskills theoretical framework requires continuous updating in the light of new knowledge about human development and change. Second, lifeskills counsellors endeavour to keep abreast of relevant research findings into the processes and outcomes of counselling. When working in a speciality area (for example, career counselling or marriage and family counselling), they focus on pertinent research literature. Third, lifeskills counsellors learn from their practical counselling experience. They actively seek to counsel more effectively by evaluating their counselling and, where necessary, modifying what they do. Fourth, lifeskills counsellors are alive and vibrant human beings who learn from personal experience outside of counselling. This capacity to learn from personal experience is especially important for counsellors operating within a framework that assumes that fundamentally both counsellors and clients require the same skills of living. If you can acquire, maintain and develop your lifeskills, you are likely to be better placed to help clients with theirs.

Lifeskills counsellors are developmental educators (Nelson-Jones, 1988). Taking into account the state of readiness, expectations and skills levels of each client, they flexibly use both relationship and training skills. The focus of counselling includes nurturing and healing vulnerable clients, assisting clients with specific problems and decisions, crisis management work and preventive and developmental lifeskills training. The clientele for lifeskills counselling may be an individual, a group or an organization (Murgatroyd, 1993). Lifeskills counsellors are always conscious of ways to 'seed' or disseminate counselling skills. Furthermore, they realize that sometimes 'upstream' counselling focusing on organizational policies, practices and personalities that create and sustain problems may be necessary either instead of or in addition to 'downstream' counselling with individuals or groups of clients (Egan and Cowan, 1979).

Within an educational framework, lifeskills counsellors use a range of training interventions focusing on feeling, thinking and action. Lifeskills counsellors tend not to be archaeologists or historians – instead choosing to focus mainly on clients' presents and futures. In particular, counsellors collaborate with clients to identify specific skills deficits that sustain difficulties. Then, counsellors assist clients in shifting the balance of deficits more in the direction of skills strengths. Always lifeskills counsellors heavily emphasize clients taking away trained skills as self-helping skills.

What lifeskills counsellors are not

Another way of presenting what lifeskills counsellors are is to indicate what they are not. First, lifeskills counsellors are not different from other people, except that they possess better counselling skills. They still have their own struggles, imperfections and difficulties in affirming their positive rather than negative potentials. Second, they are not superficial manipulators. They genuinely care for the growth and development of clients. Third, lifeskills counsellors are neither magicians nor snake-oil doctors promising instant cures. Clients usually come to counselling with long-established skills deficits as well as strengths. Counsellors emphasize that, frequently, relinquishing lifeskills deficits and developing lifeskills strengths requires much work and practice.

Lifeskills counsellors cannot do clients' work and discourage dependency. Rather, they quietly and sometimes more forcefully challenge clients with their existential responsibility to create their lives. Lifeskills counsellors do not encourage conformity. Rather, they assist clients to think through which choices have the highest probability of being best for them in their unique life circumstances. Lifeskills counsellors do not view themselves as having a monopoly on counselling skills. Many counselling skills are similar to skills needed for other roles, such as being a partner, friend, parent or supervisor. In addition, many counselling skills can be used for self-helping. The more people who possess good counselling skills the better (Charles-Edwardes, 1989).

CHAPTER HIGHLIGHTS

* *Four main categories of counsellors and helpers are: counselling and helping professionals; voluntary counsellors and helpers; those using counselling and helping skills as part of their jobs; and informal counsellors and helpers.*

* *Reasons for preferring the term counsellor to helper include greater clarity and avoidance of connotations of dependency and of downgrading the importance of self-help.*

* *Dimensions for defining counselling include viewing it in terms of a relationship, a*

repertoire of interventions, a psychological process, the people who counsel, its goals, its clienteles and its relationship to psychotherapy.

- *Lifeskills counselling is a people-centred approach for assisting clients to develop self-helping skills.*

- *Lifeskills counselling is based on a psychological education theoretical framework and lifeskills counsellors are primarily developmental educators.*

- *Lifeskills counsellors hold humanistic values either within or outside religious frameworks. They are practitioner researchers who constantly make, implement and evaluate client change hypotheses. They possess a range of interventions focused on feeling, thinking and action.*

- *Lifeskills counsellors always encourage clients to become their own best helpers.*

EXERCISE 1.1   WHAT IS COUNSELLING?

Answer the following questions on your own, with a partner or in a group.

1. What does the term counselling mean to you?

2. How, if at all, might you distinguish counselling from helping?

3. How, if at all, might you distinguish counselling from psychotherapy?

4. What do you view as the goals for counselling?

5. Critically discuss the idea that counsellors are primarily developmental educators.

TWO

Lifeskills Theory

Everything should be made as simple as possible, but not simpler.

Albert Einstein

CHAPTER QUESTIONS

- *What are the elements of a counselling theory?*

- *What are lifeskills?*

- *What are thinking skills and action skills?*

- *What are some assumptions of lifeskills counselling?*

- *How do people acquire lifeskills strengths and deficits?*

- *How do people maintain lifeskills strengths and deficits?*

- *How do lifeskills deficits become activated?*

INTRODUCTION

Though still in the process of development, lifeskills theory fulfils each of the three main functions of counselling theories (Nelson-Jones, 1995). First, it provides a conceptual framework in which counsellors can think systematically about human

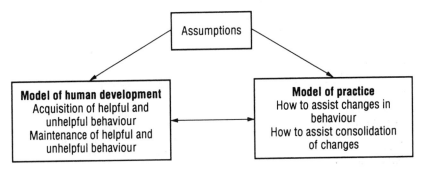

Figure 2.1 *The elements of a theory and their interrelationships*

development and counselling practice. Second, it offers a language or vocabulary in which the counselling conversation can take place. Third, lifeskills counselling may be viewed as a series of research hypotheses. For instance, research may be conducted on the processes and outcomes of counsellors and clients using lifeskills language during counselling and of clients using it after counselling to maintain self-helping skills.

Counselling theories may be viewed as possessing four main elements if they are to be stated adequately. These elements are: (1) a statement of the basic *assumptions* underlying the theory; (2) an explanation of the *acquisition* of helpful and unhelpful behaviour; (3) an explanation of the *maintenance* of helpful and unhelpful behaviour; and (4) an explanation of how to help clients *change* their behaviour and *consolidate* their gains when counselling ends. Figure 2.1 shows how counselling theories can be viewed as containing a model of human development and a model of practice. In this chapter I overview the assumptions and model of human development of lifeskills counselling. In Chapter 3 I overview lifeskills counselling's model of practice.

ASSUMPTIONS

Following are some assumptions of lifeskills counselling.

Biological and psychological life

Most commonly life is regarded as a biological concept. However, the main concern of lifeskills counselling is with psychological rather than biological life. The two concepts overlap and psychological existence takes place within biological life. Moreover, biological life can influence psychological life (for instance, the effects of fatigue on feelings of well-being) and psychological life can influence biological life, an extreme example being suicide. In addition, with physical illnesses such as cancer, treatment frequently needs to focus on both biological and psychological lives.

Having noted a few areas of overlap, we can ask: what are some distinguishing characteristics of psychological as contrasted with biological life? Figure 2.2 summarizes some of these differences.

The following discussion elaborates the distinctions made in Figure 2.2. Most often, despite the use of the word versus, the differences are of degree rather than either/or distinctions.

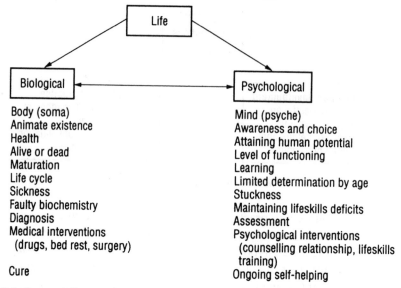

Figure 2.2 *Some differences between biological and psychological life*

- *Body versus mind.* The primary focus of psychological life is the mind rather than the body.

- *Animate existence versus awareness and choice.* By definition, any form of biological life has animate existence. From birth, people's vital organs exist at a sufficient level to sustain this existence. They can obtain energy by breathing and obtaining food. However, human psychological life goes beyond animate existence in that humans have a unique capacity for self-awareness and choice. They can remember their pasts, make choices in their presents and plan their futures. Psychological life is a continuous process of struggling to make life-enhancing rather than life-constricting choices. A psychological life-against-death struggle permeates biological life.

- *Health versus attaining human potential.* The primary goal of biological life is good physical health. The primary goal of psychological life is attaining human potential. Psychological life concerns people's ability to use their minds for the purpose of enhancing the quality of their existence by fulfilling their unique potentials.

- *Alive/dead versus level of functioning.* The opposite of biological life is death, ceasing to exist in animate form or non-being. There are some debatable areas regarding when people are clinically dead. However, for most humans, even when sick, the issue is polarized into being either alive or dead. The purpose of psychological life is to enhance existence rather than survival. People are at different levels of functioning in terms of their ability to affirm their psychological lives. Psychological life is relative (there are varying degrees of it) rather than dichotomous (such as being alive or dead).

- *Maturation versus learning.* Maturation is an important concept in the acquisition of biological abilities, such as the ability to reproduce. The quality of psychological life is based more on learning than maturation, on nurture rather than nature. However, there are areas of overlap: for instance, cognitive capacities biologically mature and people possess biological tendencies to sabotage their psychological lives.

- *Life cycle versus limited determination by age.* There is a biological human life cycle of conception, birth, growing up, maturity, decline and death. However, there is no fixed relationship between psychological life and biological age. Young people's potentials can be stunted and old people can be actively in control of their lives.

- *Sickness versus stuckness.* Though a simplification, when people come to see medical doctors they are physically or biologically sick and do not know how to get better. When they come to see counsellors they are psychologically stuck and do not know how to think and act better.

- *Faulty biochemistry versus maintaining lifeskills deficits.* Frequently, sickness may be viewed as the individual's body acquiring and then maintaining faulty bio-chemistry. Psychological stuckness may be viewed as the individual's mind acquiring and then maintaining lifeskills deficits or faulty ways of thinking and acting.

- *Diagnosis versus assessment.* Sickness requires medical diagnosis to identify the faulty biochemistry that interferes with biological health. Stuckness requires psychological assessment to identify the lifeskills deficits that interfere with attaining human potential.

- *Medical versus psychological interventions.* Medical interventions for attaining health include drugs, bed rest and surgery. Counselling interventions for attaining psychological lifeskills include offering good counselling relationships and training clients in relevant lifeskills.

- *Cure versus ongoing self-helping.* Often the concept of cure is used in relation to overcoming sickness. The concept of cure is inappropriate to psychological life. Psychological life is reversible, in that people can go backwards as well as forwards in ability to make choices. Lifeskills counselling is concerned to provide clients with the skills to enhance and maintain psychological life. Because maintenance of psychological life cannot be assumed, and given the certainty that most clients end counselling, lifeskills counselling's prime objective is to impart self-helping skills.

Skills language

WHAT ARE SKILLS? One meaning of the word skills pertains to *areas* of skill: for instance, listening skills or disclosing skills. Another meaning refers to *level of competence*: for instance, skilled or unskilled in an area of skill. A third meaning of skill relates to the *knowledge and sequence of choices* entailed in implementing the skill. The essential element of any skill is the ability to make and implement sequences of choices to achieve objectives. For instance, if clients are to be good at asserting themselves or at managing stress, they have to make and implement effective choices in these lifeskills areas.

The concept of skill is best viewed not as an either/or matter in which people either possess or do not possess a skill. Rather it is preferable to think of people as possessing *skills strengths* or *skills deficits* or a mixture of the two. Good choices in skills areas are skills strengths. Poor choices are skills deficits. The criterion for good or poor client choices is whether or not they affirm psychological life. In all lifeskills areas people are likely to possess skills strengths and deficits in varying degrees. For instance, in the skills area of listening, they may be good at understanding talkers, but poor at showing their understanding. The object of lifeskills counselling is to help clients, in one or more skills areas, to move more in the direction of skills strengths rather than skills deficits.

WHAT ARE LIFESKILLS? Apart from such obviously biological functions as breathing, virtually all human behaviour is viewed in terms of learned lifeskills. The term lifeskills in itself is a neutral concept. Lifeskills may be strengths or deficits depending on whether or not they help people to survive and to maintain and develop potentials. A neutral definition of the term lifeskills is: *lifeskills are sequences of choices that people make in specific skills areas*. A positive definition of the term lifeskills is: *lifeskills are sequences of choices affirming psychological life that people make in specific skills areas*.

WHAT IS SKILLS LANGUAGE? Skills language means consistently using the concept of skills to describe and analyse people's behaviour. With regard to counselling, skills language means conceptualizing and conversing about clients' problems in terms of lifeskills strengths and deficits. Skills language provides a relatively simple way for both counsellors and clients to analyse and work on problems. Many clients find it easier to look at their problems in terms of the skills they need to work on them rather than having to admit personal inadequacy or blame. In particular, skills language involves identifying the specific thinking skills and action skills weaknesses that maintain clients' problems. Feelings too are important. However, feelings represent people's animal nature and are not skills in themselves. People can influence their feelings for good or ill through their use of thinking and action skills.

A difference exists between the vernacular, the descriptive language of ordinary conversation, and the functional language required for people trying to help themselves. Since the goal of counselling is to help people adopt a lifelong philosophy of self-helping, the language of counselling needs to lend itself to client self-instructing. However, counselling's language should still be as close as possible to the vernacular to help clients to understand and use it. Skills language provides a psychologically functional way of communicating that is close to the vernacular.

In any helping contact, at least four possible languages are involved: namely, helper and client private and public talk (Nelson-Jones, 1986). Lifeskills counselling is based

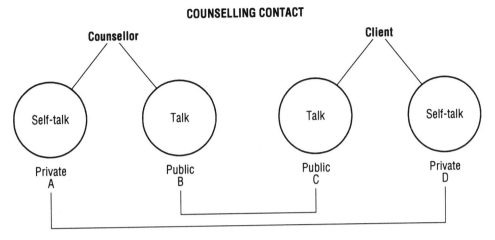

Figure 2.3 *Public and private talk in counselling*

on an educational theoretical framework, expressed in skills language, that counsellors can use both for private and public talk. Counsellors do not need to talk one language to themselves and another to clients. Lifeskills counsellors use their own and their clients' public talk to develop clients' private talk, so that the latter can understand their own problems and instruct themselves through sequences of choices to cope with them.

Figure 2.3 illustrates public and private talk in counselling. Much counselling is educationally inefficient. It focuses insufficiently on moving beyond counsellor and client public talk at points B and C. In lifeskills counselling, counsellors use public talk at points B and C not just to develop a counselling relationship, but actively to work from counsellor private self-talk at point A to influence client private self-talk at point D. By communicating from an educational framework expressed in skills language, counsellors can help clients to acquire relevant private self-talk to monitor, maintain and develop targeted skills. Hence, the language of lifeskills helping becomes the people-centred language of self-instructing and self-helping.

Three forms of self

A person's self is what she or he calls 'I' or 'me'. It is the centre of her or his personal universe. As depicted in Figure 2.4, the self has three major components.

THE NATURAL SELF Each person has a fundamental biological inner nature, or inner core of genetic aptitudes, drives, instincts, instinct remnants and human potentialities. This is their animal nature. The Natural Self incorporates characteristics such as energy, sexuality, feelings and anxiety. It possesses needs shared by the entire human species: for instance, for food, shelter, physical safety, belonging and love. However, the Natural Self is also unique to each individual in terms of his or her specific aptitudes, inner valuing process, energizing drive and thresholds for conditioning and anxiety. The Natural Self is a person's inner nature or the biological core of his or her personhood. Unfortunately, this inner nature can work against as well as for the person:

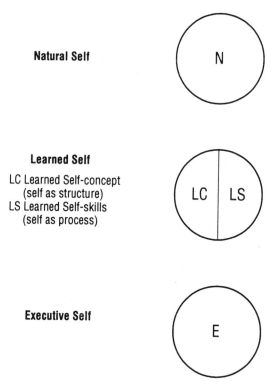

Natural Self

Learned Self

LC Learned Self-concept
(self as structure)
LS Learned Self-skills
(self as process)

Executive Self

Figure 2.4 *The three forms of self*

for instance, in terms of a universal biological propensity to think irrationally as well as rationally (Ellis, 1995).

THE LEARNED SELF The Learned Self is the product of people's learning experiences. The self-concept is the traditional way of viewing the learned self. In Figure 2.4 it is depicted as the LC or Learned Self-concept. The LC consists of people's self-conceptions in numerous different areas: relationships, sexuality, work, leisure, tastes and preferences, values and so on.

Another way of looking at the learned self is in terms of people's lifeskills strengths and deficits in different skills areas. In Figure 2.4, this is depicted as the LS or Learned Self-skills. People's self-concepts (LC) do not necessarily reflect their lifeskills strengths and deficits (LS). First, they may not think about themselves in skills language. Second, they may not know what are the different specific lifeskills they require. Third, they may inaccurately perceive their strengths and deficits in various lifeskills areas.

Viewing the Learned Self in skills terms has advantages. The LC relates to the self as structure, whereby people describe their self-concepts in static terms: for instance, 'I'm depressed.' The LS relates to the self as process, whereby people are in process of using, maintaining, developing or losing skills: for instance, 'I'm using certain skills deficits that contribute to my depressing myself.' The LS has the advantages of skills language, in that counsellors and clients can then try to pinpoint the skills for becoming less depressed. Furthermore, once clients know what the sequences of choices are for the skills of depressing themselves less, they can use these skills again when on their own.

THE EXECUTIVE SELF Whereas people's Natural Self represents their biological endowment and their Learned Self reflects their past learning history, their Executive Self represents their capacity to *make* their lives through their choices in the present and future. Thus people not only have selves but also continuously create selves. People can choose those aspects of their Natural and Learned Selves that they wish to develop. This is particularly important in lifeskills counselling, where clients choose to develop specific skills to attain personal goals. The Executive Self provides a means whereby people can choose to work on relinquishing the misperceptions and skills deficits of their Learned Selves that block the fulfilment of their Natural Selves.

Energizing drive

Ordinary people may have difficulty understanding terms like the organism's 'actualizing tendency' (Raskin and Rogers, 1995, p. 128) or self-realizing. All people possess an energizing drive towards surviving, maintaining and developing themselves. However, humans possess weak instinctual remnants (Maslow, 1970): unlike that of other animals, human behaviour is not strongly programmed by instincts. Consequently, people can have fortunate or unfortunate experiences in both acquiring and learning how to maintain and develop lifeskills. The long human learning process and humans' ability for symbolic thought offer much scope for acquiring and maintaining lifeskills deficits as well as strengths.

The energizing drive is neither good nor bad: nature does not operate in such terms. Humans are animals first and people second. If anything, instinctually people are more likely to operate in ways that protect themselves and the species than not. However, biologically, both as individuals and as a species, humans have predispositions for both life affirming and life destructive behaviours. Consequently, both for biological reasons and as a result of faulty learning, the energizing drive may turn against itself.

The goals of the energizing drive may be viewed on at least three dimensions: first, the basic animal survival dimension; second, the pleasure dimension, or what Ellis terms 'short-range hedonism' (Ellis, 1995, p. 173); third, the dimension of higher level and often more socially oriented involvements and commitments. Terms like 'self-actualizing' (Maslow, 1962, 1970, 1971) and 'propriate striving' have been used to describe 'the integrity that comes only from maintaining major directions of striving' (Allport, 1955, p. 51). Lifeskills are required for each of the above three ways of expending energy. However, most humans are probably more spontaneously driven by survival and short-range hedonism than by longer-term and higher level strivings, although they can learn to forgo short-term goals in the pursuit of longer-term goals.

Meanings of anxiety

SURVIVAL ANXIETY The existential counselling viewpoint is that fear of biological death, non-being or destruction is the underlying fear from which all other fears are derived (May and Yalom, 1995; Yalom, 1980). The term survival anxiety seems preferable to that of death anxiety. The notion of survival anxiety focuses more than death anxiety on the continual fears of the living. Survival anxiety relates both to people's fear of biological death itself and to their fears of not being competent to meet their survival needs, which they perceive in psychological as well as biological terms.

Survival anxiety can be conscious, preconscious and unconscious. In varying degrees people can be aware of their anxiety as it happens. Preconscious anxiety may surface in relatively safe situations, such as counselling or loving relationships. Much anxiety is repressed because it is too threatening to the organism and because other people collude in the repression. For instance, repressed fears of death may appear in disguised form in dreams and nightmares.

NORMAL AND DEBILITATING ANXIETY Anxiety is viewed as a normal part of life in a number of ways. First, anxiety is a basic animal survival mechanism that signals some danger or threat to the organism. Second, humans cannot escape the anxiety connected with confronting the givens of existence: death, suffering, freedom, isolation and meaninglessness. Third, anxiety is part of learning, deciding and changing, each activity requiring relinquishing something to gain something. For example, a degree of psychological independence from parents is a developmental task of all humans, yet most often this entails giving up some security to become more secure.

For many reasons, humans learn skills deficits that contribute to normal anxiety being transformed into debilitating anxiety (Alpert and Haber, 1960). In varying degrees, all humans acquire and maintain an exaggerated sense of danger and threat, either general or in relation to specific situations, that interferes with full psychological life. This view is echoed by Beck, who conceptualizes anxiety disorders 'as excessive functioning or malfunctioning of normal survival mechanisms' (Beck and Weishaar, 1995, p. 240). Debilitating anxiety can be both cause and effect of lifeskills deficits. People with anxiety disorders maximize the chances of negative and minimize the chances of positive outcomes instead of realistically appraising situations and having an optimal level of anxiety. As part of this process, they may distort their sense of competence about performing at a level to achieve desired outcomes or, to use Bandura's term, their self-efficacy beliefs (Bandura, 1986).

Personal responsibility

Focusing on personal responsibility is almost like focusing on one's nose. Though right in front of the face, the concept is not always easy to observe (Nelson-Jones, 1984). Lifeskills counselling adopts the existential notion of people as responsible for the authorship of their lives (May and Yalom, 1995; Sartre, 1956; Yalom, 1980). Another metaphor is that people are responsible for inventing their lives. Authorship or invention requires a continuous process of choosing. Personal responsibility is an inner process in which people work from 'inside to outside'. This process starts with people's thoughts and feelings and leads to their observable actions. Furthermore, especially as people grow older, many if not most of the significant barriers to assuming responsibility are internal rather than external. However, both inside and outside of counselling, people 'differ enormously in the degree of responsibility they are willing to accept for their life situation and in their modes of denying responsibility' (May and Yalom, 1995, p. 274).

Courage

The word courage is derived from the Latin word *cor*, meaning heart. Paul Tillich, in his inspiring book *The Courage to Be* (1952), wrote: 'The courage to be is the ethical act in which man affirms his own being in spite of those elements of his existence which conflict with his essential self-affirmation' (p. 3). May, a long-standing friend of Tillich's, distinguished between physical, moral, social and creative courage (May, 1975).

Here I distinguish between three different, yet overlapping, kinds of courage. First, there is the courage to confront and relinquish lifeskills deficits. Though lifeskills deficits may offer the illusion of security, by definition they constrict psychological life. It can take courage to acknowledge one's human frailty. Second, there is the courage to develop lifeskills strengths. The development of lifeskills strengths is frequently carried out despite many factors that make it hard to do so. Such 'despite' factors include the work involved and anxieties about learning and change. Third, there is the courage to maintain and develop lifeskills. There is no magic or concept of cure. Nor is there any automatic 'pat on the back' for good use of lifeskills. Instead, counsellors and clients need to work on the skills of having the courage to be 'centred' and authentic people. Inner strength is another term to describe the sort of courage to which I refer.

ACQUISITION

The lifeskills approach to human development seeks to answer two important and interrelated questions. First, how do people acquire lifeskills strengths and deficits? In particular, how do they acquire thinking skills and action skills strengths and deficits? Second, how do people acquire skills language, the ability to think about and analyse their behaviour in skills terms? In this section, the focus is more on the processes of acquiring lifeskills strengths and deficits, though the same processes apply to learning skills language. I start by describing what I mean by thinking skills and action skills.

Inner and outer games

If humans are to control their behaviour, they need to think and act effectively. A simple way of highlighting the distinction is to talk about people's inner and outer games of living. The inner game relates to what goes on inside them, how they think, or their thinking skills. The outer game relates to what goes on outside them, how they act, or their action skills. Thinking is covert, action is overt. Feelings are not ignored. Humans need to be able to experience, express and manage their feelings. However, as mentioned earlier, feelings represent humans' animal nature and are not skills in themselves.

THINKING SKILLS Below are brief descriptions of 12 thinking skills areas. By using skills language, lifeskills counsellors can draw upon the insights of various cognitive theorists, such as Beck and Ellis, without getting trapped in the different languages of their theoretical positions. The thinking skills are presented in 'you' language, both to heighten readers' awareness of their meaning and to make the point that counsellors and clients require the same lifeskills.

- *Owning responsibility for choosing.* You are aware that you are the author of your existence and that you can choose how you think, act and feel. You are aware of the limitations of existence, such as your death.

- *Understanding the relationships between how you think, feel and act.* You possess insight into how you can influence how you feel and act through how you think. You are aware that your feelings and actions in turn influence your thoughts.

- *Getting in touch with your feelings.* You acknowledge the importance of getting in touch with how you feel. You are able to access significant feelings (for instance, your wants and wishes) and accurately state them as thoughts.

- *Using coping self-talk.* Instead of talking to yourself negatively before, during and after specific situations, you can make self-statements that calm you down, coach you in how to cope, and affirm the skills you possess.

- *Choosing realistic personal rules.* Your unrealistic personal rules make irrational demands on yourself, others and the environment: for instance, 'I must be liked by everyone,' 'Others must not make mistakes' and 'Life must be fair.' Instead you can develop realistic rules: for instance, 'I prefer to be liked, but it's unrealistic to expect this from everyone.'

- *Perceiving accurately.* You avoid labelling yourself and others either too negatively or too positively. You distinguish between fact and inference and make your inferences as accurate as possible.

- *Explaining cause accurately.* You explain the causes of events accurately. You avoid assuming too much responsibility by internalizing ('It's all my fault') or externalizing ('It's all their fault').

- *Predicting realistically.* You are realistic about the risks and rewards of future actions. You assess threats and dangers accurately. You avoid distorting relevant evidence with unwarranted optimism or pessimism. Your expectancies about your level of competence to perform tasks are accurate.

- *Setting realistic goals.* Your short-, medium- and long-term goals reflect your values, are realistic, are specific and have a time frame.

- *Using visualizing skills.* People think in pictorial images as well as in words. You use visual images in ways that calm you down, assist you in acting competently to attain your goals and help you to resist giving in to bad habits.

- *Realistic decision-making.* You confront rather than avoid decisions and then make up your mind by going through a rational decision-making process.

- *Preventing and managing problems.* You anticipate and confront your problems. You assess the thinking and action skills you require to deal with them. You set goals and plan how to implement them.

ACTION SKILLS Action skills involve observable behaviours. They are what you do and how you do it rather than what and how you feel and think. Action skills vary by area of application: for instance, relating, study, work, leisure, health and social participation.

There are five main ways in which people can send action skills messages. Again, I list these in 'you' language.

- *Verbal messages.* Messages that you send with words.

- *Voice messages.* Messages that you send through your voice volume, articulation, pitch, emphasis and speech rate.

- *Body messages.* Messages that you send with your body through your gaze, eye contact, facial expression, posture, gestures, physical proximity and clothes and grooming.

- *Touch messages.* A special category of body messages. Messages that you send with your touch through the part of body that you use, what part of another's body you touch, how gentle or firm you are and whether or not you have permission.

- *Action messages.* Messages that you send when you are not face-to-face with others: for example, sending flowers or a legal writ.

Following this brief introduction to viewing how people think and act in skills terms, below are some processes by which people acquire lifeskills strengths and deficits.

Supportive relationships

Children require supportive relationships. Bowlby (1979) talks of the concept of a secure base, otherwise referred to as an attachment figure. He notes accumulating evidence that humans of all ages are happiest and most effective when they feel that standing behind them is a trusted person who will come to their aid should difficulties arise. Rogers has also stressed the need for supportive parent–child relationships characterized by high degrees of respect, genuineness and empathic understanding, whereby children can feel sensitively and accurately understood (Rogers, 1951, 1959). Supportive relationships can be provided by many people other than parents: for instance, relatives and teachers. When growing up, most people seem to need at least one primary supportive relationship.

Many reasons exist why the presence of supportive and absence of unsupportive or hostile relationships can help children to develop lifeskills strengths. First, supportive relationships provide children with the security to engage in exploratory behaviour and risk trial-and-error learning. Such exploratory behaviour represents a series of personal experiments in which children collect information about themselves and their environments. Second, supportive relationships help children to listen better to themselves. By feeling prized and accurately understood, children can get more in touch with their wants, wishes and personal meanings. Third, children may feel freer to bring out into the open and show others emerging lifeskills without risk of ridicule. Fourth, instruction in specific skills is frequently best conducted in the context of supportive relationships in which the anxiety attached to learning is diminished. Fifth, the presence or absence of supportive relationships can either affirm or negate children's sense of worth. They may be helped to become confident to face life's challenges or they may become inhibited, withdrawn and afraid to take risks. Alternatively, they may mask their insecurity by excessive attention-seeking.

Learning from examples

Learning from observing is a major way in which people acquire lifeskills strengths and deficits (Bandura, 1986). How to think, feel and act can be learned from others' examples. Frequently people remain unaware of behaviours they demonstrate to children. If either or both parents are emotionally inexpressive, children miss opportunities for observing how to express emotions. If parents and others use ineffective thinking skills, such as blaming and overgeneralizing, children may be quick to do likewise. In addition, children may acquire from parents' examples poor action skills for relationships, work, leisure and health care. The converse is also true, in that lifeskills strengths in how to feel, think and act may be acquired from the role-modelling of parents and significant others. Significant others may include peers, teachers, siblings, other relatives and even people in the media.

Just as teaching by example is often unintentional, so is learning by example. For instance, the effects of modelling are less direct when thinking skills rather than action skills are involved. Not only are thinking skills not observable in the sense that action skills are, they are seldom clearly verbalized. People may absorb from example deficient skills for thinking, feeling and action, and then possess the added barrier of remaining unaware this has happened.

The following vignettes illustrate learning from examples.

Sarah grew up in a house where neither parent

talked openly about sex. Further, she never saw her parents being openly affectionate to one another. The message that Sarah received from her parents' example was that sex was something of which to be ashamed.

On occasions when he was growing up, Roger and his father would have disagreements and argue. However, once tempers had cooled, Roger's father would sit down with him, listen to his side of the story, state his own viewpoint calmly and try to reach a mutually acceptable solution to their problems. Roger now tries to adopt the same approach in his marriage.

Learning from consequences

Lifeskills learning from observation of role models is frequently intermingled with learning from rewarding or unrewarding consequences. For example, parents poor at showing emotions may also be poor at receiving children's emotions. Rewarding consequences can be either primary or secondary. Primary rewarding consequences are those that people find rewarding independent of their learning histories: for instance, food, shelter, sex and human warmth. Skinner considers that all rewards eventually derive their power from evolutionary selection and that it is part of human nature to be rewarded by particular things (Skinner, 1971). However, only a small part of behaviour is immediately reinforced by rewards of evident biological significance. Most behaviour is emitted in response to secondary rewards, such as approval or money, that have become associated with or conditioned to primary rewards.

People receive consequences in two main ways. First, there is *classical conditioning*, where consequences are independent of operating on the environment. For example, a person who has been in a serious car accident may feel anxious about either being in a car or about other characteristics of the accident, such as its location. Many aversions appear to result from classical conditioning (Lazarus, 1995). Second, there is *operant conditioning*, where consequences result from behaviours that operate on the environment. For example, the behaviour of requesting dates may lead to acceptance or rejection. However, people do not just receive consequences, they think about past consequences they have received and present consequences they are receiving, and make rules and predictions to guide their future behaviour (Bandura, 1986). Thus, people's cognitive processes may strengthen, weaken or otherwise alter the impact of rewarding consequences. In addition, there are biological differences in people's propensity to be conditioned by rewarding consequences.

Rewarding consequences play a large part in helping or hindering people in acquiring lifeskills strengths. Virtually from birth, humans receive messages about how 'good' or 'bad' their actions are. Usually, with the best of intentions, adults try to reward children for developing the skills necessary to cope with the world. However, often adults provide rewards in deficient ways. For example, most people learn their relationing skills and thinking skills from a mixture of observing others, unsystematic feedback and trial and error. Rarely, either inside or outside the home, are people systematically rewarded as they develop these lifeskills. Furthermore, sometimes children are rewarded for exhibiting skills deficits rather than strengths. For instance, they may find that they are more likely to get their way if they shout aggressively rather than take a more reasonable approach. In addition, skills deficits can be acquired by people becoming too dependent on the need for external rewards rather than trusting their own judgement and skills. Furthermore, skills deficits can be developed by people receiving the message that their whole personhood is bad rather than a specific behaviour insufficiently skilled. Last but not least, many people acquire skills deficits through receiving negative consequences because of their biological sex, race, social class or culture.

The following is an example of learning from consequences.

> When Frank was a child he would cry easily, both when he got into fights with other children and when he saw something sad on television. When Frank cried during a fight, other children were quick to put him down as a 'sissy' and a 'cry baby'. Charlie, Frank's father, was afraid his son might become a homosexual. Charlie told Frank how wet he was to cry watching television and that he was behaving like a little girl. After a time, Frank began to think of crying in boys and men as a sign of weakness.

Instruction and self-instruction

Psychologists researching animal behaviour stress the importance of learning from example and consequences. However, humans possess the capacity for symbolic thought and communication. Consequently, instruction is a major transmitter of lifeskills strengths and deficits. Much lifeskills instruction takes place informally in the home. Some of this instruction is very basic: for instance, asking children to say 'please' and 'thank you'. Children are frequently being told by their parents how to relate, how to study, how to look after their health and so on. Relatives and peers are other providers of instruction outside educational settings.

Much informal lifeskills instruction takes place in schools and colleges. However, systematic attempts to train children in a range of relating skills are probably still more the exception than the rule. Nevertheless, lifeskills programmes are run in many schools in such areas as career education and drug and alcohol education. In addition, a range of lifeskills programmes may be offered in colleges and universities inside or outside the formal curriculum. The lifeskills targeted include relating skills, study skills, managing test anxiety, career development skills, anxiety and stress management skills and effective thinking skills. Most often participation in such programmes is voluntary.

Instruction can be for better or worse. Skills deficits as well as strengths can be imparted. For various reasons, those instructed may resist instructors. Sometimes instructors are poor at drawing out learners and just tell them what to do. Frequently instruction contains sex bias: for instance, teaching only girls cooking and parenting skills. In addition, lifeskills may not be communicated clearly enough for learners to instruct themselves afterwards. If learners are unable to talk themselves through the relevant sequences of choices, many lifeskills have been inadequately imparted and learned. Much instruction falls far short of this self-instructional objective.

Information and opportunity

People require adequate information to develop lifeskills. For example, keeping children in ignorance about basic facts of sexuality and death impedes self-awareness and emotional responsiveness. Intentionally or unintentionally, adults often relate to their children on the basis of lies, omissions of truth and partial truths (Steiner, 1974). Furthermore, necessary information may not be readily available outside the home. For instance, schools differ greatly in the adequacy of the career information they provide.

Children, adolescents and adults alike need available opportunities to test out and develop lifeskills. Ideally such opportunities are in line with their maturation and state of readiness. People may have different opportunities on account of their sex, race, culture, social class, financial position and schooling, to mention but some barriers. Furthermore, people can be fortunate and unfortunate in having parents who open up rather than restrict learning opportunities. Children and adults also have a role in seeking out information and opportunities. Some have better skills at this than others.

Anxiety and confidence

Children grow up having both helpful and harmful experiences for developing self-esteem. The fortunate acquire a level of anxiety that both protects against actual dangers and motivates them towards realistic achievements. Those less fortunate may acquire debilitating anxieties through role-modelling, instruction and the provision of faulty consequences. Even parents who communicate carefully can bruise children's fragile self-esteem. Far worse are parents who communicate hostilely and then become defensive. Here children's feelings and perceptions are doubly discounted: first by the initial aggression and second by being subjected to further aggression when they react. However, children differ biologically in the extent to which they are vulnerable to negative parental behaviour and also in terms of the coping skills they possess.

Deficient behaviours resulting from as well as manifesting anxiety include: unwillingness to take realistic risks; tense and nervous rather than relaxed learning; a heightened tendency to say and do the wrong things; unnecessary aggression; excessive approval seeking; and underachieving, with or without overstriving. Inadequate performance in different skills may further raise anxiety and make future lifeskills learning even more difficult. However, people who are helped or who help themselves to acquire anxiety management skills may learn lifeskills more easily than those without such skills.

MAINTENANCE

People can maintain both lifeskills strengths and deficits. This section focuses only on how people maintain lifeskills deficits. Especially for children, *acquiring* lifeskills strengths and deficits is more a matter of 'what the environment does to me' than 'what I do to myself'. Young people are frequently at the mercy of their elders. However, *maintaining* lifeskills strengths and deficits is a different matter. Here, partly because lifeskills are maintained into adulthood, shifts take place more in the direction of 'what I do to myself' than 'what the environment has done or does to me'. Following are processes maintaining lifeskills deficits.

Insufficient use of skills language

Though this is offered as a hypothesis, a contributing factor to people maintaining skills deficits is that they think insufficiently about their behaviour in lifeskills terms. Already, drawbacks of not using lifeskills language have been indicated. People can go round in circles talking about their problems in descriptive language rather than analysing them in skills language. Few people think rigorously about how they think, including being familiar with the various thinking skills. In addition, most people do not know how to restate everyday problems in skills terms so that they can work for change.

Thinking skills deficits

Lifeskills counselling focuses on stuckness rather than sickness. Thinking skills deficits are a major reason why people maintain poor lifeskills. Too much anxiety tends to be a common theme in faulty thinking. Below are some illustrative thinking skills deficits.

NEGATIVE SELF-TALK Negative self-talk may be contrasted with coping self-talk (Meichenbaum, 1986; Meichenbaum and Deffenbacher, 1988). Negative self-talk statements inhibit people working on a range of lifeskills deficits. Such negative statements include: 'I'm never going to be able to do it,' 'I'm starting to feel anxious and this is a signal that things may get out of control' and 'The future is hopeless.'

Coping self-talk has three main functions: calming, coaching and affirming. A sample calming self-instruction might be 'Keep calm.' A sample coaching self-instruction might be 'Break the task down.' A sample affirming self-instruction is 'I have some skills to deal with this situation.' Frequently, calming, coaching and affirming statements are combined: 'Keep calm. Break the task down. I have some skills to deal with the situation.'

UNREALISTIC PERSONAL RULES Personal rules are the 'do's' and 'don'ts' by which people lead their lives. Each person has an inner rulebook of standards for himself or herself and for others. Sometimes these standards are realistic and appropriately flexible. On other occasions the standards may be unrealistic and inappropriately rigid. Ellis has coined the term 'musturbation' to refer to rigid internal rules characterized by 'musts', 'oughts' and 'shoulds' (Ellis, 1980, 1995). These unrealistic rules are not only lifeskills deficits in themselves, but may help to maintain other lifeskills deficits. Below are illustrations of musturbatory personal rules in different lifeskills areas.

Feeling: 'I must never get angry.'

Sex: 'I must always perform at a high level.'

Thinking: 'All women are less smart than men.'

Relationships: 'I must always win an argument.'

Study: 'I must write the perfect essay.'

Work: 'I must always be stimulated by my job.'

Leisure: 'I must always earn my leisure time.'

Health: 'I must always push myself to the limit of my endurance.'

Possessing unrealistic personal rules about change – that it always should be easy, effortless and painless – contributes to low tolerance of the frustrations entailed in changing. People's low frustration tolerance can contribute to their maintaining their lifeskills deficits.

PERCEIVING INACCURATELY A Chinese proverb states: 'Two-thirds of what we see is behind our eyes.' People erroneously maintain lifeskills deficits if they rigidly perceive their skills to be either better or worse than they are. They may find it difficult to accept contrary feedback if they overestimate how intelligent, affectionate, competent at work or good in bed they are. Further, people may misperceive positive feedback to sustain a negative self-picture as well as negative feedback to sustain a positive self-picture (Rogers, 1959). In both instances, the faulty perceiving contributes to maintaining lifeskills deficits as well as being a lifeskills deficit in itself.

'Defence mechanisms', 'defences' or 'security operations' are terms for the ways that people operate on incoming information that differs from their existing self-pictures (Freud, 1936; Sullivan, 1953; Yalom, 1980). Defensive processes involve people diminishing awareness for short-term psychological comfort. Defensive processes range from denying incoming information to distorting it in various ways: for example, rationalizing, making excuses when your behaviour causes you anxiety, or projecting, i.e. externalizing thoughts and feelings on to others rather than owning them.

EXPLAINING CAUSE DEFICITS How people explain cause influences the degree to which they maintain lifeskills deficits. The following are possible explanatory errors that may sustain lifeskills deficits. A common theme is that these explanations of cause tend to convert partial truths into whole truths by missing out relevant aspects of personal responsibility.

- *'It's my nature.'* Such an explanation inadequately acknowledges the large learned component in most lifeskills deficits.

- *'It's my unfortunate past.'* For people who have left home, explanations of inadequate pasts are largely irrelevant to how they maintain their skills deficits in the present.

- *'It's my bad luck.'* People often make their luck by developing relevant skills.

- *'It's my poor environment.'* Many people have learned to overcome the skills deficits contributed to by their poor environments.

- *'It's all your fault.'* Why bother to change when negative events are someone else's fault?

- *'It's all my fault.'* Quite apart from being inaccurate, overinternalizing cause may erode the confidence people require to deal with difficulties in their lives.

UNREALISTIC PREDICTIONS ABOUT CHANGE Once acquired, lifeskills deficits can become well-established habits resistant to change (Ellis, 1987). Possible areas for unrealistic predictions about changing include the following:

Fear of the unknown

Fear of the discomfort in making the effort to change

Fear of losing the payoffs from existing behaviours

Fear of inner conflict between the old and the emerging self

Fear of conflict with others arising from changing

Fear of failure

Fear of the consequences of success

Especially if unrealistic, perceived self-inefficacy or lack of confidence in being able to enact the level of performance necessary to produce a desired outcome can be a major prediction that blocks change (Bandura, 1986). Many people fail to try out changed behaviours or, if they try, they do not persist in them in face of setbacks. All learning involves giving up the safety of the known to develop new or different skills. Some people are better able to confront fears about change and setbacks than others. Some of the thinking skills mentioned earlier – for example, perceiving accurately and using coping self-talk – help people to manage rather than to avoid change.

Unchanged environmental circumstances

Lifeskills deficits are usually maintained both by how people think and by how the environment constrains them. Most factors mentioned in the section on how people acquire lifeskills can help to maintain lifeskills deficits. People may continue to have insufficiently supportive relationships. They may still be exposed to examples of poor thinking and action skills. They may continue to receive inappropriate rewarding consequences. They may fail to receive or find adequate lifeskills instruction and also continue instructing themselves in their deficits. In addition, they may still be exposed to insufficient or faulty information and lack suitable opportunities to develop their skills and human potential.

Activation of deficits

Lifeskills deficits may be both latent and manifest. People may possess thinking skills and actions skills deficits that leave them vulnerable to specific situations. However, the deficits may not become strongly activated because people's life circumstances do not trigger them. The concept of activation relates to the worsening of an existing skills deficit in response to adverse life events. Let us take the example of a woman who finds difficulty in asserting herself because she possesses a thinking skills deficit, 'Women must not assert themselves', and a corresponding action skills deficit, difficulty saying 'no' to unwanted requests. If this woman marries a considerate husband, who encourages her to express what she thinks and feels, her deficits may be ameliorated rather than worsened. However, if the same woman were to marry a domineering husband, her deficits might become much worse.

People's lifeskills deficits and vulnerabilities tend to be activated by stressful life events or a series of negative experiences. Often these events are stressful because they relate to previous negative experiences. For instance, a young man who when growing up felt rejected by his mother may be hypersensitive to signs of rejection from girlfriends and lovers. The skills deficits and vulnerabilities relating to previous events feed forward into the present and contribute to more biased perceptions and more negative actions than warranted by the behaviour of the women to whom the young man now relates. Further, once one partner's deficits become activated, his behaviour can activate and worsen the deficits of the other partner, thus increasing the likelihood that the original partner's deficits will be further activated. Thinking can become even more biased, demanding and rigid and actions even more hostile and counter-productive.

CHAPTER HIGHLIGHTS

- *Lifeskills counselling is an integrative approach for assisting clients to develop self-helping skills. The approach distinguishes between biological and psychological life. Lifeskills are sequences of choice affirming psychological life that people make in specific skills areas.*

- *The theory and practice of lifeskills counselling is expressed in skills language. Skills language consistently uses the concept of skills to describe and analyse how people think and behave. In each skills area people can possess skills strengths and skills deficits.*

- *There are three forms of self: the Natural Self; the Learned Self, consisting both of self-concept and of lifeskills; and the Executive Self, or choosing self. All people possess an energizing drive towards surviving, maintaining and developing themselves.*

- *Survival anxiety is a normal part of life, though it may become transformed into debilitating anxiety. People are personally responsible for making their psychological lives. They require courage to confront and relinquish lifeskills deficits and to acquire, maintain and develop lifeskills strengths.*

- *Lifeskills theory focuses on the acquisition of both lifeskills and skills language.*

- *The presence or absence of supportive relationships is important in helping children to develop lifeskills strengths or deficits.*

- *Learning from examples is a major way that people acquire lifeskills. Frequently, people remain unaware of the full impact of what they have learned.*

- *Observational learning is frequently intermingled with learning from rewarding or unrewarding consequences. People think about the consequences provided for their behaviour and develop rules and predictions that guide future behaviour.*

- *People also learn lifeskills strengths and deficits from instruction and self-instruction.*

- *Adequate information and opportunities are important to developing lifeskills strengths.*

- *Poor parental relating skills may cause children to possess debilitating anxiety, which in turn may interfere with their acquiring lifeskills strengths and make it easier for them to acquire lifeskills deficits.*

- *A contributing factor to people maintaining relating skills deficits is that they think insufficiently about their behaviour in skills terms.*

- *Thinking skills deficits that help people to stay stuck in self-defeating patterns of behaviour include negative self-talk, unrealistic personal rules, perceiving inaccurately, explaining cause deficits and unrealistic predictions about change.*

- *Unchanged environmental circumstances can also contribute to people maintaining relating skills deficits.*

- *People's thinking and action skills deficits can be activated or worsened by stressful life events.*

EXERCISE 2.1   LIFESKILLS THEORY

Answer the following questions on your own, with a partner or in a group.

1. List some differences between psychological life and biological life.

2. What are lifeskills?

3. Why does lifeskills counselling emphasize the importance of skills language?

4. Describe each of the three forms of self. How are they related?

5. What is the energizing drive?

6. What is survival anxiety?

7. Why is normal anxiety an inevitable part of life?

8. What are the inner and outer games of lifeskills counselling?

9. Describe each of the five ways of sending action skills messages.

10. Why are supportive relationships important in helping children to acquire lifeskills?

11. Apart from supportive relationships, what other processes are important in helping children to acquire lifeskills strengths and avoid acquiring lifeskills deficits?

12. How do people maintain lifeskills deficits?

EXERCISE 2.2   MY PAST EXPERIENCES OF SUPPORTIVE RELATIONSHIPS

First do this exercise on your own. Then, if appropriate, discuss your answers with a partner or in a group.

Select the two most important childhood relationships you had with parents or other significant adults. For each relationship, specify behaviours that supported or hindered you in acquiring relating skills strengths.

1. Details of relationship 1:
   (a) supportive behaviours;
   (b) unsupportive behaviours.

2. Details of relationship 2:
    (a) supportive behaviours;
    (b) unsupportive behaviours.

3. Based on your answers to questions 1 and 2, rank order the supportive behaviours, listing the most supportive behaviour first.

4. Based on your answers to questions 1 and 2, rank order the unsupportive behaviours, listing the most unsupportive behaviour first.

EXERCISE 2.3 LEARNING LIFESKILLS FROM PARENTAL EXAMPLES

First do this exercise on your own. Then, if appropriate, discuss your answers with a partner or in a group.

1. What were the examples set by your parents in each of the following relating skills areas. In most instances 'parents' refers to your biological parents. However, if a step-parent or surrogate parent has been more important to you, answer in respect of him or her.

Sender skills	Your mother	Your father
Talking about their experiences		
Showing their feelings		
Standing up for themselves		

Receiver skills	Your mother	Your father
Paying attention		
Understanding another person's communications		
Showing understanding of another's communications		

Solving relationship problems skills	Your mother	Your father
Managing anger constructively		
Confronting problems assertively		
Working for rational solutions		

2.   Summarize the effects on your current relating skills strengths and deficits of your parents' examples in each of the following areas: (a) sending information, (b) receiving information and (c) solving relationship problems.

EXERCISE 2.4 LEARNING LIFESKILLS FROM PARENTAL CONSEQUENCES

First do this exercise on your own. Then, if appropriate, discuss your answers with a partner or in a group.

1.   Indicate the extent to which you were rewarded by your parents for each of the following behaviours by putting an M in the box that best describes your mother's reaction and an F in the box that best describes your father's reaction. Try to give one or two specific examples of the consequences they provided for you. If answering in terms of a biological parent is inappropriate, answer for a step-parent or surrogate parent.

Reward from parents

Your behaviour	Much	Little	None	Punished	Example(s)
Expressing affection to him or her					
Expressing anger to him or her					
Expressing your opinions on current affairs					
Expressing negative feelings about yourself (e.g. depression)					
Expressing positive feelings about yourself (e.g. happiness)					
Saying you wish to be left out of parental disagreements					
Being prepared to listen to him or her					
Responding helpfully to him or her					
Requesting participation in decisions involving you					
Wanting to discuss a conflict between you					
Stating your position in the conflict					
Trying to understand his or her position					
Placating and giving in to him or her					
Working for a rational solution to a conflict with him or her					

2.   Summarize the effects on your current relating skills strengths and deficits of the consequences provided for your behaviour by your parents.

EXERCISE 2.5   HOW I MAINTAIN A LIFESKILLS DEFICIT

First do this exercise on your own. Then, if appropriate, discuss your answers with a partner or in a group.

1. Select a specific action skills lifeskills deficit that you are currently maintaining (for example, either poor showing affection skills or poor saying 'no' skills).

2. Assess the contribution of each of the following thinking skills deficits to maintaining your action skills deficit:
    (a) negative self-talk
    (b) unrealistic personal rules
    (c) perceiving inaccurately
    (d) explaining cause deficits
    (e) unrealistic predictions about change

3. Specify ways and assess the extent to which unchanged environmental circumstances contribute to maintaining your action skills deficit.

4. What stresses activate or might activate (worsen) your action skills deficit? You may repeat this exercise for another action skills deficit.

EXERCISE 2.6   GROUP DISCUSSION: LEARNING LIFESKILLS

This is intended as a group exercise, though it may be done individually or in pairs. For each part:

1. Spend 10 to 15 minutes answering the question in groups of three or four.

2. Each group shares its answers with the whole group.

3. Then the whole group ranks the six most important points from the most to the least important.

Part A   Acquiring lifeskills
List the six most important ways or processes by which people acquire lifeskills strengths and/or deficits.

Part B   Maintaining lifeskills
List the six most important ways or processes by which people maintain lifeskills strengths and/or deficits.

THREE
Lifeskills model of practice

To make the growth choice instead of the fear choice a dozen times a day is to move a dozen times a day towards self-actualization.

Abraham Maslow

CHAPTER QUESTIONS

- *What are lifeskills counselling's goals?*

- *What is the difference between a problem management and a problematic skills model of practice?*

- *What are the five stages of the DASIE lifeskills counselling model of practice?*

- *What counsellor skills and client behaviours illustrate each stage of DASIE?*

- *What are the issues in applying the DASIE lifeskills counselling model of practice?*

GOALS

Lifeskills counselling has triple goals: managing current problems, developing skills to manage and prevent these problems now and in future, and developing the skilled person. As such, lifeskills counselling goals can be overall or focused, elegant or inelegant. Focused or inelegant goals entail helping clients to develop skills to manage specific problems. The elegant application of lifeskills counselling aims to develop the skilled person.

The skilled person

The skilled person possesses the knowledge and skills to live effectively in all the main areas of life. Terms like 'self-actualizing', 'self-realizing' and 'fully functioning person' are regarded as too vague and alien to the everyday language of most clients. Given time and client commitment, lifeskills counselling seeks to empower the skilled person rather than the person who is only skilled in specific areas. The skilled person can make appropriate choices in a range of areas as well as confront new situations effectively. Below, illustrative lifeskills required by the skilled person are grouped according to the five Rs of affirming psychological life.

- *Responsiveness*. Responsiveness skills include existential awareness, awareness of feelings, awareness of inner motivation and sensitivity to anxiety and guilt.

- *Realism*. Realism refers to the thinking skills listed earlier, such as coping self-talk and visualizing.

- *Relating*. Relating skills include initiating, conversing, disclosing, listening, showing caring, cooperating, assertion, managing anger and solving relationship problems.

- *Rewarding activity*. Rewarding activity skills include identifying interests, work skills, study skills, leisure skills and looking after physical health skills.

- *Right-and-wrong*. Right-and-wrong skills include social interest that transcends one's immediate environment and ethical living.

Problem management and problematic skills goals

Lifeskills counselling goals encompass assisting clients both to manage problems and to alter the underlying problematic skills that sustain problems. D'Zurilla and Maydeu-Olivares (1995) distinguish between problems and solutions. Problems are life situations 'in which no effective or adaptive coping response is immediately apparent or available to the individual, thus requiring problem-solving behavior' (p. 410). Solutions are the products or outcomes of the problem-solving process when applied to specific problematic situations.

Problem management or problem solving models, such as those of Carkhuff (1987) and Egan (1994), are useful, since frequently clients require help to manage or solve immediate problems. However, a big drawback of such models is that they inadequately address the *repetition phenomenon*, the repetitive nature of many clients' problems. In the past clients may have repeated underlying self-defeating behaviours, or lifeskills deficits, and they are at risk of continuing to do so in future. An example of such repetition across time – *vertical* repetition – is that of people who keep losing jobs because of poor relating to employers skills. Clients may repeat self-defeating behaviours, or lifeskills deficits, across a range of current situations – *horizontal* repetition.

For example, the same people may be non-assertive at home, at work, in leisure activities and so on.

Clients require assistance in developing lifeskills strengths that last into the future and not just in managing or solving specific current problems. However, frequently practical considerations limit counsellor contact with individual clients: for example, heavy counsellor case loads and clients being content with short-term problem amelioration. Nevertheless, counsellors who only aim to help clients to manage or solve immediate and specific problems when they could work more thoroughly with clients to alter problematic skills do clients a disservice. In reality, often counsellors and clients compromise on the amount of time and effort they take to address underlying patterns of skills deficits that predispose and position clients for further problems.

Following is a vignette illustrating the difference between identifying a problem and identifying a problematic skill or skills deficit.

> Mary was a middle-aged divorcee with custody of her 15-year-old son Rick. For just over a year she had been dating George, a divorcee with custody of two boys, aged 8 and 10. For some months Mary had been planning a camping holiday. Repeatedly Mary had tried to talk Rick round to having George and his two children on the holiday. Rick adamantly refused. Mary was very reluctant to bring Rick's refusal to the attention of George because he might be hurt and react angrily. The date for the proposed holiday was getting nearer and nearer. When asked, Mary told the counsellor that she had difficulty bring up difficult issues across a range of relationships and that she disliked any form of conflict. The counsellor pointed out to Mary the difference between managing a problem – levelling with George about Rick's refusal – and using this problem to build skills for confronting issues in this and other relationships both now and in future. Mary agreed that developing her confronting problems skills would help her not only with George but also with others, such as Rick.

DASIE: THE FIVE-STAGE MODEL

The practice of lifeskills counselling is structured around DASIE, a systematic five-stage model (see Figure 3.1). The model provides a framework or set of guidelines for counsellor choices. DASIE is a five-stage model not only for managing or solving problems but also for addressing underlying problematic skills. DASIE's five stages are:

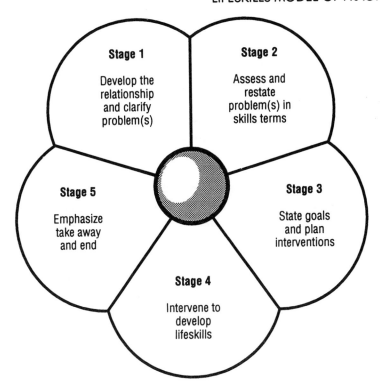

Figure 3.1 *DAISIE: the five-stage lifeskills counselling model*

D DEVELOP the relationship and clarify problem(s)
A ASSESS and restate problem(s) in skills terms
S STATE goals and plan interventions
I INTERVENE to develop lifeskills
E EMPHASIZE take-away and end

Stage 1 Develop the relationship and clarify problem(s)

Stage 1 starts with pre-helping contact with clients and either ends at some time in the initial interview or takes longer. It has two main overlapping functions: developing supportive counselling relationships and working with clients to identify and obtain fuller descriptions of problems. Supportive counselling relationships go beyond offering empathy, non-possessive warmth and genuineness, to fostering more actively client self-support. The nature of the supportive relationship differs according to the stage of the model. In stage 1 counsellors use relating skills to provide emotional support as clients tell and elaborate their stories. In subsequent stages, counsellors use relating skills to support training interventions.

Many of the counsellor skills used in stage 1 are the same as those used in other approaches: for example, reflective responding, summarizing and confronting. Counsellors collaborate with clients to explore, clarify and understand problems. Together they act as detectives to 'sniff out' and discover clients' real problems and agendas. Then they break them down into their component parts. An analogy for the role of questioning in initial sessions is that of plants and their root system. For example, a client comes to counselling saying, 'I am depressed. Help me.' This statement about depression represents the part of the plant above ground. However, by listening, observing and effective questioning, the counsellor starts identifying roots of the client's problem in five different areas: relates poorly to spouse, has a difficult parent, is short of friends, has few pleasant activities and gets little satisfaction from work. Now both counsellor and client have information about the overall problem's sub-structure, so that they can develop hypotheses about how the client contributes to sustaining each problem area.

Counsellors can use skills language when structuring initial sessions. One possibility is to start the session by giving clients an open-ended permission to tell their stories. After they respond, the following statement might structure the remainder of the session.

> 'You've given me some idea of why you've come. Now I'd like to ask some more questions to help us to clarify your problem(s) (specify). Then, depending on what we find, I will suggest some skills to help you cope better. Once we agree on what skills might help you, then we can look at ways to develop them. Does this way of proceeding sound all right?'

When structuring, counsellors can briefly state reasons for adopting a lifeskills approach. Following is an example.

> 'It can be useful to think of problems in terms of the skills you need to cope better. This way you get some 'handles' or 'keys' to work for change.'

Homework in the form of 'take-away' assignments is a feature of lifeskills counselling. Between-session learning is enhanced by clients listening at home to audio-cassettes of their counselling sessions. In addition, counsellors may negotiate other homework assignments with clients: for instance, completing monitoring logs.

Stage 2   Assess and restate problem(s) in skills terms

The object of this stage is to build a bridge between *describing* and *actively working on* problems and their underlying skills deficits. In stage 1, problems were described, amplified and clarified largely in everyday language. The description of clients' problems represents an expansion of their internal viewpoints rather than providing them with different insights. In stage 2, counsellors build upon information collected in stage 1 to explore hypotheses about how clients think and act to sustain difficulties. Counsellors add to and go beyond clients' present perceptions to look for 'handles' on how to work for change. They collaborate to break down clients' problems into their component skills deficits. Whereas stage 1 might end with descriptive summaries of problems in everyday terms, stage 2 ends with a redefinition of at least either the main or the most pressing problem in skills terms.

In stage 2, the nature of the supportive relationship changes. In stage 1, counsellors support clients in telling their stories in their own terms. In stage 2, counsellors support clients in making sense of their stories. A critical ingredient of stage 2 is for counsellors to maintain a skills focus. Maintaining a skills focus does not mean that counsellors immediately translate everything clients say into skills language. However, the question at the back of counsellors' minds in stage 2 is always: 'What skills deficits sustain clients' problems?' Most clients do not think of their problems in skills language, so counsellors require sensitivity in when and how they convey that clients may have specific thinking and action skills deficits.

The emphasis in counsellors' questions differs in stage 2 from that in stage 1. In stage 1, counsellors ask questions to clarify clients' existing frames of reference. In stage 2, counsellors are likely to question as much from their own as from their clients' frames of reference. Much questioning is based on information wittingly or unwittingly provided by clients: clues, hunches, how things are said, what is left unsaid and overt and subtle indications of underlying thought patterns. While the major focus is on pinpointing skills deficits, attention is also paid to identifying skills strengths and resources. Strength reviews both identify skills for coping with problems and prevent assessments from becoming too negative. Following is an example where the counsellor attempts to help a middle-aged client, Tania, who gave up an office management job in a university department, to identify her strengths.

Counsellor: Uh-uhm. So, I'm first going to ask you something which may seem a little bit strange. But what do you think were your strengths in how you handled the problems both at the office and as a worker?
Client: Um. How I handled the problems? My strengths were ... that's hard because I keep focusing on what I didn't do right.

If they have not already done so, counsellors can suggest the value of breaking down problems into the component skills that sustain them. Furthermore, they introduce clients to the distinction between thinking skills and action skills, possibly using the inner and outer game analogy. In the following excerpt, the counsellor lays the groundwork for identifying two of Tania's thinking skills deficits: an unrealistic rule about perfection and choosing not to perceive her strengths and others' positive feedback.

Counsellor: There was a little more of the negative, it sounds to me, than there should have been.
Client: That's true. And I think too that was based on the fact that I thought I should be able to do everything absolutely perfectly.
Counsellor: And that gets into a rule about perfection.
Client: Yes.
Counsellor: Yes.
Client: Cause I wouldn't have been happy with anything less than them saying she's the best office manager we've had.
Counsellor: Right, right, right.

Client: I mean, in fact, I met one of the staff members in the street the other day and he said, 'You're an absolute legend and we keep saying we need another Tania.' And I keep saying, 'Oh dear.'

Counsellor: Right, so it's partly your rule about perfection, that you felt you may not have measured up to perfection, but it's also that you didn't perceive your strengths and the fact that the academic staff did think you were super.

Client: Yeah.

Counsellor: But Tania wasn't thinking she was super.

Counsellors need to develop good skills at restating problems in skills terms and communicating these working definitions to clients. A good restatement succinctly suggests clients' main skills deficits that sustain problems. Counsellors need to distinguish important from less important material. Restatements that are too comprehensive confuse. Write restatements in skills terms on whiteboards. Visual presentation makes it easier for clients to retain what you say; if necessary suggest alterations, and make written records.

Counsellors use a simple diagram to present thinking and action skills weaknesses for sustaining each problem (see Table 3.1). At the top of the table there are headings for 'Thinking skills deficits/goals' and 'Action skills deficits/goals'. These headings are divided by a long vertical line down the middle to allow specific deficits to be listed on either side.

Restatements of problems in skills terms need to be negotiated with clients. Counsellors require good questioning and facilitation skills when checking restatements with clients. If counsellors, in stages 1 and 2, have competently gathered information, skills restatements should flow reasonably logically from this material. Clients who share their counsellors' conceptualizations of problems are more likely to commit themselves to developing self-helping skills than clients resisting counsellors' conceptualizations. Restatements of problems in skills terms are essentially hypotheses, based on careful analysis of available information, about clients' thinking and action skills deficits. As hypotheses they are open to modification in the light of further or better information.

Table 3.1 *Restatement in skills terms of Tania's office management problem*

Thinking skills deficits/goals	Action skills deficits/goals
Insufficiently owning responsibility for being a chooser at work	Giving instructions non-assertively (poor verbal, voice and body messages)
Unrealistic personal rules: for example, everyone must approve of me, I must be the perfect manager	Getting support skills: for example, from department head
Inaccurately perceiving for example, not acknowledging own strengths, discounting positive feedback	
Negative self-talk for example, about confronting difficult colleagues	

Restating problems in skills terms can be difficult. Mistakes in restating not only lead to time and effort being wasted, but may contribute to clients being even less able to manage problems.

Table 3.1 is a restatement of Tania's office management problem in skills terms. Even though she had given up this job, Tania wanted to understand the issues raised by it because they were undermining her confidence in getting another job.

Stage 3   State goals and plan interventions

Stage 3 builds on counsellors' restatements in skills terms to focus on the question: 'What is the best way to develop the required self-helping skills?' Stage 3 consists of two phases: stating deficits as goals and planning interventions.

STATING DEFICITS AS GOALS Goals can be stated at different levels of specificity. First, goals can be stated in overall terms, such as 'I want to feel less depressed,' 'I want to improve my marriage' or 'I want to come to terms with my disability and get back into life.' Such overall goal statements give clients visions about what they want from counselling. However, overall statements refer more to ends than to means.

Second, goals can be stated in terms of the skills required to attain ends. Stage 3 requires this level of specificity to establish working goals. In stage 3 counsellors should state goals clearly and succinctly. Assuming that counsellors succeed in restating problems in skills terms, stating goals becomes a relatively simple matter. Working goals are the flip-side of restatements: positive statements of skills strengths to replace existing skills deficits. For instance, Tania's thinking skills goals are to develop her skills of: owning responsibility for being a chooser at work; possessing realistic personal rules about perfection and approval; accurately perceiving her strengths and others' feedback; and coping self-talk for confronting difficult colleagues. Tania's action skills goals are to develop her skills of giving instructions assertively and of getting support. Counsellors can easily change, on the whiteboard, statements of deficits into statements of goals. Counsellors should ensure that clients understand and agree with goals. Then client and counsellor record this statement as a basis for their future work.

Third, goals can be stated still more precisely. For example, Tania's giving instructions assertively skills can be broken down still further into specific verbal, voice and body message goals for different target people. Each case needs to be treated on its merits. Clients can only cope with so much information at any one time. A risk of getting into too much detail in an initial session is that clients retain little if anything. Usually detailed descriptions of skills goals are best left to later sessions.

PLANNING INTERVENTIONS Stating deficits as goals provides the bridge to choosing interventions. Counsellors hypothesize not only about goals, but also about ways to attain them. An important distinction exists between interventions and plans. Interventions are intentional behaviours, on the part of either counsellors or clients, designed to help clients to attain problem management and problematic skills goals. Plans are statements of how to combine and sequence interventions to attain goals.

Clients come for counselling with a wide variety of problems, expectations, motivations, priorities, time constraints and lifeskills strengths and deficits. Counsellors tailor intervention plans to individual clients. In very focused counselling, say anxiety about an imminent test, counsellors are likely to plan to manage the immediate problem, with less emphasis on altering underlying problematic skills. With more time to alter problematic skills, counsellors may choose between structured plans and open plans.

Structured plans are step-by-step training and learning outlines of interventions for attaining specific goals. Sometimes structured plans involve using existing material: for instance, developing relaxation skills using a programme based on Bernstein and Borkovec's (1973) *Progressive Relaxation Training: A Manual for the Helping Professions.*

Counsellors and clients can also design partially structured plans to attain goals. For instance, in the case of a recently fired executive, certain sessions might be set aside for testing to assess interests and aptitudes and for attending a brief course to develop specific action skills, such as resumé writing and interview skills. Agendas for the remaining sessions are negotiated at the start of each session.

Open plans allow helpers and clients, without predetermined structure, to choose which interventions, to attain which goals, when. Open plans have the great advantage of flexibility. Clients may be more motivated to work on skills and material relevant at any given time than to run through predetermined programmes independent of current considerations. Furthermore, owing to the frequently repetitive nature of clients' skills deficits, work done in one session may be highly relevant to work done on the same or different problems in other sessions.

Stage 4   Intervene to develop lifeskills

The interventions stage can have three objectives: first, to help clients manage their presenting problems better; second, to assist clients in working on problematic skills and in developing skills strengths for preventing and coping with specific situations; third, to help clients become more skilled persons. Counsellors are developmental educators or, in more colloquial terms, user-friendly coaches. To intervene effectively they require good relating skills and good training skills. It is insufficient to know *what* interventions to offer without also being skilled at *how* to offer them. Skilled counsellors strike appropriate balances between relationship and task orientations; less skilled helpers err in either direction.

Table 3.2 depicts methods of psychological education or training and methods of learning in lifeskills counselling. Counsellors work much of the time with the three training methods of 'tell,' 'show' and 'do'. They require special training skills for each. 'Tell' entails giving clients clear instructions concerning the skills they wish to develop. 'Show' means providing demonstrations of how to implement skills. 'Do' means arranging for clients to perform structured activities and homework tasks.

Individual sessions in the intervention stage may be viewed in four, often overlapping, phases: preparatory, initial, working and ending. The preparatory phase entails counsellors thinking in advance about how best to assist clients. Counsellors ensure that, if appropriate, they have available session plans, training materials (for instance, handouts) and audiovisual aids (for instance, whiteboards and audio-cassette

Table 3.2 *Methods of psychological education or training and of learning*

Psychological education or training method	Learning method
Facilitate	Learning from self-exploring and from experiencing self more fully
Assess	Learning from monitoring and evaluating
Tell	Learning from hearing
Show	Learning from observing
Do	Learning from doing structured activities and take-away assignments
Consolidate	Learning from developing self-helping skills in all the above modes

recorders). The initial phase consists of meeting, greeting and seating, then giving permission to talk. Though it is a skill not restricted to the initial phase, early on counsellors may wish to negotiate session agendas. For instance, counsellors may go from checking whether the client has any current pressing agendas, to reviewing the past week's take-away assignments, to focusing on one or more problematic skills and/ or problems in the client's life. As necessary, agendas may be altered during sessions.

Within a supportive relationship, the working phase focuses on specific thinking skills and action skills interventions designed to help clients manage problems and develop lifeskills strengths. Whenever appropriate, counsellors assist clients to use skills language. The ending phase lasts from towards the end of one session to the beginning of the next. This phase focuses on summarizing the major session learnings, negotiating take-away assignments, strengthening commitment to between-session work and rehearsing and practising skills outside counselling.

Thinking skills interventions vary according to which skill is targeted. Common themes are increasing awareness of deficits in the targeted skill, challenging faulty thinking and training in effective thinking. For example, a counsellor working with a client, one of whose working goals is to develop a more realistic rule about approval, can intervene in the following sequence: introduce and raise awareness of the skill of choosing realistic personal rules; identify the current unrealistic rule and its consequences; dispute the unrealistic rule; restate the unrealistic rule into a more realistic rule (for instance, 'Though I would prefer to be liked by my colleagues, what is more important is that I respect myself and do my job as well as I can.'); encourage the client to change his or her actions to accord with the changed rule (for instance, by being more assertive); and emphasize practice and self-helping.

Action skills interventions include developing clients' self-monitoring skills, sequencing graded tasks, conducting rehearsals and role-plays, timetabling activities, using exercises and games, using counsellors' aides and assisting clients to identify supports in their home environments for their changed actions. Often lifeskills counsellors work with clients to set up personal experiments in which clients use new action skills in real-life settings on a try-out basis. Clients develop 'If . . . then . . . ' statements. In the 'If' part of the statement they stipulate a specific situation and the targeted skills they will use in it. In the 'then' part of the statement they predict the consequences of using their changed behaviours. After a period of rehearsal and practice, clients try out their changed action skills in real life. Then, together with their counsellors, they evaluate the consequences.

Interventions for focusing on feelings emphasize developing clients' thinking skills and action skills. In restating problems and stating working goals, counsellors need to distinguish between experiencing feelings, expressing feelings and managing unwanted feelings. Interventions for assisting clients to *experience* their feelings include legitimizing the importance of feelings, active listening, using feelings questions, role-play methods, confronting unauthenticity, training in inner listening and developing appropriate thinking skills. Interventions for *expressing* feelings are the same as the interventions for developing action skills described above. Interventions for *managing* feelings vary according to the feeling to be managed. For instance, thinking skills interventions for managing depression can target negative predictions, unrealistic personal rules, unnecessarily negative self-perceptions and apportioning too much of the cause for negative events to oneself. Action skills interventions for managing depression can target relating, assertion and engaging in pleasant activities skills.

Consolidation of learned skills as self-helping skills takes place during, at the end of and between each session. Frequently clients are asked to fill out 'take-away' sheets on which they record skills work done on the whiteboard during the session. Either counsellor or client can write down on a 'take-away' sheet any mutually agreed homework assignments. Providing written assignment instructions for clients serves the following purposes: giving a message that take-away assignments are important; clarifying and helping clients remember what is required; and providing something in writing that can be posted as a reminder.

Stage 5   Emphasize take-away and end

Most often either counsellors or clients bring up the topic of ending before the final session. This allows both parties to work through the various task and relationship issues connected with ending the contact. A useful option is to fade contact with some clients by seeing them progressively less often. Certain clients may appreciate the opportunity for booster sessions: say, one, two, three or even six months later. Booster sessions provide both clients and counsellors with the chance to review progress and consolidate self-helping skills. Scheduling follow-up telephone calls can perform some of these functions too.

Lifeskills counselling seeks to avoid the 'train and hope' approach (Goldstein and Keller, 1987; Stokes and Osnes, 1989). For instance, prior to the ending stage, counsellors structure realistic expectations when discussing with clients restatements in skills terms and working goals. The concept of lifeskills gets away from notions of magic and cure. Counsellors explicitly and repeatedly state that clients have to work and practise not only to acquire but also to maintain the targeted lifeskills.

Counsellors attempt to build clients' self-observation and assessment skills. Transfer and maintenance of skills is encouraged by such means as developing clients' self-instructional abilities, working with real-life situations during counselling and using between-session time productively to listen to session cassettes and to rehearse and practise skills. Often counsellors make up short take-away cassettes focused on the use of specific skills in specific situations, for instance, the use of coping self-talk to handle anxiety when one is waiting to deliver a public speech. Counsellors can encourage clients to make up similar coping self-talk cassettes for other situations, for instance, participating in meetings. Thus, clients not only possess cassettes they can use to maintain skills in future, they have also acquired the skills of making new cassettes, if needed.

In addition, counsellors work with clients to anticipate difficulties and setbacks to taking away and maintaining lifeskills. Then together they develop and rehearse coping strategies for preventing and managing lapses and relapses. Sometimes clients require help in identifying people to support their efforts to maintain skills. Counsellors also provide information about further skills building opportunities.

DASIE: CASE EXAMPLE

Following is a case example illustrating each stage of the DASIE lifeskills counselling model of practice. I present only the bare bones of the case. Not all cases fit so neatly into the five stages of the DASIE model as this one.

Stage 1   Develop the relationship and clarify problem(s)

Rob, a married man in his mid-forties, decides to see a counsellor, Sue Clark, because he is afraid his marriage may break up because of his temper outbursts. Sue starts the initial session by telling Rob that this is an exploratory interview to find out what concerns him and to see if together they can identify possible options and skills for dealing with his problems. Sue encourages Rob to tell his story about why he has come and to describe his concerns more fully. Sue's verbal, voice and body messages convey both person-orientation and task-orientation. Within the context of a supportive relationship, this is a working session. Early on, Rob reveals that his wife Betty knows he has come for counselling and approves, but does not wish to come herself. Rob and Betty are the parents of three girls, aged 15, 13 and 11.

The precipitating crisis was that Rob struck his oldest daughter, Ruth, whom he has often found hard to handle. Rob cares deeply for family life and is scared that the family may disintegrate unless he gets on top of his temper. Sue encourages Rob to describe how he and Ruth relate, including focusing on the recent physical violence. Rob also shares his perceptions of how he and the other family members relate. He expresses mixed feelings about his wife, who dislikes trouble at home and does not always support his discipline attempts. Rob has a short fuse, people stir him. He has had trouble outside the home too, such as rows with employers and colleagues. Rob recalls that his father was very strict and had a bad temper. Sue facilitates Rob's description of his problem and of how he and others think and behave. Sue is alert for clues concerning Rob's thinking and action skills deficits. For instance, when Rob says that people stir him he gives the impression that he has no choice over how he reacts.

As the initial stage proceeds, Rob experiences Sue as helping him to clarify and understand his problem more fully. After a series of exploratory questions, interspersed with empathic reflections, Sue summarizes the content of the interview so far and checks on Rob's reactions to the summary. By now not only does Sue have a greater knowledge of Rob and his problem, but Rob has broadened his perspective too. Nevertheless, Sue is aware that further work remains to be done in moving beyond a descriptive summary of Rob's problem to restating it in skills terms.

Stage 2 Assess and restate problem(s) in skills terms

Sue Clark, after checking her descriptive summary with Rob, said she would now like to explore some specific areas of how Rob thought and acted to see if they could find ways in which he could improve his situation. Sue observed that some things Rob said indicated that he thought that he had little choice over how he behaved. Rob agreed that he had little control over his temper. As far as he was concerned, he had always been that way and he wondered if it were his nature. Sue also explored what Rob said to himself when faced with provocations: for example, his daughter Ruth coming home later than agreed after being out with her boyfriend. Rob's self-talk appeared to fire him up rather than calm him down. The realism of his rules concerning family behaviour was another thinking skills area that, in an initial way, Sue explored with Rob. Because the action skills of how Rob communicated to his family had already been covered in stage 1, Sue did not repeat this exploration.

Using the whiteboard, Sue suggested a tentative restatement in skills terms of Rob's anger management problem. Her restatement included the following *thinking* skills deficits: (1) inadequately acknowledging that he was always a chooser and responsible for his thoughts, feelings and actions; (2) using negative anger-engendering self-talk when faced with provocations; and (3) possibly having rigid and unrealistic personal rules concerning standards of behaviour in the family. *Action* skills deficits included: (1) poor listening skills, especially when angry; (2) poor assertion skills (verbal, voice and body), such as in how he stated his wishes about his daughter's behaviour; and (3) poor solving relationship problems skills. Sue checked with Rob each part of this restatement to see whether he understood it and also whether he agreed with it. Rob expressed relief when the restatement in skills terms was explained to him, since, for the first time, he thought he could learn to control his temper.

Stage 3 State goals and plan interventions

Sue Clark clarified with Rob that his overall goal was to improve his relationship with Ruth and hence improve his marriage. Now Sue turned the previously agreed restatement in skills terms of Rob's anger management problem into a statement of goals. Rob's *thinking* skills goals were to: (1) acknowledge that he was a chooser and responsible for his thoughts, feelings and actions; (2) use coping self-talk when faced with provocations; and (3) develop realistic personal rules concerning standards of family behaviour. Rob's *action* skills goals included developing: (1) good listening skills; (2) assertion skills, with specific reference to how he stated his wishes about Ruth's behaviour; and (3) solving relationship problems skills.

Sue realized that Rob's objective was to develop some skills as quickly as possible rather than to participate in long-term counselling. Instead of designing a step-by-step training plan, Sue suggested that the best way to proceed was to help Rob to develop thinking and action skills in relation to material brought into each session. Sue required homework, including listening to audio-cassettes of sessions. Sue also gave Rob a 'take-away' sheet on which she asked him to log how he thought, felt and acted before, during and after specific anger provocations.

Stage 4   Intervene to develop lifeskills

Sue Clark saw Rob for a total of seven sessions over a two-and-a-half month period. The intervention stage lasted from the second to the sixth session. At the start of each session, Sue checked whether Rob had any pressing concerns and how he progressed with take-away assignments. Sue approached each session flexibly within the context of the agreed skills restatement and goals. Sue's considerations in establishing session agendas included both where Rob wanted to focus and how best to develop Rob's self-helping skills.

Sue trained Rob in the thinking skills goal that he was a chooser partly by articulating this as a skill, partly by encouraging Rob to become more aware of the consequences of his choices, partly by reframing his language – for example, 'Ruth made me so angry' was reformulated into 'I chose to get very angry with Ruth' – and partly by reflective responses that continuously and unobtrusively emphasized personal responsibility. Sue trained Rob in coping self-talk skills by spending part of an early session directly teaching him by instruction, demonstration and coached practice. In subsequent sessions, Sue checked out how well Rob used his coping self-talk skills outside counselling. Sue trained the skill of choosing realistic personal rules by getting Rob to identify and examine his rules regarding his own and Ruth's behaviour in relation to specific situations that Rob brought into helping. Then, using the whiteboard, Sue helped Rob to dispute unrealistic rules and restate them more realistically.

In regard to attaining action skills goals, Sue taught Rob some simple listening skills: for instance, not interrupting and checking out how well he understood his daughter's position. Sue also trained Rob in action skills for being more assertive in stating wants and wishes and in solving relationship problems. She reviewed with him different ways of acting in specific family situations and their consequences. When role-playing the targeted action skills with Rob, Sue emphasized voice and body messages as well as verbal messages. Often, she used the whiteboard for working on both thinking and action skills.

Within sessions, Sue ended each skills training segment by asking Rob to record the main learning points on take-away sheets. Sue ended each session by negotiating 'take-away' assignments. Rob listened to the cassettes of preceding sessions as part of his homework. Since Rob was surrounded by his family, Sue encouraged him to start using his skills at home and to 'learn on the job'. Rob's wife and daughters appreciated his efforts to work on his temper. Even early on, Rob's efforts were rewarded by less family tension.

Stage 5   Emphasize take-away and end

Throughout counselling, Sue Clark worked to consolidate Rob's managing anger skills as take-away self-helping skills. During the sixth session, Sue and Rob decided that they would probably have one more session in four weeks' time when Sue came back from an overseas trip. In this session, Rob mentioned that he felt he had lost some of his influence in the family by adopting a more reasonable approach to provocations. Using the whiteboard, Sue developed with Rob a balance-sheet of positive and negative consequences of using his skills. As a result, Rob perceived the balance to be heavily in favour of maintaining them.

Rob started the seventh and final session by stating that his life was going much better. Sue helped Rob to provide specific evidence for this assessment. Together Rob and she explored each of Rob's main relationships to see how well he was using his skills and with what consequences. Rob was definitely attaining his initial goal of an improved relationship with his oldest daughter, Ruth. Rob affirmed his decision to end counselling. Sue helped him to review his learnings from the sessions. Rob mentioned how he was more prepared to think first, talk things over and play the game of life more with his head. Rob thought that there were still problems in his marriage, but he did not wish to work on them at present. Sue Clark left it open for Rob to return for counselling, if necessary.

APPLYING THE MODEL

Counsellors, in the best interests of clients, need to apply the DASIE counselling model flexibly. Managing problems and altering problematic skills rarely proceed according to neatly ordered stages. The stages tend to overlap. Counsellors may revert to earlier stages as more information or new problems emerge.

Short-term counselling

DASIE is a model of central tendency. The model assumes that much counselling is relatively short-term, say three to ten sessions, focused on one or two main problems and problematic skills areas. However, counselling can also be very short-term (say one or two sessions), medium-term (say 11 to 20 sessions) or long-term (more than 20 sessions). Whatever the length, counsellors adjust how person-oriented or task-oriented to be. For example, in short-term counselling an early skills focus may be inappropriate with recently bereaved clients needing space to tell their stories and experience their grief. On the other hand, an immediate skills focus may be highly appropriate with clients anxious about imminent examinations, public speeches, meetings with estranged spouses or job interviews.

Medium-term and long-term counselling

Since different reasons exist for medium-term and long-term counselling, there are no simple answers to how best to go about it. Vulnerable clients may require more gentle and nurturing relationships than robust clients and take longer to attain insight into how they sustain problems. However, it is possible to overgeneralize. From the initial session some vulnerable clients may appreciate identifying and working on one or two specific skills deficits.

Counselling may go more slowly where clients' starting off points are low in specific skills areas. Counsellors may have to break down skills more, spend more time on instruction and demonstration, and offer clients more support as they rehearse and practice skills. In extended counselling, much session time is spent on working through the application of targeted skills to specific issues in clients' lives, including their fears about using the skills. Where clients possess multiple problems and skills deficits, counsellors and clients face the issue of prioritizing those skills most in need of attention. In extended contacts, counsellors and clients also have to prioritize between initial and emerging problems and problematic skills areas. Emerging problems may arise through clients themselves changing or through changes in their environments. Restatements in skills terms and working goals may require reformulation. Clients' progress may be slowed down by others in their environments: for example, teachers, parents or spouses. If so, counsellors need to consider whether it is worth broadening counselling to include them.

Counselling existential concerns

Lifeskills counselling can be used to help clients to confront existential concerns as well as immediate problems. Take the case of people suffering from terminal cancer. Such people may require assistance in at least four areas: confronting and coming to terms with death anxiety; dealing with problems that arise from the cancer experience, such as changes in physical appearance and declining health; coping with problems that they have independent of their cancer, such as a stressful lifestyle or poor communication with a spouse; and finding genuine meaning for the remainder of their lives (Nelson-Jones and Cosolo, 1994). A skilled lifeskills counsellor is alert to and prepared to work in all these areas.

Adapting to the model

Beginning counsellors are likely to find that it takes time to become proficient in the lifeskills counselling model. This training model requires counsellors to go beyond offering good counselling relationship skills to also offering good assessment and training skills. The model requires counsellors to possess effective inner game or thinking skills as well as effective outer game or action skills. Many beginning counsellors experience difficulty in making the transition from *talking* relationships, based on good facilitation skills, to *training* relationships, based on assessment and specific interventions designed to assist clients to manage problems and problematic skills patterns.

The lifeskills counselling model requires counsellors to step outside their everyday language to conceptualize problems in skills terms. Some beginning counsellors do not find this congenial and take much time to make the transition, if at all. Further, the lifeskills counselling model requires counsellors to develop a range of specific interventions related to clients' problem and problematic skills. Again, it takes time to build up a repertoire of interventions. In fact, there is always room for improvement. Proficiency in lifeskills counselling is a lifetime challenge.

CHAPTER HIGHLIGHTS

- *Lifeskills counselling has triple goals: managing or solving current problems; developing skills to prevent and manage specific problems now and in future; and developing skilled persons.*

- *Beyond a presenting problem, problematic skills can manifest themselves both horizontally, across a range of similar current situations, and vertically, in future similar situations.*

- *The skilled person possesses significant lifeskills strengths in each of the five Rs of affirming psychological life: responsiveness, realism, relating, rewarding activity and right-and-wrong.*

- *DASIE is a five-stage model for helping clients to manage or solve problems and alter problematic lifeskills patterns.*

- *In stage 1, develop the relationship and clarify problem(s), counsellors develop supportive relationships with clients and work with them to identify and clarify problems.*

- *In stage 2, assess and restate problem(s) in skills terms, counsellors and clients collaborate to pinpoint thinking and action skills deficits that sustain problems.*

- *In stage 3, state goals and plan interventions, counsellors translate skills restatements into goals and plan interventions to attain them.*

- *In stage 4, intervene to develop lifeskills, within the context of supportive relationships counsellors apply a range of interventions to develop clients' self-helping skills.*

- *In stage 5, emphasize take-away and end, the counselling contact ends with further attention paid to clients' ability to take away lifeskills, a process that is built into lifeskills counselling from its start.*

- *Counsellors should apply the stages of the DASIE lifeskills counselling model flexibly, for instance, their sequencing may overlap.*

- *Counsellors require flexibility in adapting DASIE to short-term, medium-term and long-term counselling. Counsellors can help clients to address existential concerns.*

- *Beginning counsellors are likely to take time to become proficient in the lifeskills counselling model. Proficiency in lifeskills counselling is a lifetime challenge.*

EXERCISE 3.1 LIFESKILLS COUNSELLING PRACTICE

Answer the following questions on your own, with a partner or in a group.

Counselling questions

1. What is the skilled person and what are the five Rs for affirming psychological life? What are your reactions to viewing goals for counselling and living in this way?

2. What is the difference between a problem management goal and a problematic skills goal? Do you consider this a useful distinction for counselling practice and, if so, why?

3. What do you consider are the advantages and disadvantages of counsellors working within systematic stage models of the counselling process?

4. What is the role of the counsellor–client relationship in lifeskills counselling?

5. What are the goals of stage 1 of the DASIE model? Describe some counsellor skills for attaining them.

6. How do lifeskills counsellors go about assessing clients' problems?

7. Describe some important skills for restating clients' problems in skills terms.

8. What are the different levels of specificity for stating clients' goals and which level applies to stating working goals?

9. What is the difference between an intervention and a plan? Describe some different kinds of plans.

10. What are 'trainer skills' and what is their role in lifeskills counselling?

11. Describe some interventions for developing clients' thinking skills.

12. Describe some interventions for developing clients' action skills.

13. Describe some interventions for helping clients:
    (a) to experience feelings;
    (b) to express feelings;
    (c) to manage unwanted feelings.

14. What skills do lifeskills counsellors use for consolidating clients' trained skills as take-away self-helping skills?

15. What are your initial thoughts and feelings about the DASIE lifeskills counselling model of practice?

Self-referent questions
1. How skilled a person are you? Answer with respect to each of the five Rs.

2. Identify a problem in your life and restate it in skills terms, stipulating at least one thinking skills deficit and one action skills deficit.

3. Translate the thinking skills deficits and the action skills deficits stipulated above into a statement of goals and develop a plan to attain them.

4. Implement your plan and evaluate the consequences of doing so.

5. What relevance, if any, has the theory and practice of lifeskills counselling for how you live?

FOUR
Counsellors as persons

I am simply a human being, more or less.
Saul Bellow

CHAPTER QUESTIONS

- *What are your motives for counselling?*

- *How emotionally responsive are you?*

- *How confident are you?*

- *What anxieties and fears do you possess?*

- *What is your physical health?*

- *What is your sexuality?*

- *What sex-role identity and expectations do you possess?*

- *What are your values?*

- *What are your ethics?*

- *What culture and cross-cultural skills do you bring?*

- *What race and racial skills do you bring?*

- *What social class and social class skills do you bring?*

Counsellors and clients are made from the same human clay. Counsellors are persons first and counsellors second. Each brings various skills, characteristics and attributes to the task. This chapter focuses on *you*, what you bring to counsellor training and to counselling. Some characteristics, such as your biological sex, you cannot change. Other characteristics, such as cross-cultural sensitivity, you can improve. In all instances, your personal characteristics influence how you counsel.

Counselling differs from most other occupations in that the tools are *people* who use various *people* skills to help *people* to help themselves. Contrast this with dentists, who use tools, such as drills, to work on teeth, or with car mechanics, who use tools, such as spanners, to work on cars. In counselling the self is the main instrument or tool. The self that you bring to counsellor training possesses both strengths and deficits. Skilled counsellors enhance strengths and try to overcome personal blocks.

Counselling interviews are ever-changing processes between two people who influence one another. Counsellors and clients bring many characteristics into interviews and experience many thoughts and feelings during them. What transpire between counsellors and clients are not just matters of fact, but also matters of perception. For example, counsellors may perceive their race positively, but their clients may perceive it negatively. Figure 4.1 shows some characteristics that both counsellors and clients bring to interviews.

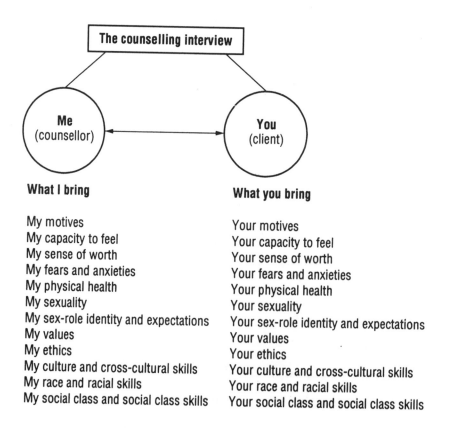

Figure 4.1 *Some characteristics both counsellors and clients bring to counselling*

YOUR MOTIVES

The area of people's motives for counselling is complex and provides fertile soil for self-deception. Apart from the obvious requirements for professional recognition, many applicants give vague reasons for wanting to join counsellor training courses. Such reasons include 'I like helping people' and 'People find me a good person with whom to talk over problems.' Counselling students can hardly be expected to have the diamond hard commitment of skilled and experienced counsellors. Nevertheless, some soul-searching concerning reasons for entering counselling can highlight beneficial motives and unearth harmful motives. The criterion for a beneficial motive is whether its consequences are in the best interests of clients. Needless to say, the categories of beneficial and harmful motives overlap. Specific motives may be both beneficial and harmful. Counsellors possess profiles of both beneficial and damaging motives. Furthermore, counsellors' profiles of motives can change over time and also between individual clients.

Possible beneficial motives

Following are some suggestions concerning the rewards and values that motivate counsellors to pursue clients' best interests.

ALTRUISM Altruism means unselfish concern for the welfare of others. It entails 'viewing and pursuing another person's welfare as an ultimate goal' (Batson, 1990, p. 336). A debate exists as to whether people are capable of altruism, where helping others is an ultimate goal, or only of social egoism, where the primary purpose of helping others is what is in it for you. Counsellor altruism resembles the concept of *agape* or unselfish love. Clients are prized for themselves and helped to unfold their unique potentials. Counselling is genuinely people-centred rather than a means of pursuing counsellor self-interest. Some writers view altruism as a fragile flower (Batson, 1990) and a weak instinctual remnant (Maslow, 1970). Maslow makes the further points that the capacity for a wide identification with the human species is a character-istic of self-actualizing people and that many people repress altruistic instincts. However, even counsellors possessing altruism require 'tough minds' to accompany their 'tender hearts' (King, 1963, p. 13).

HUMANISM Humanists believe in the possibility of reason overcoming anxiety, fear and destructive tendencies. Individuals can find the courage to affirm the self 'in spite of the elements of nonbeing threatening it' (Tillich, 1952, p. 120). Humanism involves empowering others by fostering their personal development (Kelly, 1995). Counsellors espousing humanistic values are likely to gain strength from their belief in the possibility for human improvement. Such a belief does not ignore human fallibility and destructiveness. Instead, humanism allows counsellors to commit themselves to the struggle to make themselves and others better people for the sake of a better world.

PEOPLE ORIENTATION Holland's theory of personality types asserts that the special heredity and experiences of people lead to the characteristics of six main personality types: realistic, investigative, artistic, social, enterprising and conventional (Holland, 1973). The social personality type in particular is found in the helping professions. Illustrative characteristics of the social personality type are responsible, helpful, friendly, idealistic, feminine, insightful and kind. People may be attracted to counselling by a good matching between the demands of the role and their personality type. Holland acknowledges that a simple six-category scheme of personality types is unrealistic and talks in terms of profiles of personality types. Nevertheless, the social personality type is still likely to predominate in counsellors' personality type profiles.

INTELLECTUAL CURIOSITY Effective counsellors tend to have a great interest in 'what makes people tick'. They enjoy the challenge of making and testing hypotheses about human behaviour. They are in a constant process of revising their models of the person and of counselling practice. They are creative people who continue learning. As such, they acknowledge mistakes. Effective counsellors experience excitement out of developing their knowledge and competence. Yalom observes that ideological schools of therapy tend to assuage the therapist's rather than the patient's anxiety. He states that 'The creative members of an orthodoxy, any orthodoxy, ultimately outgrow their disciplines' (Yalom, 1989, p. 36).

WORKED-THROUGH EMOTIONAL PAIN Many people are influenced to become counsellors by having experienced significant emotional pain. This pain may be associated with relationships in their families of origin or regarding any one or more of a number of specific circumstances: divorce, sexual abuse, racial discrimination, physical disability, to mention some. Emotional pain can be for good or ill. Counsellors who have worked through their pain and attained some distance from it may have extra sensitivity to the needs of others. In addition, from being in the client role, they may have acquired some useful counselling skills and insights.

COMMITMENT TO COMPETENCE Effective counsellors like to do things well and are prepared to work at it. They take pride in their work and resist taking short cuts that are not in clients' best interests. Egan observes that studies show that competent helpers add value to clients' lives, whereas 'incompetent helpers usually are not neutral; they actually do harm' (Egan, 1994, p. 50). Both counselling trainees and trained counsellors differ in the extent to which they are prepared to work at *being*, as contrasted with *seeming*, competent. Counsellor competence has many dimensions: honestly evaluating your counselling processes and outcomes; keeping abreast of the literature; being prepared to work on professional and personal problems; and, where necessary, obtaining and learning from supervision. Professional integrity is another term for a commitment to competence.

The above are only some potentially beneficial counsellor motives. You may be able to think of others. Some motives (for instance, money and client goodwill) may help or hinder, depending on how they are pursued.

Possible harmful motives

Harmful motives have the common thread that, in varying degrees, they lead to clients being treated as objects for counsellors' gratification rather than respected as unique human beings. Counsellors make inadequate distinctions between 'me' and 'you'. Emotional boundaries get blurred, to clients' detriment. Though the issues are rarely black and white, potentially harmful motives include the following.

UNRESOLVED EMOTIONAL PAIN Many counsellors require personal counselling to become fully effective. Without acknowledging it, some enter counselling as a way of working on their own concerns at one remove. Their underlying agenda is to seek help rather than to provide it. Their attraction to nurturing others stems from their own need to be nurtured. A possible consequence of unresolved emotional pain is that counsellors provide clients with the kinds of help that they rather than their clients need. The attraction of helping for people with problems seems widespread. For instance, Yeo observes: 'When the Samaritans of Singapore first started advertising, they had an overwhelming response. Soon after the selection and screening process was complete, it was discovered that about half the people who volunteered actually needed help with their problems' (Yeo, 1981, p. 24).

DO-GOODING Do-gooding may be contrasted with altruism. With altruism, the ultimate agenda is another's welfare. With do-gooding, the ultimate agenda is your own feelings of satisfaction at what a good person you are. Do-gooders need others in dependent roles. They may wish to take charge and, by so doing, treat clients as objects and infantilize them. Though not alone in this tendency, do-gooders may overly concern themselves with obtaining clients' approval and appreciation for their good works.

SEEKING INTIMACY AND SEX Some people are attracted to counselling because it provides opportunities for psychological closeness they find difficult to obtain otherwise. Afraid to take the risks of authentic living, they are attracted to the limited nature of the counselling role. This way of gaining emotional closeness was one of Carl Rogers's motivations for becoming a counsellor (Rogers, 1980). In addition, some people see counselling as a way of spending time with sexually attractive people, even though they may stop short of dual relationships outside counselling. A small minority of counsellors may be motivated by the possibility of finding attractive sexual partners among clients.

TRUE BELIEVERISM True believers are those who enter counselling rigidly committed to causes. True believerism implies lack of openness to conflicting evidence and to the specific needs of individual clients. For example, true believers in the rights of minority groups may view individual clients in terms of larger political agendas, such as gay rights, rather than as individuals. Once in helping, some become true believers in terms of theoretical positions: for example, hard line rational emotive behaviour therapy or Gestalt therapy advocates. Then, whether it is appropriate or not, clients risk getting pigeon-holed in terms of the concepts of the theoretical position.

EXPEDIENCY Some people choose to become counsellors out of expediency rather than from genuine commitment. An example might be physical education teachers tempted to become school counsellors once their joints start aching. Some are motivated towards counselling as an easy way of making a living. Unfortunately, some counsellor trainers fall into this category too. In addition, some people may be thrust by administrators into counselling roles because they have underperformed in positions perceived as more sensitive.

As for beneficial motives, the suggestions for possible harmful motives are not exhaustive. You may be able to think of others. What are your motives for entering or being in the field of counselling? Which beneficial and harmful motives apply to you? Are you satisfied that your motives for helping will always work for rather than against your clients' best interests?

YOUR EMOTIONAL RESPONSIVENESS

Question: Why do they bury counsellors 300 feet down in the ground?
Answer: Because deep down they are really good people.

You bring to counselling your capacity to experience your feelings. Many reasons exist why it is important for counsellors to be responsive to their flow of feelings. These reasons include being genuine, spontaneous and able to resonate and appropriately to respond to clients' feelings. In counselling you are continuously required to listen to your own as well as to clients' feelings. Your feelings are good guides to issues in your relationships with clients that may be similar to issues they experience outside counselling. For instance, if you feel bored and distant from some clients, they may have the same effect on others.

Inhibiting and repressing feelings

As you grew up you learned, in varying degrees, that it is unsafe to acknowledge, experience and express all feelings. Consequently, an editing process takes place about which you may remain unawares. Some people find it difficult to express any feelings. They are emotionally flat and lifeless. In all families people learn permissions and inhibitions regarding how to feel, though change is possible. For instance, different families may inhibit or dilute the experiencing of specific emotions like sensuality, anger, sadness or death anxiety. In addition, families vary in the extent to which they encourage children to experience and show altruistic feelings. Furthermore, families can influence the degree to which children inhibit wants and wishes.

You also learned permissions and inhibitions according to your social characteristics. For instance, females and males may find it easier to express affectionate and competitive feelings, respectively. If anything, male conditioning is more likely to lead to emotional inexpressiveness than female conditioning. The 'strong, silent' type is a male stereotype. Culture also influences the degree to which feelings are experienced and expressed: for instance, the British 'stiff upper lip' contrasts with southern European emotional expressiveness. Social class is another influence on which feelings get acknowledged and on how they are expressed.

Internalizing others' feelings as if your own

How many of your feelings are truly your own and how many are 'hand-me-downs' from your parents and culture? Especially where parental affection has been conditional, children may internalize the feelings of significant others as if they were their own. Rogers gives the example of a child, who enjoys hitting his baby brother, learning to deny his feelings of enjoyment. 'The accurate symbolization would be: "I perceive my parents as experiencing this behaviour as unsatisfying to them." The distorted symbolization, distorted to preserve the threatened concept of self, is: "I perceive this behaviour as unsatisfying" ' (Rogers, 1951, p. 500). The main thrust of Rogers's person-centred therapy is to assist clients to experience their own inner valuing process rather than to deny and distort their feelings.

Homosexual feelings provide an example where many people deny and distort what they truly feel. Many gay people go through a process of acknowledging and coming to terms with their gayness. This process can be more difficult because of the internalized loathing about homosexuality that they may have learned and may still face from both parents and culture (Rhoads, 1995).

> When, as an adolescent, Alice noticed that she was attracted to other girls, she did her best not to take any notice of these feelings. Instead, to affirm her heterosexuality, she engaged in an active social life of dating boys. Hard as she tried to be affectionate, Alice's heart was not in these relationships. Then Alice became friendly with a slightly older girl, Marcia. When they kissed and embraced, Alice felt so guilty that she told Marcia it was wrong and she could no longer be her friend. Alice is now a counsellor in her late twenties and still feels ambivalent about being a lesbian. She has 'come out' to a few close friends, but has yet to tell her parents or her professional colleagues, who wonder why she is not married.

In counsellor training, as in life, it is important for people to work through what they really feel and think as contrasted to what they have been taught to feel and think. Many damaging or mixed messages in counselling originate in counsellors internalizing the feelings of significant others in their pasts as if they were their own and then not examining their validity in the light of present circumstances.

Transferring unfinished business

Both counsellors and clients can distort their perceptions and feelings towards one another by transferring perceptions from past relationships and conflicts and then reacting emotionally and behaviourally on the basis of these distortions (Gelso and Carter, 1994). Usually the term transference is used when clients distort their perceptions and feelings towards counsellors, with the term countertransference being used when counsellors distort perceptions and feelings towards clients. Many people transfer significant unfinished emotional business from past relationships into present relationships. Transferred feelings can be positive as well as negative. However, the fact that a counsellor's feelings are transferred may create problems if the feelings are inappropriate to current circumstances.

YOUR SENSE OF WORTH AND ANXIETIES

No one can make you feel inferior without your consent.
Eleanor Roosevelt

You bring to counselling your feelings of security and insecurity, your pain and unfinished business, and your fears and anxieties. Vulnerability can be an attractive quality in counselling relationships. Acknowledging your vulnerability to yourself can make you more understanding of clients' vulnerabilities. Furthermore, appropriate disclosure of vulnerability to clients may be viewed as a token of caring and that you too are a part of the human race.

Your sense of worth

Confidence and self-esteem are both general characteristics and characteristics that vary across specific situations that people face. Some people find difficulty in acknowledging that they lack confidence. Others admit it all too readily. Sometimes, by disclosing under-confidence, they seek to manipulate the environment to look after them. Insecurities and fears, if not confronted and managed, can be the breeding ground for distorted communication.

No one's upbringing is perfect. In varying degrees you have learned to feel 'Not OK' as well as 'OK', even though these 'not OK' feelings may be difficult for you to acknowledge. Carkhuff (1987) categorizes families into two main groupings, facilitative and retarding. The members of facilitative families help each other to become persons. The members of retarding families are in the process of becoming non-persons. In facilitative families, parents are likely to have a secure sense of their own worth, which is transmitted to their children. In retarding families, either or both parents feel insecure. Lacking a true sense of their own worth, they send messages that undermine the sense of worth of their children.

In varying degrees, all counsellors possess some unresolved pain and unfinished business from their families of origin. Many have overcome significant obstacles to become more confident and effective people. As a counsellor, associated with how confident you feel, you may send either affirming or negating messages to clients. Effective counsellors send many more affirming messages than ineffective counsellors.

Your fears and anxieties

The late American psychiatrist Harry Stack Sullivan reportedly said that 90 per cent of human communication was specifically designed not to communicate. Both counsellor and client anxiety are always present in counselling encounters (Sullivan, 1954). Part of it comes from being human, part from starting as strangers, part from clients admitting problems and part from work undertaken in counselling. The words anxiety and fear are interchangeable. Anxiety may be defined as your fears about your capacity to cope adequately with the future. Anxiety may be viewed either as a general *trait* or as a *state* that applies to specific situations. There is a close connection between your sense of worth and feelings of anxiety. Insecurity both manifests and engenders anxiety. People who feel worthwhile are relatively free from debilitating anxieties.

Counselling students bring their general level of anxiety to counselling as well as their specific fears and anxieties about it. Counsellor anxiety may be facilitating, debilitating or both (Alpert and Haber, 1960). Excessive levels of debilitating anxiety tend to be associated with unrealistic counselling rules. For example, the rule 'I must always have my clients' approval' leads to over-sensitivity to cues of rejection. Along with their fears and anxieties, beginning counsellors bring into counselling their skills strengths and deficits in dealing with them.

Specific fears and anxieties

Below is an illustrative list of just a few of the fears and anxieties that people bring to counselling. These fears represent subjective rather than objective reality. However, often they are exaggerated and result in unhelpful feelings and actions. Sometimes you may be more afraid of getting what you want than not getting it. Consequently, I group fears into three categories: fear of failure, success and change.

Fear of failure

Fear of rejection
Fear of losing clients
Fear of being incompetent
Fear of hurting clients emotionally
Fear of being seen through
Fear of silences
Fear of not formulating satisfactory restatements in skills terms of clients' problems
Fear of not possessing enough interventions
Fear of clients making no progress

Fear of certain client feelings, such as anger
Fears about coping with certain kinds of clients, such as those in crisis
Fears that certain clients may highlight unfulfilled areas in your life
Fear of what your supervisor thinks

Fear of success

Fears about attaining psychological closeness
Fear of not being able to maintain success
Fears about dealing with expressions of gratitude and appreciation
Fear of other's envy
Fear of losing clients once they become stronger

Fear of change

Fear that you may be challenged or touched deeply by clients and forced to re-examine how you live
Fear that you may have to change how you counsel
Fear of practical changes, such as the consequences of building up a caseload

Some consequences of counsellor anxiety

Anxiety can have positive and negative consequences. Counsellors able to experience and cope with their own anxieties may be more sensitive to clients' anxieties. A certain degree of anxiety is necessary to tone counsellors up and motivate them to give skilled performances. Further, counsellors' anxiety can serve as a signal that issues regarding themselves, their clients or their helping relationships merit exploration.

Many negative consequences flow when counsellor anxiety becomes debilitating rather than facilitating. Counsellors may cease to listen accurately. They may perceive and relate to clients in terms of their own needs and fail to keep adequate psychological boundaries between 'me' and 'you'. The psychoanalysts call this phenomenon counter-transference. Counsellors may assume too much responsibility both for the content of helping sessions and for their clients' lives. In addition, counsellors may use their defensive processes both to distort feedback from clients and to misperceive the extent of client progress. Specific behaviours that may result from excessive counsellor anxiety include asking too many questions, offering superficial reassurance and being too directive in telling clients how to behave.

Personal counselling

How can counselling students become more aware of their levels and cues of anxiety and of what might be the consequences for clients? What can students do to overcome debilitating anxieties? Some of the anxiety may dissipate with experience, practice and good supervision. In addition, the lifeskills approach to counsellor training includes, where possible, teaching skills in self-referent ways. For instance, a good way to learn how to use thinking skills with clients is to use them on yourself. However, the question remains as to whether students still require the more intense focus on their skills and anxieties that personal counselling provides. Debilitating anxiety affects counselling students to varying levels of intensity and in many different ways. Assuming the availability of skilled counsellors, most students profit from personal counselling.

Likeskills counselling does not assume that a single course of counselling is necessarily enough. During their careers, counsellors may supplement their self-helping by further focused work with other counsellors on problematic issues and skills. They may also seek peer support, possibly in groups.

YOUR PHYSICAL HEALTH

Biology and psychology overlap, and below are listed just a few physical health considerations that counselling students and counsellors can bring to their work.

- *Energy level.* How much physical and mental energy do you have? To what degree do you possess vitality or seem apathetic? How physically resilient are you? If your energy level is very low, check with your doctor for possible medical explanations. Your energy level can influence how many clients you can see and how well you listen to them.

- *Fitness.* Counsellors differ greatly in how fit they are and how well they look after their bodies. They also differ in how much they expose themselves to health risk factors, such as obesity, smoking, alcoholism and drug abuse.

- *Sickness and sickliness.* Counsellors may bring their sickness into a counselling relationship. For instance, you may suffer from cancer or a heart problem. In addition, counsellors vary in how prone they are to various ailments, be they minor or more serious.

- *Managing stress skills.* Counsellors differ in how good their skills are at acknowledging and managing stress. Some counsellors are very poor at listening to the signals that their body is over-stressed. At worst, poor stress management skills can result in terminal heart attacks. Poor stress management skills can also result in inappropriate counselling behaviours: for instance, tense body posture and heightened irritability.

- *Physical disability.* To what degree are you physically disabled: for instance, with impairments of vision, hearing or mobility? If you are physically disabled, your thinking and actions skills strengths and deficits in coping with your disability become very important. Some physically disabled people can turn their disability into a counselling strength, since they may possess greater insight into disabled clients' thought and feelings than ordinary counsellors.

- *Mental disorders.* Some mental problems have a biological component to them: for instance, schizophrenia and manic depression (American Psychiatric Association, 1994). Certain counsellors may have to work around a mental disorder: for instance, taking time out during manic-depressive episodes.

YOUR SEXUALITY
Your sexual feelings

All counsellors are sexual beings. However, you have a choice as to whether or not you bring your sexuality into counselling, and if so, how much. Counsellors differ in their levels of sexual energy or libido. In their relationships they have varying preferences for how, when and how many times they like to have sex. In a British national survey of nearly 20, 000 respondents aged 16–59, sex was defined as vaginal intercourse, oral sex or anal sex (Wellings *et al.*, 1994). For both males and females, the median of the distribution never exceeded five acts of heterosexual sex in the past four weeks (the median divides a set of values, in this case heterosexual sex acts, into two groups of equal size – half of the values are larger and half are smaller than the median). An indication of how frequency of sex acts varied is shown in the 95th centile (95 per cent reporting lower frequency), being 20 for males and 25 for females. Frequency of sex varied substantially with age for both males and females, ranging from a median of five acts per month for women aged 20–29 and for men aged 30–34, thereafter declining to a median of two for men aged 55–59, with more than 50 per cent of women in this age group reporting no sex acts in the past four weeks.

Despite the strength of their sexual urges, counsellors differ in their capacity to experience themselves as sexual beings. Faulty thinking can lead counsellors to underemphasize or overemphasize their sexuality. Counsellors may have picked up parental inhibitions about being sexual. A major area for counsellors and therapists working with sexually dysfunctional couples is that of helping either or both partners work through thoughts interfering with performance: for instance, 'sex is dirty' or 'sharing sexual fantasies is wrong'. In addition, counsellors may possess counter-productive fears about their bodies: for instance, that either their breasts or their penises are too small. Especially for males, poor thinking skills may lead to an exaggerated emphasis on sexual performance. They may boast about their sexual conquests to their peers and treat women as objects rather than persons. Fears underlie both inhibited and exaggerated sexuality. These fears include: acknowledging the strength of sexual feelings; fears about physical attractiveness; performance fears; and fears about being seen to be sufficiently 'masculine' or 'feminine'.

Counsellors possess thoughts and feelings not only about their own but also about their clients' sexuality. Many counsellors experience great difficulty avoiding dual relationships and sexual intimacy with clients (Corey *et al.*, 1993; Egan, 1994; Yalom,

1989). Professional codes for psychologists and counsellors clearly state that such relationships are unethical (Australian Psychological Society, 1986; British Association for Counselling, 1993; British Psychological Society, 1993, 1995).

Your sexual orientation

Are you straight, gay or in between? You bring your sexual orientation to your counselling relationships. I use the term sexual orientation rather than sexual preference. Many, if not most, people's sexual orientation is a fact of life, based on genetics and social learning, and not a preference, based on free choice. The word homosexual is derived from the Greek word *homos*, meaning same. Researchers experience difficulty obtaining accurate data on the extent of homosexual attraction and experience. If anything, the amount of homosexuality gets under-reported. Until 1967, male homosexuality was a criminal offence in Britain. At the time of writing, homosexuality is still a criminal offence in some Australian states, such as Tasmania. Only as recently as 1974 did the American Psychiatric Association remove homosexuality from its list of psychiatric disorders. In Western societies there is still widespread stigma attached to being gay. Consequently, gay people may select themselves out of survey samples. Once in samples, some gay people may be inhibited from revealing full details of their behaviour. Further, some survey respondents may find it difficult to acknowledge consciously any homosexual attraction or experience and, if they do, can find it easy to forget afterwards.

In the late 1940s and early 1950s, pioneering studies on American sexual behaviour were conducted by Alfred Kinsey and his colleagues (Kinsey *et al.*, 1948, 1953). They found that in the large, predominantly white, middle-class population that they surveyed, 4 per cent of males and between 1 and 3 per cent of females were exclusively homosexual. Furthermore, 10 per cent of males were more or less exclusively homosexual for at least three years between ages 16 and 65 and 37 per cent had participated in at least one homosexual experience which led to orgasm. Though heterosexuality was very much the predominant sexual orientation for both males and females and exclusive homosexuality was very much the minority orientation there was a considerable amount of bisexuality.

More recent data exist regarding homosexual attraction and experience in Britain. Wellings and her colleagues (1994) found that, in face-to-face interviews, of their large sample of 16–59-year-olds, 5.5 per cent of men and 4.5 per cent of women admitted to having been *attracted* to a person of the same sex. In addition, 5.2 per cent of men and 2.7 per cent of women reported some homosexual *experience*. Sexual experience was defined as 'any kind of contact with another person that you felt was sexual (it could be just kissing or touching, or intercourse or any other form of sex)' (p. 181).

Wellings and her colleagues also collected data from a self-completion booklet. Based on booklet responses, 6.1 per cent of men reported some homosexual experience and 3.6 per cent genital contact with a man. The corresponding figures for women were 3.4 and 1.7 per cent, respectively. These British findings for men are similar to American data, which estimate the lifetime prevalence of male homosexual experience within the range 4.8–4.9 per cent (Rogers and Turner, 1991).

Though heterosexuality is very much the predominant orientation, many counsellors are confronted with choices in their personal lives about how to handle homosexual feelings, whether to engage in homosexual sex and whether openly to admit to homosexual feelings. In addition, in their professional lives, homosexual and bisexual counsellors are faced with choices regarding whether or not to 'come out' to colleagues and clients.

All counsellors have attitudes about clients' sexual orientations, whether they be the same as or different to their own. Furthermore, they possess varying degrees of knowledge about the feelings, thoughts and actions of people with different sexual orientations. Especially if you plan to work in such areas as marital counselling, sexual dysfunction counselling or counselling gay and bisexual people, you need to review the adequacy of your knowledge and attitudes about sexuality and sexual orientation.

YOUR SEX-ROLE IDENTITY AND EXPECTATIONS

Sex-role and gender issues are relevant to all counselling relationships and to many counselling problems. A fundamental value of this book is equality between females and males. Equality between the sexes means that females and males should have the same opportunity to develop their potential and express their humanity. Apart from realistic constraints stemming from biological differences, both sexes should have the same opportunity to exercise choice in their lives. Equality between the sexes is an ideal towards which progress is being made in Western societies. In the past, both females and males have related both to their own sex and to the other sex in traditional ways that needlessly constricted choice. You are in a transitional period now, where perhaps females especially, but also many males, are challenging conventional wisdoms about sex-related attitudes and behaviours. This poses threats and risks as well as exciting opportunities. Gender is now on the agenda in all but the most unaware of male–female relationships.

Following are some definitions of terms relevant to your exploring the sex-role identity and expectations that you bring to counsellor training and counselling.

- *Sex.* In this context refers to biological differences between males and females: for instance, difference in genitals, reproductive functions, bone structure and size.

- *Gender.* Gender refers to the social and cultural classification of attributes, attitudes and behaviours as 'feminine' or 'masculine'.

- *Sex-role identity.* Your sex-role identity is how you view yourself and behave on the dimensions of 'masculinity' and 'femininity'.

- *Sex-role expectations.* These are your thoughts and feelings about how you and others should think, feel and behave on account of differences in biological sex.

- *Gender awareness*. Gender awareness relates to how aware you are of the processes of and consequences of gender scripting on both males and females.

- *Sexism*. Individual sexism relates to any feelings, thoughts and actions that assume the superiority of one sex over the other. Institutional sexism relates to institutional structures that discriminate against and devalue a person on the grounds of sex.

- *Heterosexism*. Heterosexism refers to the assumption that everyone is or should be heterosexual. Schreier (1995, p. 19) defined heterosexism as 'a belief in the inherent superiority of demonstrating love toward members of the opposite sex, and therefore a belief in the right to dominate others and set societal standards and norms' (p. 19).

Masculinity, femininity and androgyny

In Western societies, certain psychological characteristics have been traditionally viewed as either 'feminine' or 'masculine'. Feminine characteristics have included being affectionate, gentle, sensitive to the needs of others, tender and warm. Masculine characteristics have included being aggressive, ambitious, assertive, analytical and dominant (Bem, 1974). The predominant traditional roles of women have been those of the nurturer and social harmonizer within the home. Men's traditional roles have focused on being the breadwinner outside the home and the enforcer of discipline within the home.

Because of their sex-role learning, males and females develop different relating skills strengths and deficits. Argyle (1984) states that the research evidence suggests that there are a number of areas where females may be more socially competent than males. These include: being better at sending and receiving body language; being more rewarding and polite; and disclosing more and forming closer friendships. However, he notes that being assertive is an area where women appear to have more problems than men. Both masculine and feminine sex roles may have costs. The traditional feminine sex role has created problems for many women in such areas as expressing anger, being autonomous and obtaining power and status (DeVoe, 1990). The traditional masculine role has created problems for many men through excessive concern with success, power and competition, being emotionally inexpressive and restricting affectionate behaviour between men (Good *et al.*, 1989). Furthermore, the help seeking behaviour of the sexes differs in that 'men come into therapy less frequently than women, are less aware of their feelings, and present more work-related issues' (Stevens-Smith, 1995, p. 288).

Underlying the 'femininity–masculinity' dimension is the issue of nature versus nurture. Moir and Jessel (1989) review research indicating that from birth males and females are different. The main behavioural difference is the natural, innate aggression of men. Moir and Jessel observe that the sexes are different because their brains are different, and observe: 'To maintain that they are the same in aptitude skill or behaviour is to build a society based on a biological and scientific lie' (p. 5). On the other hand, some social scientists consider that humans have weak instinctual remnants tending towards either a male or a female sex-role identity, and that such biological predispositions may be easily overwhelmed by the strength of their learning experience (Oakley, 1972). Another perspective is that of Buss (1995), who offers an explanation of psychological differences between the sexes based on the fact that, in many domains, 'men and women have faced substantially different adaptive problems throughout human evolutionary history' (p. 164).

There are three interesting possibilities in how the nature–nurture controversy can be positively resolved. One possibility is that 'masculinity' and 'femininity' become outmoded concepts because further research indicates that the sexes are biologically similar. The second possibility is that further research supports Moir and Jessel's position that the sexes possess important biological differences and manage to utilize each other's strengths for everyone's benefit. A third possibility is that human evolutionary history moves in the direction of fostering even greater biological similarity between the sexes.

Related to the issue of nurture or nature is the increasing popularity of the concept of psychological androgyny. The androgynous male or female 'is flexibly masculine or feminine as circumstances warrant' (Bem, 1981, p. 362). Thus, females and males can be brought up with the capacity to express a range of characteristics independently of whether they have traditionally been viewed as 'masculine' or 'feminine'. For instance, men can be tender and women assertive.

As long as males and females increasingly adopt the strengths rather than the deficits of the other sex's gender characteristics, androgyny offers much promise for enriching people's lives. This is true for gay as well as for heterosexual counsellors and clients. Already there are many counsellors and clients of both sexes who, in varying degrees, are flexible in exhibiting masculine and feminine characteristics. We can hope that there will be a continuing trend towards bringing up and encouraging more people to acknowledge and share the full range of their psychological characteristics. Such sharing is likely to lessen the amount of loneliness and alienation in Western countries.

You learned your current sex-role identity in many different ways. Your gender scripting started at the cradle with pink for a girl and blue for a boy. You may have observed your parents undertaking different household tasks: for instance, mending clothes and looking after the car. Probably your parents and significant others gave you different toys according to your sex and rewarded different behaviours and characteristics. The books you read showed boys and girls in different roles, as did the films and television programmes you watched. When you went to school, you may have been treated differently according to your sex. Furthermore, the subjects you were encouraged to study and the occupations thought appropriate for you varied by sex. No one can grow up in Western society without a considerable amount of gender brainwashing. However, there are risks to oversimplifying male and female experiences of sex-role socialization. Your current sex-role identity is the internalized sum of individual differences, personal situational factors and cultural, social and environmental influences, plus any modifications from thinking for yourself (Enns, 1991). Also, if you are part of a dual career couple, both of you may confront sex-role conflicts that can create personal stresses and contribute to relationship instability (Heppner, 1995; Wilcox-Matthew and Minor, 1989).

Your sex-role expectations

Based on your gender socialization and sex-role identity, you bring sex-role expectations to counselling. Your sex-role identity also influences behaviour. For example, a consistent research finding is that female therapists are more oriented towards their clients' affect than male therapists (Mintz and O'Neil, 1990). Female therapists experience and express more feelings in interactions with clients than male therapists (Maracek and Johnson, 1980). Sex-role identity and its associated behaviours can also provide a way of categorizing counsellors: for example, non-sexist humanist, liberal feminist or radical feminist (Enns and Hackett, 1990). Good and his colleagues have proposed gender aware counselling. They state: 'Counsellors must not only be non-sexist in their work with clients, but they must also understand clients' difficulties within a gender perspective' (Good et al., 1990, p. 377).

Sex-role expectations can permeate counselling in a number of ways. You may assess clients differently according to whether or not they fit into traditional sex roles (Robertson and Fitzgerald, 1990). You may bring to counselling inflexible and sexist assumptions for appropriate behaviour in dating, marital and partner relationships and parenting. Your attitudes to sexual harassment, rape and domestic psychological and physical violence may be sexist. You may also possess unexamined sexist assumptions about the place of males and females in the home or workforce and about jobs and careers appropriate for each sex. In addition, you may engage in simplistic over-generalizations about the characteristics of males and females and insufficiently acknowledge within-group differences. Some students bring to counselling such strong feelings about sex-role and gender issues – for instance, about physically violent males – that they interfere with their ability to formulate accurate restatements of clients' problems in skills terms.

YOUR VALUES

Values are principles that guide your life. The earlier section on motives explored some values underlying your choice to become a counsellor. However, you bring many other values too. Your values influence how you work with clients. Further, in counselling you may be subject to value conflicts within your own values and between your and your clients' values.

A prominent measure of Western values is the Rokeach Value Survey (Rokeach, 1967). Rokeach saw values as conceptions of the desirable means and ends of action. The Rokeach value survey distinguishes between terminal values, or the ultimate end-goals of existence, and instrumental values, or the behavioural means for achieving such end-goals. Between 1968 and 1981, American terminal values were highly stable. In 1981 the six most highly ranked terminal values were a world at peace, family security, freedom, happiness, self-esteem and wisdom. Rokeach last surveyed American instrumental values in 1971, when the six most highly ranked values were being honest, ambitious, responsible, forgiving, broad minded and courageous (Rokeach and Ball-Rokeach, 1989).

Schwartz is another prominent researcher in the area of values (Schwartz, 1992; Schwartz and Bilsky, 1990). Schwartz classified values into ten types: power, achievement, hedonism, stimulation, self-direction, universalism, benevolence, tradition, conformity and security. Based on information from 20 countries in six continents, Schwartz (1992) confirmed that each of the ten values was found in at least 90 per cent of the countries he surveyed, suggesting that his value types are near universal.

Using the Schwartz Universal Values Questionnaire (Schwartz, 1992), Kelly (1995) surveyed a national sample of nearly 500 American counsellors. Items were rated on a nine-point scale from -1 (opposed to my values) to 7 (of extreme importance), with the middle score of 3 (important). The average scores of the value items within each type were: benevolence, 5.27; self-direction, 5.08; universalism, 4.89; achievement, 4.63; hedonism, 4.14; security, 4.07; conformity, 4.07; stimulation, 3.59; tradition, 3.17; power, 2.09. Similar information is not available for British and Australian counsellors.

You can view yourself as possessing a profile of values or guiding principles for your life. This profile is composed of your values and the importance you attach to each. Below are some values that you and others, consciously or otherwise, bring to your life and to your counselling relationships (Allport *et al.*, 1951; Holland, 1973; Maslow, 1970; Rokeach and Ball-Rokeach, 1989; Schwartz, 1992).

- *Survival*. Biological survival is the primary instinctive value, though other values sometimes override it: for example, patriotism or religious belief.

- *Love*. Loving and being loved; appreciating others for what they are and not just for what they do.

- *Friendship*. Being joined to others outside your family by mutual intimacy and interests.

- *Family life*. Having and being part of a family; valuing parenthood.

- *Religion*. Acknowledging the need for connectedness to some ultimate and super-human power.

- *Achievement*. Being ambitious; valuing success, status and influence.

- *Materialism*. Valuing the accumulation and control of money.

- *Security*. Valuing financial security and social order.

- *Aesthetics*. Appreciating beauty and good taste, with special reference to the arts, such as music, literature and painting.

- *Intellect.* Valuing analytical and rational pursuits.

- *Social interest.* Helping others; being benevolent and showing social concern.

- *Hedonism.* Valuing fun, pleasure and having a good time.

- *Excitement.* Valuing being daring and a varied and stimulating life.

- *Conformity.* Being obedient; respecting and honouring parents and authority figures.

- *Tradition.* Appreciating the status quo; accepting your position in life.

- *Career.* Valuing having a career and the work entailed.

- *Practical.* Valuing practical pursuits and, where practical matters are concerned, self-reliance.

- *Nature.* Appreciating and valuing being outdoors and in communion with nature.

- *Health.* Valuing being healthy and engaging in pursuits conducive to good health.

- *Self-direction.* Valuing autonomy, choosing your goals and personal freedom.

- *Personal growth.* Being committed to personal development.

You can look at your career choice and wish to counsel in terms of work values. Work values resemble many of the values mentioned above. Harrington and O'Shea have developed a Career Decision-Making System that lists 14 work values. In alphabetical order, these work values are creativity, food/salary, high achievement, independence, job security, leadership, physical activity, prestige, routine activity, supervised work, variety/diversion, work with hands, work with mind and work with people (Harrington and O'Shea, 1993; Lebo *et al.*, 1995).

Value conflicts

Counsellors bring their value conflicts to counselling. For instance, counsellors may feel conflict between wanting to help others and at the same time charging fees. Counsellors experience many value conflicts similar to those of clients: for instance, between home and career and between religious teachings and liberal-pragmatic values, such as regarding abortion.

The values you bring to counselling may put you in conflict with clients. Sexual behaviour constitutes a potential area of value conflict (Corey *et al.*, 1993). For instance, what are your attitudes to pre-marital sex, extra-marital sex, casual sex, group sex, teenage sex and homosexuality? For Catholic counsellors, issues of contraception, abortion, divorce and intentional single parenting create value conflicts. Value conflicts are not restricted to personal counselling. For instance, in academic counselling, how might you feel about clients consciously choosing not to try hard when their parents sacrifice to keep them in college? In vocational counselling, how might you feel about clients drawing unemployment benefits for as long as possible?

You may bring to counselling skills strengths and deficits in the handling of value conflicts. For instance, some counsellors may want to 'push' their values irrespective of their clients' wishes. Other counsellors may consider that the way to handle severe value conflicts is to refer clients on to counsellors with more similar values. Yet another option is to keep quiet about your values. A further option is to declare your values as your own and, possibly, use this as a springboard for helping clients to clarify their values.

Questioning your values

You may find it fruitful to question your values. When I interview applicants for counsellor training, many experience difficulty answering my question: 'What are your core values?' How might you answer that question? Would you find it helpful to formulate either a hierarchy or a profile of your values or both? Other questions that you might ask yourself are: 'How did I acquire my values and to what degree do they represent my inner valuing process rather than being "hand-me-downs" of others' values?'; 'What are my key areas of value conflict?'; 'In what areas, if any, do I anticipate I might have significant value conflicts with clients?'; 'To what degree are my values open to modification and how might they influence my work with clients?'

YOUR ETHICS

Your ethics and values are interrelated. Numerous ethical issues are connected with counselling: for example, competence, obtaining consent for interventions, confidentiality and appropriate personal conduct. Here the emphasis is on counsellor training rather than on counselling practice.

Many of the ethical issues of counselling practice pertain to both counsellor trainers and students. Especially if teaching counselling skills, counsellor trainers require competence as both teachers and practitioners. I think it important that trainers continue working with clients so that they maintain and develop their counselling skills.

Ethical issues abound in the learning of counselling skills. Though this is not an either/or matter, students who learn counselling skills differ greatly in how diligent they are. Students have varying degrees of commitment to competence as well as varying abilities to explore the adequacy of their learning behaviours. Below are a few examples of less than ethical student behaviour.

> As part of the contract in a counselling skills class,
> Ken is required to confirm that he has done 30

hours of independent interview practice. Ken does only 10 hours, but confirms that he has done 30 hours.

Lucia is required to read up on different approaches to working with depressed clients, prior to having such clients referred to her. Lucia fails to do most of her reading homework.

Julie has been told by her supervisor that she intrudes too much by 'pushing' her own values on to her clients. Julie thinks that she knows better than her supervisor and just becomes more subtle in how she goes about altering her clients' values.

In a counselling skills class, there is a clear requirement that students attend all sessions. Paul misses a number of sessions, claiming pressure of other business. Paul becomes aggressive when his supervisor raises reservations about Paul's skills level for seeing clients as part of the subject.

All counselling students need to address specific tendencies to unethical behaviour: be it breaking confidentiality for the sake of telling a good story or taking a prurient interest in clients' sexual lives. Allied to ethics is the area of personal development or of working on potentially damaging aspects of yourself that you bring to counselling. Awareness of areas of fallibility is the first step in preventing ethical lapses. A genuine commitment to becoming competent is essential for students. Issues of professional ethics start with counsellor training. Some counselling students seem more interested in acquiring certificates than competence. To what extent are you open to learning and working on your counselling skills? How committed to competence in counselling are you?

YOUR CULTURE AND CROSS-CULTURAL SKILLS

You bring cultural rules and assumptions to counsellor training and to counselling. Culture refers to the predominant pattern of a given group during a given period. Culture pervades every aspect of living: values, ethics, religion, language, food, table manners, music, clothing, attitudes towards democracy, sporting activities, family structures and relations, social relations and body language, to mention only some. Ho (1995) distinguished between internalized culture, the culture operating in the individual through enculturation and the external culture or cultural group membership. Especially in a multicultural migrant country like Australia, your internalized culture may be influenced by parents who came from a different culture as well as by Australian culture.

Examples of cultural differences abound. For example, Ho (1985) observes that important Western values include emphasis on youth, assertiveness, independence and competition, whereas the corresponding Eastern values emphasize maturity, compliance, interdependence and cooperation. Argyle (1986) studied common rules in 22 social relationships in four different cultures: Britain, Hong Kong, Japan and Italy. He found: 'In Japan virtually all highly endorsed rules were conflict-regulating ones. In contrast, Italy endorsed intimacy-reward rules more, especially compared to Japan' (p. 313). Cultures differed on both verbal and non-verbal dimensions. Addressing the other person by first name was highly endorsed in only three Japanese relationships, a much lower figure than in the other three cultures. Looking the other person in the eye during conversation was highly endorsed in virtually all British and Italian relationships, but in under half of Japanese and Hong Kong relationships. Yet another example is that eye contract by young people is a sign of disrespect among some Native American groups (Ivey, 1994).

Your cultural and ancestral roots

What are your cultural and ancestral roots? In Britain, there is a majority British culture, though there are many sub-cultures within it as well as many minority ethnic groups. The 1991 British census showed that the non-white ethnic minority population was just over 3 million or 5.5 per cent of the total population of 54.9 million. The largest individual ethnic minority group was Indian, constituting 1.5 per cent of the total population, or 27.9 per cent of the ethnic minority population as a whole. Pakistanis formed 0.9 per cent of the total population, or 15.8 per cent of the total ethnic minority population. Three black categories – Black Caribbean, Black African and Black other – combined formed 1.6 per cent of the total population, 29.5 per cent of the total ethnic minority population. Bangladeshis and Chinese each formed 0.3 per cent of the total population (Teague, 1993).

The 1991 Australian census found 265,000 people who identified themselves as being of Aboriginal or Torres Strait Islander origin out of Australia's then total population of 17.28 million. Though Australia's population is still primarily Anglo-Celtic, the census counted 3.8 million people born overseas who were classified to 224 countries. A further 3.3 million people had one or both parents born overseas. Between 1947 and 1991, the proportion of the population born overseas increased from 10 to 23 per cent. In the period 1947 to 1961, there was more than a sevenfold increase in migrants from continental Europe, while the number from the UK and Ireland increased by less than half.

More recently, there has been an increase in immigration from other countries, especially New Zealand, Vietnam, China and the Philippines (Castles, 1993). In 1994, there were 77,490 permanent (settler) arrivals in Australia, of whom 19 per cent were born in Southeast Asia (Malaysia, Philippines, Vietnam), 11 per cent in Northeast Asia (China, Hong Kong, Taiwan) and 8.2 per cent in Southern Asia (India, Sri Lanka) (Australian Bureau of Statistics, 1995). Asians are now the main migrant group, which reflects Australia's geographic location. In 1994, only 12.3 per cent of permanent (settler) arrivals were born in the United Kingdom. The Australian Bureau of Statistics estimated that, at the end of 1994, the resident population of Australia was nearly 18 million people.

Settler New Zealand culture also has its origins in Anglo-Celtic culture. New Zealanders are sometimes called the 'Poms of the Pacific'. However, Maoris constitute about 10 per cent of New Zealand's population of approximately 3.5 million. In 1994, 11.5 per cent of Australian permanent (settler) arrivals came from New Zealand.

Your cross-cultural awareness and skills

The message from the above figures is simple. Though there are undoubtedly national characteristics common to most Britons, Australians and New Zealanders, awareness of cultural differences and the ability to build bridges across them are important counselling skills. You bring your knowledge and awareness of your own culture to counsellor training and to counselling (Sue *et al.*, 1992). Counsellors differ to the extent to which they are aware that how they think, feel and behave has been conditioned by their cultural upbringing. You may possess cultural tunnel vision without knowing it. Some counsellors gain knowledge of other cultures by having relatives, friends and acquaintances from them. Overseas travel may have heightened your awareness of cultural differences and increased your sensitivity to migrants experiencing culture shock and disorientation.

You also bring your knowledge and awareness of clients' cultures to counselling. A useful distinction is that between culture-deficit and culture-sensitive assumptions. The culture-deficit model assumes that the rules and values of the dominant or mainstream culture are normal. Variations observed in minorities are deficits (Rogoff and Morelli, 1989). The culture-deficit counselling model incorporates oppression even by those 'trying to help' minorities. For example, patronizing attitudes and 'missionary zeal' are two kinds of majority group insensitivity experienced by many American Indians (LaFromboise *et al.*, 1990). The culture-sensitive counselling model avoids the assumption that dominant group practices are proper and superior. Respect is shown for cultural differences and positive features of cultural variation may be emphasized. Furthermore, counsellors show sensitivity to minority group members' differing levels of and wishes for acculturation (LaFromboise *et al.*, 1990).

You also bring your cross-cultural skills to counsellor training and to counselling. How good are you at helping people from different cultures to share their cultural differences with you? Cross-cultural skills include: understanding the cultural meaning of verbal, voice and body messages; giving others permission to talk about their culture; and helping others to work through cross-cultural mistrust and alienation.

YOUR RACE AND RACIAL SKILLS

You also bring your race to your counselling relationships – whether you are Caucasian, Aboriginal, African, Asian, Polynesian or of mixed race. The 1991 British census showed that 94.5 per cent of the population were Caucasian, with the remaining

5.5 per cent being predominantly Asian and African (Teague, 1993). Though the majority of Australians are Caucasian, with immigration the proportion of Asians steadily increases. This development points to the possibility of Australia having a Eurasian future. New Zealanders are also predominantly Caucasian. However, the Maoris are Polynesian.

Your racial attitudes and skills

When you counsel people outside your racial group, you bring your attitudes towards your own and other races. You may have a racial learning history in which you have acquired negative thoughts and feelings about your own or other races or both. In Western societies, the main kind of racism is the belief in white genetic superiority over other racial groups. Racist assumptions and behaviours by whites can contribute to second-order racism, whereby members of oppressed minority groups react with simplistic racial stereotypes of whites: for instance, calling them 'potatoes'.

Frequently, racial differences are highlighted by cultural differences. Much behaviour labelled racist stems from cultural rather than solely from racial differences. On the other hand, racial differences can disguise cultural similarities, as in the case of second- and third-generation Asian-Australians, sometimes known as 'bananas' (yellow on the outside and white on the inside).

Whether members of racial majority or minority groups, counsellors possess different levels of awareness about the impact of race on their own and others' identity and life chances (Christensen, 1989). Furthermore, they possess different levels of racial mistrust and attraction. In addition, counsellors possess different skills at demonstrating racial empathy. In multiracial societies, it is important that you possess race-sensitive as well as culture-sensitive counselling skills: for instance, giving people permission to share their views on the role of race in their lives and in their relationship with you.

YOUR SOCIAL CLASS AND SOCIAL CLASS SKILLS

Every society throughout the globe has its pecking order or status system. These are open to varying degrees of vertical mobility. Many people migrated to the Antipodes to get away from what they perceived as the stultifying traditional social class systems of Europe based on old money, landed estates, titles, schooling and accent.

Income, educational attainment and occupational status are currently three of the main measures of social class in Britain, Australia and New Zealand. Other indicators include schooling, accent, clothing, manners, nature of social networks and type and location of housing. The social class into which you are born and raised influences your chances of surviving at birth, your educational and occupational opportunities, whom you are likely to meet and to marry, how much money you are likely to make, how well your health is looked after and the quality of your funeral. The same holds true for your clients.

Each of you brings your social class to your counselling relationships. A common stereotype is a middle-class counsellor who lacks the language, life experience and skills to relate to lower-class clients. You also bring your sensitivity to the effects of others' social class on you and your social class on them. Furthermore, you bring your skills at understanding people from different social classes and of forming counselling relationships with them. One skill may be handling resistances and negative messages resulting from clients' social class insecurities. Another skill is that of using language appropriate to your client group. If you possess feelings of either inferiority or superiority on account of your social class, work to eliminate them. Being an effective counsellor is difficult enough without the intrusion of avoidable social-class agendas.

CHAPTER HIGHLIGHTS

- *Counselling differs from most other occupations, in that its main tools are people.*

- *Your motives for counselling can be beneficial or harmful. Beneficial motives include altruism, humanism, people-orientation, intellectual curiosity, worked-through emotional pain, and commitment to competence. Harmful motives include unresolved emotional pain, do-gooding, seeking intimacy, true believerism and expediency.*

- *You bring to counselling your capacity to experience feelings. Dimensions of this capacity include inhibiting and repressing feelings, internalizing others' feelings as if your own and transferring unfinished business.*

- *You bring your sense of worth to your counselling relationships. You also bring some debilitating anxieties, which may include fears of failure, success and change.*

- *Depending on your sense of worth, you may send either affirming or negating messages to clients about their worth. Most counselling students can benefit from personal counselling.*

- *Aspects of physical health for counsellors and counselling students include: energy level, fitness, sickness and sickliness, managing stress skills, physical disability and mental disorders.*

- *Counsellors differ in the strength of sexual feelings, capacity to experience themselves as sexual persons, preferred sexual activities, prior sexual experience and sexual orientation.*

- *Your sex-role identity is how you see yourself on the dimensions of 'masculinity' and 'femininity'.*

- *Your sex-role expectations may free or restrict you and your clients.*

- *Your bring your values or guiding principles for your life to counselling. You may be subject to value conflicts both within your values and between your and clients' values.*

- *You need to become aware of how ethically you approach counsellor training, especially regarding gaining competence.*

- *You bring your culture and cross-cultural skills to your counselling relationships. You can either see minority cultures as inferior to the mainstream culture or value cultural diversity.*

- *You bring to counselling your racial attitudes and skills in relating to racially different people. Frequently, racial differences are highlighted by cultural differences.*

- *Your social class may make it hard for you to understand and work with clients whose life experiences are very different to yours. In addition, you may have to cope with your own and your clients' social class insecurities.*

EXERCISE 4.1 MY MOTIVES FOR COUNSELLING

Motives for counselling are potentially either beneficial or harmful. The criterion for a beneficial motive is whether its consequences are likely to help rather than harm clients. The criterion for a harmful motive is the reverse. This exercise challenges you to explore and become more aware of your motives.

Answer the following questions on your own, with a partner or in a group.

1. Assess how applicable each of the following motives for counselling is for you.

   Potentially beneficial motives

   Altruism
   Humanism
   People-orientation
   Intellectual curiosity
   Worked-through emotional pain
   Commitment to competence
   Others not mentioned above (list and explain)

   Potentially harmful motives

   Unresolved emotional pain
   Do-gooding

Seeking intimacy and sex
True believerism
Expediency

Others not mentioned above (list and explain)

2. Summarize your profile of beneficial and harmful motives.

3. If appropriate, identify areas on which you need to work and write out a plan for change.

EXERCISE 4.2   MY SENSE OF WORTH

The goal of this exercise is to raise your awareness of how confident a person you are and how this might affect how you counsel.

First do this exercise on your own. Then, if appropriate, discuss your answers with your partner or in a group.

1. Take a piece of paper and head it LEARNING MY SENSE OF WORTH. Draw a line down the centre underneath this heading. At the top of the left column write HELPFUL EXPERIENCES, at the top of the right column write HARMFUL EXPERIENCES.

2. List five experiences that you consider were *helpful* in developing your sense of worth and confidence and that you would like to *repeat* with your children.

3. List five experiences that you consider were *harmful* in developing your sense of worth and confidence and that you would like to *avoid* with your children.

4. Summarize how secure and confident a person you feel you are now and how this might influence how you counsel.

EXERCISE 4.3   MY FEARS AND ANXIETIES ABOUT COUNSELLING

Answer the following questions on your own, with a partner or in a group.

1. What fears and anxieties might you bring to your counselling relationships in each of the following areas (if they apply to you)?
    Fear of failure
    Fear of success
    Fear of change

2. What fears and anxieties have you noticed clients bringing into their counselling relationship with you?

3. How do your and your clients' fears and anxieties influence those of one another?

4. What have been or might be the effects of your fears and anxieties on how you counsel? Provide specific illustrations.

5. If you have identified some fears and anxieties that might interfere with how you counsel, what can you do about them?

EXERCISE 4.4   MY SEXUALITY

First do this exercise on your own. Then, if appropriate, discuss your answers with your partner or in a group. Answer the following questions.

1. To what extent are you satisfied or dissatisfied with your capacity to experience and express your sexuality?

2. Think of your body image. To what extent are you satisfied or dissatisfied with your body from the viewpoint of sexual relating?

3. What is your sexual orientation and how do you know? If you are bisexual, identify the extent to which you are heterosexual or homosexual.

4. Take a piece of paper and at the top write HOW I LEARNED ABOUT MY SEXUALITY. At the top of the left-hand column write HELPFUL EXPERI-ENCES and at the top of the right-hand column write HARMFUL EXPERI-ENCES. List important experiences that have helped or harmed you to experience and express your sexuality.

5. Do you or might you bring any fears and anxieties about your sexuality into a counselling relationship? If so, be as specific as possible in identifying them.

6. In what ways, if any, do you think your sexuality poses or may pose problems for you in the counsellor role? How might you prevent such problems occurring?

EXERCISE 4.5 MY SEX-ROLE IDENTITY AND EXPECTATIONS

The way you think of yourself as 'masculine' or 'feminine' has been largely learned. Think back over your experiences as you were growing up and answer the following questions on your own, with a partner or in a group.

Part A Learning my sex-role identity
1. Did you get different toys on account of your sex? Illustrate with examples.

2. Did you get different clothes, including their colour, on account of your sex? Illustrate with examples.

3. What roles did your mother and father play in caring for you as a child?

4. Who did the following household tasks in your family?
    Vacuum cleaning
    Dusting
    Shopping for food
    Cooking meals
    Washing dishes
    Making beds
    Polishing furniture
    Washing clothes
    Ironing
    Mending clothes
    Changing a fuse
    Interior decoration
    Exterior decoration
    Mowing the lawn
    Looking after the car

5. Either in your home or among your friends, were you ever called a 'sissy' or a 'tomboy'? If so, provide an example.

6. Which of the following psychological characteristics do you consider each of your parents either encouraged you or discouraged you to show:
    Being analytical
    Gentleness
    Ambition
    Dominance
    Feelings of vulnerability
    Concern with your clothes
    Competitiveness
    Being nurturing
    Career orientation
    Home orientation

7. Did the books and magazines you read when growing up show males and females as having different psychological characteristics, interests and activities? Provide examples.

8. Did the TV programmes you watched when growing up show males and females as having different psychological characteristics, interests and activities? Provide examples.

9. Did the advertising you saw when growing up show males and females as having different psychological characteristics, interests and activities? Provide examples.

10. Which of the following activities were you encouraged to participate in at elementary/primary school?
      Football
      Netball
      Cooking
      Needlework

11. If you went to a co-educational elementary/primary school, did your teachers treat girls and boys differently?

12. If you went to a co-educational secondary school, do you think boys and girls were encouraged differently in relation to choosing the following subjects?
      Physics
      Home economics
      Computer studies
      Languages
      Mathematics

13. In your secondary school, assuming it was mixed, did boys and girls obtain (a) popularity and (b) high status from their peer group for the same or for different reasons? If different, specify in what ways.

14. Do you consider that your choice of occupation either has been or is being influenced by your sex? If so, specify how.

15. Summarize how you see your current sex-role identity. To what extent does it work either for or against you?

Part B   My sex-role expectations
1.   Below are a number of areas in female–male relationships where either or both of you may take the initiative:
      Asking for a date
      Ordering a meal

Paying the bill after eating out
Arranging to go to a movie
Arranging a vacation
Driving
Verbally expressing affection
Touching
Making love
Asking for support

(a) To what extent are you prepared to take the initiative in each of the above areas?

(b) To what extent do you have a double standard between yourself and the other sex in regard to taking initiatives in each of these areas?

2.   In each of the following areas relevant to sexual equality:

(a) What is your perception of the current situation?

(b) How would you prefer the situation to be?
Being the breadwinner
Having a career
Nurturing children
Disciplining children
Doing housework
Looking after the garden
Looking after the car(s)
Sexual behaviours
Explaining the facts of life to girls and boys
Showing feelings
Offering emotional support
Being able to dress in many colours
Getting custody of children after divorce
Engaging in professional and managerial work
Engaging in manual work, for example, repairing roads
Being conscripted into the forces in time of war

3.   Summarize the sex-role expectations that you bring to female–male relationships with people roughly your own age.

4.   Do you think your current sex-role expectations help you or harm you in relating effectively with the other sex?

Part C   My sex-role identity and expectations and how I counsel
1.   What do you consider is an appropriate sex-role identity for counsellors? Does your sex-role identity reality match your counsellor ideal?

2.   To what extent do you consider that males and females bring different expectations and problems to counselling?

(a) List mainly female expectations
(b) List mainly female problems
(c) List mainly male expectations
(d) List mainly male problems

3.   To what extent and in what ways do you think your sex-role identity and expectations influence or might influence how you counsel? Please be specific.

EXERCISE 4.6   MY VALUES AND VALUE CONFLICTS

Answer the following questions on your own, with a partner or in a group.

Part A   My values
1.   Using the following seven-point scale, rate the importance of each of the following values as a guiding principle in your life.

Rating scale

Of supreme importance	5
Very important	4
Important	3
Moderately important	2
Slightly important	1
Not important	0
Opposed to my values	-1

My rating	Value
_____	Survival
_____	Love
_____	Friendship
_____	Family life
_____	Religion
_____	Achievement
_____	Materialism
_____	Security
_____	Aesthetics
_____	Intellect
_____	Social interest
_____	Hedonism
_____	Excitement
_____	Conformity
_____	Tradition
_____	Career
_____	Practical
_____	Nature
_____	Health
_____	Self-direction
_____	Personal growth

2. Group your values according to your ratings and summarize what you see as your key values in life.

3. To what extent are you satisfied with your values?

Part B   My value conflicts
1. What are the main areas of conflict between your values? Please be specific.

2. When you counsel, what are the main areas of conflict you either experience or anticipate experiencing between your values and those of clients? Please be specific.

EXERCISE 4.7   MY CULTURE, RACE AND SOCIAL CLASS

Answer the following questions on your own, with a partner or in a group.

Part A   My culture and counselling
1. Other than your national culture, from which ancestral culture(s) are you?

2. What distinctive values, behaviours and expectations do you possess stemming from your ancestral culture(s)?

3. What are the main problems that you experience in your everyday relationships with people from different cultures?

4. What attitudes do you possess towards people from other cultures that might either assist or hinder you in forming effective counselling relationships with them?

5. What observable skills strengths and deficits do you possess for forming counselling relationships with people from different cultures? Please be specific.
   (a) Skills strengths
   (b) Skills deficits

Part B   My race and counselling
1. From which race(s) are you?

2. What behaviours and expectations have you learned that are related to your race(s)?

3. To what extent and in what ways have you been the victim of racism in your life?

4. What attitudes do you possess towards people from other races that might either assist or hinder you in forming effective counselling relationships with them?

5. What observable skills strengths and deficits do you possess for forming counselling relationships with people from different races? Please be specific.

    (a) Skills strengths
    (b) Skills deficits

Part C   My social class and counselling
1. To what social class do you belong? How do you know?

2. What distinctive values, behaviours and expectations do you possess related to your social class?

3. What are the main problems that you experience in your everyday relationships with people from different social classes?

4. What attitudes do you possess towards people from other social classes that might either assist or hinder you in forming effective counselling relationships with them?

5. What observable skills strengths and deficits do you possess for forming effective counselling relationships with people from different social classes? Please be specific.

    (a) Skills strengths
    (b) Skills deficits

EXERCISE 4.8   GROUP DISCUSSION: WHAT I BRING TO COUNSELLING

This is intended as a group exercise, though it may be done individually or in pairs. For each part:

1. Spend 10 to 15 minutes answering the question in groups of three or four.

2. Each group shares its answers with the whole group.

3. Then the whole group ranks the six most important points from the most important to the least important.

Part A Most important characteristics
List the six most important characteristics that you and the other counselling students in your group bring to counselling.

Part B Characteristics most difficult to change
List the six characteristics that you and the other counselling students in your group bring to counselling in order of how difficult each is to change.

PART TWO

Stage 1: Develop the Relationship and Clarify Problem(s)

Chapters 5 and 6 present skills for developing the counselling relationship by listening and showing understanding. Chapter 7 reviews skills counsellors can use to expand and clarify their own and clients' understanding of problems.

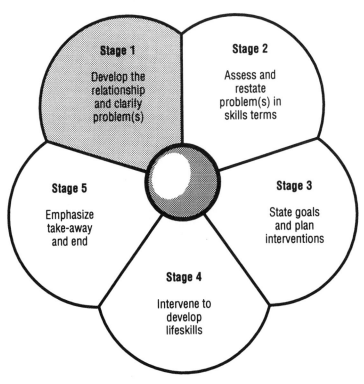

FIVE
Listening skills

Don't walk ahead of me,
I may not follow.
Don't walk behind me,
I may not lead.
Just walk beside me,
And be my friend.

Anon

CHAPTER QUESTIONS

- *What are the goals for the initial counselling session?*

- *What is the counselling relationship?*

- *What messages do counsellors and clients send and receive?*

- *Why are perceptions of messages important?*

- *What is active listening and why is it important?*

- *What does it mean to possess an attitude of respect and acceptance?*

- *How can you tune in to a clients' internal viewpoint?*

- *How can you send good voice messages?*

- *How can you show interest through body messages?*

- *How can you use opening remarks, small rewards and open-ended questions?*

GOALS FOR THE INITIAL COUNSELLING SESSION

Before reviewing specific skills, I outline the four main goals of the first three stages of the lifeskills counselling model. Where clients' problems have a limited focus, you can attain these goals in the initial session. You may require more than one session where clients' problems are complex or there are other factors – for example, ventilating strong feelings or verbosity – that slow the process down. These goals apply to clients as well as to counsellors.

1. DEVELOP A RELATIONSHIP From the start, counsellors convey understanding and support as a basis for developing clients' skills. The relationship in lifeskills counselling is rarely an end in itself, but a vehicle for assisting clients to work on problems and problematic skills. I discuss the counselling relationship in the next section of this chapter.

2. DEVELOP A WORKING MODEL Clients tend to be stuck at present levels of understanding problems. Both counsellors and clients collaborate to develop working models. A working model consists of a set of hypotheses about how clients function in problem areas. Working models are statements of how individual clients feel, think and act.

Many advantages stem from counsellors and clients working together in the detective work of developing working models. First, clients can provide valuable insights if allowed to do much of the work themselves; their contributions are greater when treated as active rather than passive partners. Second, clients as well as counsellors are hypothesis makers and testers. Collaborating with counsellors improves both parties' skills as practitioner-researchers. Third, clients are more likely to own responsibility for possessing and altering skills deficits that they have played some part in discovering. Fourth, collaborating to understand clients' problems can develop the counselling relationship more than active listening alone. Clients may perceive counsellors as more empathic when active than when passive.

3. DEVELOP A WORKING RESTATEMENT IN SKILLS TERMS Counsellors assist clients to identify not only problems, but also the component parts of problems. However, it is insufficient to leave clients hanging. Counsellors need to assist clients to restate their problems in skills terms so that they then have 'handles' for working on them. Here the earlier distinction between *descriptive* summaries and *skills* restatements of problems becomes important. Descriptive summaries clarify problems, but do not move much outside clients' existing concepts and internal viewpoints. Skills restatements identify the specific action and thinking skills deficits sustaining problems. Where possible, reach agreement with clients on how to restate their problems in skills terms.

4. DEVELOP WORKING GOALS AND INTERVENTIONS By the end of the initial session, or if necessary initial sessions, counsellors and clients should agree on prelimi-

nary statements of working goals to guide future work. Furthermore, counsellors can indicate how the goals might be attained. As part of this process, they may discuss the appropriateness of different interventions. Bordin (1979) has suggested that there are three main elements that determine the quality and strength of the counsellor–client working alliance. In addition to the development of a personal bond (relationship), helpers and clients require agreement on treatment goals (goals) and on the tasks to achieve these goals (tasks). Counsellors and clients who achieve each of these three elements in the initial session or sessions have a strong foundation for continuing to develop the working alliance. Sometimes counsellors can start implementing interventions during as well as at the end of initial sessions. Counsellors make such decisions in the light of progress made in sessions and individual clients' needs.

THE COUNSELLING RELATIONSHIP

What exactly is the counselling relationship? Gelso and Carter (1985, 1994) suggest that, regardless of theoretical orientation, all counselling relationships consist of three components: a working alliance, a transference configuration and a real relationship. The working alliance consists of the joining of the client's reasonable self with the counsellor's 'therapizing' self for the purpose of the work. Gelso and Carter (1994, p. 287) 'view the strength of the working alliance as both affected by and affecting the extent to which the therapist and client agree on the goals of their work, agree on the tasks that are useful to attain the goals, and experience an emotional bond with each other.' The transference configuration represents both counsellor and client distortion of one another by transferring perceptions, feelings and behaviours from past relationships on to their current relationship. The real relationship has two defining characteristics: genuineness and realistic perceptions. These different components can change over the course of counselling. The components also overlap and interact with one another.

Beutler and Sandowiz (1994) criticize the Gelso and Carter model of the counselling relationship by observing that the difference between 'real', 'unreal' and 'working alliance components' is difficult to maintain both rationally and empirically. Hill (1994) regards the Gelso and Carter counselling relationship model as too broad. In her framework, 'The relationship can be defined as the feelings and attitudes that participants have toward each other' (p. 91).

Lazarus (1993) asserts that the counselling relationship should not be the same for all clients. On the assumption of 'different strokes for different folks', he argues for interpersonal and inter-session diversity. 'Relationships of choice' are as important as 'techniques of choice' for effective counselling. The counsellor should be an authentic chameleon who selects different relationship stances or styles with different clients at different stages of counselling. The counsellor–client relationship is 'on a continuum extending from a rather formal, businesslike investment at the one end to a close-knit, dependent bonding at the other' (Lazarus, 1995, p. 336). Counsellors need to decide 'when and how to be directive, supportive, reflective, cold, warm, tepid, formal, or informal' (Lazarus, 1993, p. 404). Furthermore, counsellors should take clients' expectations into account. Too great a discrepancy between counsellor style and client expectation makes positive outcomes unlikely.

Clients come to counselling in pain, with problems, with decisions, in crisis and in need of support. They need to relate to or become connected to counsellors as a means of working on their concerns. I define the counselling relationship as the quality and strength of the human connection that counsellors and clients share. Listening and showing understanding skills are central to building quality relationships with clients. In reality, all counselling relationships consist of two relationships: the counsellor's relationship with the client and the client's relationship with the counsellor. Each of these separate relationships consists of how the counsellor or client actually behaves, how the counsellor or client perceives and feels about his or her own behaviour, and the perceptions and feelings that the counsellor or client have about one another.

Throughout all five stages, the lifeskills counselling model heavily emphasizes the importance of the counsellor–client relationship. However, unlike in the person-centred approach, where the counselling relationship is considered both necessary and sufficient for client change to occur (Rogers, 1957), I consider it necessary, but for the most part insufficient or, in many cases, just too slow. Furthermore, I endorse Lazarus's view that skilled counsellors adapt their counselling relationships to their clients. Within limits, join with clients in modes of conversation that lessen discomfort and discrepancy: for example, not focusing extensively on feelings with emotionally inexpressive clients or those expecting practical solutions.

Though it is a simplification, a useful distinction exists between counsellors possessing relationship orientations and task orientations. However, unlike the illustration below, relationship and task orientations are not opposite ends of a continuum.

Relationship ——————————————————————— Task
orientation   orientation

Effective counsellors focus both on relationships and on the tasks of helping clients to develop lifeskills. They go beyond establishing *talking* relationships, where the relationship overshadows the task, to forming supportive *working* relationships, where the relationship facilitates the task. Though this is overstating the point, an analogy may be made with school teaching, where good teacher–student relationships are insufficient substitutes for rigorous teaching and learning. In each of DASIE's five stages, counsellors use relationship skills for supporting both counsellor–client rapport and the tasks of that stage. Counselling relationships support clients as they learn self-support. As such, they contain the seeds of their own destruction.

Counsellors and clients as senders and receivers of messages

Messages are encoded by senders and decoded by receivers (Argyle, 1983). As mentioned in Chapter 2, both counsellors and clients can send five main kinds of messages: verbal, voice, body, touch and action messages. Counsellors and clients are not only senders of messages; they are perceivers of how they send messages. For

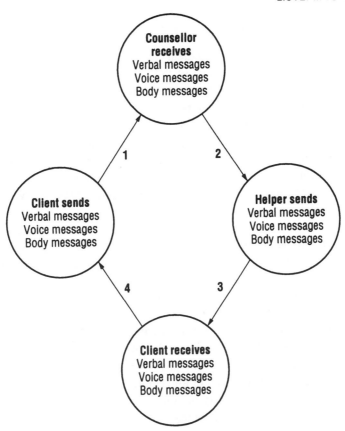

Figure 5.1 A basic 'client communicates, counsellor responds' interaction cycle

instance, counsellors may rightly or wrongly perceive that they send supportive messages to clients. Furthermore, they are perceivers of each other's reactions to their messages. For instance, counsellors may consider that clients misunderstand their supportive messages. In addition, since counsellors and clients can send messages in so many different ways, genuineness is important. For example, how something is said needs to be congruent with what is said.

Effective communication entails counsellors both receiving and sending messages. On the surface, a 'client communicates, counsellor responds' unit of interaction may seem simple. However, this is not the case. As depicted in Figure 5.1, at each of the four points of the cycle – client sends, counsellor receives, counsellor sends, client receives – communication difficulties or 'static', which impair rapport and trust, can arise.

ACTIVE LISTENING

Two counsellors meet in the bar at the end of a working day. One looks fresh, the other tired.

> **Tired-looking counsellor**: I don't know how you can look so fresh after all that listening.
>
> **Fresh-looking counsellor**: Who listens?

Defining active listening

A distinction may be made between hearing and listening. *Hearing* involves the capacity to be aware of and to receive sound. *Listening* involves not only receiving sounds but, as much as possible, accurately understanding their meaning. As such it entails hearing and memorizing words, being sensitive to vocal cues, observing body language and taking into account the personal and social context of communications. However, you can listen accurately without being a rewarding listener. *Active listening*, a term popularized by Thomas Gordon in his 1970 book *Parent Effectiveness Training*, entails not only accurately understanding speakers' communications, but also showing that you have understood. As such, active listening involves receiver and sender skills.

You may wonder why active listening is so important when there are so many opportunities for people to be listened to in everyday life. Here, it is possible to distinguish between social and counselling conversations. *Social* conversations are geared towards meeting the needs of both participants; they have facetiously been described as 'two people, both of whom are taking turns to exercise their ego'. Often listening, let alone rewarding listening, becomes lost along the way. *Counselling* conversations primarily emphasize meeting clients' needs. As such, they place a high premium on rewarding clients by listening and showing understanding to them.

Four kinds of listening take place in any one-to-one counselling conversation. Listening takes place between counsellor and client and within each of them (Gendlin, 1981; Nelson-Jones, 1986). The quality of your inner listening, or being appropriately sensitive to your own thoughts and feelings, may be vital to the quality of your outer listening. If either you or your client listen poorly or too much to yourselves, you listen less well to one another. Conversely, if you listen well to one another, this may help the quality of your inner listening (though counsellors should be skilled at this already). The following saying of Lao-Tse beautifully illustrates the unfolding and healing effect of outer listening on inner listening.

> It is as though he listened
> and such listening as his enfolds us in a silence
> in which at last we begin to hear
> what we are meant to be.

Importance of active listening

Active listening is probably the central skill in developing and maintaining counselling relationships. For clients who come to counselling, occasionally not being listened to may have created mild psychological pain; often not being listened to, moderate pain; and mostly not being listened to, severe pain. Never being listened to is like a psychological death penalty.

Active listening by counsellors has a number of important consequences.

ESTABLISHING RAPPORT You are more likely to develop rapport with clients if they feel understood by you than if this is not the case. For example, a study of helpful and non-helpful events in brief counselling identified eight kinds of events perceived as helpful by clients (Elliott, 1985). These helpful events were grouped into two super-clusters corresponding to interpersonal and task aspects of counselling. Understanding was the predominant cluster in the interpersonal grouping.

ESTABLISHING TRUST Trust is a major issue throughout any relationship (Nelson-Jones, 1996a). Dictionary definitions of trust focus on a firm belief in the honesty, integrity and reliability of another. Many clients come to counselling perceiving that significant others in their past or present lives have been untrustworthy. In addition, life teaches most people to be wary of being taken advantage of. In the face of clients' inevitable mistrust, counsellors need to establish their credentials of honesty, integrity and reliability.

An important way of looking at trust in counselling relationships centres on clients' fears of rejection. The question becomes: 'Deep down can I trust this counsellor to accept me and not to hurt me intentionally?' Here the underlying issue is that of acceptance. A second way of looking at trust is in terms of respect. Here relevant questions are: 'Can I trust this counsellor to continue seeing me as a separate individual and not to distort his or her perception of me to meet her or his own needs?' and 'Can I trust this counsellor to encourage my growth as a separate person within the independence of our relationship?' A third way of looking at trust is in terms of duty of care and competence: 'Can I trust this counsellor to act in my best interests?'

Trust in a counselling relationship is an interactive process. The degree to which counsellor and client trust themselves, one another and the relationship influences the other person's trust. Counsellors can expedite the process of establishing trust and dissolving mistrust by listening carefully to clients and showing them that they understand them on their own terms.

BRIDGING DIFFERENCES Every counsellor has a potential set of blinkers depending upon her or his circumstances. How can you know what it is like to be old, dying, female, male, gay, physically disabled, an immigrant, White, Black, Asian, Aboriginal or Maori etc., if the description does not fit you? However, if you counsel someone with a different set of life's circumstances, she or he can greatly assist you to understand them if you use good listening skills. By showing your understanding you build bridges, not walls.

HELPING CLIENTS TO DISCLOSE Clients are often shy and anxious. They may be divulging highly sensitive information. Even if the information is not highly sensitive, clients may perceive disclosure as risky. Many clients are like boxers who have learned to keep their guards up for fear of getting hit if they reveal themselves. Previously they may have received much overt and subtle rejection for disclosing. Good listening helps clients to feel accepted, safe and understood. This in turn helps clients to choose to tell their stories and share their inner world with you.

HELPING CLIENTS TO EXPERIENCE FEELINGS Many clients have been inadequately listened to in their pasts. Consequently, they may have relinquished, temporarily at least, some of their capacity for emotional responsiveness (Rogers, 1959, 1961; Raskin and Rogers, 1995). Rewarding listening can help clients to tune into and acknowledge the inner flow of their emotions. The message some clients may require is that it is OK to experience and express feelings. They can become stronger and more centred if they can face and learn to deal with feelings than if they either block them out or only partially acknowledge them.

GATHERING INFORMATION A facetious remark about a psychologist colleague was that he had to ask everyone whether they were male or female since he was incapable of gathering information without asking questions. If you listen well, most clients collaborate in providing relevant information about themselves. You do not have to interrogate them. Together you build a working model of their problems and problematic skills patterns. At later stages of counselling, clients provide you with knowledge about how they use their skills in their daily lives. Many beginning counsellors question too much and listen too little. However, some ask too few or the wrong sorts of questions.

CREATING AN INFLUENCE BASE The lifeskills counsellor is a developmental educator actively influencing clients to develop self-helping skills. Active listening is one way you can build your influence base so that clients are more likely to listen to you. Showing understanding to clients from different cultural groups contributes to your ascribed status and credibility (Sue and Zane, 1987).

Social influence research points to active listening contributing to clients perceiving you as competent, trustworthy and attractive (Strong, 1968, 1978). Studies of the counselling process indicate that successful counselling relationships start with high agreement, pass through a period of disagreement and end with high agreement. The middle or disagreement stage results from counsellor efforts to generate change and client resistances to such efforts (Strong *et al.*, 1992). Building social influence early on increases clients' willingness to accommodate your efforts to generate change.

HELPING CLIENTS TO ASSUME RESPONSIBILITY Clients who are listened to sharply and supportively are more likely to assume responsibility for working on their problems and problematic skills than those who are not. One reason is that active listening may reduce defensiveness. Another reason is that active listening provides a base for offering well-timed challenges that encourage clients to assume rather than to avoid responsibility. Furthermore, active listening provides a climate in which clients can assume greater personal agency for constructing their actions and meanings (Strong *et al.*, 1995).

BASIC SKILLS OF ACTIVE LISTENING

This and the next chapter describe ten basic skills of active listening for counselling. Some of the skills overlap. Each of these skills requires counsellors to make choices. As a practitioner-researcher, become aware of your active listening choices and evaluate their consequences.

Ten skills of active listening

Skill 1	Possess an attitude of respect and acceptance
Skill 2	Tune into the client's internal viewpoint
Skill 3	Send good voice messages
Skill 4	Send good body messages
Skill 5	Use openers, small rewards and open-ended questions
Skill 6	Paraphrase
Skill 7	Reflect feelings
Skill 8	Show understanding of context and difference
Skill 9	Manage initial resistances
Skill 10	Avoid unrewarding 'don'ts'

SKILL 1: POSSESS AN ATTITUDE OF RESPECT AND ACCEPTANCE

An accepting attitude involves respecting clients as separate human beings with rights to their own thoughts and feelings. Such an attitude entails suspending judgement on clients' goodness or badness. All humans are fallible and possess lifeskills strengths and deficits that may result in good or bad consequences for themselves and others. Fromm (1956) notes that respect comes from the Latin word *respicere*, meaning to look at. Respect means the ability to look at others as they are and to prize their unique individuality. Respect also means allowing other people to grow and develop on their own terms without exploitation and control. Rogers, the founder of person-centred therapy, which heavily emphasizes counsellor acceptance, grew up afraid that if he said anything significant to his mother she would judge it negatively (Heppner *et al.*, 1984).

Though an accepting attitude involves respecting others as separate and unique human beings, this does not mean that you agree with everything they say. However, you are secure enough in yourself to respect what they say as their versions of reality. You do not need to use barriers and filters to protect you from listening to the full range of their messages. These barriers can be internal and external. Internal barriers operate on, distort and filter out certain elements of the messages you receive. At worst you may deny or block out the whole message. External barriers manifest themselves in subtle and not so subtle voice and body cues to others that they should edit what they say. Barriers also manifest themselves in the more obvious verbal 'don'ts' of being an active listener, listed in Chapter 6.

Barriers to an accepting attitude

Counsellors need to be psychologically present to clients. This entails absence of defensiveness and a willingness to allow clients' expressions and experiencing to affect you. Ideally, you should be 'all there' – with your body, thoughts, senses and emotions. Psychological accessibility entails an accepting attitude not only to clients, but to yourself. Put simply, a confident person's acceptance of self translates into acceptance of others, whereas the reverse is also true.

What are some of the main barriers and filters that act as sources of interference to your receiving another loud and clear? All of them are related to your sense of worth and to how much debilitating anxiety you possess. The stronger you are emotionally, the less need there is for you to use barriers and filters, so the more open you are to others. Following are some barriers likely to influence how you listen.

ANXIETY-EVOKING FEELINGS Clients can express feelings that counsellors find hard to handle: for instance, apathy, depression, happiness or sexuality. Counsellors may feel threatened by feelings directed towards them, such as hostility or liking. Alternatively, counsellor anxiety may be evoked by the intensity of clients' feelings about others: for instance, envy at a sibling or grief over a bereavement.

> Anita, 25, a beginning counsellor, listened to Stan pour out his resentment over his girlfriend Eva's behaviour. Anita was uncomfortable when people became angry in her life outside counselling. Even though none of Stan's anger was directed towards her, she started feeling very anxious and wondered whether the session would get out of control.

ANXIETY-EVOKING CLIENTS Counsellors may feel threatened by certain categories of clients: for example, clients of the opposite sex, seriously disturbed clients, highly successful clients, very intelligent clients and clients who hold strong feelings with which the counsellor disagrees.

> Penny, 29, a trainee counsellor, became uncomfortable when faced with Henry, a sexually active homosexual client. Her discomfort stemmed not from prejudice about gays, but because she felt out of her depth in being able to relate to his life experiences. She was aware that her anxiety about coping made it even harder to empathise with Henry.

ANXIETY-EVOKING SITUATIONS Anxiety and threat are present in all counselling situations. The following are some common situations where counsellors may feel vulnerable – their own agendas may preclude fully listening to clients.

- The first few minutes of an initial session.

- Concentrating on developing new counselling skills as well as on the needs of clients.

- Feeling insecure about restating problems in skills terms.

- Thinking that progress is too slow.

- Clients coming late for appointments.

- Recording interviews for supervision.

TRIGGER WORDS, PHRASES AND ATTITUDES Trigger words and phrases raise a 'red flag' for you. Each counsellor has his or her own emotionally charged triggers. For example, counsellors can allow themselves to be triggered by sexist comments, prejudice against gays, cross-cultural put-downs and racist comments. Trigger phrases can also be 'you' messages from clients to helpers: for example, 'You screwed up,' 'You don't understand' or 'You're not helping me enough.'

> Imran, 31, a Pakistani counsellor, has to struggle to control his emotions with anyone who expresses racist attitudes. Recently Imran had a client, Wayne, who started using the term 'wog' and said he thought Asian immigrants should be repatriated. Imran became so angry that, for some moments, he lost sight of his client's vulnerability.
>
> Sarah, a trainee group therapist who had been raped, allowed herself to be triggered by Carlos, an advanced cancer patient who was a new entrant to her group. Carlos belittled the experiences of rape victims and ended by saying he would welcome a rape attempt by any woman in the group. At this last remark, Sarah said 'If you believe that, you're fucking ignorant!' (Yalom, 1989, p. 70)

Positive words and phrases can also trigger feelings that interfere with your listening: for example, flattery like 'Gee, you're wonderful, Mr/Ms Murgatroyd.'

PREJUDICES Counsellors are not immune from varying degrees of prejudice. For reasons connected with your upbringing, you may tune out to people different from you because of age, sex, sexual orientation, culture, race, social class, physical disability or intelligence level, among other possible differences.

> Megan, 27, dislikes working with elderly clients. She not only tries to avoid seeing them, but also withdraws from forming close counselling relationships with them. She rationalizes her behaviour by saying that she is of much more use spending time with younger clients.

CURRENT UNFINISHED BUSINESS Unfinished business can interfere with your being open to clients. For instance, if you have just come from a heated staff meeting, you may be less ready to listen and accept your next client. If you have just rushed to get to a counselling session, you may not listen adequately until you have calmed down. Furthermore, you can think about something said earlier in this or a previous session and fail to attend to the present. In addition, you may have intrusive personal worries.

> Marita is a successful counsellor in private practice. However, she is going through a very difficult period in her marriage. She and her husband, Roland, have frequent rows. Marita is uncertain whether she wants to stay in the marriage. Hard as she tries to concentrate in her counselling sessions, Marita has intrusive thoughts about her resentment with Roland and her anxiety about the future of their marriage.

PRESENTING A PROFESSIONAL FAÇADE Genuineness is an important characteristic for counsellors (Raskin and Rogers, 1995; Rogers, 1957). A difference exists between being genuine and seeming genuine. Some counsellors are too concerned with maintaining a smooth professional façade. Their concern with how clients perceive them may interfere with perceiving their clients accurately. Such counsellors are too busy listening to their own needs to accept clients fully. Maintaining a professional facade is especially difficult when clients directly challenge your professional adequacy.

> Danny, 26, a counselling psychology student on placement at his university's student counselling service, worries that clients will see that he is not yet fully competent. He puts on an act, being too friendly and trying to appear too expert. He takes control rather than forms cooperative working relationships with clients.

EMOTIONAL EXHAUSTION AND BURNOUT Frequently counsellors possess a combination of difficult environments, demanding clients and poor skills at setting limits on their involvement. Freudenberger defines burnout: 'To deplete oneself. To exhaust one's physical and mental resources. To wear oneself out by excessively striving to reach some unrealistic expectation imposed by one's self or by the values of society' (Freudenberger, 1980, p. 17). Emotionally exhausted counsellors may be less accepting of clients than those who feel well. Their energy level and sense of personal accomplishment are low. Counselling relationships, instead of being positive challenges, can become endurance tests.

> Patricia, 43, is a social worker with a heavy caseload. She is highly conscientious and worries a lot about what happens to her clients. Recently she has been feeling depressed, irritable and very tired. Patricia has to drag herself to work and feels anxious much of the time. She is not doing her best work.

INSUFFICIENT ADMINISTRATIVE SUPPORT Counsellors in organizations and institutions may spend much time securing budgets, ensuring their role is understood and dealing with other administrative matters. Frequently, they lack adequate administrative support. Insufficient administrative support can undermine morale, increase caseloads and involve counsellors in routine secretarial and administrative chores. A casualty can be how accepting counsellors are of clients.

> Brad, 53, is the staff counsellor in an insurance company. He reports to Greg, 35, the personnel manager. Greg is very smooth on the surface, but underneath possesses an unpleasant shadow side. He consistently sends Brad messages that his work is not good enough and that clients and staff complain about him. The reality is that Brad's work is of a very high standard and almost all his clients find him very helpful. Recently Brad has been feeling run down. Greg jumps on this as evidence of his weakness rather than supports him. Greg's behaviour further undermines Brad's energy level and concentration.

PHYSICAL BARRIERS Physical barriers may contribute to your being less accepting of clients than desirable. For example, you may be too hot or too cold, you may lack privacy, your room may be dreary, your chair may be uncomfortable, the lighting may be poor or there may be too much noise.

> Helen is a nursing student who is required to interview patients assigned to her. There is a shortage of suitable interview rooms. On some occasions the

only room available is one that has glass windows facing the corridor. On other occasions Helen has to interview patients in open wards. Helen feels distracted by the lack of genuine privacy for herself and her patients.

So far I have discussed ten barriers and filters to your adopting an attitude of respect and acceptance for your clients. Some of the barriers stem solely from you. Some originate in the environment. The list is far from exhaustive. You may think of other relevant barriers and filters.

SKILL 2: TUNE INTO THE CLIENT'S INTERNAL VIEWPOINT

Don't judge any man until you have walked two moons in his moccasins.

American Indian Proverb

If clients are to feel that you receive them loud and clear, you need to develop the ability to 'walk in their moccasins', 'get inside their skins' and 'see the world through their eyes'. At the heart of active listening is a basic distinction between 'you' and 'me', between 'your view of you' and 'my view of you', and between 'your view of me' and 'my view of me'. Your view of you and my view of me are both inside or internal viewpoints, whereas your view of me and my view of you are both outside or external viewpoints. The skill of listening to and understanding another person is based on your choosing to acknowledge the separateness between 'me' and 'you' by getting inside the other's internal viewpoint rather than remaining in your own external viewpoint.

If you respond to what clients say in ways that show accurate understanding of their viewpoints, you respond as if inside their internal viewpoints. Such responses do not mean you agree with them, but that you acknowledge that what they say is their subjective reality. However, if you choose not to show understanding of your clients' viewpoints or lack the skills to understand them, you respond from your external viewpoint. In short, if you respond to clients as if inside their internal viewpoints, you respond to them from where they are. If you step outside your clients' internal viewpoints, you respond more from either where you are or where you think they should be.

The following are examples of counsellor responses *external* to clients' viewpoints.

'What can I do for you?'

'You should get out of the relationship.'

'Women can be very manipulative.'

'You are going to be all right.'

'I think you're feeling too sorry for yourself.'

'Consider taking tranquillizers over your exam period.'

'Let me tell you about a similar experience to yours.'

Tuning into clients' internal viewpoints involves understanding them on their terms. You listen carefully and allow clients the psychological space to say what they wish. In addition, you need to decode their messages, taking into account voice and body as well as verbal messages.

Following are examples of counsellor responses as if in clients' *internal* viewpoints.

'You feel betrayed by your company.'

'You're delighted at passing your statistics test.'

'You feel that often people don't look beyond your disability to discover what sort of a person you are.'

'You have mixed feelings about accepting the promotion.'

'You're pleased that your parents-in-law live nearby.'

'You feel unsettled since returning from visiting home.'

'You feel appreciated and happy because your daughter phoned on your birth-day.'

Think of a three-link chain: client statement–counsellor response–client statement. Counsellors who respond from clients' internal viewpoints allow them either to continue on the same path or to choose to change direction. However, if counsellors respond from the external viewpoint, they influence clients to divert from paths they would otherwise have chosen. Sometimes such external influence is desirable, but frequently it is not. Always consciously choose whether or not to respond as if inside clients' internal viewpoints.

SKILL 3: SEND GOOD VOICE MESSAGES

Your voice messages can greatly enhance the emotional climate of your listening. When supervising beginning counselling students, I pay great attention to how they use their voices to frame their verbal responses to clients. The two most common faults are speaking either too quickly or too softly – both indicate anxiety. Your voice can speak volumes about what you truly feel and how emotionally responsive you are to clients' feelings. Counsellors may use voice messages little during clients' verbal utterances, perhaps restricting them to 'uh-hmms'. However, voice messages always accompany verbal responses. As such, they are an integral part of active listening.

The following five dimensions of voice messages form the acronym VAPER: volume, articulation, pitch, emphasis and rate.

VOLUME Volume refers to loudness or quietness. You need to respond at a decibel level that is comfortable and easy to hear. Some counsellors have the bad habit of fading, letting their voices trail away at the end of sentences. Sometimes counsellors unnecessarily quieten their voices to match those of clients. While a booming voice overwhelms, speaking in too quiet a voice may make you appear weak.

ARTICULATION Articulation refers to the distinctness and clarity of speech. Counsellors may speak with adequate loudness, but still be difficult to understand. Enunciate words clearly. Poor enunciation can interrupt the client's train of thought. Heavy accents can be very difficult to listen to, especially if accompanied by poor use of grammar and language. Again, this may interfere with the client's train of thought. Some counsellors need to modify strong regional or overseas accents. Counsellors possessing excessively nasal, guttural or throaty voices might consider speech therapy.

PITCH Pitch refers to the highness or lowness of voice. An optimum pitch range includes all the levels at which a pleasing voice can be produced without strain (Kruger, 1970). Errors of pitch include being either too high-pitched or too low-pitched. High-pitched and shrill voices can disconcert. A harsh tone can threaten. Counsellors' voices may be higher pitched when they feel anxious than when they feel calmer.

EMPHASIS It is important that your voice is expressive in picking up the major feelings and feeling nuances of clients. Counsellors may use emphasis in the wrong places. You can speak with too much variation in emphasis and seem melodramatic or with too little variation and appear wooden. If you speak with too little emphasis, clients may perceive you as weak; with too much emphasis, as controlling.

RATE Try to achieve a speech rate that is comfortable for both you and your clients. Speech rate is often measured in words per minute and depends on how quickly words are spoken and also on the frequency and duration of pauses between them. Counsellors who speak very quickly may contribute to keeping clients anxious rather than calming them down. Often it is a good idea for counselling students to speak more slowly. A slower speech rate helps you appear less nervous and also provides more time to think of what to say.

Your use of pauses and silences can also enhance your capacity to be a rewarding listener. If you want to make it easier for clients to tell their stories, you can pause each time they stop speaking before responding, to see if they wish to continue. Good use of silences can also allow clients more psychological space to think things through before speaking and to get more in touch with feelings. Some counselling students find silences threatening – they have to work on tendencies to interrupt too soon.

SKILL 4: SEND GOOD BODY MESSAGES

Counsellors always send messages to clients. Your body messages as a listener are important when both clients and you speak. Here the emphasis is on the former. To be a rewarding person with whom to talk you need physically to convey your receptiveness and interest. Often this is referred to as attending behaviour. Body messages are the main helper responses *during* a client's verbal utterances. A simple example may highlight the point. Imagine a counsellor looking out of the window at the start of a session when the client describes a sensitive personal problem.

The following are some of the main body message skills that demonstrate interest and attention (Argyle, 1992; Egan, 1994; Ivey, 1994). In varying degrees, they provide non-verbal rewards for talking.

AVAILABILITY It may seem obvious, but counsellors may sometimes rightly or wrongly be perceived as insufficiently available to help. You may be overworked. You may be poor at letting your availability or limits on it be known. Intentionally or unintentionally you may send messages that create distance. For instance, teachers may physically edge away from pupils wishing to discuss personal concerns. Send clear messages to clients and others about availability and access.

RELAXED AND OPEN BODY POSTURE A relaxed body posture, without slumping or slouching, contributes to the message that you are receptive. If you sit in a tense and uptight fashion, your clients may consciously or intuitively feel that you are too bound up in your personal agendas and unfinished business to be fully accessible to them.

Sit openly facing your clients, so that you can easily see one another. Trainers such as Carkhuff and Egan recommend sitting square to clients – your left shoulder opposite their right shoulder (Carkhuff, 1987; Egan, 1994). However, another option is to sit at a slight angle to clients. Here, both of you can still receive all of each other's significant facial and bodily messages. The advantage of this is that it provides each of you with more discretion in varying the directness of your contact than if sitting opposite each other. Highly vulnerable clients may especially appreciate this seating arrangement.

How you use your arms and legs can enhance or detract from an open body posture. For example, crossed arms can be perceived as barriers – sometimes crossed legs can too. Research suggests that postural similarity, where two people take up mirror-image postures, is perceived as a sign of liking (Argyle, 1992).

SLIGHT FORWARD LEAN Whether you lean forwards, backwards or sideways is another aspect of your body posture. If you lean too far forward you look odd and clients may feel you invade their personal space. However, in moments of intimate disclosure, a marked forward lean may build rapport rather than be perceived as 'imposing' (Sharpley and Sagris, 1995). If you lean too far back, clients may find this distancing. Especially at the start of counselling, a slight forward trunk lean can encourage clients, without threatening them.

GOOD USE OF GAZE AND EYE CONTACT Gaze means looking at people in the area of their faces. Good gaze skills indicate your interest and enable you to receive important facial messages. Women are usually more attentive than men on all measures of gaze (Henley, 1977; Argyle, 1983). Gaze can give you cues about when to stop listening and start responding. However, the main cues used in synchronizing conversation are verbal and voice messages rather than body messages (Argyle, 1983). Good eye contact skills involve looking in the client's direction so that you allow the possibility of your eyes meeting reasonably often. There is an equilibrium level for eye contact in any counselling relationship, depending on the degree of anxiety in client and counsellor, how developed the relationship is and the degree of attraction involved. Staring threatens clients: they may feel dominated or seen through. Some clients even feel threatened at seeing their reflections in shop windows! Clients may perceive you as tense or bored if you look down or away too often.

APPROPRIATE FACIAL EXPRESSIONS Your face is perhaps your main vehicle for sending body messages. Ekman *et al.* (1972) identified seven main expressions of emotion: happiness, interest, surprise, fear, sadness, anger and disgust or contempt. Much facial information is conveyed through the mouth and eyebrows. A friendly, relaxed facial expression, including a smile, usually demonstrates interest. However, as the client talks, your facial expressions need to show that you are tuned into what they say. For instance, if the client is serious, weeping or angry, adjust your facial expression to indicate that you observe and hear what they communicate.

APPROPRIATE GESTURES Perhaps the head nod is the most common gesture in listening: 'small ones to show continued attention, larger and repeated ones to indicate agreement' (Argyle, 1992, p. 11). Head nods can be viewed as a rewards to clients. On the negative side, selective head nods can also be powerful ways of controlling clients. Then unconditional acceptance becomes conditional acceptance. Arm and hand gestures can also be used to show responsiveness to clients. However, counsellors using expressive arm gestures too much or too little can be offputting. Other negative gestures include: fidgeting with pens and pencils, hands clenched together, finger drumming, fiddling with your hair, your hand over your mouth, ear tugging and scratching yourself, to mention but some.

APPROPRIATE USE OF TOUCH Use of touch may be appropriate in counselling, though care needs to be taken that it is not an unwanted invasion of personal space (Bacorn and Dixon, 1984). For example, demonstrations of concern may include touching a client's hands, arms, shoulders and upper back. The intensity and duration of touch should be sufficient to establish contact yet avoid discomfort and any hint of sexual interest. Part of being an active listener includes picking up messages about the limits and desirability of your use of touch. As porcupine parents advise their offspring regarding making love, when contemplating touching clients, 'proceed with caution'.

SENSITIVITY TO PERSONAL SPACE AND HEIGHT Active listening entails respecting clients' personal space. Counsellors can be too close or too far away. Perhaps a comfortable physical distance for counsellors and clients is sitting with their heads about 5 feet apart. In Western cultures clients might perceive any less distance as too personal (Hall, 1966; Pease, 1981). On the other hand, if counsellors are physically too far away, not only do clients have to talk louder, but they may perceive you as emotionally distant. The most comfortable height for counselling conversations is with heads at the same level. This fact is forgotten by some counsellors, who sit in higher and more elaborate chairs than clients.

CLOTHING AND GROOMING Counsellors' clothes send messages which may influence how much and in which areas clients reveal themselves. These messages include social and occupational standing, sex-role identity, ethnicity, conformity to peer group norms, rebelliousness and how outgoing you are. While maintaining your individuality, you need to dress appropriately for your clienteles: for example, delinquent teenagers probably respond better to informally dressed counsellors than do stressed business executives. Your personal grooming also provides important information about how well you take care of yourself: for instance, you may be clean or dirty, neat or tidy. In addition, the length and styling of your hair sends messages about you.

The concept of rules is very important for understanding the appropriateness of body messages (Argyle and Henderson, 1985; Argyle, 1986). For example, mention has been made of differing physical proximity rules depending on whether you are in a personal or counselling relationship. Relationship rules also differ across cultures. For instance, Arabs and Latin Americans stand very close by Western standards. You require sensitivity to the body message rules of the social and cultural contexts in which you work as well as to your own and clients' individual needs.

Counsellors require flexibility in making active listening choices. As your counselling relationships develop, clients get to know whether and when you are receptive to them. For instance, clients may know from past experience that when you lean back you still attend. Counsellors need to use attending body messages selectively. When appropriate, you can choose to make your body messages less rewarding: for instance, when you want to check your understanding of what clients say, stop them from rambling or make your own points.

Both *within* your body messages and *between* your body messages and your voice and verbal messages, consistency increases the chances of clients perceiving you as a rewarding listener. For instance, you may be smiling and at the same time either fidgeting or tapping your foot. Your smile may indicate interest, your foot tapping impatience and your overall message may appear insincere.

SKILL 5: USE OPENING REMARKS, SMALL REWARDS AND OPEN-ENDED QUESTIONS

Opening remarks, small rewards and open-ended questions tend to require a few words as well as good voice and body messages. They make it easier for clients to talk.

Opening remarks

Lifeskills counselling always starts with acknowledging the client's name, saying who you are, and checking 'where the client is at'. Counsellors are not all-knowing. Opening remarks, openers or permissions to talk are brief statements indicating that counsellors are prepared to listen. Counsellors start initial sessions with opening remarks that build rapport and encourage clients to share why they have come. Counsellors can leave until later a statement about how they work. Opening remarks are 'door openers' that give clients the message 'I'm interested and prepared to listen. Please share with me your internal viewpoint.'

I avoid the common opening remark 'Please tell me how I can be of help,' and similar opening statements. Such remarks can get initial sessions off to unfortunate starts by connoting that clients are dependent on me rather than on helping themselves. Examples of opening remarks that might be used in initial lifeskills counselling sessions include:

When meeting the client outside your office

Hello (state client's name), I'm (state your name). Please come in.

When the client is seated

'Please tell me why you've come.'

'Please tell me why you're here.'

'Please tell me what's concerning you.'

'Please tell me what's the problem.'

'Please put me in the picture.'

'You've been referred by ... Now, how do you see your situation?'

Sometimes counsellors make opening remarks in response to client body messages.

'You seem upset. Would you care to say what's bothering you?'

'You seem very nervous.'

The opening remark 'You seem very nervous' gives clients the opportunity to talk about either a problem they bring to counselling or how they feel here-and-now in the interview. Counsellors can sometimes give permission to talk by body messages alone, for instance a look, possibly accompanied by an arm gesture.

On occasion you may sense that clients want to talk, but have difficulty doing so. In such instances, if you follow up your opening remark with another, this may make it easier for them to talk. Examples of 'lubricating' comments include:

'It's pretty hard to get started.'

'Take your time.'

'When you're ready.'

Some counsellors have contacts with clients outside formal interviews: for instance, correctional officers in facilities for delinquents; residential staff in halfway houses for former drug addicts; or nurses in hospitals. Here you may use permissions to talk when you sense that someone has a personal agenda that bothers him or her, but requires that extra bit of encouragement to share it. Opening remarks for use in informal counselling include:

'Is there something on your mind?'

'You seem tense today.'

'I'm available if you want to talk.'

Small rewards

Small rewards are brief verbal and non-verbal expressions of interest designed to encourage clients to continue speaking. The message they convey is 'I'm with you. Please go on.' Wrongly used small rewards can encourage clients to respond to counsellor agendas rather than to their own. For instance, you may say 'Tell me more' whenever clients talk about topics of interest to you. Many small rewards are body rather than verbal messages: for example, facial expressions, head nods and good eye contact. The following are examples of verbal small rewards, though perhaps the most frequently used 'uh-hmm' is more a voice than a verbal message.

Uh-hmm	Sure
Please continue	Indeed
Tell me more	And ...
Go on	So ...
I see	Really
Oh?	Right
Then ...	Yes
I hear you.	You're not kidding.

Another kind of small reward is to repeat the last word a client has said:

Client: I'm feeling nervous.
Counsellor: Nervous.

Open-ended questions

Counsellors may use questions in ways that either help clients to elaborate their internal viewpoints or lead them out of their viewpoints, possibly into yours. Open-ended questions allow clients to share their internal viewpoints without curtailing their options. A good use of open-ended questions is when, in the initial session, you wish to assist clients to tell why they have come. In subsequent sessions too, you are likely to find open-ended questions useful. Open-ended questions include: 'Tell me about it,' 'Please elaborate' and, slightly less open-ended, 'How do you feel about that?'

Open-ended questions may be contrasted with closed-ended questions that curtail speakers' options: indeed, they often give only two options, 'yes' or 'no'.

Open-ended question: How do you feel about your relationship?
Closed-ended question: Is your relationship good or bad?

Open-ended questions may also be contrasted with leading questions that put answers into clients' mouths:

Open-ended question: What do you think about her?
Leading question: She's a great person, isn't she?

Closed-ended and leading questions may have various negative outcomes. You may be perceived as controlling the conversation. You may block clients from getting in touch with and listening to themselves and responding to their internal viewpoint rather than to your external viewpoint. You may set the stage for an interrogation. Since closed-ended and leading questions can be disincentives to talking, they can create silences in which the stage is set for further closed-ended questions.

Be careful not to use leading questions. However, I do not mean to imply that counsellors never use closed-ended questions. It depends on the goals of your listening. Closed-ended questions can be useful for collecting information. However, show restraint if you wish to help others share their worlds. You may also need to use open-ended questions sparingly.

CHAPTER HIGHLIGHTS

- *Four main goals for the initial counselling session(s) are developing a relationship, a working model, a working restatement in skills terms and working goals and interventions.*

- *The counselling relationship can be defined as the quality and strength of the human connection that counsellors and clients share. Lifeskills counselling heavily emphasizes the importance of the counselling relationship.*

- *Active listening entails not only accurately understanding speakers' communications, but showing them that you have understood. Active listening is the central skill in the development of supportive counselling relationships.*

- *Functions of active listening include establishing rapport, establishing trust, bridging differences, helping clients to disclose, helping clients to experience feelings, gathering information, creating an influence base and helping clients to assume responsibility.*

- *Counsellors should possess an attitude of respect and acceptance towards clients as separate human beings with rights to their own thoughts and feelings.*

- *Barriers to possessing an attitude of respect and acceptance include: anxiety-evoking feelings, clients and situations; trigger words, phrases and attitudes; prejudices; current unfinished business; presenting a professional facade; emotional exhaustion and burnout; insufficient administrative support; and physical barriers.*

- *Tuning into clients' internal viewpoints involves understanding them on their terms and not yours. Counsellors always need to be aware of whether they respond inside or outside their clients' internal viewpoints.*

- *You require skills of sending good voice messages when responding to clients. Five dimensions of sending good voice messages are volume, articulation, pitch, emphasis and rate (VAPER).*

- *When listening, you can reward speakers by showing interest through body messages, including your relaxed and open body posture, slight forward lean, good use of gaze and eye contact, facial expressions, gestures, use of touch and sensitivity to personal space and height.*

- *You need a repertoire of opening remarks that communicate that you are available to listen.*

- *Small rewards are brief verbal messages that encourage speakers to continue: for instance, 'Go on,' 'Then' and 'I hear you.'*

- *Open-ended questions, unlike closed or leading questions, allow speakers to share their internal viewpoints without curtailing their options.*

EXERCISE 5.1   ASSESSING MY BARRIERS TO AN ACCEPTING ATTITUDE

Complete this exercise on your own, with a partner or in a group.

1. Assess how much each of the following barriers either does or might interfere with your possessing an accepting attitude when counselling.

    (a) anxiety-evoking feelings
    (b) anxiety-evoking clients
    (c) anxiety-evoking situations
    (d) trigger words, phrases and attitudes
    (e) prejudices
    (f) current unfinished business
    (g) presenting a professional facade
    (h) emotional exhaustion and burnout
    (i) insufficient administrative support
    (j) physical barriers
    (k) others (please specify)

2. Summarize the main barriers to your adopting an attitude of respect and acceptance for your clients when you counsel.

EXERCISE 5.2   TUNING INTO THE CLIENT'S INTERNAL VIEWPOINT

As appropriate, complete parts of this exercise on your own, with a partner or in a group.

Part A   Assess how counsellors respond
Below are some statement–response excerpts from formal and informal counselling situations. Three counsellor responses have been provided for each statement. Write 'IN' or 'EX' by each response according to whether it reflects the client's internal viewpoint or comes from the counsellor's external viewpoint. Some of the responses may seem artificial, but they have been chosen to highlight the point of the exercise. Answers are provided at the end of this chapter.

Example: Client to marital counsellor

Client: 'We seem to be growing apart. Jim spends more and more time at the office and I'm worried for the kids.'

Marital counsellor:

EX   (a) 'Have you talked over your concerns with Jim?'
EX   (b) 'You deserve more support from Jim.'
IN   (c) 'You and Jim are becoming more distant and you're concerned how this affects your kids.'

1. Pupil to school counsellor

Pupil: 'I've got this big test coming up and I don't seem to be able to concentrate. I'm worried sick.'

School counsellor:

(a) 'This is a case of test anxiety.'
(b) 'You're scared because your lack of concentration prevents you from revising properly.'
(c) 'You will be all right on the day.'

2. Client to social worker

Client: 'I hate being on welfare. It strips me of all pride and dignity.'

Social worker:

(a) 'You loathe being dependent on handouts with the loss of pride and self-esteem it involves.'
(b) 'The recession is hurting a lot of people.'
(c) 'How much money do you get?'

3. Client to career counsellor

Client: 'I'm getting to the point where I don't want to continue with my law course. I think I'm mainly doing it to please my parents.'

Career counsellor:

(a) 'You've invested a lot of time and effort in getting so far and should think very carefully before quitting your course.'
(b) 'Many students change directions when at college.'
(c) 'You're thinking of quitting your law course since you're doing it more to please your parents than yourself.'

Part B Summarize another's internal viewpoint
Work with a partner.

1. Person A talks for at least two minutes about what he or she considers important in a counselling relationship (Person A's internal viewpoint). Person B does not interrupt.

2. When Person A finishes, Person B summarizes the main points of what Person A was saying. Person A does not interrupt.

3. When Person B finishes summarizing, Person A comments on how accurate Person B was in understanding his or her internal viewpoint. Person B can respond to this feedback.

4. Then reverse roles and repeat 1, 2 and 3 above.

Part C Observe how you and others respond
1. Watch and listen to TV and radio interviews and talk shows. Observe when interviewers respond from either interviewees' internal or from their own external viewpoints.

2. Monitor your own behaviour for a week and become more aware of when you respond to speakers from your own or their viewpoints.

    (a) in counselling sessions
    (b) in your daily life

EXERCISE 5.3 HOW REWARDING ARE MY VOICE MESSAGES WHEN I LISTEN?

As appropriate, complete parts of this exercise on your own, with a partner or in a group.

Part A Self-assessment
1. On each of the following dimensions, assess how rewarding your voice messages are when you listen as a counsellor.

    (a) volume
    (b) articulation
    (c) pitch
    (d) emphasis
    (e) rate
    (f) others (please specify)

2. Summarize how rewarding or unrewarding your voice messages are when you listen as a counsellor.

3. Identify specific skills deficits in your voice messages when you listen and set goals for change.

Part B   Use terrible and good voice message skills when counselling
Your partner shares a concern, with you acting as counsellor.

1. First two minutes: use terrible voice message skills when counselling.

2. Second two minutes: use good voice message skills when counselling.

3. Evaluation period: discuss what it felt like receiving and sending terrible and good voice messages. Your evaluation session may be more educational and fun if you play back a cassette of your four-minute conversation.

4. Reverse roles and repeat 1, 2 and 3 above.

Part C   Observe and assess your voice messages
Record on audio-cassette a brief interview, say five minutes, in which you play the counsellor and your partner shares a concern with you. Do your best to use good voice messages when you respond. Play back the cassette and, using the VAPER categories, evaluate with your partner your voice messages. Observe not only what you do, but also the consequences of what you do. Note if your and your partner's voice messages are related. Afterwards, reverse roles. Repeat the exercise as often as necessary and, if appropriate, vary the length of the role plays.

Part D   Experiment with changing a specific voice message
In this experiment, pick a specific voice message area that you think you could improve: for instance, you may have a tendency to respond too quietly. Then role-play with a partner a brief interview in which you respond too quietly and evaluate with your partner the consequences of how you respond. You then conduct a second brief role-play in which you respond with good volume and, afterwards, evaluate the consequences of your different behaviour. Playing back audio-cassettes of role-plays helps you to evaluate voice messages.

Part E   Obtain feedback from your environment
1. If you are currently in a counselling skills training group, obtain feedback from the other students and from your trainer on your use of voice message skills when you counsel.

2. If you are recording your interviews for supervision purposes, you and your supervisor can assess your use of voice message skills.

3. Obtain feedback from colleagues, friends and relatives about how they find your voice messages: how you communicate with your voice and what they think and feel about it.

EXERCISE 5.4   HOW REWARDING ARE MY BODY MESSAGES WHEN I LISTEN?

As appropriate, complete parts of this exercise on your own, with a partner or in a group.

Part A   Self-assessment
1. On each of the following dimensions, assess how rewarding your body messages are when you listen as a counsellor.

   (a) relaxed and open body posture
   (b) slight forward lean
   (c) use of gaze and eye contact
   (d) facial expressions
   (e) gestures
   (f) use of touch
   (g) sensitivity to personal space and height
   (h) clothing and grooming

2. Summarize how rewarding or unrewarding your body messages are when you listen in counselling.

3. Identify specific skills deficits in your body messages when you listen and set goals for change.

Part B   Use terrible and good body message skills when counselling
Your partner shares a concern, with you acting as counsellor.

1. First two minutes: use terrible body message skills when counselling.

2. Second two minutes: use good body message skills when counselling.

3. Evaluation period: discuss what it felt like receiving and sending terrible and good body messages. Your evaluation session may be more educational and fun if you play back a videotape of your four-minute conversation.

4. Reverse roles and repeat 1, 2 and 3 above.

Part C   Observe and assess your body messages
Videotape a brief interview, say five minutes, in which you play the counsellor and your partner shares a concern with you. Do your best to demonstrate attentiveness, interest and emotional responsiveness with body messages. Playback the videotape and, using the categories above, evaluate with your partner your body messages when you listen. Observe not only what you do, but also the consequences of what you do. Note if yours and your partner's body messages are related. Afterwards, reverse roles. Repeat the exercise as often as necessary. If appropriate, vary the length of the role-plays.

Part D   Experiment with changing a specific body message
In this experiment, pick a specific body message area that you think you could improve: for instance, you may have a tendency to sit with your arms crossed. Then role-play with a partner a brief interview in which you sit with your arms crossed and evaluate with your partner the consequences of how you behaved. You then conduct a second brief role-play in which you sit with a relaxed and open body posture and, afterwards, evaluate the consequences of your different behaviour. Playing back videotapes of role-plays helps you to evaluate body messages.

Part E   Obtain feedback from your environment
1.   If you are currently in a counselling skills training group, obtain feedback from the other students and from your trainer on your use of body messages skills when you counsel.
2.   If you are video-recording your interviews for supervision purposes, you and your supervisor can assess your use of body message skills.
3.   Obtain feedback from colleagues, friends and relatives about how they find your body messages: how you communicate with your body language and what they think and feel about it.

EXERCISE 5.5   HELPING CLIENTS TO TELL THEIR STORIES

Work with a partner.

1.   Each partner spends a few minutes in inner listening to identify a concern on which he or she is willing to work in counselling. During this inner listening or focusing period, attend to emerging feelings as well as to emerging thoughts.
2.   As a counsellor, conduct a five-minute interview with your partner during which you help him or her to share his or her internal viewpoint. You can only use the following skills:

> opening remark(s)
> small rewards
> open-ended questions
> good voice messages
> good body messages

Allow your partner total responsibility and control over what material he or she presents. Under no circumstances try to lead him or her out of his or her internal viewpoint. Avoid giving verbal responses beyond small rewards. It may help if you audiotape or videotape your session and play it back.

3. At the end of your session, discuss and evaluate what skills the counsellor used and what the consequences were for the client.

4. Reverse roles and go through steps 2 and 3.

5. Repeat this exercise to the point where you are confident that you have some proficiency in basic skills of helping clients tell their stories.

EXERCISE 5.6 GROUP DISCUSSION: USING LISTENING SKILLS IN COUNSELLING

This is intended as a group exercise, though it may be done individually or in pairs. For each part:

1. Spend 10 to 15 minutes answering the question in groups of three or four.
2. Each group shares its answers with the whole group.
3. The whole group ranks the six most important points or skills from the most important to the least important.

Part A   Functions of active listening
List the six main functions of active listening in counselling.

Part B   Barriers to an accepting attitude
List the six main counsellor barriers to an attitude of acceptance and respect for clients.

Part C   Voice message skills
List the six main voice message skills for active listening in counselling.

Part D   Body message skills
List the six main body message skills for active listening in counselling.

ANSWERS TO EXERCISE 5.2 (PART A)

1. (a) EX; (b) IN; (c) EX.
2. (a) IN; (b) EX; (c) EX.
3. (a) EX; (b) EX; (c) IN.

SIX

Showing understanding skills

Understanding is the beginning of approving.
André Gide

CHAPTER QUESTIONS

- *What is empathy?*

- *What are paraphrasing skills?*

- *How can you use reflecting feelings skills?*

- *How can you show understanding of context and difference?*

- *What are some skills for managing initial resistances?*

- *How can you avoid blocking clients from talking?*

SHOWING UNDERSTANDING

Active listening entails showing understanding by tuning into and reflecting with your verbal, voice and body messages the crux of the meaning contained in the verbal, voice and body messages of clients. Counsellors provide the gift of their listening so that clients genuinely feel understood.

Sometimes responding as if within clients' internal viewpoints is called empathy (Rogers, 1957, 1962, 1975, 1980; Raskin and Rogers, 1995). Rogers described empathy likewise: 'To sense the client's inner world of private personal meanings as if it were your own, but without ever losing the "as if" quality, this is empathy' (Rogers, 1962, p. 419). Rogers emphasized the importance of counsellors 'communicating your sensings of his/her world as you look with fresh and unfrightened eyes at elements of which the individual is fearful' (Rogers, 1975, p. 4). Furthermore, clients need to perceive that counsellors empathically understand them or at the very least communicate the intent to understand (Barrett-Lennard, 1962, 1981; Rogers, 1962). Rogers preferred not to think of empathy as a skill, but as an attitude (Rogers, 1951) or way of being (Rogers, 1975).

Rogers's counselling goal was to help people become more in touch with their inner valuing process rather than to develop specific lifeskills. His use of empathy particularly focused on the construct of experiencing (Gendlin, 1962). He attempted to improve the quantity and quality of his clients' inner listening to the ongoing flow of experiencing within them. This flow is a referent to which clients can repeatedly turn to discover the meaning of their experience so that they can move forward in it.

In Rogers's person-centred counselling, empathic reflections are the counsellor's major tool. One study showed that over 53 per cent of Rogers's verbal responses fell in the reflection/restatement category, whereas Lazarus, a more eclectic and task-oriented helper, had only 10 per cent of responses in this category (Lee and Uhlemann, 1984). In lifeskills counselling, the proportion of reflections changes according to the stage of the model and to the agendas within specific sessions.

Before we discuss paraphrasing and reflecting feelings, the main skills for actively showing understanding, here are some examples of reflections.

Patient to nurse
Patient: 'When I first heard I had terminal cancer, my world fell apart. I'm still reeling and frightened at the thought of death.'
Nurse: 'You still feel shaken and scared by the diagnosis of terminal cancer.'

Woman to career counsellor
Woman: 'With the children coming to the end of their education I want to build more of a life for myself. I don't want to hang around the house all the time.'
Career counsellor: 'You're determined to carve something outside the home for yourself and not keep brooding over an empty nest.'

When counselling students are first introduced to the skill of reflecting, many express reservations.

'It's so unnatural.'

'Clients will just think I'm repeating everything they say.'

'It gets in the way of my being spontaneous.'

'It makes me too self-conscious.'

When you are learning any new skill, from driving a car to driving a golf ball, there is a period where you are likely to have to concentrate extra hard on making the correct sequence of choices that make up the skill. Active listening is no exception. If you work at and practise a skill, you ultimately are likely to own it as a 'natural' part of you. It is natural to the extent that it feels natural.

Be careful about using reflections all the time. Flexibly incorporate them in your repertoire of responses. On occasion you may gain from either not using active listening or using it sparingly.

Following are some occasions when reflecting may assist counselling.

- When creating a safe emotional climate for clients to tell their stories.

- When you need to show that you have understood.

- When you need to check out that you have understood.

- When clients struggle to get in touch with thoughts and feelings.

- When clients need to experience their thoughts and feelings as valid.

- When you want to ensure that clients assume responsibility for their thoughts and feelings independently of what you may think.

- When clients need a reward or emotional stepping stone to continue talking.

- When you check out clients' understanding of specific points you make.

SKILL 6: PARAPHRASE

Along with reflecting feelings, paraphrasing is one of the component skills of how you show understanding in active listening. It is important that you paraphrase because you drive people crazy if you parrot them. As a frustrated husband once said to his wife: 'If I had wanted someone to repeat everything I said after me, I would have married a parrot.' Another example of the importance of not mechanically parroting is the joke (probably apocryphal) about a prominent American therapist who was counselling a suicidal client in his office near the top of a tall building.

Client: I feel terrible.
Counsellor: You feel terrible.
Client: I feel really terrible.
Counsellor: You feel really terrible.

Client: For two cents I would jump out of that window there.
Counsellor: For two cents you would jump out of that window there.
Client: Here I go.
Counsellor: There you go.
Client: (Lands on the pavement below with a thud.)
Counsellor: Thud!

Paraphrasing means rewording speakers' verbal utterances. However, it excludes showing understanding of their voice and body messages. Focusing only on the verbal content of clients' messages is a first step in learning to respond to their combined voice, body and verbal messages. When you paraphrase, you may sometimes use clients' words, but sparingly. You try to stay close to the kind of language they use. Here are a few basic examples.

Patient to speech therapist
Patient: I'm finding swallowing difficult.
Speech therapist: You're having trouble swallowing.

Parishioner to priest
Parishioner: I'm delighted that you've come back to our church.
Priest: You're very pleased to have me back in the parish.

Parent to family counsellor
Parent: I told my kids to go to hell.
Family counsellor: You told your children to get lost.

Employee to manager
Employee: Some of the time I like working here, but on other occasions I'm not too sure.
Manager: You have mixed feelings about being employed here.

A good paraphrase can provide mirror reflections that are clearer and more succinct than original statements. If so, clients may show appreciation with comments such as 'That's right' or 'You've got me.' A simple tip for paraphrasing is to start your responses with the personal pronoun 'you' to indicate that you reflect clients' internal viewpoints. Another tip is to slow your speech rate down to give you more time to think. You need a good memory and a good command of vocabulary to paraphrase well. Confidence and fluency in the skill require much practice.

SKILL 7: REFLECT FEELINGS

Skilled counsellors are very sharp at picking up clients' feelings. In counsellor training, I emphasize the importance of reflecting clients' feelings at the start of initial sessions to show that you are tuned into them as 'human animals'. Reflecting feelings from the beginning, rather than reflecting thoughts alone, can establish a climate for initial and subsequent sessions where clients share rather than bury feelings.

Reflecting feelings is both similar to, yet different from, paraphrasing. Both reflecting feelings and paraphrasing involve mirroring. Reflecting feelings usually involves paraphrasing. However, the language of feelings is not words. Feelings are bodily sensations which may then have word labels attached to them. Consequently, paraphrasing alone has distinct limitations. For example, clients may send voice and body messages that qualify or negate verbal messages. Lauren says 'I'm OK,' yet speaks softly and has tearful eyes. A good reflection of feelings picks up these other messages as well. Reflecting feelings entails responding to clients' music and not just to their words. To do this, counsellor responses incorporate appropriate voice and body messages.

Reflecting feelings involves feeling with a client's flow of emotions and experiencing and communicating this back. Often counselling students have trouble in reflecting feelings. They may just talk about feelings rather than offer an expressive emotional companionship. Inadequately distinguishing between thoughts and feelings can be another problem for both clients and counsellors. For example, 'I feel that equality between the sexes is essential,' describes a thought rather than a feeling. On the other hand, 'I feel angry when I see sex discrimination,' labels a feeling. This distinction between thoughts and feelings is important in reflecting feelings and also when you are helping clients to influence how they feel by altering how they think. Constant reflections of feelings run the risk of encouraging clients to wallow in feelings rather than to move on to how best to deal with them.

Reflecting feelings involves both receiver and sender skills.

Receiver skills

- Understanding clients' face and body messages.

- Understanding clients' voice messages.

- Understanding clients' verbal messages.

- Tuning into the flow of your own emotional reactions.

- Taking into account the context of clients' messages.

- Sensing the surface and underlying meanings of clients' messages.

Sender skills

- Responding in ways that pick up clients' feelings words and phrases.

- Rewording feelings appropriately, using expressive rather than wooden language.

- Using voice and body messages that significantly neither add to nor subtract from the emotions conveyed.

- Checking the accuracy of your understanding.

Pick up feelings words and phrases

Let us start with the obvious. A good but not infallible way to understand what clients feel is to listen to their feelings words and phrases. Feelings phrases are colloquial expressions used to describe feelings words. For example, 'I've got the blues' is a feelings phrase describing the word depressed. Picking up feelings words and phrases is similar to paraphrasing, but with a heightened focus on feelings rather than informational content. Sometimes counselling students ask, 'Well, what did you feel?' after clients have just told them. They need to discipline their listening more. On occasion, feelings words are not the central message. For instance, Emma may say, 'It's just great' that she is living on her own again after the break-up of a relationship, but at the same time her voice chokes, her face is sad and the corners of her mouth are turned down.

Table 6.1 *List of feelings words*

accepted	dependent	involved	supported
adventurous	depressed	irresponsible	suspicious
affectionate	discontented	jealous	tense
aggressive	embarrassed	joyful	tired
ambitious	energetic	lonely	trusting
angry	envious	loved	unambitious
anxious	excited	loving	unappreciated
apathetic	fit	optimistic	unassertive
appreciated	free	outgoing	unattractive
assertive	friendly	pessimistic	underconfident
attractive	frightened	powerful	uneasy
bored	grieving	powerless	unfit
carefree	guilt-free	rejected	unfree
cautious	guilty	relaxed	unfriendly
cheerful	happy	resentful	unloved
competitive	humiliated	responsible	unsupported
confident	hurt	sad	unwanted
confused	indecisive	secure	uptight
contented	independent	shy	vulnerable
cooperative	inferior	stressed	wanted
daring	insecure	strong	weak
decisive	interested	superior	worried

Table 6.1 provides a list of feelings words. Incidentally, it is cumbersome, when reflecting feelings, always to put 'You feel' before feelings words: sometimes 'You're' is sufficient': for example, 'You're sad' instead of 'You feel sad.'

Following are some dimensions of the reflecting of feelings words and phrases.

INTENSITY Mirror the intensity of clients' feelings words in reflections. For example, Jack has just had a negative experience about which he might feel 'devastated' (strong intensity), 'upset' (moderate intensity) or 'slightly upset' (weak intensity). Corresponding mirroring words might be 'sent reeling' (strong intensity), 'distressed' (moderate intensity) or 'a little distressed' (weak intensity). You may err on the side of either adding or subtracting intensity.

MULTIPLE AND MIXED FEELINGS Sometimes clients use many words to describe their feelings. The words may form a cluster around the same theme, in which case you may choose only to reword the crux of the feeling. Alternatively, clients may have varying degrees of mixed feelings, ranging from simple opposites (for instance, happy/sad) to more complex combinations (for instance, hurt/angry). Good reflections pick up all key elements of feelings messages. For instance:

Client: I'm sorry, but relieved not to have got the promotion.
Counsellor: You're upset, but feel a weight off your shoulders at not being promoted.

Client: I both like being with her, yet also like being on my own.
Counsellor: You appreciate her companionship, but enjoy your own personal space too.

ASSIST LABELLING OF FEELINGS Sometimes counsellors assist clients in finding the right feelings words. Here reflecting feelings goes beyond reflecting feelings to helping choose feelings words that resonate for them.

Client: I don't quite know how to express my reaction to losing my job ... possibly angry ... upset, no that's not quite it ... bewildered.
Counsellor: Hurt, anxious, confused, devastated ... are any of those words appropriate?
Client: Devastated, that's what I really feel.

Pick up voice and body messages

Much information about clients' feelings does not come from what they say, but from how they say it. Sometimes clients' verbal, voice and body messages are consistent. In such instances, it is relatively easy to label feelings and their intensity accurately. However, frequently clients' messages are heavily encoded. Clients may struggle to express what they *truly* feel in the face of their conditioning about what they *should* feel. It also takes time for clients to trust counsellors. Consequently, many emotional messages 'come out sideways' rather than loud and clear. Effective counsellors are skilled at listening with the 'third ear' to clients' voice and body messages and to what is left unsaid or camouflaged. They realize that certain clients take time to develop skills of clearly identifying and articulating feelings. Be sensitive to the pace at which clients can work. Clients may require patience rather than pressure.

Counsellors unclear about clients' real or underlying feelings can check with them. For instance, you may make comments like 'I think I hear you saying (state feelings tentatively) ... Am I right?' or 'I would like to understand what you're feeling, but I'm still not altogether clear. Can you help me?' Another option is to say: 'I'm getting a mixed message from you. On the one hand you are saying you do not mind. On the other hand you seem tearful.' After a pause, you might add: 'I'm wondering if you are putting on a brave face?'

A further consideration in picking up feelings is to understand whether and to what extent clients possess insight into their feelings. For instance, as a counsellor you may infer that a parent is absolutely furious with a child. However, the parent may not be able to handle such an observation since it clashes with his or her self-image of being a loving parent. Consequently, you may need to pick up three feelings: first, the parent's stated feeling of unconditional love for the child; second, the underlying anger with the child; third, the feeling of threat were the parent's self-picture to be challenged by your reflecting how intensely angry he or she was.

Sender skills of reflecting feelings

When reflecting feelings, you may wonder how best to respond to the numerous verbal, voice and body messages you have received. There are no simple answers. What you try to do is (1) decode the overall message accurately, and (2) formulate an emotionally expressive response that communicates back the crux of the client's feelings. Here are a few guidelines for sending reflecting feelings messages.

SEND BACK THE CRUX OF THE CLIENT'S MESSAGE Where possible, show that you have understood the client's main message or messages. Whatever else you do, communicate back the core feeling.

> **Client:** We just argue and argue and don't seem to get anywhere. I don't know what to do. It's so frustrating. I wish I knew the answer. I don't seem to be able to handle our relationship.
> **Counsellor:** You're extremely frustrated with constant unproductive arguments and not knowing how to improve matters.

STATE THE CLIENT'S MAIN FEELING AT THE FRONT OF YOUR RESPONSE Even though the clients may not start with their main feeling, they may feel better understood by you if you reflect their main feeling at the front of your response than if you reflect information first.

> **Client:** I've failed my statistics exam and have to repeat it. I'm so disappointed.

Counsellor: You're bitterly disappointed at having to resit your stats exam.

In the above example, the counsellor has tuned into feelings immediately. However, imagine that the counsellor had replied: 'You failed your stats test and are bitterly disappointed.' The counsellor has started by responding from the head to the client's head. By the time the counsellor reflects the feeling of disappointment, it may be too late for the client to experience being emotionally understood.

BE SENSITIVE TO CLIENTS' UNDERLYING FEELINGS AND AGENDAS Sometimes there are no hidden agendas in what clients communicate. On other occasions, you may help them to articulate underlying feelings. However, sometimes you may intentionally not respond to underlying feelings and agendas. For example, clients may require more space to acknowledge the feelings on their own. Alternatively, they may not be ready for a deeper reflection. When you are making deeper reflections, you run a greater risk of being wrong than when making surface reflections.

KEEP YOUR RESPONSE APPROPRIATELY SIMPLE Use simple and clear language. Avoid unnecessary words and qualifications. However, be prepared to state different parts of multiple and mixed messages.

USE VOICE AND BODY MESSAGES TO ADD EXPRESSIVENESS TO YOUR VERBAL MESSAGE(S) You are not just talking about feelings, you are reflecting feelings. For instance, if, hypothetically, a suicidal client says 'I feel terrible', you can adjust your voice and facial expression to mirror, to some extent, a sense of desperation. Consistency between your verbal, voice and body messages is important. If you send mixed messages clients may perceive you as insincere.

CHECK YOUR UNDERSTANDING You respond to client statements with different degrees of tentativeness depending on how clearly they have communicated and how confident you are about receiving their messages accurately. However, all reflections should contain an element of checking whether you accurately understand clients' internal viewpoints. Sometimes you can check by slight voice inflections. On other occasions you can check more explicitly.

Reflect feelings and reasons

A useful variation in active listening is to reflect both feelings and the reasons for them. Reflecting back reasons does not mean that you make an interpretation or offer an explanation from your external viewpoint. Instead, where clients have already provided reasons for a feeling, you reflect these feelings back in a 'You feel ... because ...' statement that mirrors the internal viewpoint. Here is an example:

Tom: I've struggled so hard to get to the end of the course and now I'm afraid I'm going to fail the last semester.

Counsellor: You're worried *because* you might fail after all that effort.
Tom: Yes. I get anxious just thinking of all the time I may have wasted.

Here the counsellor's 'You feel ... because ... ' response showed more understanding of Tom's predicament than if the response had stopped after 'You're worried.' Todd was able to emphasize that the meaning of passing was not only getting through the course, but avoiding wasting so much time and effort. Put another way, the because part of the counsellor's response identified the thinking contributing to Tom's feeling. Thus, 'You feel ... because ... ' reflections are useful not only for helping clients to tell their stories, but also for assessing how clients' thinking contributes to unwanted feelings.

SKILL 8: SHOW UNDERSTANDING OF CONTEXT AND DIFFERENCE
Understand clients in context

Counsellors require skills of understanding the contexts of clients and their problems. Issues of context and of clients' differences from counsellors pervade counselling. Clients with problems do not exist in vacuums. Rather, they exist in networks of contextual variables whose relevance differs in each instance. Figure 6.1 gives just some of the possible contexts pertinent to understanding clients and their problems. These contexts are also relevant to negotiating areas of difference between counsellors and clients.

CULTURAL CONTEXT This refers to the value and communication patterns of clients' cultures. Involved here are exposure of clients to mainstream cultures, wishes for assimilation and cross-cultural issues of culture shock, alienation, mistrust and loneliness. Cross-cultural issues can be relevant to both native-born and migrant clients. In addition, both native-born and migrant clients can have issues of internalized culture. Ho (1995) defines internalized culture 'as the cultural influences operating within the individual that shape (not determine) personality formation and various aspects of psychological functioning' (p. 5). For example, frequently native-born children of migrants to Australia and Britain feel torn between two cultures. Both native-born and migrant clients also differ in cultural autonomy: how able they are to choose those aspects of different cultures that work for them rather than being entrapped by mainstream culture.

RACIAL CONTEXT Here include: the extent of clients' racial identity and pride; exposure to racial discrimination and skills at handling it; and values, communication patterns and family structures that differ from the culture of the racial majority.

SOCIAL CLASS CONTEXT Rules for behaviour differ widely among social classes. Counsellors need to understand many client behaviours – for instance, manners, dress and language – in the context of their social classes.

FAMILY OF ORIGIN CONTEXT Here family of origin refers to parents and step-parents. The family of origin context may be direct or indirect. Take the example of Jock and Nancy, a couple in their twenties who have a distressed marriage. Up to four natural parents, and possibly some step-parents too, may directly tell them how to behave. They may also receive advice from relatives. In addition, families of origin indirectly influence Jock's and Nancy's relationship through parental 'voices in the head', many of which go unrecognized. In multicultural societies, such as Australia, cultural and family of origin context intermingle: in the extreme all four of a couple's natural parents may be culturally different.

WORK/STUDY CONTEXT The work/study context can be relevant to both work-related problems and non-work problems. For instance, workers whose companies are being rationalized after take-overs may experience additional work stress and psychological bullying (Rennie-Peyton, 1995). This stress may then manifest itself in increased

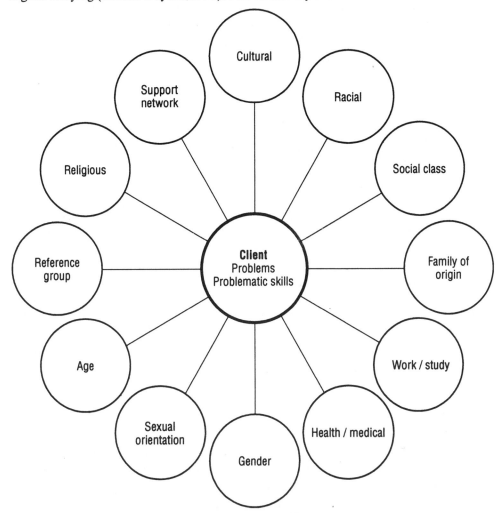

Figure 6.1 *Areas for understanding context and difference*

irritability at home, creating problems there too.

HEALTH/MEDICAL CONTEXT Clients' states of physical health can in varying degrees contribute to psychological problems: for example, glandular problems causing apathy. Furthermore, clients may behave differently when on medication and when not. Frequently, counsellors need to explore the past and current medical contexts of clients' problems. Often opinions from medical practitioners are essential. Clients' prior experiences of seeking and receiving psychiatric and psychological help can also merit exploration.

GENDER CONTEXT Feminist counsellors and gender aware counsellors (Good *et al.*, 1990) consider that most, if not all, problems need to be understood within gender perspectives. Counsellors require sensitivity to differences in biological functioning and experiencing: for instance, in regard to menstruation and the menopause. However, the main area of gender sensitivity relates to learned sex-role behaviour and expectations: for instance, in relationships and career choice. Furthermore, gender aware counsellors frequently emphasize understanding the historical, social and political contexts of gender learning and discrimination.

SEXUAL ORIENTATION CONTEXT Homosexual clients may or may not live within the context of the rules and values of the gay and lesbian communities. The attitude of mainstream or straight culture towards homosexual or bisexual orientation provides a further context for understanding certain clients' problems. In addition, changing attitudes towards homosexuality within the helping professions, whereby the stigma of mental illness is no longer attached to it, provide still another context.

AGE CONTEXT The physical process of ageing may contribute to some clients' problems. Others may face deprivations – for instance, companionship and employment – on account of age. In addition, the respect accorded to age differs greatly across cultures. Ageism, discrimination on the basis of age, may be more a feature of Western than of Asian cultures.

REFERENCE GROUP CONTEXT Humans are social animals who tend to associate much of the time in groups. Frequently, valuable understandings about clients' behaviours may be gained by placing them in the context of reference group norms. For example, a different understanding of a problem may stem from the counsellor discovering that a teenager stole a car in response to a delinquent peer group dare rather than on his own.

RELIGIOUS CONTEXT Clients' religious faiths can be sources of strength. Furthermore, sharing the same religious beliefs and ethics can strengthen the counselling relationship. However, religious faiths, albeit sometimes misunderstood, can be sources of self-oppression. In addition, some skills deficits may be sustained on religious grounds: confusing lack of assertion with humility. Since religion forms such a central part in many clients' lives, counsellors need to be sensitive to the religious context and its influence. Some counsellors require awareness of their limitations in understanding religiously motivated people.

SUPPORT NETWORK CONTEXT A valuable insight for understanding clients and their problems may come from exploring their support networks. Murgatroyd (1985, p. 151) observes: 'When a person seeks help from a stranger it is often a sign that their own helping networks are inadequate.' Support networks can consist of spouse, family, friends, work colleagues, church ministers and helping professionals, to mention but some. How isolated are clients? Who is available to offer support and how useful is or might that support be? What are the clients' skills of accessing and using a support network?

Possess understanding context and difference skills

Clients vary in the number of contextual considerations relevant to identifying and clarifying their problems. Counsellors also vary in the range of clients they see. Most counsellors require a range of understanding context and difference skills, some of which are presented below.

DEVELOP A KNOWLEDGE BASE If counsellors work with specific groups – for instance, migrants from a certain country or gay and lesbian clients – they should be familiar with the assumptions, values and shared experiences of these groups. Understand what are the major counselling problems for any minority group you target. Also understand the ways in which stereotyping and feelings of powerlessness may leave major scars. If you are not in possession of such knowledge, find it out. Even counsellors possessing a good understanding of specific cultures and minority groups always need to update their knowledge. For example, counsellors working with homosexual groups require the most up-to-date information about legislation concerning homosexual behaviour and about the transmission and treatment of HIV/AIDS.

Be conscious of the assumptions underlying the sources from which you gain information. For instance, information and investigations about minority cultural groups may primarily reflect the perspective of members from the majority culture (LaFromboise and Foster, 1992). The same may hold true for some, if not much, of the literature in other areas. You can also gain knowledge by speaking to leaders and members from the minority cultures or groups that you wish to target. Here, the risk is that the information may overly reflect the perspective of the minority culture. However, knowing what a predominant minority group perspective is, including its main variations, in itself is valuable for understanding clients who come from that group.

DEMONSTRATE CONTEXTUAL EMPATHY Counsellors can show contextual empathy with their voice, body, verbal and action messages. Take demonstrating cultural empathy as an example. British people tend to speak more softly than many Australians. Japanese people do not use eye contact as much as people from Western cultures (Pease, 1981). In the Arctic, 'it may be best to sit side by side rather than opposing with a forward trunk lean' (Ivey, 1987, p. 169). Counsellors dealing with people from different cultures need the ability 'to *send* and *receive* both *verbal* and *non-verbal* messages *accurately* and *appropriately*' (Sue *et al.*, 1992). Do not assume that good intentions lead to good cross-cultural results.

In responding to verbal messages, counsellors need to be sensitive to topics that may have particular meaning to people from different cultures. For instance, a desire for harmonious family relationships contains a much stronger cultural message when expressed by Asians than Anglo-Saxons. Sometimes high levels of empathy can only be offered by counsellors speaking clients' primary language. Counsellors whose linguistic skills do not match those of clients can either seek the services of translators with cultural knowledge or refer to bilingual counsellors, if appropriate people are available. Often cross-cultural sensitivity is far more important that the cultural matching of clients and counsellors. On occasions, migrant clients may prefer counsellors from the majority culture who can assist their integration into it.

An important skill in understanding clients' contexts and differences is that of assessing whether their 'problem' stems from others' personal biases or from discriminatory bias in institutional structures. If so, counsellors can assist clients not to personalize problems inappropriately and then blame themselves. Counsellors can also consider using institutional intervention skills on behalf of clients.

A related skill in understanding the impact of clients' contexts is the ability to assess when clients are using the context as a way of avoiding critically looking at their own behaviour. For instance, migrants who make little or no attempt to understand the language of their host country contribute to their feelings of cultural alienation. In showing understanding you may have to strike a delicate balance between acknowledging clients' internal viewpoints and not colluding in erroneous efforts to simplify themselves as victims of oppressive majority cultures. Even when majority cultures are oppressive, counsellors can empower clients with skills to manage their lives better in them. In addition, counsellors can train clients in skills of counteracting institutional oppression.

Each client has a unique life history and way of interpreting the cultural and minority group influences that have affected her or him. Be careful to avoid pigeon-holing clients into your versions of their cultural and minority group contexts rather than understanding them as individuals.

GIVE PERMISSION TO DISCUSS COUNSELLOR–CLIENT DIFFERENCES Counsellors and clients come from different contexts. Counsellors may quickly become aware that they differ on significant characteristics from clients. One possibility is to acknowledge the difference – for instance, racial or cultural – and ask what clients think and feel about this. A possible advantage of being direct is that it provides clients with opportunities to air and work through mistrust. A risk is that such questions may reflect more counsellors' than clients' concerns and, hence, defocus clients. Possibly a more neutral way to unearth clients' concerns about obvious differences is to say: 'Are there any questions you would like to ask me?'

GIVE PERMISSION TO DISCUSS PROBLEMS IN TERMS OF THEIR BROADER CONTEXTS Despite an absence of counsellor–client matching, counsellors can show sensitivity to contextual issues in clients' problems. One way to do this is to acknowledge a possible deficiency in your understanding of the context of clients' problems and ask them to fill in gaps (Poon *et al.*, 1993). The following is a simplified illustration.

> **Asian student:** My father wants me to go into the family building business and I feel under a lot of pressure to continue on my building course to please him.
> **Counsellor:** It sounds as though you have mixed feelings. You have reservations about continuing your building course, yet don't want to go against your father's wishes. Cultural considerations are often important in understanding such problems and if you feel they are relevant to your case, please feel free to share them.

ASK QUESTIONS TO UNDERSTAND BROADER CONTEXTS As part of their attempts to elicit relevant information, counsellors may use questions to understand the broader contexts of clients and their problems. Depending on what seems potentially relevant, you can ask questions focused on one or more of the contexts depicted in Figure 6.1: cultural, racial, social class, family of origin, work/study, health/medical, gender, sexual preference, age, reference group, religion and support network. This list is far from exhaustive. The earlier presentation of these broader contexts indicates topics for questions within each context.

SKILL 9: MANAGE INITIAL RESISTANCES
What are resistances?

Resistances may be broadly defined as anything that gets in the way of counselling. Clients can both bring resistances to counselling and have them activated during it. Resistances can be present at any stage of counselling. At best, most clients are ambivalent when they come for counselling. At the same time as wanting change, they may have anxieties both about changing and about the counselling process: for instance, talking about themselves. Some clients come reluctantly: for example, 'problem' children sent to school counsellors for disrupting class.

Sullivan (1954) observed that there were cultural handicaps to the work of the psychiatrist. These 'anti-psychiatric' elements in the culture can also lead to resistances in non-medical counselling. Such culturally handicapping norms include: people ought not to need help; people should know themselves; and people 'should have "good natural instincts" and "good intuition" which ought to govern them in choosing the "right" way to act and think' (Sullivan, 1954, p. 37). Other cultural thinking errors contributing to resistances are that people who need helping are 'sick' and that you should be able to solve all problems by 'common sense'.

Counsellors may wrongly attribute the sources of clients' resistances by being too quick to blame them for lack of cooperation and progress. Clients' resistances may be the consequence of poor counselling skills: for instance, unrewarding listening. Furthermore, some counselling models, especially if incompetently applied, may engender resistances: for instance, the lack of structure of the person-centred counselling or the didactic nature of the rational emotive behaviour counselling. Clients may resist counsellors whose behaviour is too discrepant from their expectations and perceived requirements (Lazarus, 1993).

Counsellors may also bring resistances to their work: for example fatigue, burnout and prejudices. Yalom mentions his difficulty, when faced with a huge female client, in overcoming his resistances to fat ladies (Yalom, 1989). When writing this book, I counselled a 59-year-old female client whose manipulative manner triggered anxieties in me because she reminded me of how my mother sometimes controlled how I should feel and think when a child. Counsellor resistances may interact with client resistances to impede the counselling relationship and slow down or stop progress.

Deal with initial resistances

Following are skills for understanding and dealing with resistances in initial sessions. Since there are so many variations and reasons for resistances, it is impossible to cover all contingencies.

USE ACTIVE LISTENING SKILLS Beginning and even more experienced counsellors may both sustain and create clients' resistances through poor listening skills. Resistances are a normal part of initial sessions. By using good active listening skills, you do much to build the trust needed to lower resistances. Some clients' resistances manifest themselves in aggression. Rather than justify yourself or allow yourself to be sucked into a competitive contest, one approach to handling such aggression is to reflect it back, locating the feelings clearly in the client, but indicate that you have picked them up loud and clear. Where clients provide reasons for their hostility, you can reflect these too. Just showing clients that you understand their internal viewpoints, especially if done consistently, may diminish resistances.

JOIN WITH CLIENTS Sometimes counsellors can lower clients' resistances by helping them to feel that they have a friend at court. For instance, counsellors can initially listen and offer support to children expressing resentment about parents.

> **Client:** I think coming here is a waste of time. My parents keep picking on me and they are the ones who need help.
> **Family counsellor:** You feel angry about coming here because your parents are the people with problems.
> **Client:** Yeah (and then proceeds to share his/her side of the story).

In the above instance you can focus on parental deficiencies prior to, possibly, focusing the client back on himself or herself. You use your client's need to talk about parental injustices to build the counselling relationship.

Another example is that of a pupil referred to the school counsellor by a teacher. Here the counsellor responds more to voice and body than to verbal messages.

> **Pupil:** (looks down and sighs).

School counsellor: I sense that you are uncomfortable about being here ... (if no response after a pause). Would you care to tell me how you view the situation? I'd really like to understand your viewpoint.

GIVE PERMISSION TO DISCUSS RELUCTANCE AND FEARS If you receive overt or subtle messages from clients that they have reservations about being in counselling, you can bring the agenda out into the open and give clients permission to elaborate. In the following example, a parole officer responds to a juvenile delinquent's seeming reluctance to disclose anything significant.

Parole officer: I detect an unwillingness to open up to me because I'm your parole officer. If I'm right, I'm wondering what specifically worries you about that?

In the previous section, mention was made of giving permission to discuss differences in counsellor–client characteristics – for instance, culture and race – that may create reluctance to participate in counselling.

INVITE COOPERATION The cooperative nature of the relationship in lifeskills counselling both prevents and overcomes many client resistances. Initial statements by counsellors aim to create the idea of a partnership, a shared endeavour in which clients and counsellors can together perform the detective work of finding out how clients can better attain goals.

ENLIST CLIENT SELF-INTEREST Help clients to identify reasons for participating in counselling. For instance, children who perceive their parents as picking on them and as the ones with problems can be assisted to see that they themselves might be happier with better coping with parents skills. Questions that challenge clients with the adequacy of their own behaviour may enlist self-interest. Such questions include 'Where is your current behaviour getting you?' and 'How is that behaviour helping you?' (Glasser, 1984; Glasser and Wubbolding, 1995). Questions that encourage clients to think about goals are also useful: for example, 'What are your goals in the situation?' and 'Wouldn't you like to be more in control of your life?'

REWARD SILENT CLIENTS FOR TALKING Some clients find it difficult to talk, whether in or out of counselling. Others may find it particularly difficult to talk to counsellors. Without coming on too strong, counsellors can respond more frequently and more obviously. For example, counsellors may use more small rewards when clients talk. Counsellors can offer encouragement by reflecting and making the most of what clients say. In addition, counsellors can reflect the difficulty certain clients have in talking, even though they may not have verbalized this themselves.

The above are just some ways of working with resistances and reluctance. Counsellors need to be sensitive to the pace at which different clients work. Clients who feel pressured by counsellors may become even more resistant. Furthermore, if attacked prematurely and clumsily, clients may reinforce their defences. When dealing with client resistances, counsellors require sensitivity, realism, flexibility and tact.

SKILL 10: AVOID LISTENING BLOCKS

Client: My problem is that everyone thinks I'm a liar.
Counsellor: Go on ... I don't believe you.

Client: My problem is that I have an inferiority complex.
Counsellor: Lots of people have *important* problems and you come and bother me with your inferiority complex.

If clients are going to self-disclose, explore problems and problematic skills areas, and experience their feelings more fully, they require psychological safety and space. Here the emphasis is on how not to spoil your listening by sending clumsy verbal messages that block or inhibit clients from talking. Psychological safety and space are both quantitative and qualitative. If you are rarely physically accessible, or if, when present, you monopolize or keep interrupting, you scarcely give clients the quantity of psychological safety and space they need. However, counsellors can also deprive clients of the quality of safety and space they need by responding in ways that show lack of respect for their internal viewpoints. Showing such lack of respect not only makes it more difficult for clients to talk to you, it also interferes with their inner listening. Clients may both repress material from awareness and be more inclined to edit what they disclose for fear of disapproval.

Below are some ways that counsellors communicate to clients that they are not totally safe and free to talk. Avoiding these blocks does not mean you should never use any of them. You simply need to be aware of their possible negative consequences before choosing to use them.

- *Directing and leading.* Taking control of what the client can talk about: for example, 'I would like you to start with what happened to you when you were a child.'

- *Judging and evaluating.* Making evaluative statements, especially ones implying that the client does not live up to your own standards: for example, 'You are overpossessive of your children.'

- *Blaming.* Assigning responsibility for what happens to clients in a finger-pointing way: for example, 'It's all your fault.'

- *Moralizing, preaching and patronizing.* Telling clients how they should be leading their lives: for example, 'People who help others are usually happier than those who live for themselves.'

- *Labelling and diagnosing.* Placing superficial diagnostic categories on clients and their behaviour: for example, 'You're paranoid' or 'You have an inferiority complex.'

- *Reassuring and humouring.* Trying to make clients feel better, yet not acknowledging their true feelings: for example, 'You'll be all right ... Don't worry.'

- *Not accepting clients' feelings.* Telling clients that their positive or negative feelings should be different from what they are: for example, 'You've got no reason to be so depressed.'

- *Advising and teaching.* Not giving clients the space to arrive at their own solutions: for example, 'Why don't you go around to see her and try to make things up?'

- *Interrogating.* Using questions in ways that threaten clients with unwanted probing: 'Tell me about your weaknesses. Be specific.'

- *Overinterpreting.* Offering explanations that come from your internal viewpoint and that bear little similarity to what clients might have thought: for example, 'Your indecision about choosing a career is related to your fear of failing to live up to your father's perfectionist standards.'

- *Inappropriately self-disclosing.* Talking about yourself in ways that interfere with clients' disclosures: for example, 'You have troubles. Let me tell you mine.'

- *Putting on a professional facade.* Trying to make yourself seem an expert and thereby communicating in a defensive or otherwise inauthentic way: for example, 'I've had a lot of training and experience with problems such as yours.'

- *Faking attention.* Part listening and insincerely pretending to be more interested and involved in what is being said than you are: for example, 'That's so interesting.'

- *Placing time pressures.* Letting clients know that your availability for listening is limited: for example, 'You had better be brief.'

A major 'don't' not mentioned above is breaking confidences. Quite apart from damaging specific helping relationships, breaking confidences represents a serious breach of ethics. All the above listening blocks focus on verbal responses, but as mentioned earlier, counsellors' voice and body messages can also create a lack of psychological safety.

CONCLUDING COMMENT

Active listening is the fundamental skill of developing supportive counselling relationships. Without this basic skill of getting inside clients' internal viewpoints and showing that you understand and care about what they say, you severely if not fatally limit your capacity to help. Furthermore, you may just add to clients' pain and distress by sending negative messages. In lifeskills counselling, active listening is central to assisting clients in managing problems and overcoming problematic skills patterns. Counselling students need to work and practise to develop the fluency of skilled counsellors. Experienced counsellors should pay close attention to whether they maintain high listening standards or let bad habits interfere. In most instances, active listening needs to be accompanied by other skills for managing problems and developing lifeskills.

CHAPTER HIGHLIGHTS

- *Showing understanding in active listening entails tuning in to and 'mirroring' with your verbal, voice and body messages the crux of the meaning contained in your clients' verbal, voice and body messages.*

- *Paraphrasing involves rewording clients' key words. Good paraphrases can be clearer and more succinct than clients' original statements.*

- *The language of feelings is not verbal. Consequently, good reflections of feelings both pick up and communicate back non-verbal as well as verbal messages.*

- *Counsellors require good skills at picking up feelings messages, including their intensity and whether they are multiple or mixed feelings. Sometimes counsellors assist clients in labelling feelings.*

- *Counsellors can reflect back feelings and the reasons for them. Reflecting feelings and reasons identifies thoughts contributing to feelings.*

- *Counsellors require skills of understanding clients' contexts and differences. Areas of context and difference include cultural, racial, social class, family of origin, work/study, health/medical, gender, sexual orientation, age, reference group, religious and support network.*

- *Skills for managing initial resistances include active listening, joining, inviting cooperation and enlisting client self-interest.*

- *You create unsafe emotional climates for clients by sending clumsy verbal messages. Listening deficits that block or inhibit clients from talking include directing and leading, judging and evaluating, blaming, moralizing, preaching and patronizing, labelling and diagnosing, reassuring and humouring, not accepting clients' feelings, advising and teaching, interrogating, overinterpreting, inappropriately self-disclosing, putting on a professional facade, faking attention and putting unnecessary pressures on clients.*

- *For most clients, active listening needs to be accompanied by other counsellor skills focused on managing problems and developing lifeskills.*

EXERCISE 6.1   PARAPHRASING SKILLS

As appropriate, complete each part of this exercise on your own, with a partner or in a group. Suggested answers to Parts A and B of this exercise are provided at the end of this chapter.

Part A   Single paraphrasing
Paraphrase the content of each of the following client statements into clear and simple language. Use 'you' or 'your' where the speaker uses 'I', 'me' or 'my'. There is no single correct answer.

> *Example*
> **Client:** I'm always getting hassled by my boss.
> **Counsellor:** You're continually getting pressured by your employer.

Client statements
1. 'I can't stand it when she ignores me.'
2. 'I get fed up working with that lazy bastard.'
3. 'I'd like to give up drinking so much.'
4. 'Guys like that really turn me on.'

Part B   Multiple paraphrasing
Think of at least three different ways to reword the following statements.

1. 'I've always been shy in social situations.'
2. 'I don't perform to the best of my ability.'

Part C   Practise in pairs and in a group
1. *In pairs.* You 'feed' each other statements. Listeners paraphrase speakers' statements and speakers provide feedback on their reactions to each paraphrase.

2. *In a group.* Members take turns to make statements – they may write them on whiteboards or blackboards. After each statement, all group members formulate a paraphrase and then share them with the group.

EXERCISE 6.2   REFLECTING FEELINGS SKILLS

As appropriate, complete each part of this exercise on your own, with a partner or in a group. Suggested answers to Parts A, B and C of this exercise are provided at the end of this chapter.

Part A   Identify and reflect feelings words and phrases
For each of the following statements: (a) identify the words and phrases the client has used to describe how he or she feels; and (b) reflect the client's feelings, starting your responses with either 'You feel' or 'You're'.

Example

Bruce to counsellor: I find being without a job depressing. I'm so anxious about my future.

(a) Bruce's feelings words and phrases: depressing, anxious.

(b) Reflection of feeling: 'You feel low and are very anxious about your job prospects.'

1. **Martina to counsellor:** I've always envied women who manage to stay slim. I worry a lot about my weight.
   (a) Martina's feeling words and phrases
   (b) Your reflection of feeling

2. **Sarah to counsellor:** I was sexually abused by my father when I was nine. I've never forgiven him for betraying my trust and I'm still angry.
   (a) Sarah's feelings words and phrases
   (b) Your reflection of feeling

3. **Jimmy to helper:** I hate it when my folks argue. I'm afraid the family is going to split up and I don't want that to happen.
   (a) Jimmy's feelings words and phrases
   (b) Your reflection of feeling

Part B   Pick up feelings from voice and body messages

Indicate what voice and body messages might serve as cues for you to pick up each of the following emotions.

Anger
(a) voice messages
(b) body messages

Anxiety
(a) voice messages
(b) body messages

Depression
(a) voice messages
(b) body messages

Part C   Reflect feelings and reasons

For each of the following client statements formulate a reflective response that strictly uses the 'You *feel ... because ...*' format.

Example

> **Tom:** I've struggled so hard to get to the end of the course and now I'm afraid I'm going to fail the last semester.
>
> **Counsellor:** You *feel* worried *because* you might fail after all that effort.

Your responses

1. **Tracey to teacher:** I hate being teased. I just hate it. I'm really no different from the other girls and yet they seem to enjoy ganging up on me.
    (a) You feel
    (b) because

2. **Diana to social worker:** I've got this neighbour who wants her little girl to play with my son. I would like to please her, yet her girl is very naughty. I'm confused about what to do.
    (a) You feel
    (b) because

3. **Lee to parole officer:** I don't want to smoke dope no more. It costs too much.
    (a) You feel
    (b) because

4. **Simon to counsellor:** I'm really happy that Sally and I don't fight so much. I feel much better about our relationship.
    (a) You feel
    (b) because

Part D   Practise in pairs and in a group

1. *In pairs.* Each of you takes turns to be speaker and listener. When listening, help your speaker to talk about his or her feelings by reflecting them accurately. Pay attention to voice and body as well as verbal messages.

2. *Group exercises.*
    (a) The group picks a feeling. Then members identify and demonstrate the verbal, voice and body messages required to express that feeling mildly, moderately and strongly. Repeat the exercise for other feelings.
    (b) This exercise may be done with a beach ball or tennis ball. Members sit in a circle. The member holding the ball (the speaker) expresses a feeling by means of verbal, voice and body messages. He/she pauses to allow all members to formulate a reflection of feeling response (or a reflection of feeling and reasons response) and then throws the ball to one member (the listener) who attempts to reflect the feeling accurately. Then the listener becomes the speaker and so on.
    (c) One member sits in front and acts as a speaker who is trying to share and explore his feelings on a topic. The remaining group members sit in a semi-

circle around him/her. The speaker states a feeling to each member of the group in turn. After each statement, the member who is 'listener' reflects the speaker's feeling (with or without reflecting reasons) as accurately as possible. Members take turns in being the speaker.

EXERCISE 6.3   UNDERSTANDING CONTEXT AND DIFFERENCE SKILLS

As appropriate, do parts of this exercise on your own, with a partner or in a group.

Part A   Analyse a counselling setting
Analyse the importance of the following context and difference consideration in terms of the client population of a counselling setting in which you either work or might like to work.

1. Culture
2. Race
3. Social class
4. Family of origin
5. Work/study
6. Health/medical
7. Gender
8. Sexual orientation
9. Reference group
10. Religion
11. Support network
12. Other important contexts (please specify).

You may carry out the above analysis for the contexts of individual clients' problems. In addition, you may use the categories to identify counsellor–client differences and to assess their implications for counselling.

Part B   Use understanding context and difference skills
Try to find partners who differ from you on one or more significant context variables. Conduct at least one mini-session with each partner in which the counsellor uses one or more of the following understanding context and difference skills:

- demonstrate contextual empathy;

- give permission to discuss counsellor–client differences;

- give permission to discuss problems in terms of their broader contexts;

- focus questions on broader contexts.

Have a feedback and discussion session after each mini-session, then reverse roles. Use audio or video feedback if helpful.

EXERCISE 6.4   MANAGING INITIAL RESISTANCES SKILLS

As appropriate, do each part of this exercise on your own, with a partner or in a group.

Part A   Identifying and responding to resistances
1.   For a counselling setting in which you work, or might work, list the main ways clients might show resistances in initial counselling sessions.
2.   Formulate the following kinds of managing resistances responses:

   (a) joining response
   (b) permission to discuss reluctance and fears response
   (c) enlisting client self-interest response.

Part B   Practise with a partner
Conduct mini interviews in which the client engages in resistant behaviour and the counsellor uses active listening plus one or more of the following managing initial resistances skills:

- join with clients

- give permission to discuss reluctance and fears

- invite collaboration

- enlist client self-interest

- reward silent clients for talking

At the end of each interview have a feedback and discussion session prior to reversing roles. If it is helpful, play back recordings of your mini interviews.

EXERCISE 6.5   WHAT ARE MY LISTENING BLOCKS?

For Part A, first answer on your own. Then, if appropriate, discuss with a partner or in a group. As appropriate, do Part B in pairs or in a group.

Part A   Assess my listening blocks
Using the scale below, rate each of the following listening blocks according to how much you respond that way in *either* a specific counselling relationship *or* counselling relationships generally.

Always	3
Frequently	2
Sometimes	1
Never	0

Your rating	Listening blocks
_____	Directing and leading
_____	Judging and evaluating
_____	Blaming
_____	Moralizing, preaching and patronizing
_____	Labelling and diagnosing
_____	Reassuring and humouring
_____	Not accepting clients' feelings
_____	Advising and teaching
_____	Interrogating
_____	Over-interpreting
_____	Inappropriately self-disclosing
_____	Putting on a professional facade
_____	Faking attention
_____	Putting time pressures on client(s)
_____	Others (please specify)

Starting with your 'worst' tendency, rank order your five main tendencies to be an unsafe listener to clients and assess the consequences of each.

Part B   Practise in pairs and in a group
1. *In pairs.* Both partners identify what they consider to be their main listening block. The one partner speaks while the 'listener' responds with the speaker's main listening block to let him or her experience what it feels like to be on the receiving end of it. Afterwards, discuss and reverse roles. This exercise can be repeated for other listening blocks.
2. *In a group.* One person sits out in the front as the speaker and the rest of the group sit in a semi-circle around him or her. The speaker tries to talk to each member in turn, who responds with his or her (the group member's) own main listening block. After each response, the group tries to identify the listening block. Members take turns at being speakers.

EXERCISE 6.6 CONDUCTING AN INITIAL COUNSELLING SESSION USING ACTIVE LISTENING SKILLS

Work with a partner. Each of you thinks of an area in your personal or work life that you are prepared to share in an initial counselling session. One of you acts as counsellor and conducts a 20-30-minute initial session using the following active listening skills: stay in the client's internal viewpoint; send good body and voice messages; use an opening remark, small rewards and open-ended questions; paraphrase verbal content; reflect feelings; and reflect feelings and reasons. Preferably video-record or, failing that, audio-record your session. At the end of the session obtain feedback from your client on your active listening skills. Then play back the video-recording or audio-recording and stop it when either of you wishes to comment. After a suitable interval, reverse roles.

Variation of the above exercise: make a training video
Work with a partner and together make a training video-tape or audio-cassette as though it might be used for instructional purposes with a target audience of people learning counselling skills. Each video-tape or audio-cassette consists of three parts: (1) an introduction to the skills of active listening (5–10 minutes); (2) a demonstration of an initial session in which the counsellor demonstrates only active listening skills (20–30 minutes); (3) a sharing and feedback session with counsellor and client discussing the session (5–10 minutes).

ANSWERS TO EXERCISES

EXERCISE 6.1

Paraphrases other than those suggested may be appropriate.

Part A Single paraphrasing
1. 'You dislike it when she takes no notice of you.'
2. 'You're exasperated working with that idle idiot.'
3. 'You want very much to get off the booze.'
4. 'You feel randy about those sorts of men (boys).'

Part B Multiple paraphrasing
1. 'You've always been bashful in company.'
   'You've always been timid when socializing.'
   'You've always been anxious mixing with people.'

2. 'You underachieve.'
   'You don't do as well as you're able.'
   'You're more competent than your results show.'

EXERCISE 6.2

Part A
Identify and reflect feelings words and phrases
1. Martina's feelings words and phrases: 'envied', 'worry a lot'.
   Reflection of feeling: 'You're very anxious about your size and are jealous of women who keep their figures.'
2. Sarah's feelings words and phrases: 'never forgiven', 'betraying my trust', 'still angry'.
   Reflection of feeling: 'You're still mad and unforgiving because of your father's extreme breach of faith in sexually abusing you.'
3. Jimmy's feelings words and phrases: 'hate', 'afraid', 'don't want'.
   Reflection of feeling: 'You get very upset when your parents fight and worry that your worst fears about the family breaking up might come about.'

Part B
   Anger
   Illustrative voice messages: loud volume, even shouting and screaming, harsh pitch, fast speech rate.
   Illustrative body messages: clenched teeth, raised posture, glaring eyes, clenched fists, finger pointing, chopping arm and hand gesture.

   Anxiety
   Illustrative voice messages: quiet and timid volume, either quickened or haltering speech rate, sometimes poor articulation, mumbling, sometimes lack of emphasis.
   Illustrative body messages: poor gaze and eye contact, strained facial expression, tense body posture, drumming fingers, biting fingernails, tugging hair, bouncing leg.

   Depression
   Illustrative voice messages: sighing, soft voice, lack of emphasis, slow speech rate.
   Illustrative body messages: averted gaze, poor eye contact, tearful, corners of mouth turned down, slouched posture, holding head in hands.

Part C
1. '**You feel** you loathe being played about with and picked on **because** you see yourself the same as your peers.'
2. '**You feel** torn both ways about your son playing with your neighbour's little girl **because** you want to get on with her, yet fear her daughter may be a bad influence.'
3. '**You feel** you want to give up snorting **because** it's too expensive.'
4. '**You feel** delighted **because** you and Sally don't row so much and now you're more optimistic about staying together.'

SEVEN
Clarifying problems skills

A matter that becomes clear ceases to concern us.
Friedrich Nietzsche

CHAPTER QUESTIONS

- *How can counsellors use structuring skills?*

- *How can counsellors use questioning skills?*

- *How can counsellors use focusing skills?*

- *How can counsellors use challenging skills?*

- *How can counsellors use self-disclosing skills?*

- *How can counsellors use summarizing skills?*

- *How can counsellors use referral skills?*

- *What are some counsellor thinking skills for the initial session?*

EXPANDING UNDERSTANDING

Counsellor: Would you care to tell me what your problem is?
Client: My problem is that I have difficulty remembering things.
Counsellor: When did your problem start?
Client: What problem?

Definition of having a problem: Loving yourself more than your analyst.
Definition of overcoming a problem: Loving your analyst more than yourself.

Clients bringing problems to counsellors want to move beyond their stuckness, but are unclear how best to proceed. In Stage 1 of the lifeskills model, counsellors go beyond developing the relationship to identifying and clarifying clients' problems. The previous chapters on active listening skills heavily emphasized staying within clients' internal viewpoints. This chapter emphasizes using a range of skills to elaborate and clarify clients' internal viewpoints. In reality, frequently the identifying and clarifying work of Stage 1 overlaps with the assessing and restating problems in skills terms work of Stage 2. Counsellors also use many identifying and clarifying skills both when intervening and when emphasizing take-away of lifeskills and ending, Stages 4 and 5 of the model.

STRUCTURING SKILLS

Objectives of structuring

Clients come to counselling in various states of knowing what to expect. Even those who think they know may be misinformed. Structuring is a term used to describe how counsellors let clients know their respective roles at different stages of counselling. Cormier and Cormier (1991, p.51) state: '*Structuring* refers to an interactional process between counselors and clients in which they arrive at similar perceptions of the role of the counselor, an understanding of what occurs in counseling, and an agreement on which outcome goals will be achieved.' Structuring occurs throughout counselling and even prior to counselling: for example, through the publicity, image and reputations of counsellors and counselling agencies. Here the focus is on structuring skills for initial sessions.

Effective structuring leads to positive outcomes and prevents or minimizes the chances of negative outcomes. The functions of structuring in initial sessions include: reducing anxiety by clarifying roles; explaining the purpose of the initial session; establishing expectancies conducive to clients' working on rather than just talking about problems; providing an introductory rationale for working within the lifeskills counselling model; establishing the possibility of change; and, if necessary, communicating limitations concerning the counselling relationship, for instance, restrictions on confidentiality.

When structuring in initial sessions, counsellors begin the process of assisting clients to assume responsibility for developing their skills. Counsellors can establish cooperative alliances with clients as partners in developing their skills rather than doing things either to or for them. In the medical model of counselling, physicians might think: 'What can I do to cure my patients?' In the lifeskills counselling model, counsellors think: 'How can I best cooperate with clients to develop their self-helping skills?'

Too much and too little structure

Counsellors can provide both too much and too little structure (Osipow *et al.*, 1984). If you provide too much structuring, clients may feel stifled by your agendas and reluctant or unable to reveal their own. You may establish a 'teacher knows best' emotional climate that is conducive to dependency and resistances. Clients may perceive you as too set on fitting them into your way of working whether it suits them or not. Furthermore, if you talk too much at the beginning of sessions, not only do you make it difficult for clients to talk, but you may structure the counselling process in too intellectual a way. Too little structuring also has dangers. Clients may feel anxious and confused. You too may be anxious and confused. In addition, clients may perceive that you have nothing of value to offer.

Counsellors' voice and body messages may enhance or impede structuring. Again, negative outcomes may arise if counsellors come on either too strong or too weak. For instance, clients may feel overwhelmed and put off by counsellors who structure in loud voices and gesticulate too much. On the other hand, counsellors who structure in diffident voices, with minimal use of gesture and eye contact, may convey insufficient commitment.

Some structuring skills

VERBAL MESSAGE SKILLS A choice that counsellors face is how much to structure at the start of sessions. Already, I have mentioned that lifeskills counselling always starts with checking out 'where the client is at'. You can perform initial session structuring with at least two statements. The first statement gets the session started and allows clients to say why they have come or 'tell their stories'. The second statement establishes the agenda for the remainder of the session. Below is an example of a possible opening statement providing structure for a session's start.

> 'Hello, Jeff, my name is Debbie Roberts and I'm one of the student counsellors here. We have about forty minutes and everything you say is confidential. Would you please tell me why you're here?'

You then give the client a chance to state why he or she has come for counselling and you use active listening skills to show him or her that you have received the messages 'loud and clear'. Following are two examples of statements that might provide structure for the rest of the session.

> 'You've given me some idea why you've come. Now what I'd like to do is to ask some more questions to help us understand more fully your problem(s) (specify). Then, depending on what we find, I will review with you some skills to help you cope better. Once we agree on what skills might be useful, then we can look at ways to develop them. Does this way of proceeding sound all right?'

> 'You have mentioned three main areas that bother you (specify). Which of these would you like to spend time on first? (The client states her or his choice.) I'd now

like to ask you some questions to clarify for us both what's going on and then use the whiteboard to make some suggestions – in a sense give you a print-out – of some possibly unhelpful ways you may be thinking and acting. Then we can discuss what to do next.'

One reason for not amalgamating both parts of the structuring in your opening statement is that the second part may be inappropriate for certain clients: for example, those requiring either specific information or referral. Furthermore, lengthy opening statements may show lack of empathy to clients' immediate needs to say why they have come. Some clients may seek emotional release and feel blocked by your talking too much too soon. Sometimes, when sessions start, you may notice from body language that clients are experiencing strong emotions, such as distress or anxiety. You can reflect such feelings and give clients permission to discuss them.

Following are some guidelines for verbal messages when structuring in initial sessions.

- Be flexible. Considerations include: your clients' expectations and problems; their emotional state; their age and intelligence level; at what stage of the initial session you are; how much time you have; and the context in which you counsel.

- Break your structuring down into more than one statement.

- Pay attention to timing.

- Use simple language.

- Where appropriate, use skills language.

- Be clear and relatively brief.

- Be consistent. Make your structuring consistent with the theoretical position you adopt.

- Emphasize counsellor–client cooperation.

- Establish an agenda. You can start initial sessions by allowing your clients psychological space to tell their stories. However, at some point, you may need to establish an agenda by targeting a specific problem to clarify and restate in skills terms. Establishing an agenda helps to prevent rambling and unfocused sessions.

- Emphasize work. Counselling is not magic. Clients need to work to acquire and maintain skills.

- Check for questions and reservations. Do not assume that what you say is understood and agreed upon by clients.

VOICE AND BODY MESSAGES How you send voice and body messages is important when you structure. Your voice messages should indicate your commitment to what you do. Good voice message skills include easy audibility, comfortable speech rate, firm voice, clear articulation and appropriate variations in emphasis. Your body messages should support your verbal and voice messages: for example, by appropriate gaze, eye contact and use of gestures. A theme throughout this book is the importance of counsellors paying great attention to voice and body messages. Structuring is a clear instance where ineffective voice and body messages can countermand verbal messages.

QUESTIONING SKILLS
Goals of questioning

Viktor Frankl (1975, p.94) tells the following psychiatrist joke:

Are you a psychiatrist?
Why do you ask?
You're a psychiatrist.

Here, instead of unmasking, the psychiatrist has been unmasked. Often, as in this instance, counsellors ask questions inappropriately. A major reservation about using questions is that they take clients out of their internal viewpoints. Some questions are asked more to make counsellors feel secure that to help clients. However, judicious questioning can help clients better to explore, clarify and understand their internal viewpoints. Furthermore, questions assist counsellors to identify what clients' problems are and to break them down into component parts. Then you both possess more information for developing hypotheses about how problems are sustained. In this chapter the primary focus is on the use of questions to identify, clarify and break problems down into their component parts.

The iceberg provides a good analogy for understanding the role of questioning in Stage 1 of lifeskills counselling. Much relevant information lies below the surface. In general, clients responding to permission to tell their stories reveal useful information. Area A in Figure 7.1 depicts this information. However, effective counsellor questioning enables clients to provide much additional information for identifying, clarifying and breaking down problems. Area B depicts this further information. In addition, there may be additional information that clients may be either unaware of or unwilling to disclose. Counsellor questions may not tap this information. Area C depicts this either highly private or unconscious information.

Another analogy for the role of questioning in initial sessions of lifeskills counselling is that of plants and their root system. Counsellors use questions to identify different roots of problems. For example, earlier a hypothetical client came to counselling saying, 'I am depressed. Help me.' This represents the part of the plant which is above ground. However, by listening and effective questioning, the counsellor starts identifying roots of the client's problem in five different areas (see Figure 7.2). Then the counsellor may ask further questions to clarify each root area and its relative importance. Alternatively, the counsellor may ask the client on which problem root she or he wants to focus and then ask questions relevant to expanding his or her own and the

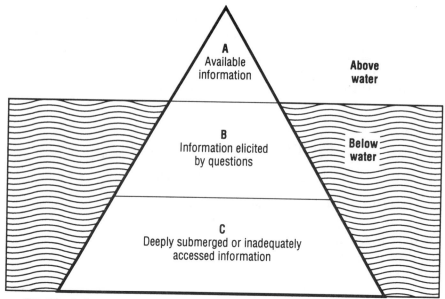

Figure 7.1 *The information about problems iceberg*

client's understanding of it. Often in initial sessions, but not invariably, I work this latter way.

In this depressed client example, the roots of the problem are located in the present rather than in the past. Questions concerning clients' childhoods may illustrate origins of problems and help them to work through and understand painful events. Nevertheless, the focus of questioning in lifeskills counselling is not on how clients arrived at their present problems, but on how they sustain them now and possibly in future.

Strategies for questioning

Spitzer and Williams (1984) classify clinical interviewing approaches into three types: smorgasbord, checklist and canine. In the smorgasbord approach counsellors sample whatever seems interesting. In the checklist approach, counsellors ask a series of closed

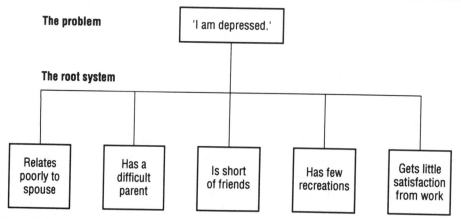

Figure 7.2 *Identifying the roots of a problem*

questions about particular symptoms 'without getting the patient to describe spontaneously the symptoms that are being talked about' (Spitzer and Williams, 1984, p.6). In the canine approach the counsellor is like a dog sniffing around for a buried bone. The counsellor continues to sniff around until the goal of that portion of the interview is reached and then moves on in search of another 'bone'.

In lifeskills counselling, initial session questioning takes the detective approach. Counsellors cooperate with clients first to ask questions that describe, clarify and break down their problems and then to ask further questions that assist the restating of at least one problem area in skills terms. The detective approach contains elements both of inquiring systematically and of sniffing around looking for bones or 'handles'. Counsellors try to create safe emotional climates in which clients feel free to offer information spontaneously and not just when questioned.

Choices when questioning

Counsellors have numerous choices when questioning, including the following.

- *Purpose of questions.* Effective counsellors ask questions that contribute to expanding their own and their clients' understanding of problems and problematic skills patterns. They do not just ask questions for questioning's sake.

- *Present versus past focus.* Questioning in lifeskills counselling tends to focus more on clients' presents than their pasts.

- *Number of topics covered.* An issue is that of whether just to ask questions in the area of the presenting problems(s) or conduct a broader reconnaissance (Sullivan, 1954). Practical considerations – for instance, what the client wants from counselling – often influence how many topics you cover.

- *Amount of detail.* How detailed should inquiries into each topic area be? When should counsellors move on? Partly by intuition, effective counsellors assess when areas may continue to yield valuable information and when to move on.

- *Intimacy level.* Counsellors need be sensitive to the intimacy and threat level of questions. They still tactfully ask intimate questions, if appropriate.

- *Timing.* Counsellors require caution regarding the timing and ordering of questions. You may defer some intimate or probing questions pending the establishment of greater trust.

- *Number of questions.* Egan observes: 'When in doubt as to what to say or do, inept helpers tend to ask questions, as if amassing information were the goal of the helping interview' (Egan, 1994, p.124). Be careful not to conduct interrogations that may lead to defensiveness or dependence, or both.

- *Confirmatory questions.* Beware of asking questions designed to elicit responses fitting pet theories. Sometimes counsellors prematurely decide what are clients' problems and skills deficits and then only ask questions to confirm their judgements.

Types of questions

Counsellors also need choose among different types of questions, including the following.

OPEN-ENDED VERSUS CLOSED-ENDED QUESTIONS Open-ended questions give clients considerable choice in how to respond, whereas closed-ended questions restrict choice. When working with new clients many helpers use open-ended questions prior to asking more focused questions.

> **Open-ended question:** What do you think of your previous experience in counselling?
> **Close-ended question:** Was your previous counsellor good or bad?

CLARIFICATION QUESTIONS Clarification questions seek information about and clarify your perception of clients' words and phrases. Examples include:

> 'When you say ... what do you mean?'
> 'Sounds to me like you're saying ... ?'

ELABORATION QUESTIONS Elaboration questions are open questions that give clients the opportunity to expand on what they have already started talking about. Examples include:

> 'Would you care to elaborate?'
> 'Is there anything more you wish to add?'

SPECIFIC DETAIL QUESTIONS Specific detail questions aim to collect concrete information about clients' problems and problematic skills patterns. Specific detail questions focus on how, what, when, and where.

- *How questions* include: 'How do/did you think, feel or act (or a combination of these)?', and 'How often does it happen?' How questions are particularly useful for eliciting details of how clients act.

- *What questions* include: 'What happened?' or 'Give me an example of what happened?', 'What do you perceive as the problem?' and 'What are the likely consequences of doing that?'

- *When questions* include: 'When did it start?' and 'When is your next public speech?'

- *Where questions* include: 'Where does it happen?' and 'Where in your body do you experience the tension?'

'SHOW ME' QUESTIONS 'Show me' questions ask clients to show the counsellor how they acted. Sometimes the counsellor will act the other person in a role-play. Examples include:

'Show me how you actually spoke to . . .'
'Imagine I am . . . Show me how you behaved to me.'

ELICITING PERSONAL MEANING QUESTIONS The information clients provide often has personal or symbolic meaning for them. For example, whenever a husband would come home late without having called her, his wife would think he did not care about her (Beck, 1988). Eliciting personal meanings questions should be open and tentative, since the client should, but not always will, know the answer better than anyone else. Illustrative questions include:

'I'm wondering about what the meaning of . . . is for you.'
'What do you make of that?'
'Why is it so important for you?'

SEARCHING FOR STRENGTHS QUESTIONS Ivey uses the term positive asset search to describe searching for clients' strengths. He observes: 'People grow from their strengths. The positive asset search is a useful method to ensure a more optimistic and directed interview' (Ivey, 1994, p. 144). Illustrative questions include:

'What do you see as your strengths?'
'What are your assets?'
'Was there anything good in the way you behaved?'
'What skills do you bring to this problem?'

SOLUTION-FOCUSED QUESTIONS Solution-focused questions ask clients to provide information concerning the extent to which they have tried or are trying to do something about their problems.

'What have you attempted to do about the problem to date?'
'What are your options?'
'What are you planning to do?'
'How can you change your behaviour?'

Areas of information for questions

Once beginning counsellors agree with clients on a specific problem to address, I encourage them to cover the following areas of information in their questioning. In each area, start open-ended and then, if appropriate, become more specific. There is no set ordering, though I prefer finding out information about clients' feelings early on. Let us take the example of exam-anxious Lisa, a 20-year-old university student.

BRIEF HISTORY OF PROBLEM Sample questions include:

'How long have you had this problem of getting anxious over exams?'
'Can you briefly describe what has happened when you took exams in the past?'
'Have you ever sought help for this problem before?'
'What course are you on and how well have you been doing?'
'How have you attempted to cope in the past?'

FEELINGS Sample questions include:

'When you say you get anxious, how exactly do you feel?'
'On a scale of one to ten, how anxious do you feel?'
'When do you feel anxious? Is it before, during or after exams?'
'Are there any subjects about which you get particularly anxious?'

PHYSICAL REACTIONS Sample questions include:

'What happens to your body when you feel anxious?'
'Do you have any distressing physical symptoms of anxiety?'
'Where exactly do you feel the tension in your body?'

THOUGHTS Sample questions include:

'What goes through your mind before, during and after an exam?'
'What thoughts and images accompany your anxiety?'
'What are the consequences for you of not doing well in exams?'
'Where is the evidence that you do not do well in exams?'

ACTIONS Sample questions include:

'When will you sit your next exam?'
'How do you act when you are anxious?'
'What are your revision skills like?'
'What are your exam-taking skills like?'
'Where do you study?'
'Have you discussed the problem with your lecturers?'
'What recreation are you taking?'

MISCELLANEOUS Sample questions include:

'Are there any other current stresses in your life?'
'Are you on any medication?'

'To whom can you turn for support?'

At the end of a series of questions such as the above, both the counsellor and Lisa should have a clearer picture of the nature and extent of her exam anxiety problem. The counsellor might ask further questions depending on the answers Lisa provided. In addition, a counsellor working within the lifeskills model would have some hypotheses about what were Lisa's thinking and action skills deficits that sustained her exam anxiety. The counsellor might ask further questions to confirm or negate hypotheses as the information suggesting a hypothesis became available or later.

Throughout this process of asking questions, the counsellor should take brief notes. Some counselling students dislike taking notes since they fear it blocks their relationships with clients. I discreetly take notes for three reasons (I use an A4 pad). First, note-taking enables me to be more, not less, psychologically present to clients – it relieves the pressure for me to memorize information. Second, when later I come to restate clients' problems in skills terms, I draw the evidence for my suggestions from my records of what clients tell me. Third, I have a record to which I can refer back, if necessary, for use in subsequent sessions.

Work in partnership with clients

In lifeskills counselling, questions are to provide information as much for clients as for counsellors. Counsellors try to avoid questioning in ways that create dependency, passivity and resistance. Below are some skills for cooperating with clients when asking questions.

ASK ESTABLISHING AGENDA AND TRANSITION QUESTIONS Establishing agenda and transition questions have the advantage of getting clients involved in the detective work of identifying and clarifying problems. Clients are invited to participate in working in areas important for them. Illustrative questions include:

> 'You've mentioned three areas (specify). Which one would you like to focus on first?'
> 'Is there anything you would like to add before we move on to ... ?'

INTERSPERSE ACTIVE LISTENING WITH QUESTIONS Clients feel interrogated when counsellors ask a series of questions in quick succession. When counselling, you can greatly soften your questioning if you pause to see if clients wish to continue responding and then reflect each response. Interspersing active listening has the added advantage of ensuring that you check the accuracy of your understanding. The following excerpt shows what you should avoid.

> **Lisa:** I'm getting very anxious over my upcoming exam.
> **Counsellor:** What makes you so anxious?
> **Lisa:** The fact that I may fail.
> **Counsellor:** Why are you so afraid of failing?

Lisa: Because then it will be harder to get a job.
Counsellor: What sort of job do you want?

Below is a gentler approach to the same initial statement.

Lisa: I'm getting very anxious over my upcoming exam.
Counsellor: You're very worried about your exam ... Would you say more about this?
Lisa: Yes. It's in three weeks' time and I feel overwhelmed.
Counsellor: So you experience this vital exam as overpowering.
Lisa: My whole future depends on it.
Counsellor: You think it is make-or-break. Can you explain this further?

Though these are only short excerpts, in the first the counsellor controls and dominates the client, whereas in the second the counsellor facilitates Lisa's description of her internal viewpoint. The emotional climate in the first excerpt is 'in the head'. The second excerpt encourages expressing feelings as well as thoughts.

ASK FOLLOW-ON QUESTIONS Avoid jackrabbitting, in which you quickly hop from one topic to another. Always listen carefully to and respect what clients have just said. Frequently, your next question can follow on from and encourage clients to build upon their last response. Questioning that is logically linked to clients' responses creates a feeling of working together rather than of being directed by you.

ENCOURAGE CLIENTS TO DO THEIR OWN WORK Often clients can both ask and answer their own questions. Interspersing reflections with questions provides clients with the psychological space to do their own work. If you establish good relationships, your clients will give you much information without being asked. You can also use silences to encourage clients to engage in self-exploration and move beyond superficial answers. Furthermore, you can ask questions that encourage clients to think and feel for themselves. Illustrative questions are:

'What information is important for helping you to understand your problem?'
'Just stay with the problem and try to get in touch with what you truly think and feel about it.'

CAREFULLY OBSERVE HOW QUESTIONS ARE ANSWERED Much of the art of questioning lies in decoding clients' answers. Much information is conveyed by what is left unsaid or only partially said and by voice and body messages. Effective counsellors are finely tuned to subtle client messages. They use tact both in asking questions and in responding to clients' answers. Clients with anxieties, confusions and vulnerabilities that counsellors sensitively pick up are more likely to answer questions honestly than clients listened to clumsily.

USE GOOD VOICE AND BODY MESSAGES How you question is very important in addition to what you say. For example, clients may feel overwhelmed if your voice is loud and harsh. If you use little eye contact and have a stiff body posture, they may also feel less inclined to answer your questions. When questioning use good volume, articulation, pitch, emphasis and speech rate. Furthermore make your body messages clearly show clients your interest in their answers.

Example of questioning to identify and clarify problems

Below is an excerpt from the start of an initial session between a student counsellor and an exam-anxious client, the previously mentioned Lisa. Introductions have taken place in the waiting area. The counsellor and Lisa are now seated in the counsellor's office.

Counsellor: We have about 45 minutes together. Please tell me why you've come.

Lisa: I'm getting very anxious over my upcoming exam.

Counsellor: You're very worried about your exam ... Would you say more about this?

Lisa: Yes. It's in three weeks' time and I feel overwhelmed.

Counsellor: So you experience this vital exam as overpowering.

Lisa: My whole future depends on it.

Counsellor: You think it is make-or-break. Can you explain this further?

Lisa: If I fail the exam it will show on my record and make it harder for me to get a good job.

Counsellor: So failure will jeopardize your prospects of good employment.

Lisa: Yes. Is there anything you can do to help me?

Counsellor: I appreciate your worry. However, before answering that question I would like to become clearer regarding your problem. Perhaps we can explore it further and then I should be in a better position to suggest some skills that you might develop to cope better.

Lisa: Where do we start?

Counsellor: Well can you give me some basic information about what course you are on and what subject or subjects you are afraid of failing?

Lisa: I'm in the final year of a Business Studies course and I'm afraid of failing Accounting 2.

Counsellor: What specifically about Accounting 2 bothers you?

Lisa: I got very nervous about my Accounting 1 exam and nearly failed the subject. My grades are generally above average, but I just scraped through. If it hadn't been for the marks on my take home assignments I would have failed.

Counsellor: You're wondering whether history may repeat itself and you'll do badly in your Accountancy 2 exam. How much of the grade does the exam account for?

Lisa: Fifty per cent. I think I'm doing OK on my homework assignments. I just don't want to mess up the exam.

Counsellor: You're worried about messing the exam up. I'm wondering if you're more concerned with how well you actually take the exam, your exam-taking skills, or how well you prepare for it, your revision skills, or both?

Lisa: What I'm most afraid of is that I will go to pieces during the exam.

Counsellor: So you're worried about falling apart during the exam. What precisely are you afraid you might do?

Lisa: Well in my last accountancy exam I could scarcely hold my pen. My hand was shaking and my heart was pounding. At times I felt faint as though I might blank out.

Counsellor: Last time you had numerous distressing physical symptoms – hand shaking, difficulty holding your pen, heart pounding, feeling faint. In what ways did these reactions affect how you actually behaved during the exam?

Lisa: I couldn't think clearly and I didn't leave enough time to answer all the questions.

Counsellor: When you say you couldn't think clearly, what do you mean?

Lisa: At times my head felt like cotton wool. I had to struggle to concentrate. These feelings of panic kept coming. I can't work with numbers under pressure.

In this brief excerpt, the counsellor has identified that a major concern of the client, Lisa, relates to not being able to handle her Accountancy 2 exam. The counsellor is still in the early stages of discovering the dimensions of Lisa's accountancy exam-taking difficulties and also whether there are other roots to the problem outside the exam-taking situation. The counsellor uses questions not only to discover the client's surface feelings and behaviours, but also to probe for the roots of the problem.

Sometimes when they are questioning, counsellors store away information for future use without responding to it directly. For example, counsellors might note that Lisa perceived her whole future resting on this exam as an example of black and white or polarized thinking (Beck, 1988). This observation might form the basis for questions in Stage 2 of the lifeskills model as the counsellor gathers more information to restate Lisa's problem in skills terms.

FOCUSING SKILLS

Ivey (1994) states that the main function of focusing is 'to direct the client conversational flow into the areas you want' (p.215). Other reasons for focusing include broadening clients' perspectives on problems by examining them from different points of view and helping clients to focus on important issues that they might otherwise avoid facing. Be conscious of when, why and how you choose to influence or direct the counselling process. Focused responding and focused exploration are two important focusing skills.

Focused responding

Client statements often have many parts to them. Consequently, you can choose where to focus. Take the following statement by Cheryl.

'I've just had the most terrible row with my mother-in-law. I can't seem to control my temper. OK, there are many problems between me and the kids, but why does she have to interfere? Right now I feel as though I could kill her.'

The above statement provides a challenge even for experienced counsellors trying to reflect all of it accurately. Depending upon what you wish to achieve in your interview, you may choose to respond by focusing on one or more from many options.

1. *Focus on the feeling.* 'You feel like murdering your mother-in-law.'
2. *Focus on the feeling and the thinking behind it.* 'You feel like murdering your mother-in-law because ... '
3. *Focus on one or more of the problems.* For instance, focus on controlling anger, coping with interference and/or dealing better with the kids. You may also choose to focus on problematic skills.
4. *Focus on the other person or persons.* For instance, focus on the mother-in-law or the kids.
5. *Focus on the counsellor.* The counsellor might share a reaction to Cheryl's statement: for instance, 'What do you want from me?'
6. *Focus on the environment context.* There may be broader social, cultural, racial, sex-role and economic issues that might provide an insight into the problem (Ivey, 1994).

Approach focused responding with caution. You may block clients from exploring and experiencing material that is important for them rather than for you. You may also get in the way of clients doing their own work. For instance, an excessive focus on Cheryl's mother-in-law's behaviour might block Cheryl from looking at her own behaviour. However, Cheryl might better examine her own behaviour if assisted to focus on her mother-in-law's perspective as well as her own. A further danger is that counsellors focus on areas of special interest to them: for example, paying excessive attention to sexual material. A reverse problem is that counsellors may not focus sufficiently on some topic areas.

Focused exploration

Focused exploration can follow from focused responding. Take the above example of Cheryl. The counsellor might respond to a specific part of Cheryl's statement: for instance, her perceptions of her mother-in-law, and explore them further before moving on to repeating the same process with another part of her statement: for instance, controlling her temper.

One way to establish focus is to ask clients to prioritize areas for exploration. However, counsellors may also wish to initiate explorations of specific areas. Furthermore, counsellors may wish to focus further when exploring specific areas. For example, when attempting to clarify Ron's stress difficulties, the counsellor may focus on related areas such as Ron's recreational activities and attention to keeping fit. Within the area of recreational activities, the counsellor may focus on why Ron no longer participates in a specific activity, say bike riding, that he previously enjoyed. Counsellors can use focusing skills to collect information on parts of problems not mentioned by clients. Counsellors also require skills of knowing when they reach diminishing returns. Furthermore, counsellors require skills of shifting the focus from one topic to another.

CHALLENGING SKILLS

Challenging is an alternative word for confronting. Challenges focus on discrepant, inconsistent and mixed messages that counsellors perceive that clients send. Egan (1994, p. 158) observes: 'Put most simply, challenge is an invitation to examine internal (cognitive) or external behavior that seems to be self-defeating, harmful to others, or both – and to change that behavior.' Egan's observation consists of two parts: first, developing new perspectives; second, translating these new perspectives into action. Here I review some skills of challenging clients' existing perceptions.

Challenging clients to speak for themselves

Frequently clients require help in speaking for themselves. By failing to send 'I' messages, clients may distance themselves from their feelings, thoughts and actions (Gordon, 1970). 'I' messages involve the use of the first person singular. Ways in which clients avoid speaking for themselves include making statements starting with words like 'you', 'people', 'we', and 'it'. Sometimes clients avoid sending 'I' messages by asking questions, in the hope that they can agree with the answer.

Here are examples of non-'I' messages transposed into 'I' messages.

- *Owning a feeling*
  Client's 'non-I' message: 'He is impossible when he behaves like that.'
  Client's 'I' message: 'I feel hurt and frustrated at his behaviour.'

- *Owning a thought*
  Client's 'non-I' message: 'What do you think about women serving in the forces in combat roles?'
  Client's 'I' message: 'I think women should/should not serve in the forces in combat roles.'

- *Owning an action*
  Client's 'non-I' message: 'The car crashed into the garage door.'
  Client's 'I' message: 'I crashed the car into the garage door.'

Counsellors require skills of challenging clients to speak for themselves. Following are three ways to encourage your clients to send 'I' messages.

RESPOND AS THOUGH CLIENTS SEND 'I' MESSAGES You can respond to clients in ways that use the word 'you' as though they had sent an 'I' message, even when they have not. For instance, if a client says 'He is impossible when he behaves like that', you might respond with 'You feel hurt and frustrated at his behaviour.' Your response implicitly challenges the client to express feelings directly.

REQUEST THAT CLIENTS SEND 'I' MESSAGES If clients fail to send 'I' messages consider openly drawing this to their attention. Following is an example of a discreet approach to challenging clients to speak for themselves: 'You're asking me what I think about women in combat roles, but I get the impression you have your own ideas on this matter.' Even more direct is to ask clients: 'Please use the word "I" when you wish to own a feeling, thought or action.' Where appropriate, you can educate clients to the distinction between 'I' messages and 'non-I' messages. Your doing so may challenge their existing perception that they speak for themselves.

Even after you request clients to send 'I' messages, they may revert to their old ways. Then both of you require persistence – counsellors in challenging clients and clients in challenging their old habits. Be careful not to threaten clients prematurely.

DEMONSTRATE SENDING 'I' MESSAGES If you are open in your own behaviour and use 'I' messages to own your feelings, thoughts and behaviour, your example may help clients to do likewise.

Challenging mixed messages

You may experience discrepancies in messages your clients send, including the following.

- *Discrepancy between verbal, voice and body messages.* 'On the one hand you say that you are nervous, but you smile.'

- *Discrepancy within verbal messages.* 'You say you are doing poorly, but report being in the top 25 per cent of your class.'

- *Discrepancy between words and actions.* 'You say you love your children from your former marriage, but you are behind on your maintenance.'

- *Discrepancy between past and present statements.* 'You now say you hate her, but about ten minutes ago you were saying how much you loved her.'

How you challenge involves verbal, voice and body messages. A common counsellor response when challenging mixed messages is 'On the one hand you say ... but on the other hand ... ': for example, 'On the one hand you say you are fine, but on the other hand I catch a note of pain in your voice.' This way of challenging is often shortened to 'You say ... but ... ': for example, 'You say that you are fine, but I catch a note of pain in your voice.' Sometimes, counsellors may wish to verbalize that they are receiving a mixed message: 'I'm getting a mixed message. You say that you are fine, but I catch a note of pain in your voice.' Counsellors can also explore the consequences of clients sending mixed messages in their relationships outside of counselling.

Challenging possible distortions of reality

When clients talk to counsellors they may make statements like the following.

'They are all out to get me.'

'I have no friends.'

'I'm a terrible mother.'

'I'm no good with women (or men).'

'She (or he) doesn't love me any more.'

All of these may be examples of unrealistic perceptions that can harm rather than help clients. Clients' perceptions are of varying degrees of accuracy. Sometimes counsellors need either to challenge such perceptions directly or to assist clients to test the reality of their own perceptions (Beck, 1976, 1988; Beck and Weishaar, 1995). Clients often jump to conclusions on insufficient evidence ('I have no friends'), and use black and white thinking ('Either I'm perfect or no good at all'). They may also fail to own responsibility for their thoughts, feelings and actions ('They made me do it'). Use your judgement about whether to continue listening within their internal viewpoints or to challenge their possible distortions of reality.

A useful format for challenging possible distortions of reality is 'You say ... but where's the evidence?' An example is, 'You say that you have no friends, but where's the evidence?' Such a response reflects the client's internal viewpoint and then invites him or her to produce evidence to support it. The client may then make a remark like 'Well, Leanne never calls me any more.' Then the counsellor may challenge the client again with a question like 'Is there any other way of looking at that?' With the questions 'Where's the evidence?' and 'Is there any other way of looking at that?', you invite speakers to produce their own evidence or provide different perceptions to confirm or negate their version of reality. On other occasions you may suggest some evidence from your external viewpoint.

Challenging not acknowledging choice

Lifeskills counselling heavily emphasizes personal responsibility. You can confront clients with their role as choosers in their lives. One way to do this is to highlight their choice processes. For example, clients who say 'I must send my children to private schools' might be challenged with the fact that they have some choice in the matter. Another example is that of Serena, aged 37, who says of her father: 'I resent having to visit him every weekend.' Here the counsellor responds by both reflecting her resentment and challenging her seeming failure to assume responsibility for being a chooser: 'You feel resentful, but I wonder whether you sufficiently acknowledge that you *choose* to visit him every weekend.' Such a challenge might open the way to exploring both how Serena thinks – for instance, not always acknowledging that she has choices – and how she acts, possibly not asserting herself enough with her father. Yet another way of challenging clients with their choices is to focus on the verbs that they use. For example, if a client says 'I *can't* do that', the counsellor may ask 'Can you say "I *won't* do that"?'

Challenging by reframing

Counsellors may also challenge clients' existing perceptions by offering new perspectives. Geldard observes: 'Sometimes a skilful counsellor can change the way a client perceives events or situations by "reframing" the picture which the client has described' (Geldard, 1989, p. 58). Though the facts may remain the same, the picture may look different in a new frame. Beck observes of relationships going downhill that partners begin to see each other through negative frames: for instance, 'He's mean and manipulative' or 'She's irresponsible.' He states: 'Reframing consists of seeing these negative qualities in a different light' (Beck, 1988, p. 267).

Below is an example of a counsellor confronting a client with a reframe.

> Tim, 16, perceived his mother as disliking him because she was always nagging him about doing household chores. The counsellor acknowledged his anger, but offered the reframe that his mother was a single parent who had to go to work to support the family and got very tired because she had more on her plate than she could handle. When she felt exhausted, she became irritable.

In the above example, 'the nagging mother who dislikes me' gets reframed as 'the overtired and overwhelmed single parent'. Reframing is integral to the lifeskills counselling model. Most clients do not perceive how they think and act in skills terms. In Stage 2 of the model, counsellors reframe the 'pictures' of clients' problems by stating them in skills rather than in descriptive language.

How to challenge

The following are some guidelines on how to challenge.

- *Start with reflecting.* Always start your response by showing that you have heard and understood clients' messages. Then build on this understanding with your challenging response. This way you are more likely to keep clients' ears open to your viewpoint.

- *Where possible, help clients to challenge themselves.* By reflecting mixed messages, you allow clients to choose their own conclusions about them. Similarly, by asking clients to search for evidence to back their statements, you help them to challenge themselves. Assisting clients in self-challenging often leads to less resistance than directly challenging them from your external viewpoint. Strategies that clients can use to resist challenges include: discrediting challengers, persuading challengers to change their views, devaluing the issue, seeking support elsewhere for views being challenged and agreeing with the challenge but then not acting accordingly (Egan, 1994).

- *Do not talk down.* Keep your challenges at a democratic level. Remember, challenges are invitations for exploration. Be careful not to send 'you' messages. A major risk in challenging clients is that they perceive what you say as put-downs.

- *Use a minimum amount of 'muscle'.* Only challenge as strongly as your goal requires. Strong challenges can create resistances. Although sometimes necessary, such challenges are generally best avoided – especially in initial sessions where rapport and trust are not yet established.

- *Avoid threatening voice and body messages.* Try to avoid threatening voice and body messages – raising your voice and pointing your finger are extreme examples.

- *Leave the ultimate responsibility with clients.* Allow clients to decide whether your challenges actually help them to move forward in their explorations. Often your challenges are only mildly discrepant to clients' existing perceptions. If well timed and tactfully worded, such challenges are unlikely to elicit a high degree of defensiveness.

- *Do not overdo it.* No one likes being persistently challenged. With constant challenges you create an unsafe emotional climate. If you challenge skilfully, you can help clients to enlarge their understanding and act more effectively. However if you challenge too often and too clumsily you can block clients and harm your relationship.

SELF-DISCLOSING SKILLS

Patient: Doctor, I've got a boil on my bottom. Let me show it to you.
Doctor: Let me show you my bottom too.

As the above travesty indicates, counsellor and helper self-disclosure can be for good or ill. Counsellor self-disclosure relates to the ways in which you let yourself be known to clients. Usually the term refers to intentional verbal disclosure. However, there are numerous other ways in which counsellors disclose, including voice and body messages, availability, office decor, written communications and size of fees! Though the following discussion mainly focuses on intentional verbal disclosure in initial sessions, it has much relevance to later sessions.

A useful distinction exists between self-involving responses and self-disclosing responses. McCarthy observes: 'Self-disclosure responses are statements referring to the past history or personal experiences of the counselor, and self-involving responses are direct present expressions of a counsellor's feelings about or reactions to client statements and/or behaviors' (McCarthy, 1982, p. 125). Another way of stating this is that there are at least two major dimensions of counsellor self-disclosure: showing involvement and disclosing personal information.

Showing involvement

There is a story about Dr Ida Libido, a psychoanalyst who would go down to the coffee shop leaving her cassette recorder on in her office to listen to her patients' free associations and dreams. One day, Amy Guilt, a patient who was meant to be on the couch, came into the coffee shop and the following dialogue took place.

> **Dr Libido:** What are you doing down here? You're meant to be in psycho-analysis.
> **Ms Guilt:** Don't worry, doc. I've left my cassette player on up there speaking into your cassette recorder.

Unlike Dr Libido, who is totally detached, you can show involvement to assist the counselling relationship. In particular, positive self-involving statements, expressing positive rather than negative feelings about clients, draw favourable reactions (Watkins, 1990). Self-involving disclosures can personalize counselling so that clients feel they relate to real people. Even negative reactions can be used constructively as invitations for exploration. There is a 'here and now' quality about reacting to clients. The following are three areas for self-involving statements.

- *Responding to specific disclosures.* Such comments include 'I'm delighted', 'That's great', 'That's terrible'.

- *Responding to clients as people.* Illustrative positive comments are 'I admire your courage', 'I appreciate your honesty', 'I like your sense of humour'.

- *Responding to the counselling relationship.* Illustrative comments are 'I'm uneasy because I sense that you want to put me on a pedestal', 'I find my attention wavering and wonder why', 'I'm pleased at your willingness to cooperate and work hard'.

Disclosing personal information

Research has yet to offer any definite conclusions on counsellors' sharing personal information (Watkins, 1990). Edwards and Murdock (1994) surveyed nearly 200 American psychologists licensed at the doctoral level and practising psychotherapy. Overall, respondents reported disclosing most often about professional qualifications and experience. The two main reasons endorsed for self-disclosing were to increase perceived similarity and to model self-disclosure as a desired behaviour.

Disclosing personal information and experiences may help clients feel that you understand what they go through. For instance, unemployed clients may not only feel more positively about counsellors who share past unemployment experiences, but also talk more readily about their own current experiences. Following is an example:

> **Counsellor:** Keith, as you've been talking of your experiences of being unemployed, it reminds me of a period in my life when I was out of a job and really scared that I would never find another one. Though clearly our experiences differ, I think I do have some idea of what you're going through.
>
> **Keith:** Thanks for that. One of the hardest things about being unemployed is feeling so bloody alone and useless. It's as if I'm burdening people by talking about it.

In some types of counselling, disclosure of shared experiences forms part of the helping process: for instance, disclosure of experiences by ex-alcoholics and ex-addicts in Alcoholics Anonymous and in certain drug treatment programmes. Such disclosures provide testimonials that people can beat substance abuse, though often it is an agonizing journey and one requiring constant vigilance to prevent and, if necessary, manage relapses.

Counsellors have many choices in disclosing personal information: first, whether to mention it or not; second, how honest to be; third, whether to go beyond disclosing facts to disclosing feelings (for instance, not only being unemployed but also having to struggle against depression and feelings of uselessness); fourth, how you coped with your experience; fifth, how you feel about it now.

Dimensions of self-disclosure that counsellors need to consider include: topic area, amount of disclosure in a topic area, intimacy level of disclosure, frequency of disclosure, positive or negative disclosure, degree of reciprocity, timing of disclosure, accompanying voice and body messages, client expectations and preferences, and cultural considerations (Edwards and Murdock, 1994; Jourard, 1964; Nelson-Jones, 1996a).

Following are some tentative guidelines for appropriate counsellor disclosure of personal information and experiences. Appropriateness means counsellor disclosure that benefits clients.

- *Be self-referent.* Be careful about disclosing third parties' experiences.

- *Be to the point.* Do not slow down or defocus the interview through irrelevance or talking too much.

- *Use good voice and body messages.* Be genuine and consistent. Your voice and body messages should match what you say.

- *Be sensitive to clients' reactions.* Have sufficient sensitivity to realize when your disclosures may help clients and when they may be unwelcome or a burden. For instance, if you are currently heavily emotionally involved in getting divorced, you must judge whether you have sufficient detachment to disclose the experience constructively. Be sensitive to how clients receive your disclosures and decide whether to continue accordingly.

- *Be sensitive to counsellor–client differences.* Expectations for counsellors differ across cultures, social class, race and gender and so do expectations regarding appropriateness of counsellor self-disclosure.

- *Do not overdo it.* With most clients, use self-disclosure judiciously rather than frequently. Counsellors who keep talking about themselves risk switching the focus of their work from their clients to themselves.

- *Beware of countertransference.* Countertransference refers to negative and positive feelings towards clients based on unresolved areas in counsellors' lives. Intentionally or unintentionally some counsellors use both involving and information self-disclosures to manipulate clients to meet needs for approval, intimacy and sex. This highlights the importance both of awareness of your motivation and also of behaving ethically.

SUMMARIZING SKILLS
Purposes of summaries

Summaries are brief statements of longer excerpts from counselling sessions. Summaries can pull together different parts of extended communications and may take place at any stage of counselling. Much of the time counsellors summarize what clients communicate. However, since lifeskills counselling has didactic as well as relationship emphases, some counsellor summaries relate to previously communicated educational content. Clients also use summaries: sometimes of their own accord and sometimes at the request of counsellors. For example, clients can be asked to summarize the main points in a skills sequence they learn.

Here I focus on counsellor summaries in initial sessions. Such summaries serve numerous purposes. If clients have had a lengthy period of talking, counsellors summarize to establish their presence and make the interaction more two-way. Furthermore, if clients are telling their stories very rapidly, counsellors may deliver summaries at a measured speech rate to calm clients down. Where possible, counsellor summaries serve to move the session forward. Such summaries may clarify what clients have communicated, identify themes and problem areas, and form the basis for establishing session agendas.

Types of summaries

The following are different types of summaries, albeit interrelated.

BASIC REFLECTION SUMMARY Basic reflection summaries can take place at any stage of counselling. They are short summaries that counsellors make after clients have spoken for more than a few sentences. Such summaries pull together the main feelings and content of what clients say. Basic reflection summaries serve a bridging function for clients, enabling them to continue with the same topic or move on to another. Other functions include making sure counsellors listen actively, rewarding clients for talking, showing understanding, checking your own understanding and possibly clarifying clients' understanding. Sometimes summaries highlight each of feelings, thoughts and actions.

> **Counsellor:** You feel very unhappy with your boss. You think he does not appreciate you and manipulates people all the time to get his way. Your relationship has got to the point where you speak to each other only when absolutely necessary.

REFLECTING FEELINGS AND REASONS SUMMARY Clients may convey one or more central feelings. At the same time they may either directly or indirectly suggest reasons for their feelings. Clients do not always speak in tidy and logically sequenced sentences. You may be faced with making order out of client statements varying in length and coherence. A reflecting feelings and reasons summary can usefully link emotions with their perceived sources.

> **Counsellor:** You feel tense and anxious all the time because you have your divorce coming up in three weeks and there still is considerable acrimony between you and Mick in many areas: child custody, division of property and even who gets the dog.

CLARIFICATION SUMMARY In clarification summaries, counsellors seek to ensure that they understand clients' internal viewpoints correctly. Clarification summaries are stated tentatively and allow clients to correct or add to what helpers say.

> **Counsellor:** Can I run what you have been telling me back to check that I understand you correctly. You have a drinking problem, but much of the time find this hard to admit. Your wife has told you that if you keep up your present level of drinking she will leave you. You feel guilty about sometimes coming home drunk and abusing her. You find her both emotionally and sexually unresponsive. You're unsure of whether you want to stay in the marriage. Is that about right?

THEME SUMMARY Theme summaries are reflections in which counsellors piece together what clients communicate to identify themes. You may note recurring patterns of thoughts, feelings and behaviours: for instance, fear of intimacy, preoccupation with homosexuality, avoidance of decisions or need for approval. A theme summary puts together the different pieces of information that constitute a theme.

> **Counsellor:** Sophie, as you've been talking I've noticed a number of occasions where you have emphasized how important it is to you that others like you. At times it comes over so strongly that it is almost as though your psychological survival depends on it. You've mentioned how vital it is for you to be popular with

the other girls at school, how upset you were when you thought your history teacher was not interested in you and how you always make a big effort to please your parents and be nice to their friends.

IDENTIFICATION OF PROBLEM AREAS SUMMARY Imagine that a client comes to counselling and starts describing a number of different problems. Summaries that overview or identify different problem areas mentioned can provide clients with clearer statements than they managed on their own. Furthermore, such summaries can provide a basis for asking clients to prioritize either which problems are most important or which ones they want to work on first.

> **Counsellor:** You started by talking about your problems with your housemate over keeping the place tidy. You then moved on to discuss your problems with your mother whom you perceive as excessively controlling and interfering even though you have moved out of home. You then talked about your mixed feelings about whether or not to stay in your relationship with Scott. You also expressed some dissatisfaction with your nursing studies and wonder if it is the right career for you. Which of these areas would you like to focus on first?

DETAILS OF PROBLEM SUMMARY In the initial session many questions seek to 'flesh out' details of clients' problems. For instance, a client who reports difficulty sleeping may have difficulty first going to sleep, spend the night tossing and turning or wake up early and not be able to get back to sleep, or a mixture of these. This pattern may happen every night or less frequently. Numerous different possibilities need to be checked to arrive at an accurate clarification. The same holds true for most other problems: for instance, marital conflict, job indecision, exam anxiety and specific phobias such as to spiders. The following is an illustrative details of problem summary. When gathering information, you can take notes to assist your memory. Furthermore, you can collect further descriptive information later.

> **Counsellor:** We've now spent some time exploring your sleep problem and these seem to be some of its main characteristics. Your problems with sleep started three months ago when you moved out of home and into an apartment at the time you took up your first social work position. You have difficulty getting to sleep practically every night. You like to get eight hours sleep a night, but currently get about six hours. When you can't get to sleep your brain becomes very active. You start worrying about everything that has happened during the day. You also worry about not being on top form the next day. You just lie there feeling uncomfortable, angry with yourself and somewhat depressed until exhaustion takes over. A consequence of not sleeping properly is that you feel tired the next day. Most late afternoons when you get home you lie down for about an hour. Is there anything important that I've left out?

OTHER TYPES OF SUMMARIES Other types of summaries include the following.

- *End-of-session summary.* Some counsellors favour end-of-session review summaries in which they go over the ground covered in the session and highlight accomplishments.

- *Beginning of next session summary.* Counsellors may summarize the previous session at the start of the next one. These summaries provide continuity. However, take care to allow space for clients to mention current as well as previous concerns.

- *Problems restated in skills terms summary.* As shown in Chapter 10, restating problems in terms of the thinking and action skills deficits sustaining them entails clearly and concisely summarizing diverse information.

- *Educational content summary.* Even in initial sessions, counsellors may start teaching skills. Summaries consolidate the main points. Furthermore, counsellors can request clients to summarize and, if necessary, correct their misunderstandings.

- *Take-away assignments summary.* At the end of sessions, counsellors can summarize what they and their clients have agreed upon as appropriate between-session take-away assignments.

REFERRAL SKILLS

In initial sessions, and also in subsequent sessions, you may face decisions about referring clients elsewhere. Even experienced counsellors have types of clients with whom they feel more competent and comfortable and others less so. Lazarus states that an important counselling principle is to 'Know your limitations and other clinicians' strengths' (Dryden, 1991, p. 30). He considers that referrals should be made where other counsellors have skills that the counsellor does not possess or more appropriate personal styles for particular clients. Important ethical issues surround referral, especially where other counsellors are more expert than you with specific problems: for instance, schizophrenia or traumatic stress disorders.

Referral may not be an either/or matter. Sometimes counsellors continue working with clients but also refer to other counsellors and helping professionals. Alternatively, counsellors may be the recipients of referrals from other helping professionals who continue working with them. I have worked as a sessional counsellor in a leading career outplacement company. All my clients were referred by other professionals who continued seeing them for job search counselling. I acted as a 'back-stop' for clients whose problems were more severe than or different from their normal clientele.

Sometimes you can refer clients to gain additional knowledge about their problems. For example, refer clients with thought-blocking problems or sexual dysfunctions for medical checks. Then, depending on the outcome of these checks, you have relevant information about whether or not to continue seeing them.

On other occasions you can refer the client's problem rather than the client to other counsellors and helping professionals. For example, you can discuss with colleagues or supervisors how best to assist certain clients. Occasions when you may refer the client's problem rather than the client include: when you are the only counsellor available in an area; when clients state a clear preference for continuing working with you; and when clients are unlikely to follow through on referrals.

Following are some skills for making referrals.

- *Know your strengths and limitations.* Be realistic about the kinds of clients with whom you work well and those with whom you are less skilled. Also be realistic about your work-load and set appropriate limits on it.

- *Build a referral network.* Get to know the resources available in your area so that you may make good referrals. Where possible, avoid referring 'blind' to someone about whose competence you are unsure. You should check whether another counsellor or helping professional has time available to see your client.

- *Build a support network.* Your support network provides professional support for you when you want to refer clients' problems rather than the clients themselves. Your support network is likely to overlap with your referral network.

- *Where possible, refer early on.* If you defer referrals longer than necessary, you waste clients' and your own time. It is preferable to refer clients before they emotionally bond with you.

- *Avoid unnecessary referrals.* Sometimes it is better for clients to continue working with you. Tune into your own anxieties and fears about seeing certain clients. You build your confidence and skills by expanding the range of clients with whom you can work. However, wherever possible, ensure that you have adequate supervision and support.

THINKING SKILLS

I deal briefly here with the important topic of counsellor thinking skills for initial sessions. This brevity is because I discuss assessing clients' thinking skills in Chapter 9 and interventions focused on clients' thinking in Chapters 14 and 15. All of this later material is also relevant to how counsellors think. Following are areas of counsellor thinking skills pertinent to the initial session and, frequently, to later sessions as well.

Owning responsibility for choosing

Counsellors need always be conscious that they are choosers (Nelson-Jones, 1982, 1995). They make choices in regard to their verbal, voice, body, touch and action messages. They choose how they think and how they feel. Throughout counselling they continually make decisions about how to respond to clients' communications. In addition, in initial sessions there is a heavy emphasis on choosing how best to identify, clarify and break down problems. Counsellors should own responsibility not only for choosing, but also for the consequences of choices. Counselling choices are best viewed as hypotheses modifiable in the light of feedback.

Using coping self-talk

In initial sessions counsellors can use negative self-talk in ways that create anxiety in themselves and their clients. Trish is a beginning counsellor. After a semester-long skills class, she is about to see her first client and videotape the session for her supervisor. Trish is highly nervous and worsens matters with the following self-talk.

> **Trish:** Help! I've got this important interview coming up. I wonder whether I'm going to do all right. I'm scared the client will notice that I'm anxious and lacking in skills. What if the client has a problem that is out of my depth? How will I manage then? Also, my supervisor will listen and hear all my mistakes.

A more constructive way for Trish to approach her first real session would be to use coping self-talk. Coping self-talk consists of calming, coaching and affirming self-statements: calming statements to relax herself, coaching statements to stay focused on how best to proceed, and affirming statements to remind herself of her strengths and support factors. Trish could use the following coping self-talk.

> **Trish:** Help! I'm feeling anxious because this is my first time with a real client. Now calm down and take a few deep breaths. I'm pretty certain I can cope with the situation. I've done a lot of practising and received good feedback. My supervisor just wants me to do as best I can and does not expect me to be perfect. I can start the interview with a good opening statement and speak calmly and clearly. Then I can use my active listening skills. I do not have to control everything that happens. Already, I'm starting to feel better by using my coping self-talk skills.

Counsellors can also use coping self-talk during and after their sessions. For instance, they can calm themselves down and think how best to act if clients get hostile during sessions. They can talk to themselves constructively after sessions: for instance, by acknowledging what went right and not overly focusing on what went wrong.

Choosing realistic personal rules

Counsellors can place unnecessary pressures on themselves by their unrealistic personal rules (Nelson-Jones, 1995), irrational beliefs or 'musturbations' (Ellis, 1962, 1995). The term 'musturbation' refers to rules that often contain words like 'must', 'ought' or 'should'. Counsellors can place demands on themselves ('I *must* be perfect'), their clients ('My clients *must* always appreciate me'), the counselling process ('Counselling *must* always go smoothly') and the environment ('Other people *must* always understand and support my counselling endeavours').

Counsellors need to identify unrealistic personal rules and restate them as more realistic or rational rules. The main objective is to replace demanding or 'musturbatory' thinking with preferential thinking.

Unrealistic rule: 'I must be perfect.'
Realistic rule: 'I would prefer to perform as competently as I can.'

Unrealistic rule: 'I must have my client's approval.'
Realistic rule: 'Though I would prefer to have my client's approval, my main task is to help him or her to the best of my ability.'

Unrealistic rule: 'Counselling must always go smoothly.'
Realistic rule: 'Counselling is somewhat unpredictable and I can handle this.'

Perceiving accurately

Counsellors perceive themselves, others, their clients and events with varying degrees of accuracy. Take care not to distort your perceptions of clients to fit your own needs and agendas. It is important not to jump to conclusions when attempting to identify and clarify problems. Rather, you need carefully to sift fact from inference and, if appropriate, accumulate more information to build and test your inferences. Below are some specific perceiving errors to avoid (Beck, 1976, 1988; Beck and Weishaar, 1995).

- *Arbitrary inference.* Drawing conclusions without adequate supporting evidence or in the face of conflicting evidence.

- *Tunnel vision.* Focusing on only a portion of the available information regarding a problem rather than taking into account all significant data.

- *Magnifying and minimizing.* Magnifying or exaggerating the qualities and significance of events, or minimizing them.

- *Black and white thinking.* Perceiving in either/or and polarized terms: 'Clients are either very cooperative or very uncooperative'; 'Clients either continue having problems or are cured.'

- *Negativeness.* Overemphasizing negative aspects of clients and yourself and minimizing the positive aspects. Always searching for deficits rather than for strengths. Applying negative labels to yourself and others: for example, 'I'm a loser' or 'That client is impossible.'

- *Selective inattention.* Overlooking or being inattentive to material that may cause you anxiety (Sullivan, 1954). Denying and distorting information through defensive thinking.

- *Overgeneralizing.* Making sweeping generalizations unsupported by evidence: 'All my initial sessions go well'; 'My clients never stick to the point'; 'She failed in one relationship and therefore she has failed in all her previous relationships.'

- *Catastrophizing.* Making highly negative predictions unsupported by evidence: 'My first session this afternoon did not go well, so all my other sessions will go badly too.'

Explaining cause accurately

Counsellors may err in the directions of explaining too much or too little cause and responsibility to themselves. Here are some counsellors' statements explaining *too much* responsibility to themselves.

'I'm responsible for everything that happens in my counselling sessions.'

'I'm solely responsible for the outcomes of counselling.'

'Everything that goes wrong in counselling is my fault.'

Below are counsellor statements explaining *too little* cause and responsibility to themselves.

'Jenny is not saying much because she is a shy person.' (Jenny may be shy but the counsellor also has poor active listening skills.)

'Boris has a lot of resistances to being helped.' (The counsellor may also have contributed to these resistances.)

CHAPTER HIGHLIGHTS

- *Counsellors can use a range of skills to clarify and expand their own and clients' understanding of problems.*

- *Structuring describes the behaviours by which counsellors let clients know their respective roles at various stages of counselling.*

- *Structuring statements in initial sessions may be made more than once: voice and body as well as verbal messages are important.*

- *Questions can help to identify and clarify the roots of problems.*

- *Counsellor choices when questioning include its purpose, past or present focus, amount of topics covered, degree of detail, intimacy level and timing.*

- *Types of questions include open-ended versus closed-ended, clarification, elaboration, specific detail (how, what, when and where), show me, eliciting personal meaning, searching for strengths and solution-focused.*

- *Areas of questions to clarify problems include brief history of problem, feelings, physical reactions, thoughts, actions and miscellaneous.*

- *Questioning skills for working in partnership with clients include establishing agenda and transition questions, interspersing active listening, asking follow-on questions and encouraging clients to do their own work.*

- *Focusing entails directing and influencing the helping conversation into specific areas.*

- *Focusing skills include focused responding to parts of clients' communications and focused exploration.*

- *Challenges can expand clients' existing perceptions so together you can work with new and better information.*

- *Counsellors can challenge clients to speak for themselves, mixed messages, possible distortions of reality and not acknowledging choice. Counsellors can use challenging skills to reframe problems by offering new perspectives.*

- *Showing involvement and disclosing personal information are two important areas of counsellor self-disclosure.*

- *Self-involving disclosures can be in response to specific disclosures, clients as people and the counselling relationship.*

- *Judicious disclosing of personal information can increase perceived similarity and demonstrate desired behaviour.*

- *Summarizing skills entail making brief statements of longer excerpts from counselling sessions.*

- *Types of summaries include basic reflection, reflecting feelings and reasons, clarification, theme, identification of problem areas, and details of problems.*

- *Counsellors can refer clients elsewhere or seek additional information, supervision and support about clients – referring the problem, but not the client.*

- *Referral skills include knowing your strengths and limitations, building referral and support networks, where possible referring early on and avoiding unnecessary referrals.*

- *Thinking skills for identifying and clarifying problems include: owning responsibility for choosing, using coping self-talk, choosing realistic personal rules, perceiving accurately and explaining cause accurately.*

EXERCISE 7.1   INITIAL STRUCTURING SKILLS

As appropriate, complete the parts of this exercise on your own, with a partner or in a group.

Part A   Formulating structuring statements
Answer the following questions.

1. What are the main verbal message choices you need to consider when making structuring statements in initial sessions?
2. What are the main voice and body message choices counsellors need to consider when making structuring statements in initial sessions?
3. Formulate at least one initial structuring statement to say at the beginning of the initial session.
4. Formulate at least one structuring statement to say after clients have had a chance to say something about why they have come for counselling. Your statement should establish some structure for the remainder of the session.
5. Rehearse; then audio-record your structuring statements and play them back. Repeat this activity until you are satisfied with your verbal and voice messages.

Part B   Practising structuring
Suggestions for practising with a partner include the following.

1. Work through the items in Part A together.
2. Counsel each other for brief periods, consisting of: counsellor initial structuring; facilitating the 'client' who responds to the initial structuring by sharing his or her reasons for coming; and then a second counsellor statement to establish some structure for the remainder of the session (end session here). At the end of each counselling session, the 'client' gives the counsellor feedback on his or her structuring statements. It can help to play back audio-recordings or video-recordings of your work.

EXERCISE 7.2   QUESTIONING SKILLS

As appropriate, complete this exercise on your own, with a partner or in a group.

Part A   Exploring the role of questions in initial counselling sessions
Answer the following questions.

1. Describe some of the main reasons for and against asking questions in initial counselling sessions.

    (a) reasons for
    (b) reasons against

2. Describe some of the main considerations for counsellors when asking questions in initial sessions.

Part B   Formulating questions
Formulate two examples of each of the following types of questions.

1. Open-ended
2. Closed-ended
3. Clarification
4. Elaboration
5. Specific detail
    (a) how question
    (b) what question
    (c) when question
    (d) where question
6. 'Show me'
7. Eliciting personal meaning
8. Searching for strengths
9. Solution-focused

Part C   Practising in pairs or in a group
1. *In pairs.*

    (a) Together go through Parts A and B of this exercise.
    (b) Counsel each other for sessions consisting of:
    - counsellor initial structuring;
    - counsellor facilitating the 'client', who responds to the initial structuring by sharing his or her reasons for coming;
    - a second counsellor statement to establish the structure for asking questions to identify and clarify the 'client's' problem or an aspect of it;
    - interspersed with active listening, ask appropriate questions for your client and you to gain greater clarification and understanding of the problem.

    At the end of each session, the 'client' gives the 'counsellor' feedback on his or her questioning skills. It can help to play back audio-recordings or video-recordings of your work.

2. *In a group.* One person acts as client, and presents a problem to the group, who sit in a semi-circle facing him or her. Each member takes turns in responding to the

client, first by reflecting what he or she has just said and then by asking a question that helps to clarify his or her problem. When the client answers, the next member reflects the answer and then asks a question and so on. When finished, the client provides feedback on the 'session'. Members take turns as clients.

EXERCISE 7.3 FOCUSING SKILLS

As appropriate, complete this exercise on your own, with a partner or in a group.

Below are two client statements. For each you are asked to formulate responses that focus in different ways. You are not asked to assess the appropriateness of each response. To do this properly you need know more about the context of each client's statements within his or her counselling sessions.

Vera, aged 63, is a married client talking to a social worker

'I'm exhausted. I don't know if I can go on much longer. I used to feel I had a husband, but over the past three years as Josh's Alzheimer's disease has got worse, he has progressively withdrawn from me. It's not just the lack of companionship... it's being on edge all the time over what he may do next. Last night he was wandering about after midnight on the road. I wish his relatives would help out more.'

1. Your focusing on feeling response.
2. Your focusing on feeling and the thinking behind its response.
3. Your focusing on one or more of the problems response.
4. Your focusing on other person or persons response.
5. Your focusing on counsellor (social worker) response.
6. Your focusing on environmental context response.

Drew, aged 18, a client talking to a career counsellor

'I just can't seem to get my work done. My heart isn't in it. I'm thinking of quitting university. I thought going into engineering would provide me with a safe career. However, I've wanted all my life to be a pilot. My parents are divorced and my father is an alcoholic whom I don't see much of. I live with my mother who is very concerned about my future. I've done some flying already and she is prepared to pay for me to go to flying school.'

1. Your focusing on feeling response.
2. Your focusing on feeling and the thinking behind it response.
·3. Your focusing on one or more of the problems response.
4. Your focusing on other person or persons response.
5. Your focusing on counsellor response.
6. Your focusing on environmental context response.

EXERCISE 7.4   CHALLENGING SKILLS

As appropriate, complete this exercise on your own, in pairs or in a group.

Part A   Formulating challenges
1. *Challenge clients to speak for themselves.*
   Formulate illustrative counsellor requests for clients to speak for themselves.
   (a) indirect request
   (b) direct request

2. *Challenge mixed messages.*
   Formulate illustrative counsellor challenges in each of the following areas.
   (a) discrepancy between verbal, voice and body messages
   (b) discrepancy within verbal messages
   (c) discrepancy between words and actions
   (d) discrepancy between past and present statements

3. *Challenge possible distortions of reality.*
   Give two examples of counsellor responses that challenge possible distortions of reality.
   (a) example 1
   (b) example 2

4. *Challenge not acknowledging choice.*
   Give two examples of counsellor responses that challenge clients with insufficiently acknowledging choice.
   (a) example 1
   (b) example 2

5. *Challenge by reframing.*
   Give two examples of counsellor responses that challenge clients by reframing or offering new perspectives.
   (a) example 1
   (b) example 2

Part B   Practising in pairs or in a group
1. *In pairs.* Suggestions include:

   (a) Together work through the items in Part A of this exercise.
   (b) Conduct mini interviews with each other. Focus each mini interview on a particular challenging skill. Counsellors should ensure that they make at least one response of the targeted challenging skill in the interview. Pay attention to voice and body as well as to verbal messages. After each mini interview, the

'client' gives feedback on the use of the challenging skill, followed by discussion. Play back recordings if helpful.

(c) Conduct longer interviews with each other, say for 15 minutes or more, in which the counsellor attempts to incorporate challenges. Again pay attention to voice and body as well as verbal messages. Debrief and give feedback after each session.

2. *In a group.* One person acts as client and presents a problem to the group, who sit in a semi-circle facing him or her. The client deliberately introduces discrepancies into what he or she says. Each member takes turns in responding to the client, first by reflecting what he or she has just said and then, when a discrepancy occurs, making a challenging response. When finished, the client provides feedback on the 'session'. Members take turns as clients.

EXERCISE 7.5   SELF-DISCLOSING SKILLS

As appropriate, complete each part of this exercise on your own, with a partner or in a group.

Part A   Formulating self-disclosures
Self-involving disclosures
1. With respect to your present or future counselling work, write down the sorts of situations in which it might be appropriate for you to show involvement to clients.

2. Formulate one or more appropriate *self-involving disclosures* in each of the following areas.

   (a) responding to specific client disclosures
   (b) responding to clients as people
   (c) responding to the counselling relationship

Personal information disclosures
1. With regard to your present or future counselling work, write down the sorts of situations in which it might be appropriate for you to disclose personal information and experiences to clients.

2. For each situation formulate one or more *disclosing personal information* responses.

Part B   Practising self-disclosing
1. *In pairs.* Suggestions include:
   (a) Counsel a partner who discusses a personal concern or role-plays a client. During the course of a mini session, try on a few occasions to make

self-involving disclosures. Afterwards your partner gives you feedback on the impact of your disclosures, followed by discussion. Then reverse roles.

(b) Counsel your partner for a mini session, but this time on one or more occasions *disclose personal information*. Afterwards your partner gives you feedback on the impact of your disclosures, followed by discussion. Then reverse roles.

(c) Conduct a brief session in which, where appropriate, the counsellor uses both self-involving disclosures and disclosures of personal information and experiences. After discussion and feedback, reverse roles.

2.   *In a group*. One person acts as client and presents a problem to the group, who sit in a semi-circle facing him or her. One member of the group acts as counsellor and the remaining members act as observers. The counsellor has permission to disclose self-involvement or personal information or both when he or she considers it appropriate. After each disclosure, the session stops for discussion of the appropriateness and impact of the disclosure. Then another member of the group takes over as counsellor and so on.

EXERCISE 7.6   SUMMARIZING SKILLS

As appropriate, complete Part A of this exercise on your own and Part B with a partner.

Part A   Formulating summaries
Imagine that you conduct an initial interview with a client. Formulate and write out a summary statement for each of the following types of summaries.

1.   Basic reflection summary
2.   Reflecting feelings and reasons summary
3.   Clarification summary
4.   Theme summary
5.   Identification of problem areas summary
6.   Details of problem summary
7.   End-of-session summary

Audio-record each of the above statements, paying attention to voice and body as well as verbal messages. Play back your recordings and modify them if necessary.

Part B   Practising summarizing
Suggestions for practising with a partner include the following.
1.   You and your partner communicate each of your summary statements formulated in Part A, one type at a time, to each other. Pay attention to voice and body messages. Give each other feedback.

2. Conduct mini interviews, say 5 minutes, in which the counsellor
    *   provides an initial structuring;
    *   facilitates the client telling his or her story, including making brief summaries every now and then – for example, basic reflection and clarification summaries;
    *   ends by providing a summary of the session so far.
    After the mini interview, the client provides feedback on the counsellor's summarizing skills, followed by discussion. Afterwards, reverse roles. Playing back recordings of mini interviews may help you to assess your skills.

3. Conduct longer interviews in which the counsellor
    *   provides an initial structuring;
    *   facilitates the client initially telling his or her story, including using one or more brief summaries;
    *   after about 5 minutes summarizes the session so far and makes a structuring statement for the remainder of the session;
    *   conducts the next part of the session using questions, active listening and summaries;
    *   ends by providing a summary identifying and clarifying the client's problem or problems.
    After the session, the client provides feedback on the counsellor's summarizing skills, followed by discussion. Afterwards, reverse roles. Again, playing back recordings of sessions may help you assess your skills.

EXERCISE 7.7   REFERRAL SKILLS

Answer the following questions on your own, in pairs or in a group.
1. When might you refer clients to other counsellors or helping professionals?
2. What categories of counsellors and helping professionals do you require in your referral network?
3. What categories of counsellors and helping professionals do you require in your support network, when you refer problems but not clients?
4. What are some considerations in making good referrals?
5. When might you be at risk of making unnecessary referrals?

EXERCISE 7.8   ASSESSING MY THINKING SKILLS AS A COUNSELLOR

First do this exercise on your own. Then, if appropriate, discuss with a partner or in a group.

1. Assess your strengths and deficits on each of the following thinking skills relevant to developing counselling relationships and clarifying problems. Then state how your strengths and deficits influence how you counsel.

Owning responsibility for choosing
(a) skills strengths
(b) skills deficits
(c) influence on my counselling

Using coping self-talk
(a) skills strengths
(b) skills deficits
(c) influence on my counselling

Choosing realistic personal rules
(a) skills strengths
(b) skills deficits
(c) influence on my counselling

Perceiving accurately
(a) skills strengths
(b) skills deficits
(c) influence on my counselling

Explaining cause accurately
(a) skills strengths
(b) skills weaknesses
(c) influence on my counselling

2. Summarize:
    (a) what you perceive to be your thinking skills strengths and deficits for conducting initial counselling sessions;
    (b) how your thinking strengths and deficits might influence how you counsel in initial sessions.

PART THREE

Stage 2: Assess and Restate Problem(s) in Skills Terms

Chapter 8 reviews how counsellors can assess feelings and physical reactions. Chapter 9 covers assessing thinking and actions. Chapter 10 addresses how counsellors can restate information obtained from assessing clients' problems into skills terms, so that clients have 'handles' for future work.

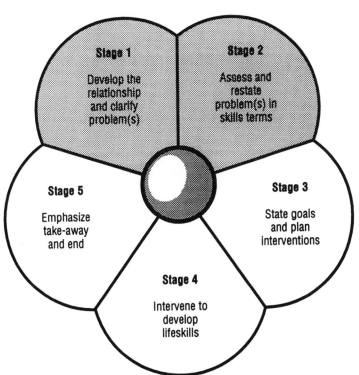

Stage 1

Develop the relationship and clarify problem(s)

Stage 2

Assess and restate problem(s) in skills terms

Stage 5

Emphasize take-away and end

Stage 3

State goals and plan interventions

Stage 4

Intervene to develop lifeskills

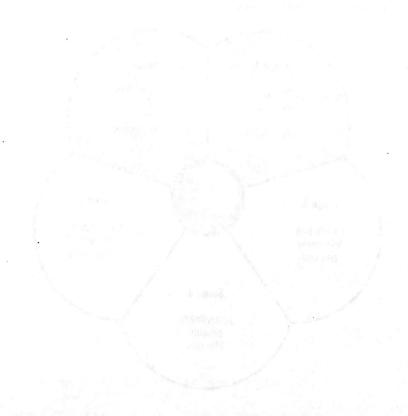

EIGHT

Assess feelings and physical reactions

Seeing's believing, but feeling's the truth.
Thomas Fuller

CHAPTER QUESTIONS

- *What is the role of assessment in lifeskills counselling?*

- *Why assess feelings and physical reactions?*

- *What are physical reactions?*

- *What are some dimensions of feelings?*

- *How can counsellors elicit and assess feelings and physical reactions?*

ROLE OF ASSESSMENT

Assessment in lifeskills counselling is performed both with clients and for clients. During Stage 1, develop the relationship and clarify problem(s), counsellors develop working models of clients' problems and problematic skills. Clients come to counselling with hypotheses, albeit inadequate, of what their problems are and how they are sustained. During the clarifying problems process, clients may start revising their models. Often the process of systematically eliciting descriptive information about clients' problems loosens existing conceptualizations.

During Stage 2, assess and restate problem(s) in skills terms, counsellors continue loosening clients' conceptualizations of problems. However, the process does not stop there. The desired outcome of Stage 2 is to reconceptualize problems so that clients now have 'handles' for change – what Egan (1994) calls 'leverage'. Counsellors use skills both to elicit basic descriptive information and to explore hypotheses about problematic skills sustaining problems. Counsellors assess information that is both volunteered and elicited. Together counsellors and clients reform descriptive summaries of problems into skills restatements.

The counsellor's role

Counsellors should always offer supportive relationships when assessing and restating clients' problems in skills terms. Active listening skills are fundamental. Furthermore, many skills used for clarifying problems – for instance, focusing and summarizing – are relevant for assessing and restating problems.

Counsellors are practitioner-researchers who formulate hypotheses about how clients sustain problems. Sources of such hypotheses are descriptive information provided by clients, information elicited as counsellors 'try on' initial hypotheses, counselling theory, knowledge of relevant research and previous experiences with clients. Where possible, work openly with clients. Treat them as intelligent people who, despite defences and anxieties, wish to help themselves by gaining greater self-understanding. Assist clients to do much of their own assessing rather than do all of it for them. Never lose sight of the fact that counselling is temporary. Especially where client contact extends over a number of sessions, counsellors can train clients in how to restate their own problems in skills terms.

Can assessment be overdone? The answer is a resounding 'yes'. Be sensitive to the amount of information required for assessing problems. Furthermore, take into account clients' perceptions of when 'enough is enough'. Collect information and also restate problems in skills terms as parsimoniously as possible.

The client's role

Like counsellors, clients are hypothesis makers and testers. To date, their hypotheses about how to solve their problems are inadequate. Frequently, they are stuck in faulty definitions of problems. Clients can actively collaborate with counsellors to generate hypotheses, provide information for assessing hypotheses and evaluate conceptualizations of problems. They can participate in various attempts to assess their feelings, thoughts and actions. For example, they can strive for honesty in experiencing and expressing feelings. They can be open about how they think, even if in socially undesirable ways. They can assist in exploring and evaluating hypotheses about how they think. In addition, they can share specific details of how they have acted in the past, monitor their current actions and participate in role plays.

Assessment is for clients' even more than for counsellors' benefits. Clients can engage in testing the adequacy of original conceptions of problems and make corrections. They can provide confirmatory, corrective or negative feedback about counsellors' hypotheses. Clients can cooperate with counsellors to develop more accurate and parsimonious skills restatements of problems. If they are active in assessing and restating problems, clients can become more motivated to change. Furthermore, active participation in assessing and restating problems assists clients to develop these skills for later self-helping.

WHY ASSESS FEELINGS AND PHYSICAL REACTIONS?

The following examples are of clients who make feelings and physical reactions statements.

'I get panic attacks.'

'I have suicidal thoughts.'

'I have high blood pressure.'

'I shake with fury.'

'I never know what I want.'

'I lack energy.'

'I'm sexually unresponsive.'

Counsellors assess feelings and physical reactions, the physical manifestations of feelings, for numerous reasons. Some of these reasons are mentioned below.

PROTECT CLIENTS Counsellors have an ethical duty to protect clients. At the back of most counsellors' minds when meeting new clients is the question: 'Is this client a suicide risk?' Counsellors also seek to understand the intensity and nature of clients' pain. Such understanding is partly to protect clients, but also to make appropriate skills restatements of problems.

EVALUATE EMOTIONAL RESPONSIVENESS Always be mindful of clients' ability to experience feelings. Feelings may be viewed as the core of human personhood and identity. Counsellors seek to assess how responsive clients are both to themselves and others. To what extent are clients in touch with their valuing process? Are clients in touch with significant feelings or do they deny and distort such feelings? To what extent are clients in touch with wants and wishes?

CLARIFY REAL AGENDAS Attending closely to feelings and physical reactions may assist counsellors to clarify what clients' real agendas are. Sometimes clients give feelings clues that more substantial problems underlie their 'calling card' explanations for coming. For example, by voice and body messages a woman who presents wanting to discuss a 'problem' child may indicate that her real agenda is marital dissatisfaction. Sometimes counsellors need to allow clients space to clarify feelings prior to knowing which problem to work on in skills terms.

> Dave, 50, had been divorced for five years and had custody of three children: Jan, 17, Beth, 15, and

Marty, 13. For the past year, Dave had been seeing Maria, 45, a divorcee who also had three children, with ages ranging from 6 to 17. Dave came to counselling confused about whether or not he wanted to develop his relationship with Maria further or get out of it. Dave's counsellor, Mel, spent much of the initial session assisting Dave to get in touch with and explore his feelings concerning: his past, present and possible future with Maria; his fears of commitment after the pain of his divorce; his anxieties about how good he was at communicating in close relationships; his needs for companionship; and his fears of being lonely for the remainder of his life. As the session progressed Dave became clearer regarding his wish to work on his skills at relating to Maria.

OBTAIN LEADS ABOUT THINKING AND ACTION SKILLS DEFICITS Another reason for assessing feelings and physical reactions is to assist clients in regulating unwanted feelings and in expressing appropriate feelings. Since feelings and physical reactions reflect humans' animal nature they are not in themselves skills. Nevertheless, assessing feelings accurately can be a major route to identifying thinking and action skills deficits. For example, clients admitting their anger, hurt and guilt – and what this does to their bodies – have better starting points for developing the thinking and action skills to manage these feelings than clients denying or distorting them. Assess clients' skills at expressing feelings. For example, Betsy knows what she feels about her boyfriend Wassim, but is too inhibited to reveal it.

SCREEN FOR MEDICAL AND PSYCHIATRIC CONSIDERATIONS A simple mind–body split is erroneous. Nevertheless, you need to be aware that medical considerations can influence how clients feel. Non-medically trained counsellors should acknowledge their limitations and seek appropriate medical or psychiatric advice. Occasions to take medical and psychiatric considerations into account include where clients: are on medication; have a physical illness, such as cancer, that affects how they feel; show psychophysiological symptoms, such as peptic ulcers and migraine headaches; exhibit the effects of substance abuse; and suffer from mental disorders (American Psychiatric Association, 1994).

DEVELOP CLIENTS' SELF-ASSESSMENT SKILLS Counsellors work together with clients to assess feelings and physical reactions. In their pasts many clients have had their feelings and physical reactions invalidated. Skilled assessment can both affirm the importance of awareness of feelings and help clients to experience, identify and explore significant feelings. Clients' feelings may take time to emerge and be shared with you. Revealing and assessing feelings occurs throughout counselling. Where possible, you can assist clients to develop skills at assessing feelings after counselling.

PHYSICAL REACTIONS

Physical reactions both represent and accompany feelings and, in a sense, are indistinguishable. I talk about physical reactions prior to reviewing dimensions of feelings. This ordering emphasizes that feelings are located in the body.

Bodily changes

The following are some bodily changes before, during and after feelings.

- *Galvanic skin response.* Detectable electrical changes take place in the skin.

- *Blood pressure, distribution and composition.* Blood pressure can rise. The distribution of blood may alter: for instance, in blushing (going red) or blanching (going white) the blood vessels near the skin's surface dilate or constrict respectively. In addition, there can be changes in blood composition, for instance, blood sugar, acid–base balance and adrenaline content.

- *Heart rate and pulse rate.* A pounding heart and a rapid pulse characterize intense emotion.

- *Breathing.* Shallow, rapid breathing can characterize anxiety.

- *Muscular tension.* Muscular tension is associated with intensity of feeling. Clients can feel tension in different parts of their bodies. Sometimes trembling accompanies muscular tension.

- *Psychomotor retardation.* Slowing down of bodily movements: for instance, when depressed.

- *Dry mouth.* Emotional excitation can produce a decrease in saliva.

- *Dilation of eye pupils.* In moments of heightened feeling, such as anger or sexual attraction, the eye pupils tend to dilate.

- *Stomach problems.* Emotional excitation may contribute to nausea or diarrhoea. Persistent emotional excitement may lead to ulcers. Appetite may become poor.

- *Goose pimples.* Pilomotor response is the technical name for goose pimples, in which the hairs of the skin stand on end.

- *Thought blocking.* Tension may contribute to clients' minds going totally or partially blank.

- *Speech difficulties.* Heightened excitation can lead to stammering, speaking rapidly and slurring words. In extreme instances, the ability to speak may be temporarily lost.

- *Sleep difficulties.* Sleep difficulties include time taken to get to sleep, disturbed sleep and early morning waking.

- *Sex difficulties.* Complete or partial loss of desire is a common sex difficulty associated with tension.

Physical reactions and feelings

Word labels or linguistic symbols describing feelings are attached to different clusters of physical reactions. For example, physical reactions associated with the word shyness include dry mouth, blushing, nausea, feeling faint, perspiring, knotted stomach, pounding heart, shaking, mind going blank and shallow, rapid breathing. Most, if not all, of these feelings characterize anxiety. Often in the psychological literature, shyness gets called social anxiety. Sometimes clients react to their physical reactions. For example, in anxiety and panic attacks, clients may first feel tense and anxious and then become even more tense and anxious because of this initial feeling. Counsellors need to develop skills at empathically describing with appropriate words clients' physical reactions.

Energy level

Related to clients' ability to experience feelings is their energy level. Changes in energy level may precede, be concurrent with or follow from changes in how clients feel and think. For example, energetic clients may feel more confident. However, once clients lose their confidence, they may feel less energetic. Counsellors can assess how much mental and physical energy clients have and how vital or apathetic they are. If clients' energy levels are very low counsellors should ask them to check with their doctors for medical explanations.

Mood

A mood is a state of mind or feeling associated with physical reactions. Moods may last for two weeks or more. For instance, 'The essential feature of a major depressive disorder is a period of at least two weeks during which there is either depressed mood or the loss of pleasure or interest in nearly all activities' (American Psychiatric Association, 1994, p. 320). However, often moods are relatively transient in duration: for instance, a few months, a day or a week. McNair *et al.*'s (1981) *Profile of Mood States* (POMS) provides scores on six identifiable mood states: tension-anxiety; depression-dejection; anger-hostility; vigour-activity; fatigue-inertia; and confusion-bewilderment. Counsellors can assess severity, direction, duration and fluctuations in clients' moods.

Psychophysiological disorders

Psychophysiological or psychosomatic disorders are physical reactions caused and maintained primarily by psychological and emotional rather than physical or organic factors. Psychophysiological disorders can affect the skin (for instance, acne) and the body's musculoskeletal, respiratory, cardiovascular, blood and lymphatic, gastrointestinal and endocrine systems. The more common psychophysiological disorders include peptic ulcers, migraine headaches, asthma and high blood pressure. Psychophysiological disorders may be distinguished from somatoform disorders, the latter being phoney or imitative rather than actual physical disorders.

DIMENSIONS OF FEELINGS

Dimensions of feelings overlap with physical reactions. In the section on reflecting feelings in Chapter 6, I discussed some ways of identifying feelings by picking up feelings words and by attending to voice and body messages. Now I review dimensions of feelings from the viewpoint more of assessing problems than making active listening responses.

Capacity to feel

Counsellors need to be aware of clients' abilities to experience feelings (Rogers, 1951, 1959, 1961, 1975). Some clients lack emotional responsiveness across a wide range of feelings. Other clients may have difficulty experiencing specific feelings: for example, sexuality or anger. Clients' difficulties in experiencing feelings can be at different levels. An extensive and long-standing incapacity to experience feelings may have different implications for how counselling might proceed than a more focused and less severe problem of experiencing feelings. One of the outcomes of any extended counselling contact is that clients should become better at experiencing and expressing feelings.

Self-esteem

Counsellors need to be aware of clients' confidence levels. Clients with very low self-esteem are potential suicide risks. Clients with reasonable self-esteem possess a useful asset for working on problems and problematic skills. Words to describe low self-esteem include worthlessness, hopelessness, helplessness, pessimism and despair. Self-statements indicating lack of self-esteem include 'I'm no good,' 'I never do anything right' and 'I can't cope.' Adjectives to describe high self-esteem include confident, strong, self-accepting, worthwhile, optimistic and emotionally resilient.

Anxiety and defensiveness

Counsellors need to assess how anxious clients are and in what areas of their life anxiety occurs. Is their anxiety a pervasive trait or is it a state attached to specific situations? Counsellors also need to assess how clients show anxiety, both in obvious ways and in terms of their less obvious defensive processes or security operations (Clark, 1991; Sullivan, 1953, 1954). The American Psychiatric Association's (1994) *Diagnostic and Statistical Manual of Mental Disorders* states: 'Defense mechanisms (or coping styles) are automatic psychological processes that protect the individual against anxiety and from the awareness of internal or external dangers or stressors. Individuals are often unaware of these processes as they operate' (p. 751). Pay attention to ways in which clients' anxieties – and yours too – can distort the counselling process.

Psychological pain

Effective counsellors are skilled at locating clients' areas of psychological pain and assessing their severity. Sometimes during counselling clients acknowledge major areas of psychological pain which they have hitherto either repressed or suppressed. Counsellors also need to be conscious of the pain and distress that clients may experience when discussing certain material: for instance, a bereavement, rape or sexual abuse.

Predominant feelings

Sometimes clients present with a specific feeling that they wish to handle better: for example, anxiety in exam or public speaking situations. In other instances, a predominant feeling may emerge as counselling progresses: for instance, self-pity, resentment, anger or wariness. Teyber (1989, p. 84) uses the term 'characterological feeling' to describe these central feelings that clients experience as their fate, because they have 'always been there and it seems like they always will be.' Counsellors need to keep an eye and ear out for repetitive and central feelings that clients handle with difficulty. Prior to and even during counselling clients may find it hard to acknowledge such feelings.

Strength and persistence of feelings

Often feeling intensity is described by words like 'mild', 'moderate' or 'severe'. For example, clients may be mildly depressed, moderately depressed or severely depressed. There can be different perceptions of what is mild, moderate or severe both among counsellors and between counsellors and clients. Persistence of feelings may be described by words like chronic and acute. Chronic implies persistent, whereas acute implies sharp and short. In addition, disorders like schizophrenia may be in partial remission or full remission (American Psychiatric Association, 1994).

Complex and conflicted feelings

Clients' feelings are frequently complex. Counsellors require skills at eliciting, clarifying and articulating the different elements of what may be multiple and mixed feelings. Clients may need to learn to avoid thinking about their feelings in static, rigid and simplistic terms. Feelings often come in twos and threes. For example, anger may be accompanied by hurt and guilt or depression by anxiety and sadness. Though not always with the same intensity, frequently feelings are accompanied by their opposites. Ambivalent feelings include: happy–sad, love–hate, pleased–displeased and approach–avoidance. Sometimes clients experience ambivalent feelings simultaneously and sometimes sequentially.

Unclear feelings

Clients may be unclear about feelings or communicate feelings unclearly, or both.

Sometimes feelings are masked: for instance, depression may mask anger. On other occasions feelings are displaced: anger at failing an exam may be 'taken out' on a room-mate, spouse or parent. Sometimes the real agenda is unclear. For instance, married couples may argue over little things and avoid confronting more serious differences and relationship fears. Frequently, expression of feelings is inhibited or diluted.

Some clients obscure feelings by going to the other extreme: they dramatize and magnify feelings. Social desirability considerations pervade the early stages of counsel-ling: clients may play out social roles to please counsellors. Clients may also have acquired poor skills at using feelings words and framing their verbal feelings messages with appropriate voice and body messages. Many feelings take time to emerge. As mentioned previously, counsellors require sensitivity to the pace at which clients both can and wish to reveal their emotional selves.

Antecedents and consequences of feelings

When assessing feelings, counsellors may assess their antecedents and consequences. The antecedents of feelings can stretch back into clients' childhoods. For example, the pain of a present loss may reactivate the pain of an earlier loss. Anger may be hard to express now because such feelings were suppressed in clients' families of origins. Frequently, counsellors explore current antecedents and consequences of feelings: for example, clients' thoughts prior to experiencing feelings and the positive and negative consequences that follow from expressing certain feelings.

Appropriateness of feelings

Often counsellors and clients attempt to assess appropriateness of feelings. Did the client experience an appropriate quantity of an appropriate feeling and was this appropriately expressed? Counsellors and clients assessing the appropriateness of feelings must take into account clients' unique styles of expressing feelings and numerous situational, contextual and cultural considerations. One way of assessing appropriateness of feelings is to assess what were their consequences for clients and others. To what extent and in what ways were there positive or negative emotional and behavioural consequences? Another way is to assess certain feelings in terms of psychiatric classification.

Feelings about counselling and counsellors

Clients invariably have feelings both about counselling and counsellors. Clients may resist or cooperate in the counselling process. They may feel pleased or frustrated with their progress. In addition, clients may have a range of feelings about counsellors, on dimensions such as like–dislike, trust–mistrust, competent–incompetent and dependent–independent. Sometimes clients express feelings that counsellors find diffi-cult to handle, for example, liking, sexual attraction, anger and sadness. Often there is a reciprocity of feeling between counsellors and clients, for example, mutual like or dislike.

SKILLS FOR ELICITING AND ASSESSING FEELINGS AND PHYSICAL REACTIONS

Feelings are central to clients' abilities to function effectively and to grow and develop as persons. Many skills for assessing feelings entail enlisting clients' cooperation in sharing feelings. Below are some skills useful for eliciting and assessing feelings.

Active listening

In supportive and trusting relationships, clients assist counsellors to understand how they feel. Active listening provides a safe emotional climate for clients to experience and share feelings. Counsellors sensitive to clients' feelings and feeling nuances legitimize the importance of experiencing and discussing feelings. You require good skills at picking up and reflecting back feelings messages. Receiver skills include paying attention to feelings words, observing voice and body messages, and being keenly attuned to any mismatch between voice, body and verbal messages. Sometimes you can infer feelings from what is left unsaid or partially said. Sender skills that you can use to help clients to share feelings include showing attention with voice and body messages, reflecting feelings, reflecting feelings and reasons and offering companionship as clients explore new and sometimes unexpected feelings.

Use tact and sensitivity when clients encounter feelings difficult either to experience or to share. Always remain aware of the pace at which clients wish to reveal feelings. Often a box of Kleenex helps! You can make the following remarks to encourage but not pressure clients to share feelings.

'I realize that this may be a painful area for you to discuss.'

'You seem upset. Just take your time in sharing what you feel.'

Probably clients' voice and body messages provide the most valid source of information about how they feel. From the moment of first contact, skilled counsellors closely watch out for body messages and listen for voice messages. Clients differ in how clearly they send messages. However, both consciously and intuitively, effective counsellors listen 'with the third ear' and observe 'with the third eye' for deviations, omissions and discrepancies in communications. They look out for feeling fragments or glimpses that are clues to more substantial and as yet unshared feelings. Skilled counsellors have highly developed capacities for sensing out what seems false. Their ability to tune into their own feelings as well as experience of numerous previous clients provides a base for formulating feelings hypotheses.

Advanced reflection of feelings

As a result of observing and listening, you may sense clients' underlying messages. Frequently clients repress, suppress or otherwise inhibit feelings. Advanced reflection of feelings, what Egan (1994) calls advanced empathy, entails making exploratory responses that help clients to articulate more personally relevant, emotionally tinged and threatening areas of their experiencing. Relevant questions that counsellors can ask themselves include: 'What is this person only half saying? What is this person hinting at? What is this person saying in a confused way? What messages do I hear behind the explicit messages?' (Egan, 1994, p. 180).

You require sensitivity to reflect partially hidden agendas. Sometimes you may choose not to mention such agendas for fear of upsetting clients. Advanced reflections of feelings check out your 'hunches' or feelings hypotheses. Such responses generally require humility and tentativeness. Inaccurate, clumsily worded and badly timed responses can do more harm than good.

EXAMPLE A The counsellor gets the impression that the client talks around the area of lesbian feelings.

>**Counsellor:** You've mentioned a couple of people you know who do not find lesbian life easy. I'm wondering whether lesbianism may be an issue for you too?

EXAMPLE B The counsellor senses that the client is very taken with a woman he has recently met, yet keeps expressing reservations about her.

>**Counsellor:** You seem to be stating numerous reasons why you should be careful about starting a relationship with Brenda. However, the overriding feeling I get is that you're swept off your feet by her and can't get her out of your mind ... nor do you want to.

EXAMPLE C The counsellor has a hunch that a client who recently had a blazing row with her mother either is feeling or soon will feel guilty about how she behaved.

>**Counsellor:** On the one hand you have a sense of triumph at giving Mum a piece of your mind, but I catch an undercurrent of guilt and sorrow at how you behaved. Am I correct?

Questions about feelings and physical reactions

Questions can assist clients in being specific about feelings and physical reactions. Frequently, since you cannot assume common meaning, you need to clarify labels clients attach to feelings. For instance, follow-up questions to a client who says 'I am very depressed' might be: 'When you say you are very depressed, what exactly do you mean?', 'When you say you are very depressed what are your specific feelings and physical reactions?' or 'You feel very depressed. Tell me more about that feeling.' Then you assist the client in pinpointing feelings and physical reactions. Sometimes counsellors check specific feelings or physical reactions: for instance, 'Do you feel suicidal sometimes?' or 'How is your appetite?'

Counsellors assist clients to distinguish between feelings and thoughts. If clients respond to focusing on feelings questions with how they think, you may choose to keep them focused on feelings.

>**Client:** I feel very depressed.

Counsellor: When you say you feel very depressed what exactly do you mean?

Client: I am having problems in my job and in my marriage.

Counsellor: You're having problems at work and at home. These are thoughts or reasons why you may be very depressed. However, could you tell me more about the actual depressed feelings you experience?

Counsellors may need to assist clients in expanding and elaborating their feelings and physical reactions (Teyber, 1989). Open-ended focusing on feelings questions can be helpful: 'Describe the feeling more fully.' Further questions that helpers may use to elicit and clarify feelings and physical reactions include the following.

'Tell me more about the feeling.'

'Describe how your body experiences the feeling.'

'In which part of your body do you experience the feeling?'

'Do you have any visual images that capture the feeling?'

'Are there any metaphors that illustrate the feeling?'

'How has your mood been and how is it today?'

'How confident a person are you?'

'Are there any other feelings that accompany that feeling?'

'How do you feel here and now?'

Counsellors may need to ask follow-up questions that encourage clients to expand on their feelings and physical reactions. For example, 'You say you experience tension in your stomach. Can you describe the experience more fully?' Depending on how clients respond to such open-ended questions, counsellors may ask specific questions, for example, 'How persistent?' and 'On a scale of one to ten, how much tension?'

Emotion-eliciting techniques

Sometimes counsellors deliberately attempt to induce feelings so that both they and clients can acknowledge and assess them.

- *Live observation.* Counsellors can take clients into difficult situations, observe their reactions and listen to what they say about how they feel.

- *Visualizing.* Clients can be asked to shut their eyes, visualize a scene and re-experience the emotions attached to it.

- *Role-play.* Counsellors may role-play scenes with clients, for example, arguments with parents. Then counsellors can assist clients to process emotions elicited in role-plays.

- *Task assignment.* Counsellors and clients may agree on between-session tasks for clients, for instance, asking someone for a date. Clients are asked to monitor and record feelings before, during and after these tasks.

Encouraging clients to monitor feelings

Without setting specific tasks, counsellors can encourage clients to monitor their feelings and physical reactions. Such monitoring can raise self-awareness as well as help clients to learn a valuable skill, namely, listening closely to their feelings.

DAILY RATING FORMS Clients can be asked to rate themselves daily on feelings such as mood (very happy to very depressed), anxiety level (not anxious at all to very anxious), feelings of stress (very relaxed to very stressed) and so on. Ratings may be on scales ranging from 1 to 3, 5, 7, 9 and 10. In the example below clients are asked to give themselves a daily mood score using the following scale.

Very happy   1   2   3   4   5   6   7   8   9   **Very depressed**

SPECIFIC INCIDENT LOGS Clients can keep logs of how they feel in relation to specific difficulties they experience. For example, shy clients can keep logs that record their feelings and physical state before, during and after being in company. Below is a possible format for such a log.

Date and time	What happened	My feelings and physical reactions

Administering questionnaires

Though I do not advocate this approach for most clients, counsellors can administer questionnaires to assess feelings and physical reactions. Some questionnaires exclusively focus on assessing feelings: for example, the *Beck Depression Inventory* (Beck, 1978; Kendall *et al.*, 1987); the *State-Trait Anxiety Inventory* (Spielberger, 1983); and the *Profile of Mood States* (POMS) (McNair *et al.*, 1981). Other questionnaires have sections on feelings, for example, Lazarus's *Multimodal Life History Questionnaire* (Lazarus and Lazarus, 1991). Questionnaires may also focus on the stimuli that elicit feelings. For example, Wolpe's *Fear Inventory* asks respondents to indicate how disturbed they are by each of a range of 'things and experiences that may cause fear or other unpleasant feelings' (Wolpe, 1973, p. 283). Counsellors may also devise their own questionnaires focused on feelings and physical reactions.

Being sensitive to cultural and other differences

The most recent version of the *Diagnostic and Statistical Manual for Mental Disorders* has as one of its sections for each disorder 'Specific culture, age, and gender features' (American Psychiatric Association, 1994, p. 9). Cultures differ greatly in the ways in which they express feelings. In addition, somatic symptoms – or physical reactions –

associated with distress differ across cultures. In some cultures depression is experienced largely in somatic terms rather than with sadness or guilt. For example, in Chinese and Asian cultures, depressed people may complain of weakness, tiredness or 'imbalance'. Western counsellors should be particularly careful in assessing feelings of people from non-Western cultures. Clients' perceptions of counsellors as dissimilar on cultural, racial, gender and social class characteristics may influence the degree to which they disclose feelings and physical reactions to you.

Waiting and seeing

Even with skilled counsellors, clients' feelings may take time to unfold. Clients brought up to deny feelings may change slowly. Allow clients to share feelings and physical reactions at a pace comfortable for them. Invariably initial session assessments of feelings require updating. Sometimes such assessments require substantial modification as you get to know more about clients and clients more about themselves.

Forming feelings and physical reactions hypotheses

When assessing feelings and physical reactions, counsellors form hypotheses both to guide collection of information and to state conclusions. Feelings hypotheses are open to modification as helping progresses. Below is a case study of a company executive who sees a counsellor after being fired.

Case study: Jim Blake

Description of Jim Blake's problems

Jim Blake, 45, was a divisional finance controller of a large conglomerate before being fired a week ago, when his division was closed down. Jim is married with two teenaged children, both at private school. He was earning a package of over £100,000 and has a substantial mortgage. Jim's wife Lyn is not in the workforce. Jim had 20 years of service with the one company and has received a six-month severance package to tide him over while he finds another job. In addition, Jim's company has arranged for him to have the services of an external outplacement counsellor, Sam Rushton. The initial counselling session is held on company premises immediately after Jim receives the news of his severance, which is effective immediately. Jim expresses shock, disbelief and anger at being fired. He is also highly anxious about his future prospects, dreads a long period of unemployment and is worried that his family's standard of living may be drastically curtailed. Sam allows Jim to share these feelings, discusses strategies for breaking the news to his family and makes an appointment for them to meet next day in Sam's external office.

In this second session, Jim reports that he spent a sleepless night with worry and feels very depressed. He feels in crisis and overwhelmed at his misfortune. He still feels extremely bitter at his rejection after so many years of loyal service and fantasizes giving those responsible for his firing a sharp piece of his mind. Sam accepts Jim's feelings and then assists him in identifying and clarifying the main areas of his problem. To some extent, the *financial* area is dealt with by Jim's expertise in the area. However, Jim still has catastrophic predictions of financial disaster and inability to cope with this.

Regarding *getting another job*, Jim swears he never wants to go through the experience of being fired again. He thinks of setting up his own business, though he is vague about the nature of this. Jim admits to great indecision regarding what he wants to do for the rest of his life. He feels that all his life he has been doing the 'right' thing first for his parents and later as a male wage slave for his wife and family. Having worked for the same company for 20 years, he has little idea about how to get another job. Part of him wants to rush back into the workforce to ease the anxiety of unemployment. Jim wonders how good he will be at presenting himself in interviews. He also worries about what kind of references his former employers will give him.

Jim's *work difficulties* emerge during the session. Jim sees himself as better with figures than with people. He finds it difficult to tell people working under him what to do and even more difficult to confront them with their mistakes. Frequently, because of his financial knowledge and analytical skills, he would have good ideas for directions the company might take. However, often either he inhibited sharing his ideas or they were discounted because of his poor presentation skills and inadequate persuasive powers.

Jim acknowledges *family difficulties* and fears that these will worsen with his unemployment, especially if, as is probable, his job search lasts for more than three months. His wife, Lyn, has very mixed feelings about him. On the one hand, she respects his reliability, industry and obvious concern for the children. On the other hand, she feels that he is emotionally inexpressive, avoids rather than confronts marital issues and is no longer fun to be around. Apparently there are no third parties in the relationship. Jim cares for Lyn, but does not find her nearly as supportive as before. At times he thinks that, after the children, Lyn cares for her horses more than him. She stays with him partly as a means of maintaining her lifestyle. Jim said that he loves his children, Chris aged 14 and Mark aged 17, but that they see him as too ready to pick on wrongdoings rather than as prizing them for themselves. Jim also mentions that he is the only son of an elderly widowed mother who lives nearby. He visits her regularly and feels responsible for her well-being.

Jim's *health and stress difficulties* are uncovered when identifying and clarifying problems. Jim is a compulsive worker, often staying late at the office and working weekends. He suffers from tension headaches when overworked. A recent medical examination showed that his blood pressure was too high. Jim mentions that he was becoming increasingly aware of how stressed his body feels much of the time. He finds it hard to switch off and relax. Jim used to enjoy tennis and golf, but gave golf up as too time-consuming and tennis as too much effort. Jim has few recreational outlets, though he enjoys music and gardening. He feels he was reasonably sociable at the time of his marriage, but became less so after the advent of children. Now he sees himself in company as the strong, silent type. Jim observes that, without a job, he will not know what to do with his time.

Jim has never seen a counsellor before. Though desperate, he sees receiving help as a sign of weakness. He wants to stand on his own two feet as soon as possible. Sam detects Jim's resistance in talking about himself and gathers that he does not disclose much in personal and work dealings. Jim is not on medication, nor does he want to be.

Feelings and physical reactions hypotheses

During the two initial sessions the counsellor, Sam Rushton, formed a series of feelings and physical reactions hypotheses about Jim. Sam had the advantage of observing Jim's voice and body messages. Below I systematically present Sam's feelings and physical reactions hypotheses. In real life, counsellors may not take these items into account in such a thorough and ordered way.

Physical reactions Jim reports spending a sleepless night. Undoubtedly he experiences other physical reactions not mentioned in the case study.

Energy level Jim's energy level seems lower than usual. Even before he was fired, Jim diverted too much energy into worrying. Effective counselling should be able to raise both his short-term and long-term energy level and zest for life.

Mood Immediately after being fired, Jim masked the full extent of his depression. By the second session, Jim felt very depressed. However, in neither session did Jim appear a suicide risk.

Psychophysiological disorders Jim suffers from tension headaches and high blood pressure. Further questioning is required to establish their severity and health risk.

Capacity to feel Jim is somewhat out of touch with his capacity to feel. He does not know his wants and wishes regarding employment and has difficulty expressing emotions at home. Jim might require long-term counselling to develop good skills at experiencing and listening to his feelings.

Self-esteem Prior to his being fired, Jim's self-esteem was only moderate. Though he derived some self-esteem from family, much came from work. Jim's fragile self-esteem has taken a major knock and his confidence is very low.

Anxiety and defensiveness Even prior to being fired, Jim was an anxious person, especially with people. He dealt with many anxiety-evoking problems by denial and avoidance. Now Jim admits to being highly anxious, though his anxiety may lessen as he comes to terms with his changed circumstances.

Psychological pain Jim is in considerable psychological pain as his work world falls apart. Other areas of psychological pain include relationship difficulties at home and work. Jim may also experience pain as he becomes aware of how much of his life has been spent living other people's 'shoulds', 'oughts' and 'musts'.

Predominant feeling In the first session, Jim's predominant feelings were shock and anger; in the second session, depression and anger. In both sessions he was very anxious.

Strength and persistence of feelings Jim's anger towards his company is strong and his depression moderately severe. Though this is not fully revealed in the initial sessions, Jim may also be very angry with Lyn. Persistence of feelings remains to be seen.

Complex and conflicted feelings Jim's feelings towards his future career are complex and conflicted. Jim also appears to have very mixed feelings about his marriage. The full complexity of his feelings in both career and marital areas has yet to emerge.

Unclear feelings Sometimes Jim communicates feelings poorly: for instance, voice and body messages are insufficiently congruent with verbal messages. Furthermore, Jim needs more time and psychological space to become clearer about underlying feelings.

Antecedents and consequences of feelings How Jim thinks contributes to the negativeness of his feelings. A possible consequence of Jim's anger towards his former company is that he may behave in self-defeating ways: for instance, harming his reputation with them.

Appropriateness of feelings Jim's strong initial feelings of anger, anxiety and depression at being fired may be appropriate. In fact, Sam would worry more if Jim covered up his feelings. However, if such strong feelings persist, they may be disproportionate and unhelpful to Jim.

Feelings about counselling and counsellors Jim is

highly ambivalent about receiving counselling, seeing his wish for support as a sign of weakness. Jim finds it difficult to talk about himself. Jim respects Sam's competence and sincere wish to help him. By the end of the second session, Jim and Sam have established reasonable rapport and trust.

CHAPTER HIGHLIGHTS

- *Assessment in lifeskills counselling is performed with clients and for clients. Counsellors and clients are hypothesis makers and testers.*

- *Counsellors should always offer supportive relationships when assessing and restating clients' problems in skills terms.*

- *Reasons for assessing feelings and physical reactions include protecting clients, evaluating emotional responsiveness, clarifying real agendas, obtaining leads about thinking and action skills deficits, screening for medical and psychiatric considerations and developing clients' self-assessment skills.*

- *Dimensions of physical reactions include bodily changes, their relationship to feelings, energy level, mood and psychophysiological disorders.*

- *Dimensions of feelings overlap with physical reactions and include capacity to feel, self-esteem, anxiety and defensiveness, psychological pain, predominant feelings, strength and persistence of feelings, complex and conflicted feelings, unclear feelings, antecedents and consequences of feelings, appropriateness of feelings and feelings about counsellors and counselling.*

- *Skills for eliciting and assessing feelings and physical reactions include active listening, advanced reflection of feelings, questions about feelings and physical reactions, emotion-eliciting techniques, encouraging clients to monitor feelings, administering questionnaires, being sensitive to cultural and other differences, waiting and seeing, and forming feelings and physical reactions hypotheses.*

EXERCISE 8.1 DIMENSIONS OF FEELINGS AND PHYSICAL REACTIONS

As appropriate, do parts of this exercise on your own, in pairs or in a group.

Part A Meaning and importance of dimensions
For each of the following dimensions of feelings and physical reactions, briefly explain
(a) the meaning
(b) the importance
when you conduct initial counselling sessions:

1. Bodily changes
2. Relationship of physical reactions to feelings
3. Energy level
4. Mood
5. Psychophysiological disorders
6. Capacity to feel
7. Self-esteem
8. Anxiety and defensiveness
9. Psychological pain
10. Predominant feelings
11. Strength and persistence of feelings
12. Complex and conflicted feelings
13. Unclear feelings
14. Antecedents and consequences of feelings
15. Appropriateness of feelings
16. Feelings about counsellors and counselling

Part B Practising and discussing
1. *In pairs.* Suggestions for practising with a partner include the following:

    (a) Work through the items in Part A together.
    (b) Counsel each other for a minimum of 15 minutes, if possible in a problem area involving strong feelings. After each counselling session, partners discuss how they perceived the 'client' on each of the dimensions listed in Part A of this exercise. Video-tape or audio-cassette recording and playback may assist learning how to assess feelings.

2. *In a group.*

    (a) List the six most important physical reactions that counsellors should look out for when assessing clients.
    (b) List the six most important dimensions of feelings that counsellors should consider when assessing clients.

EXERCISE 8.2 ELICITING AND ASSESSING FEELINGS AND PHYSICAL REACTIONS

As appropriate, do the parts of this exercise on your own, with a partner or in a group.

Part A Formulating responses

Think of a problem, in either your or a client's life, involving strong feelings. Regarding this problem, give examples of the following skills:

1. Active listening
2. Advanced reflection of feelings
3. Questions about feelings and physical reactions
4. Emotion-eliciting techniques (e.g. live observation, visualizing, role-play, and/or task assignment)
5. Use of monitoring feelings measures (e.g. daily rating forms and/or critical incident logs)
6. Use of questionnaires
7. Sensitivity to cultural and other differences
8. Waiting and seeing
9. Forming feelings and physical reactions hypotheses

Part B Practising eliciting and assessing feelings

1. *In pairs.* Ways in which you can practice with a partner include the following.

    (a) Work through the items in Part A of this exercise together.
    (b) Conduct counselling sessions with one another in which the counsellor focuses mainly on helping the client experience, disclose, explore and assess her or his feelings about a problem. The counsellor uses skills such as active listening, advanced reflection of feelings, questions focusing on feelings and physical reactions, and forming feelings and physical reactions hypotheses. At the end of each counselling session, the counsellor shares and discusses his or her feelings and physical reactions hypotheses about the client on each of the dimensions listed in Part A of this exercise.
    (c) Counsel a partner using two experimental modes. Practice each mode prior to conducting the experiment.
    The focusing on information mode. Here the counsellor mainly reflects and asks questions about information or content. You consciously try not to help the client experience, disclosure and explore feelings. You attempt both to interview 'from the head' and to get the client responding 'from the head'.
    The focusing on feelings and physical reactions mode. Here the counsellor demonstrates great sensitivity in helping the client to experience, disclose and explore feelings and physical reactions. You and your client work together to understand and assess the client's feelings. You use interventions such as reflection of feelings and physical reactions, advanced reflection of feelings

and questions focusing on feelings and physical reactions. You aim to help the client respond 'from the heart' rather than 'from the head'.

Spend at least three minutes counselling in each experimental mode. Then, together with your partner, evaluate the consequences of the differences in your behaviour. Playing back a video-tape recording of the session may help you to assess the consequences of the experimental modes. Afterwards, reverse roles. Has this experiment taught you something about how you can be a more effective counsellor? If so, what?

2. *In a group.* One person acts as client. The remainder of the group sit in a semi-circle round the client and counsel the client in such a way as to assess his or her feelings about a problem. Every now and then stop and discuss both what's happened and where to go next. Repeat this exercise with other 'clients'.

NINE

Assess thinking and actions

Most folks are about as happy as they make up their minds to be.

Abraham Lincoln

CHAPTER QUESTIONS

- *What is the point of assessing thinking and actions?*

- *What is the product from assessing thinking and actions?*

- *What areas of thinking do lifeskills counsellors assess?*

- *How can counsellors elicit and assess thinking skills?*

- *How can counsellors elicit and assess action skills?*

INTRODUCTION

Assessing clients' thinking skills and helping clients to think about how they think is central to the lifeskills counselling approach. Feelings and physical reactions differ from thoughts. In the previous chapter, I deliberately did not refer to feelings and physical reactions in skills terms. Clients' feelings and physical reactions reflect their animal nature. Clients can think about how they think, feel and act, but they can only feel how they feel. If clients wish to change how they experience, express and manage their feelings and physical reactions, they need to focus on the thinking and action skills choices influencing them.

Skilled counsellors, who discover much about clients' feelings and physical reactions, still face the problem of what to do next. For the lifeskills counsellor knowledge about inhibited, troublesome and unwanted feelings is insufficient in itself. Rather, such knowledge raises questions about what thoughts and actions contribute to sustaining the inappropriate and unwanted feelings and physical reactions. Assuming that many feelings and physical reactions can be influenced by how clients think and act, the lifeskills counsellor asks: 'What thoughts and actions engender or fail to engender feelings and physical reactions conducive to clients' well-being rather than causing them distress?' or, put another way, 'What thinking skills deficits and what action skills deficits sustain the problem?'

The product of assessing thinking and actions is a restatement in skills terms of a problem that both counsellor and client identify as meriting attention. Often clients bring problems to initial sessions with numerous roots or sub-problems. However, once the component sub-problems are clarified, counsellors and clients can agree upon an agenda in which one of these sub-problems becomes the problem targeted for assessment. On numerous other occasions, clients may have only one main problem that they wish to target. The product of an assessment of any targeted problem or situation is a restatement in skills terms that is not only presented and negotiated verbally, but also shown visually on a whiteboard.

In restating problems the counsellor identifies the main thinking skills deficits/goals and the main action skills deficits/goals sustaining the problem. Previously, I used the term skills weakness instead of skills deficits/goals. In response to student and colleague feedback, I have changed the terminology to make it less negative and more encouraging right from the start. Even when stated negatively, deficits have the potential to become goals. Goals are deficits stated in the positive.

When you are assessing thinking and action skills, avoid the trap of black and white thinking. Clients can have skills strengths as well as deficits in a problem area. Specific deficits in a skills area can be partial strengths. For such specific skills deficits, the skill of the counsellor is to assist the client to retain the useful 70 per cent or so and discard or amend the harmful 30 per cent.

THINKING SKILLS AREAS

Always counsellors need to be conscious of not just what clients think, but how they think. Lifeskills counsellors help clients to think about how they think, alter thinking skills deficits and develop self-helping skills for working independently on their thinking. Few counselling students think about how they think in skills terms. Consequently, you may acquire a new way of thinking about yourself as well as your clients. Assessing and working with your own thinking skills is one of the best ways to learn to work effectively with clients' thinking skills.

The following is an overview of some thinking skills areas that you may assess and subsequently work on with clients. In all thinking skills areas people can make choices about how and what they think. I illustrate each thinking skill with an example of deficit thinking. In Chapters 14 and 15, I review methods of altering the balance of thinking skills deficits more in the direction of strengths.

Owning responsibility for choosing

I choose, therefore I am.
Adaptation from Descartes

In their waking hours clients are always choosers. Clients can make choices in relation to themselves, others and the environment. Within limits they can choose how they think, feel and act. Clients can be the authors or architects of their lives (May and Yalom, 1995; Yalom, 1980). However, often clients are unaware of the full extent of their existential responsibility to make their lives. They may also knowingly or unknowingly relinquish some of this responsibility. Many clients deceive themselves into thinking they have more insight about and ability to make choices in their lives than is the case. They may possess an illusion of autonomy that masks a constricted approach to life. Below is a vignette of a woman who has just come for counselling.

> Katie is in her early forties, the mother of four children aged from 4 to 16 years. Six months ago her husband, Peter, left her, to set up house with his secretary, Penny. Katie is furious with him for 'abandoning' her and the children. Additionally, Katie is now having a difficult time with her eldest daughter, Sandra, age 16, who has decided for the time being to live with her father. Katie, who used to have a good relationship with Sandra, is now very angry with her and says that she has become 'selfish' and 'hard'. Her relationship with her other children is deteriorating too, not least because they see her pushing and shoving Peter when he comes round unannounced to visit them. Katie has a huge chip on her shoulder and feels herself very much the victim of others' bad behaviour. She feels angry, anxious, depressed, confused and powerless.

Katie is similar to many people of both sexes who come for counselling. They feel that their lives are out of their control. They have relinquished, temporarily at least, their capacity to make effective choices within the constraints of reality. Even assuming that her husband Peter has behaved very badly, in the final analysis Katie is *choosing* to allow her emotions to be controlled by his bad behaviour rather than *choosing* to work to free herself from his negative influence. Furthermore, she has probably *chosen* to allow her relationship with Sandra to deteriorate. An important part of counselling with people like Katie is to help them become more aware that: (1) they are always choosers; (2) their choices always have costs and consequences; (3) within the constraints of reality, they can develop skills to increase the odds that their choices will have good rather than bad results.

Understanding the relationships between how you think, feel and act

Frequently clients need to learn how their thinking mediates how they behave (Ellis, 1991, 1995). By gaining more ability to examine their thinking, they become more able to choose both how they think and how they act. Increasingly I regard the ability to see the relationships between situations, thoughts and consequences as a fundamental thinking skill in its own right as well as a skill permeating all other thinking skills. The STC framework provides a simple way of understanding the effects of skilful and unskilful thinking (Nelson-Jones, 1996b). The framework is as follows:

S   The situation
T   Your thoughts relating to the situation, including visual images
C   Your feelings, physical reactions and actions that are the consequences of S and T

> Whenever Karen, 26, goes over to see her dad, Danny, she finds herself getting very upset. She resents the fact that Danny split up with her mother when she was 10. She is jealous of Danny's current family situation – he has a new wife and two teenage daughters. Karen and Danny are fond of each other, but communication between them is strained. Karen thinks that her dad will never give her the kind of relationship she would really like.

In the above example, Karen regards her feelings as the consequences (C) of her father's situation and behaviour (S). She insufficiently realizes that she is upsetting herself by what she is thinking (T). Consequently, she reduces her freedom to become less upset and more happy by thinking differently and then perhaps acting and feeling differently.

A variation of STC is to take a client's thoughts at T and group them according to the different thinking skills they represent. This latter approach is taken by lifeskills counsellors when they restate clients' problems in skills terms (Nelson-Jones, 1996b).

Getting in touch with feelings

Being in touch with feelings is important, since feelings are often the parents of thoughts. Furthermore, clients out of touch with their valuing process lack a firm base for assessing inner and outer information. Clients may experience difficulty sorting out what are their real feelings as contrasted with how they have been taught to feel and think. Furthermore, clients may acknowledge specific feelings but dilute or distort their strength. Clients badly out of touch with feelings lack a firm sense of their own identity. They may experience themselves as 'leaves in the breeze' waiting to be blown around by what others think. They may also be indecisive, since they lack a clear inner referent for assessing decision options.

Stu, 16, has been brought up in a family where he has learned to put on an act of compliance to keep his demanding parents at bay. His father, Ross, has strict ideas about how he wants his son to be a man. His mother, Eileen, is very unhappy in her marriage and persistently turns for support to Stu, whether Stu wants to give it or not. Stu thinks that all the good is being sucked out of him at home. He is uneasy with girls and tries to cover this up by being extra nice to them. Stu finds it a strain having to adjust his behaviour all the time to gain approval. He lacks a clear sense of his own identity and devalues himself. Stu feel too afraid to acknowledge his real thoughts and feelings and to share them with other people.

Using coping self-talk

My view is that people who talk to themselves are not crazy. It is what they choose to keep telling themselves that determines sanity or insanity. Here self-talk refers to how people talk to themselves before, during and after difficult situations (Meichenbaum, 1977, 1983, 1985, 1986; Meichenbaum and Deffenbacher, 1988). Often clients use negative self-talk that has the effect of creating or worsening self-defeating feelings, physical reactions and actions. The following are characteristics of negative self-talk.

* *Emphasizing mastery rather than coping.* Clients setting unrealistically high standards are prone to worrying about whether and how they can attain them.

* *Catastrophizing.* Clients can convince themselves that the worst will happen.

* *Adversely reacting to physical symptoms.* Clients can worsen their feelings of anxiety even to the extent of full-blown panic attacks by negatively talking to themselves about their bodily sensations, such as tension, nausea, breathlessness, palpitations, choking, hot-and-cold flushes and sweating.

* *Being overly self-conscious about what others think.* Clients can freeze up with anxiety by talking to themselves as though they are the centre of other people's attention.

* *Putting oneself down.* Clients can erode their confidence with statements like 'You fool' or 'I can't do anything right'.

* *Focusing on past setbacks rather than successes.* Clients can tell themselves what went wrong and ignore what went right.

> Val, 56, works for a local council and gets very anxious over public speaking. Three years ago, Val had a heart operation. Then, two years ago, she had to hand over the rostrum when her mind went blank. The time in which Val experiences most anxiety is the 30 to 60 seconds before she is due to speak, whether it be a formal speech or waiting for her turn to contribute at committee meetings. During this period, her self-talk consists of statements like: 'Don't be so stupid', 'My anxiety may get out of control like two years ago' and 'I may have a heart attack.' Apart from the occasion two years ago when she could not continue, Val speaks in public very competently – no one would know how anxious she feels.

Coping self-talk is the contrast to negative self-talk. In coping self-talk, clients make self-statements that calm themselves down, coach them in the skills needed to perform tasks and affirm their strengths and support factors.

Choosing realistic personal rules

Personal rules provide the standards by which clients judge themselves and others. Ellis (1980, 1995) coined the term *musturbation* to refer to rigid personal rules characterized by 'musts', 'oughts' and 'shoulds'. He identifies three major clusters of irrational beliefs that create inappropriate feeling and action consequences (Ellis, 1980, pp. 5–7).

1. I *must* do well and win approval for all my performances.
2. Others *must* treat me considerately and kindly.
3. Conditions under which I live *must* be arranged so that I get practically everything I want comfortably, quickly and easily.

Some of the main characteristics of unrealistic or self-oppressing personal rules include:

- *Demandingness.* Clients think of wants and wishes as demands rather than preferences.

- *Perfectionism.* Clients put pressure on themselves and others to be perfect. No one is perfect.

- *Self-rating.* Clients rate themselves on their total worth as persons rather than on how functional are specific characteristics for achieving goals.

- *Awfulizing.* Clients think it is absolutely awful if they, others or the environment are not as they should be.

> Louise, 43, is an accountant who was made re-
> dundant from a very senior position three years
> ago. She now works for a relatively low salary in a
> position whose status is below where she was two
> moves ago. In the past three years Louise has been
> for numerous interviews for very senior positions.
> However, she receives consistent feedback that,
> while selection panels find her technical skills to be
> excellent, they have reservations about her people
> skills and find her too pedantic. When Louise an-
> swers questions she does so in a bombastic, long-
> winded and far too detailed way. Contributing to
> her answering questions skills deficit is the unreal-
> istic rule that she must give the perfect answer.

Perceiving accurately

Clients, like most humans, are prone to perceive themselves and others with varying
degrees of distortion (Beck, 1976; Beck and Weishaar, 1995). Clients' negative self-
labels are unrealistically negative perceptions either of specific characteristics or of
themselves as persons. More clients seem to make unrealistically negative than positive
inferences about themselves. They are much better at listing what is wrong than what is
right. This perceiving error of ignoring personal strengths and focusing on deficits
perpetuates feelings such as anxiety, depression and lack of confidence.

Clients may also allow their feelings to influence how they perceive others, including
counsellors. They jump to conclusions without adequately taking into account available
evidence. Subjective inferences can get treated as objective facts. Central to all marital
counselling is assisting partners to perceive each other more accurately and usually
much less negatively. Beck (1988) uses the term 'negative cognitive set' for the ways in
which partners can systematically bias their interpretations of one another's intentions
and behaviour for the worse. He observes: 'When a husband has framed his wife within
this set, for example, he will interpret virtually everything she says or does in a negative
way' (Beck, 1988, p. 31).

> Judy, 59, has been married for 31 years to George,
> 57. They have three children, all of whom have left
> home. Four years ago, Judy took voluntary retire-
> ment from a very good job as executive assistant to
> a company managing director. George is now the
> sole breadwinner. When Judy talks about George,
> she complains that he 'always' thinks of himself and
> 'never' does anything around the house without

> being asked. When George talks about Judy, he says that she gives him long lists of jobs to do around the house and garden. Then she is quick to notice what remains undone, without giving him any credit for what he has accomplished. George also reports that after they come home from an evening out together, Judy always manages to find fault with something he has said or done.

In the preceding chapter I listed some perceiving errors for counsellors to avoid. These are also perceiving errors for clients to avoid: for instance, tunnel vision, magnifying and minimizing, negativeness, selective inattention, overgeneralizing and polarized thinking.

Explaining cause accurately

Clients can stay stuck in problems through wholly or partially explaining their causes inaccurately. Possible faulty explanations for the causes of problems include: 'It's my genes', 'Its my mental illness', It's my unfortunate past', 'It's my bad luck', 'It's my poor environment', 'It's all their fault' or 'It's all my fault'. Frequently clients succumb to the temptation to externalize problems: they are the victims of others' inconsiderate and aggressive behaviours. Such clients explain cause from outside to inside. However, change requires explaining cause from inside to outside.

> Ian, 38, is a bus conductor who comes to see a counsellor because of stress problems. Ian reports having frequent rows with bus passengers. Ian admits that he has a short fuse. However, he explains that the main cause of the rows is that many passengers are too pushy and aggressive. As long as Ian locates the cause of his anger outside of himself, he allows passengers to have the power over whether he gets angry or not. Unless he changes his explanation of cause, he is unlikely to work on developing anger-management skills.

Clients can adversely affect their confidence and mood by inaccurately explaining the causes of negative and positive events. For instance, depressed people may overestimate their responsibility for negative events in their own and others' lives (Beck *et al.*, 1979; Beck, 1991). In addition, they may fail to own their contribution to successful experiences and events.

Clients can influence their motivation to achieve by how they explain the causes of their successes and failures. For instance, they may rightly or wrongly assign the causes for their academic successes and failures to such factors as ability, effort, anxiety, task difficulty, staff competence or luck.

Predicting realistically

In a sense all client problems contain disorders of prediction. Many clients predict risk inaccurately by overestimating bad consequences. They may fear change, failure or success. However, some clients underestimate the risk of bad consequences, for instance, in excessive gambling or grandiose business ventures.

Clients can also predict reward inaccurately by either overestimating or underestimating good consequences. Two trends are common in underestimating reward. First, clients may be poor at perceiving the potential rewards of proposed courses of action. Second, even when rewards are identified, they may not give them the weight they deserve. Predicting realistically entails accurately thinking about future consequences. Independent of notions of risk and reward, some clients are poor at consequential thinking: for instance, they may remain unaware of and fail to predict how their behaviour affects others.

> Dean, 22, is an attractive young man who goes to a gay counselling service to discuss 'coming out'. Dean works on a farm. Whenever he gets the opportunity he goes to the city and visits gay bars and saunas. Dean is sexually active, has many partners and particularly enjoys being penetrated in unprotected anal intercourse. Dean does not like his partners to wear condoms because he thinks using them lowers pleasurable sensations and interferes with intimacy. He considers that he is at little risk of becoming HIV-positive.

Setting realistic goals

Some clients have difficulty articulating goals and consequently relinquish much opportunity to create their futures. Goals can be short-term, medium-term or long-term and in various areas: for instance, relationships, study, work, recreation, health, and finances. When they are in close relationships, clients' goals may need to be negotiated so that they become shared goals. Apart from not possessing goals, errors in goal setting include not reflecting values, insufficient realism, inadequate specificity and unclear time frames. Clients' goals in relation to problem areas may suffer from not being expressed in skills language. Moreover, clients may not focus on how to think as well as on how to act.

> Anna, 18, drifted through her first semester at university. After the regimentation of her secondary school, Anna experienced difficulty in adjusting to the relatively unstructured nature of her university course. She knew she was doing poorly, but when she received her grades she was shocked at how bad they were. On the advice of a friend, Anna

went to the counselling service to see how she might get more control over her study. During the initial session, the following information emerged relevant to Anna's goal-setting deficits: she had gone to university because that's what all her friends were doing; she had no real commitment to the course she was on; she did not prioritize her work, but left everything to the last moment; and, often when she did study, she allowed herself to become sidetracked by answering phone calls and going out with her friends.

Using visualizing skills

People whose most highly valued representational system is visual tend to respond to the world and organize it in terms of mental images (Lazarus, 1984, 1992, 1995). Clients may use mental images or pictorial thinking to support or to oppress themselves. Negative images can influence feelings towards self and others. For instance, in one research study, some 90 per cent of anxious patients reported visual images prior to and concurrent to their anxiety attacks (Beck *et al.*, 1974). Absence of the capacity to visualize calming images can contribute to tension and anger. Clients who visualize themselves as socially incompetent may feel shy.

How clients visualize others influences their feelings towards them. For instance, angry clients may be poor at using visualizing to understand others' positions and take a balanced view of them. In addition, some clients are poor at communicating visual images, for instance, sharing sexual fantasies. Frequently clients' negative visual images impede their performance: for example, imagining acting incompetently in either social or academic situations can lead to self-fulfilling prophecies. Clients may also be poor at visualizing positive and negative consequences of their behaviour: for instance, clients engaged in job searches may be poor at visualizing what it is actually like working for specific employers.

Edna, 66, is a retired physiotherapist who goes to see a counsellor to help her feel less lonely. Her husband, Ron, died two years ago. The counsellor explores with Edna what she does in the way of recreational activities. At the moment, Edna is doing little outside the house. However, she mentions that she has thought of joining a neighbourhood social club, but is afraid because she gets images of going there and being socially clumsy, with no one wanting to make friends with her.

Realistic decision-making

Clients may possess decision-making styles that lessen their effectiveness. For instance, they may be hypervigilant, and try too hard to take every consideration into account. Conversely, they may be impulsive and rush into major and minor decisions. Some clients do their best to avoid decisions altogether. Sometimes decisions are best made in collaboration with others. In such instances, decision errors include being overly competitive or compliant. Rational decision-making can be viewed as taking place in two main stages: first, confronting and making decisions; second, implementing and evaluating them. Clients may have weaknesses in either or both stages. An illustrative weakness when making decisions is failure to generate sufficient decision options. An illustrative weakness when implementing decisions is poor planning.

> Rachel, 32, is a clinical psychologist who considers going into private practice as a counsellor because she is dissatisfied with the petty politics of working for a government organization. Despite counselling other people all the time, Rachel has relatively poor skills at identifying and gathering the information she requires to make a balanced decision about where to go next in her career.

Preventing and managing problems

Frequently clients seek counselling because of poor skills at preventing and managing problems. Skills deficits may be in such areas as confronting problems, assessing and restating problems in skills terms, setting goals, planning, implementing plans and evaluating consequences. People can have positive or negative orientations towards managing or solving problems (D'Zurilla and Maydeu-Olivares, 1995; Seligman, 1991). A positive orientation towards problems includes perceiving problems as challenges, being optimistic about being able to solve them and persisting despite set-backs. A negative orientation towards problems includes perceiving them as threats, being pessimistic about being able to handle them adequately and becoming easily upset by set-backs. Where possible clients should develop skills for either preventing problems or catching them early: for instance, not allowing stress to endanger health.

> Josh, 29, is a graduate student in chemistry who continually procrastinates about handing in his work. He is very skilled at identifying how much flexibility there is in the system and then taking full advantage of it. Josh's grades and future prospects suffer because of his procrastination. He gets very distressed over having to fight a battle about getting down to and completing every piece of work. To date, Josh has failed to confront the full implications of his procrastination problem. Furthermore,

he has failed to do anything about it, for instance, developing self-help strategies or seeing a counsellor. He says he does not go for counselling because his problem is so entrenched that he does not think it will do any good.

SKILLS FOR ELICITING AND ASSESSING THINKING

When assessing thinking, counsellors and clients work together to establish clients' thinking skills strengths and weaknesses. It is important to help clients become more aware of their thought processes (Beck and Emery, 1985). With increased self-awareness, clients may start correcting their own thinking errors. Furthermore, they are better accomplices in the detective work of uncovering faulty thinking. You aim to train clients in how to think about how they think. Following are some skills for eliciting and assessing thinking.

Build a knowledge base

It is essential that counsellors wishing to work with clients' thinking skills develop their knowledge of how people think. You cannot help clients if you do not know what to look for. In addition, you may limit your effectiveness if you only focus on one or two thinking skills. How can you develop your knowledge base? First, you can read the works of cognitive therapists such as Ellis (1962, 1980, 1995), Beck (1976, 1988; Beck and Weishaar, 1995) and other therapists who work with clients' thinking: for instance, Frankl (1959, 1967, 1969), Glasser (1965, 1984; Glasser and Wubbolding, 1995), Lazarus (1984, 1992, 1995), Meichenbaum (1977, 1983, 1985, 1986) and Yalom (1980; May and Yalom, 1995). Second, you may read secondary sources: for instance, counselling theory textbooks and self-help books. Third, you can work on your own thinking skills, independently, with counsellors or in training groups. Fourth, you can work with clients, preferably at first under supervision.

Think in skills terms

Important cognitive theorists like Beck, Ellis and Meichenbaum rarely use skills language when thinking about how clients think. However, you are encouraged to do so. Failure to think in skills terms may cause you to focus on only one or two rather than on many potential thinking skills deficits. In addition, Stage 2 requires you to restate clients' problems in skills terms. You will find difficulty doing this if you are not already assessing clients' skills. However, when eliciting and assessing thinking you may choose not to use skills language openly with clients, but leave this until you restate their problems.

Gather information

Active listening skills are always important when counsellors gather information about how clients think. Other ways of eliciting and gathering information about clients' thinking include the following.

CLIENT SELF-REPORT Clients may have insight into their own thought processes – for example, tendencies to rigid personal rules or negative self-labelling – without knowing what to do about them.

THINK ALOUD Think aloud involves encouraging clients to speak aloud their thought processes in relation to specific situations (Blackwell *et al.*, 1985). For instance, clients can be asked to take counsellors in slow motion through their thoughts and feelings in relation to specific anxiety-evoking experiences. Additionally, clients can use think aloud when confronted with real or simulated situations.

THOUGHT LISTING Clients can be asked to list, and possibly rank order in terms of importance, thoughts in relation to specific problems. Clients can list thoughts within the STC framework. Alternatively, clients can use Ellis's ABC framework, where A is the activating event, B is the client's thoughts about the activating event, and C is the feelings and action consequences of the client's thoughts (Ellis, 1991, 1995). At B, Ellis asks clients to distinguish between rational and irrational thoughts.

THOUGHT CHARTING Thought charting entails clients keeping a record of the thoughts associated with specific situations involving negative feelings. Beck and Emery (1985, pp. 194–5) observe: 'The most common method by which a patient can become aware of his thinking between sessions is the thought record. At its simplest, thought charting involves the double-column technique: recording situations in one column and thoughts and feelings in the other column. Thought charts may also use the STC framework: a column each for (S) situations, (T) thoughts and (C) feelings, physical reactions and actions consequences. Thought charting encourages clients to see links between how they think, feel and act.

COUNTING Counsellors can ask clients to count the frequency of specific types of thoughts, for instance, negative self-labels. Clients may use index cards to make frequency records. Counting may help clients to become aware of the repetitive nature of their thinking.

FOCUSING ON THINKING QUESTIONS Clients can be asked what they think about themselves, their behaviour, others and specific situations. Then counsellors can ask follow-up questions that encourage clients to elaborate, specify and reveal personal meanings. Before leaving an area you may ask the open-ended question: 'Can you think of anything else that might be relevant?' Such a question may elicit further information that might have been lost had you moved on prematurely. Intersperse reflective responding with focusing on thinking questions. Remember that sometimes focusing on feelings and physical reactions questions opens up the way for focusing on thinking questions.

> **Counsellor:** And how did you feel when that happened?
> **Client:** I felt mad as hell.
> **Counsellor:** You felt hopping mad? Why do you think that was?

Counsellors can also use questions that challenge clients' thinking, for example, 'Where's the evidence?' However, resist the temptation to answer your own questions. Rephrase questions that clients seem not to understand.

THOUGHT-ELICITING TECHNIQUES Thought-eliciting techniques are similar to feelings-eliciting techniques; the same techniques may be used to elicit thoughts and feelings.

- *Live observation*. Counsellors can accompany clients into situations that cause them difficulty – for instance, returning something to a store or driving a car after an accident – and ask them to recount their thoughts.

- *Visualizing*. Clients can be asked to conjure up images that elicit feelings and asked to identify the accompanying thoughts. Clients can visualize past, present or future scenes and get in touch with harmful and helpful thoughts.

- *Role-play*. Counsellors can conduct role-plays with clients – for instance, tele-phoning someone for a date – and then explore their thoughts and feelings.

- *Task assignment*. Counsellors can encourage clients to perform feared tasks and afterwards record their thoughts and feelings. Clients can view such tasks as personal experiments to collect evidence about themselves.

QUESTIONNAIRES There are numerous self-report measures to assess thinking: for example, the *Anxious Self-Statements Questionnaire* (Kendall and Hollon, 1989), the *Attributional Style Questionnaire* (Petersen *et al.*, 1982; Petersen and Villanova, 1988), the *Test for Optimism* (Seligman, 1991) and the *Fear of Negative Evaluation Scale* (Watson and Friend, 1969). Regarding problem-solving questionnaires, D'Zurilla and Maydeu-Olivares (1995) identify and evaluate many of the major instruments. In addition to using existing measures of how clients think, counsellors can develop their own.

Make inferences and form hypotheses about thinking skills deficits/goals

Clients rarely, if ever, tell counsellors: 'Look, I've got this thinking skills deficit!' (and then proceed to name it). Consequently, counsellors make inferences and form hypotheses about possible deficits. Inferences about thinking may stem from clients' words, feelings and actions. You may obtain clues from how clients use language. For example, use of words like 'should', 'ought' or 'must' may indicate unrealistically rigid personal rules. Use of verbs like 'I can't' and expressions like 'I had no choice' may indicate insufficient ownership of responsibility for choosing. Use of terms like 'What will people think of me?' and 'I wonder if I look as stupid as I feel' represent negative self-talk and also indicate an unrealistic rule about needing others' approval.

Both counsellors and clients require skills at making linkages between feelings and underlying thoughts. Often, strong, persistent negative feelings indicate thinking difficulties. You require sensitivity to more subtle clues that come from voice messages, body messages or what is left unsaid. You and your clients should also make linkages between self-defeating actions and thinking. Clients need to develop skills at doing this for themselves.

Counsellors identify and collect evidence that helps them to form hypotheses about clients' thinking skills deficits. Counsellors may generate many more hypotheses than they eventually share with clients when restating problems in skills terms. As part of the process of assessing thinking, you may collect further information that either supports or negates your hypotheses. Conversely, you may choose not to collect further information about some hypotheses.

When you are making hypotheses, remember that a deficit can be the absence of a skills strength as well as the presence of a skills deficit. For example, a client suffering from hypertension might just have the deficit of failing to use relaxing imagery rather than the added deficit of using anxiety-engendering imagery. Another reminder is given about inappropriately stating deficits in black and white terms: for example, with some clients insufficient use of relaxing imagery may be more accurate than failure to use any relaxing imagery at all. As mentioned earlier, even when stating deficits, I state them as deficits/goals to help keep my counselling sessions from becoming unnecessarily negative.

Case study: Jessica Henderson

Form thinking skills deficits/goals hypotheses

The client's problem

Jessica Henderson comes to see a counsellor, Lauren Fulton, feeling very depressed about what is going on in her job. Jessica has worked for a leading insurance company since she left secondary school 30 years ago. Starting as a clerk, she made her way up to managerial positions and finally to be a well paid systems analyst in the insurance company's electronic data processing section in London. Until recently, Jessica, married with three children, had planned to stay with the insurance company until she retired.

Last month, Jessica, now 47, was told that her job would no longer exist. The insurance company is offering her a much less senior position as a relieving manager, albeit with no drop in pay. Jessica is considering turning down the offer, seeing it as too big a step backwards. She says the company would term her departure 'early separation', but she calls it being made redundant. Jessica, who needs employment to help support her family, has not been looking elsewhere for a job.

Jessica explains to Lauren: 'I had not seen it coming the way it came. I saw the particular area I was in going to be amalgamated with other areas. But I didn't see that they were going to be offering early separations at that stage.' She says that although she is unhappy with the way the insurance company is trying to squeeze her out, at least she is being given the chance to make a 'respectable departure' by being able to choose when she leaves. She believed she would never lose her job with the insurance company, given her years of service and loyalty. Jessica says: 'I had always considered myself a career person with the company. My work performance appraisals have always indicated that my performance was satisfactory. I've certainly found that all my loyalty to it has virtually stood for nothing. I'm shocked and disappointed.'

The counsellor's hypotheses

Following are the counsellor Lauren Fulton's hypotheses about Jessica's thinking skills deficits. Here, for teaching purposes, I provide many hypotheses. When Lauren restates Jessica's problem, she would only mention her hypotheses about Jessica's main deficits. During her assessment, Lauren takes brief notes to help to remember significant material for later use in forming and illustrating hypotheses.

Owning responsibility for choosing Jessica seems to possess insufficient awareness of herself as a chooser who can be proactive in finding meaning and fulfilment in her career and life. For example, she planned to stay with the company for the rest of her working life – even in the good times, such insufficient choice awareness may restrict career fulfilment.

Understanding the relationships between how you think, feel and act Jessica does not realize that her interpretations of how she views her situation contribute to her feeling depressed, shocked and disappointed. An alternative interpretation to Jessica's view that the company is trying to squeeze her out is provided in the perceiving accurately section below.

Getting in touch with your feelings For some time Jessica may have been insufficiently in touch with her feelings and possible reservations about the insurance company. Jessica seems unaware of any positive feelings towards the company. Furthermore, Jessica may inadequately acknowledge her underlying feelings of strength and of confidence. In addition, Jessica may inhibit her real wants and wishes about her career.

Using coping self-talk Jessica may use negative self-talk which could contribute to negative feelings – for instance, increased anger and anxiety – and negative actions – abruptness when discussing with management her future in the company. Lauren would need to check for evidence of this possibility.

Choosing realistic personal rules Possible unrealistic rules that Jessica may have include: 'I must stay with the same company until retirement,' 'My loyalty and service must always be appreciated,' 'My career must always move forwards' and 'I must make a respectable departure.'

Perceiving accurately Jessica perceives that she is being undervalued by the insurance company. An alternative perception or interpretation is that she is being so highly valued by the company that, despite their downsizing, they are still offering her employment at the same salary. In addition, Jessica appears to perceive that she is losing her job with the company – in reality, she is changing her position, but staying employed.

Explaining cause accurately Jessica explains the cause of her possible departure as the company trying to squeeze her out. This may or may not be true in the medium to long term. However, if she were to leave in the short term or immediately, she herself would be the cause of her departure. She voluntarily would take 'early separation' *from* the company rather than compulsorily be made redundant *by* the company.

Predicting realistically In today's climate of greater economic rationalism and rapid technological change, Jessica's prediction of never losing her job is questionable. Furthermore, Jessica may be inadequately predicting the difficulty of getting another job if and when she leaves the company.

Setting realistic goals Jessica may need to establish clearer goals concerning what she wants from her career and from life. Jessica may also require greater clarity about her goals within the insurance company so that she focuses on what she can achieve without alienating management unnecessarily.

Using visualizing skills Jessica may be insufficiently using visualizing skills to help to clarify goals, to anticipate the consequences for herself and her family of giving up her job without having another to go to, and to relax herself and stay task-oriented.

Realistic decision-making At present, Jessica is just thinking in terms of either staying on at or leaving the insurance company. She appears to be insufficiently considering other options, when she is still employed, so that she can make a systematic and realistic decision about whether to stay or go.

Preventing and managing problems Jessica is on the verge of creating a problem for herself by leaving the company with no other job lined up. Jessica needs to confront her present situation as a problem to be managed in her own best interests. Then, with Lauren's help, Jessica can identify the thinking and action skills she needs to prevent unnecessary unemployment and develop her career effectively.

ASSESS ACTIONS

Action skills are observable behaviours. Pay close attention to assessing action skills because, if clients are to manage most problems better, they must act better. Action skills interact with thinking and feeling. Improved thinking needs to be followed by effective action. Furthermore, if clients are to feel better, they frequently need to take action to achieve their goals: for example, developing friendship skills so as to become less lonely.

Generally counselling students find it easier to think in terms of action skills than thinking skills. However, a common mistake is to focus only on verbal skills. Action skills involve five main message categories: verbal, voice, body, touch and action. The first four message categories usually assume face-to-face contact. The fifth category, action messages, does not require direct contact: for instance, sending flowers to someone you love.

SKILLS FOR ELICITING AND ASSESSING ACTIONS

When counsellors assess actions they seek both to identify which skills are important and to evaluate how skilfully clients perform in them. Below are some counsellor skills for assessing clients' actions and for helping clients to observe themselves.

Build a knowledge base

As with thinking, when they are assessing actions counsellors need to think in skills terms. In addition, counsellors require knowledge of the relevant action skills for client populations they service. Needless to say, counsellors also require knowledge of the relevant thinking skills. If you do not know what constitutes skilled behaviour in an area you cannot assess it properly. For example, counsellors working with aggressive children require knowledge of action skills for managing aggression and behaving assertively. Counsellors working with the unemployed require knowledge of action skills such as making resumés, seeking employment information and handling interviews. Counsellors working with clients with sexual difficulties require knowledge of action skills for managing different sexual problems and disorders. Finally, counsellors working with school and university students' study and examination problems require knowledge of how to study and sit exams effectively.

Gather information in interviews

Counsellors can gather information about observable actions either inside or outside interviews. Here are some ways you can collect information in interviews.

CLIENT SELF-REPORT Clients can tell you how they behave outside counselling. Limitations of client self-report include your not observing their behaviour and so being reliant on their versions of events. Clients may edit what they say to protect their self-pictures.

OBSERVING CLIENTS Depending on the areas of clients' problems, you may learn much from observing their verbal, voice and action messages as they relate to you. For example, shy clients may perform shyness behaviours right in front of you.

FOCUSING ON ACTIONS QUESTIONS Focusing on actions questions aims to elicit specific details of personal actions and of interactive patterns of actions. 'How' questions are useful: for example, 'How did you behave?' and 'How did he or she react when you did that (specify)?' You may need to direct clients to provide details of voice and body as well as of action messages. Furthermore, you may need to assert yourself to ensure that clients provide you with specific behavioural information. 'How' questions go beyond the question 'What actually happened?' to identify participants' specific skills strengths and deficits. 'How' questions also include probing to discover how clients avoid carrying out desired behaviours: for instance, 'How do you actually behave when you put off studying?'

Frequency is a dimension of focusing on action questions: for example, 'How many ... ?', 'How many times did you ... ?' or 'How many times a day/week/month do you ... ?' Duration is another dimension: for example, 'Over what period were you ... ?', 'How long does it take you to ... ?', or 'How many minutes/hours do you ... each day ?' Kazdin (1994, p. 78) observes: 'In most behaviour modification programs, the goal is to increase the frequency of a response rather than its duration. There are notable exceptions, of course.'

In addition, counsellors can ask questions about situational and environmental circumstances contributing to specific actions. For example, 'In what specific situations, do you find yourself shouting at him or her?', 'Where do you shout at him or her?' or 'Are there any other circumstances that influence when and how you shout at him or her?'

ROLE-PLAY A further focusing on actions request is 'Show me.' Clients can be invited to illustrate the verbal, voice and body messages they used in an interaction, either on their own or in a role-play with you playing the other party. For instance, parents having difficulty disciplining children can show you how they attempt this. Role-play allows the possibility of exploring interactive patterns that extend beyond an initial 'show me' response focused on just one unit of interaction. You can video-record role-plays and play them back to clients to illustrate points and develop clients' skills of observing themselves.

Gather information in natural settings

Counsellors may wish to supplement interview information with that gathered in clients' natural or home environments.

- *Counsellors as observers.* You can go with clients into situations in which they experience difficulty and observe how they behave: for instance, requesting a drink in a bar or relating to children at home.

- *Clients as observers.* Always encourage clients to become more aware of how they behave in problem areas. More formally, clients can take away and fill in behaviour monitoring sheets and thinking, feeling and action logs. Furthermore, you can set clients tasks – for instance telephoning to ask a girl out – and get them to record how they behave.

- *Third parties as observers.* With permission, you may also collect information about how clients act from third parties: for instance, spouses, parents, siblings, peers or supervisors. Note, and possibly explore, differences between third parties' and clients' observations. You may need to train third parties in what to look for and in how to observe systematically.

Explore the antecedents and consequences of actions

Counsellors can encourage clients to understand inner and outer events preceding actions. For instance, how did they think and feel before they acted? What events in their outer environment influenced their actions? You can also assist clients to become much more aware that their actions always have consequences and what they are. Furthermore, you can assist clients to see the extent to which consequences of actions influence subsequent behaviours.

Form hypotheses about action skills deficits/goals

As counsellors listen to clients and collect information, they form action skills hypotheses. You may feel confident about some hypotheses at the end of an initial session. You may make other hypotheses more tentatively. Still other hypotheses emerge as counselling progresses. Clients may also share ideas about unhelpful actions. Such observations always merit attention, not least because clients show some responsibility for their problems and problematic skills.

Counsellors may formulate many hypotheses concerning broad areas in which clients may need to develop skills. Often counsellors leave detailed assessment of specific skills deficits until subsequent sessions, when there is more time to do the job thoroughly. By then, counsellors and clients may have prioritized which skills require detailed attention.

Case study: Jessica Henderson

Form action skills deficits/goals hypotheses

The counsellor, Lauren Fulton, formed the following hypotheses concerning Jessica Henderson's possible action skills deficits/goals. For teaching purposes, I have provided more detail than desirable for a restatement in skills terms.

Discussing her future with management skills

Jessica is at risk of allowing her feelings of rejection to become translated into action skills deficits whenever she discusses her future with the managers of her insurance company – in fact, she thinks she has already acted inappropriately. In discussion with Jessica, Lauren specifies the following as actual or potential deficits.
Verbal messages Not indicating clearly enough that she has heard what management is saying.

Insufficiently using 'I' statements – instead, using 'you blame' statements that leave the impression that she is the victim of management's persecution. Failing to express appreciation for positive actions by management. Not clearly enough stating her contribution to helping the company achieve its performance targets.

Voice messages Allowing her voice to have a whiny quality about it. Speaking too quickly. De-powering herself by not speaking sufficiently clearly and firmly.

Body messages Waving her arms around too much when making points. Slouching slightly by not having her shoulders sufficiently back. Making insufficient eye contact.

Systematic job search skills

In conjunction with her career decision-making thinking skills deficits, Jessica appears to have action skills deficits in the following areas:

- making a resumé;

- information-seeking about advertised job opportunities;

- creating and using an informal contact network to find out about unadvertised job opportunities;

- creating and implementing a marketing plan, if necessary;

- interview skills (e.g. verbal, voice, and body messages).

CHAPTER HIGHLIGHTS

- *Counsellors and clients can assess the following thinking skills: owning responsibility for choosing; understanding the relationships between how you think, feel and act; getting in touch with your feelings; using coping self-talk; choosing realistic personal rules; perceiving accurately; explaining cause accurately; predicting realistically; setting realistic goals; using visualizing skills; realistic decision-making; and preventing and managing problems.*

- *Skills for eliciting and assessing thinking include building a knowledge base and thinking in skills terms.*

- *Counsellors and clients can gather information about thinking skills from client self-report, thinking aloud, thought listing, thought charting, counting, focusing on thinking questions, questionnaires and thought-eliciting techniques, such as live observation, visualizing, role-playing and task assignment.*

- *Counsellors make inferences and form hypotheses about clients' thinking skills deficits/goals.*

- *In counselling sessions counsellors and clients can gather information about action skills: for instance, from client self-report, observing clients, focusing on actions questions and role-plays.*

- *Counsellors and clients can also gather action skills information from clients' natural or home settings.*

EXERCISE 9.1   GATHERING INFORMATION ABOUT THINKING

Complete Part A of this exercise on your own and Part B with a partner.

Part A   Gathering information about my thinking
Collect information by each of the following methods about how you think in relation to a problem in your life:
1. Think aloud
2. Thought listing
3. Thought charting
4. Counting (indicate how you might use it)
5. Focusing on thinking questions (indicate what questions might help)
6. Thought-eliciting techniques (where possible try them out)
   (a) live observation
   (b) visualizing

(c) role-play
(d) task assignment

7.   Questionnaire (where possible self-administer the questionnaire)

Part B   Gathering information in pairs
Work together through Part A of the exercise, focusing on a problem for each of you in turn.

EXERCISE 9.2   FORMING THINKING SKILLS HYPOTHESES

As appropriate, do parts of this exercise on your own, in pairs or in a group. Look back at the case example of Jessica Henderson earlier in this chapter for further ideas on how to hypothesize about thinking skills deficits/goals.

Part A   Hypothesizing about thinking skills deficits/goals
Read the following case example and answer the questions about how each partner thinks.

Case example

Rob and Mary have been married for a year. Both think that their relationship is headed for the rocks.

Mary thinks

'Rob is no longer the person I married. We used to have such fun together. He is often late home from work and never does anything around the house. All he cares about is his career. I want a man who can openly express affection and knows what I want without having to be told. It seems as though I am doing all the giving in our relationship. Rob is uncaring. I think it is Rob's fault that our relationship is in such deep trouble. What is the point of trying to improve it? He will never change.'

> *Example of one of Mary's possible deficits/goals*
> Deficit: Inaccurate perceiving (black and white thinking)
> Statement suggesting deficit: 'Rob never does anything around the house.'

Your hypotheses

What are your hypotheses about Mary's thinking skills deficits/goals and what statement(s) suggests each one as a deficit/goal?

Rob thinks

'Mary has little respect for me. We married for companionship and now we are in a power struggle. She seems to enjoy putting me down. She is controlling and critical. At times I think that underneath she hates men. If I were to talk to her about our problems, she would leave the room in a huff. At times I want to have a serious talk with her, but I get anxious just thinking about it. Good relationships don't have conflict. Her family are very cool toward me. I want a wife that I can be proud of and who is fun to be around. Our problems are mainly Mary's fault.'

Your hypotheses

What are your hypotheses about Rob's thinking skills deficits/goals and what statement or statements suggests each one as a deficit/goal?

Part B   Practising forming thinking skills hypotheses
Look for evidence of one, two or three thinking skills deficits/goals

You counsel your partner for ten minutes about a specific problem that he or she brings to counselling. You may take brief notes. At the end of the ten minutes, share with your partner any evidence that suggests that he or she might possess a thinking skills deficit/goal in one or more of the following three skills areas.

1.   Using negative self-talk
2.   Choosing unrealistic personal rules
3.   Perceiving inaccurately

Afterwards, reverse roles.

Look for evidence of any relevant thinking skills deficits/goals

Counsel your partner in relation to a problem for as long as it takes to make an initial assessment of what thinking skills deficits/goals sustain his or her problems. Do not restrict yourself to focusing on the above three skills. At the end of the session summarize your main conclusions and check these with your client. Afterwards, reverse roles.

EXERCISE 9.3   USING ROLE-PLAY TO ASSESS ACTION SKILLS

Work with a partner and conduct the following experiment.

Part A   Experimental variations
This experiment involves two variations.

- *Variation 1.* Finding out about how clients act in a relationship problem by a mixture of active listening and focusing on actions questions.

- *Variation 2.* Engaging the client in one or more brief role-plays designed to elicit information about how the client acts in the same relationship problem. The client sets the scene and gives you sufficient information to play the 'other person' in the problem.

Make sure that you understand how to perform each variation.

Part B   Making an 'If ... then ... ' statement

Make an 'If ... then ... ' statement along the lines of '*If* I counsel a client about a relationship problem for five to ten minutes using active listening and focusing on actions questions alone and then conduct one or more brief role-plays, *then* the role-play variation will provide (a) more and better information about verbal messages, (b) more and better information about voice messages and (c) more and better information about body messages.'

   If (part of statement)
   then (part of statement)
(a)
(b)
(c)
(d)

Part C   Trying out and evaluating

Working with a partner who discusses a relationship problem with you as counsellor, try out the variations in how you collect action skills information. Together with your partner, evaluate the consequences of the differences in your behaviour. Have your predictions been confirmed or negated? Has this experiment taught you something about how you can use role-play to collect action skills information? If so, what?

EXERCISE 9.4   GATHERING INFORMATION ABOUT ACTIONS AND FORMING ACTION SKILLS HYPOTHESES

Complete this exercise with a partner.

Part A   Collecting information in interviews

Counsel a partner who discusses a problem entailing how he or she behaves towards another person. Your focus in this session is work with your client in identifying and assessing his or her action skills. Counsel in an open-ended manner for the first two or three minutes and then intersperse focusing on action questions with reflective responses. As you proceed, incorporate role-play into your information-gathering. Aim to obtain a clear picture of how he or she behaves. During this process, form skills hypotheses about how he or she may contribute to his or her relationship problem. Remember to focus on voice and body as well as on verbal messages. End the session by summarizing and discussing with your client your action skills hypotheses.

Part B   Collecting information in natural settings

Assume that you wish to collect further information to assess the clients' action skills from natural or home settings. Work out, with your client, how such information might be collected in each of the following ways.

1. Counsellor as observer
2. Client as observer
3. Third party (specify) as observer

Afterwards, reverse roles and do both Parts A and B of this exercise.

TEN

Restate problems in skills terms

No problem is so big or complicated that it can't be run away from.

Charles Schultz, *Peanuts* caption

CHAPTER QUESTIONS

- *How does restating problems in skills terms add value to counselling?*

- *What are the three main steps in restating problems?*

- *What are some counsellor skills for restating problems?*

- *How can the whiteboard be used in restating problems?*

- *How can counsellors construct shared meaning with clients?*

- *What can clients take away from restatements?*

- *What are some examples of restatements across different areas of counselling?*

INTRODUCTION

The desired outcome of the second stage of the lifeskills counselling model is a clear initial statement of the skills deficits that sustain a problem targeted by both client and counsellor. Good restatements of problems in skills terms break problems down and identify specific thinking and action skills areas in which clients can make better choices. During later sessions, problems may be still further broken down into their component skills. However, such detail may be inappropriate for initial sessions. Initial skills restatements pinpoint or flag areas for later work.

Skills restatements are sets of hypotheses about skills deficits sustaining clients' problems. Though forming the basis for goal setting and intervening, they should be open to modification in the light of feedback and new information. In short, initial restatements of problems in skills terms are subject to continuous testing and also to major or minor reformulations as counselling progresses.

RESTATEMENTS AS ADDING VALUE

Following are some ways that restatements in skills terms, if well done, can add value to counselling. First, restatements that use skills language normalize or 'depathologize' counselling. Some clients become visibly relieved when they hear that the object of the initial session is to identify some lifeskills to help them to cope better with their problem. Many clients feel threatened by going to counsellors – some think they will be psychoanalysed. Some clients devalue themselves for not standing on their own two feet. Skills language can reduce threat and self-disparagement. Second, restatements in skills terms identify the underlying skills deficits/goals that sustain problems. Thus, restatements have added value over descriptive summaries that focus on coping with a current problem. Such summaries may fail to pinpoint deficits/goals even for managing the current problem, let alone preventing and managing future similar problems.

Third, clarifying problems by good restatements in skills terms can reduce clients' anxiety and increase their self-efficacy, optimism, confidence and motivation for change. Whereas previously clients may have felt stuck, now they gain some glimpses of how to proceed. Fourth, the process of restating problems in skills terms involves the social construction between counsellors and clients about which skills deficits/goals sustain problems. Restatements are constructed with clients rather than imposed on them. They are creative constructions of reality that provide meaning for both clients and counsellors (Lyddon, 1990; Strong *et al.*, 1995). Such restatements can include skills deficits/goals for dealing with depowering forces in clients' environments (Sue *et al.*, 1992). Lifeskills counselling does not assume that clients are the sole source of their problems.

Fifth, restatements in skills terms provide bridges for setting goals, intervening and developing lifeskills after counselling. Good restatements summarize the past and present in such a way as to provide a crossing to a better future. Sixth, restatements in skills terms add value by providing a focus for monitoring and evaluating progress.

STEPS IN RESTATING PROBLEMS

The process of restating problems in skills terms can be broken down into three steps.

Step 1: Laying the groundwork

A good restatement, clearly summarizing the skills required to address a problem, requires thorough prior preparation. Your restatement logically draws together threads covered in your earlier work. In addition to good active listening skills, you require skills of establishing a focus or setting an agenda. You cannot adequately restate a problem if you and the client are unclear about which problem you are working on. This may seem obvious, but many counselling students allow initial sessions to drift aimlessly. All the skills previously mentioned for clarifying and assessing problems and forming hypotheses are also relevant to laying the groundwork. Take notes to refresh your memory.

Step 2: Presenting and socially constructing restatements

Having laid the groundwork, the next step is to present your hypotheses to the client and negotiate a restatement of their problem. Together you construct a restatement that resonates and possesses meaning for them. I always use a whiteboard for this process (see Figure 10.1). I ask clients for a minute or so to allow me to go over my notes and pull together the threads of what they have said so that I can suggest a break-down or 'print-out' of skills deficits on which they may need to work. I do not get into lengthy explanations of what deficits are, other than to say that another way of looking at deficits is that we are establishing goals. Once specific action skills or thinking skills deficits are presented, most clients easily comprehend what constitutes a deficit/goal. If clients do not understand what you mean by a specific deficit, explain it more clearly. If a deficit still fails to possess meaning for clients, either reword it to an acceptable form or remove it altogether. Once counsellors and clients construct mutually agreeable restatements of problems on whiteboards, they may then reword deficits to become more clearly goals.

Figure 10.1 *An interview room set up with a whiteboard*

Step 3: Recording restatements in take-away form

Much of the value of counselling sessions can be lost if clients and counsellors fail to memorize information accurately. Consequently, the next step is to make permanent records of restatements. When clients are clear about how skills deficits can become goals, counsellors and clients each write out restatements from whiteboards on to standard assessment of deficits/statement of goals forms (see Figure 10.2). In lifeskills counselling, both clients and counsellors keep records. The client's records consist of the initial assessment of deficits/statement of goals form, plus additional take-away sheets on which he or she records work performed on specific skills in subsequent sessions.

LIFESKILLS COUNSELLING
ASSESSMENT OF DEFICITS/STATEMENT OF GOALS

PROBLEM OR SITUATION

_____

_____

_____

ASSESSMENT OF DEFICIT/STATEMENT OF GOALS

Thinking skills deficits/goals	Action skills deficits/goals

Figure 10.2 *Assessment of deficits/statements of goals take-away form*

SOME SKILLS FOR RESTATING PROBLEMS

The following are some counsellor skills for restating clients' problems in skills terms.

Take notes

I think it extremely difficult to make sharp restatements in skills terms unless you take notes as you go along. During your clarification and assessment time. clients will provide you with much valuable information for your restatements. Why lose much of this information by not taking notes? Your memory is incomplete. selective and fallible. If I wanted to be even less kind or even more accurate. I would say that relying on it was unprofessional. Strong words, but you cannot do a professional job of restating problems unless you have gathered and stored information properly.

Storing information properly means being able to retrieve it accurately and easily to form the basis of your skills deficits/goals hypotheses. Clients are much more likely to acknowledge the validity of your hypotheses if they are backed up by specific thoughts or actions they have told you than if your hypotheses appear solely or mainly to come from your external viewpoint. When later intervening, you can refer back to the information in your notes. I am not advocating slavishly taking down everything clients say. Rather, when clients provide you with important clues as to possible deficits and statements that illustrate specific deficits, write them down.

Following is a vignette whose point is to illustrate that you simply cannot remember the detail of what clients say unless you write important points down. Then you can use this information to form hypotheses for your restatements. The client, reported here with his permission, is providing the counsellor with a goldmine of information for later use.

> Paul, aged 48, came to see a counsellor, Richard (me) because of a pause at the top of his golf swing. Golf was his big passion in life as a pastime and as a release from the stress and concentration of being possibly the leading engraving artist in Melbourne. Paul's pause was so serious that this whole body became contorted when he attempted to hit the ball. This ugly contortion produced disastrous results in terms of where the ball ended up. Paul's confidence was shattered. When he came for counselling, Paul, who had struggled with this problem for six years, had not been on a golf course for over a year nor in the club house of his golf club for over six months. When I started to probe Paul about his thinking, numerous thoughts and images emerged that helped me to understand how he sustained his problem. I present some of these thoughts and images below.

'If I panic once, the problem is perpetually there.'

'I'll make a fool of myself.'

'I'm silly.'

'This is a complete failure on my part.'

'When someone watches me, I think I cannot come down.'

'Other people are going to say "Poor bloke, hasn't he got a problem?".'

'A mental picture of not being relaxed over the ball and in a paralysis of analysis.'

'An image of contorting myself to hit the ball and other people thinking I've had a seizure.'

Make a transition statement

When making initial structuring statements counsellors can indicate to clients that their problems will be broken down later into thinking and action skills terms. Below are possible transition statements that counsellors might make when starting to offer skills restatements.

'Well, Rebecca, for the past 30 minutes or so we've been exploring in some detail the difficulties in your relationship with your daughter Chloe. I'm now about to test out on you a way of viewing your problem in skills terms. I'll put this up on the whiteboard. I'll make two columns: one for thinking skills deficits/goals and the other for action skills/deficits goals. I call them deficits/goals because any skill that we agree requires development can then become a goal for our work. If possible, we need to agree on the main skills areas in which you experience difficulty. Your feedback is vital since you are unlikely to work on skills where you do not see the point.'

'Louise, I've now asked you a number of questions about your going for senior job interview problems. Time is moving on and, if it's all right with you, I'd now like to give you a print-out on the whiteboard of some skills that may help you. Can you give me a moment or two to look at my notes and pull together the threads? (Louise agrees and counsellor looks at notes and pulls together threads.) I'm now ready to make some suggestions. We can discuss each of them as I write them up. If you are unhappy with anything I put up, let me know and I can either reword it or remove it. (Counsellor starts writing on the whiteboard.) I use the term deficits/goals to indicate that deficits are really goals for developing skills.'

Make clear and parsimonious restatements

Counsellors should remember that restatements of problems in skills terms are mainly for clients' benefit. Unless clients understand them, restatements are useless. Always use simple and clear language. Aim to summarize key thinking and action skills deficits in the targeted problem area or situation. Furthermore, be sensitive to the amount of material clients can absorb. It is much preferable that clients are comfortable with a small amount of material than confused about a lot. Moreover, it is far easier for counselling students to put up simple restatements than to try to do too much and then do it poorly. In later sessions you can elaborate your restatements either by breaking down the skills you initially presented or by adding other skills deficits/goals.

Besides clarity and parsimony, following are some other characteristics of good restatements.

- They bear a clear relationship to information clients provide.

- They are illustrated with material or statements provided by clients.

- They are formulated in conjunction with clients.

- They relate to a problem or problems of high priority to clients.

- They are stated as hypotheses.

- Clients are likely to perceive them as relevant and own them as a basis for working on their problems.

- They lend themselves to setting helpful and realistic goals.

Use a whiteboard

When you are restating problems in skills terms, using a whiteboard has many advantages. The discipline of writing up your restatement – a column each for thinking and action skills deficits/goals – imposes a degree of discipline on you. The visual image may increase clients' understanding and retention of what you communicate. Clients can clearly see the component parts of how you are breaking down their problem. They do not have to struggle to remember previous skills deficits/goals as you move on to introduce new ones.

The whiteboard provides a useful vehicle for the social construction of restatements. Restatements are not only presented, but negotiated. Having written restatements before their eyes makes it easier for clients to provide feedback. For example, you can ask clients what wording or examples they would like to use when illustrating particular skills deficits. Word deficits/goals in language that has meaning for clients. Openly work together on the whiteboard to formulate mutually agreeable restatements of problems. Be prepared to remove any deficit/goal with which clients remain uncomfortable. In addition, once agreed, having restatements on whiteboards makes it easy for both counsellors and clients to record them. Such recording may take place either before or after the deficits have been reworded to become working goals.

Why use the whiteboard instead of other visual aids? Whiteboards are cleaner than blackboards – you do not get your hands chalky. You can erase material more easily and get a clearer picture. Some modern whiteboards can even provide print-outs of what has been written on them. Notepads have the huge disadvantage of restricting the degree to which clients can participate in the joint work in progress. First, counsellors usually control notepads, which they often place on their laps. Second, when counsellors write on notepads, they can lose some contact with clients. Third, it is harder to make changes on notepads than on whiteboards.

Construct shared meaning

Restating problems in skills terms is a creative process involving constructing problems into statements of skills deficits/goals that resonate and have meaning for both counsellors and clients. Skilled counsellors take clients below the descriptive surfaces of their problems to understand their underlying structure of skills strengths and deficits. Good restatements of problems provide conceptualizations of problems that counsellors and clients can share. Counsellors usually possesses a deeper understanding of how skills deficits impede clients. Nevertheless, if the restatement phase is properly negotiated, clients have participated sufficiently to construct a shared meaning of their problem with their counsellors.

Following are some ways in which counsellors can enhance the likelihood of restatements possessing shared meaning. I do not mean to imply that you follow these suggestions all the time.

- Use the client's material.

- Use the whiteboard to create shared space.

- Use the client's language, where appropriate.

- Explain tactfully and carefully what you mean by suggesting specific skills deficits.

- Invite contributions and feedback: for example, by questions like 'Is that clear?', 'Do you agree?' or 'How would you like me to word that?'

- Check clients' satisfaction with the restatement: for example, by asking 'Is there anything that I've left out?', 'Are you happy with that restatement?' or 'What do you feel about that restatement?'

- Allow clients the right to veto what goes into the restatement.

- Acknowledge significant environmental factors.

Where appropriate, let clients know that you appreciate that their problem may be how best to develop skills for dealing with other people's problems and with broader social and organizational structures. However, be careful not to collude with clients who cast themselves as victims and then act as victimizing victims.

Attend to feelings

Always, when restating problems, pay attention to clients' feelings. The following are among areas in which you require sensitivity to clients' feelings. First, you should look out for any client reservations regarding taking a skills approach to their problems. If possible, work through these reservations together. Second, be aware that often you deal with highly sensitive material and that you always require tact. Often clients find it difficult to accept responsibility for their problems and not externalize them. Do not make it harder for them by being clumsy. Third, good restatements can improve clients' morale and motivation. Whereas previously they may have been stuck, now they have 'handles' with which to work. A glimmer of light appears. Problems formerly experienced as insurmountable may now seem manageable. However, take note of any signals that clients have not found the restatements useful, either in part or in whole. For example, clients may acquiesce and later sabotage your work together. Had you caught the mixed messages contained in their acquiescence, you might have addressed their reservations sooner.

Encourage between-session learning

From the start of lifeskills counselling, you can encourage clients to take an active role in learning. Already, I have mentioned working closely with clients during the initial sessions, including using a whiteboard. You can cassette-record sessions and ask clients to play them back prior to subsequent sessions. Many clients find this useful for further exploring problems and understanding restatements. They find that there is too much material to remember and absorb first time around without again listening to sessions. You can use between-session time to build clients' self-assessing skills. For instance, you may request that clients keep records of how they think, feel and behave in targeted skills areas.

EXAMPLES OF RESTATEMENTS IN SKILLS TERMS

Example 1. Louise Donovan

Problem: Consistently bad feedback from job interviews

Already mentioned in Chapter 9, Louise Donovan, 43, is an accountant who was made redundant from a very senior position three years ago. Louise now works for a relatively low salary in a position whose status is below where she was two moves ago. In the past three years Louise has been for numerous interviews for very senior positions. However, she receives consistent feedback that, while selection panels find her technical skills to be excellent, they have reservations about her people skills and find her too pedantic. When Louise answers questions she does so in a bombastic, long-winded and far too detailed way. Her counsellor constructs with Louise the following restatement in skills terms of her job interview problem.

Thinking skills deficits/goals	Action skills deficits/goals
Unrealistic personal rule • 'I must give the perfect answer.' *Perceiving inaccurately* • interviews for senior positions are knowledge exams • others' reactions to personal style not picked up adequately • own strengths insufficiently acknowledged *Negative self-talk* • 'I don't know how to improve.' • 'Things are going to go wrong again.'	*Poor interview skills* • verbal: answers too long, unfocused and lecturing • voice: booming, overpowering • body: stiff posture, eyes glaring, unsmiling (not user-friendly)

Example 2. Paul Fleming

Problem: Golf swing anxiety

Most often, restatements of a targeted problem can be completed in the first session. However, Paul had much pent-up frustration and wanted to give the full history of his problem, including his numerous attempts over the past six years to seek help (including flying over 1500 kilometres to Brisbane for a session with Greg Norman's coach). The clarification and assessment phases lasted into the second session for two additional reasons: Richard, the counsellor, asked many questions in order to make sound hypotheses about the real deficits 'driving' Paul's problem; and Paul tended to give lengthy answers. The restatement took place towards the end of the second session. By this time, it was clear that there was nothing physically wrong with Paul. He had potentially a very good golf swing – he jumped up to demonstrate this as well as to give a graphic demonstration of how his swing became contorted. During the assessment, Richard discovered that Paul's problems were both on the course and in the clubhouse, where he felt very embarrassed about his 'problem'. With Paul's help, Richard composed the following restatement.

Thinking skills deficits/ goals	Action skills deficits/ goals
Negative self-talk • 'I'm silly.' • 'I'm going to mess up.' *Unrealistic personal rules* • competence: 'I must be perfect.' • approval: 'I must be approved.' • control: 'I must always be in control.' *Perceiving inaccurately* • black and white: 'I'm a complete failure.' *Predicting unrealistically* • 'If I panic once, the problem is perpetually there.' *Negative visualizing* • contortions, others' negative reactions	*Insufficient relaxation skills* • muscular • mental • breathing *Poor assertion skills (verbal, voice and body) in the clubhouse* • drawing attention to problem • insufficiently limiting discussion of problem

Example 3. Anita Walton

Problem: Managing shyness

Anita Walton, a 19-year-old college student came to see a counsellor, Maureen Perrone, because she thought she was too shy. During Stages 1 and 2 of the lifeskills counselling model, Maureen formulated many thinking and action skills deficits/goals hypotheses. However, Maureen used only some of the main hypotheses in her restatement of Anita's shyness problem in skills terms. After some discussion and minor changes, Anita and Maureen shared the following conceptualization of her problem.

Thinking skills deficits/ goals	Action skills deficits/ goals
Insufficiently owning responsibility for choosing • always waiting for others to initiate contact *Unrealistic personal rule* • 'I must have everybody's approval.' *Perceiving inaccurately* • jumping to conclusions about others' negative reactions to me *Negative self-talk before, during and after social exchanges* • e.g. 'I'm uninteresting.'	*Poor initiating contact skills* *Poor self-disclosure skills* • revealing little personal information *Poor voice message skills* • voice too diffident and quiet *Poor telephone skills* • what to say, how to say it

Example 4. Jordan McKay

Problem: Relating better to dad

Jordan McKay, 15, comes to counselling worried about his deteriorating relationship with his dad. Jordan is disturbed about the aggressive way his dad sometimes relates to his mum. He handles his difficulties with his dad by alternating aggression with withdrawal. Jordan admits that his dad does a lot for him and might respond favourably to moves to improve the relationship. He wants to get on better, but fears his own resentment will get in the way. He is also unclear how best to proceed. Jordan and his counsellor, Charlotte, agree on the following restatement of his problem.

Thinking skills deficits/ goals	Action skills deficits/ goals
Possessing unclear goals for relationship with dad *Unrealistic personal rule* • demanding approval from dad *Inaccurately explaining cause* • assuming too much responsibility for dad and mum's relationship *Perceiving inaccurately* • negatively labelling dad • insufficiently owning personal strengths *Negative self-talk* • 'I'm going to put my foot in it.'	*Active listening skills* • not showing understanding *Showing appreciation skills* • not saying thank-you *Self-disclosing skills* • not letting dad into my world *Sharing pleasant activities skills* • not going to the footie with dad

Example 5. Sophia Romano

Problem: Cancer patient with negative attitude to life

Sophia Romano is a 59-year-old Italian woman who has cancer. She is married to Benno and they have three children in their twenties. Despite the fact that, in normal circumstances, Sophia would have a life expectancy of about two-and-a-half years, she focuses all the time on the fact that she is dying. Sophia finds it increasingly difficult to cope round the house, yet gets very angry with her family when they try to help. In addition, Sophia is terrified of chemotherapy to the point of seriously delaying investigations, such as a myelogram. Below the counsellor attempts a restatement of Sophia's negative attitude to life problem.

Thinking skills deficits/ goals	Action skills deficits/ goals
Insufficiently owning responsibility for being a chooser • poor life awareness stemming from death anxiety *Poor goal-setting skills* • setting priorities for remainder of life *Unrealistic personal rules* • 'I must not die.' • 'I must always look after my family.' *Explaining cause inaccurately* • 'My family has negative reasons for offering to help.' • 'Cruel fate is responsible for my misery.'	*Poor active listening skills* • understanding family members *Poor showing appreciation skills* • acknowledging help graciously *Insufficient assertion skills* • setting limits on attempts to help *Poor pleasant activities skills* • finding meaning in activity

Example 6. Hannah Mee

Problem: *Stopping unwanted attention*

Hannah Mee, aged 18, is a first-year nursing student. Two months ago, Hannah met James, a 22-year-old science faculty student. Shortly after, James offered Hannah a part-time job in a shop selling books. She accepted the job, needing the money. James fell in love with Hannah. Since then Hannah has received much unwanted attention from James. James persists in telling Hannah how much he loves her and how much he needs her to be his girlfriend. To date James has made no overtly sexual advances. However, for the past couple of weeks, he has been coming round to Hannah's flat every evening around dinner time and inviting her out for dinner and entertainment. Hannah opens the door and each time talks to

Thinking skills deficits/ goals	Action skills deficits/ goals
Insufficiently owning responsibility for choices • how I think and act *Unrealistic personal rules* • 'I must not hurt James.' • 'James must understand what I feel.' *Explaining cause inaccurately* • 'James is the problem' rather than 'I have a problem with James.' *Negative self-talk* • 'I can't handle James.' • 'I'm weak.'	*Poor assertion skills* • verbal: not saying 'No, go away' • voice: not firm • body: staying talking with door open

James for about half-an-hour to an hour, while he pours out his feelings. Hannah has told him she already has a boyfriend and she has left the job at the book shop. Hannah is afraid that James will continue to visit her and may start stalking her and sexually abusing her. Opposite is a restatement in skills terms of Hannah's problem.

Example 7. Val White

Problem: Public speaking anxiety

As mentioned in Chapter 9, Val White, 56, works for a local council and gets very anxious over public speaking. Three years ago Val had a heart operation. Then, two years ago she had to hand over the rostrum when her mind went blank. The time in which she experiences most anxiety is the 30 to 60 seconds before she is due to speak, whether it be a formal speech or waiting for her turn to contribute at committee meetings. During this period, Val's self-talk consists of statements like 'Don't be so stupid,' 'My anxiety may get out of control like two years ago' and 'I may have a heart attack.' Apart from the occasion two years ago when she could not continue, Val speaks in public very competently – no one would know how anxious she feels. Jerry, the counsellor, constructs the following restatement with Val.

Thinking skills deficits/ goals	Action skills deficits/ goals
Negative self-talk • 'Don't be so stupid.' • 'My anxiety may get out of control.' • 'I may have a heart attack.' *Unrealistic personal rules* • 'I must be perfect.'	*Insufficient relaxation skills* • pre-talk breath control • progressive muscular relaxation

Thinking skills deficits/ goals	Action skills deficits/ goals
• 'I must have everybody's approval.' *Perceiving inaccurately* • others are looking for my faults • forgetting my own strengths and past successes *Visualizing insufficiently* • not using visualized rehearsal of performing calmly and competently	

CHAPTER HIGHLIGHTS

• *Good restatements of problems in skills terms break problems down and identify specific thinking and action skills areas in which clients can make better choices.*

• *Restatements in skills terms add value to counselling by normalizing it, pinpointing specific deficits/goals, reducing anxiety and increasing motivation, developing shared meaning, providing bridges for future work and providing a focus for monitoring and evaluating progress.*

• *The three main steps in restating problems are laying the groundwork, presenting and socially constructing a restatement, and recording the restatement in take-away form.*

• *Skills for restating problems in skills terms include taking notes, making transition statements, clarity and parsimony, using a whiteboard, constructing shared meaning and attending to feelings.*

• *Counsellors can encourage clients to work between sessions on their understanding of both problems and restatements of problematic skills.*

EXERCISE 10.1   USING A WHITEBOARD FOR RESTATING PROBLEMS

Complete Part A of this exercise with a partner and Part B in a group.

Part A In pairs
1. *Discussion and practice.* Hold a discussion with your partner, who presents a very specific situation that he or she perceives as a problem (for example, getting started with a particular essay or starting a counselling session with a new client). Together clarify, assess and restate the problem in skills terms. Limit yourselves to up to three thinking skills deficits/goals and one action skills deficit/goal (though, for the action skill, stipulate verbal, voice and body components, if appropriate). Then one of you writes the restatement on the whiteboard and together you discuss issues of how best to go about this. Afterwards, the other partner takes a turn at writing the restatement on the whiteboard, accompanied by another discussion of the skills involved in presenting and negotiating restatements. At the end, each of you writes the restatement out on an assessment of deficits/statement of goals form.

2. *Counselling practice.* Allow yourself 15 to 20 minutes in which you counsel your partner, who presents a very specific problem or situation. During this period, clarify and assess your client's problem. Using the whiteboard, negotiate a simple restatement of your client's problem in skills terms. At the very least, identify and illustrate one thinking skills deficit/goal and one action skills deficit/goal. Do not try to do too much in the time. Afterwards, discuss the session with your partner. At the end, each of you writes the restatement out on an assessment of deficits/ statement of goals form. Playing back a video of the session may help you assess your skills. Afterwards, reverse roles.

You can repeat this exercise either with the same or with other partners.

Part B In a group
1. *Group discussion.* Hold a group discussion on restating clients' problems in skills terms. Issues that you can focus on include:

- whether or not restating problems in skills terms adds value to counselling

- taking notes

- using a whiteboard

- constructing shared meaning

- what clients remember and take away from initial sessions

2. *Group practice*. One member of the group acts as 'client', while the others act as counsellors or, if in a large group, some may be observers. The client presents a very specific situation or problem. The group members counsel him or her, clarify and assess the problem and negotiate a restatement in skills terms (here one 'counsellor' takes responsibility for writing thinking and action skills deficits/goals on the whiteboard). Keep the restatement very simple. During the exercise stop every now and then to assess what you are doing, where to go next, and why. At the end of the session, each group member writes the restatement out on an assessment of deficits/statement of goals form.

Afterwards, repeat the exercise with another 'client'.

EXERCISE 10.2   CONDUCTING INITIAL SESSIONS

Work with one or more partners and practise initial 40- to 50-minute counselling sessions in which you complete Stages 1 and 2 of the lifeskills counselling model. 'Clients' can present problems that require breaking down into different component areas, but these problems should not be too complex. If you are presented with a complex problem, agree with your client to target a specific part of the overall problem as an agenda. Afterwards, discuss with your client. At the end of each session the client fills out the assessment of deficits/statement of goals form and the counsellor fills out the following worksheet. Playing back a video of the session may help you to assess your skills.

Worksheet for Stages 1 and 2 of the lifeskills counselling model
Client _____ (protect confidentiality)
Date _____
Client's presenting problem(s)
_____
_____
_____

Identification and clarification of targeted problem
_____
_____
_____
_____
_____
_____

Client's feelings
1.
2.
3.
4.

Client's physical reactions
1.
2.
3.
4.

Restatement of client's problem in skills terms

Thinking skills deficits/goals	Action skills deficits/goals

Identify your strengths as a counsellor
1.
2.
3.
4.

Indicate the counselling skills on which you need to work
1.
2.
3.
4.

PART FOUR

Stage 3: State Goals and Plan Interventions

Chapter 11 reviews how counsellors and clients translate restatements of problems in skills terms into statements of goals. Chapter 12 reviews skills of choosing and planning interventions to develop clients' lifeskills.

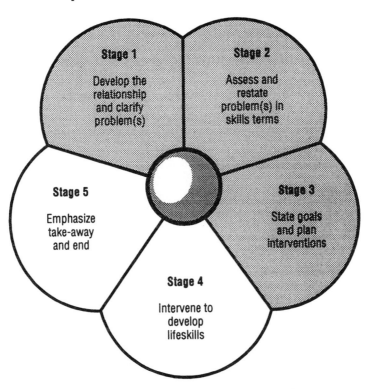

Stage 1

Develop the relationship and clarify problem(s)

Stage 2

Assess and restate problem(s) in skills terms

Stage 5

Emphasize take-away and end

Stage 3

State goals and plan interventions

Stage 4

Intervene to develop lifeskills

ELEVEN

State deficits as goals

It is not enough to take steps which may some day lead to a goal; each step must be itself a goal and a step likewise.

Goethe

CHAPTER QUESTIONS

- *What differences are there between stating goals for problem management and stating goals for altering problematic skills?*

- *What are some advantages and risks of stating goals?*

- *What are some considerations in goals decisions?*

- *How do counsellor thinking skills influence goals?*

- *What are some counsellor action skills for stating goals?*

PROBLEM MANAGEMENT AND PROBLEMATIC SKILLS GOALS

Though they overlap, a distinction exists between problem management and problematic skills goals. Short-term problems dominate much of counselling. Clients want help to cope with immediate problems or crises: be they getting a job, dealing with a disruptive child, sleeping better, giving up excessive drinking, passing an exam or feeling less anxious. Statements of problem management goals can be general or specific. Often clients' *general* problem goals are obvious from their presenting concerns, for instance, feeling less depressed or sleeping better. On other occasions, counsellors may need to probe and spend time with clients to discover their real agendas or underlying problems. *Specific* problem management goals entail stating the outcomes by which counsellors and clients can evaluate whether or not clients are adequately managing problems. Frequently, counsellors need to work with clients in shaping general statements of outcome goals into more specific statements. For instance, 'I want to lose weight' needs to be translated into weight loss objectives stated in terms of pounds or kilograms. Effective counsellors would also specify a period for maintaining weight loss.

Where possible, lifeskills counselling goes beyond stating problem management goals to stating problematic skills goals. Even if clients are to attain problem management goals they require assistance in developing skills strengths. In Chapter 3, I mentioned that clients' problems often extend both *horizontally*, or to other current similar situations, and *vertically*, or to future similar situations. Problematic skills goals stem from restatements of clients' problems in skills terms. Such goals can encompass thinking and action skills for managing a specific current problem, other similar current problems and similar future problems. Ideally lifeskills are for life, not just for managing immediate problems.

ADVANTAGES AND RISKS OF STATING GOALS

Establishing skills goals has both advantages and risks. Following are some advantages of collaborating with clients to state goals.

- *Helping clients to become authors of their lives.* Stating goals helps clients assume rather than avoid personal responsibility for managing problems and problematic skills. Goals negotiated with clients enable them to become authors of their lives rather than to drift or live out other people's goals as if they were their own.

- *A bridge to working.* A great risk in counselling is that counsellors and clients talk rather than work. Counselling may become directionless without working goals (Cormier and Cormier, 1991). Stating goals clearly establishes an expectancy that counsellors and clients expend effort to attain them.

- *Clarity of focus.* Well-stated goals clearly identify the problematic skills on which clients need to work. Where before confusion and aimlessness may have reigned, now clients have reasonably clear objectives towards which to strive. Skills focus on what is important and, thus, economize client effort by excluding or de-emphasizing peripheral activities.

- *Increased motivation.* Goals can increase clients' motivation and persistence because they provide clients with something tangible to attain. Goals may also increase counsellors' motivation because they too have objectives to attain.

- *A basis for planning interventions.* If working goals are neither stated nor clear, counsellors and clients have an inadequate base for selecting strategies and planning interventions.

- *A basis for evaluation.* Despite goals differing in how easy they are to measure, statements of goals provide a basis for clients and counsellors to evaluate progress and success. Clients can monitor and evaluate targeted skills at the start of, during, at the end of and after counselling.

- *An impetus for self-helping.* Statements of goals identify skills strengths that clients require both now and in future. After counselling, clients are more likely to remember what went on if there are clear statements of skills strengths than if no such statements exist. They can use this knowledge to consolidate targeted skills.

There are also risks to stating goals. Such risks usually happen if goals are set and stated the wrong way or prematurely. Most risks are not inherent in setting goals.

- *Insufficient emphasis on feelings.* Some clients require time, space and support to get in touch with their capacity to feel and with their wants and wishes. A risk of stating goals is that clients are insufficiently helped to experience themselves as feeling persons. There can be an overemphasis on thinking and doing at the expense of feelings.

- *Premature restriction of focus.* Goals stated too rigidly early on interfere with counsellors and clients dealing with emerging problems and problematic skills. The die has been cast too soon. Furthermore, some problems are so complex that simple statements of goals in initial sessions do not do them justice.

- *Inaccuracy and superficiality.* Counsellors may wrongly assess problems and problematic skills and this inaccuracy is reflected in goals statements. Furthermore, counsellors may only focus on parts of problems and on less rather than more important problematic skills.

- *Eliciting resistances and rejection.* Statements of goals may elicit resistances, 'Yes … but' responses and even open defiance. Skills goals that may be intellectually tidy to counsellors may be emotionally untidy to clients who ultimately have to implement them. Clients' resistances and reservations may be openly aired or later become manifest in lack of commitment.

- *Controlling and pressuring clients.* Counsellors may state goals more to meet their own needs for certainty and achievement than to help clients. They may have their own agendas and pet theories that they work into goal statements. In addition, counsellors may state goals in ways that pressure clients: for instance, unrealistically high goals or stating them in a demanding manner.

CONSIDERATIONS IN GOALS DECISIONS

Besides the distinction between problem management goals and problematic skills goals, there are many other considerations when deciding on goals.

Elegant and inelegant goals

In Chapter 3 I distinguished between the elegant goal of lifeskills counselling, the skilled person, and inelegant goals, specific lifeskills. When focused on the elegant goal, counsellors train clients in the lifeskills counselling model as a self-helping skill for managing problems and altering problematic skills. Consequently, clients can apply the model to problems and problematic skills different from those for which they originally requested counselling. The inelegant application of the model primarily aims to assist clients to use specific targeted skills in current situations and in future similar situations. Though my lifeskills model and Egan's problem management model differ, Egan too regards his problem management model not just as a counsellor tool, but also as a client self-helping tool (Egan, 1994).

Goals as hypotheses

Counsellors and clients are each practitioner-researchers: counsellors in how best to counsel; clients in how best to live. Counsellors and clients need to view problematic skills goals scientifically. They are really a series of 'If ... then ... ' hypotheses. For instance, '*If* I develop my career decision-making skills, *then* I will make better career decisions both now and in future.' Career decision-making skills might then be broken down into a series of sub-hypotheses contributing to the main hypothesis. Another example is that of a shy teenager wishing to be more outgoing: '*If* I possess a more realistic personal rule concerning others' approval, *then* I am likely to become more outgoing.' Though not always using the language of research, counsellors and clients hypothesize which skills deficits contribute to sustaining problems. Then these deficits are stated as working goals in which to develop skills strengths. As hypotheses, such goals are open to modification in the light of feedback and changing circumstances. For instance, clients and counsellors may find that other skills deficits/goals are more important to achieving desired outcomes than those initially agreed upon.

Initial and emergent goals

In initial sessions, counsellors can identify, clarify and restate some problems in skills terms and then negotiate goals that stand throughout counselling. Goals are more likely to be stable where problems are relatively focused and have brief time frames: for instance, passing an upcoming driving test. However, on other occasions counsellors take into account emergent goals in addition to, as modifications of or even instead of initial goals.

Situations where counsellors need to pay attention to emerging goals include the following. First, some clients may be highly anxious and badly out of touch with their valuing process. Highly vulnerable clients may require nurturing relationships to lower their defences to the point where they are prepared to accept some responsibility for working on their problems. Until they have had more time to share feelings and trust counsellors, it may be premature to negotiate thinking skills and actions skills goals. Second, some problems, such as marital problems, may be so complex that counsellors are either unwilling or unable to state a full range of goals at the end of an initial assessment. Too full a statement of problematic skills goals may only confuse clients and risks turning counselling into an arid intellectual exercise. Too rigid an early skills restatement of clients' problems may exclude much valuable information emerging during counselling. Third, both for focused and also for more complex problems and problematic skills, counsellors need always to be prepared to alter and fine tune goals in the light of feedback and changed client circumstances.

Imposed or negotiated goals

A basic question is 'Whose goals are these?' Goals can be counsellor-centred or client-centred. Ideally goals represent shared meaning. Counsellors and clients cooperate to identify, clarify, assess and restate problems in skills terms. When counsellors sensitively and thoroughly conduct Stages 1 and 2 of the lifeskills counselling model, statements of goals in Stage 3 should seem the logical outcome of this earlier work. The negotiations involved in conceptualizing clients' problems and problematic skills essentially mean that goals based on this shared meaning have been negotiated too.

The risk of counsellors imposing their own agendas as goals is ever-present. Sometimes counsellors are insufficiently thorough in assessing and restating problems in skills terms and rush into goal statements to meet their own needs for certainty and achievement. Counselling students may be especially prone to this. Some counsellors may work within a narrow range of thinking and action skills, and so suggest a more restricted or lop-sided range of goals than desirable. Counsellors may present skills restatements and goals to clients in ways that leave little room for discussion. In addition, clients may be prone to acquiesce and say 'yes' to goals when they mean 'no' or 'maybe'. Counsellors may fail to recognize cues that further negotiation and explanation are necessary.

Commitment to goals

Clients can have varying degrees of commitment to goals (Janis and Mann, 1977; Watson and Tharp, 1989). Sometimes clients openly express doubts about their commitment. On other occasions clients may talk commitment, but later fail to act it. It is one thing for counsellors to state goals, another for clients to agree to them, and still another for clients to work to implement them both now and in future. Client ambivalence is almost always a feature of commitment to goals. One the one hand, they wish to be problem free, yet, on the other hand, they resist fully admitting personal responsibility for changing problematic skills. In varying degrees, they still believe in magical solutions. Fear of change, fear of failure and fear of success can all interfere with commitment (Ellis, 1985, 1987; Nelson-Jones, 1995). Commitment to working goals may entail giving up the pay-offs and secondary gains of previous patterns of behaviour: for instance, blaming others or substance abuse. In addition, clients may go back to environments that reward skills deficits rather than help develop strengths.

Counsellors need to pay close attention to clients' degrees of commitment to goals. Generally, clients commit themselves more to goals that are negotiated rather than imposed. Goals expressed in skills terms may require further explanation and clarification, both initially and later. It is difficult for clients to be committed to working goals that they do not fully understand. You can explore with clients the rewards for change as well as the losses in not changing. Clients may perceive the costs of giving up long-established habits of self-defeating thinking and acting to be heavy. Identify and discuss with clients potential difficulties and setbacks that may lower confidence and self-efficacy expectations about achieving the desired level of performance in targeted skills. In addition, when planning interventions, build in rewards if you can. For instance, early alleviation of psychological pain or early success in achieving sub-tasks may strengthen commitment to goals. Supportive counselling relationships in which clients are valued as persons and not just for their achievements can strengthen clients' commitment to attaining skills goals.

Defining and measuring goals

One way of defining goals is in terms of progress in altering problematic skills rather than in coping with specific problems. However, even when focusing on problematic skills, counsellors and clients need to consider criteria for measuring progress and outcome. In reality, since clients have to maintain skills strengths throughout their lives, problematic skills deficits are never cured. Nevertheless, counsellors can consider how best to observe and measure changes in problematic thinking and action skills, even if somewhat imprecisely. For instance, the overall goal of a quitting smoking treatment programme is in its title. However, counsellors also need to think of how to measure the component skills of quitting smoking and of maintaining this change. For instance, a smoker may have a thinking skills predicting weakness that 'Lung cancer cannot happen to me.' For a given period, the client might keep a log of how many times the thought occurred and also whether he or she disputed it and then made a more realistic predictive self-statement. The problematic skills goal might be, by the end of the period, either to eliminate any occurance of the false prediction or, if it occurs, always to dispute and replace it.

COUNSELLOR THINKING SKILLS

How counsellors think influences how you set goals. Following are some thinking skills relevant to setting and stating goals.

Using the lifeskills conceptual framework and language

Counsellors stating goals in the lifeskills model need to assess and conceptualize problems within it. Counsellors think not just about problems, but about identifying problematic skills sustaining problems. In Stage 2, assess and restate problem(s) in skills terms, lifeskills counsellors break problems down into their thinking and action skills components. Counsellors state both overall goals and problematic skills sub-goals necessary to attain and maintain overall goals.

Choosing realistic personal and counselling rules

Unrealistic personal and counselling rules can negatively influence how counsellors set goals. Here are some unrealistic counsellor rules that may contribute to faulty statements of working goals.

'I must get quick results.'

'I must always help clients to set high goals.'

'I must be the person in control.'

'I must always state working goals comprehensively.'

'Clients must always be treated as though they are highly vulnerable.'

'I must always state goals before the end of the initial session.'

'I must never revise initial statements of goals.'

'All counselling must be short-term.'

'All counselling must be long-term.'

'I must always be liked by my clients.'

'I must never make mistakes when stating goals.'

Counsellors may need to identify, dispute and reformulate unrealistic rules that place unnecessary demands on themselves and clients. Unrealistic rules can rigidify the counselling process as well as pressure or infantilize clients. Furthermore, counsellors may be excessively vulnerable to client feedback and 'things needing to go right'. Ideally, counsellors formulate and state skills goals solely in clients' best interests, without distortion from their own irrational thinking.

Perceiving accurately

In many ways, how accurately you perceive may influence how you state goals. First, you may have ignored or distorted significant information when identifying, clarifying and assessing clients' problems. For instance, your perceptions of your clients' problems may be coloured by your own past struggles and present circumstances. Hence your skills restatements and statements of goals may suffer. Second, you may misperceive how realistic your goals are for clients. Third, you may misperceive how well your clients comprehend statements of goals, even though you may have checked. Fourth, you may misperceive cues of resistance and lack of commitment and thus not address them. Perceiving your clients accurately is always difficult, since counsellors bring so much of their own 'stuff' into counselling. Nevertheless, remain aware that you are always at risk of distorting clients and endeavour to identify and correct the specific ways in which you might do this.

Explaining cause accurately

'Who owns the goals?' or rather 'Who owns responsibility for setting the goals?' and 'Who owns responsibility for attaining the goals?' If counsellors and clients cooperate well in the detective work of Stages 1 and 2 of the lifeskills model, then restatements of their problems in skills terms should be reasonably clear to clients. Statements of goals follow easily from shared constructions of problematic skills. Goals need to be realistic for clients, perceived as important for managing their problems, consistent with their values and comprehensible. Setting and stating working goals is a shared responsibility between counsellors and clients.

Responsibility for attaining goals can be owned by both clients and counsellors, though in different ways. Clients own the goals for themselves, whereas counsellors own the goals as guides for how to help. The counsellor's is a 'professional' responsibility to assist clients in attaining goals. The client's is a 'personal' responsibility to attain and then maintain the stated goals.

Predicting realistically

Statements of goals assume the prediction that if clients develop some or all of the targeted skills they make progress in managing problems. Counsellors can overpredict or underpredict clients' capacities to develop skills strengths. Goals may be unrealistically high or low. Furthermore, counsellors can inaccurately predict the rewards and costs of clients' efforts to change their behaviours. In predicting reward inaccurately, counsellors may overestimate or underestimate good consequences. Similarly, in predicting cost inaccurately, counsellors may underestimate or overestimate bad consequences. Predicting reward and cost accurately is relevant to predicting clients' persistence in working towards targeted goals. To counteract tendencies to inaccurate predictions when setting goals, counsellors can more stringently review probability and assess clients' coping capacities and support factors. Counsellors can also plan interventions to assist clients in handling difficulties and in recovering from setbacks.

COUNSELLOR ACTION SKILLS

Statements of working goals are the 'flip side' of restatements of clients' problems in skills terms. Counsellors take the restatements expressed in terms of thinking skills and action skills deficits hypotheses and turn them into statements of positive counselling and self-helping objectives. Much overlap exists between the skills for restating problems in skills terms and stating skills goals. I deliberately use the term skills deficits/goals to highlight this overlap.

Once you have restated clients' problems into skills terms, basically there are two main ways to state goals: verbal presentation or both verbal and written presentation.

Verbal presentation

Let us take the example of Louise Donovan from Chapter 10. The counsellor has made the following transition statement to introduce restating her problem of consistently bad feedback from job interviews in skills terms. Note how the counsellor verbally introduces the idea of deficits as being goals as well as writing deficits/goals on the whiteboard.

> 'Louise, I've now asked you a number of questions about your going for senior job interview problems. Time is moving on and, if it's all right with you, I'd now like to give you a print-out on the whiteboard of some skills that may help you. Can you give me a moment or two to look at my notes and pull together the threads? (Louise agrees and counsellor looks at notes and pulls together threads.) I'm now ready to make some suggestions. We can discuss each of them as I write them up. If you are unhappy with anything I put up, let me know and I can either reword it or remove it. (Counsellor starts writing on whiteboard.) I use the term deficits/goals to indicate that deficits are really goals for developing skills.'

The counsellor has then constructed with Louise the following restatement of her problem in skills terms.

Thinking skills deficits/goals	Action skills deficits/goals
Unrealistic personal rule • 'I must give the perfect answer.' *Perceiving inaccurately* • interviews for senior positions are knowledge exams • others' reactions to personal style not picked up adequately • own strengths insufficiently acknowledged *Negative self-talk* • 'I don't know how to improve.' • 'Things are going to go wrong again.'	*Poor interview skills* • verbal: answers too long, unfocused and lecturing • voice: booming, overpowering • body: stiff posture, eyes glaring, unsmiling (not user-friendly)

The groundwork for seeing deficits as goals has already been laid. Assuming that the counsellor thinks the client sufficiently understands the connection, one option for how to proceed is just to re-emphasize that the deficits are in fact goals.

> 'Louise, I'd just like to say again that areas shown on the whiteboard as deficits are really skills that we can work to develop. In other words, the deficits are our goals. Is that clear?'

Another option is for the counsellor to indicate more clearly how deficits are goals.

> 'Louise, I'd just like to say again that areas shown on the whiteboard as deficits are really skills that we can work to develop. In other words, the deficits are our goals. For example, your thinking skills goals are developing a realistic personal rule, accurate perceptions and replacing negative with coping self-talk. Your action skills goals are developing good interview skills by focusing on improving your verbal, voice and body messages. Is that clear?'

Another option is for the counsellor to check with the client whether he or she would like the deficits reworded as goals. Often the client says 'no'. However, if the client says 'yes', you can then use the whiteboard to reword the goals into a mutually satisfactory form.

> 'Louise, we've now arrived at a restatement of your job interview problem in skills terms. In subsequent sessions we can work to develop your skills in each of these areas. If you think it would be useful, I could change some of the wording on the whiteboard to make the deficits more readily identifiable as goals. Would you like me to do that?'

Verbal plus written presentation

Sometimes counsellors of their own accord may decide that they should spell out for clients how deficits can be translated into goals. On other occasions, counsellors may do so at clients' requests. Usually, it is sufficient just to change the wording of the skills labels. This can be easily done on whiteboards by rubbing out words and replacing them. Following is an example of a rewording of Louise's restatement into something that more clearly indicates that the deficits are goals. Rewording the whole restatement into the positive is both unnecessary and time-consuming. There is merit in retaining illustrations of deficits so that you can specifically target them in later sessions.

Thinking skills deficits/goals	Action skills deficits/goals
Develop a realistic personal rule • 'I must give the perfect answer.' *Perceive accurately* • interviews for senior positions are knowledge exams • others' reactions to personal style not picked up adequately • own strengths insufficiently acknowledged *Develop coping self-talk* • 'I don't know how to improve.' • 'Things are going to go wrong again.'	*Develop good interview skills* • verbal: answers too long, unfocused and lecturing • voice: booming, overpowering • body: stiff posture, eyes glaring, unsmiling (not user-friendly)

Where counsellors use the whiteboard to reword client's skills deficits so that they become goals, this should be done before each of you fills out an assessment of deficits/ statement of goals form.

Using checking skills

Even though you have checked your restatement with your client and, if necessary, modified it, still check his or her reactions to seeing the problematic skills deficits expressed as positive working goals. Clients may require further clarification regarding some of the skills. Though you may try to clarify skills goals, you may choose to defer more detailed explanations to subsequent sessions. Furthermore, clients may not fully grasp the meaning of certain skills, especially thinking skills, until they become proficient in using them.

Attend to feelings

Most clients feel positive about statements of goals and see them as motivating. However, statements of goals may threaten others. Goals connote the need for effort and change. A degree of ambivalence is inevitable with regard to goals. Pay attention to resistances and reservations. Note voice and body cues of inadequate commitment. Even though clients may verbalize commitment and confidence, their non-verbal messages may indicate otherwise. If possible, work through with clients their reservations and commitment difficulties. Some clients feel more comfortable about goals when they become clearer about how to attain them.

Be flexible

Many reasons exist why you require flexibility in stating working goals. Always take client and problem considerations into account. Some clients may only come for one session – for instance, for assistance in how to ask for a promised pay rise – and seek more a strategy for handling their problem rather than a more detailed skills analysis. Children may require brief and simple statements of goals focused more on action skills rather than on thinking skills, though the latter may be relevant. With clients with complex problems, you can state goals for problem areas of priority to them. You can indicate that other problem areas can be dealt with in similar fashion. Another occasion for flexibility is that people in crisis may require goals and plans to deal with immediate predicaments. Helping these clients think about problems in skills terms and stating working goals may come later, if at all.

CHAPTER HIGHLIGHTS

- *Though they overlap, a distinction exists between problem management and problematic skills goals.*

- *Problem management goals can focus on both general and specific desired outcomes.*

- *Problematic skills goals entail targeting for development the thinking and action skills that sustain problems.*

- *Statements of working goals are restatements of clients' problems in skills terms stated as goals to be worked towards both now and in future.*

- *Advantages of stating goals include helping clients become authors of their lives, building a bridge to working, clarity of focus, increased motivation, providing a basis for evaluation, providing a basis for planning interventions and being an impetus for self-helping.*

- *Risks in stating goals include insufficient emphasis on feelings, premature restriction of focus, inaccuracy and superficiality, eliciting resistances and rejection, and controlling and pressuring clients.*

- *Considerations in goal decisions include elegant or inelegant goals, goals as hypotheses, initial and emergent goals, imposed or negotiated goals, commitment to goals and how to define and measure goals.*

- *Counsellor thinking skills for setting and stating goals include use the lifeskills conceptual framework and language, choose realistic personal and counselling rules, perceive accurately, explain cause accurately and predict realistically.*

- *Counsellors can verbally state and illustrate how deficits may be regarded as goals. Alternatively, counsellors can accompany verbal explanations by using the whiteboard to reword deficits into goals.*

- *When stating goals, counsellors require checking skills, attention to clients' feelings and flexibility.*

EXERCISE 11.1   CONSIDERATIONS IN STATING GOALS

As appropriate, answer the following questions on your own, with a partner or in a group.

1. What are the differences between problem management goals and problematic skills goals?
2. What are elegant and inelegant goals for lifeskills counselling?
3. Why should counsellors and clients regard goals as hypotheses?
4. Why should lifeskills counsellors attend to both initial and emergent goals?
5. Why is the issue of imposed or negotiated goals so important?
6. What is meant by commitment to goals and why is it important?
7. What are some of the main issues in defining and measuring goals?

EXERCISE 11.2   COUNSELLOR THINKING SKILLS AND GOALS

As appropriate, do this exercise on your own, with a partner or in a group.

For each of the following thinking skills areas, assess whether and how your strengths and deficits might influence how you set counselling goals.

1. Using the lifeskills conceptual framework and language

    (a) my strengths
    (b) my deficits

2. Choosing realistic personal and counselling rules

    (a) my strengths
    (b) my deficits

3. Perceiving accurately

    (a) my strengths
    (b) my deficits

4. Explaining cause accurately

    (a) my strengths
    (b) my deficits

5. Predicting realistically

    (a) my strengths
    (b) my deficits

6. Summarize how you see your thinking skills influencing, for better or worse, how you decide upon and state goals in counselling.

EXERCISE 11.3   TRANSLATING SKILLS DEFICITS INTO GOALS

As appropriate, complete this exercise in pairs or in a group.

Part A In pairs

1. Reword each of the restatements of problems in skills terms in examples 2 to 7 at the end of Chapter 10 into statements of goals.

2. Take each of the restatements in skills terms you and your partner constructed in Exercise 10.1 and reword them into statements of goals.

3. Conduct 40- to 50-minute initial counselling sessions as in Exercise 10.2, but include the step of translating the restatement of the client's problem in skills terms into a statement of working goals.

Part B In a group

1. Reword each of the restatements of problems in skills terms in examples 2 to 7 at the end of Chapter 10 into statements of goals.

2. Take each of the restatements in skills terms that the group constructed in Exercise 10.1 and reword them into statements of goals.

TWELVE
Plan interventions

Little by little does the trick.
Aesop

CHAPTER QUESTIONS

- *What do the terms interventions and plans mean?*

- *What are some criteria for choosing interventions?*

- *What are different types of plans?*

- *What are some considerations in developing plans?*

- *What are skills for working with clients when choosing and planning interventions?*

INTRODUCTION

Statement of goals provide the bridge to choosing interventions. Counsellors as practitioner-researchers hypothesize not only about goals, but also about ways to attain them. This chapter focuses on some of the many issues and skills in choosing and planning interventions. Though the focus of this chapter is on initial sessions, counsellors also choose and plan interventions for goals that emerge during counselling.

Some readers might consider that this chapter on choosing and planning interventions might be better placed after the chapters on the different interventions. I start with this chapter on planning interventions for two main reasons. First, in counselling, choosing and planning interventions comes before intervening. Second, readers may find it easier to understand the five stages of the DASIE lifeskills model if they are presented in the order in which they occur rather than jumping forwards and then backwards. You can still choose to read or reread this chapter after reading the subsequent chapters on interventions.

INTERVENTIONS AND PLANS

Counsellors make choices concerning specific interventions and also about interventions used in combination. An important distinction exists between interventions and plans.

Interventions

In lifeskills counselling, interventions are intentional behaviours designed to help clients to attain problem management and problematic skills goals. In the context of this and subsequent chapters, interventions mean 'helping strategies' (Cormier and Cormier, 1991), 'effective procedures' (Hutchins and Cole, 1992) or techniques.

Interventions or strategies for change can be either counsellor-centred or client-centred. With counsellor-centred interventions, counsellors do something to or for clients: for instance, counsellors may give clients advice on how to behave. With client-centred interventions, counsellors develop clients' capacities to intervene in their own problem and problematic skills areas: for instance, counsellors may assist clients in how to monitor their thinking. Both counsellors and clients can intervene. The object of all counsellor interventions should be to strengthen clients' self-helping interventions: 'I as a counsellor am of most use to you as a client if I help you to intervene, at first with my assistance but later on your own, to develop and maintain *your* skills to manage *your* problems now and in future.' Counsellors require a repertoire of interventions or intervention skills to cover a range of clients' lifeskills deficits. Because of the enormous range of clients' problems and skills deficits, you may need to specialize in the most useful interventions for the client populations with which you deal.

Plans

Plans are overall statements of how to combine and sequence interventions for managing problems and attaining goals. They are the outlines, maps or diagrams that enable counsellors and clients to get from where they are to where they want to be. The term treatment plan is sometimes used. A possible risk of using the term treatment plan is that it may connote counsellor-centredness rather than counsellors developing clients' skills to help themselves. The term working plan may be more appropriate, since plans provide frameworks within which both helpers and clients work. Plans arrange interventions beforehand. However, as the Roman writer Publilius Syrus observed in the first century BC: 'It is a bad plan that admits of no modification.'

CHOOSING INTERVENTIONS

Many counselling students, after stating goals, experience a sense of emptiness about their ability to do anything useful to help clients to attain them. The requirement to choose and plan interventions creates pressure to 'deliver the goods'. Counsellors require time and experience to build a repertoire of interventions that they can apply confidently and competently. Frequently, even experienced counsellors find that decisions about interventions are not clear cut and involve trade-offs between conflicting considerations. Counselling students' anxieties about choosing interventions are not in themselves detrimental – how you handle your anxieties determines this.

Criteria for choosing interventions

This section focuses more on how to choose interventions than on choosing how to implement interventions. Having stated goals, your next step is to choose appropriate interventions. You do not start from scratch in doing this. Even as you clarified, assessed and restated clients' problems in skills terms, you were probably thinking about possible interventions. Now is the time to clarify and refine these hypotheses. Below are some criteria to consider when deciding about interventions.

Importance of maintaining a supportive relationship

Whatever other interventions you choose, always offer them within the context of supportive counselling relationships. A risk for some counsellors when breaking down problems, stating goals and specifying interventions is that they become too technique-oriented. For some vulnerable clients, until they gain more confidence and insight, the emphasis on them as persons derived from supportive counselling relationships may be the major intervention. For all clients, supportive relationships can contribute to the working alliance and facilitate motivation. Furthermore, supportive relationships can assist more task-oriented interventions: for instance, by providing better emotional climates for role-plays and coached performance of skills.

Emphasis of interventions on managing problems or altering problematic skills

You and your client may choose to focus more on managing an immediate problem than on altering problematic skills. How you intervene will be heavily influenced by such a decision. Situations where there may be more emphasis on problem management than on problematic skills interventions include the following. First, clients may be in crisis. They may feel overwhelmed by the intensity of their emotions and be in shock, disoriented, highly anxious, extremely depressed, very angry, contemplating suicide and fearing insanity or nervous breakdown. The objectives of counsellor interventions in crisis include protecting clients, calming them down and assisting them in here-and-now problem-solving and planning, so that they regain a sense of control over their lives. A clear focus on problematic skills is deferred until later, or not made at all.

Second, clients may be faced with coping with immediate problems: for instance, upcoming exams, public speaking engagements or confrontations with difficult people. Together counsellors and clients develop 'game plans' for dealing with immediate situations rather than emphasize self-helping skills for afterwards. Third, clients may have limited goals. Dealing with an immediate problem may be all that they have the time or inclination for. Fourth, your own schedule as a counsellor may be so busy that all you can offer is 'band aid' problem management assistance.

Relevance of interventions for attaining goals

Lifeskills counselling heavily emphasizes both thinking and action goals rather than either on its own. Having taken the trouble to assess clients and negotiate restatements, counsellors have laid the basis for selecting interventions. For instance, with Louise Donovan (see Chapters 10 and 11), who has a thinking skills goal of possessing a realistic personal rule about the need to give perfect answers, the counsellor might consider a range of interventions focused on developing this personal rule skill: for instance, providing a rationale for the intervention, using the STC (situation–thoughts–consequences) framework to show how Louise's rule influences how she feels and acts, demonstrating disputing and restating the rule, rehearsing and coaching her, and setting appropriate take-away assignments. For Louise's action skills goal of speaking with a less booming voice, the counsellor could also consider a range of interventions: for instance, playing back cassette recordings of Louise answering questions to increase her voice awareness, encouraging Louise to speak more calmly during counselling, exploring how Louise thinks and feels when she speaks calmly or with a booming voice and setting Louise systematic speaking more calmly tasks outside of counselling. Your choice of goals provides a good framework for your choice of interventions, with each intervention having many sub-choices in how you actually apply it.

Counsellor competence

If your only tool is a hammer, you will probably treat everything as if it were a nail. Wise counsellors know their limitations and strengths. Acknowledge the range of interventions within which you can work effectively. Initially, counselling students need to focus on building a repertoire of central interventions. For example, the intervention of helping clients to build the thinking skill of identifying, disputing and restating unrealistic personal rules is pertinent to numerous client problem areas (Ellis, 1995). Similarly, the intervention of helping clients to learn skills of delivering verbal, voice and bodily assertive messages has widespread relevance (Alberti and Emmons, 1990). Another criterion for developing your repertoire of interventions is to focus on those of most use to the client populations with which you either work or are likely to work. As time goes by, most counsellors acquire a fund of practical knowledge concerning what goals and interventions to use for which kinds of problems and skills deficits.

Counselling students cannot expect to perform interventions competently without adequate training, practice and supervision. A small number of interventions performed thoroughly generally helps clients much more than a greater number performed superficially. You also put much less pressure on yourself if you aim to achieve limited agendas well rather than attempting too much. Though some counselling students are overambitious, many underestimate their potential to help. This under-estimation may lead students either not to suggest interventions or not to implement them confidently. Self-consciousness and a degree of discomfort are inevitable when learning new interventions. If underconfident, you require good training and super-vision coupled with realistic self-appraisal. You need to be open to client feedback about how well you implement interventions. Experienced counsellors too may doubt themselves as they take risks to develop their repertoire of interventions. Nevertheless, it is important that they continue to build their skills.

Theoretical and research support

Skilled counsellors operate within theoretical frameworks. The interventions you offer should be based on psychological principles of learning, maintaining and changing behaviour. The lifeskills framework presented in Chapter 2 provides an introductory theoretical statement for assessing interventions. Keep abreast of the practitioner and research literature in the areas in which you counsel or intend to counsel. In this way you can find out about both existing and new interventions. You can also assess their empirical support. Lazarus and his colleagues observe that empirical data exist for documenting treatments of choice across a variety of conditions, including 'bulemia nervosa, compulsive rituals, social skill deficits, bipolar depression, schizophrenic delusions, focal phobias, tics and habit disorders, pain management, hyperventilation, panic disorders, autism, enuresis, vaginismus and other sexual dysfunctions, and a variety of stress-related disorders' (Lazarus *et al.*, 1992, pp. 13–14).

Sometimes you may come across findings in the literature which indicate that interventions used in combination are more effective than interventions used in isolation. For instance, in marital counselling, focusing on increasing the exchange of rewarding behaviours between partners is more helpful in combination with commun-ication training than on its own (Jacobson, 1989). However, for some clients, also including a focus on assisting them to be more accepting of their partners' behaviours may add even more value to counselling (Jacobson, 1992). On other occasions, you may find research studies indicating that different interventions each proved effective in achieving similar outcomes. For instance, Moon and Eisler (1983) conducted a study on anger control with undergraduate subjects randomly assigned to cognitive stress inoculation, problem-solving, social skills or minimal attention groups. At post-treatment, all treatment groups reported significantly fewer anger-provoking incidents and had significantly lower scores on an anger inventory than the control group. However, there were also between group differences: the problem-solving and social skills groups displayed more socially skilled assertive behaviour in the presence of anger-provoking stimuli than the cognitive stress inoculation group. Reasons why different interventions may lead to similar outcomes include the contribution of the counselling relationship and the increases in clients' self-efficacy beliefs across each intervention. When reading research studies, pay particular attention to the main-tenance of treatment gains. Always read the research literature critically.

Client considerations

Numerous client considerations influence both choosing and implementing interventions. Client considerations include the following.

ANXIETY LEVEL AND SENSE OF WORTH Always take into account how psychologically vulnerable clients are and how badly their anxieties interfere with how they feel, think and act. For example, interventions focused on improving marital communication assume that clients can accept some responsibility for contributing to marital distress. Specific interventions for building career decision-making skills may be premature for clients badly out of touch with their valuing process. Action skills interventions to assist highly anxious clients to initiate friendships may need to await their obtaining sufficient confidence to implement them.

MOTIVATION AND RESISTANCES With its emphasis on developing clients' self-helping skills, motivation is a critical issue in lifeskills counselling. As with goals, clients can say 'yes' to interventions when they mean 'no' or 'maybe'. Assess clients' motivation for implementing interventions and explore potential difficulties and resistances. Clients need to own interventions both intellectually and emotionally in order to exhibit commitment to attaining them. Interventions that bring early rewards, including relief of psychological distress, enhance motivation.

EXPECTATIONS AND PRIORITIES Related to motivation is the degree to which interventions are geared to outcomes that clients want and expect from counselling. Always take client expectations and priorities into account. For instance, clients who enter counselling wanting to manage an immediate problem may not want interventions focused on longer-term skills building. Clients seeing career issues as the main focus for counselling may resist interventions focused on their personal lives.

AGE AND MATURITY Adjust interventions to the age of clients. For example, though friendship skills for adults and pre-teen children have similarities, children and adults require somewhat different skills for relating to peer and friendship groups. Also take into account how much both children and adults know about relationships. Deliver interventions according to the age and maturity of clients: for instance, by varying use of language.

INTELLIGENCE LEVEL AND ABILITY TO COMPREHEND INTERVENTIONS Depending on their intelligence level, some clients may find difficulty comprehending certain interventions: for instance, the thinking skill of identifying possible misperceptions, generating alternatives and choosing best-fit perceptions. Work with interventions that clients can comprehend. Ultimately clients have to understand the choices involved so that they can implement lifeskills on their own.

CULTURE Take into account clients' cultures when choosing and implementing interventions. For instance, the rules for work and personal relationships differ greatly across cultures (Argyle, 1986). Consequently, relationship skills interventions need to take into account relevant cultural rules.

SEX AND GENDER Depending on their biological sex, clients may have learned different skills strengths and deficits. However, be careful to avoid fitting clients into masculine and feminine stereotypes. Nevertheless, assess where inappropriate sex-role conditioning interferes with the development of clients' lifeskills and choose interventions accordingly.

SUPPORT FACTORS Families, peer groups, friendship groups and work colleagues can support or interfere with skills acquisition. Sometimes clients can be trained to identify and use environmental supports better. As part of this process they may also learn skills of being more supporting to others. On other occasions interventions may focus on helping clients to develop skills to protect themselves from environmental pressures.

PRACTICAL CONSIDERATIONS Practical considerations may influence choice of interventions: for instance, pressing current difficulties, threatening upcoming tasks, unexpected challenges and stresses, time available for counselling, whether or not the client lives locally, financial circumstances and so on.

Development of self-helping skills

Where possible, select and implement interventions that develop clients' self-helping skills. Some interventions may directly address issues of clients maintaining skills: for instance, helping clients to develop realistic expectations and explanations of cause about the difficulty of acquiring and maintaining skills. Counsellors may also choose to implement interventions in ways that emphasize self-helping: for instance, by ensuring that clients understand and can verbalize the sequence of choices involved in specific skills – an example is self-administered relaxation as contrasted with counsellor-administered relaxation.

Appropriateness of group interventions

Consider whether clients might best attain some or all their working goals by attending one or more lifeskills training groups (Nelson-Jones, 1991). Other clients might benefit from joining longer-term interactional groups, if possible incorporating a skills focus (Corey and Corey, 1992; Gazda, 1989; Yalom, 1985). Considerations relevant to selecting group interventions include the nature of the clients' problems, availability of appropriate groups and clients' willingness to participate in group work instead of, concurrently with or after individual work.

Appropriateness of third-party involvement

Sometimes you may choose to work with clients' environments. For instance, with depressed and acting out pupils, school counsellors may choose to work with clients' parents or families as well. You can also involve third parties as counsellor's aides. For instance, you can enlist parents, teachers or peers to help shy clients to develop confidence and skills. In a work setting, you can enlist the help of supervisors and managers: for example, in developing employees' public speaking skills. On other occasions your interventions with third parties may involve advocacy on clients' behalf.

Appropriateness of referral

Making referrals generally implies your assessment that other counsellors or helping professionals can deal with clients' problems and problematic skills better than you can. You may start making referral hypotheses early in Stage 1 of the lifeskills counselling model. Whether or not you implement them then or in subsequent stages depends on whether and when you become sufficiently clear that referral is in your clients' best interests. If problems and problematic skills emerge that would be better dealt with by others, you can refer later in counselling.

PLANNING INTERVENTIONS

Almost invariably counsellors use interventions in combination rather than in isolation. Consequently, as well as developing hypotheses about interventions, counsellors develop hypotheses about how interventions might best be used in combination. In short, they develop plans of varying degrees of structure to attain goals.

TYPES OF PLANS

Clients come to counselling with a wide variety of problems, expectations, motivations, priorities, time constraints and lifeskills strengths and deficits. In lifeskills counselling, counsellors tailor interventions and plans to individual clients. Following are types of plans that counsellors might consider.

Problem management plans

Problem management plans are outlines of interventions and steps required to assist clients to manage specific problematic situations. Often, in brief counselling, plans emphasize managing problems rather than altering problematic skills. Counsellors who wish to focus on problematic skills may make treatment compromises to be practical. All that clients may have the time or motivation for is to plan for managing immediate situations: for instance, requesting pay rises, imminent public speaking engagements, statistics exams or visits from in-laws. Even in longer-term counselling, counsellors and clients can develop plans to deal with specific situations. However, in longer-term counselling planning for specific situations is more likely to take place within the framework of altering problematic skills deficits in the direction of strengths. Below are two examples of problem management planning.

Example A   Brief counselling: Mohammed Kahn

Mohammed Kahn was a part-time student majoring in medical radiation. He was referred to the student counselling service by a lecturer after failing a mid-term exam in pathology, a subject he was already repeating. During the initial assessment, the counsellor assessed Mohammed as having limited motivation both for study and for counselling. However, Mohammed was interested in obtaining his medical radiation qualification. He needed to pass the pathology course to do this. Mohammed and the counsellor agreed that the best way to spend the remainder of the first session was to develop a plan or 'survival kit' that would assist him to pass pathology. Here, as is often the case in brief counselling, the statement of goals merged into planning interventions to attain them. Using the whiteboard, the counsellor and Mohammed outlined the following problem management plan.

1.   Obtain accurate and specific feedback on my strengths and deficits in the pathology mid-term exam I failed (within the next week).
2.   Do weekly essays on major topics and get teaching assistant's feedback (for remainder of semester).
3.   Attend *all* pathology lectures (for remainder of semester).
4.   Attend *all* pathology tutorials (for remainder of semester).
5.   Define the pathology syllabus more precisely (within the next week).
6.   Review what might be possible final test questions (within the next three weeks).
7.   Take properly structured notes (starting immediately).
8.   Keep in contact with full-time classmates, so as not to miss tips about important areas for study and revision (starting immediately).
9.   Organize study time systematically (prioritizing and time charting to be done as homework assignment).

At the end of the session, Mohammed wrote down this plan.

A month later, Mohammed returned for a follow-up session. He reported he had made progress in items 1 to 8 of his plan. Much of the second session was spent developing Mohammed's skills of systematic time charting.

Example B   Extended counselling: Emily McPherson

Emily McPherson came for counselling with numerous presenting concerns, including depression, low self-esteem, difficulty holding down relationships and anxieties about being a female engineer. Emily's working goals included thinking and action skills for being more assertive. During her fifth weekly session, Emily and her counsellor, Andre, planned how best to manage a specific current problem in Emily's life. Emily's first job after graduation was with a leading construction engineering company. When hired, she was promised a salary review after her first year's service. The company had not conducted this review three months into her second year. Emily and Andre formulated her overall problem management goal, which was, before the end of two weeks, to ask her boss for a salary review. They then stated thinking and action skills working goals. For instance, an illustrative thinking skills goal was to develop a more realistic personal rule about discussing money. Illustrative action skills goals focused on verbal, voice and body messages for raising the issue of her salary review and then requesting that it be conducted. Emily and Andre then developed a plan for how to make a salary review request when face-to-face with her boss. This plan included strategies for handling possible countermoves by her boss. Andre demonstrated, coached and rehearsed Emily in the component skills of the plan.

Problematic skills: structured plans

Counsellors and clients may consider a highly structured approach the best way to obtain some working goals. Structured plans or programmes are step-by-step training and learning outlines of interventions for attaining specific goals. Structured plans are commonly used in lifeskills training groups: for instance, in assertion or stress management groups (Gazda, 1989; Hopson and Scally, 1981; Nelson-Jones, 1991). Structured plans may also be used to train individual clients in skills where working goals are clear and specific. Three variations of structured plans are predetermined programmes, tailor-made structured plans and partially structured plans.

STRUCTURED PROGRAMMES Counsellors may work with clients using existing or modifications of existing packages or programmes to develop skills. Such skills development programmes may be in areas like parenting, career decision-making and weight control. Below are examples of counsellors and clients using structured programmes.

> Herb suffered from hypertension. A central working goal was to develop his relaxation skills, both physical and mental. Herb's counsellor decided that the best way to develop her relaxation skills was to use a programme based on Bernstein and Borkovec's (1973) *Progressive Relaxation Training: A Manual for the Helping Professions.*

> Amy suffered from agoraphobia. Working goals included developing Amy's self-talk skills for coping with feelings of panic and being able to leave home and perform feared tasks, such as going on buses and into stores. Amy's counsellor negotiated with her that treatment interventions would be based on Mathews *et al.*'s (1981) *Programmed Practice for Agoraphobia: Clients' Manual.*

TAILOR-MADE STRUCTURED PLANS Structured plans combining interventions can be tailor-made to specific problems or to specific persons. When tailor-made to specific problems, such plans resemble predetermined packages. For instance, when Jim Blake see the outplacement counsellor Sam Rushton about getting another job, Sam can fit Jim into an existing job skills programme, design a programme specifically to address Jim's skills deficits or combine the two approaches. In the tailor-made approach Sam develops a step-by-step outline to attaining Jim's working goals. Here Jim can be part of the planning process, with his specific goals, wishes and circumstances taken into account. The structured plan is negotiated rather than prescribed.

PARTIALLY STRUCTURED PLANS Counsellors and clients can design plans that have elements of structure, yet fall short of step-by-step structured plans. For instance, in the case of the unemployed executive Jim Blake, another option for his counsellor Sam Rushton is to set aside certain sessions for testing to assess interests and aptitudes and also for developing specific action skills, such as resumé writing and interview skills. The agendas for the remaining sessions are open for negotiation at the start of each session. Below is another example of a partially structured programme, a continuation of the Anita Walton case study from the end of Chapter 10.

Anita Walton's main presenting concern was shyness. Her counsellor Maureen Perrone worked out with Anita the following goals. Anita's thinking skills goals were to: own more responsibility for initiating; choose a realistic personal rule about approval; perceive others' reactions to me more accurately; and use coping self-talk. Anita's action skills goals were to: speak with a louder, more confident voice; develop my initiating contact skills; develop my self-disclosure skills; and develop my telephone skills. Maureen Perrone had an extremely heavy client load, which rarely allowed her to do long-term counselling. She assessed Anita as not being seriously underconfident and suggested that they work for three further sessions at fortnightly intervals.

Maureen's aim was to give Anita the maximum amount of self-helping skills within a limited time span. Maureen suggested the following plan to Anita. The first session had already been spent on assessment and stating goals; the second session would mainly focus on interventions for Anita's thinking skills; the third session would mainly focus on interventions for Anita's action skills; the fourth session would be spent filling learning gaps and consolidating trained skills as self-helping skills. During the fourth session, Maureen and Anita would review the advisability of holding a follow up session, say three months later. Anita agreed to the plan, which allowed for flexibility within sessions, but ensured that attention was clearly paid to both thinking and action skills rather than to one set of skills at the expense of the other.

Problematic skills: open plans

Open plans allow counsellors and clients without a predetermined structure to choose which interventions to use to attain which working goals, when. Many considerations influence decisions to adopt open plans. Some clients may require nurturing relationships to help them to get more in touch with their feelings and to reduce their anxieties. They may not be able to work effectively on thinking and action skills deficits until feeling less vulnerable. Some cases are complex and difficult to understand. Counsellors risk prematurely deciding on interventions if they opt for too much structure too soon. Open plans allow counsellors and clients to cooperate in setting session agendas. Such session agendas can emphasize material and the skills on which clients and counsellors currently want to work. Open plans have the great advantage of flexibility. Clients may be more motivated to work on skills and material that have relevance at any given time than to run through existing programmes independent of current considerations. Below is how an open plan was applied in working with Louise Donovan (see Chapters 10 and 11).

Richard (me), the counsellor, and Louise Donovan decided to use an open plan to address her interview skills deficits. In reality her interview skills deficits were just the tip of the iceberg in a well-entrenched cumbersome, pedantic and off-putting style of professional relating. The initial impression given by Louise was that she would be best placed in back rooms well away from important clients. The counsellor suggested to Louise that she needed not only to work on specific action skills, but to work on her thinking skills deficits that contributed to her being highly anxious in interviews.

Near the start of each session, Richard and Louise would establish an agenda for that session's work. Early sessions focused mainly on building Louise's interview skills. Counsellor and client made a list of questions she was likely to be asked at interviews, and Richard engaged in cassette-recorded question and answer sessions with her. Afterwards, both client and counsellor assessed the cassettes, looking for specific evidence to confirm or negate guidelines. During the evaluation of cassettes, Louise became more aware of the effect that differing her verbal, voice and body messages could have on interviewers and clearer that interviews for senior positions had an important relationship as well as knowledge agenda. In the third session, using the whiteboard, Richard assisted Louise to dispute her rule that she must give the perfect answer and then developed with her a statement of a more realistic rule.

Subsequent sessions incorporated the following interventions: more practice in the verbal, voice and body message skills of answering questions; making up a cassette in which Louise was relaxed and then taken by Richard through appropriate calming, coaching and affirming self-talk for waiting outside the interview room and then going in and answering the first few questions competently; and identifying and listing Louise's competencies and then cassette recording them twice – first with Richard's voice and then with Louise's voice.

During counselling, Louise was given a series of take-away assignments both to prepare for sessions and to consolidate skills targeted in sessions. In addition, Louise was encouraged to practise her skills in her daily professional life, which she did with increasing success. This daily practice was especially important, since Louise was not going for interviews as she did not want to leave her present job unless it was for a substantial improvement. Louise is still in counselling after 15 sessions, but now comes monthly.

CONSIDERATIONS IN PLANNING

Some counsellors are good at designing and leading lifeskills groups, but poor at planning training interventions for individual clients. They find it advantageous to combine interventions sequentially and systematically for groups, but omit to use the same disciplined approach with individual clients. Even when adopting open plans, some effective lifeskills group leaders still inadequately use training skills to deliver specific interventions. In the above section I emphasized varying degrees of structure for plans. Here I focus on plans for clients so that clients can develop lifeskills from systematic learning sequences. Most considerations mentioned below are also relevant to plans for managing specific problem situations.

Preparation time

If you decide to design treatment plans for individual clients, when do you do it? Though you may discuss with clients possible interventions for attaining goals, you may find it difficult to develop systematic plans during the same sessions. Instead, you can take time to do this before the next session. Some counsellors do not develop systematic plans because they are unwilling to spend out of session time doing this task.

Involvement of clients and others

Counsellors need to consider at what stage and how much to involve clients in planning. Counsellors' prior discussions about goals provide some protection against plans unacceptable to clients. In addition, always check that clients understand and are comfortable with proposed plans. If necessary, modify plans in the light of client feedback. Sometimes it helps to involve clients early in the planning process. Advantages of such involvement include taking clients' wishes and priorities into account and clients being more likely to implement plans that they have had some say in making.

With clients' permission, you may sometimes involve significant others when planning: for instance, partners, care-givers or parents.

Sequencing of interventions

What is the best way to sequence activities to attain goals? Sometimes the logic in sequencing interventions is clear. For instance, with most unemployed executives, there are three logically sequenced steps in assisting them in becoming re-employed: (1) evaluation and career planning; (2) developing a job marketing plan; and (3) implementing a job marketing plan (Davidson, 1988). Within an individual intervention like choosing realistic rules, the sequence of sub-interventions is clear: namely, identifying unrealistic rules, disputing them and restating them into more realistic rules. Here the learning tasks are cumulative. In action skills interventions, counsellors often use step-by-step graded tasks to develop clients' skills and confidence.

Time frame for plan

Counsellors, clients and the learning process may each influence time allocated for carrying out plans. For instance, counsellors may have restricted amounts of time to work with clients. In addition, you may want clients to participate in learning activities offered by others (for instance, workshops) that are only available on specific dates. Client considerations include varying degrees of urgency in acquiring skills and different abilities to pay, if fees are involved. Learning process considerations include the degree to which sessions and planned activities should be intensive rather than spaced out, or a combination of the two. Further, should you plan for one or more follow-up or booster sessions?

Management of learning considerations

What is the best way to put interventions across? For each intervention, when should counsellors use the following training and learning methods: assessment and facilitating client self-assessment, facilitation, verbal presentation, demonstration, coaching and take away assignments? Counsellors need to make decisions concerning the overall balance between facilitation and didactic input. Other considerations include the availability of written training materials, such as training manuals and handouts, and of audiovisual materials and equipment. A further set of learning considerations includes sensitivity to the costs and rewards for clients of carrying out plans. How difficult are the plans' various elements? Where are clients' support factors, including how supportive their counsellors are? When do clients obtain rewards from implementing planned activities?

Emphasis on maintaining and developing skills

Always, when initially planning interventions, consider how to help clients to take away and maintain trained skills as self-helping skills for afterwards. Both structured and open plans should emphasize clients learning to use skills on their own. You can emphasize client thinking skills relevant to maintenance. As mentioned, examples of pertinent client thinking skills are possessing realistic expectations about the difficulty of maintaining change, and understanding the sequences of choices in targeted skills well enough to instruct themselves and, if necessary, make corrections. You can also plan interventions in ways that help clients to maintain action skills. Ways of doing this include emphasizing overlearning, practice in real-life settings, and anticipating and working through difficulties in applying skills.

Counsellors may leave developing more formal maintenance plans to Stage 5 of the lifeskills model, emphasize take-away and end. At that stage you can take clients' end of counselling skills levels into account as well as their current estimations of obstacles to maintaining skills. In brief counselling, planning interventions, intervening and consolidating self-helping skills and ending may become compressed into one another. In such circumstances, counsellors and clients have to plan for maintenance as best they can.

Monitoring and evaluating outcomes

In Chapters 8 and 9 I discussed ways of assessing feelings, physical reactions, thoughts and actions. When making plans, keep in mind the importance of clients developing self-assessment skills and monitoring their progress. When stating goals in skills terms, you have defined the areas in which it is important to observe change. Plans are successful to the extent that they efficiently help clients to develop and maintain self-helping skills. If plans do not produce desired results, examine closely the reasons and, if necessary, modify plans. Be prepared to modify plans in the light of important information emerging during counselling.

Outlining plans

Especially where plans involve some detail, consider writing outlines of plans. Such outlines may guide both your own and your client's work. Below is an outline of a structured plan by the counsellor Sam Rushton for his client Jim Blake, the recently fired executive, to develop Jim's getting another job skills.

> Sam has already seen Jim twice, the first time on company premises immediately after Jim was fired and the second time in Sam's office a few days later. In this second session, Sam and Jim agreed on a statement of job search skills goals. Sam said that at the start of their next session he would present a plan to help Jim to attain these goals. Sam mentioned that this plan would have three elements: counselling sessions; planned activities, both to assess Jim's aptitudes and interests and to develop specific skills; and take away assignments. Sam and Jim agreed that, though the job search might well take longer, a month should be the time

frame for developing basic effective job search skills.

Draft of plan to assist Jim Blake develop job search skills

Session	Goals	Illustrative content
Week 1 Session 3 Counselling	Greater realism about job search Own more responsibility for choices Become more in touch with wants and wishes Possess more realistic achievement rules	Presentation and discussion of plan in context of realities of job searching Checking current state of being a chooser Facilitate self-exploring Further discussion and challenging of unrealistic achievement rules *Take-away assignments* Positive asset search Reading on career planning Write own occupational history focusing on choices
Planned activity – testing	Perceive self more accurately Collect data relevant to job search goals	Complete interest, aptitude and occupational self-evaluation measures

Week 2 Session 4 Counselling	Perceive self more accurately Get in touch with wants and wishes Further work on job search goals Possess more realistic achievement rules	Review current functioning and take-away assignment progress Feedback and discuss test results Facilitate self-exploring *Take-away assignments* Thinksheet on rules Career planning exercise
Planned activity – all-day workshop	Creating a job-marketing plan Utilizing informal networks Resumé skills	Presentation, demonstration coaching and practice in each skills area *Take-away assignments* Further develop job marketing plan Work on resumé
Week 3 Session 5 Counselling	Develop goal-setting skills Develop skills at creating job marketing plan Own more responsibility for choices Be more in touch with wants and wishes	Review current functioning and take-away assignment progress Develop job-marketing plan Facilitate self-exploring Assess thinking and action skills for managing

	Managing time when unemployed	non-work time and set goals Work on thinking skills as needed *Take-away assignments* Refine job-marketing plan Collect information for job plan Exercise on using non-work time
Planned activity – all-day workshop	Use coping self-talk skills Improve interview skills Improve skills at using informal network	Presentation, demonstration coaching and practice in thinking and action skills for interviews *Take-away assignments* Continue data collection Visualize rehearsal of job interviews using coping self-talk
Week 4 Session 6 Counselling	Thinking and action interview skills Other thinking and action skills as needed	Review current functioning and take-away assignment progress Coach and rehearse interview skills as needed

		Anticipate difficulties and setbacks in implementing job-marketing plan
		Take-away assignments Implement job-marketing plan Exercise: anticipating difficulties
Week 5 Session 7 Counselling	Thinking skills for maintaining behaviour Maintaining action skills	Review current functioning and take-away assignment progress Facilitate self-exploring Develop thinking and action skills strategies for maintaining and consolidating self-helping skills
		Take-away assignments Implement job-marketing plan Monitor progress in using skills and make corrections as needed

Follow-up sessions and telephone support as needed.

SKILLS FOR WORKING WITH CLIENTS

So far this chapter has mainly explored how counsellors think when making interventions and planning hypotheses. Where detailed plans are not involved, counsellors tend to discuss plans immediately after agreeing on goals. Below are some working with client skills.

Make transition statements

You may have signalled moving on to discussing interventions as part of your rationale for presenting goals: for instance, with a sentence like 'Also, stating goals gives us a focus for discussing how best to attain them.' The following are examples of possible transition statements after you have finished presenting and checking your client's agreement to goals.

'Now that we have agreed on goals, let's spend some time in discussing how best to attain them.'

'Can we now move on to discuss approaches to building your skills?'

'Now let's look at some ways to attain your goals.'

Enlist cooperation and commitment

Since the purpose of any intervention or combination of interventions is to develop client self-helping skills, it is crucial that you encourage them to cooperate. One way of encouraging cooperation is to involve clients from the start in the process of choosing interventions and planning their sequencing. You may jointly develop a plan using a whiteboard. On occasions when you present plans, you can do so in ways that imply that plans are a series of suggestions for discussion that, if necessary, can be modified or fine tuned. Check your client's comprehension and feelings about proposed plans. Explore reservations and, if necessary, negotiate changes in plans. You can explore with clients the payoffs and rewards as well as the costs of implementing plans.

Give simple explanations and answers

Without insulting your clients' intelligence, offer clear and simple explanations for suggested interventions and plans. You can give clients too much information so that they feel confused rather than motivated to work. Be prepared to answer questions, but again keep your answers simple and to the point. In initial sessions, the purposes of discussing interventions and plans are as much emotional and motivational as instructional. Clients feel better if they perceive that counsellors know ways to approach their problems and skills deficits. Often you do best to leave describing the detail of interventions until later, when clients require this information to develop specific skills.

Discuss expectations and contract

You and your clients can discuss your expectations of yourselves and each other in implementing plans. For instance, you may indicate that you expect regular attendance over a specified number of sessions, with possibly a joint review of progress at the end of this period. You may stress the necessity of diligently carrying out take away assignments. Sometimes counsellors give clients written plans. These plans can assume the status of contracts of varying degrees of formality. One approach is to turn the plan into an informational treatment contract. Informational contracts possess five elements: (1) information about interventions; (2) statements about (goal) outcome expectations; (3) client intention statements agreeing to participate fully in important aspects of interventions; (4) duration (weeks or sessions) of the contract; and (5) an informed consent statement (Cormier and Cormier, 1991; Seidner and Kirschenbaum, 1980).

Start implementing plans

After counsellors state goals and discuss plans, they can then negotiate take away assignments. One type of take away assignment is for clients to observe and monitor feelings, thoughts and actions in targeted skills areas. Sometimes clients can be instructed to start developing specific skills: for instance, speaking louder or taking a few gentle risks in disclosing more information about themselves. Getting clients started on implementing plans right away has many advantages. First, it reinforces the idea of working rather than talking relationships. Second, clients may feel better for working on problems and problematic skills that have worried them for some time. Third, implementing plans may lead to short-term rewards that build motivation and commitment. Fourth, getting started enables profitable use of between first and second session time. Ultimately this may mean one or more fewer sessions.

CHAPTER HIGHLIGHTS

- *A useful distinction exists between interventions, or helping strategies, and plans, or how to use interventions in combination.*

- *Criteria for choosing interventions include the importance of maintaining supportive relationships, emphasis of interventions on managing problems or altering problematic skills, relevance for attaining working goals, counsellor competence, and theoretical and research support.*

- *When choosing interventions, client considerations include anxiety level and sense of worth, motivation and resistances, expectations and priorities, age and maturity, intelligence level and ability to comprehend interventions, culture, sex and gender, support factors, and practical considerations, such as availability.*

- *Three types of plans are problem management plans, structured plans for problematic skills and open plans for problematic skills.*

- *Considerations in planning include preparation time, involvement of client and others, sequencing of interventions, time frame for plan, how to manage learning, emphasizing maintaining and developing skills and monitoring and evaluating outcomes.*

- *Counsellors may need to outline plans for their own and clients' benefits.*

- *Skills for working with clients when choosing and planning interventions include make transition statements, enlist cooperation and commitment, give simple explanations and answers, discuss expectations and contract and start implementing plans.*

EXERCISE 12.1   CHOOSING INTERVENTIONS

As appropriate, complete this exercise on your own, with a partner or in a group. Discuss the importance of each of the following criteria in choosing interventions. State reasons for your observations.

1. Maintaining a supportive relationship
2. Emphasis on managing problems or on altering problematic skills
3. Relevance for attaining goals
4. Counsellor competence to administer interventions
5. Theoretical and research support for interventions
6. Client considerations
   (a) anxiety level and sense of worth
   (b) motivation and resistances
   (c) expectations and priorities
   (d) age and maturity
   (e) intelligence level and ability to comprehend interventions
   (f) culture
   (g) biological sex
   (h) support factors
   (i) practical considerations (for instance, time, pressing current difficulties)
   (j) other client considerations not mentioned above
7. Development of self-helping interventions
8. Appropriateness of group interventions
9. Appropriateness of interventions involving third parties
10. Appropriateness of referral
11. Other criteria for choosing interventions not mentioned above

EXERCISE 12.2   MAKING PLANS FOR INTERVENTIONS

As appropriate, complete this exercise on your own, with a partner or in a group.

Part A   Types of plan
What is the meaning to you of each of the following kind of plans and what might be their advantages and disadvantages?

1.   Problem management plans

   (a) description
   (b) advantages
   (c) disadvantages

2.   Structured plans for attaining problematic skills goals

   (a) description
   (b) advantages
   (c) disadvantages

3.   Open plans for attaining problematic skills goals

   (a) description
   (b) advantages
   (c) disadvantages

Part B   Considerations in making plans
State how you might take each of the following considerations into account in making structured or partially structured plans to attain goals.

1.   Preparation time
2.   Involvement of client and others
3.   Sequencing of interventions
4.   Time frame for plan
5.   Management of learning considerations
6.   Emphasis on maintaining and developing skills
7.   Monitoring and evaluating outcomes

Part C   Choosing and planning interventions for a typical problem and client
Select a typical problem for a typical 'client' whom you might counsel, either when in training or afterwards. For instance, exam anxiety is a common problem among secondary and tertiary students. Answer the following questions.

1.   What is the typical problem you have selected for your typical 'client'?

2. What might be up to three thinking skills goals for the client's problem?
    Thinking skills goal A
    Thinking skills goal B
    Thinking skills goal C

3. What intervention or interventions would you choose to develop the client's skills
    for each of these goals?
    Intervention(s) for thinking skills goal A
    Intervention(s) for thinking skills goal B
    Intervention(s) for thinking skills goal C

4. What might be up to three appropriate action skills goals for the client's prob-
    lem?
    Action skills goal A
    Action skills goal B
    Action skills goal C

5. What intervention or interventions would you choose to develop the client's skills
    for each of these goals?
    Intervention(s) for action skills goal A
    Intervention(s) for action skills goal B
    Intervention(s) for action skills goal C

6. What type of plan would you choose to assist your client to attain the above
    thinking skills and action skills goals? Give reasons for your choice.

7. If appropriate, outline your plan.

Part D Conduct role-play interviews
Conduct a series of role-plays with one or more partners based on the cases on which
you worked in Exercise 11.3 (question 3 of Part A and/or question 2 of Part B). In each
role-play you, as a counsellor, suggest and discuss with your client interventions and
plans to attain goals. Skills to bear in mind include:

*   make a transition statement;
*   enlist cooperation and commitment;
*   give simple explanation and answers;
*   discuss counsellor and client role expectations and any contract involved.

After each role-play hold a sharing and feedback session with your 'client'. Afterwards,
reverse roles. Playing back video- or audio-recordings of role-plays may help you to
learn skills faster.

PART FIVE

Stage 4: Intervene to Develop Lifeskills

Chapter 13 reviews some central skills for conducting post-initial sessions and delivering interventions. Chapters 14 and 15 focus on interventions for developing clients' thinking skills. Chapter 16 examines interventions for developing clients' actions skills. Chapter 17 reviews how developing clients' thinking and action skills can assist them to experience, express and manage feelings more effectively.

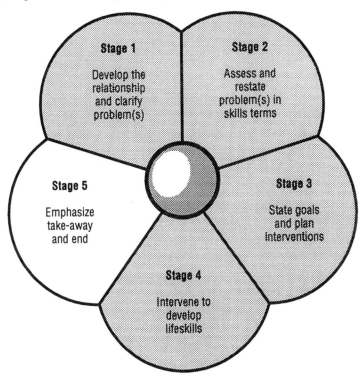

THIRTEEN

Delivering interventions skills

I hear, I forget
I see, I remember
I do, I understand

Chinese proverb

CHAPTER QUESTIONS

- *What are training skills?*

- *What are reconnect and catch-up skills?*

- *What are establishing session agenda skills?*

- *What are speaking skills for presenting interventions?*

- *What are demonstrating skills?*

- *What are coaching and feedback skills?*

- *What are negotiating take-away assignment skills?*

- *What are ending sessions skills?*

THE COUNSELLOR AS TRAINER

In this chapter I focus on some central skills of conducting sessions in which you deliver interventions. In much of counsellor training the emphasis is on receiver or listening skills rather than on sender skills or training skills. Counsellors as developmental educators also require educational or training skills. Counselling is an educational process in which counsellors flexibly use both relationship and training skills to assist clients to attain learning goals for now and later. Lifeskills counselling encourages clients to learn for themselves and to understand, retain and use what they have learned.

Clients as learners require counsellors as trainers to guide learning. Counsellors as trainers require not only knowledge of what interventions provide, but also skills of how to intervene. The *what* of intervening needs to be supplemented by the *how* of intervening.

Following are counsellors who sabotage their effectiveness through poor training skills.

Sophie is a rehabilitation counsellor trainee on placement. She attempts to explain the thinking skill of identifying, disputing and restating unrealistic personal rules to a client, Les, who devalues himself because of the after-effects of an industrial accident. Sophie's presentation is muddled and she answers Les's questions poorly. She also speaks in a monotone and keeps tugging at her hair. Les is little the wiser about the skill Sophie tries to communicate and feels frustrated with both himself and her.

Lee is a counsellor who tries to teach Tuan, a refugee from Vietnam, assertion skills. Lee spends a lot of time discussing with Tuan what he might say when he faces racial discrimination. However, at no stage does Lee demonstrate the voice and body messages that might accompany Tuan's assertive verbal messages. Consequently, Tuan does not really know how to be assertive.

Rod is a careers counsellor who thinks that Barb requires better interview skills to increase her employability. Rod talks about interview skills and demonstrates some of them. However, Rod never encourages or helps Barb to rehearse and practise interview skills. Barb tells her friends that she still goes to pieces in job interviews and devalues herself for not using the skills Rod has shown her. At no

stage has Rod suggested to Barb that she do specific take-away assignments to build skills.

Counsellors as trainers require good skills in three broad areas central to most interventions: namely, *tell, show* and *do*. In Chapter 3 I mentioned that the corresponding learning modes were learning from hearing, observing and doing. In the above examples, Sophie exhibited skills deficits in the area of tell, or helping Les learn from hearing; Lee, in the area of show, or helping Tuan learn from observing; and Rod, in the area of do, or helping Barb learn from doing. You are more likely to impart lifeskills and clients are more likely to learn them if you use all three modes. When you are initially presenting a lifeskill, 'tell' may be accompanied by 'show' and then 'do'. On many occasions all three modes interact. For example, when clients rehearse skills, 'do' may be interspersed with 'show' and 'tell'. Figure 13.1 shows the interrelationships between learning from hearing, observing and doing.

Importance of the counselling relationship

Counsellors as trainers require both good counselling relationship skills and good training skills. Counsellors who possess only good relationship skills are unable to impart specific skills clearly and efficiently. For instance, person-centred counsellors operate on the assumption that all clients have lifeskills strengths latent in their repertoires that will be unblocked by empathic counselling relationships (Rogers, 1951, 1959, 1961, 1980). While such an assumption may be appropriate for some clients, it is not true for most. Imagine trying to learn how to drive a car with an instructor who only provided you with an empathic relationship. The relationship might support your learning, but would be insufficient on its own for learning the required skills. Most clients do not have sufficient skills strengths latent in repertoires so that you and they can rely on the quality of the counselling relationship alone.

The majority of clients are stuck and require more active help to provide them with the skills to move forward. Nevertheless, the counselling relationship is central to this learning process in many ways, including strengthening the working alliance, helping assessment and client self-assessment, assisting client self-exploration and experiencing

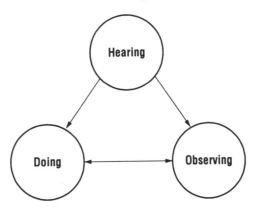

Figure 13.1 *Interrelationships between learning from hearing, observing and doing*

of feelings, providing the emotional climate for clients to take risks and look more closely at the consequences of their behaviours, and allowing clients to be open about difficulties in implementing skills. Clients are likely to gain most from counsellors who both offer good relationships and impart skills effectively. The counselling relationship supports an active approach to training and learning.

RECONNECT AND CATCH-UP SKILLS

When you meet clients for sessions in Stage 4 of the lifeskills counselling model, start by re-establishing your relationship with them. In other words, you reconnect and catch up with one another. Sessions focused on interventions are a process. For instance, you might engage in minimal small talk with clients as you usher them into your office. Then ask an open-ended question that checks 'where the client is at'. You deliberately give some control of the content of the first part of the session to clients. Sample opening questions are:

'How's your week been?'

'How have you been getting on?'

'Is there anything you would like to share?'

'What's on your mind today?'

'Where would you like to start today?'

When the client responds, use active listening skills to show your understanding. Use questioning skills to show your interest and elicit relevant information.

Why do I advocate such a 'softly, softly' approach to starting post-initial sessions? First, you need to re-establish that you offer person-to-person relationships. Clients' views and agendas are important and to be treated with respect. Second, you re-establish your influence base as a rewarding person for clients. Third, right from the start you encourage clients' active participation by valuing their contribution. Fourth, you allow clients the psychological safety and space to bring you up to date with information that they select as important to them. By not 'pushing your agenda', you avoid talking over or suppressing significant events that they may wish to share with you. Fifth, you allow the opportunity for amending the session's agenda in the light of new information provided by clients. Sixth, you help to create safe emotional climates for subsequent more focused work on developing specific lifeskills. Seventh, you minimize the chance of resistances through clients feeling unheard and misunderstood.

Once you have allowed clients some initial session space, you may still require further information to help you assess their progress regarding specific skills and take-away assignments. As appropriate, you can ask additional questions pinpointing feelings, physical reactions, thoughts, actions and interactive patterns to illuminate the pictures already provided.

There are not easy answers to how long this reconnect and catch-up phase of post-initial sessions should last. You can err on the side of being either too abrupt or too lenient. Take into account what kind of relationship the client expects and is comfortable with (Lazarus, 1993). Assuming no significant new developments or crises, a rough guide is to spend the first five to ten minutes of 45- to 50-minute sessions on this phase. However, this suggestion can be adjusted upwards or downwards as circumstances warrant. Often, in practice the dividing line between re-establishing relationships and delivering interventions becomes blurred.

ESTABLISHING SESSION AGENDA SKILLS

Near the start of each session in the interventions stage, it is generally desirable for counsellors and clients to establish agendas for the session's work. Often the best time to establish session agendas is after you have reconnected and caught up with your client. If you are working with a highly structured plan, your session agenda might be outlined in the plan. However, if you are conducting sessions with an open plan, each session requires an agenda. Agendas may be for all or part of sessions. For example, you may decide where you will work first and then, later, make another decision regarding the next agenda area. Alternatively, as part of your initial agenda-setting discussion, you may target one area to start and then agree to move on to another area. However, once session agendas are established, remain flexible so that you can respond to developments during sessions.

An issue in establishing session agendas is how client-centred or how counsellor-centred to be. I favour paying considerable attention to clients' wishes, since I want their involvement and motivation. For instance, with a client like Louise Donovan, when establishing agendas in second sessions, I might produce her assessment of deficits and statement of goals form, and say:

> 'In the last session we stated a number of goals for developing your interview skills. For instance, your thinking skills goals were to develop skills of choosing a more realistic rule about giving perfect answers, perceiving interviews and yourself more accurately and using coping self-talk. Your action skills goals were to develop your verbal, voice and body messages skills for interviews. Where would you like to work first?'

If I thought there was some important reason for starting with a particular skill, I would share this observation with clients. However, my inclination would be to allow clients the final say in where we worked. However, if necessary, I set limits: for instance, I rarely participate in long unfocused conversations.

In third and subsequent sessions, often at least part of the session agenda flows or feeds forward from previous sessions. For example, at the end of a previous session you may have broken off working on a skill and want to resume your work now. Another possibility is that you agreed on a take-away assignment that would provide information for working on a specific skill in this session. Another option is to ask the client where he or she would like to work. Still another option is to make some suggestions yourself.

SPEAKING SKILLS

In turn, I now discuss the central delivering intervention skills of tell, show and do. Whether you listen actively or train you require effective speaking skills. For instance, when listening, you require speaking skills to communicate reflections and summaries. Here I emphasize using speaking skills when training clients in specific lifeskills. Following are some occasions when you might require speaking skills.

- When offering reasons for developing a skill.

- When initially describing component parts of skills.

- When providing commentaries for skills demonstrations.

- When coaching clients as they rehearse skills.

- When answering client questions about skills.

- When negotiating take-away assignments.

Speaking skills for training are somewhat different from those for active listening. Some counselling students experience difficulty switching from the more passive role of active listening to the more active role of imparting information. You cannot feed off your clients' most recent utterances. Without overwhelming clients, communicate information as clearly and as interestingly as possible. Furthermore, remain conscious that the best learning requires clients to develop their own self-talk about how to implement skills.

Manage speech anxiety

Whether presenting to individuals or groups, counselling students may suffer from debilitating speech anxiety for three main reasons. First, as a beginner you still need time to become comfortable in your knowledge of the skill. Second, your delivering interventions skills require developing. Third, you may possess thinking skills deficits that interfere with the relaxed concentration required to present lifeskills well.

Speech anxiety has many dimensions. Feelings that may be associated with speech anxiety include tension, insecurity, vulnerability, embarrassment and confusion. Physical reactions include nausea, a dry mouth, butterflies in your stomach and your mind going blank. Verbal messages include using confused and rambling sentences. Your vocal messages may convey anxiety; for instance, too many 'uhms' and 'ers', and speaking too quickly or softly. Your body messages may be inappropriate: for instance, hair tugging, scratching or excessive smiling.

Following are some illustrative thinking skills weaknesses associated with speech anxiety even in individual counselling.

- *Owning responsibility for choosing.* You may inadequately own responsibility for working on presentation skills. You may pay considerable attention to developing counselling relationship skills without realizing the need also to develop training skills. Consequently, albeit unwittingly, you choose to ignore an important area of your development as a counsellor.

- *Getting in touch with your feelings.* You may deny or dilute your feelings of anxiety about the training aspect of counselling. This 'tuning out' may impede your working on this problem. In addition, when it comes to the more didactic aspects of counselling, you may feel vulnerable and insufficiently acknowledge any feelings of strength and competence.

- *Using coping self-talk.* You may use negative self-talk, fail to use coping self-talk or both. Negative self-talk statements include: 'I can't cope', 'I can't do anything right' and 'I feel totally confused' (Kendall and Hollon, 1989). You may fail to use the calming, coaching and affirming dimensions of coping self-talk.

- *Choosing realistic personal rules.* You may place unrealistic 'musts', 'ought' and 'shoulds' on yourself and clients: for instance, 'I must be an excellent presenter of skills immediately' or 'Clients must always understand me.'

- *Perceiving accurately.* You may overemphasize your skills deficits in presenting lifeskills and inadequately acknowledge skills strengths. You may be hyper-sensitive to any cues of negative feedback from clients.

- *Explaining cause accurately.* You may assume too much responsibility for clients' learning. You may also wrongly ascribe the causes of your speech anxiety: for instance, to your genes or to your unfortunate previous attempts to present skills to clients. Some counsellors insufficiently ascribe the cause of their anxiety about presenting lifeskills to their own lack of preparation.

- *Predicting realistically.* Counselling students may be beset by undue pessimism or undue optimism, or oscillate between the two regarding presentation skills.

- *Setting realistic goals.* If you suffer from anxiety when presenting lifeskills to clients, make overcoming this anxiety a goal. Some counsellors increase their anxiety by having unrealistic goals about what is attainable both in individual presentations and in counselling.

- *Use visualizing skills.* You may be visualizing the worst when you describe skills to clients. Negative and catastrophic imagery may interfere with competent performance. Much better is to use your imagination to rehearse and practise relaxed competence (Lazarus, 1984).

The skills you require to manage speech anxious thinking are the same skills clients require to manage their thinking skills deficits. In Chapters 14 and 15 I describe ways in which you and your clients can work to develop your thinking skills.

Prepare clear content

Clients cannot be expected to comprehend poorly presented skills, let alone know them well enough to instruct themselves once counselling ends. Many counselling students experience difficulty in explaining skills clearly. Some are aware of this, others less so. In some cases, anxiety is a factor. Unfortunately, all too often neophyte counsellors do not properly understand the skills they present. Consequently, their explanations are either muddled or clearly inaccurate. On other occasions, counsellors may understand the skills, but communicate them insufficiently clearly.

When leading training groups, counsellors may give lecturettes of five or ten minutes. Individual counselling lends itself to a more informal and interactive approach than is sometimes possible in training groups. Nevertheless, counsellors still require the skills of introducing and describing the key points of any lifeskills they impart. Systematic preparation is desirable, especially for beginners. Such preparation should not lead to rigid presentations. Rather, when clear in their own minds, often counsellors better address individual clients' needs and learning rates.

Counsellor presentations of lifeskills focus on the mechanics of how to perform a skill or sub-skill. They are not academic discourses. In addition to preparing clear content use clear language: for instance, *active listening* is better than *empathic listening*. Be concise and specific. Aim to describe skills as simply as possible, so that clients can easily describe the skills to themselves. Avoid long sentences – the language of speech uses shorter sentences than written language (Bernstein, 1988). The longer your sentences, the fewer the clients who comprehend them (Goddard, 1989).

The language of lifeskills helping is not the language of boredom. If rightly used, humour can illustrate points and make learning fun. Furthermore, humour can relax clients and lower defensiveness and resistances. However, if wrongly used, humour can divert both clients and counsellors from goals.

Consider using visual as well as aural presentation. Audiovisual aids, such as the whiteboard, may help you to present information more clearly than if it is just spoken. Think carefully about how to integrate audiovisual aids into your presentations so that they are not disruptive.

Develop delivery skills

If you prepare clear content you are only part way to introducing and describing skills effectively. You still need to put your message across. Presenting information to individuals or couples does not require the theatrical performance skills of presenting information to larger numbers. Nevertheless, even in individual counselling, your voice and body are delivery tools for holding interest, emphasizing points and enlisting motivation.

SEND EFFECTIVE VOICE MESSAGES Perhaps even more when you send messages than when you receive messages, you need to develop an awareness of your voice as a delivery tool. For better or worse, your voice messages frame your verbal messages. Let us take the VAPER acronym (Nelson-Jones, 1991) and suggest how you may use volume, articulation, pitch, emphasis and rate when you deliver content rather than respond to clients.

Volume When you are presenting skills, you are under less obligation to adjust your volume to reflect that of clients than when you are responding as a listener. Without overwhelming clients, you need to speak reasonably loudly, possibly louder than when you respond. Some counsellors may be better at being gentle listeners rather than outgoing talkers. If this is true of you, you may need to project your voice when presenting skills in individual counselling.

Articulation Clear articulation may be more important when you present than when you respond. If you enunciate poorly when sending listening responses, clients at least are able to put what you say in the context of their previous utterances. They do not have this opportunity when you present information for the first time. Instead they may be struggling to understand both delivery and content. The longer speakers talk, the more poor enunciation distracts.

Pitch Any pitch errors you possess – for instance, uncomfortable highness, lowness or narrowness of range – may be more pronounced when you present information than when you respond. One reason is that, when responding, you may modify your pitch to match your client's pitch. Another reason is that, when presenting information, you may be less conscious of pitch because you are thinking of what to say. Furthermore, you have more scope for pitch errors since you are likely to speak for longer when presenting material than when responding.

Emphasis When as a listener you use reflections, you emphasize the same words and phrases that clients emphasize. As a presenter of information you emphasize words and phrases highlighting your main points. Your use of emphasis should convey interest and commitment.

Rate As with responding, when you are describing skills speak fairly slowly. A slow, but comfortable, speech rate gives you time to think and gives clients time to comprehend. Effective use of pauses can both clarify and emphasize what you say and allow clients to ask questions. Pause errors include too many, too few, too long, too short and making extraneous sounds such as 'uhms' and 'ers'.

SEND EFFECTIVE BODY MESSAGES Sending effective body messages when describing a lifeskill is partly a matter of avoiding interfering messages and partly a matter of sending good messages. Unlike when presenting skills in training groups, in individual counselling you are likely to be seated. Many body messages for attending to clients when listening are still appropriate when delivering content: for instance, relaxed body posture, physical openness, sensitivity to physical proximity and height, appropriate clothing and grooming and appropriate facial expressions. Following are some additional suggestions for using effective body messages when you present.

Gestures Use gestures economically to help to explain what is being said. Fischer (1972) states that there are three main types of gestures: *emphatic* gestures, such as pointing the finger, designed to make it clear that what is being said is important; *descriptive* gestures, such as stretching your arms out when you say that marital partners are poles apart, designed to help illustrate your points; and *symbolic* gestures to which a commonly understood meaning has been ascribed, such as shaking your head to say no. Another broad category of gestures is that of *distracting* gestures: touching your head, scratching your nose, pulling lint off your cuff, waving your arms around, tugging your hair and so on. Learn to use gestures to work for rather than against your training messages.

Gaze and eye contact Talkers tend to use much less gaze and eye contact than listeners. Nevertheless, when presenting, you require an adequate gaze level to read clients' reactions. Present lifeskills as though you converse with clients rather than talk at them. Your use of gaze and eye contact is a most important way of relating directly to clients when making learning points. Gaze and eye contact errors include looking down too much and keeping turned away as you write on whiteboards, rather than checking client reactions.

Put content and delivery together

So far I have focused on managing speech anxiety, preparing clear content and using good voice and body message delivery skills. You may have practised long and hard to develop your active listening skills so that clients want to talk to you. Show the same conscientiousness in developing sender skills of imparting information so that clients want to hear you. An analogy may be made with effective parenting: parents not only need to listen so that their kids will talk, they also need to talk so that their kids will listen (Gordon, 1970). You may need to rehearse and practise gaining fluency in describing different lifeskills to clients. Furthermore, effective counsellors combine talking and listening skills in such a way that clients feel valued parts of the training process and not just receptacles of others' knowledge – the so-called *jug-and-mug* approach. Skilled counsellors develop emotional climates where clients are motivated to learn, ask questions and take risks.

At the risk of repetition, use speaking skills to help clients to develop self-instruction skills. Ideally, when learning new skills, clients start by being receptive to your voice in their heads. However, they then need to replace your voice with their voices. Your public speech becomes their private speech.

DEMONSTRATING SKILLS

By demonstrating skills, effective counsellors add 'show' to 'tell'. One of the main ways in which people learn is from observational learning or learning from models (Bandura, 1986). Rosenthal and Steffek (1991, p. 70) write: 'The processes by which information guides an observer (often without messages conveyed through language), so that conduct is narrowed from "random" trial-and-error toward an intended response, are collectively termed *modeling*.' In real life, much modelling is unintentional. However, counsellors can consciously promote observational learning of desired skills and sub-skills. I prefer the more everyday word *demonstrating* to modelling.

Goals for demonstrating

Demonstrating may be used to initiate new skills strengths, develop existing skills strengths, disinhibit existing skills strengths, and inhibit and weaken existing skills deficits. Goals for demonstrating and observational learning can be viewed in the following categories.

THINKING SKILLS Thinking skills include using coping self-talk, choosing realistic rules and perceiving accurately.

> Naomi, a human relations consultant, works with Vince on his public speaking skills. As part of her plan, she aims to train Vince to use coping rather than negative self-talk before, during and after speaking situations. Naomi demonstrates coping self-talk by verbally giving examples of appropriate coping self-talk statements and also by giving Vince a handout with examples of public speaking coping self-talk statements.

ACTION SKILLS Action skills demonstrations focus on observable behaviours. In action skills demonstrations, counsellors emphasize voice and body as well as verbal messages.

> Naomi and Vince have working sub-goals to develop Vince's public speaking delivery skills by: (a) speaking at a comfortable rather than a rapid rate; (b) being easy to hear rather than too quiet; (c) making good gaze and eye contact with his audience; and (d) using gestures to emphasize points. Naomi demonstrates one skill at a time, then coaches and rehearses Vince in it before moving on to the next skill. Ultimately Naomi demonstrates and coaches Vince in all four skills together. Naomi also

> encourages Vince either to audio-record or, if possible, to video-record his own competent performance of the skills so he can use himself as a model in future. In addition, she encourages Vince to observe good public speakers and assess how they use the targeted skills.

ACTION SKILLS WITH ACCOMPANYING SELF-TALK Here the demonstrator focuses both on action skills and on accompanying self-instructions.

> To speak effectively in public, Vince needs to combine both thinking and action skills. Naomi demonstrates to Vince in slow motion how he can use calming and coaching self-instructions when speaking. Naomi's demonstration intersperses 'think aloud' self-instructions with demonstrating action skills.

Methods of demonstration

Counsellors have many options when presenting demonstrations. These options, which are not mutually exclusive, are summarized in Table 13.1.

WRITTEN Thinking skills in particular lend themselves to written demonstration. Counsellors can demonstrate thinking skills on whiteboards and clients can record these examples on take-away sheets. Counsellors can also demonstrate lifeskills through the written page – be it handouts or passages in books and training manuals. Written demonstrations can be supplemented by visual images such as cartoons. Written demonstrations can be easily stored and retrieved by counsellors and clients. Furthermore, written examples can introduce subsequent written or live exercises.

LIVE Probably most counselling demonstrations are live. Counsellors may demonstrate live when initially presenting skills, when coaching clients afterwards and when

Table 13.1 *Methods of demonstrating lifeskills*

Methods of demonstrating lifeskills	Skills Areas		
	Thinking skills	Action skills	Action skills plus self-talk
Written demonstration	✓	Difficult	Difficult
Live demonstration	✓	✓	✓
Pre-recorded demonstration	✓	✓	✓
Visualized demonstration	Less suitable	✓	✓

working with current material that clients bring into later sessions. Live demonstrations have the advantage of here-and-now communication. Clients can receive verbal, voice and body messages as they occur. You can interact with clients and, if appropriate, show different or simpler ways to enact skills.

Live demonstrations have limitations as well as advantages. Unless demonstrations are recorded, clients have no copies to listen to or watch on their own. Another limitation is that in live demonstrations it can be difficult to portray scenes involving more than one or two persons.

A variation of live demonstration is to encourage clients to observe good and poor demonstrators of targeted skills in their everyday lives. For instance, clients with public speaking problems can monitor the skills of good and poor public speakers. Clients with difficulty initiating contact with others can look out for how socially skilled people do this. Clients with poor parenting skills can be asked to observe parents they admire.

RECORDED Recorded demonstrations can use audio-cassettes and video-tapes. Audio-cassettes and video-tapes can either be integral parts of initial skills demonstrations or used for take-away assignments. Advantages of audio-cassette and video-tape demonstrations include that they can be reproduced and loaned to clients, and they lend themselves to playback and to repeated listening or viewing.

Audio-cassettes are particulary useful for demonstrating thinking skills. With audio-cassettes as contrasted to video-tapes, clients can be taken through the sequences of choices entailed in targeted skills without visual distractions. Initial audio-cassette demonstrations of thinking skills are best done by counsellors. It is unreasonable to expect clients to demonstrate skills that they do not properly understand. However, later in the learning process, counsellors can assist clients to make up their own demonstration cassettes. If clients switch to using themselves as demonstrators during counselling, they may be more likely to maintain skills afterwards. Clients probably require repeated listenings to their demonstrations for the thinking skills to become part of their everyday repertoires (Ellis, 1987). Disadvantages of audio-cassette demonstrations are that they are not always as spontaneous as live demonstrations and that they may be insufficiently geared to individual clients' needs. Often a combination of audio-cassette, written and live demonstration is the most effective way to impart thinking skills.

A major advantage of video-tape demonstration over audio-cassette demonstration is that clients observe body messages. During sessions you can use video-tapes to demonstrate action skills: for instance, excerpts of how to make an assertive request for a behaviour change, demonstrate attention and interest when listening, or answer questions at job interviews. Clients may also self-administer demonstration video-tapes without counsellors present (Webster-Stratton *et al.*, 1989). Many lifeskills training video-tapes are already on the market. However, commercial video-tapes may not suit your needs. If you make your own demonstration video-tapes, you have the choice of whether or not to bring in outside resources.

VISUALIZED Visualized demonstration is sometimes called covert modelling (Cautela, 1976; Cormier and Cormier, 1991; Kazdin, 1994). Counsellors ask clients to visualize or imagine the demonstration scenes that they describe. Depending on the instructions, clients visualize either themselves or persons similar to themselves demonstrating targeted action skills. Visualized demonstration has the advantage of flexibility. Different situations can be readily presented to clients' imaginations depending on their needs and how fast they learn. Clients can follow up visualized demonstration in counselling sessions with visualized demonstration and rehearsal at home. Visualized demonstration has potential disadvantages. It is only appropriate for clients who can visualize scenes adequately. Moreover, clients never actually see skills demonstrated. Consequently, even when instructions are well given, there may be important gaps between what you describe and what clients imagine.

In general, clients visualize best when relaxed (Kazdin, 1976). Counsellors can develop different visualized demonstrations around targeted skills. For instance, visualizations may be graduated by threat or difficulty. In addition, clients can visualize themselves coping with different consequences when using targeted skills.

Demonstrator skills

Beyond speaking well, the following are some demonstrator skills. Prepare adequately. Even live demonstrations require adequate preparation. You must know your material thoroughly to integrate good demonstrations into skills presentations. Pay attention to characteristics of the demonstration and not just of the demonstrator. One issue is whether to demonstrate incorrect as well as correct behaviours. You may plan briefly to demonstrate negative behaviours as a way of highlighting positive ones. However, make sure not to confuse clients and always have the major emphasis on correct rather than incorrect skills.

Take care how you introduce demonstrations. Your initial demonstration of a skill is likely to be part of a 'tell', 'show', 'do' sequence. You may increase clients' attention by telling them what to look out for and also informing them that afterwards they will perform demonstrated behaviours (Perry and Furukawa, 1986).

During and at the end you may ask clients whether they understand the points you demonstrate. Also, clients can summarize the main points of demonstrations. Research suggests that observers actively summarizing the main points of demonstrations are better able to learn and retain this information (Bandura et al., 1966; Perry and Furukawa, 1986). Probably, the best way to check clients' learning is to observe and coach them as they perform demonstrated behaviours.

COACHING SKILLS

Here I focus on coaching clients to perform skills after initial presentations. Learning from hearing and observing must be translated into learning from doing. I have listened to the supervision tapes of many counselling students who describe and demonstrate thinking and action skills, but then omit to coach clients in how to perform them. Following are some counsellor skills for coaching clients in lifeskills.

BALANCE DIDACTIC AND FACILITATIVE COACHING In *didactic* coaching, counsel-lors give a series of explicit instructions to clients on how to perform skills. The counsellor's comments take the form: 'First you do this, then you do that, then you do that' and so on. The counsellor is the expert taking clients through sequences of performance choices.

In *facilitative* coaching, counsellors have two important objectives: first, to draw out and build upon clients' existing knowledge and skills; second, to help them to acquire the skills of self-coaching. Counsellor comments may include: 'I'm going to ask you to perform the skill now and then get you to evaluate your performance. Afterwards, I'll give you some feedback too', and 'How did you think you went in that practice?'

When coaching, counsellors require both facilitative and didactic skills. For example, counsellors might start with trying to build on the existing knowledge and skills of learners, but then intersperse didactic instructions when clients go badly wrong. Didactic coaching alone can produce resistances. Coaching without using facilitative skills lessens the likelihood of targeted skills being owned and integrated into clients' daily routines.

GIVE CLEAR INSTRUCTIONS Include clear instructions for coached performance in your initial presentations and demonstrations of skills. When coaching, you may need to give specific instructions, tips and prompts that build targeted skills (Karoly and Harris, 1986). Coaching should always emphasize ways in which clients can help themselves: for instance, by translating clear instructions into clear self-instructions.

BREAK TASKS DOWN AND CONSIDER NUMBER OF TRIALS When initially getting clients to perform them, you may decide to break skills and sub-skills down. Consider how much clients can assimilate in each learning trial. For example, with a teenager wishing to return a defective compact disc to a shop, one trial might focus on verbal messages, another on voice messages, another on body messages and another on putting it all together. Another way of breaking learning trials down is to include graded steps. Here you coach clients in using targeted skills in progressively more difficult situations. With or without graded steps, clients may require many coached attempts before performing skills competently within, let alone outside, helping ses-sions.

USE BEHAVIOUR REHEARSAL AND ROLE-PLAY By definition, when you coach you also rehearse clients in targeted skills. Behaviour rehearsal and role-play are not always the same. Clients can rehearse action skills on their own without role-plays: for instance, rehearsing relaxation skills. They can mentally rehearse thinking skills and visually rehearse action skills plus accompanying self-talk. Role-plays are especially useful for rehearsing action skills. Behaviour rehearsal and role-play skills are covered in more detail in Chapter 16.

USE FEEDBACK SKILLS When coaching, counsellors are managers of feedback. Follow-ing are some feedback dimensions to bear in mind (Egan, 1994; Gazda, 1989; Gilbert,

1978; Hopson and Scally, 1981; Kazdin, 1994; National Training Laboratory, 1967; Osipow *et al.*, 1984).

- *Client self-feedback or counsellor feedback.* Throughout, encourage clients to develop skills of monitoring and assessing their behaviour and its consequences for self and others. As a guideline, after each behaviour rehearsal, clients should be the first to comment on their learnings and reactions to their performance. Nevertheless, your feedback is still essential because of your special knowledge of targeted skills.

- *'I' message or 'you' message feedback.* Take responsibility for your feedback and send, or at least imply, 'I' messages. For example, 'Tim, I think Jeremy would appreciate your request for a date more if your voice were louder' is different from 'Your voice should have been louder when asking Jeremy for a date.' However, Tim might still have received the latter statement as an 'I' message if you had established the ground rule that your feedback always represented perception rather than fact and was open for discussion.

- *Specific or non-specific feedback.* Feedback should always be specific and concentrate on targeted actions. For instance, in the previous example, suggesting to Tim that his voice might be louder is far preferable to telling him his voice quality is poor.

- *Verbal or demonstrated feedback.* Feedback may be given largely by means of words. Often, however, you may communicate feedback even more clearly if you accompany verbal description with demonstration. For instance, in the Tim and Jeremy example, you could demonstrate Tim's present voice loudness and then demonstrate a more appropriate loudness.

- *Confirmatory or corrective feedback.* Feedback can be confirmatory or corrective. Confirmatory feedback reinforces correct behaviours, whereas corrective feedback lets clients know which specific behaviours require altering and in what ways. Much feedback is both confirmatory and corrective: for example, 'Tim, when you asked Jeremy to go out I thought that you gave a good verbal "I" message (confirmatory), but that your voice was too quiet' (corrective). Persistent corrective feedback, without some confirmatory feedback, can weaken clients' motivation to work and change.

- *Audiovisual feedback.* Cassette feedback may be especially useful when helpers coach verbal messages, voice messages and thinking skills. Putting how clients think on whiteboards can provide useful visual feedback since it highlights clients' thought processes. Video-tape feedback is especially beneficial when counsellors coach body messages. Audiovisual feedback lends itself to client self-assessment. Furthermore, it provides a factual basis for counsellor–client discussions.

- *Feedback or reward.* You may provide feedback in the form of reward. You can say 'good' or 'well done' in response to specific behaviours that clients implement well. You can use non-verbal forms of reward such as head nods and smiles. However, beware of clients only performing targeted behaviours under conditions of external reward rather than self-reward.

- *Verbal or non-verbal feedback.* Much feedback, for good or ill, is non-verbal. Uninterested looks and voice messages can greatly interfere with good verbal coaching messages. Conversely, good voice and body messages when you are giving feedback increase the likelihood of clients receiving the verbal message positively. Whether or not you speak, show interest when clients perform demonstrated skills.

- *Cultural feedback considerations.* Counsellors coming from different cultural backgrounds to clients require sensitivity to differences in cultural rules concerning giving and receiving feedback. You can give clients permission to relate how feedback is handled in their cultures.

NEGOTIATING TAKE-AWAY ASSIGNMENT SKILLS

After presenting, demonstrating and coaching clients in new skills, counsellors can negotiate relevant between-session take-away assignments. Many reasons exist for assigning such tasks (Cormier and Cormier, 1991; Egan, 1994; Hutchins and Cole, 1992). These reasons include: speeding up the learning process; encouraging clients to monitor, rehearse and practise skills; helping the transfer of trained skills to outside life; finding out about difficulties in using skills in real life; and increasing the client's sense of self-control and of personal responsibility for developing targeted skills.

Following are some central skills for negotiating take-away assignments. These skills can increase the chances of clients complying to do agreed-upon activities.

OFFER REASONS FOR ASSIGNMENTS Counsellors can often enhance clients' motivation for completing take-away assignments if they explain their importance. At the start of tell, show and do sequences, you can introduce the idea of outside counselling practice.

> 'Now, Gill, first I am going to describe ... (specify which) skills, then I am going to demonstrate it for you, then I am going to coach you in it, and then, if agreeable, we will discuss some ways to practise your ... (specify which) skills in real life. To gain competence in developing any skill requires practice.'

NEGOTIATE REALISTIC ASSIGNMENTS I use the word negotiate to highlight the importance of client participation in take-away assignment decisions. I assume that clients are more likely to comply with assignments that they have had a say in designing. Following are three key aspects of realistic assignments. First, such assignments either consolidate earlier learning or set the stage for the learning activities of the next

LIFESKILLS COUNSELLING
TAKE-AWAY SHEET

Figure 13.2 *Standard lifeskills counselling take-away sheet*

session. Do not introduce any new skills and ideas that clients will have insufficient time to assimilate before the session ends.

Second, the assignments are of appropriate difficulty. The tasks take into account clients' understanding of and readiness to perform targeted skills. Where appropriate, suggest graded steps. Third, the amount of work entailed in the assignments is realistic for the client's circumstances and motivation. It is preferable for clients to make a definite commitment to a small amount of homework than to make a vague commitment to a larger amount. Encourage clients to view homework in terms of learning contracts not just to you but, more importantly, to themselves (Wehrenberg, 1988).

GIVE CLEAR INSTRUCTIONS IN TAKE-AWAY FORM How can clients know precisely what to do? What, when, how often, and how recorded are each pertinent questions. Sometimes clients have already received handouts summarizing the main learning points of a skill. Where possible, give instructions in take-away form. I use a standard lifeskills counselling take-away sheet (Figure 13.2). You may either fill out the form yourself or supervise clients as they do this. If you require clients to fill out forms such as monitoring logs, specific worksheets and thinksheets and homework record logs, provide these forms yourself. This practice ensures clear instructions and saves clients writing out forms before filling them in – an activity sometimes too difficult to do and too easy to avoid.

ANTICIPATE DIFFICULTIES AND SETBACKS Explore with clients their motivation for completing take-away assignments. Where possible, identify and help clients to work through resistances. Also identify rewards for completing assignments. If you have negotiated realistic amounts, it is likely that clients will comply. Sometimes, implementing a skill requires asking clients to give up long-established habits. Here, it can be especially important not to assign too difficult an assignment too soon. Some clients return to unsupportive, if not downright hostile, environments. Here you may need to prepare clients more thoroughly prior to suggesting that they implement targeted skills in real-life settings. Such preparation is likely to include devising strategies for coping with negative feedback.

SIGNAL A JOINT PROGRESS REVIEW Let clients know that at or around the start of the next session, together you will review progress with assignments. In your reconnect and catch-up periods at the start of subsequent sessions, remember to ask clients how they fared.

ENDING SESSION SKILLS

This section focuses on ending sessions in the interventions stage of the lifeskills counselling model. My assumption is that the counselling process will continue for at least one more session and, possibly, many more sessions. You have a number of tasks when ending sessions in Stage 4 of the DASIE model. A useful ending skill is to plan sessions so that you can end promptly. Develop a norm or rule with clients that sessions end on time. If you are rigorous over time-keeping, you encourage clients to take full advantage of available time. You also protect subsequent clients from delayed appointments. In addition, ending sessions promptly provides you with the opportunity for note-taking or 'having a breather' before your next client.

Often, especially if you remember time limits, you can finish intended interventions by the end of sessions. On other occasions, you may start an intervention knowing that you will have to break it off and resume it again in the next session. Whether finishing interventions or breaking them off, do this smoothly so as to maximize clients' learning. For example, rather than end abruptly, you can signal, say five to ten minutes in advance, that the session is coming to its close. Your signalling gives both you and the client the opportunity to address points in a relaxed manner before ending the session rather than in a rushed manner when finishing it. For example, you may want to negotiate take-away assignments or summarize the work of the session. Clients may have questions to ask or disclosures to make. Other ending session tasks include arranging the next appointment and saying goodbye.

CHAPTER HIGHLIGHTS

- *Counsellors as developmental educators require training skills. Three broad areas are central to delivering most interventions: speaking, demonstrating and coaching, or 'tell', 'show' and 'do'.*

- *Start Stage 4 intervention sessions by reconnecting and catching up with clients.*

- *Where there is no predetermined structure, counsellors require skills of establishing session agendas.*

- *Speaking skills include managing speech anxiety, preparing clear content and the delivery skills of sending good voice and body messages.*

- *Observational learning is an extremely important method of acquiring and developing applied lifeskills.*

- *Demonstrations can focus on thinking skills, action skills and action skills with accompanying self-talk.*

- *Methods of demonstration include written, live, recorded and visualized.*

- *Demonstrator skills include preparing adequately, telling clients what to look out for, checking clients' learning and summarizing.*

- *Learning from hearing and observing must be translated into learning by doing.*

- *Assist clients to become their own coaches for acquiring, maintaining and developing targeted lifeskills.*

- *Coaching skills include balancing didactic and facilitative coaching, giving clear instructions, breaking tasks down, paying attention to the number of learning trials, using behaviour rehearsal and role-play, and using feedback skills.*

- *Consolidate initial learning from inside counselling by negotiating take-away assignments for outside of counselling.*

- *Negotiating take-away assignment skills include offering reasons for assignments, negotiating realistic assignments, giving clear instructions in take-away form, anticipating difficulties and setbacks, and signalling a joint progress review.*

- *End sessions smoothly so as to maximize clients' learning. By signalling that sessions are coming to a close, you provide opportunities for clients and yourself to raise outstanding issues before, rather than when, ending.*

Note to reader

A problem for some readers may be that you do not have sufficient knowledge about interventions to do the exercises in this chapter properly. If this is the case, before doing the exercises for this chapter, read Chapters 14 to 17 which review specific interventions.

EXERCISE 13.1   DEVELOPING SPEAKING SKILLS

As appropriate, do the parts of this exercise on your own, with a partner or in a group.

Part A   Managing speech anxiety
1. If you suffer from any level of debilitating speech anxiety when counselling, assess the contribution of skills deficits you may have in each of the following thinking skills areas.

   (a) owning responsibility for choosing
   (b) getting in touch with your feelings
   (c) using coping self-talk
   (d) choosing realistic personal rules
   (e) perceiving accurately
   (f) explaining cause accurately
   (g) predicting realistically
   (h) setting realistic goals
   (i) using visualizing skills

2.   Make a plan to develop your thinking skills in each of the areas you have targeted as in need of change.

Part B   Preparing clear content

Choose a skill or sub-skill to present to a client. Thoroughly prepare the content of your initial presentation of the skill. Pay attention to the following guidelines:

*   know your material;

*   outline your presentation;

*   use appropriate language;

*   where appropriate, use humour;

*   consider using the whiteboard.

Part C   Developing delivery skills

1.   Either on your own or with a partner acting as client, practice your voice message delivery skills as you present your content. Pay attention to your:

*   volume
*   articulation
*   pitch
*   emphasis
*   rate

If possible, obtain feedback from audio-recording your efforts and from your client.

2.   Either on your own or with a partner acting as client, practise your body message skills as you present your content. Pay attention to your:

*   gestures
*   facial expressions
*   posture
*   gaze and eye contact

If possible, obtain feedback from video-recording your efforts and from your client.

Part D   Putting content and delivery together

Practise your speaking skills as you give initial descriptions of skills to partners who act as clients. Focus on:

*   managing speech anxiety;

*   preparing clear content;

- using appropriate audio-visual aids;

- sending effective voice messages;

- sending effective body messages.

Playing back audio-recordings or video-recordings of how you perform may assist learning.

EXERCISE 13.2   DEVELOPING DEMONSTRATING SKILLS

As appropriate, do the parts of this exercise on your own, with a partner or in a group.

Part A   Demonstrating a thinking skill
Work through those parts of the following sequence that you find useful.

1. *Write out a demonstration.* Think of a specific thinking skill or sub-skill you might like to demonstrate to a client. Write out an instructional handout for your chosen thinking skill or sub-skill in which you:

    - state the targeted skill;
    - identify the key learning points to observe in your demonstration;
    - provide one or more demonstrations of the targeted thinking skill or sub-skill.

2. *Record a demonstration.* Either for the thinking skill or sub-skill you worked on above or for another thinking skill or sub-skill, make a demonstration cassette in which you:

    - state the targeted skill;
    - identify the key learning points to observe;
    - provide one or more demonstrations.

Before making your recording, develop a script (or use the script from section 1) and then rehearse it using either your own or someone else's voice(s). When ready, audio-record your script, play back your cassette, and modify it as many times as necessary to attain a polished performance. Think through how you might incorporate a recorded cassette demonstration into your overall presentation of your chosen thinking skill or sub-skill.

3. *Demonstrate live.* Work with a partner. Either for a thinking skill or sub-skill for which you prepared a script above or for another thinking skill or sub-skill,

rehearse and give a live demonstration. Afterwards obtain feedback from your partner on the effectiveness of your demonstration.

Assess the main advantages and disadvantages, when initially presenting lifeskills, of live, written and recorded thinking skills demonstrations.

Part B   Demonstrating an action skill
Work through those parts of the following sequence that you find useful.

1. *Video-record a demonstration.* Think of a specific action skill or sub-skill that you might want to demonstrate to a client. Make up a video-tape demonstration that focuses on the verbal, voice and body message dimensions of your chosen skill or sub-skill. You may make your video-tape either with one demonstrator (probably yourself) or with two demonstrators using dialogue. Perform the following tasks:

    •   set clear verbal, voice and body message goals for your demonstration video-tape;
    •   develop a brief script that indicates the verbal skills you want to convey – in the margin indicate appropriate voice and body messages;
    •   if appropriate, coach and rehearse your demonstrator(s) in the verbal, voice and body aspects of your demonstration;
    •   make at least one pilot video-tape and then, if necessary, keep altering and re-recording your demonstration until satisfied with it.

Indicate how you might incorporate instructions in your video-tape demonstration so that clients know what to observe: for instance, will you pre-record instructions?

2. *Demonstrate live.* Work with a partner. Either for the action skill or sub-skill that you worked on above or for another action skill or sub-skill, rehearse and give a live demonstration either with or to your partner. Afterwards, obtain feedback from your partner.

3. *Use visualized demonstration.* Work with a partner. Either for an action skill or sub-skill that you have worked on above or for another action skill or sub-skill, give a visualized demonstration. Perform the following tasks:

    •   Develop a visualized demonstration involving an interaction between two people. The demonstration should contain three elements: (a) set the scene; (b) describe the appropriate action skill(s); (c) depict favourable consequences for using the action skill.
    •   Rehearse your visualized demonstration.
    •   Ask your partner to visualize your scene as you describe it. Afterwards get feedback regarding how realistic he or she found your demonstration.

Part C   Demonstrating an action skill with accompanying self-talk
Rehearse and practise a live demonstration in which the demonstrator talks himself or herself through an action skills sequence. You may use a partner as a confederate in your demonstration.

EXERCISE 13.3   DEVELOPING COACHING SKILLS

As appropriate, do the parts of this exercise on your own, with a partner or in a group.

Part A   Considerations in coaching
Imagine that you have just given to a client a verbal presentation of a specific lifeskill or sub-skill followed by a demonstration. You are now about to coach the client in how to perform the skill. How might you take into account each of the following considerations?

- Balancing didactic and facilitative coaching

- Giving clear instructions

- Breaking tasks down

- Choosing the number of learning trials

- Using behaviour rehearsal and role-play

- Using feedback skills

Part B   Rehearsing and practising how to coach
1.   Work with a partner. Give him or her a verbal presentation that includes demonstration of a specific skill or sub-skill. Do not attempt too much. Afterwards, coach him or her to the point where, within the limits of this exercise, he or she performs the skill competently. Playing back video-tapes of your coaching efforts may enhance learning.

2.   Work with one or more partners. Repeat the exercise until you have coached another person in (a) a thinking skill, (b) an action skill and (c) an action skill plus self-talk.

EXERCISE 13.4   DEVELOPING NEGOTIATING TAKE-AWAY ASSIGNMENT SKILLS

As appropriate, do the parts of this exercise on your own, with a partner or in a group.

Part A   Considerations in negotiating take-away assignments
Imagine that you have just coached a client in a specific skill or sub-skill that you have presented and demonstrated. You are now thinking about setting the client one or more take-away assignments. How might you take into account each of the following negotiating take-away assignment considerations?

- Offering reasons for assignments
- Negotiating realistic assignments
- Giving clear instructions in take-away form
- Anticipating difficulties and setbacks
- Signalling a joint progress review

Part B   Rehearsing and practising negotiating take-away assignments
Work with a partner, possibly on a skill for which you coached him or her in Exercise 13.3. Now rehearse and practise how best to go about negotiating take-away assignments so that your client can use between-session time to good effect.

FOURTEEN

Interventions for thinking
1

There is nothing either good or bad, but thinking makes it so.

William Shakespeare

CHAPTER QUESTIONS

- *Why is it important that clients think about how they think?*

- *Why is it important that counsellors attend to feelings when focusing on thinking?*

- *What are some interventions for developing owning responsibility for choosing skills?*

- *How can counsellors help clients to understand the relationships between thinking, feeling and actions?*

- *What are some interventions for developing coping self-talk skills?*

- *What are some interventions for developing realistic personal rules skills?*

- *What are some interventions for developing perceiving accurately skills?*

INTRODUCTION

The late Abraham Maslow reportedly said that most clients were not sick, but just cognitively wrong. In other words they possessed poor thinking skills. Here is an example of such a person.

There was a young lady from York
Whose life was increasingly fraught.
Rather than thinking,
She turned to hard drinking,
With aggressive self-pity for thought.

The importance of focusing on how both counsellors and their clients think is a major theme of this book. In Chapter 8, I discussed assessing how clients think. In this chapter, I review interventions for five thinking skills: owning responsibility for choosing; understanding the relationship between how you think, feel and act; using coping self-talk; choosing realistic personal rules; and perceiving accurately. In the next chapter, I review interventions for six thinking skills: explaining cause accurately; predicting realistically; setting realistic goals; using visualizing skills; realistic decision making; and preventing and managing problems. I defer the discussion of getting in touch with your feelings, another thinking skill, to Chapter 17. My coverage of thinking skills is neither exhaustive nor in any set order of importance. Some of the skills overlap and are interrelated. Which skills you and clients focus on depends on your restatement and goals. At all times, assist clients to understand the thinking skills well enough to instruct themselves outside of counselling.

Counsellors should focus on their own as well as on their clients' thinking. Unless you develop skills at understanding and working with how you think, you risk ignorance and ineffectiveness when focusing on how your clients think. Paraphrasing the old adage 'Physician, heal thyself', 'Counsellor, think realistically yourself'.

THINKING ABOUT THINKING

Both counsellors and clients are hypothesis makers and testers who have the reflective capacity to think about how they think. Why do both counsellors and clients need to develop such skills? Unless clients can think about how they think, they risk condemning themselves to repetitive patterns of thinking skills deficits. They require the tools to take responsibility for how they think. If they develop a language categorizing different thinking skills, they can target specific skills for development.

Counsellors and clients capable of thinking about how they think are better able to define themselves and make their lives. For example, those capable of understanding how their thinking has been affected by parental and cultural rules can free themselves from unwanted 'voices in the head'. In addition, those able to think about how they think are capable of learning and instructing themselves in how to think more effectively.

ATTEND TO FEELINGS

Working with clients' thinking skills should not be an arid intellectual exercise. Always, counsellors require sensitivity to clients' and their own feelings. Following are some reasons why, when focusing on thinking, it is important to attend to feelings.

- *Assess readiness and motivation.* Counsellors need to take into account client readiness to work on thinking skills. For instance, vulnerable clients may wish to use the early phases of counselling to discharge and discuss feelings of hurt and pain. Some clients may be so anxious and distort information so badly that they may have insufficient insight to explore thinking difficulties until they are less anxious. Clients take differing lengths of time to trust counsellors. Until trust is established, they may be neither willing nor able to deal with their faulty thinking choices.

- *Elicit thoughts and feelings.* Working with clients' thinking can be a delicate process in which counsellors create safe emotional climates for clients' thoughts and feelings to emerge. Counsellors and clients collaborate in unearthing and detecting both thinking skills deficits sustaining unwanted feelings and self-defeating actions. Insufficient counsellor empathy blocks clients from experiencing, identifying and exploring their feelings and thoughts.

- *Distinguish clients' own thoughts.* Counsellors need to attend closely to clients' feelings to help them distinguish what they think from what they have been taught to think. Permit clients to articulate their thoughts and, where necessary, support them through the pain and guilt of going against significant others' ways of thinking.

- *Acknowledge defences and resistances.* Counsellors require awareness of barriers and resistances to acknowledging and working with specific thoughts and thinking skills deficits. Frequently, clients do not readily share their worlds. You require sensitivity to the degree of threat in focusing on certain areas of clients' lives. Then, you have various options: for example, helping clients to acknowledge and work through resistances or backing off, either temporarily or permanently.

- *Check the emotional validity of thinking skills hypotheses.* Counsellor hypotheses about clients' thoughts and thinking skills deficits must have emotional validity to enlist clients' motivation for change. Clients can overtly agree, but covertly disagree, with your hypotheses. Check the emotional validity for clients of your thinking skills deficits/goals hypotheses. Furthermore, help clients to do their own work. Hypotheses that clients arrive at for themselves are more likely to feel right for them.

- *Offer support during learning, rehearsal and practice.* Attend to clients' feelings as you train them in thinking skills. Client feelings requiring attention include confusion, insecurity and disappointment: for instance, when unsuccessfully practising the skill outside counselling.

When you are working to develop clients' thinking skills, active listening skills are central. The desirable counselling relationship is one of mutual cooperation in pursuit of goals. Counsellors support clients in many ways: emotionally, facilitating exploration, helping them to analyse information and encouraging their learning.

OWNING RESPONSIBILITY FOR CHOOSING

How can counsellors assist clients to attain the goal of owning more responsibility for being choosers in their lives? Four dimensions of owning responsibility for choosing are choice awareness, responsibility awareness, existential awareness and feelings awareness. Choice awareness consists of awareness of the fact that people are always choosers in their lives, even in relation to suffering and genuinely adverse external circumstances: for instance, poverty, racial discrimination or concentration camp internment (Frank, 1959). Responsibility awareness entails awareness that people are responsible for making their lives through their choices. Thus clients may need to become more effective authors or architects of their lives (May and Yalom, 1995). Existential awareness consists of awareness of the existential parameters in which all humans lead their lives: for example, death, isolation, freedom and meaninglessness (Yalom, 1980). Feelings awareness entails the capacity to listen to your bodily sensations and to your inner valuing process.

Assisting clients to make better choices permeates counselling. Clients may resist owning responsibility for choosing. Sometimes these resistances are very deep-rooted. Below are some suggestions for helping clients to become more responsible for their choices.

RAISE CONSCIOUSNESS Some clients may need to be told in simple language that they are responsible for their choices. They may require help in seeing that they can choose not only how they act, but also how they think and feel. In the past they may have taken a passive stance to life and waited for things to happen to them. You can encourage them to see that they can be active agents in shaping their lives.

ENCOURAGE CHOICE LANGUAGE Counsellors can assist clients to become more aware of how their use of language restricts their choices. You can encourage: sending 'I' messages, using verbs that acknowledge choice (for example, 'I won't' rather that 'I can't'); and avoiding static self-labelling (for example, 'I choose to be a poor letter writer' rather than 'I am a poor letter writer').

Borrowing from reality therapy, you can use active language to describe feelings. For instance, clients are not depressed but 'depress-ing'. Other active language terms for feelings include: 'anxiety-ing', 'guilting', 'phobicing', 'compulsing', 'headach-ing' and 'sick-ing'. Glasser and Wubbolding (1995, p. 302) observe: 'To reframe such phenomena from conditions to behaviours is to see them as more controllable.' Active rather than static language encourages clients to own responsibility for either sustaining or ameliorating unwanted feelings.

FACILITATE EXPLORING CHOICES Skilled counsellors assist clients in exploring choices and their consequences. Always clients are choosers. Spending time exploring choices is valuable for developing their skills of owning responsibility for their choices.

Be careful not to make clients' choices for them, but assist them in choosing for themselves.

EXPLORE OPPOSITES You may help some clients to become more aware of their capacity for choice by getting them to explore opposite ways of thinking and behaving. For example: 'Think of someone who makes you feel angry. Now imagine yourself going out of your way to do something to make that person happy. How might he or she react?' Sometimes clients can gain insight into choices sustaining their problems by exploring opposite ways of viewing the same problems.

CHALLENGE NOT ACKNOWLEDGING CHOICE Clients may make statements like 'I had no choice but to ... ' You can either challenge such statements or help clients to challenge themselves. Not only challenge clients with how they restrict choice, but help them to explore the consequences for themselves and others of this behaviour. Sometimes clients insufficiently acknowledge that they have choices. Here you may need to strengthen clients' perceptions and will to be choosers: for instance, in regard to resisting peer group pressure.

CHALLENGE EXTERNALIZING All clients and counsellors, in varying degrees, externalize thoughts, feelings, actions and responsibility for problems on to others. Looking at others' shortcomings is easier than looking at our own. Skilled counsellors resist colluding with clients who consistently see themselves as the victims of others' persecution. Use both challenging and active listening skills in assisting clients to look at their own behaviour and choices.

EXPLORE DEFENCES Counsellors can assist clients to acknowledge and become aware of the impact of any characteristic 'security operations' or 'defensive processes' they possess (Arlow, 1995; Clark, 1991; Freud, 1936; Sullivan, 1953). Defensive processes diminish choice awareness in the interest of making life more psychologically comfortable in the short term. Illustrative defensive processes include denying or distorting information, rationalizing or making excuses while unawares, and projecting unwanted aspects of yourself on to others. Assisting exploration of defences requires skill and caution. Clients' defences alleviate their anxiety and may protect highly sensitive areas.

RAISE CONSCIOUSNESS CONCERNING DEATH, DYING AND FINITENESS Counsellors may assist some clients by increasing their death awareness (Feifel, 1990; Yalom, 1980; May and Yalom, 1995). Relevant interventions include: (1) assisting clients in imagining the process of dying and their own deaths; (2) encouraging clients to write their own obituaries; (3) facilitating clients in reminiscing about their contacts with dying people and with death; and (4) encouraging clients to make contact with dying people: for instance, by visiting hospices.

UNDERSTANDING THE RELATIONSHIPS BETWEEN HOW YOU THINK, FEEL AND ACT

How can counsellors assist clients to become more aware of the relationships between how they think, feel and act? Ellis (1962, 1991, 1995) developed an ABC framework for thinking about thinking: A represents the activating event; B, a person's rational and/or irrational beliefs about the activating event; and C, the emotional and behavioural consequences of both A and B. Ellis reckons that much of the time people are only aware of what happens at points A and C. However, what happens at point C is mediated by beliefs at point B.

The STC framework extends Ellis's ABC framework by allowing more room for other thoughts than beliefs and by incorporating skills language (Nelson-Jones, 1996b). The STC framework applies to specific problematic situations.

S   The situation.
T   Your thoughts and images relating to the situation.
C   Your feelings, physical reactions and actions that are the consequences of both S and T.

One way of introducing the STC framework is by general examples. For instance, you can ask clients to imagine the situation of someone treading on their toe (S), and then assess how their feelings, physical reactions and actions consequences (C) might differ if they thought the action was either hostile or unintentional (T). Another example is the sharp noise of a window banging at night (S). How might the client's feelings, physical reactions and actions differ (C), depending on whether he or she thought the noise resulted either from a burglar entering the house or from a failure to shut the window properly before going to bed (T)?

Another option is to take a specific example from clients' lives and put it in the STC framework. Here I would use the whiteboard. Daniel, 15, gets very nervous before telephoning girls to ask for a date. In this example, Daniel is thinking of phoning Charlotte. Together Daniel and his counsellor might create on the whiteboard the following STC to depict his current thinking.

S   Phoning Charlotte for a date.
T(1)   'I'm going to screw up.' 'I'm no good at this.'
C(1)   High anxiety, sweaty palms, stammering and hesitant speech when phoning.

The counsellor might work with Daniel to identify some more constructive thinking at T and then ask what consequences this might have for him at C. The S on the whiteboard remains the same, but now the original T and C are replaced with revised Ts and Cs.

S   Phoning Charlotte for a date.
T(2)   Calm down. Speak slowly and clearly. Though I like Charlotte, she is not the only girl in the world.
C(2)   Manageable anxiety, no sweaty palms, clear and calm speech.

Counsellors can assist clients to see that unwanted feelings and self-defeating actions can be signals to alter how they think. For instance, Daniel can be helped to see that once he starts feeling anxious, he can substitute his self-empowering for his self-destructive thinking. Even more elegant is for clients to learn the self-helping skill of identifying the specific thinking skills they can use to prevent and manage problematic situations in future. Here the T in STC stands for thinking skills rather than just thoughts (Nelson-Jones, 1996b).

USING COPING SELF-TALK

Counsellors skilled at training clients in coping self-talk possess an intervention applicable to most of them. Meichenbaum and others have trained many groups of clients in coping self-talk. Targeted problems include managing anger, managing stress, being creative, curbing impulsiveness, managing pain, and controlling weight (Meichenbaum 1977, 1983, 1985; Meichenbaum and Deffenbacher, 1988). One way to help clients understand that they engage in self-talk is to ask them to close their eyes for 30 seconds and think of nothing. Most become highly aware that they cannot rid themselves of self-talk.

Let us assume that you and a client have targeted developing coping self-talk skills to manage a particular situation as one of your counselling goals. When you come to intervene, what can you do?

Highlight negative self-talk

As part of your assessment you may have noted or elicited negative self-talk statements by the client regarding a particular situation. You can retrieve these statements from your notes. For example, Val, 56, the client mentioned in Chapter 8 with public speaking anxiety, used the following negative self-talk statements in the 30 to 60 seconds before she was due to speak:

'Don't be so stupid.'

'My anxiety may get out of control like two years ago.'

'I may have a heart attack.'

You can work with your client, using the whiteboard, to identify further negative self-talk statements that engender anxiety and/or disrupt performance in the specific situation you have targeted. Use the STC framework to emphasize the consequences of using negative self-talk.

Educate clients about coping self-talk

Educate clients about the skill of coping self-talk. Below is an example of the kind of statement introducing the skill of coping self-talk to a client like Val.

'Coping self-talk is a useful thinking skill for managing public speaking anxiety. The idea is that during your waking hours you continuously engage in an internal dialogue, or perform self-talk. The goals of coping self-talk are to calm your anxieties and to help you deal effectively with the task at hand. Thus, coping self-talk contains three major elements: calming, coaching and affirming. Coping self-talk is about coping or "doing as well as I can" rather than about mastery or "being perfect" and "having no anxiety". Coping is a much more realistic goal than mastery. You can use coping self-talk before, during and after public speaking.'

Point out to clients that calming, coaching and affirming statements tend to be interspersed in coping self-talk.

- *Calming statements.* Simple statements include 'keep calm', 'relax' and 'take it easy'. In addition, you can instruct yourself to 'take a deep breath' or 'breathe slowly and regularly.'

- *Coaching statements.* One kind of coaching statement is to remind yourself of your goals. For instance, for a shy person going to a party a goal might be 'I will go up and talk to a minimum of three new people at the party.' Most coaching statements involve breaking tasks down and identifying the steps needed to attain goals. Clients then instruct themselves in the specific elements of competent behaviour.

- *Affirming statements.* Clients may have strengths and prior successes about which they can remind themselves. They can focus on support factors in specific situations. In addition, they can make statements like 'I can handle this situation.'

Elicit coping self-talk from clients

Frequently, for each category of coping self-talk, I ask clients to supply their own statements which I write on the whiteboard. Following is an example of how to do this.

Val's counsellor first put the word 'calming' on the whiteboard and then helped Val to identify statements she would find useful to calm herself down in the 30 to 60 seconds before speaking in public. The counsellor and Val repeated this process for coaching and affirming self-statements. They ended with the following categories and statements written on the whiteboard.

Calming
Calm.
It's not the end of the world.

Coaching
Rehearse my opening ideas and remarks.

No last-minute changes.
My anxiety is a signal for me to use my coping
skills.
I can retrieve mistakes.

Affirming
I've done this very well many times before.

Emphasize take-away

Following are ways whereby clients can consolidate their coping self-talk skills. First, they can write down on lifeskills counselling take-away sheets their tailor-made statements from the whiteboard. Second, counsellors can make cassettes in which they relax clients and then take them through guided imageries of competently dealing with targeted stressful situations by using their coping self-talk skills. Clients can play these cassettes as often as necessary to learn the skills thoroughly. They have the cassettes available for use in future, should they need them. Third, clients can make cue cards, or reminder cards, that they can carry with them and read just before they face their specific anxiety-evoking situations. Fourth, counsellors can set clients take-away assignments in which they seek out and practise their coping self-talk skills in real life situations.

CHOOSING REALISTIC PERSONAL RULES

The Golden Rule is that there are no golden rules.
George Bernard Shaw

Albert Ellis has been particularly prominent in highlighting the importance of realistic personal rules, or what he terms rational as contrasted with irrational beliefs (Ellis, 1962, 1980, 1995). Personal rules represent a form of self-talk, much of which goes on below conscious awareness, for judging one's own and others' behaviour. Many clients possess rules representing the internalization of others' standards rather than rules thought through by themselves. Such rules can be benign and realistic as long as they help clients to meet their preferences. However, unrealistic rules can cause clients to be tyrannized by their 'musts', which contribute to negative emotions (for instance, anger and anxiety) and self-defeating actions (for instance, withdrawal and temper tantrums).

Assist clients to identify danger signals

Counsellors can assist clients to develop the skills of identifying danger signals that they possess one or more unrealistic personal rules.

- *Attend to inappropriate feelings.* Persistent inappropriate feelings are one signal alerting clients to unrealistic personal rules. Clients can ask themselves questions like 'Is this feeling appropriate for the situation?' and 'To what extent does this feeling have unnecessary negative consequences for me?'

- *Attend to inappropriate actions.* Inappropriate feelings and actions are interrelated. Clients can ask themselves questions like 'Are my actions helping or harming me and others?', 'Am I overreacting?' and 'Is my behaviour self-defeating?'

- *Attend to inappropriate language.* Rigid personal rules are characterized by 'must' 'ought', 'should' and 'have to'. Such language signals the 'musturbatory' or demanding thinking involved in irrational beliefs or rules.

- *Look for the real agenda.* Assist clients in the skills of identifying which rules are most important. For example, it may be more important for clients whose anger at home is related to self-induced stress at work to focus on stress rules than anger rules.

Help clients to put unrealistic rules into the STC framework

Assuming adequate initial explanation, counsellors should encourage clients to do their own work rather than spoon feed them. Below are two examples of clients' rules put into the S, situation, T, thoughts, and C, feelings and action consequences, framework. The first example focuses on an unrealistic *personal* rule and the second example on an unrealistic *relationship* rule.

Ryan is a family man with two children.

S Ryan's children do not overtly show appreciation for how hard he works to support them.
T(1) I must always have my kids' approval or else I am less of a person.
C(1) Hurt, self-pity and anger. Curtness with children that creates emotional distance.

Emma and Luke are a newly married couple.

S Emma and Luke disagree over how much time to spend with the in-laws.
T(1) We must never have conflict in our marriage.
C(1) Both Emma's and Luke's negative feelings persist. The in-law issue in their relationship is not openly worked through.

Assist clients to dispute unrealistic rules

Ellis (1995) considers disputing to be the most typical and often-used method of his rational emotive behaviour therapy (REBT). Disputing means challenging unrealistic rules. An issue for counsellors is whether to dispute clients' rules or assist clients in doing their own disputing. One approach is to demonstrate the skill first, then coach clients in developing disputing skills. Take the earlier example of Ryan, whose personal rule was 'I must always have my kids' approval or else I am less of a person'. Following are questions that Ryan might ask himself or be asked.

'What evidence exists that I cannot survive without my kids' approval?'

'Does the fact that my kids do not overtly show approval for what I do mean that they do not notice it?'

'Is it realistic to expect children to be aware of what their father does for them outside the home, let alone always to appreciate it?'

'Would I expect the children of my friends to show approval in the same way that I expect my kids to, or do I have a double standard?'

'Did I always show appreciation for what my parents did for me?'

'What is it about me that may make me vulnerable to not having shows of appreciation from my kids?'

'How exactly does not having constant appreciation from my kids make me less of a person?'

Following is an example of the product of a counsellor and client working together in a session to challenge an unrealistic rule.

> Richard, the counsellor, and Louise Donovan agreed that the first item on their agenda for this particular session was to dispute her unrealistic rule for interviews that 'I must give the perfect answer.' Richard encouraged Louise to challenge her own thinking, but also gave feedback and made suggestions along the way. Sometimes, Richard's feedback was aimed at helping Louise to be more specific. Sometimes, he suggested additional challenges. Towards the end of the session, Louise and Richard formed a more realistic restatement of Louise's previous perfect answer rule. Throughout, Richard wrote on the whiteboard the information shown below. Afterwards, Louise and Richard recorded on lifeskills counselling take-away sheets all that was written on the whiteboard.

Unrealistic rule
I *must* give the perfect answer.

Challenges/disputations
In my application I've already demonstrated meticulous attention to detail, so I need to add value with human relating skills.

There is no perfect answer.

The panel at my level is more concerned about style than substance.

I may have to sacrifice detail for conciseness.

I need to keep communication two-way, but also allow each panel member to have his or her allocated time.

Pressure for perfection lowers performance.

Excessive attention to technical detail lowers perception of personal relations skills.

I'm limiting my opportunity to gain marks on other questions.

Rational/realistic restatement
I'd prefer to give highly competent technical answers, but to achieve my goals it is also very important for me to come over well as a person.

Assist clients to restate more realistic rules

As in the above example of Louise Donovan, restating means substituting more realistic for unrealistic rules. Counsellors can assist clients in understanding some of the main characteristics of realistic personal rules.

* Expressing preferences rather than demands: for example, 'I'd PREFER to do very well but I don't HAVE TO' (Sichel and Ellis, 1984, p. 1).

* Emphasizing coping rather than mastery or being perfect.

* Being based on clients' own valuing process rather than rigid internalizations of others' rules.

- Flexibility or, where appropriate, being amenable to change and updating.

- Absence of self-rating: for example, 'I am a PERSON WHO acted badly, not a BAD PERSON' (Sichel and Ellis, 1984, p. 1).

Then counsellors can assist clients to restate unrealistic into more realistic rules. Get them to do much of the work. Make sure the restatements are in clients' own language, since they have to live with their new rules. In addition to Louise Donovan, I illustrate restating with the examples of Ryan's unrealistic personal rule and Emma's and Luke's unrealistic relationship rule.

Ryan
T(1) Unrealistic personal rule: 'I must always have my kids' approval or else I am less of a person.'
T(2) Realistic personal rule: 'I would prefer to have my kids' approval much of the time. However, it is more important that I take responsibility for how well I behave to them and approve of what I do.'

Emma and Luke
T(1) Unrealistic relationship rule: 'We must never have conflict in our marriage.'
T(2) Realistic relationship rule: 'We would prefer not to have serious conflicts in our marriage. However, differences and conflicts are part of all close relationships. When faced with important relationship problems, we want to solve them cooperatively rather than avoid dealing with them.'

Emphasize take-away

Remind clients that, since they possess well-established habits of re-indoctrinating and recontaminating themselves, they need to practise challenging the same unrealistic rule again and again. If you have used the whiteboard when working together, ask clients to take down both disputations and restatements on lifeskills counselling take-away sheets. Encourage clients to remember and practise restatements of rules. Clients can prominently post reminder cards with their restated rules. Also, clients can make cassettes of their restatements and keep playing them back until they sink in. Emphasize that maintaining restated rules requires practice, practice, practice.

Counsellors can encourage clients to practise implementing their more realistic rules in real life situations. Effective thinking should lead to effective action. Psychologists differ over whether practice is best approached gradually, from the less to more difficult tasks, or 'floodingly', going straight to a difficult assignment. With either approach, encourage clients to develop relevant action skills: for instance, unappreciated Ryan might need to improve his showing affection skills. Ellis asks clients to do practice assignments repetitively and floodingly (1980, 1995). He believes that, by jumping in at the deep end over and over, clients find that their worst fears rarely materialize. Other psychologists, myself included, generally advocate a more gradual approach. For instance, I might ask a woman afraid of saying 'no' to people to say 'no' to less threatening people before repeating the behaviour with more threatening ones. Often clients do not have much choice. A difficult encounter or an imminent exam is the reality they face.

PERCEIVING ACCURATELY

Aaron Beck of the University of Pennsylvania is a prime advocate of helping clients to influence their feelings by choosing more realistic perceptions. In particular, Beck has focused on the thoughts that precede depression, anxieties and phobias and anger in relationships (Beck, 1988; Beck and Emery, 1985; Beck *et al.*, 1979; Beck and Weishaar, 1995). You can assist numerous clients with a wide range of problems to develop skills of testing the reality of their perceptions. I view Beck's approach as encouraging 'propositional thinking', in contrast to Ellis's approach, which encourages 'preferential thinking'.

Help clients to become aware of the influence of perception on feelings

Let clients know that they may have tendencies to jump to unhelpful conclusions that contribute to negative feelings. Earlier I gave examples of using the STC framework to help clients see relationships between thoughts, feelings and actions. You can also encourage clients to monitor upsetting perceptions. Ideally, they should monitor them as they happen. Clients need to develop the skill of becoming aware of the thinking that accompanies inappropriate feelings. You can get clients to set aside some time each day to monitor and record upsetting perceptions. Clients can fill in a log with the following three column headings. In the feelings column, they can rate intensity of their feelings on either a 1 to 10 or a 1 to 100 scale.

S The situation (with date and time)	T My perceptions	C My feelings

Assist clients to identify characteristic perceiving errors

Counsellors can assist clients to become aware of characteristic errors which distort how they perceive. With regard to distressed couples Beck observes: 'These cognitive distortions occur automatically, often in a fraction of a second, and the number of distortions that can take place in that short period is considerable' (Beck, 1988, p. 159). Especially under stress, clients are likely to activate their perceptual 'fault lines'. Awareness of characteristic distortions provides clients with information with which to check specific perceptions. They have a start in knowing where to look and what to avoid.

Using the STC framework, the following are some perceiving errors that clients may make at T that lead to negative feelings and action consequences at C. These perceiving errors mirror the errors for counsellors listed in Chapter 7.

- *Arbitrary inference.* Drawing conclusions without adequate supporting evidence or in the face of conflicting evidence. For instance, an unemployed man who engages in many activities yet views himself as achieving little.

- *Tunnel vision.* Focusing on only a portion of the available information in a situation rather than taking into account all significant data.

- *Magnifying and minimizing.* Seeing things as far more important or less important than they really are. For instance, magnifying minor upsets into disasters or minimizing negative events, such as viewing a relative's cancer as a cold (Beck and Weishaar, 1995).

- *Black and white thinking.* Perceiving in either/or or polarized terms: for example, 'Either I am a total success or I am a total failure.'

- *Negativeness.* Attaching negative and critical labels to yourself, and others. Over-emphasizing the negative at the expense of the positive or neutral. Going beyond a functional rating of a specific characteristic to devaluing your whole person-hood.

- *Selective inattention.* Overlooking or being inattentive to material that may generate anxiety (Sullivan, 1954). Denying and distorting information through defensive thinking.

- *Personalizing.* Perceiving causal connections to oneself on the basis on inadequate evidence: for example, 'The two people who are sitting there talking are talking about me.'

- *Overgeneralizing.* Making global comments that are probably untenable if the evidence is checked. For example, 'My daughter *never* does anything for me' and 'I *always* try to understand my employees' viewpoints.'

- *Catastrophizing.* Making catastrophic predictions: for instance, when not succeeding in making a date, 'All women are the same. I'll never find love.'

Assist clients to understand the difference between fact and inference

Clients' perceptions of themselves, others and the world are their subjective 'facts'. Often, however, they fail to realize that these perceptions may be based on inference rather than fact. A favourite illustration of this point by one of my Stanford University professors was: 'All Indians walk in single file: at least the one I saw did.' That one Indian was seen is a fact; that they all walk in single file is inference. Facts are the true data of experience; inferences are deductions and conclusions drawn from the data. Inferences are both necessary and useful as long as their assumptions are both recognized and accurately evaluated. However, all too often, clients treat inferences as facts. This deprives them of accurate information on which to base further thoughts, feelings and actions. Below is an example.

> **Fact:** Husband comes home very late from work three nights in a row.
> **Wife's inference:** He does not love me any more and has a girlfriend.

Assuming the husband had genuine reasons for staying late, which he may even have explained to her, his wife was making an erroneous inference that could have serious repercussions for their relationship. However, we don't know the husband's previous track record: this may have supported his wife's inference!

Assist clients to reality test their perceptions

Clients can be encouraged to think of thoughts as testable hypotheses capable of investigation to see how far they are supported by evidence. Beck and Weishaar (1995, p. 252) give the example of a resident who insisted 'I am not a good doctor.' Counsellor and client then listed criteria for being a good doctor. The resident then monitored his behaviour and sought feedback from supervisors and colleagues. Finally, he concluded, 'I am a good doctor after all.'

Below is another example of the importance of helping clients to reality test their perceptions.

> George, a 59-year-old unemployed client of the author's, had come for counselling severely depressed. At that time he was spending much of the day drained of energy and sitting staring into space. During a session two and a half months later, George reported that, in the previous week, he had slept during the day and gave the impression of dissatisfaction with what he was achieving. When I asked how much he was sleeping during the day, he replied '10 minutes'. At the end of the session we negotiated a take-away assignment to test the hypothesis, which I considered was undermining his confidence, that he was not doing very much with his time. At the start of the next session, George enthusiastically read out to me a long list of accomplishments and activities that he had undertaken in the previous week. By reality testing his negative thinking, he had amassed much positive evidence to the contrary. Not only did this evidence negate his 'I am not doing much' hypothesis, but it served two further functions. First, the positive evidence made George much more aware

of his tendency to depress himself through the skills deficit of arbitrarily judging his actions negatively without adequately considering the evidence. Second, the positive information George generated helped him to realize that he was well on the way back to his previous energetic level of functioning and so further contributed to his confidence and empowerment.

Sometimes the best way for clients to reality test perceptions is for them to change how they behave and then assess what happens rather than to wait for others to change. For instance, clients who complain about others can try acting more positively towards them and see if any change occurs.

Assist clients to stop, think, generate, evaluate and choose the 'best fit' perception

A man walks into a psychiatrist's office with a duck on his head.

> **Psychiatrist:** What's your problem?
> **Duck:** Can you get this man off my bum?

As the above joke shows, there is usually more than one way of perceiving a situation. Another joke, illustrating that situations can be perceived differently, is about the psychiatrist, Dr Fritz Anal-Angst, who had been using the Rorschach test when treating a sex offender. The Rorschach is a projective test, presenting ten ambiguous ink-blot pictures in succession. To each picture subjects are asked to respond saying what they see. After the test was administered, the following dialogue took place.

> **Dr Anal-Angst:** I am unable to help, but my assessment is that you are an inveterate sex pervert.
> **Sex offender:** Come off it, doc. You're the one who's been showing me the dirty pictures.

A further joke about different perceptions is based on the Freudian Oedipus complex, in which the son, in love with his mother, competes with and has murderous fantasies about his father.

> **Mum:** Oedipus, Oedipus, come back ... all is forgiven.
> **Dad:** Over my dead body.

Counsellors can assist clients to realize that they have choices in how they perceive. Help clients to check the accuracy of their information base when they become aware that they either feel and act, or are at risk of feeling and acting, in inappropriate ways. Clients can ask themselves the following kinds of questions.

'Stop ... think ... am I jumping to conclusions in how I perceive?'

'Are my perceptions based on fact or inference?'

'If based on inference, are there other ways of perceiving the situation more closely related to the facts?'

'What further information might I need to collect?'

'Does my way of perceiving this situation reflect any of my characteristic perceiving errors?'

'What perception can I choose that best fits the available facts?'

GENERATE DIFFERENT PERCEPTIONS Clients are often very poor at generating alternative ways of viewing people and situations. Below is an example in the STC framework.

S   Craig has cooked a nice dinner for his girlfriend Shannon, who is 30 minutes late.
T   Craig thinks: 'Shannon is very inconsiderate of my feelings.'
C   When Shannon finally arrives, Craig verbally attacks her and they have a row.

Tactfully suggest to Craig that he requires the skill of perceiving accurately rather than jumping to conclusions. One element of this skill is acknowledging that you have choices in how you perceive and looking for alternative perceptions. You could help him to generate alternative perceptions at T. For example: 'Shannon may have had a flat tyre', 'Shannon may have been forced to stay late at work', 'Shannon may have stopped off to buy me a present' and 'Shannon and I may not have made our arrangement clearly enough.'

EVALUATE DIFFERENT PERCEPTIONS Another element of the skill of perceiving accurately is evaluating different perceptions and choosing the 'best fit' perception. For instance, you might assist Craig in evaluating the perception that 'Shannon is very inconsiderate of my feelings.' How closely does the inference fit the facts? What is the evidence for and against this hypothesis. Then you encourage Craig to evaluate the other perceptions he has generated. Craig decides that the 'best fit' perception in this case is 'Shannon and I may not have made our arrangements clearly enough.' The feelings consequence of this perception is that Craig is not angry with Shannon. The action consequence is that Craig welcomes Shannon and they calmly talk over what went wrong.

Reframing

Reframing is a variation of the skill of generating and evaluating different perceptions and choosing the best fit perception. Either the counsellor or the client places a situation, feeling or behaviour within a different frame. Reframes should not be rationalizations. Often reframing focuses on one alternative perception rather than generating and evaluating a series of different perceptions. Counsellor-offered reframes confront clients with new ways of perceiving events. However, clients can also develop skills of generating and evaluating their own reframes. Below is an example of a counsellor offered reframe.

> **Shane:** I feel guilty that, since returning from being off work with stress problems, I'm not performing my supervising job to my full ability. I like to do as well as I can by the company.
>
> **Counsellor:** I get the impression that what you do is really important to your company and that, even though you don't feel 100 per cent, your being back at work has saved them from a lot of problems.

How can counsellors assist clients to develop reframing skills? First identify reframing as a useful self-helping skill. The concept of reframing may be easier for certain clients to grasp than that of generating and evaluating different perceptions. Second, as in the above example, use the client's material to demonstrate how to reframe. Third, where appropriate, encourage clients to suggest their own reframes: for instance, by questions such as 'Can you think of a way to reframe that?' Fourth, encourage clients to practise the skill of reframing in their daily lives. Fifth, assist clients to assess not only the consequences of individual reframes on how they feel and act, but also the longer-term consequences for developing reframing as a self-helping skill.

Emphasize take-away

Following are some ways that counsellors can enhance consolidation of perceiving accurately skills. Clients can write down on lifeskills counselling take-away sheets everything relevant put up on whiteboards during sessions. In addition, clients can listen to recordings of counselling sessions focused on training them in perceiving accurately. Furthermore, clients can do take-away assignments in which they are encouraged to produce evidence to affirm or negate their perceiving hypotheses. Clients can also complete take-away assignments focused on generating alternative perceptions and choosing the perception that best fits the available facts. In addition, counsellors can encourage clients to develop the habit of reality testing their perceptions, rather than jumping to conclusions, in their daily lives.

CHAPTER HIGHLIGHTS

- *Developing your own thinking skills is a good way to learn how to work with clients' thinking skills.*

- *When focusing on how clients think, you always require sensitivity to how they feel.*

- *Interventions for helping clients own responsibility for choosing include raising consciousness about being a chooser, encouraging choice language, facilitating exploring choices, exploring opposites, challenging not acknowledging choice and externalizing, exploring defences, and raising consciousness concerning death, dying and finiteness.*

- *Using the STC (situation, thinking, consequences) framework, counsellors can assist clients to understand the relationships between their thoughts, feelings, physical reactions and actions.*

- *In order that clients can manage specific situations better, counsellors can train them in the calming, coaching and affirming dimensions of coping self-talk.*

- *Interventions for choosing realistic personal rules emphasize assisting clients to identify unrealistic rules, put unrealistic rules into the STC framework, dispute unrealistic rules, restate unrealistic into more realistic rules and change actions along with restated rules.*

- *Interventions for helping clients perceive more accurately include assisting them to become aware of the influence of perception on feelings, identify their characteristic perceiving errors, understand the difference between fact and inference, test the reality of their perceptions, learn to stop, think, generate, evaluate and choose the 'best fit' perception, and develop reframing skills.*

EXERCISE 14.1   INTERVENING FOR OWNING RESPONSIBILITY FOR CHOOSING

As appropriate, complete parts of this exercise on your own, with a partner or in a group.

Part A   Developing your owning responsibility for choosing skills
1.   Assess your strengths and weaknesses in owning responsibility for your choices in each of the following areas.

  (a) how you feel
  (b) how you think
  (c) how you act

2.   To what extent do you consider that you are the author or architect of your life?

Part B   Assisting clients to develop skills of owning responsibility for choosing
1.   How might you incorporate, if at all, each of the following interventions into your work as a counsellor?

  (a) raising consciousness concerning being a chooser in life – for instance, by pointing this out in simple language

(b) encouraging choice language
(c) facilitating exploring choices
(d) exploring opposites
(e) challenging not acknowledging choice
(f) challenging externalizing
(g) exploring defences
(h) raising consciousness concerning death, dying and finiteness

2. Counsel a partner, who discusses an issue of concern to him or her in such a way as not fully to own responsibility for his or her choices regarding it. Become aware of when he or she does this and, where appropriate, use one or more of the above interventions to assist your client to own more responsibility for his or her choices. Afterwards, reverse roles. End by discussing some of the issues and problems in directly intervening to assist clients to own more responsibility for their choices.

EXERCISE 14.2   INTERVENING FOR UNDERSTANDING THE RELATIONSHIPS BETWEEN HOW YOU THINK, FEEL AND ACT

As appropriate, complete parts of this exercise on your own, with a partner or in a group.

Part A   Developing your using the STC framework skills
Identify a situation in your life where you think you may possess unwanted feelings and physical reactions and may act in self-defeating ways. Preferably using a whiteboard, use the STC framework to break down the relationships between how you think, feel and act.

1. **S**   What is the situation?

2. **T(1)** What are your thoughts about the situation?

3. **C(1)** What are the consequences of both the situation and your thoughts about it?

   (a) feelings consequences
   (b) physical reactions consequences
   (c) actions consequences

4. Identify the strengths and deficits of how you think (T).

   (a) strengths
   (b) deficits

5. **T(2)** What might be more realistic thoughts about the situation (S)?

6. **C(2)** What, if any, are the revised consequences of both the situation and more realistic thought about it?

    (a) feelings consequences
    (b) physical reactions consequences
    (c) action consequences

Part B   Using the STC framework to assist a client
Counsel a partner, who identifies a very specific situation in his or her life where he or she thinks he or she possesses unwanted feelings and physical reactions and acts in self-defeating ways. Preferably using a whiteboard, together use the STC framework to break down the relationships between how your 'client' thinks, feels and acts.

1. **S**   What is the situation?

2. **T(1)** What are your client's thoughts about the situation?

3. **C(1)** What are the consequences for your client of both the situation and his or her thoughts about it?

    (a) feelings consequences
    (b) physical reactions consequences
    (c) actions consequences

4. Identify the strengths and deficits of how the client thinks (T).

    (a) strengths
    (b) deficits

5. **T(2)** What might be more realistic thoughts about the situation (S)?

6. **C(2)** What, if any, are the revised consequences of both your client's situation and his or her more realistic thought about it?

    (a) feelings consequences
    (b) physical reactions consequences
    (c) action consequences

Afterwards, reverse roles.

EXERCISE 14.3   INTERVENING FOR USING COPING SELF-TALK

As appropriate, answer the parts of this exercise on your own, with a partner or in a group. If possible, use a whiteboard.

Part A   Developing your using coping self-talk skills

1.   Identify a specific situation in your life where using coping self-talk might be appropriate.

2.   Identify any negative self-talk statements you may have.

3.   Formulate at least one statement in each of the following categories.

   (a) calming self-talk
   (b) coaching self-talk
   (c) affirming self-talk
   (d) a composite statement consisting of calming, coaching and affirming self-talk

4.   How can you change how you act along with your coping self-talk?

Part B   Assisting clients to develop coping self-talk skills

Work with a partner who either uses a personal concern or role-plays a client with a working goal of developing coping self-talk skills to manage a specific situation better. Within the context of a good counselling relationship:

• use speaking skills to describe the skill of coping self-talk;

• use demonstrating skills;

• assist the client to identify any current negative self-talk;

• use coaching skills to help the client to formulate calming, coaching and affirming statements;

• use negotiating take-away assignment skills.

Afterwards, discuss and reverse roles. Playing back audio-recordings or video-recordings of rehearsal and practice sessions may assist learning.

EXERCISE 14.4   INTERVENING FOR CHOOSING REALISTIC PERSONAL RULES

As appropriate, complete parts of this exercise on your own, with a partner or in a group. If possible, use a whiteboard.

Part A   Developing your choosing realistic personal rules skills

1.   Identify a specific situation in your life where you may be hindering your effectiveness because of one or more unrealistic personal rules.

2.   Put the situation into the STC framework.
   S   The situation

T   Your unrealistic rule or rules regarding the situation
C   The consequences of both the situation and your unrealistic rule(s) regarding it

(a) feelings consequences
(b) physical reactions consequences
(c) action consequences

3.   Dispute each of your unrealistic rules.

(a) dispute unrealistic rule 1
(b) dispute unrealistic rule 2

4.   Restate each unrealistic rule into a more realistic rule.

(a) restatement of unrealistic rule 1
(b) restatement of unrealistic rule 2

5.   How can you change how you act along with your more realistic rules?

Part B   Assisting clients to develop choosing realistic personal rules skills
Work with a partner, who either uses a personal concern or role-plays a client with a goal of developing realistic personal rules skills to manage a specific situation better. Within the context of a good counselling relationship:

•   use speaking skills to describe the skill of choosing realistic personal rules;

•   use demonstrating skills;

•   cooperate with the client to identify any major unrealistic personal rule, and put the main one into the STC framework;

•   use coaching skills to assist the client to dispute the main unrealistic rule and restate it into a more realistic rule;

•   use negotiating take-away assignment skills.

Afterwards, discuss and reverse roles. Playing back audio-recordings or video-recordings of rehearsal and practice sessions may assist learning.

EXERCISE 14.5   INTERVENING FOR PERCEIVING ACCURATELY

As appropriate, complete parts of this exercise on your own, with a partner or in a group. If possible, use a whiteboard.

Part A   Developing your perceiving accurately skills

1. Identify a specific situation in your life where you may be jumping to unwarranted conclusions.

2. Monitor and record your upsetting perceptions relating to the situation by making an STC log with the column headings shown below. Fill the log out for at least the next 24 hours. Rate the intensity of your main feelings on a 1 to 10 scale.

S The situation (with date and time)	T My perceptions	C My feelings

3. To what extent does your perceiving contain any of the following errors?

    (a) arbitrary inference
    (b) tunnel vision
    (c) magnifying and minimizing
    (d) black and white thinking
    (e) negativeness
    (f) selective inattention
    (g) personalizing
    (h) overgeneralizing
    (i) catastrophizing

4. To what extent are you upsetting perceptions based on fact or inference? Pick a questionable perception and generate at least three ways of perceiving the situation differently.

    (a) alternative perception 1
    (b) alternative perception 2
    (c) alternative perception 3

5. Evaluate each of the perceptions you generated and place a star by the perception that best fits the facts.

6. If not already covered above, what might be a good way to reframe your problematic situation or some aspect of it?

Part B   Assisting clients to develop skills at perceiving accurately
Work with a partner, who either uses a personal concern or role-plays a client with a goal of developing perceiving accurately skills to manage a specific situation better. Within the context of a good counselling relationship:

• use speaking skills to describe the skill of perceiving accurately;

• use demonstrating skills;

• cooperate with the client to identify current inaccurate perceptions and their consequences;

- collaborate with your client to identify errors by which he or she distorts perceptions;

- use coaching skills to assist your client to reality test the existing evidence for a perception;

- use coaching skills to assist the client in developing stopping, thinking, generating, evaluating and choosing the 'best fit' perception skills;

- use negotiating take-away assignment skills.

Afterwards, discuss and reverse roles. Playing back audio-recordings or video-recordings of rehearsal and practice sessions may assist learning.

FIFTEEN

Interventions for thinking 2

You cannot prevent the birds of sorrow from flying over your head, but you can prevent them from building nests in your hair.

Chinese Proverb

CHAPTER QUESTIONS

- *What are some interventions for developing explaining cause skills?*

- *What are some interventions for developing predicting skills?*

- *What are some interventions for developing goal-setting skills?*

- *What are some interventions for developing visualizing skills?*

- *What are some interventions for developing decision-making skills?*

- *What are some interventions for developing preventing and managing problems skills?*

EXPLAINING CAUSE ACCURATELY

Earlier I mentioned the skill of owning responsibility for choosing. Here I elaborate on how counsellors can assist clients' motivation by helping them to explain more accurately the causes of what happens in their lives. Explanations of cause are the reasons that clients give themselves for what happens. Explanations of cause can influence how clients think about their pasts, presents and futures. They also influence how clients feel, physically react and act. Frequently, clients make explanatory errors that interfere with their motivation and effectiveness. Let us take the example of the women's movement. When women explained their lack of status as owing to male dominance, they were relatively powerless. However, when women also ascribed their lack of status to their own insufficient assertion, they empowered themselves.

Following is a more tongue-in-cheek example of an explanatory error.

> After work, a man picks up a woman at a singles bar and they go to a motel and make mad, passionate love. In the early hours of the morning the man gets up, dresses and, as he does so, takes out a piece of chalk and makes a chalk mark on his cuff. When he returns home the following dialogue takes place.
>
> **Wife:** Where on earth have you been?
> **Husband:** I cannot tell a lie . . . I cannot tell a lie. I picked up a woman, we went to a motel, and we've been making mad, passionate love all night.
> **Wife:** Liar. You've been playing snooker all night.

Assist clients to identify inaccurate explanations

Often clients' explanations of cause convert partial truths into whole truths. For instance, a partial cause of Sharon's boyfriend difficulties may be that she was rejected by her father. However, Sharon can immobilize herself from changing if she ascribes the whole cause of her difficulties to her father's past behaviour. Counsellors can use the STC framework to help clients to identify not only explanatory errors, but their negative consequences. Following are some explanatory errors for different areas.

CAUSES OF PROBLEMS Explanation of cause errors can cause clients to remain unnecessarily stuck with problems. Following are some examples.

* *It's my genes.* Though genetic endowment does limit capacities, clients also limit themselves. For instance, clients who say that they are 'naturally' lazy obscure their own roles in sustaining their laziness.

* *It's my mental illness.* The medical profession has done ordinary people a huge disservice by fostering the concept of mental illness. For most psychological problems, the explanation of mental illness overemphasizes the role of heredity and physical factors and underemphasizes the role of learning and choice.

* *It's my unfortunate past.* As shown in the example of Sharon, unfortunate pasts may contribute to problems and skills deficits. However, clients are unlikely to change unless they assume responsibility for how they sustain problems.

- *It's my poor environment.* Adverse social, economic and psychological environments may make it more difficult for clients to fulfil themselves. However, even in Nazi concentration camps, people could change and grow (Frankl, 1959).

FEELINGS OF DEPRESSION Clients' explanations of cause for positive and negative events in their lives affect their self-esteem. Following are some inaccurate explanations that may contribute to depression.

- *I am the cause of all negative events.* Clients can overemphasize their role in negative events in their own and others' lives (Beck *et al.*, 1979).

- *I am never the cause of positive events.* Clients can deny and distort their roles in positive events in their own and others' lives.

- *I am unable to act on my environment in such a way as to produce desired results.* Frequently depressed people think of themselves as powerless or helpless to influence their environments (Schulman *et al.*, 1987; Seligman, 1991; Seligman *et al.*, 1979).

RELATIONSHIP PROBLEMS Often clients require help in acknowledging their contributions to sustaining relationship problems. Following are some common explanatory errors.

- *It's all your fault.* Instead of looking at conflicts from the inside to the outside, clients view them from the outside to inside. Disliking what they see outside provides a convenient excuse for not looking at their own behaviour.

- *It's because of his or her poor personality.* The explanation of cause becomes a permanent and pervasive negative label applied to one's partner. Why should people change if they perceive themselves, despite their own best efforts, as victims of others' personality problems? One of the values of thinking in skills terms is that it encourages specificity rather than talking in vague and general terms about 'personality'.

- *You must change first.* Here clients allow their feelings, thinking and actions to be dependent on their partner's behaviour. Unwittingly clients give up some control over their lives.

- *You deliberately want to hurt and humiliate me.* Hostile explanatory or attributional bias describes a tendency to interpret the intent of others as hostile when social cues are ambiguous. Biased explanations of hostile intent can lead to increases in anger and aggression (Epps and Kendall, 1995). People explain to themselves that malicious intentions stimulate another's negative behaviour and so justify anger towards him or her. Beck (1988, p. 166) observes: 'The attribution of negative intent is a marital barometer. When spouses consistently ascribe negative motives, especially malice to one another, their relationship is troubled.' Beck acknowledges that insidious motives do occur. However, often people in distressed relationships exaggerate one another's negative motives and sanitize their own.

- *You do not love me.* A partner may say, 'If you loved me, you would not act like that.' This level of explanatory simplification can ignore interactive patterns: for instance, your unlovable behaviour may be in response to mine. It also assumes that love is a black and white phenomenon rather than an emotion difficult to define, fluctuating and frequently tinged with ambivalence. In addition, partners may fail to understand differences between them in the symbolic meaning they attach to certain behaviours: for example, remembering birthdays and anniversaries.

- *I cannot trust you.* Irrational jealousy or misplaced mistrust is a clear case of explaining cause inaccurately. Here, rather than locating the cause of insecure feelings in oneself, you externalize cause on to your partner and then punish him or her for your own disloyal fantasies.

BECOMING AND STAYING UNEMPLOYED Depending on clients' specific situations, the following explanations may be inaccurate.

- *It was my fault.* Numerous external reasons contribute to unemployment: for instance, recessions, takeovers, restructurings, downsizings and technological change. Clients may either genuinely not be responsible for their job loss or be only partially so.

- *It was their fault.* Some clients may fail to acknowledge that they may have personal and work-related skills deficits that increase the chances of their being fired.

- *The state should provide for me.* Whatever clients' political persuasions, the reality is that they are likely to receive limited welfare payments.

- *My work skills are adequate.* Clients may need to review the accuracy of this assumption. For example, their work skills may be in demand, but they perform them poorly. Alternatively, their work skills may be obsolete.

ACADEMIC SUCCESSES AND FAILURES Counsellors can assist both underachieving and overstriving students to be more realistic about their explanations of cause for their academic successes and failures. Following are some causes to which students may explain academic success and failure (Nelson-Jones, 1989; Weiner and Kukla, 1970) Needless to say, there is a subjective element in what students perceive as success or failure.

- *Aptitude.* Aptitude is an internal and stable explanation.

- *Effort.* Effort is an internal explanation largely within a client's control.

- *Task difficulty.* Task difficulty is composed of the task's realistic level of difficulty and any perceiving errors: for example magnifying or minimizing.

- *Luck.* Academic results owing to chance are outside clients' control. Unfortunately some clients explain their academic successes to luck, but are quick to blame themselves for their academic failures.

- *Anxiety.* Anxiety can both help and hinder academic performance (Alpert and Haber, 1960). The effects of debilitating anxiety may be inadequately recognized.

- *Staff competence.* Good or poor teaching and supervision may help or hinder achievement.

- *Student group norms.* The degree to which the student peer group values or does not value academic success.

- *Student group attraction.* The degree to which the student group is attractive to you and you like studying with your peers.

- *Socio-economic considerations.* Some students need to take outside work to support themselves. Some live in inadequate housing and so on.

Assist clients to alter inaccurate explanations

Counsellors can use some of the skills already described in the section on perceiving accurately to help clients to become more realistic in explaining cause. For example, you can encourage clients to examine the evidence for their explanations and see how closely they fit the facts. Then clients can generate and evaluate alternative explanations. In addition, clients can dispute explanations and restate them into more realistic ones. For example, the explanation in a relationship conflict that 'It's all my partner's fault' can be restated to 'Even though I may not like how my partner behaves, I may be happier if I examine how I behave to my partner and, if necessary, change how I act rather than wait for him or her to change first.' Assist clients to conduct behavioural experiments in which, for specified periods, they change their actions in line with altered explanations. For example, a husband's 'It's all my partner's fault' explanation can be disproved if he acts more positively towards his wife, who in turn acts better towards him.

Counsellors can provide new information that challenges existing explanations: for example, informing clients wrongly diagnosing themselves as schizophrenic that they do not possess any of its key symptoms. Counsellors can encourage clients to test the accuracy of their explanations by collecting additional information. For instance, clients attributing their maths problems to insufficient aptitude can collect additional information by taking a maths aptitude test.

Emphasize take-away

Remember to emphasize take-away. Ways discussed previously for consolidating other thinking skills as self-helping skills are relevant to consolidating the skills of explaining cause accurately: namely, taking work down off the whiteboard, using reminder cards, making cassettes, and encouraging clients to discipline themselves to practise the skills in daily life. In addition, where clients are in relationships, they can demonstrate explaining cause accurately skills to one another and reward each other's honesty. To avoid repetition, I will assume that readers understand the importance of emphasizing take-away and so not emphasize it for the remaining thinking skills covered in this chapter.

PREDICTING REALISTICALLY

Clients lead their lives into the future rather than into the past. Predictions are thoughts and images forecasting the future. George Kelly (1955) took a rational approach to prediction when he wrote: 'The two factors from which predictions are made are the number of replications already observed and the amount of similarity which can be abstracted among the replications' (p. 53). Invariably clients experience disorders of prediction of varying degrees of intensity. Anxiety is a disorder of prediction (Beck and Emery, 1985). Distorted predictions also play a large part in depression: for instance, hopelessness (Beck *et al.*, 1988b), helplessness (Abramson *et al.*, 1978) and perceived self-inefficacy (Bandura, 1986, 1989).

How clients explain cause influences whether people predict optimistically or pessimistically. Seligman (1991) considers that pessimists are more likely to explain the cause of negative events as permanent (across time) and pervasive (across different situations), whereas optimists are more likely to view positive events that way. Optimism can benefit physical well-being (Schier and Carver, 1992). One reason is that optimists are more likely than pessimists to confront stress-inducing problems directly and persist in coping with them.

Assist clients to become aware of their predictive styles

Counsellors can assist clients to become more aware of their predictive styles and their consequences, both in general and in relation to specific problems. Predicting risks and predicting rewards are interrelated. However, clients can become more aware of where specific skills deficits lie. Following are the four main options.

PREDICT RISK INACCURATELY

* *Underestimate bad consequences.* Some research in the health area indicates that people tend to underestimate their own, relative to others', risk for various illnesses and negative life events (Weinstein, 1980, 1984). Many people underestimate their risk of HIV infection. For example, a large-scale study of nearly 6000 men entering gay bars in 16 small American cities found that, excluding those in long-term

exclusive relationships, 27 per cent reported engaging in unprotected anal sex during the past two months (Kelly *et al.*, 1995). Compulsive gamblers and stock-market speculators have a similar tendency to underestimate risk.

• *Overestimate bad consequences.* Fear of change, failure and success can be powerful motivators for clients to overestimate negative consequences of actions. Many clients engage in catastrophic predictions.

PREDICT REWARD INACCURATELY
• *Overestimate good consequences.* Overestimating good consequences frequently accompanies underestimating bad consequences: for instance, in compulsive gambling.

• *Underestimate good consequences.* Many counselling clients underestimate good consequences. They have a predictive style that focuses far more on risk than reward. Two trends are common in underestimating reward. First, clients are poor at identifying rewards. Second, even when clients identify rewards, they minimize their significance.

Highlight links between clients' erroneous explanations and predictions

Clients can create and reinforce their own pessimism by the permanence and pervasiveness of certain erroneous explanations. Counsellors can work with clients to help them see how their explanatory styles can often create self-fulfilling prophesies. For instance, spouses who think their partner will never change because of their poor personality may themselves sustain their partner's negative behaviour by failing to do anything positive. By ascribing a permanent cause to a partner's negative behaviour, the spouse continues to reinforce the negative outcomes contained in the prediction.

Where necessary, assist clients to reality test the pervasiveness of their explanations. For instance, counsellors can challenge clients who have one unsatisfactory date with a man or woman then make negative predictions about their abilities in other areas: for instance, study or work.

Assist clients to become aware of current predictions and their consequences

A simple two column technique can be useful for eliciting clients' assessments of risks and rewards in specific situations. For example, using the STC framework, the S or situation is that Sean is a shy 30-year-old bachelor wondering whether to ask Suzy for a date. Sean's counsellor places the following two column headings on the whiteboard to elicit Sean's thoughts or predictions at T.

Risks (-s)	Rewards (+s)

Then the counsellor assists Sean in articulating his fears about asking Suzy out, for instance, 'This might contribute to keeping me depressed' and 'I could get hurt.' At this stage, Sean has difficulty predicting that there will be any rewards from his actions.

Counsellors can go beyond pinpointing predictions to exploring their consequences at C. Exploration can focus on consequences for clients; for instance, Sean's overemphasis on the risks rather than the gains may lead to persistent loneliness. You can also assist clients to become better at predicting consequences for others: for instance, drug-addict Jana may need to see more clearly the dangers for others of sharing her needles.

Assist clients to generate and evaluate additional risks or rewards

If clients' predictive errors lean toward underestimating risks, counsellors may need to assist them to develop skills of generating what other risks there may be. Most clients tend towards overestimating risks. Frequently, they need to develop skills of generating and evaluating potential rewards.

> Sean started by mentioning items to go in the risks column with regard to asking Suzy for a date, but had difficulty generating items for the rewards column. Sean's counsellor worked with him to generate some potential rewards for asking Suzy out, including the following: 'I might have a chance of a strong relationship', 'I might gain more experience in developing relationships' and 'I might gain confidence and a more positive self-image.' Working to generate rewards enabled Sean to obtain a more balanced picture about asking Suzy out. Sean decided that the rewards outweighed the risks and acted on his changed predictions, and Suzy later became his first steady girlfriend.

Assist clients to assess probability

Counsellors can assist clients to review their assumptions about the likelihood of risks or rewards actually occurring. Clients can wrongly assign high probability to low-probability events or low probability to high-probability events.

> Fifteen years ago, toward the end of his first year in a lecturing position, Daniel had an extremely painful nervous breakdown. Now Daniel is a professor. Recently, on doctor's orders, Daniel took sick leave for a 'holiday' because he had started experiencing his pre-breakdown symptoms of 15 years ago. A few days before returning to his university, he experienced chronic anxiety. A major contributor to

his anxiety was his prediction that he might have another breakdown. Daniel's counsellor assisted him to assess the evidence for his prediction. Once Daniel faced the facts, he realized that this time he had taken preventive action and had the skills to monitor his load and seek further assistance, if necessary. Consequently, Daniel recognized that the probability of having another full-blown break-down was close to nil. This realization lowered his anxiety, thus further reducing the likelihood of an-other breakdown.

Questions that clients might ask themselves in assessing probability fall into two categories. First, what *rational* basis do I have for making a particular prediction? Here, clients need to assess the connections between facts and inferences. Second, what *irrational* considerations might interfere with the accuracy of my prediction? The perceiving errors mentioned earlier, clients' states of emotional arousal and their physical condition might all interfere with their predictive ability.

Assist clients to assess their coping capacity and support factors

Clients may predict on the basis of inaccurate assessments of their skills at coping with particular situations. They may engage in focusing on their deficits and need to counteract this by searching for and affirming their resources. Additionally, clients may possess many support factors that they inadequately acknowledge: for example, people who can help them prepare for upcoming tasks, friends and relatives to provide emotional support, and opportunities to repeat failed tasks. Encourage clients to identify, acknowledge, use and develop appropriate supports (Emery, 1982).

Encourage clients to reality test predictions

The most conclusive way for clients to test the accuracy of their predictions is to reality test them. Here are two examples of clients whom helpers might encourage to reality test predictions.

Maureen, aged 27, is afraid to tell her husband how she would like him to make love to her. She predicts 'If I tell him, he'll be furious.'

Wayne, a widower, is reluctant to throw a party to mark his sixtieth birthday. He predicts: 'No one will want to come.'

In the above examples, each client needs to set himself or herself a specific goal. For example, Maureen's might be to tell her husband how to pleasure her better within the next month. Wayne's goal might be to throw a moderate-sized party on or within two weeks of his sixtieth birthday. You may need to assist clients to think through and develop the action skills for attaining their goals. For example, Maureen requires verbal, voice and body message action skills to make an assertive request for her husband to change his behaviour. Wayne may need skills of asking a relative or friend to help him with the catering.

SETTING REALISTIC GOALS

'Did you hear about the counsellor firing squad? They stood in a circle.'

Bandura (1989, pp. 1179–80) observes: 'Human motivation relies on *discrepancy production* as well as *discrepancy reduction*. It requires both *proactive control* and *reactive or feedback control*.' Initially, people motivate themselves through setting standards or levels of performance that create a state of disequilibrium and then strive to maintain them. Goals act as motivators by specifying the conditions of self-satisfaction with performance. Feedback control involves subsequent adjustment of efforts to achieve desired results.

Clients' goal setting errors vary. Some clients may possess goals, but these goals may be unrealistically high or low. Furthermore, their goals may be based on how others think they should be rather than on their own valuing process. Other clients may lack clear goals. Still more may require assistance in stating their goals clearly. Some of the rewards for clients of setting realistic goals include increased authorship of their lives, clarity of focus, finding increased meaning and gaining increased motivation. However, risks to clients setting themselves unrealistic goals include self-alienation, overemphasizing doing as contrasted with being, putting too much pressure on themselves and compromising their health.

Assisting vulnerable clients to formulate clear goals may entail long-term counselling. Such clients lack a clear sense of their identity. You may need to assist these clients in getting more in touch with their feelings, wants and wishes. Furthermore, you may need to caution clients against making major decisions until they are less anxious.

Many other thinking skills are relevant to assisting clients in setting realistic goals. Clients' goals need to be based on realistic personal rules. Furthermore, where clients' goals involve another person – for instance, getting engaged or married – they need to perceive her or him reasonably accurately. In addition, clients can use visualizing skills to formulate goals. When setting goals, clients can engage in the steps of rational decision making.

Assist clients to state goals clearly

Clients are more likely to attain goals that they state clearly. You can make clients aware of the following criteria for effective goals.

- *Do your goals reflect your values?* Clients' goals should reflect what they consider be worthwhile in life.

- *Are your goals realistic?* Clients' goals are realistic when they adequately acknowledge both external and personal constraints. Encourage clients to set goals reflecting potentially attainable standards.

- *Are your goals specific?* Assist clients in stating goals as specifically as possible. Ideally, clients' goals should be stated so that they can easily measure the success of attempts to attain them. For instance, when Glenys makes a goal statement, 'I will introduce myself to three new people in my ballroom dancing class,' this statement is much preferable to the more general, 'I want to meet some new people.'

- *Do your goals have a time frame?* Goals can be short term, medium term or long term. Vague intentions are insufficient. Assist clients in stating a realistic time frame for attaining goals: for instance, Glenys might set as a goal, 'By the end of this month, I will introduce myself to three new people in my ballroom dancing class.'

Once goals are stated, you may need to work with clients to identify the thinking and action skills required to attain them. In the above example, her counsellor could assist Glenys in articulating the thinking and action skills helpful for meeting three new people in the ballroom dancing class. Then, the counsellor might need to train her in some or all of these skills.

Assist clients to set sub-goals

Where appropriate, assist clients to break goals down into sub-goals. Particularly useful are progressively difficult short-term sub-goals. Such sub-goals provide incentives for action and, when attained, produce confidence to persist. In the above example, an initial goal might be for Glenys to meet one new person at her next ballroom dancing class, followed by a second goal of meeting two new people by the middle of the month, with the third goal being meeting three new people by the end of the month.

Sometimes, striving for high goals may provide evidence that clients have made significant gains. However, on other occasions, clients are at risk of relapsing into previous skills deficits because they attempt too much too soon. Then counsellors may need to support them as they work through any negative reactions to not doing as well as they would like. Counsellors can also reaffirm or renegotiate appropriate goals and sub-goals.

> Paul Fleming, the client with golf swing anxiety, was building his confidence and skills by gradually and systematically succeeding in more difficult tasks. As part of this gradual approach, his counsellor, both in the office and on various golf courses, would assist him through any mental and technical difficulties he faced. One day, when the counsellor was

not present, Paul had a particularly good score. Three weeks later Paul, with the knowledge of his counsellor, entered a Pro-Am tournament that was way beyond his experience, since entering counselling, of playing in public. He fared disastrously and came off the course physically drained and mentally depressed. Paul was afraid that he had undone all his progress to date. When they next met, Paul and his counsellor discussed how his Pro-Am experience showed he had tried too much too soon. Then they negotiated some more realistic short-term, medium-term and longer-term goals for consolidating his skills.

USING VISUALIZING SKILLS

Visual images play a large part in everyone's life, though some clients are more visually oriented than others (Lazarus, 1995). Glasser (1984) asserts that 80 per cent of the perceptions people store in their memory albums are visual. Counsellors can assist clients to develop visualizing skills for numerous purposes (Lazarus, 1984; Nelson-Jones, 1989). Visualizing skills are most effective when used in conjunction with other thinking and action skills. Here, after discussing raising awareness of visualizing, I focus on three of its main uses: namely, enhancing relaxation, enhancing competent performance and breaking bad habits.

Assist clients to develop an awareness of visualizing

Some clients may need to become more aware of the role of visual images in sustaining their problems. Following are ways that counsellors can highlight the importance of visualizing.

QUESTIONS Counsellors who ask questions about clients' visual imagery are more likely to assist clients to recognize its importance than counsellors who avoid the area. Sample questions might be: 'Were you aware of any visual images that accompanied the anxiety attack?' and 'To what extent do you use imagery to help cope with the situation?' As clients answer questions, counsellors can assess their visualizing powers. Clients can also be asked to close their eyes and recount specific instances as though they were describing slow motion replays of movies. In general, the more clients can experience sensations and feelings attached to images, the greater their potential for developing visualizing skills for self-help.

EXPLANATIONS You can incorporate visual images into the STC framework used to explain problematic situations. For instance, the T in the STC framework can emphasize visual images as well as thoughts:

S	The situation
T	Your thoughts and *visual images*
C	Your feelings, physical reactions and action consequences

EXERCISES You can use exercises to illustrate various aspects of visualizing. A simple exercise that highlights visualizing is to ask clients to think of someone they love. Almost invariably they will get a visual image. You can show the relationship between visualizing and feelings by getting clients to visualize first something that 'makes' them feel happy and then something that 'makes' them feel afraid.

Enhancing relaxation

When clients visualize, it is best that they be relaxed. In addition, relaxation can be a useful skill for clients to develop if they suffer from such problems as tension headaches, hypertension and feelings of excessive stress. Furthermore, relaxation is a useful skill for helping manage such feelings as anxiety (Deffenbacher and Suinn, 1988; Wolpe, 1982; Wolpe and Wolpe, 1988) and anger (Deffenbacher *et al.*, 1995). The most common helping approach to relaxation is probably the Jacobson progressive muscular relaxation technique (Jacobson, 1938), more fully described in Chapter 17. Visual imagery may be used independently of as well as in conjunction with muscular relaxation. You may assist clients in the following elements of visual relaxation.

IDENTIFYING RELAXING SCENES You can encourage clients to identify one or more favourite scenes conducive to their feeling relaxed: for instance, looking at a valley with lush green meadows, lying on a beach on a warm sunny day or sitting in a comfortable chair at home.

DEVELOPING SELF-INSTRUCTIONS Though counsellors may initially relax clients, the idea is for clients to develop visual relaxation as a self-helping skill. First, you can demonstrate how clients can instruct themselves in visual relaxation. Then you rehearse clients as they use their own instructions. Clients may wish to record their self-instructions for playback outside of counselling sessions. Below is a brief example.

'I'm lying on an uncrowded beach on a pleasant, sunny day, enjoying the sensations of warmth on my body. There is a gentle breeze. I can hear the peaceful noise of the sea steadily lapping against the nearby shore. I haven't a care in the world, and enjoy my feelings of peace, calm, relaxation and well-being.'

USING VISUAL RELAXATION IN DAILY LIFE You can assist clients in identifying opportunities for taking 'time-out' in their daily lives to use visual relaxation. You can encourage clients to keep visual relaxation monitoring logs of their daily practice and use of the skill. They can also record the consequences of using visual relaxation skills.

Enhancing competent performance

Though they overlap, visualized rehearsal and practice and visualizing attaining goals are two important skills for clients wishing to perform tasks more competently.

VISUALIZED REHEARSAL AND PRACTICE Following is a quotation from Jack Nicklaus, one of the most successful golfers of all time, that highlights the potential of visualized rehearsal to enhance competent performance. Nicklaus writes: 'In practice, I sometimes build into my preshot preparation a mental and sensory picture of how the end of a perfect follow-through looks. Then, when I swing, I will focus only on trying to be picture perfect' (Nicklaus, 1985, p. 22). Here Nicklaus uses visualizing immediately prior to acting partly to counteract 'ball fixation' – standing rigidly on tee staring at the ball.

Counsellors can encourage clients to use visualized rehearsal to prepare for more distant scenarios. Clients may have limited opportunity to rehearse and practise certain targeted skills in real life: for instance, going for a job interview or speaking in public. However, they have virtually unlimited opportunity to use visualized rehearsal and practice. While it is no substitute for the real thing, visualized rehearsal has many advantages. These advantages include assisting clients to: break tasks down and focus on the processes of skilled performance; identify potential setbacks and ways of coping with them; and rehearse and practise coping self-talk along with their visualizing skills. I often make up cassettes to assist clients in visualized rehearsal: for instance, waiting outside an interview room, then going in, sitting down and then answering the first question competently.

Following are instances of clients using visual rehearsal and practice.

> Wendy, 61, a recently retired widow, has a goal of asking her friend, Laura, if she can join her bridge group. Wendy visually rehearses the best way to do this, including how she might respond if Laura says 'no'.

> Bruce, 41, a car factory foreman, visualizes different ways he can assertively tell workers when their work is not up to standard.

> Duncan, 23, a police officer, visualizes how he can calmly yet firmly react to people who call him a 'pig' when he is on crowd control duty.

VISUALIZING ATTAINING GOALS Visualized rehearsal and practice focuses on the *processes* of skilled performance. However, clients may also enhance their performance if they visualize themselves being successful in attaining goals (Lazarus, 1984; Woolfolk *et al.*, 1985). For example, if clients rehearse hard and then visualize that they are going to perform very competently when speaking in public, they are more likely to do so than if they visualize lack of success. Often clients are far too good at visualizing the worst. They need to be able to counteract this tendency by visualizing success experiences. Counsellors can encourage clients, even when imagining the worst possibility, to visualize how they can cope successfully in such adverse circumstances (Emery, 1982).

Breaking bad habits

There is an Oscar Wilde aphorism: 'I can resist everything except temptation.' Visualizing can be a useful skill when you are trying to overcome bad habits. Clients with bad habits, instead of dwelling on negative consequences, often switch to dwelling on short-term rewards. If clients sincerely wish to break bad habits, the time to reward themselves is when they have resisted temptation, not when they have given in to it. Visualizing realistic negative consequences and visualizing exaggerated negative consequences are two ways in which counsellors can assist clients to break bad habits.

VISUALIZE REALISTIC NEGATIVE CONSEQUENCES How can you assist clients to visualize realistic negative consequences from such activities as smoking and engaging in unsafe gay sex? One way is to encourage clients to collect visual images of negative consequences: for instance, coloured medical photographs of the effects of smoking on lung tissue or of AIDS-related symptoms, such as Kaposi's sarcoma and malignant lymphomas. In addition, clients can be encouraged to develop visualizations, possibly including photographic images, of negative consequences of bad habits: for instance, the ability to call up on their memory screens pictures of AIDS-related symptoms. Clients can also develop the following self-helping skill. When tempted, they can shout to themselves 'Stop!' and then strongly visualize the negative consequences of giving in to the temptation. Clients may then engage either in distracting activities or in substitute rewarding activities that involve little or no risk.

VISUALIZE EXAGGERATED NEGATIVE CONSEQUENCES Cautela (1967) developed what he termed a 'covert sensitization' approach to undermining and resisting temptations. Clients are encouraged to visualize exaggerated negative consequences whenever an unwanted temptation is anticipated or experienced. For instance, if clients wish to break overeating, and they have targeted rich cakes as a food to avoid, they might practice visualizing the following sequence.

> 'I am at home, sitting around the table at dinner, and a rich cake is being served. As I see it I start getting nauseous. I accept a piece. As I take my first bite, I vomit all over the table and my clothes. I throw up all my dinner in a disgusting smelly mess. Seeing and smelling my vomit makes me retch even more violently. I feel very weak and faint. Everyone is looking at me in disgust. As I get up from the table, having made up my mind to eat no more, I feel better. I wash, change and feel great to have stopped eating rich food.'

I prefer encouraging clients to visualize realistic rather than exaggerated negative consequences. Realistic consequences can be horrific enough. However, some clients may find that exaggeration increases the power of their negative imagery, with a beneficial effect on willpower.

REALISTIC DECISION-MAKING

Frequently clients are faced with decisions. Such decisions include making choices about jobs and career, major area of study, further education, recreational activities, getting married or divorced and whether or not to give up a bad habit. Decisions produce varying degrees of conflict and anxiety. Clients may fear the consequences of making the wrong decision. Additionally, they may be under stress at the time of making the decision: for instance, leaving university. How can you assist clients to make better decisions and, even more important, to become better decision-makers? The main thrust of all counselling interventions is to assist clients to make better choices. Here I discuss two areas, decision-making styles and realistic decision-making, in which you focus specifically on clients' decision-making processes.

Explore decision-making styles

Clients have styles of decision that may be helpful or harmful (Arroba, 1977; Nelson-Jones, 1989). In reality, each client possesses a profile of decision-making styles. Furthermore, they may make different decisions in different ways. Their styles may also alter when they are making decisions in conjunction with other people.

You can assist clients to become more aware of their decision-making styles and their positive or negative consequences. Though it is far from an exhaustive listing, below are given eight styles that describe how people make individual decisions.

- *Rational.* You dispassionately and logically appraise all important information and then select the best option in light of your criteria.

- *Feelings-based.* Though you may generate and appraise different options, the basis for choice is what intuitively feels night. This style emphasizes getting in touch with what you truly feel.

- *Impulsive.* You make decisions rapidly, based on sudden impulses. You act on initial and surface feelings rather than explore and evaluate options.

- *Hypervigilant.* You try too hard. You become so anxious and aroused by the conflict and stress triggered by the decision that your decision-making efficiency decreases. You may become indecisive and fail to see the wood for the trees.

- *Avoidant.* You cope with decisions by refusing to confront them, hoping they will go away, and by procrastinating over them.

- *Conformist.* You conform to what others expect of you. You allow your decisions to be heavily influenced, if not made, by others.

- *Rebellious.* You rebel against what others expect of you. Your decisions are dependent on what others think, though in an oppositional way.

- *Value-based.* The framework for your choice is a code of values and ethics, be it religious or secular.

Sometimes counsellors can assist clients to become more aware of their styles of joint decision-making. Frequently, clients are in situations where they have differences and potential conflicts of interest with others: for instance, partners. Following are three main styles of joint decision-making (Nelson-Jones, 1996a).

- *Competitive.* You operate on an 'I win – you lose' basis and view decisions as competition for scarce resources. You think, and very likely behave, aggressively.

- *Collusive.* You are non-assertive and go along with or give in to the other person. This can be an 'I lose – you win' style. Alternatively, you both avoid decisions and problems, which may end up as an 'I lose – you lose too' solution.

- *Cooperative.* You both assertively search for a solution that best meets each person's needs. You search for an 'I win – you win too' solution. If necessary, you make rational compromises in the interest of the relationship.

You can assist clients in identifying their decision-making styles and exploring their strengths and deficits. Some clients may need to think through the consequences of their decision-making styles more thoroughly: for instance, impulsively choosing friends or buying goods on credit. You require skills such as active listening and challenging when clients explore decision-making styles and their consequences. You may need to challenge clients who distance themselves from responsibility for decisions and who do not perceive their consequences accurately.

Develop realistic decision-making skills

Some clients require assistance in learning to make decisions systematically. Realistic or rational decision-making can be viewed as taking place in two main stages: first, confronting and making the decision; second, implementing and evaluating it. Following is a seven-step framework for realistic decision-making within the context of these two main stages.

Stage 1: Confronting and making the decision

- *Step 1: Confront the decision.* Component skills include acknowledging the need for decisions and clearly stating what is the decision to be made.

- *Step 2: Generate options and gather information about them.* Some clients may be poor at generating options and thus restrict their decision effectiveness. Other skills deficits include inability to identify and gather relevant information.

- *Step 3: Assess the predicted consequences of options.* Clients need accurately to perceive and evaluate positive and negative short-term and long-term consequences of options for both themselves and others.

- *Step 4: Commit yourself to a decision.* Clients need to go beyond making rational decisions to committing themselves to implement them. Clients may have various barriers to commitment, including post-decisional anxieties and conflict (Janis and Mann, 1977).

Stage 2: Implementing and evaluating the decision

- *Step 5: Plan how to implement the decision.* Component skills of planning include stating goals and sub-goals clearly, breaking down tasks, generating and assessing alternative courses of action, anticipating difficulties and setbacks and identifying sources of support.

- *Step 6: Implement the decision.* Clients need to consider when best to implement decisions and be open to feedback during implementation. Clients may require skills of rewarding themselves for performing targeted behaviours: for instance, by positive self-talk or more tangible rewards, such as a new item of clothing or some special entertainment.

- *Step 7: Assess the actual consequences of implementation.* Realistic decision-making requires accurate perception of feedback and a willingness to act on it. Clients may stick with original decisions or modify or discard them.

Especially if you work in a decision-related area (for instance, as a career counsellor), you can make clients more aware of the steps of realistic or rational decision-making. One approach is to go through the steps, preferably using a whiteboard, and then giving clients handouts. In addition, you can request clients to identify decision-making strengths and deficits. Take into account previous decision-making skills deficits when assisting clients to deal with current decisions. Clients can also work through current decisions in terms of the steps of realistic decision-making. Here focus on developing clients' skills rather than doing the work for them. For example, rather than saying

'Your options seem to be ... ', you might ask 'What are your options and what information do you require to assess them adequately?'

PREVENTING AND MANAGING PROBLEMS AND ALTERING PROBLEMATIC SKILLS

Decision-making and problem management overlap. The previous section focused on making decisions at major and minor turning points, where clients needed to decide among different options. Here the focus is on helping clients to use thinking skills to prevent and manage thoughts, feelings, behaviours and situations that are problematic for them. This is similar to the term social problem-solving, which refers to 'problem solving as it occurs in the real world' (D'Zurilla and Maydeu-Olivares, 1994, p. 409).

Assist clients to prevent problems

Counsellors can assist clients to recognize the preventive function of thinking skilfully in their daily lives. When thinking effectively, clients may be less disposed to a range of problems. Skilful thinking can make them more confident and less prone to upset themselves with imaginary, as opposed to real, difficulties. Clients can also acquire skills of anticipating problems and 'nipping them in the bud'. For example, clients able to anticipate when they are at risk of excessive stress are in better positions to take preventive actions than those less aware. Given awareness of the risk of allowing themselves to be excessively stressed, clients may still need to use a range of thinking skills to prevent them from giving in to bad habits: for instance, possessing realistic rules about achievement. Clients who have come to helping with stress-related problems are never totally cured. They still need to think skilfully to prevent recurrences.

Assist clients to manage problems and alter problematic skills

Managing problems effectively requires clients to use many of the same skills as for making decisions. Nevertheless, there are important differences: for instance, in how problems are assessed and restated. The lifeskills counselling model is basically a self-helping model. Counsellors can train clients in how to use the model to manage future problems and problematic skills. The five-stage DASIE model can be modified to CASIE when used for client self-helping purposes.

C	*Confront* and clarify my problem
A	*Assess* and restate my problem in skills terms
S	*State* goals and plan self-helping interventions
I	*Implement* my plan
E	*Evaluate* the consequences of implementing my plan

Because of limited exposure, clients in brief counselling are unlikely to learn how to apply the lifeskills counselling model to future problems. Clients in longer-term counselling will acquire some knowledge of the model as they and their counsellors work with the problematic skills underlying their problems. Furthermore, counsellors may identify characteristic thinking skills deficits. Consequently, longer-term clients have a start in knowing where to look when assessing future problems. In addition, counsellors can systematically train clients in how to prevent and manage problems. Such training may form part of Stage 5 of the DASIE counsellor–client model, emphasize take-away and end. Here counsellors may use clients' anticipated future problems as case material for developing preventing and managing problems skills. Counsellors require both good relationship and good training skills to impart the DASE model effectively in its CASIE client self-helping format.

CHAPTER HIGHLIGHTS

- *Counsellors can assist clients to develop skills of identifying inaccurate explanations of cause and altering them to become more accurate. The skills for perceiving accurately are relevant to explaining cause accurately.*

- *Clients may predict risk, reward or both inaccurately. You can assist clients to become aware of their predictive styles, link erroneous explanations with predictions, become aware of current predictions and their consequences, generate and evaluate additional risks or rewards, assess probability, assess their coping capacity and support factors, and reality test predictions.*

- *Counsellors can assist clients to develop skills for setting goals and sub-goals. Criteria for effective goals include reflecting values, realism, being specific and having a time frame.*

- *Counsellors can develop clients' awareness of visualizing. Areas in which clients can develop visualizing skills include enhancing relaxation, enhancing competent performance and breaking bad habits.*

- *With assistance, clients can become more aware of their decision-making styles and their consequences. In addition, clients can learn to apply the steps of realistic decision-making.*

- *The five-stage DASIE lifeskills counselling model can be modified to CASIE when used for client self-helping purposes. CASIE's five stages are: (1) confront and clarify my problem; (2) assess and restate my problem in skills terms; (3) state working goals and plan self-helping interventions; (4) implement my plan; and (5) evaluate the consequences of using my plan.*

EXERCISE 15.1   INTERVENING FOR EXPLAINING CAUSE ACCURATELY

As appropriate, do parts of this exercise on your own, with a partner or in a group.

Part A   Explaining cause accurately yourself
1. Assess the relevance of each of the following explanations as causes for how well or poorly you are currently progressing in your counselling skills practical work.

    (a) aptitude
    (b) effort
    (c) task difficulty
    (d) luck
    (e) anxiety
    (f) trainer competence
    (g) student group norms
    (h) student group attraction
    (i) socio-economic considerations
    (j) others not mentioned above

2. Identify any inaccurate or partially inaccurate explanations of cause for your counselling skills progress, question them and restate them into more accurate explanations.

    (a) restated explanation 1
    (b) restated explanation 2
    (c) restated explanation 3

3. How might any explanations you have restated above influence your motivation and success in developing your counselling skills in future?

Part B   Assisting clients to develop accurately explaining cause skills
Work with a partner who either uses a personal concern or role-plays a client with a goal of explaining cause more accurately to manage a specific situation better. Within the context of a good counselling relationship:

•   use speaking skills to describe the skill of explaining cause accurately;

•   use demonstrating skills;

•   cooperate with the client to identify any current inaccurate or partially inaccurate explanations;

•   use coaching skills to assist the client to question and restate inaccurate into more accurate explanations;

- use negotiating take-away assignment skills.

Afterwards, discuss and reverse roles. Playing back audio-recordings or video-recordings of rehearsal and practice sessions may assist learning.

EXERCISE 15.2 INTERVENING FOR PREDICTING REALISTICALLY

As appropriate, complete parts of this exercise on your own, with a partner or in a group.

Part A   Focusing on your predicting skills
1.   Write down the extent to which each of the following describes your predictive style (where possible give specific illustrations).

   (a) I underestimate bad consequences (risks)
   (b) I overestimate bad consequences (risks)
   (c) I overestimate good consequences (rewards)
   (d) I underestimate good consequences (rewards)

2.   Think of a situation in which your predictions may hinder you from feeling and/or acting appropriately. What are your current predictions and their consequences?

   (a) **S** What is the situation?
   (b) **T** What are your current predictions?
   (c) **C** What are the consequences of both the situation and your current predictions about it?

3.   For the above example, review the accuracy of your predictions in the following ways.

   (a) generate and evaluate additional risks or rewards.
   (b) assess probability
   (c) assess your coping capacity and support factors

4.   If your predictions have changed as the result of the above analysis, how have you restated them?

5.   If appropriate, reality test the accuracy of your predictions.

Part B   Assisting clients to develop predicting realistically skills
Work with a partner, who either uses a personal concern or role-plays a client with a goal of developing realistic predicting skills to manage a specific situation better. Within the context of a good counselling relationship:

- use speaking skills to describe realistic predicting skills;

- use demonstrating skills;

- collaborate with the client to identify any unrealistic predictions;

- use coaching skills to assist the client to identify, assess and, where appropriate, alter unrealistic predictions;

- use negotiating take-away assignment skills.

Afterwards, discuss and reverse roles. Playing back audio-recordings or video-recordings of rehearsal and practice sessions may assist learning.

EXERCISE 15.3   INTERVENING FOR SETTING REALISTIC GOALS

As appropriate, complete parts of this exercise on your own, with a partner or in a group.

Part A   Choosing and stating your goals
1.   State at least one goal for yourself in each of the areas listed below. Your statement of each goal should reflect your values, be realistic, be specific and give a time frame.

   (a) relationships
   (b) study of work
   (c) recreation
   (d) health
   (e) finances

2.   Think of other areas of your life in which you would like to assume more responsibility for creating your future. Articulate your goals for each area.

3.   List the most important goals you want to attain during the next five years.

MY FIVE-YEAR GOALS

   1.
   2.
   3.
   4.
   5.
   6.
   7.
   8.

Part B   Assisting clients to develop setting realistic goals skills
Work with a partner who is unclear as to his/her goals in one or more areas of his/her
life or who role-plays a client with a goal of developing setting realistic goals skills in
one or more areas of his/her life. Within the context of a good counselling relationship:

* use speaking skills to describe setting realistic goals skills;

* use demonstrating skills;

* cooperate with the client to identify any current unrealistic goals;

* use coaching skills to assist the client in developing setting realistic goals skills;

* use negotiating take-away assignment skills.

Afterwards, discuss and reverse roles. Playing back audio-recordings or video-
recordings of rehearsal and practice sessions may assist learning.

EXERCISE 15.4   INTERVENING FOR USING VISUALIZING SKILLS

As appropriate, complete parts of this exercise on your own, with a partner or in a
group.

Part A   Developing your visualizing skills
When doing this exercise you should be in a quiet room with soft lighting and no
interruptions. Relax and sit in a comfortable chair. After reading the instructions for
each segment, put the book down and close your eyes. Take your time. If possible,
conjure up sound, smell and touch sensations as well as visual images. If you have
difficulty visualizing, say out loud what you are trying to see.

1. *Visualize images associated with feelings.*

    (a) Visualize something or someone that 'makes' you feel afraid.
    (b) Visualize something or someone that 'makes' you feel angry.
    (c) Visualize something or someone that 'makes' you feel sad.
    (d) Visualize something or someone that 'makes' you feel happy.

2. *Use visualizing to relax.* As you sit there, visualize a restful and relaxing scene.
    Evoke not only the sights, but the sounds, smells and other sensations that make
    this such a calm and peaceful scene for you. Stay in the scene for at least two
    minutes as you enjoy your feelings of relaxation and well-being.

3. *Use visualizing to perform better.*

    (a) Think of a specific situation that is not too difficult, but that you would like to
        handle better.

(b) Think through how you would like to act in the situation by breaking the task down into its component parts. Also think through how you might cope with setbacks.

(c) Relax and visually rehearse and practise how to manage the situation. Adjust your performance if you get better ideas. As appropriate, use coping self-talk along with visualizing. Visually rehearse performing better at least once daily.

(d) If feasible, perform your rehearsed behaviour in the real-life situation; immediately prior to your performance visualize yourself attaining realistic goals.

(e) Assess whether and how much visualizing helped you to perform better.

4. *Use visualizing to break a bad habit.*

(a) Think of a bad habit you wish to break.

(b) What graphic images of the realistic negative consequences of your bad habit might serve as a turn-off for you?

(c) Play the negative images through your mind daily. Additionally, at any other time you experience temptation, shout to yourself to 'Stop!' and switch to visualizing your negative images. If you find it helps you to exaggerate the negative consequences of your bad habit, then do so.

(d) Practise, practise and practise visualizing the negative consequences of your bad habit until you become able to resist the temptation.

Part B   Assisting clients to develop visualizing skills
Work with a partner who either uses a personal concern or role-plays a client with a goal of developing visualizing skills to manage a specific situation better. Within the context of a good counselling relationship.

- use speaking skills to describe relevant visualizing skills;

- use demonstrating skills;

- cooperate with the client to identify any current unhelpful visual images;

- use coaching skills to assist the client in developing relevant visualizing skills;

- use negotiating take-away assignment skills.

Afterwards, discuss and reverse roles. Playing back audio-recordings or video-recordings of rehearsal and practice sessions may assist learning.

EXERCISE 15.5   INTERVENING FOR REALISTIC DECISION-MAKING

As appropriate, complete parts of this exercise on your own, with a partner or in a group.

Part A   Exploring your decision-making style
Assess how much and with what consequences you use each of the following decision-making styles.

1. *When making decisions on your own*

    (a) rational (logically appraise all important information)
    (b) feelings-based (getting in touch with what you truly feel)
    (c) impulsive (decide on sudden impulses)
    (d) hypervigilant (excessively anxious)
    (e) avoidant (refuse to confront decisions)
    (f) conformist (conform to others' expectations)
    (g) rebellious (rebel against others' expectations)
    (h) value-based (adhere to moral code(s))

2. *When making decisions with another, for instance a spouse or partner*

    (a) competitive (out to win)
    (b) collusive (non-assertive)
    (c) cooperative (search for joint solutions)

Part B   Making a decision realistically
Think of a specific decision in your life that you would like to make realistically. Write out your answers for each step.

Step 1: Confront the decision (e.g. what is it?).
Step 2: Generate options and gather information about them.
    (a) option 1:
        information required to assess option 1:
    (b) option 2:
        information required to assess option 2:
    (c) option 3:
        information required to assess option 3:

Step 3: Assess the predicted consequences of options.
    (a) predicted consequences of option 1
    (b) predicted consequences of option 2
    (c) predicted consequences of option 3

Step 4: Commit yourself to a decision.
Step 5: Plan how to implement your decision.
    (a) goals and sub-goals
    (b) step-by-step plan

Where appropriate, conduct steps 6 and 7.
Step 6: Implement the decision.

Step 7: Assess the actual consequences of implementation.

Part C   Assisting clients to develop realistic decision-making skills
Work with a partner who either has a real decision to make or role-plays a client with a goal of developing his or her decision-making skills in relation to a specific decision. Within the context of a good counselling relationship:

- use speaking skills to describe realistic decision-making skills;

- use demonstrating skills;

- cooperate with the client to identify decision skills deficits;

- use coaching skills to assist the client to develop realistic decision-making skills;

- use negotiating take-away assignment skills.

Afterwards, discuss and reverse roles. Playing back audio-recordings or video-recordings of rehearsal and practice sessions may assist learning.

EXERCISE 15.6   INTERVENING FOR PREVENTING AND MANAGING PROBLEMS

As appropriate, complete parts of this exercise on your own, with a partner or in a group.

Part A   Preventing and managing your problems and altering problematic skills
Work on either preventing or managing a problem and altering underlying problematic skills in your life by working through the stages of the CASIE self-helping model.

C   *Confront* and clarify my problem.
A   *Assess* and restate my problem in skills terms:

- thinking skills deficits;
- action skills deficits.

S   *State* goals and plan self-helping interventions:

- thinking skills goals;
- action skills goals;
- plan of self-helping interventions to attain each goal.

Where possible, carry out the remaining two stages of the CASIE model.

I   *Implement* my plan.
E   *Evaluate* the consequences of implementing my plan.

Part B   Assisting clients to develop skills of preventing and managing problems and altering problematic skills

Work with a partner who has come for counselling over a specific problem and now wishes to learn how to take a systematic approach to preventing and managing future problems and altering the problematic skills associated with them. Within the context of a good counselling relationship:

- use speaking skills to describe how to use the CASIE model;

- use demonstrating skills;

- use coaching skills to assist the client to develop skills in how systematically to prevent and manage problems using the CASIE model;

- use negotiating take-away assignment skills.

Afterwards, discuss and reverse roles. Playing back audio-recordings or video-recordings of rehearsal and practice sessions may assist learning.

SIXTEEN
Interventions for actions

What we have to do, we learn by doing.

Aristotle

CHAPTER QUESTIONS

- *Why is it always important to focus on action skills?*

- *How can counsellors develop clients' skills for monitoring how they act?*

- *How can counsellors assist clients to rehearse action skills?*

- *How can counsellors and clients timetable desired activities?*

- *How can counsellors and clients plan sub-goals and sequence graded tasks?*

- *How can counsellors assist clients to generate and evaluate alternative actions and action skills?*

- *How can counsellors and clients design action skills experiments?*

- *How can counsellors and clients design and use exercises and games?*

- *How can counsellors assist clients to use self-reward?*

- *How can counsellors use third parties as aides?*

- *How can counsellors assist clients to identify and use supports?*

INTRODUCTION

However well clients feel and think, unless they act more effectively they are unlikely to attain personal goals. Did you know that the acronym NATO, the North Atlantic Treaty Organization, is held to mean 'No Action, Talk Only'? Counselling can be the same, as shown in the following Woody Allen joke.

> **Interviewer:** How long have you been in psychoanalysis?
> **Woody Allen:** Twenty-two years.
> **Interviewer:** How is it going?
> **Woody Allen:** Slowly.

Action skills provide the link from the inner to the outer world, from self to others and the environment. Counsellors and clients cannot afford to ignore action skills. Whereas Chapters 14 and 15 focused on how to develop clients' thinking skills, their inner game, this chapter focuses on how to develop clients' action skills, their outer game. Action skills entail verbal, voice, body and touch messages. They relate to how clients act when on their own and also with others. Though they are interrelated, here I focus more on learning new action skills and on developing existing action skills strengths rather than on lessening and/or extinguishing action skills deficits.

Counsellors who have inadequately assessed clients may fail to or inadequately intervene on action skills. Following are two examples of inadequate assessment.

> Andrea was a counselling student who brought a cassette of an initial interview to a supervision session. Andrea's client was Judy, who spent much of the session talking with great intensity about her relationship with Carl, a student in her home economics class. Andrea never asked questions that established how Judy and Carl actually related. At the end of the session, it emerged that Judy and Carl had never spent any time outside class on their own. The so-called relationship took place largely within Judy's head. Andrea had failed to elicit relevant information about how Judy behaved to enable her to set appropriate action skills goals for subsequent interventions.
>
> Glenn, a counselling student, brought a cassette of an initial interview with Hilary, aged 17, to a supervision session. Glenn allowed Hilary to talk at great length about how angry she was with her parents'

behaviour towards her. Every now and then Hilary would make remarks about how she behaved towards her parents: for instance, when she came home from school spending most of her time in her room and also not making the effort to socialize with her parents' friends. By allowing Hilary's main focus to be on how her parents treated her and never focusing on how Hilary behaved towards her parents, Glenn lost the opportunity to assess Hilary's action skills properly. Instead, he probably colluded in keeping Hilary stuck in her present unproductive interactive pattern.

WHEN TO INTERVENE TO DEVELOP ACTION SKILLS

Basically, there are three main options for when counsellors can intervene to develop clients' action skills: action skills before thinking skills; thinking skills before action skills; thinking and action skills together.

Action skills before thinking skills

Without necessarily using skills language, you may focus early on getting clients to change how they act. A reason for intervening on action skills first is that many clients understand the need to change how they act more easily than the need to change how they think. Throughout counselling, some clients work better with an approach focused on overt actions rather than on covert thoughts. Furthermore, some counsellors consider that 'It is much easier to change concrete actions, or to introduce new ones, than it is to change patterns of thinking' (Beck, 1988, p. 208). In addition, early successes in changing actions can instil confidence. For example, when working with severely depressed patients, Beck initially attempts to restore their functioning to premorbid levels through interventions such as scheduling activities (Beck et al., 1979). Early changes in actions can also engender goodwill in others. For instance, distressed couples who see some immediate positive changes in one another's behaviour may have created better emotional climates in which to work on deeper issues (Beck, 1988; Stuart, 1980).

Thinking skills before action skills

Sometimes both counsellors and clients may wish to intervene on thinking skills prior to action skills. For example, clients may have numerous fears about changing their outer behaviour. Changing private thoughts may seem less risky than altering outer behaviour which is mostly public. You may have to work with clients' fears about performing skills adequately, coping with the consequences of failure, coping with the consequences of success and reluctance to give up rewarding 'secondary gains'. Often in relationship conflicts, clients may externalize problems on to their partners. Assist them to see their need for change prior to working with relevant action skills.

Thinking skills and action skills together

Frequently you can simultaneously intervene with thinking skills and action skills. For example, with clients whose fears about change are not excessive, you can work to overcome such fears when training them in relevant action skills. You can also focus on thinking and action skills when targeting unwanted feelings such as anxiety, anger, shyness and stress. Sometimes using a thinking skill contributes to learning an action skill: for example, using visualized rehearsal for developing assertion skills. Thinking skills invariably form part of maintaining action skills: for instance, having realistic expectations about maintaining and developing skills after counselling. Clients need to develop the capacity for self-instruction through the sequences of choices entailed in implementing action skills. Then action skills more clearly become self-helping skills.

DEVELOP CLIENTS' MONITORING SKILLS

Following are examples of clients engaging in systematic monitoring of their actions.

> Khalid, 17, is trying to stop smoking. As part of his programme, he not only keeps a daily tally of how many cigarettes he smokes, but also keeps a log of the time, antecedents and consequences of each time he smokes.

> Joanna, 53, is receiving help for depression. Joanna has a goal of increasing the number of times she engages in pleasant activities. She keeps a daily chart of each time she engages in a number of specific pleasant activities (Lewinshon et al., 1986).

> Marty, 48, has had heart problems and is on a weight loss programme. He keeps a chart listing his daily weight. Each time he eats between meals, he records the time, what happened immediately before, what he eats and the consequences of his behaviour.

> Theo, 26, is an unemployed client searching for a job. Theo keeps a daily record of each time he engages in specific job-search activities, for instance, making phone enquiries and written applications.

Systematic self-monitoring or self-observation enables clients to become more aware of their thoughts, feelings and actions. Here the main focus is on monitoring actions. Systematic monitoring can be important at the start of, during and after interventions focused on developing specific action skills. When commencing interventions, monitoring can establish baselines and increase awareness. During interventions, monitoring can act as a reminder, motivator and progress check. After an intervention, monitoring is relevant to maintaining gains, though clients may not collect information as systematically as during counselling. Monitoring is best thought of as an adjunct to other interventions. As an intervention on its own, the effects of monitoring often do not last (Kazdin, 1994).

Monitoring methods

Following are some methods whereby clients can monitor how they act.

DIARIES AND JOURNALS Keeping a diary or journal is one way of monitoring action skills. Clients can pay special attention to writing up critical incidents where skills have been used well or poorly. Although diaries and journals may be useful, some clients find this approach too easy to ignore and too unsystematic.

FREQUENCY CHARTS Frequency charts focus on how many times clients enact a specific behaviour in a given time period, be it daily, weekly or monthly. For example, clients may tally up how many cigarettes they smoke in a day and then transfer this information to a monthly chart broken down by days. Take the earlier example of unemployed Theo recording his job search behaviours. Theo's counsellor gives him a job search activity chart and suggests that he fill it out for the next two weeks. The chart has activities on the horizontal axis and days on the vertical axis (see Figure 16.1). Where clients are only monitoring single actions, they may use wrist counters or pocket counters. However, they still need to transfer information gathered by such methods on to frequency charts.

STIMULUS, RESPONSE AND CONSEQUENCES LOGS To become more aware of their behaviour and its consequences, clients can fill in three-column stimulus, response and consequences logs.

Stimulus (what happened?)	Response (how I acted)	Consequences (what resulted?)

For example, clients who work on managing anger skills might record each time they feel angry in the stimulus column, what they did in the response column and the consequences for themselves and others in the consequences column.

SITUATION, THOUGHTS AND CONSEQUENCES (STC) LOGS Filling in three-column situation, thoughts and consequences (STC) logs can help clients to see the connections between how they think and how they felt and acted.

Activity	1 M	2 T	3 W	4 Th	5 F	6 Sa	7 Su	8 M	9 T	10 W	11 Th	12 F	13 Sa	14 Su	15 M
Written application															
Phone application															
Letter enquiry															
Phone enquiry															
Cold canvass															
Approach to contact															
Employment centre visit															
Interview attended															

Figure 16.1 *Theo's chart for recording job search activities*

Situation (what happened and when?)	Thoughts (what I thought)	Consequences (how I felt and acted)

USE OF TARGETED SKILLS LOGS Counsellors and clients need to go beyond monitoring actions to monitoring action skills. During the intervention stage, clients can usefully monitor and evaluate use of targeted skills. For instance, a counsellor works with a teenager, Vicki, on how to make assertive requests to her parents. Together, counsellor and client agree on the following verbal, voice and body message sub-skills for each time Vicki makes such a request: verbal messages, make 'I' statements and say 'please'; voice messages, speak with a calm, yet firm voice; body messages, use good eye contact and avoid threatening gestures such as finger pointing. Vicki's counsellor asks her to complete an assertive request monitoring log after each request to her parents (see Figure 16.2). In particular, the counsellor asks Vicki to record how she uses the sub-skills they have targeted.

Date and situation	How I acted		
	Verbal skills	Voice skills	Body skills
1.			
2.			
3.			
4.			
5.			
6.			
7.			
8.			

Figure 16.2 *Vicki's log for monitoring assertive requests*

Vicki's assertive request skills
Verbal messages: make 'I' statements, say 'please'.
Voice messages: speak calmly and firmly.
Body messages: use good eye contact, avoid threatening gestures.

Assisting clients to develop monitoring skills

Since monitoring mostly goes on outside sessions, counsellor skills for assisting client monitoring overlap with those for negotiating take-away assignments. Below are some ways counsellors can assist clients to monitor themselves and to develop self-monitoring skills.

OFFER REASONS FOR MONITORING Clients are not in the habit of systematically recording observations about how they act. You need to motivate them to do so. For instance, you can explain: 'Counting how many times a day you perform a behaviour not only indicates how severe your problem is but also gives us a baseline against which to measure your progress in dealing with it,' or 'Systematically writing down how you send verbal, voice and action messages after each time you go for an interview provides us with information to build your skills.'

TRAIN CLIENTS IN DISCRIMINATION AND RECORDING Clients are not naturally accurate self-observers (Thoresen and Mahoney, 1974). Consequently, counsellors may need to train them in discriminating and recording specific behaviours. Clients require clarity not only about what to record, but about how to record it. In addition, clients require awareness of any tendencies they have to misperceive or selectively perceive their actions: for instance, being more inclined to notice deficits than strengths.

DESIGN SIMPLE AND CLEAR RECORDING LOGS Always supply the log yourself. Do not expect clients to make up their own logs. They may not do so in the first place and, if they do, they may get them wrong. Simple recording systems enhance comprehension and recording accuracy.

USE REWARD SKILLS Reward clients with interest and praise when they fill in logs. This guideline is based on the basic behavioural principle that actions that are rewarded are more likely to be repeated. Furthermore, always reward clients for their efforts by debriefing them.

ENCOURAGE CLIENTS TO EVALUATE MONITORING INFORMATION When clients share monitoring logs with you, help them to use this information for self-exploration and evaluation. Assist them to understand the meaning of the information they have collected. However, do not do their work for them. When counselling ends, you will not be around to assess the implications of their frequency counts and monitoring logs. Train them to do this for themselves.

USE OTHER SKILLS BUILDING STRATEGIES Do not expect clients to develop action skills on the basis of self-observation alone. They are likely to require other interventions – for example, behaviour rehearsals and self-reward – to develop action skills. Furthermore, they require work and practice to acquire and maintain skills.

REHEARSAL AND ROLE-PLAY

Learning any skill generally requires repeated performances of targeted behaviours. Rehearsals may take place immediately after initial coached performance of skills, later in counselling, and before, when and after clients apply targeted skills in their daily lives. In role-plays, clients rehearse action skills in simulated or pretend situations involving one or more others. Most often counsellors play the part of the other person, but sometimes counsellors and clients switch roles.

Skills for assisting rehearsal

Many counsellor skills for assisting clients in rehearsing action skills overlap with those of coaching: for example, giving clear instructions, breaking tasks down and using feedback skills. Following are some counsellor skills for role-play rehearsals.

EXPLAIN REASONS FOR ROLE-PLAYS Some clients find the idea of role-playing off-putting. For example, they may be self-conscious about their acting skills. Explain reasons for role-plays to ease clients' anxieties and help motivate them. Here is a rationale for using role-play rehearsal with a client, Rob, who gets excessively angry when his teenage daughter, Ruth, comes home late.

> 'Rob, I think it would be helpful if we role-played how you might use your new skills to cope better with Ruth next time she comes home late. I realize that it may seem artificial acting the scene here. However, role-playing gives us the chance to rehearse different ways you might behave – your words, voice messages and body messages – so that you are better prepared for the actual event. It is safer to make mistakes here where it doesn't count for real. There is no substitute for learning by doing. What do you think about this approach?'

SET THE SCENE Elicit information about the physical setting of proposed scenes, what other characters are involved and how they behave. If you are to role-play someone (for instance, Ruth), collect sufficient information about Ruth's verbal, voice and body messages so that you can get into the role. Depending on what sort of office you have, you may be able to move the furniture around to create a 'stage'; for instance, a family living room.

ASSESS CURRENT ACTION SKILLS Usually, you spend time well if you conduct assessment role-plays in which clients demonstrate how they currently act in problem situations. You can elicit much relevant information about non-verbal communication that may not be apparent if clients only talk about how they act. Assessment role-plays can also reveal how clients think in situations.

FORMULATE CHANGED ACTIONS Cooperate with clients to formulate new and better ways of acting that use targeted lifeskills yet feel 'comfortable'. Facilitate clients' contributions to the discussion prior to making your own suggestions. For instance, you can ask: 'How might you use your new skills to behave differently in the situation?' Together with clients you can generate and review alternative scripts, and review appropriate voice and body messages. As part of this process counsellors can demonstrate the different verbal, voice and body message components of appropriate action skills. In addition, explore with clients how to cope with different responses by others.

REHEARSE CHANGED ACTIONS Once clients are reasonably clear of their new roles and counsellors understand their 'parts', trial enactments or rehearsals take place. Avoid trying to do too much or anything too difficult too soon. You may allow role-plays to run their course. Alternatively, you may intervene at one or more points along the way to provide feedback and coaching. Rehearsal role-plays are dry runs of how to use action skills in specific situations. Video feedback may be used as part of coaching both during and after role-plays. You may need a number of rehearsals to build clients' skills. Some of these role-plays may involve responding in different ways to clients. For example, clients asking for dates may get accepted, postponed or rejected in separate role-plays.

Role reversal and mirroring are psychodrama techniques that you may use (Blatner, 1995; Moreno, 1959). In role reversal, you get clients to play the other person in interactions. Role reversals force clients to get some way into another's internal viewpoint. With mirroring, you 'mirror back' clients' verbal, voice and body messages. Clients see themselves as others experience them.

REHEARSE THINKING SKILLS You may rehearse clients' thinking skills alongside action skills. For example, you can rehearse clients in the calming and coaching dimensions of appropriate self-talk to accompany new action skills. In addition, you can rehearse clients in other thinking skills relevant to targeted action skills.

PROCESS ROLE-PLAYS Processing involves spending time dealing with clients' thoughts and feelings generated by role-plays. Together you can discuss learning from them, and make plans to transfer rehearsed skills to daily life. You can ask clients processing questions like: 'How were you feeling in that role play?', 'How well do you think you used your skills in that rehearsal?', 'What have you learned in that role-play that is useful for real life?' and 'What difficulties do you anticipate in implementing your changed behaviour and how can you overcome them?' After processing the previous role-play, counsellors and clients may move on to the next role-play either with the same or with another problem situation.

Case example: Louise Donovan

In Chapter 12, I briefly mentioned how I trained Louise Donovan, the client who was repeatedly having unsuccessful interviews for senior positions, in interview skills. Here, I elaborate on how I rehearsed Louise in action skills for job interviews. This training concurrently addressed the thinking skills required by Louise to support her action skills.

In the restatement of Louise's getting consistently bad feedback from job interviews (for senior accounting positions) problem in skills terms, her action skills deficits/goals were to develop good interview skills. In particular her deficits/goals were: verbal messages – answers too long, unfocused and lecturing; voice messages – too booming and overpowering; and body messages – too stiff, eyes glaring, unsmiling (not user friendly).

When building Louise's interview skills, Richard and Louise first developed a list of questions that Louise was likely to be asked or that might cause her difficulty. Richard wrote each question down as Louise suggested it. Illustrative questions were:

'Why have you applied for this position?'

'Why did you leave your previous position?'

'How would you go about supplying leadership to professional accountants who work for this company?'

'What is your approach toward the supervision of support staff?'

Then, for assessment purposes, Richard and Louise conducted a cassette-recorded mini interview. When playing back this interview, Richard asked Louise to evaluate her skills along with making some suggestions of his own. As a result of this assessment, Richard wrote six answering question rules on the whiteboard (these were also taken down by Louise):

1. Home in on questions by paraphrasing/repeating their crux/key words.
2. Place conclusion at front of answer.
3. Give reasons for conclusion in point form.
4. Be brief.
5. Voice messages – comfortable, avoid booming.
6. Body messages – smile, look relaxed, use some gestures, but not too much.

Leaving these rules clearly visible on the whiteboard, Louise and Richard then conducted a series of cassette-recorded mini interviews and played them back. Louise first monitored herself, and then Richard provided her with feedback on her performance and coaching to improve it. Louise rehearsed body as well as verbal and voice messages. These rehearsals, in which Richard represented an interview panel, took place in two subsequent sessions as well.

Louise was given the take-away assignments of practising her interview skills in her present job (when interviewing clients and attending meetings) and listening to the most recent cassettes of her counselling session rehearsals. Later, Richard made Louise a take-away cassette in which he relaxed her and guided her through the imagery of waiting outside an interview room, being called in, sitting down and answering the first question competently, using all her rehearsed skills. Richard asked Louise to listen to this cassette a number of times to help the skills 'sink in'. Louise now had a cassette available to help her rehearse the targeted skills in periods just before future interviews.

TIMETABLE ACTIVITIES

Counsellors can work with clients to timetable desired activities and to build clients' skills in this area. How to assist clients in timetabling activities varies according to their needs.

Areas for timetabling

Following are some areas in which timetabling may assist clients to perform desired activities and to build action skills. Figure 16.3 shows a blank weekly timetable that can serve numerous purposes.

TIMETABLING DAILY ACTIVITIES Beck and his colleagues (Beck and Emery, 1985; Beck et al., 1979; Beck and Weishaar, 1995) stress the usefulness of developing daily activity schedules for clients who are immobilized by depression and anxiety. Counsellors and clients collaborate to plan specific activities for one day at a time. These planned activities are recorded on a weekly timetable, with days represented by columns and hours represented by rows. As clients develop skills and confidence, they can do their own activity scheduling, with the last activity for one day being the scheduling of the following day. To ease pressure, you can instruct clients to state what rather than how much they will accomplish and to realize that it is OK not to complete all activities – the important thing is to try.

TIMETABLING MINIMUM GOALS Some clients get extremely anxious over performing certain tasks and then engage in avoidance behaviour. For instance, Alison is a college student who is very distressed because she is not studying. She has lost all sense of control over her work. One approach to Alison is to assist her to timetable some minimum goals that she feels prepared to commit herself to keeping before the next session. Her minimum goals may be as little as three half-hour study periods during the week. For each study period, Alison needs to write down time, task and place. This does not mean that she cannot spend more time studying if she wishes. With certain highly anxious clients, counsellors need to be very sensitive to avoid becoming just another source of pressure. The idea of timetabling minimum goals is to show clients that they can be successful in achieving modest targets rather than to achieve large goals. Later on, Alison may increase her study periods.

TIMETABLING TO CREATE PERSONAL SPACE Many clients require timetabling skills to prioritize and create personal space. Such clients include: housewives trying to stop being at everyone's beck and call; stressed executives needing to create family and relaxation time; depressed people needing to timetable more pleasant activities; and students needing to plan their study time so that they know when they can say 'yes' rather than 'no' to requests to go out. Counsellors can assist clients to define personal space goals and to allocate time accordingly.

TIMETABLING TO KEEP CONTRACTS Clients make commitments to perform certain activities to themselves, to counsellors and to third parties: for instance, their spouses. You can assist clients to develop skills of keeping commitments by getting them to timetable when they are going to carry out these activities. For instance, Ramon is a teenager who has been resisting doing any of the household chores. He finally decides he is prepared to mow the lawn each week. Ramon may be more likely to keep this commitment if he timetables when he is going to perform this task.

Date							
Time	Monday	Tuesday	Wednesday	Thursday	Friday	Saturday	Sunday
6.00							
7.00							
8.00							
9.00							
10.00							
11.00							
12.00							
1.00							
2.00							
3.00							
4.00							
5.00							
6.00							
7.00							
8.00							
9.00							
10.00							

Figure 16.3 *Weekly timetable*

TIMETABLING TAKE-AWAY ASSIGNMENTS Certain take-away assignment activities lend themselves to being timetabled at regular times: for instance, practising progressive muscular relaxation or planning an activity schedule for the next day. Other assignments do not lend themselves so easily to regular scheduling, but are more likely to be performed if clients timetable them. For instance, Jim is an unemployed executive whose take-away assignments include developing an effective resumé, a task he has avoided. Jim is more likely to complete this assignment and to develop resumé-making skills if he blocks out specific periods of time to do it properly.

Some skills for timetabling

As shown above, many reasons exist why counsellors and clients use timetabling. Below are some counsellor skills for using timetabling to develop action skills.

- *Provide timetables.* Give clients timetables. Do not expect clients to have easy access to made up timetables or to make the effort to develop their own.

- *Offer reasons for timetabling.* For some clients the need to timetable activities and goals is obvious. Other clients require explanations. Challenge certain clients with the negative consequences of their failure to timetable.

- *Be sensitive to anxieties and resistances.* Timetabling can be very threatening to highly anxious clients – they feel failures if they do not do as agreed. Be very sensitive to how much pressure timetabling creates for vulnerable clients. Also be aware that some clients play timetabling games – either consciously or unconsciously they have little intention of achieving goals.

- *Do not overdo timetabling.* Even with less vulnerable clients, counsellors may overdo timetabling. Clients can spend too much time scheduling activities and too little time carrying them out.

- *Review progress.* At the next session, check with clients on progress in adhering to timetabled activities and on any difficulties experienced.

- *Work with thinking skills.* Often non-adherence to timetables reflects thinking skills deficits: for instance, perfectionist rules about achievement. Identify and work with any relevant thinking skills deficits.

- *Help clients to develop timetabling skills.* Always work closely with clients regarding what goes in the timetable. Aim to help clients to develop their own timetabling skills so that you can 'fade' from assisting them.

PLAN SUB-GOALS AND SEQUENCE GRADED TASKS

When helpers attempt to develop clients' action skills, planning sub-goals and sequencing graded tasks overlap. Counsellors may plan sub-goals in two main ways.

Sequencing sub-skills

When assisting clients to learn complex skills, you can break the skills down into their component parts. Then decide in what order you wish to train each component. For example, Vicki and her counsellor have the overall goal of being able to make assertive requests to her parents. However, Vicki's counsellor decides during their sessions to focus first on verbal messages, second on voice messages, third on body messages and finally on putting all three messages together.

Sequencing graded tasks

Sequencing graded tasks is sometimes called graded task assignment (Beck and Weishaar, 1995) or setting proximal sub-goals (Bandura, 1986). A useful distinction is that between setting distant and proximal or nearer goals. The research evidence is equivocal regarding the effectiveness of setting distant goals (Bandura, 1986; Whelan *et al.*, 1991). More certain appears the desirability of setting proximal goals or sub-goals (Bandura, 1986; Stock and Cervone, 1990). Bandura observes that 'Subgoals provide present guides and inducements for action, while subgoal attainments produce efficacy information and self-satisfactions that sustain one's efforts along the way' (Bandura, 1986, p. 475).

The following is an example of sequencing graded tasks to develop action skills.

Ron is a shy college student with an action skills goal of developing his dating skills. Together Ron and his counsellor draw up a sequence of graded tasks that Ron thinks he can complete before their next session.

1. Say 'hello' to the girls in my class when I see them on campus.
2. Sit down in the student union with a group of classmates of both sexes and join in the conversation.
3. Sit next to a girl in my class and initiate a very brief conversation in which I ask her what she thinks about the class.
4. Sit next to a girl in class and hold a slightly longer conversation in which I make a personal disclosure at least once.

Near the start of the next session, Ron and his counsellor review progress in attaining each task. The counsellor encourages Ron to share his thoughts and feelings about progress. The counsellor emphasizes the explanation that Ron achieves his sub-goals as a result of his willingness to take risks, his effort and his skill. As a result of feedback Ron both gets from others and gives himself about his growing skills, the counsellor and he develop further graded tasks for the next between session period. At progress reviews the counsellor rewards Ron for working to develop his skills – whether or not he is successful. For instance, when Ron eventually asks a girl for a date, the counsellor will reward him, even if she refuses. The counsellor encourages Ron to view as learning experiences all attempts to attain graded tasks.

Skills for sequencing and reviewing graded tasks

Following are some counsellor skills for sequencing and reviewing graded tasks.

RELATE GRADED TASKS TO TARGETED SKILLS Always make links between tasks and skills. The purpose of graded tasks is not only to assist clients to manage specific problems, but also to help them to develop specific skills. Encourage clients to view graded tasks as ways of developing skills for handling not just immediate but future problems.

SEQUENCE GRADED TASKS IN COOPERATION WITH CLIENTS Work with clients to assess whether they feel willing and able to work on graded tasks. Discuss with them the tasks that are important for them. When sequencing tasks, go at a comfortable pace. Start with small steps which clients think they can achieve. Be prepared to build in intermediate steps if clients think the progression of tasks is too steep. As depicted in Figure 16.4, graded tasks should be stepping stones for clients to develop skills and confidence.

ENCOURAGE REALISTIC EVALUATION OF SKILLS Before they attempt graded tasks, encourage clients to assess what skills they need to attain them. When reviewing progress, assist clients to evaluate use of targeted skills.

ENCOURAGE CLIENTS TO VIEW THEMSELVES AS PRACTITIONER-RESEARCHERS To avoid connotations of failure, encourage clients to view attempting each graded task as an experiment in which they gain valuable information about themselves. Even if unsuccessful, attempting tasks provides useful learning experiences about how clients think, feel and act.

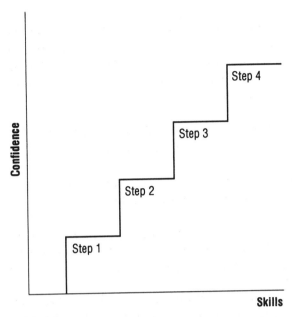

Figure 16.4 *Graded tasks as stepping stones for developing skills and confidence*

PAY ATTENTION TO FEELINGS AND THOUGHTS Help clients to share feelings and thoughts about attempting graded tasks. Where necessary, work with clients' thinking skills deficits.

ASSIST CLIENTS TO OWN SUCCESSES Not only encourage clients to acknowledge their successes, but also help them to realize that success results from willingness to take risks, expending effort and using targeted skills.

SEQUENCE NEW AND DIFFERENT TASKS AS APPROPRIATE In collaboration with clients, sequence either easier or more difficult tasks as necessary.

ENCOURAGE HOMEWORK AND PRACTICE Though some graded tasks are per-formed within counselling sessions, most are performed outside of counselling. Where feasible, encourage clients to rehearse and practise graded tasks before trying them. Repeated success experiences with specific tasks consolidate clients' skills and con-fidence.

ASSIST CLIENTS TO GENERATE AND EVALUATE ALTERNATIVE ACTIONS AND ACTION SKILLS

Many clients act in repetitive ways as if they had no choice. In Chapter 14, I discussed helping clients to stop, think, generate, evaluate and choose the best fit perception. Here I shift the focus to helping clients to generate and assess alternative actions and action skills. Clients' thinking skills deficits provide many blocks to considering alternative actions adequately: for instance, spouses continually externalizing blame to partners are likely not only to think but also to act rigidly. In such instances, counsellors need to work with relevant thinking skills as well as with action skills. On other occasions, clients may simply have developed a style of acting where they do not consider alternatives at all, do not consider enough of them or do not consider them in skills terms. Below are some examples.

> Mick, 11, thinks that the only way to act when he feels angry with another boy is to punch him.

> Becky, 32, criticizes her children vehemently whenever they leave their rooms untidy.

> Susan, 58, longs for a phone call from her son Bennie. When Bennie finally calls, Susan starts complaining that he did not call sooner.

Counsellor skills for assisting clients to generate and assess alternative actions and action skills

Following are some counsellor skills for helping clients to generate and assess alternative actions and action skills.

ASSIST CLIENTS TO DEFINE GOALS In the above examples, you could work with Mick, Becky and Susan to clarify what they wanted from their overall relationships with peers, children and son, respectively. Then you could assist them in stating appropriate goals for specific situations: for example, feeling provoked by another boy, getting frustrated over untidy rooms and feeling hurt by the lack of a phone call.

TRAIN CLIENTS IN APPROPRIATE SELF-TALK Assist clients to become aware that they always have choices in how they act. They do not have to act out their first idea of how to behave. Instead they can instruct themselves to say: 'Stop, think, what are my goals? What are alternative ways to attain them and what action skills do I need?'

MAINTAIN A SKILLS FOCUS Help clients to analyse their behaviour in skills terms. It is insufficient to think of alternative actions without also thinking of the skills entailed in such actions. For instance, if Becky decides that her best course of action is to sit down and talk to her children, she still needs to work on the verbal, voice and body message skills of doing this effectively.

ASSIST CLIENTS TO EVALUATE ACTIONS Counsellors can ask questions that challenge clients to confront how they are acting: for example, 'Is your present way of acting likely to help you attain your goals?', 'How is your current behaviour helping you?' or 'Where are your current choices taking you?' Counsellors can also ask questions that encourage clients to judge the effectiveness of specific actions. Glasser and Wubbolding provide the example of asking a parent: 'What impact did lecturing your child about school three times a day have on him? Did it help? What did it do to the family?'

(Glasser and Wubbolding, 1995, p. 305). Counsellors may also directly challenge the wisdom of actions: 'As I see it the course of action you propose is unlikely to attain your goals; are there any other approaches?'

ASSIST CLIENTS TO GENERATE ALTERNATIVES In addition to active listening, following are some counsellor skills for assisting clients to generate alternatives.

- *Use questions.* Following are some questions that counsellors might ask: 'What are your options for how you act?' and 'What action skills do you need to attain your goal?'

- *Assist brainstorming.* Counsellors can loosen clients' thinking by getting them to brainstorm options. Two rules for brainstorming are: quantity is good and suspend evaluation of ideas until later. Encourage clients to generate options, before suggesting options yourself.

- *Assist exploring opposite ways of acting.* Sometimes, though not always, clients gain valuable insights by exploring the opposite ways of acting to current intentions. For instance, the spouse who is going to give her husband a piece of her angry mind might explore being nice and taking a conciliatory approach to him.

ASSIST CLIENTS TO EVALUATE ALTERNATIVES Assist clients to evaluate the consequences for themselves and others of alternative actions. When evaluating different courses of action, counsellors and clients need to pay close attention to not only what is done, but also how it is done. As a result of evaluating alternatives, clients should choose the 'best fit' course of action that is most likely to help them attain their goals.

SUPPORT CLIENTS IN IMPLEMENTING 'BEST FIT' ACTIONS AND ACTION SKILLS Support clients as they implement their chosen actions in real life. For instance, you can work with them to identify and develop relevant skills for their 'best fit' actions. Be prepared to assist clients in developing plans. However, ensure that plans to implement actions originate with clients. Not only are clients more clearly directing their lives, they are also more likely to carry out planned actions than if the plans had originated with you (Glasser and Wubbolding, 1995). In addition, offer support and encouragement to clients developing skills for generating and evaluating alternative actions outside of counselling.

USE ACTION SKILLS EXPERIMENTS

A major concern of all effective counsellors is how best to help clients take the risks of changing their behaviours. Another major concern is how best to help them transfer trained skills to outside of counselling. Action skills experiments provide an excellent way to approach both concerns. Clients in conjunction with counsellors hypothesize about the consequences of using outside counselling the skills they learn inside. Then clients implement the skills and evaluate the consequences of their changed behaviour. An advantage of viewing changing action skills in experimental terms is that it helps clients to be detached about what they do and its results. When experiments do not work out quite as planned, clients do not have to think they have failed. Rather, each experiment is a learning experience that gathers information useful for developing action skills.

Often experiments simultaneously focus on changing both thinking and action skills. For instance, Kevin wants to increase his skills at showing affection to his girlfriend Emma. An experiment focused solely on action skills might target Kevin's skills at sending verbal, voice and body messages of affection. An experiment focused solely on thinking skills might target Kevin's skills of coping self-talk before, during and after he sends affection messages. An experiment focused on both action and thinking skills would target both how Kevin sends affection messages to Emma and his use of coping self-talk. In this section, for the sake of simplicity, I focus on changing action skills experiments.

Steps in action skills experiments

Experiments focus on the use of targeted skills in specific situations or relationships. There are six main steps in designing, conducting and evaluating action skills experiments.

1. *Assess.* Counsellors and clients assess clients' action skills strengths and deficits in problem situations.
2. *Formulate changed action skills.* Counsellors and clients work out how to behave differently in situations by using better action skills. They pay attention to voice and body messages as well as to verbal messages.
3. *Make an 'If ... then ... ' statement.* The 'If' part of the statement relates to clients rehearsing, practising and then using their changed action skills. The 'then ... ' part of the statement indicates the specific consequences they predict will follow from using their changed skills.
4. *Rehearse and practise.* Possibly with assistance from counsellors, clients need to rehearse and practise changed action skills to have a reasonable chance of implementing them properly.
5. *Try out changed action skills.* Clients implement changed action skills in actual problem situations.
6. *Evaluate.* Initially clients should evaluate their use of changed action skills on their own. This evaluation should focus on questions like 'How well did I use my changed action skills?', 'What were the positive and negative consequences for using the targeted skills for myself and for others?', 'Have my predictions been confirmed or negated?' and 'Do I want to use my changed action skills in future?' Afterwards, counsellors can assist clients in processing the learning from their experiments.

Example of designing an action skills experiment

The following is an illustrative outline for an experiment in which Kevin uses targeted action skills in how he expresses affection to Emma.

What happens when I use my action skills for expressing affection to Emma

Part A: Assessment

1. For a period of a week, monitor on a worksheet how I send expressing affection messages to Emma. Focus on strengths and deficits in each of the following sub-skills of expressing affection: verbal, voice, body, touch and action messages. Use the following column headings on my worksheet.

Date and situation	Expressing affection messages

2. List all the positive thoughts and feelings that I either fail to or inadequately convey in our relationship.

_____
_____
_____
_____

3. Based on the answers to questions 1 and 2 above, assess my action skills strengths and deficits in sending affection messages to Emma. Use the following column headings.

Expressing affection skills strengths	Expressing affection skills deficits

Part B: Make an 'If . . . then . . . ' statement

Make an 'If . . . then' statement along the lines of: 'If I use the following changed action skills (specify) to express affection to Emma during the next week, then these specific consequences (for instance, (a) I will feel better about myself for being honest, and (b) Emma will feel and act more positively toward me) are likely to follow.'

If _____

_____

then

(a) _____

(b) _____

(c) _____

(d) _____

Part C: Try out and evaluate using my action skills

During the upcoming week, try out using my changed action skills in expressing affection to Emma. What are the positive and negative consequences for myself and Emma? Have my predictions been confirmed or negated? Have I learned anything useful from this experiment? If so, what?

_____

_____

_____

_____

USE EXERCISES AND GAMES

Exercises are structured activities designed with a specific learning purpose. This book contains numerous exercises that I designed to build your lifeskills counselling skills. Whether for children or adults, exercises involving play are called games. Counsellors may assist clients to develop action skills, thinking skills, and action skills with accompanying self-talk by using exercises and games. Clients may use these materials both within counselling sessions and as take-away assignments.

There are two main sources of exercises and games: either using other people's or making up your own. Using the relating skills area as an example, existing sources of exercises include those in Johnson's *Reaching Out: Interpersonal Effectiveness and Self-actualization* (Johnson, 1993); Litvinoff's *The Relate Guide to Better Relationships: Practical Ways to Make Your Love Last from the Experts in Marriage Guidance* (Litvinoff, 1991); the author's *Relating Skills: A Practical Guide to Effective Personal Relationships* (Nelson-Jones, 1996a); and the Pfeiffer and Jones series *Structured Exercises for Human Relations Training* (1969–85).

Other people's material may not be appropriate either for the clientele or for specific clients with whom you work. If so you may need to construct some exercises. Such exercises are particularly cost-effective if they can be used repeatedly. For instance, counsellors who work with clients, many of whom have relationship difficulties, might often use exercises on making assertive requests to change others' behaviours. I encourage you not only to use existing material, but also to tap your creativity in designing learning material tailor-made to your clients' needs.

Designing exercises

Following are guidelines in designing exercises and games.

- *Set clear, specific and relevant goals.* Clients should be clear about the targeted skills they are expected to work on in the exercise. Present and demonstrate these skills prior to asking clients to do exercises in them.

- *Emphasize take-away skills.* Exercises should be highly practical and focused on learning by doing. Avoid vague exercises unrelated to the development of specific take-away skills. Many counselling students start by designing exercises that are insufficiently practical.

- *Make written instructions available.* Ensure that clients are clear about and re-member the exercise's instructions. Written instructions, as contrasted with verbal instructions, lessen the chance of slippage when clients perform exercises.

- *Demonstrate the exercise.* Demonstrate exercises between giving instructions and asking clients to perform them. Such demonstrations go beyond demonstrating skills or sub-skills to show how to do the exercise.

- *Coach and provide feedback.* Where necessary, coach clients in how to do the exercise.

- *Process the experience.* When clients have completed the exercise, give them the opportunity to share their thoughts and feelings about it. Ensure that clients understand the main learning from the exercise.

- *Pilot the exercise.* If possible, pilot your exercise to see if it works. If necessary, refine the exercise or even discard it and try again.

ASSIST CLIENTS TO USE SELF-REWARD

Counsellors may choose to use reinforcement or reward to help develop action skills. Counsellor-administered rewards include praise, encouragement, smiles and head nods. However, ultimately clients have to learn to perform targeted action skills independent of your rewards. Clients may also influence and administer their own rewards. Approaches using counsellor-administered and client-administered rewards are based on operant conditioning (Skinner, 1953, 1969). The word 'operant' emphas-izes the fact that behaviour operates on the environment to produce consequences as well as being influenced or contingent upon the responses produced by that environment. Where clients find responses rewarding, the probability of their using the action skills again increases, and vice versa.

Basic concepts

Here, I use the everyday word 'reward' in preference to the more technical term 'reinforcement'. Reward better suits the language of self-helping. Following are some basic reward concepts.

- *Positive reward.* Providing positive rewards entails presenting stimuli that increase the probability of responses occurring: for example, money increases the probability of work responses. Positive rewards can be verbal, material and imaginal.

- *Negative reward.* Negative reward also increases the probability of a response occuring through removing something from the situation: for example, removing teachers from classrooms increases the probability of pupils talking.

- *Contingencies of reward.* To consider adequately the contingencies or circumstances involved in the provision of rewards, take into account: (1) the occasion upon which a response occurs; (2) the response itself; (3) the rewarding consequences.

- *Schedules of reward.* Basically there are three reward schedules: reward each response; do not reward any response; and intermittently reward responses. Intermittent rewards can be very powerful: for instance, in sustaining gambling behaviour.

- *Self-reward.* Here clients influence how they act by administering their own rewards.

- *Prompting and fading.* Prompts are verbal, physical or environmental cues that direct clients' attention to desired actions. Fading entails progressively eliminating prompts.

- *Shaping.* Action skills may be shaped by rewarding successive approximations to targeted goals.

- *Covert conditioning.* Using clients' imaginations to provide consequences of varying agrees of reward.

Assist clients to identify suitable rewards

In many instances, clients find that using targeted action skills both is intrinsically rewarding and brings about rewards from others. For instance, clients developing appreciation skills may enjoy using paying compliments skills, give pleasure and also receive it. On other occasions clients may need to strengthen their motivation by self-administering rewards. Kazdin observes: 'In most applications of self-reinforcement, two procedures can be delineated. First, the client can determine the response require-ments needed for a given amount of reinforcement ... Second, the client can dispense reinforcement for achieving a particular criterion, which may or may not be self-determined' (Kazdin, 1994, pp. 270–1).

The basic idea in using self-reward to develop action skills is that clients make the administration of rewards contingent upon occurrence of target behaviours (Watson and Tharp, 1989). Rewards should be accessible and potent (Cormier and Cormier, 1991). Consequently, you may need to assist clients in identifying suitable rewards. There are several ways of helping clients to identify rewards, including asking them, getting them to monitor what they find rewarding, asking others who know them, though here you must be sensitive to confidentiality, observing them and asking them to fill out reward questionnaires.

MacPhillamy and Lewinsohn's *Pleasant Events Schedule* is an example of an identify-ing rewards questionnaire (Lewinsohn *et al.*, 1986; MacPhillamy and Lewinsohn, 1982). The questionnaire consists of 320 'pleasing events'. Respondents rate each item on three-point scales for frequency and pleasantness during the previous month. The authors believe that one way to combat clients' feelings of depression is to encourage them to participate in more rewarding activities. Illustrative pleasant events include being with happy people, thinking about friends, breathing clean air, listening to music, reading a good book, petting and necking, eating good meals, being seen as sexually attractive, seeing beautiful scenery and visiting friends.

For children, pictures may portray rewards. An example is Daley's 'reinforcement menu' for finding effective rewards for eight-year-old to eleven-year-old mentally retarded children (Daley, 1969). Daley enclosed 22 high-probability rewarding activ-ities drawn in colour in a single book or 'menu', with one activity per page. Children identified rewarding activities from the 'menu' book.

Assist clients to deliver self-rewards

Counsellors can assist clients in knowing how to deliver positive self-rewards. There are two main categories of reward that clients can self-administer: external and internal.

- *External reward.* External reward includes: (1) self-administration of new rewards that are outside the client's everyday life, such as a new item of clothing or a special event; and (2) initial denial of some pleasant everyday experience and later administration of it contingent upon a desired action. Kanfer and Gaelick-Buys (1991) observe that wherever possible a positive self-reward should be relevant to the target behaviour: for instance, clients achieving weight-loss goals might buy slimmer fitting clothes.

- *Internal reward.* Internal reward includes self-talk statements like 'That's great', 'I did it' or 'Well done', that clearly indicate the client's satisfaction at performing a sub-goal or goal. Clients can use their imaginations to visualize significant others praising their efforts.

Work with clients to determine the precise conditions for self-administering rewards. In the making of positive self-reward plans, several considerations may be pertinent: identification of rewards; sequencing of graded steps in developing action skills; and clear connections between achievement and reward. It is best for clients to reward themselves immediately after performing targeted action skills or sub-skills.

Counsellors can encourage clients to draw up contracts that specify the relationship between administering positive self-rewards and developing targeted action skills. Contracts should establish clear-cut criteria for achievement and specify the means whereby behaviour is observed, measured and recorded. Contracts can be unilateral or bilateral. In unilateral contracts clients obligate themselves to personal change programmes independent of contributions from others. Bilateral contracts, commonly used in relationship counselling, stipulate obligations and rewards for each of the parties. For example, partners can contract with one another to increase their exchange of caring behaviours for a specified time period (Nelson-Jones, 1996a; Stuart, 1980).

Not all clients like self-reward plans or follow them. Some clients consider the use of self-reward to be too mechanical. You may introduce self-reward ideas too soon, before clients are sufficiently motivated to change. Assess how well clients accept the idea of self-reward and their motivation for change. Often you need to intervene with clients' thinking skills deficits that hinder change.

Assist clients to modify their environments

In addition to helping clients to use self-reward, you can assist them in modifying their environments to overcome action skills deficits and develop action skills strengths. Clients can modify environments to influence action skills prior to their execution. Often self-reward plans entail clients using both positive self-reward skills and modifying environment skills.

Counsellors can assist clients to develop *stimulus control* skills (Kanfer and Gaelick-Buys, 1991; Kazdin, 1994; Thoresen and Mahoney, 1974). With stimulus control, clients learn to use the presence or absence of environmental prompts to influence behaviour. Stimulus control can be used both to develop strengths and to modify deficits. An example of the use of stimulus control to enhance an action skills strength is that of students who specify a place that they use only for study. An example of stimulus control to help overcome an action skills deficit is that of Terry, who has a goal of losing 25 pounds by the end of the next three months. Ways in which Terry modifies her environment to influence her eating skills deficit include putting food out of sight and easy reach, equipping her refrigerator with a time lock and only keeping as much food in the house as can be consumed in a short period of time. In addition, Terry tries to control her environment by associating with people who are counting calories and interested in exercise.

Terry's counsellor also encourages her to engage in *stimulus narrowing*. Stimulus narrowing involves reducing the number of stimuli associated with her eating skills deficit. Terry agrees that it is a good idea to eat only in the dining room and, where feasible, only in the presence of certain family members.

USE COUNSELLOR'S AIDES AND HELP CLIENTS TO OBTAIN SUPPORT

Counsellors can use third parties to develop clients' action skills and assist clients to identify and use third parties to support change attempts.

Using counsellor's aides

Reasons why counsellors enlist others as aides include pressure of work and the opportunity to extend interventions into clients' home environments. Counsellors may use a variety of people as aides: teachers, parents, paraprofessionals, supervisors and friends. Following are two examples.

> Janie, aged 8, is referred by her teacher, Felicity, to Anna, the school counsellor, because she is very shy and does not participate in class. As part of Janie's treatment plan, Anna enlists Felicity's help both to ask questions that draw Janie out and to reward her when she participates in class. In addition, Anna asks Felicity to monitor any changes in how well Janie relates to the other children in the playground.

> Rachel, 21, volunteers to be a student paraprofessional 'companion therapist' in a programme to support anorexic and bulimic fellow students undergoing professional treatment at the university counselling service (Lenihan and Kirk, 1990). Rachel undergoes a 25-hour training programme. She then maintains daily personal or phone contact with her allocated client. In addition, she engages in such activities as joint exercise, walking and lunching. Rachel also helps her client to monitor nutrition and assists with meal planning and shopping.

Following are skills in selecting and using counsellor's aides.

IDENTIFY SUITABLE AIDES Carefully select and screen counsellor's aides. They have the potential to do both harm and good.

OBTAIN CLIENT PERMISSION Always obtain adult clients' permissions to discuss their behaviour with 'non-professional' third parties. Clients need to accept the potential usefulness of counsellor's aides if they are to work with them. Sometimes it may be inappropriate to obtain children's permission: for instance, in the above example of Janie's teacher helping her.

INVOLVE AIDES IN PLANNING INTERVENTIONS Counsellor's aides, such as teachers, parents and supervisors, may have special knowledge of how best to support clients in developing action skills. Furthermore, if consulted, aides may be more motivated to participate in treatment plans than if they think plans are imposed on them.

TRAIN AIDES Some counsellor's aides work with many different clients. Where this is the case, effort put into training them may reap rich rewards. Even where aides work with single clients, it is essential that they understand their roles and can competently carry them out.

SUPPORT AND DEBRIEF AIDES Keep in touch with aides and make sure that they perform their functions as agreed. Give aides the opportunity to share thoughts and feelings about clients and about their contribution to treatment programmes. Where necessary, revise agreements on how your aides should assist.

WITHDRAW OR FADE COUNSELLOR'S AIDE ASSISTANCE Clients need to learn how to perform action skills without the others' assistance. Consider how best to withdraw your aide's assistance. One option is to withdraw all assistance at once. Another option is to withdraw progressively or to fade assistance.

Assist clients to identify and use supports

Counsellors may need to raise some clients' awareness about the importance of identifying and using supports and of lessening contact with unsupportive people. Counsellors and clients can work together to identify people in home environments who can support their efforts to develop targeted skills. For example, university students with study skills deficits can seek out sympathetic lecturers and tutors to help them to develop specific skills: for instance, how to write essays or prepare for examinations. Unemployed people can approach friends and relatives, who may not only offer them emotional support, but also be sources for job leads. Women working on developing assertion skills can seek out women's groups where they may find other women with similar objectives. Teachers who feel burned out can associate with colleagues relatively happy with their lot rather than those perpetually complaining. Furthermore, they can develop self-care skills by engaging in recreational activities with people unconnected with education.

An inverse approach to support is for counsellors and clients to identify unsympathetic or counterproductive people. Clients are then left with various choices: getting such people to accept, if not support, their efforts to change; seeing less of them; or stopping seeing them altogether. If these people are family members, avoiding them altogether may be difficult, especially if clients are financially dependent on them. Here, counsellors and clients may discuss damage control strategies. However, often clients can choose their friendship and membership groups. For example, if juvenile delinquents want to develop action skills that integrate them into the wider community, they may need to change the company they keep (Sarason, 1976).

CHAPTER HIGHLIGHTS

- *Action skills interventions require adequate assessments of clients' action skills deficits.*

- *Counsellors and clients may focus on action skills before, after or simultaneously with thinking skills.*

- *Diaries and journals, frequency charts and recording logs are methods of client self-monitoring.*

- *Skills for assisting client monitoring include offering reasons, training clients in discrimination and recording, designing simple and clear logs, using reward and encouraging clients to evaluate information.*

- *Skills for conducting role-play rehearsals include explaining reasons for role-playing, setting scenes, assessment, formulating changed actions, rehearsing and processing.*

- *Counsellors and clients may use timetables to schedule daily activities, set minimum goals, create personal space, keep contracts and perform homework.*

- *When assisting timetabling, always provide the timetables and be sensitive to clients' anxieties and resistances.*

- *Counsellors and clients can plan sub-goals either by sequencing sub-skills or by sequencing graded tasks.*

- *Counsellors can assist clients to be more flexible in how they act by helping them to develop skills of generating and evaluating alternatives and choosing the 'best fit' actions and action skills.*

- *Action skills experiments encourage clients to try out new skills. Six steps in action skills experiments are: (1) assess; (2) formulate changed action skills; (3) make an 'if ... then ... ' statement; (4) rehearse and practice; (5) try out changed actions; and (6) evaluate.*

- *Counsellors may either use other people's exercises and games or design their own. Exercises and games should emphasize development of practical take-away skills.*

- *Counsellors can assist clients to use self-reward by helping them to identify suitable rewards and self-administer rewards contingent on performance of targeted skills.*

- *Stimulus control, using or discarding prompts that influence behaviour, is a useful client skill for modifying their environments.*

- *Counsellors may use third parties as aides. Select aides carefully and train and support them.*

- *Counsellors can also train clients to identify and use supports in their home environments.*

EXERCISE 16.1 DEVELOPING CLIENTS' MONITORING SKILLS

As appropriate, complete parts of this exercise on your own, with a partner or in a group.

Part A   Monitoring your actions
Make out a frequency chart as shown below for the different types of beverage you drink. For the next seven days chart how many times you drink each beverage.

Beverage	Day 1	Day 2	Day 3	Day 4	Day 5	Day 6	Day 7
1.							
2.							

1. What have you learned from this monitoring exercise about your drinking behaviour?

2. What have you learned from this exercise about how to assist clients to monitor their behaviour?

Part B   Assisting a client to monitor his or her actions
Role-play a counselling session with a partner who has a goal of wanting to alter a specific action skills deficit. You decide that it would help both you and your client if he or she were systematically to observe the frequency of his or her action skills deficit over the next week. Within the context of a good counselling relationship, use the following skills:

- offer reasons for monitoring;

- train the client in discrimination and recording;

- design a simple and clear recording log.

Afterwards, discuss with your partner and reverse roles.

Part C   Assisting a client to record use of targeted action skills
Conduct a further counselling role-play with a partner. You are now training the client
in the verbal, voice and body dimensions required to develop a specific action skills
strength: for example, making an assertive request. Make a recording log in the format
below and make sure that your client knows how to fill it out for each time he or she
attempts to use the targeted skill.

Targeted skill _____

Verbal message sub-goal(s) _____
Voice message sub-goal(s) _____
Body message sub-goal(s) _____

Date and situation	How I acted		
	Verbal skills	**Voice skills**	**Body skills**
1.			
2.			

Afterwards, discuss with your partner and reverse roles.

EXERCISE 16.2   CONDUCTING ROLE-PLAY REHEARSALS

Conduct a session with a partner as 'client' in which you aim to help him or her to use
a targeted action skill in a specific problematic situation in his or her life. Conduct one
or more role-play rehearsals of the targeted action skills with your client using the
following skills:

- explain reasons for role-play;

- set the scene;

- assess current actions;

- formulate changed actions;

- rehearse changed actions;

- process each role-play.

Afterwards, discuss and get feedback on your use of role-play rehearsal skills from your
partner. Then reverse roles.

EXERCISE 16.3   DEVELOPING TIMETABLING SKILLS

As appropriate, complete parts of this exercise on your own, with a partner or in a group.

Part A   Thinking about timetabling
For each of the following areas, assess if, with what kinds of clients and why you might use timetabling to develop action skills.

1. Scheduling daily activities
2. Setting minimum goals
3. Creating personal space
4. Keeping contracts
5. Performing take-away assignments

Part B   Assisting a client to timetable
Conduct a counselling session with a partner as client. Your client has an action skills deficit for which you decide that it will benefit him or her to use timetabling between sessions. Assist your partner to timetable using the following skills:

- provide the timetable;

- offer reasons for timetabling;

- be sensitive to anxieties and resistances;

- ensure your client knows what to do.

Afterwards, discuss the exercise with your partner and obtain feedback on your use of skills when assisting timetabling. Then reverse roles.

EXERCISE 16.4   PLANNING SUB-GOALS AND SEQUENCING GRADED TASKS

As appropriate, complete parts of the exercise on your own or with a partner.

Part A   Developing a graded task plan for yourself
1. What is the difference between breaking skills down into their component parts and taking a step-by-step approach to learning and homework tasks?

2. For a specific action skill that you wish to strengthen in your life, sequence a hierarchy of progressively more difficult learning tasks to enact as take-away assignments. Start with the easiest task first. Plan a minimum of five graded tasks.

Targeted action skill:

Task 1

Task 2

Task 3

Task 4

Task 5

and so on

Part B   Developing a graded task plan for a client
Conduct a counselling session with a partner as a 'client', with a goal of developing a
specific action skills strength. You decide that the best way to help your client is for him
or her to work through a sequence of graded tasks between sessions. Sequence
progressively more difficult graded tasks using the following skills:

• relate graded tasks to targeted skills;

• sequence graded tasks in cooperation with the client;

• encourage realistic assessment of existing skills;

• encourage the client to adopt a practitioner-researcher approach;

• pay attention to feelings and thoughts;

• encourage homework and practice.

Afterwards, discuss your counselling session with your client, including obtaining
feedback on your assisting sequencing of graded tasks skills. Then reverse roles.

EXERCISE 16.5   GENERATING AND EVALUATING ALTERNATIVE ACTIONS AND ACTION SKILLS

As appropriate, complete parts of this exercise on your own or with a partner.

Part A   Developing your own alternative courses of action
Think of a specific situation in your life where you would like to act differently.

1.   Describe the situation and how currently you act.

2.   What is (are) your goal(s) in the situation?

3. Generate and evaluate at least three alternative courses of action in the situation:

    (a) course of action 1
       evaluation 1
    (b) course of action 2
       evaluation 2
    (c) course of action 3
       evaluation 3

    Star the course of action alternative that represents the 'best fit' way of acting in the situation to attain your goal(s).

4. What action skills do you need to implement your chosen course of action effectively?

Part B Assisting a client to develop alternative courses of action
Counsel a partner who wishes to act more effectively in a specific situation. Once you have identified the situation and clarified how your client currently acts, use the following skills for helping your client to generate and assess alternative actions and action skills:

- assisting defining goals;

- training appropriate self-talk;

- assisting evaluating current actions;

- assisting generating alternatives
     using questions
     brain-storming
     exploring opposite ways of acting;

- assisting evaluating alternatives and choosing the 'best fit';

- assisting identifying relevant action skills for implementing best fit alternative;

- if appropriate, assisting planning for how best to implement action skills.

Afterwards, discuss the exercise and obtain feedback on your assisting generating and evaluating alternative action skills. Then reverse roles.

EXERCISE 16.6   USING AN ACTION SKILLS EXPERIMENT

As appropriate, do sections of this exercise on your own or with a partner.

1. *Assess.* Assess your current counselling skills strengths and deficits in using action skills experiments.

    (a) strengths
    (b) weaknesses

2. *Formulate changed action skills.* Ensure that you know what is entailed in setting up an experiment with a client. I am using the six steps in this exercise to make it easier for you to remember. Work out how you might use an action skills experiment in your work with a specific client (who may be a partner acting as 'client'). Pay attention to your voice and body as well as to your verbal messages.

3. *Make an 'if ... then ... ' statement.* The 'if' part of the statement relates to you as a counsellor using your skills to use a changing action skills experiment with your client. The 'then ... ' part of the statement indicates the specific consequences for yourself and your client that you predict will follow.

    If I intervene by using a changing action skills experiment with ... (state name of client) to help him or her develop the targeted skill(s) of ... (specify targeted skill(s)), *then* I predict the following consequences (please specify):

    (a) for myself as a counsellor
    (b) for my client

4. *Rehearse and practise.* If possible rehearse and practise your designing, conducting and evaluating action skills experiments. Rehearsal and practice should ensure that you have a reasonable chance of using the intervention well.

5. *Try out changed action skills.* Interview your 'client', who has a goal of developing a specific action skill. Use your counsellor skills for intervening with an action skills experiment. Together with your client go through at least the first four steps of this outline in relation to experimenting with changing his or her action skills.

6. *Evaluate.*

    (a) How well did you use your intervening by means of an action skills experiment skills?
    (b) Were your predictions concerning the consequences for yourself as a counsellor confirmed or negated?

(c) Were your predictions concerning the consequences for your client confirmed or negated?

(d) Has doing this exercise taught you anything about how you might be a more effective counsellor? If so, what?

EXERCISE 16.7 DESIGNING AN EXERCISE OR GAME

As appropriate, complete parts of this exercise on your own, with a partner or in a group.

Part A Designing an exercise and developing written instructions
Design an exercise or game you can use for helping either individuals or couples with whom you either currently work or would like to work. Use the following skills:

• set clear, specific and relevant goals;

• emphasize take-away skills;

• write out a set of instructions to give as a handout to the client or clients covering the following points:

(a) goal of exercise or game
(b) main learning points
(c) instructions for each step of the exercise or game.

Part B Counselling a client using an exercise or game
Work with a partner who acts as a client typical of those for whom you have designed the exercise in part A above. Demonstrate how to do the exercise and, if necessary, coach the client not only in the targeted skills but also in how to do your particular exercise. Afterwards, discuss and obtain feedback on your designing and presenting an exercise or game skills. Then reverse roles.

EXERCISE 16.8 ASSISTING CLIENTS TO USE SELF-REWARD

As appropriate, complete parts of this exercise on your own, with a partner or in a group.

Part A Identifying rewards
1. Spend the next 10 to 15 minutes brain-storming as many things as possible that people might find rewarding in their lives. As you go along, record your ideas on a whiteboard or piece of paper. Then each of you independently rates each item on the following scale for how rewarding engaging in it is for you.

Rating scale

Extremely rewarding	4
Very rewarding	3
Moderately rewarding	2
Slightly rewarding	1
Not rewarding at all	0

2. Spend the next ten minutes identifying as many ways as you can think of in which counsellors and clients may either intentionally or unintentionally administer rewards to each other. Which are the most important ways? Use the following column headings.

Rewards from counsellor to client	**Rewards from client to counsellor**

Part B   Designing a plan using self-reward to develop an action skill

1. *Designing a plan for yourself.* Design a plan, either for yourself or for a real or hypothetical client, that uses self-reward to develop a specific action skill. Your plan should contain the following elements:

    (a) your overall goal
    (b) a sequence of three to five graded steps to develop the action skill
    (c) what reward(s) you intend using
    (d) how to observe, measure and record the rewards you intend using
    (e) the precise conditions for self-administering reward(s)
    (f) a time frame

2. *Designing a plan with a client.* Conduct a counselling session with your partner in which together you design a plan for helping him or her to develop a specific action skill. Afterwards, discuss and obtain feedback on your counselling skills. Then reverse roles.

SEVENTEEN
Interventions for feelings

We know too much and feel too little.

Bertrand Russell

CHAPTER QUESTIONS

• *What is the counsellor's role when focusing on feelings?*

• *Why should counsellors emphasize clients' responsibility for their feelings?*

• *What are some interventions for assisting clients to experience feelings?*

• *What are some interventions for assisting clients to express feelings?*

• *What are some interventions for assisting clients to manage feelings?*

• *What are some skills for relaxing clients?*

• *What is systematic desensitization?*

INTRODUCTION

The lifeskills counselling approach attaches great importance to influencing clients' feelings and physical reactions so that their underlying animal nature works for them rather than against them. All clients' problems involve feelings one way or another. This chapter builds on the previous chapters by showing how to influence how clients

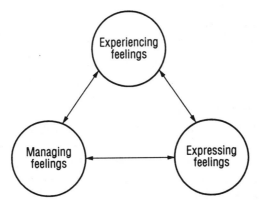

Figure 17.1 *Interrelationships between experiencing, expressing and managing feelings*

feel by intervening with their thinking skills and action skills. The area of feelings is complex. I have subdivided it into three main areas: experiencing feelings, expressing feelings and managing negative feelings. Figure 17.1 depicts the interrelationships between these areas.

Broadly speaking, counsellors can take two main approaches to clients' feelings. First, there is the facilitative approach, in which you use active listening skills to help clients to experience, disclose and explore feelings. You assume that if clients truly experience their significant feelings and self-actualizing drives they think rationally and act appropriately. Second, there is the training approach, in which you use training skills to assist clients to make better choices in how they feel. The facilitative approach emphasizes experiencing feelings, whereas the training approach emphasizes expressing and managing feelings. Rogers's person-centred therapy and cognitive-behavioural therapy are prime examples of the facilitative and training approaches, respectively.

Lifeskills counselling draws on both facilitative and training approaches to feelings. Counsellors as developmental educators need to assist clients not only to get in touch with their animal nature, but also to use what distinguishes them from lower animals, their capacity for reason and thinking, to regulate and manage that nature. Lifeskills counsellors flexibly use both the counselling relationship and training skills to assist clients to experience, express and managing feelings.

Assist clients to own responsibility for feelings

Clients are responsible not only for their thoughts and actions, but for their feelings too. Whatever other interventions you use for clients' problematic feelings, always work on the assumption that clients are responsible for feelings. Following are three examples of clients needing to assume more responsibility for feelings.

> *Experiencing feelings*
> Matt, 17, sees his school counsellor to decide what university and course he should apply for. Matt has few ideas of his own and relies mainly on others' thoughts and feelings about what he should do.

Expressing feelings
Fran, 27, is in a relationship that is heading for the rocks. She has great difficulty expressing both positive and negative feelings to her boyfriend, Josh.

Managing feelings
Paula, 43, is the headteacher of an urban school with huge staff morale and discipline problems. Over the past few weeks, Paula has been getting increasingly tense, anxious and depressed about her work and life.

Responsibility for feelings has different dimensions: for instance, 'How can I get in touch with my feelings?', 'Who or what creates my feelings?' and 'What can I do about my feelings?' Assist clients to see that they have choices in how they feel. Though past and present circumstances may influence how clients feel, such circumstances do not create how they feel. Assist clients to see that they have choices both in how they express feelings and in how they react to others' feelings. However, go beyond making clients aware that they are responsible for their feelings and feelings choices. Clients need to know how to do it. They require relevant thinking and action skills for assuming effective responsibility for their feelings both now and in future.

ASSIST CLIENTS TO EXPERIENCE FEELINGS

Question: How many counsellors does it take to change a light bulb?
Answer: One, but the light bulb has to feel like changing.

In Chapters 2 and 9, I listed getting in touch with your feelings as a thinking skill. The main reason for viewing experiencing feelings as a thinking skill is that, frequently, feelings are the parents of thoughts. I delayed discussing interventions for assisting clients to experience feelings until this chapter because I wanted to present experiencing feelings in the same chapter as expressing feelings and managing feelings. By presenting all three aspects of feelings together, I hope to give readers a clearer overall picture of the role of feelings in counselling and in life.

Experiencing feelings has at least three dimensions. First, clients need the actual sensation of experiencing feelings rather than blocking them off or distorting them. Second, clients require the skills of exploring feelings and of following feelings trails to see where they lead. Third, clients require the skills of labelling feelings accurately. Following are some interventions to assist clients to experience, explore and label feelings.

Explain reasons for focusing on feelings

You can help some clients if you legitimize the importance of focusing on feelings. How you do this depends upon the needs of individual clients. Let us take the example of Matt, the 17-year-old, whose school counsellor discovers that he relies on others' thoughts and feelings to guide his choice of university and course. Here, if you were the school counsellor, you have a number of choices, albeit not mutually exclusive. First, you can keep using active listening skills in the hope that Matt becomes more inner than outer directed. Second, you can challenge him along the lines of: 'Matt, you seem to be saying a lot about what your parents and teachers want for you, but I'm wondering what *you* think and feel about *your* choice of university and course?' Note the emphasis on you and your. Third, you can suggest to Matt that he takes an occupational interest inventory to assist self-exploration. Fourth, you can offer Matt reasons for acknowledging his own feelings more fully.

> 'Matt, you seem to say a lot about what your parents and teachers want for you. However, I get the impression that you inadequately attend to *your* feelings about what *you* want to do. Though not the only source, your feelings can provide you with a rich source of information about what might be the right choices for you. Learning to acknowledge and listen to your feelings is a skill. If you inadequately listen to your feelings, you risk making choices that you may later regret. I think you need to develop skills of focusing more on your feelings. What do you think?'

Explaining reasons for focusing on feelings may lead to a discussion with clients about how much they think they are in touch with feelings and their fears about expressing them. As an intervention for aiding emotional responsiveness, it needs to be accompanied by other interventions. However, explaining reasons may accelerate some clients in taking feelings more seriously as a basis for future feelings work.

Focus on thinking skills

Counsellors can assist clients to develop thinking skills conducive to experiencing feelings. Following are thinking skills deficits blocking experiencing feelings. I refer you to Chapters 14 and 15 on how to develop clients' thinking skills.

OWNING RESPONSIBILITY FOR CHOOSING Already I have stressed the importance of helping clients to realize that they have choices in how they feel, including how they experience feelings and what feelings they experience. Emery (1982) uses the term 'choice-ability' for people's ability to choose how they feel.

USING COPING SELF-TALK Clients can talk to themselves in ways that enhance their capacity to get in touch with feelings. They may make calming self-statements like 'Relax', 'Calm down', 'Take a deep breath'. Clients may make coaching self-statements, like 'Let's clear a space to truly get in touch with what I feel', 'Remember, my feelings are important and I need to spend time getting in touch with them' or 'Don't rush into a decision, let's feel and think this one through.' In addition, clients can make affirming self-statements: for example, 'I have a right to acknowledge my feelings' and 'My feelings are important.' Often clients can combine calming, coaching and affirming self-statements: 'Relax. Take time to get in touch with how I feel about this. My feelings are important.'

CHOOSING REALISTIC PERSONAL RULES Many clients have personal rules that get in the way of experiencing feelings. Samples of such musturbatory rules are:

I must never have strong feelings.

Women must not acknowledge feelings of ambition.

Men must be strong and silent.

Boys must be competitive rather than cooperative.

Religious people must always be self-effacing.

I must not have strong sexual feelings because they are dirty and animal.

I must never openly acknowledge that I care for others and for the welfare of the human race.

Counsellors can assist clients to become aware of rules unhelpful to experiencing feelings and dispute and restate them into more realistic rules.

PERCEIVING ACCURATELY Clients have much more choice in how they feel than most realize. Counsellors can assist clients to make links between how they perceive and how they feel. Clients can develop skills of not restricting themselves to the first feeling they experience. Instead they can generate and evaluate alternative perceptions, which in turn lead to alternative feelings. Clients can then choose the 'best fit' perceptions and feelings. Sometimes counsellors can assist clients' 'choice-ability' by getting them to explore opposite feelings to how they say they feel. For instance, clients may get more in touch with what they truly feel by exploring feelings of love towards someone they say they hate. Counsellors may assist clients in feeling less negatively about themselves and others. Searching for strengths in oneself and others in a way of attaining this outcome.

EXPLAINING CAUSE ACCURATELY Counsellors can assist clients to explain the causes of their feelings accurately. For instance, depressed clients may ascribe the cause of all negative events to themselves (Beck, 1991; Beck and Weishaar, 1995). Other clients may project negative feelings about themselves on to others: for instance, jealous clients being hypersensitive about another's jealousy. Many clients externalize the cause of their own feelings on to others: for instance, 'It's all his or her fault' or 'He or she made me feel that way.'

PREDICTING REALISTICALLY Disorders of prediction permeate how people experience negative emotions and fail to experience genuinely positive feelings. Distorted predictions play a large part in depression (Bandura, 1986, 1989; Beck, 1991; Seligman, 1991). Unrealistic predictions of physical or psychological danger are systematic biases in processing information that characterize patients suffering from anxiety disorders (Beck and Weishaar, 1995). Many who feel shy predict that they will be rejected. Other clients require help in containing feelings of optimism: for instance, manic clients or clients who do not take health risks seriously enough.

SETTING REALISTIC GOALS Clients with unrealistic goals set themselves up to feel anxious about attaining them and depressed if unsuccessful. Clients setting proximal or short-range goals enhance their motivation and feelings of self-efficacy (Bandura, 1986).

USING VISUALIZING SKILLS Counsellors can both elicit feelings and enhance many clients' experiencing of past feelings by asking them to visualize situations in which they occurred. You can also use visualizing to help clients to experience feelings about the future: for instance, taking them through a guided imagery about getting married or moving house. Furthermore, you may enhance feelings of competence by getting clients to visualize themselves performing competently.

REALISTIC DECISION MAKING Counsellors can educate clients to the importance of listening to feelings when making decisions. Assist clients' awareness of when feelings interfere with realistic decisions: for instance, being impulsive or excessively vigilant. Furthermore, assist clients to experience and explore feelings of commitment or lack of commitment to implementing decisions.

PREVENTING AND MANAGING PROBLEMS Counsellors can assist clients to listen to their early warnings signals that they may need either to prevent or to manage problems. For instance, tuning into feelings of stress early on may prevent more serious stress-related problems. You can also assist clients to see that experiencing and labelling feelings accurately is an important part of the process of managing problems and altering problematic skills.

Use active listening

In Chapters 5 and 6, I presented a range of active listening skills. Again I emphasize the importance of active listening. Active listening can be particularly useful in unfreezing or thawing clients whose experiencing of feelings is being or has been significantly frozen by adverse family of origin circumstances. The affirmation that counsellors provide with their time, attention and understanding can increase clients' sense of worth and lower anxiety and defensiveness. By being sensitively responded to, clients gain practice at listening to themselves, valuing their own experiencing and increasingly identifying and labelling it accurately. Though active listening skills are not always sufficient or sufficiently expeditious for helping clients get in touch with feelings, they are invariably necessary. However, there are limits to the pace at which clients out of touch with feelings can work. Consequently, another facet of active listening is showing sensitivity to clients' comfort zones.

Train clients in inner listening

So far I have emphasized the need for counsellors to be rewarding listeners to clients. However, clients also need to develop skills of being rewarding listeners to themselves. They need to experience, become aware of, explore and label their own feelings. Assuming that clients have a moderate degree of insight, you can impart inner listening as a self-helping skill.

Following are elements of inner listening training.

- *Explain reasons for focusing on inner listening.* Assist clients to realize that this is a useful skill for understanding both themselves and others. Clarify what you mean by experiencing feelings, exploring them and labelling them accurately.

- *Stress creating sufficient time and psychological space.* To practise inner listening, clients must give it sufficient priority in their lives. This may mean that they either spend a certain amount of time with themselves each day or make sure to clear a space when something bothers them or needs deciding.

- *Present and demonstrate the skill.* Much of the active listening material in Chapters 5 and 6 is relevant here, but with modification. For instance, the concept of internal viewpoint in this context becomes that of getting inside your own rather than another's internal viewpoint. In inner listening, it is vital that clients tune into feelings, flow with them, try to understand their messages and label them accurately. You may help clients to understand the skill if you demonstrate it by verbalizing your feelings and thoughts when attempting to listen to yourself.

- *Coach and negotiate take-away assignments.* Coach clients to ensure that they understand the skill of inner listening. Take-away assignments, in which clients practise the component parts of the skill, act as a bridge between counselling and clients relying on their own resources.

Eugene Gendlin and Fritz Perls are two writers who have stressed the need for inner listening and awareness. Gendlin (1981) developed a method termed *focusing* to help people to change and live from a deeper place than just their thoughts and feelings. In focusing, people clear a space and make contact with a special kind of internal bodily awareness called a 'felt sense'. When people get in touch with this 'felt sense' there can be a felt physical shift in their bodies as well as different perspectives on problems.

Perls, the founder of Gestalt therapy, developed a technique he called *focal awareness*. Perls observed: 'The basic sentence with which we ask our patients to begin therapy and which we retain throughout its course – not only in words, but in spirit – is the simple phrase: "Now I am aware" ' (Perls, 1973, p. 65). When using focal awareness, Perls asked clients to concentrate and become aware of their body language, breathing, voice quality and emotions as much as of any pressing thoughts. He aimed to make clients aware not only that they interrupted their contact with themselves but also how they did this. A variation of focal awareness is to ask clients to say 'Now I choose' instead of 'Now I am aware' – to raise their awareness that they are active choosers in their lives. Counsellors may train clients in both focusing and focal awareness as self-helping skills.

Use feelings and physical reactions questions

Counsellors can use feelings questions to encourage clients to experience and share feelings and physical reactions. Be careful not to get clients talking about feelings in distant ways rather than experiencing them. Another danger of using feelings questions is that clients will respond to counsellors rather than get in touch with themselves. However, if skilfully used, feelings questions can give clients useful practice at listening to and becoming more aware of their feelings. Feelings and physical reactions questions include:

'How do you feel about that?'

'I'm wondering what the emotional impact of that is on you.'

'Could you describe your feelings more fully?'

'I'm hearing that you're feeling ... '

'You seem to have conflicting feelings. On the one hand ... on the other hand ... '

'What are your physical reactions?'

'How does your body experience the feeling?'

Be authentic and appropriately self-disclose

The ability of counsellors to be real is very important for assisting clients to experience feelings. Rogers used terms like congruence and genuineness (Rogers, 1957, 1975). Existential psychologists use terms like presence and authenticity (Bugental, 1981; May, 1958). Bugental views presence as consisting of an intake side called accessibility, allowing what happens in situations to affect you, and an output side called expressiveness, making available some of the content of your subjective awareness without editing. If you are alive and present in relating to clients, you demonstrate experiencing feelings and create the climate for them to do so too. Some research suggests that female counsellors experience and express feelings more than male counsellors (Maracek and Johnson, 1980). Mintz and O'Neil (1990, p. 384) observe that research studies 'suggest that female therapists may form more effective therapeutic alliances and be more affectively oriented than are male therapists.'

Clients may perceive counsellors able to experience and express feelings and share personal information as more similar to themselves (Edwards and Murdock, 1994). Showing involvement and sharing information may make it easier for clients to experience feelings: for instance, feminist counsellors with women clients, gay counsellors with gay clients and former drug addicts with substance abuse clients.

Challenge inauthenticity

Counsellors can use their here-and-now experiencing as guides to whether clients communicate what they really think and feel. Clients may wear masks and play roles that interfere with their experiencing and expressing what they truly feel. Such roles include playing the clown, playing dumb or playing helpless. Counsellors may make clients aware of such tendencies: for example, 'I get the impression that whenever you get close to your deeper feelings, you use humour to avoid revealing them.' Counsellors can also challenge clients who externalize their own feelings on to others.

> **Client**: Jeff and Joan feel pretty angry with the way we are taught.
> **Counsellor**: I'm wondering whether focusing on Jeff's and Joan's anger is a way of protecting yourself from acknowledging that you too feel angry with your teachers and are capable of angry feelings.

Counsellors can also challenge inconsistencies between verbal, voice and body messages. For instance: 'You say you don't feel hurt by his behaviour, yet you speak with a sad tone of voice and your eyes seem weepy.'

Raise consciousness

Counsellors can use consciousness raising as a means of improving clients' capacities for experiencing and expressing feelings. In Western countries few do not need to become more in tune with feelings. Mostly counsellors use consciousness raising to raise awareness levels of specific sub-groups: for instance, women, men, gays and various ethnic and cultural minorities. Intervening to raise clients' consciousness of social, sex-role and cultural conditioning can beneficially affect how they experience feelings in many ways. First, counsellors can encourage all clients to respond to the range of feelings inherent in being human: for example, women to experience and express ambition and assertion and men vulnerability and affection. Second, counsellors can assist minority groups clients to overcome specific negative feelings (for instance, low self-esteem and guilt) attached to their minority status. Third, counsellors can suggest to clients that they seek out groups of similar people who will legitimize and support their feelings. Fourth, counsellors can raise the issue of clients engaging in social action to change institutional structures that oppress the legitimacy of their feelings.

Teach sensate focus

Relatively few counsellors specialize in sexual problems. Nevertheless, many have occasion to assist clients in experiencing and expressing sensuality. Insufficient sexual responsiveness takes many different forms and may have multiple causes. Often it forms part of a broader pattern of inadequate relating skills. However, some clients may have good relating skills in other areas, yet require specific assistance in acknowledging and exploring sensuality. Such difficulties may be independent of having specific sexual disorders: for instance, premature ejaculation.

Masters and Johnson developed the technique of sensate focus to help couples to feel and think sensuously (Masters *et al.*, 1986). Sensate focus acknowledges the importance of touch in stimulating and experiencing sexual responsiveness. Partners are asked to time their periods of sensate focus for when they feel a natural sense of warmth and compatibility. They should only continue for as long as it is pleasurable. Both partners should be naked and have a minimum of physical fatigue and tension. Avoiding specifically sexual stimulation, including genitals and breasts, the 'giving' partner massages and fondles the 'getting' partner to give pleasure. The rules of sensate focus for receiving partners are that they have to protect 'pleasuring' partners from causing discomfort or initiating sex. Receiving partners need not comment either verbally or non-verbally on their experiencing, unless such expression is completely spontaneous. Giving partners are committed not only to giving pleasure, but also to acknowledging their sensations in giving pleasure, exploring another's body by touch and receiving pleasurable reactions. After a reasonable time, partners exchange roles.

Sensate focus aims to give partners time, space and permission to respond sensually without feeling that they have to perform intercourse. Kaplan (1974, 1987) observes that, though most couples experience positive reactions to sensate focus, some individuals experience very little reaction and others negative reactions. She indicates that these negative reactions may indicate deeper inhibitions concerning sexual responsiveness and suggests how to treat them. Counsellors require sensitivity in following up clients' reactions to sensate focus.

Use role-play methods

In Chapter 16, I discussed role-play as a method of rehearsing action skills. Role-plays can also be used to allow clients to experience feelings. Role-play methods can be powerful ways of releasing and exploring feelings in various kinds of personal relationships, be they past, present or future. This unburdening may in turn generate further self-exploration and deeper understandings of underlying feelings. Clients may play both people in a relationship, either by visualizing with eyes closed or by switching chairs as they play each part. Alternatively, counsellors may play one of the parts in the relationship: for example, a parent, spouse, boyfriend or girlfriend. In role-reversal, both counsellors and clients switch roles. In addition, counsellors may heighten clients' awareness by mirroring clients' feelings-related verbal, voice and body messages. After as well as during role-plays, you can assist clients to experience, articulate and explore feelings uncovered by and associated with what happens.

Use empty chair dialogue

The resolution of 'unfinished business' can be an important task in counselling. Unfinished business refers to lingering negative feelings towards significant others. Unresolved negative feelings can contribute to anxiety and depression as well as be transferred into other relationships where they are inappropriate. Drawing on Gestalt therapy's empty chair technique (Perls, Hefferline and Goodman, 1951), Greenberg and his colleagues have devised an empty chair dialogue intervention (Greenberg *et al.*, 1993). This intervention, 'in which the client engages in an imaginary dialogue with the significant other, is designed to access restricted feelings allowing them to run their course and be restructured in the safety of the therapy environment' (Pavio and Greenberg, 1995, p. 419).

The empty chair dialogue technique, which can be used in individual or group work, helps clients to experience feelings both of unresolved anger and of weakness and victimization. During the successful application of the intervention, clients feel a greater sense of self-empowerment. Clients either view the significant other with greater understanding or hold him or her accountable for harm. Some promising research findings indicate that, both at the end of counselling and after a four-month follow up, clients receiving the empty chair intervention gained considerable relief from distressing symptoms and that their perceptions of resolution of unfinished business improved greatly (Pavio and Greenberg, 1995).

Encourage action

Frequently clients cannot fully experience and explore feelings until they take the risks of acting. For example, there are limits to how clients can know how much they like or dislike any activity or person if they have no first-hand contact with them. Already I have stressed the role of active listening in enabling clients to feel that counsellors are secure bases from which to take the risks of exploratory behaviour and action skills experiments. In addition, Chapter 16 specified interventions for developing clients' action skills.

ASSIST CLIENTS TO EXPRESS FEELINGS

Expressing feelings well requires clients to be skilled at experiencing, exploring and accurately labelling feelings. When clients reveal feelings they put themselves very much on the line. Some feelings are difficult for most clients to express, especially when they do not feel safe with another person: for example, worthlessness, incompetence and unattractiveness. Some feelings may be more difficult for female clients to express, though male clients can have difficulty expressing them too: for example, ambition, leadership and assertion. Some feelings may be more difficult for male than female clients to express, though again differences exist within each sex: for instance, vulnerability, sensitivity and affection. Many clients find it difficult to express specific feelings well: for instance, altruism. Within the context of good relationships, counsellors assisting clients to express feelings need focus on both thinking skills and action skills.

Focus on thinking skills

Here I illustrate some possible thinking skills that may interfere with or assist appropriate expression of feelings. Thinking skills deficits blocking experiencing of feelings overlap with those hindering appropriate expression of feelings. Again, I refer you to Chapters 14 and 15 for how to work with clients' thinking skills.

OWNING RESPONSIBILITY FOR CHOOSING Assist clients to know that they always are responsible for their choices in how they express feelings. Help clients to identify where their specific thinking and action skills choice points lie.

UNDERSTANDING THE RELATIONSHIP BETWEEN HOW YOU THINK, FEEL AND ACT Encourage clients to see relationships between their thoughts and how they inhibit or otherwise inappropriately express their feelings: for instance, by being aggressive. The STC framework provides a useful tool for such analyses.

USING COPING SELF-TALK As well as calming themselves down, clients can develop skills of coaching themselves through sequences of choices involved in skilled expression of feelings. For example, clients feeling strongly about obtaining promotions might use the following self-statements before and during seeing their bosses: 'Stay calm. Remember to be polite and state my case in the positive. Speak firmly and make good eye contact.'

CHOOSING REALISTIC PERSONAL AND RELATIONSHIP RULES Many personal and relationship rules interfere with appropriate expression of feelings. Following are examples.

Unrealistic personal rules
'I must have approval all the time.'

'I must always express feelings smoothly.'

'Men must keep stiff upper lips.'

Unrealistic relationship rules
'We must never have conflict in our relationship.'

'Wives must always be sexually available to husbands.'

'Children should be seen and not heard.'

PERCEIVING ACCURATELY Many clients need to develop skills allowing their feelings towards others to be based on more accurate perceptions of self and others, so that the feelings they express are what they truly feel. For instance, frequently personal insecurity or 'having a bad day' triggers unnecessary anger with others. Once clients are in touch with their feelings, they still require flexibility in perceiving various options for expressing them.

EXPLAINING CAUSE ACCURATELY Without realizing it, some clients may wait for others to make the first move in expressing feelings: for example, 'I cannot express positive feelings about him or her until he or she expresses positive feelings about me.' Counsellors may need to assist clients to take an active rather than a passive stance to expressing feelings. Counsellors can challenge clients who blame others for their feelings.

PREDICTING REALISTICALLY Many clients do not express certain feelings either at all or well enough, because they make false predictions. For instance, many shy clients are reluctant to initiate social contacts because of fears of rejection. Clients in relationships may be unwilling to bring up differences because of catastrophic predictions about the consequences. These catastrophic predictions may cause them either to underreact or to overreact when they eventually discuss differences.

SETTING REALISTIC GOALS Clients may possess unrealistic goals about what feelings to express to whom and when. For instance, insecure teenagers with unclear or unrealistic goals may come on too strong too soon with their boyfriends or girlfriends. Another example is that of males, when learning to be more emotionally expressive, coping better with discouragement from early set-backs once they realize that developing these skills takes time.

USE VISUALIZING SKILLS Clients can use visualizing skills to rehearse how to express feelings appropriately. Furthermore, they can visualize themselves attaining their goals if they use good expressing feelings skills. Clients can also visualize negative consequences stemming from poor expressing feelings skills.

Focus on action skills

Counsellors can assist clients to develop action skills of expressing feelings. I refer you to Chapter 16 for how to do this. When assisting clients to express feelings, always pay attention to verbal, voice and body messages. You may also focus on touch and action messages. Let me illustrate different action messages for showing caring skills (Nelson-Jones, 1996a). Needless to say, clients need to be sensitive to what others perceive as caring messages.

VERBAL MESSAGES Verbal messages of caring include statements like 'I love you', 'I care for you' and 'I want to help you.' Clients can also pay compliments. Furthermore, clients can show caring if they use good verbal skills when listening.

VOICE MESSAGES If clients' voice messages are wrong, they negate their verbal messages. Characteristics of caring voice messages include warmth and expressiveness.

Clients' voices should convey kindness and interest rather than harshness and uninterest.

BODY MESSAGES When clients send caring verbal messages, their gaze, eye contact, body orientation and facial expressions all need to demonstrate interest and concern for the other person. Similarly, clients need to show good attending and listening body message skills when others share problems with them.

TOUCH MESSAGES Touch can be a wonderful way to express caring. Clients can express caring by a hug, a half-embrace, an arm over the shoulder, a touch on the arm or a hand on top of or holding a hand, among other ways. With all touch messages, clients are in the close intimate zone and, consequently, must be very sensitive about another's willingness to be touched.

ACTION MESSAGES Action messages indicating caring include: making the other person a cup of tea or coffee in the morning; being prepared to do your share of the household chores; giving birthday cards and presents; initiating pleasant events, such as going out to dinner; showing affection through flowers, poems and other spontaneous gifts; and being available to help out in times of need.

ASSIST CLIENTS TO MANAGE FEELINGS

Client: I don't know whether I am a wigwam or a teepee.
Counsellor: Don't worry, either way you are too tense.

Many clients come to counselling wanting release from painful and negative feelings. Often clients lack confidence in themselves. In addition, they are subject to feelings like excessive anger, depression and anxiety. In reality, feelings tend to overlap: for instance, clients can be simultaneously depressed, anxious and excessively angry. Furthermore, success in managing one of these feelings better is likely to enhance self-esteem and, hence, handling the others better too. Clients may also use skills learned for managing one feeling for managing other feelings.

Here, rather than cover a range of feelings, I use anger, depression and anxiety to show how to approach developing clients' skills of managing feelings. The discussion of pertinent thinking and action skills is illustrative rather than comprehensive. In practice, skills restatements of clients' managing feelings problems should be tailor-made to their particular skills deficits and circumstances. Always use active listening skills when assisting clients to manage feelings.

Managing anger

Clients can identify and manage anger rather than attempt to rid themselves of it altogether. Anger can have positive uses. It can be a signal indicating that something is wrong and requires attention. It can be an energizer motivating clients to take appropriate action. In some instances, anger may also be a purge. After expressing it, clients may calm down and be more rational. Part of managing anger is to be able to

Table 17.1 *Illustrative thinking and action skills for managing anger*

Thinking skills	Action skills
Owning responsibility for choosing, e.g. 'My anger is my problem.'	Assertion: expressing anger; requesting behaviour changes
Getting in touch with your feelings, e.g. acknowledging hurt	Handling aggressive criticism
Using coping self-talk, e.g. not letting pride get in the way	Using relaxation
Choosing realistic personal rules: avoiding demandingness	Managing stress
Perceiving accurately: avoiding misinterpreting	Helping one another
Using visualizing skills: calming, rehearsing	

experience, explore and accurately label angry feelings. Table 17.1 shows some further skills for managing anger, each of which I discuss in turn.

THINKING SKILLS

- *Owning responsibility for anger.* Clients have choices in how they experience, express and manage anger. Until they own responsibility for their anger, they will have insufficient motivation to develop the skills to manage it effectively.

- *Getting in touch with your feelings.* Counsellors can create safe environments whereby some clients can become more in touch with how angry they feel. Counsellors can help clients to explore what other feelings are associated with anger: for instance, hurt pride. In addition, clients may be empowered by getting more in touch with their feelings of strength.

- *Using coping self-talk.* Simple self-instructions like 'Calm down' and 'Cool it' can often give clients more time and space to get feelings under control (Goldstein and Keller, 1987). Clients can also use longer self-statements: for instance, 'I can handle this situation if I don't let my pride get in the way' (Meichenbaum, 1983; Novaco, 1977).

- *Choosing realistic personal rules.* Ellis (1977) regards childish demandingness as the central thinking skills deficit in anger. Clients make 'musturbatory' demands on themselves (for instance 'I must never make mistakes'), on others (for instance 'Others must always let me have my way') and on the environment (for instance 'Life must be fair' and 'I must never have hassles').

- *Perceiving accurately.* Clients need to develop skills of not jumping to superficial negative conclusions about others. Beck (1988) observes of relationship difficulties that much of the friction is owing to misunderstandings stemming from differences in perspective and not from meanness or selfishness.

- *Using visualizing skills.* Clients can use visualizing skills to manage anger in many ways: rehearsing how to express angry feelings appropriately; relaxing themselves by visualizing restful scenes; and perceiving others' perspectives more accurately.

ACTION SKILLS

- *Assertion.* Skills for expressing anger assertively include using 'I' statements, speaking in a clear and firm voice and keeping good gaze and eye contact. Clients can also develop skills of requesting others to alter their behaviour before rather than after they have become thoroughly fed up with it (Alberti and Emmons, 1990; Nelson-Jones, 1996a).

- *Handling aggressive criticism.* Clients have numerous choices, other than impulsive knee-jerk reactions, in dealing with aggressive criticism. For instance, they can tell themselves to relax, calm down and breathe more slowly until they feel more under control. They can also choose from a number of verbal strategies: for example, reflecting another's anger, or partly agreeing with another's point and then putting their own, or asking another to be more specific about what they have done to upset them. Clients may also back off now and react to criticism at a later date – either requesting or, on their own initiative, taking a 'cooling off' period.

- *Using relaxation.* Clients can develop skills of muscular and visual relaxation to manage anger (Deffenbacher *et al.*, 1995). I describe relaxation skills later in this chapter.

- *Managing stress.* Frequently inability to handle life's stresses makes clients prone to anger. As well as using muscular and visual relaxation, clients may manage stress better if they develop adequate recreational outlets, actively look after their health and develop adequate support networks. Since much stress is internally generated, counsellors and clients also need to review relevant thinking skills.

- *Helping one another.* Clients can develop skills of working with their partners to help one another to manage anger. Relevant action skills for clients are: disciplining themselves to watch their tongues; expressing anger assertively; showing an awareness of what partners experience before, during and after they receive clients' expressions of anger; and using active listening and questioning skills to help partners express angry feelings. When they are helping one another to manage anger, it helps if partners possess realistic relationship rules: for instance 'When either of us expresses anger in our relationship it is a signal to explore our own thoughts, feelings and actions, and not just those of the other person.'

Table 17.2 *Illustrative thinking and action skills for managing depression*

Thinking skills	Action skills
Choosing realistic personal rules, e.g. avoiding demanding approval	Relating skills: initiating contact; self-disclosing
Perceiving accurately, e.g. owning strengths	Assertion skills: setting limits and saying 'no'
Explaining cause accurately, e.g. avoiding unnecessary self-blame	Pleasant activities skills
Predicting realistically, e.g. avoiding unnecessary pessimism	

Managing depression

Often counsellors work with clients who feel depressed. Depressed clients can be very sensitive to the quality of the counselling relationship. Experiencing difficulty affirming themselves, they seek affirmation from outside. You require good counselling relationship skills both initially, when clients may feel dependent on you, and also later, as they develop skills for emotional independence. Table 17.2 presents some common thinking skills and action skills for managing depression.

THINKING SKILLS

- *Choosing realistic personal rules.* Clients can create and sustain their depressed feelings when striving to attain and failing to live up to unrealistic rules (Ellis, 1995; Hewitt and Dyke, 1986). Depressogenic unrealistic rules include: 'I must be perfect' and 'I must always gain others' approval.'

- *Perceiving accurately.* Beck (1991, p. 372) observes of his cognitive theory of depression; 'Of all the hypotheses, pervasiveness of negative thinking in all forms of depression, symptomatic or syndromatic, has been the most uniformly supported.' Depressed clients tend to jump to negative conclusions about how others perceive them. They are also skilled at blocking out positive information about themselves (Beck, 1991; Beck *et al.*, 1979).

- *Explaining cause accurately.* Depressed clients can overemphasize their responsibility for negative events (Beck *et al.*, 1979). Depressed clients may also explain the causes of negative events not only as more owing to themselves, but also as more owing to permanent and pervasive causes than warranted (Seligman, 1991). Furthermore, clients can contribute to depressing themselves by underemphasizing their contribution to positive events in their own and others' lives.

- *Predicting realistically.* Depressed clients tend to predict the future negatively. They are more prone to feelings of hopelessness (Beck *et al.*, 1979), helplessness

(Abramson *et al.*, 1978), perceived self-inefficacy (Bandura, 1986) and pessimism (Seligman, 1991) than non-depressed people.

ACTION SKILLS

Depressed clients may have good skills in specific areas, but underrate them. The following discussion assumes that their action skills genuinely require development.

- *Relating skills.* Many depressed clients are lonely because they have insufficient as well as insufficiently high quality social contacts. Initiating contact and appropriately self-disclosing are among the relating skills such clients may need to develop.

- *Assertion skills.* Frequently, depressed clients lower their self-esteem through inability to use assertion skills. For instance, clients who do not stand up for themselves may feel doubly bad. First, they have the outer negative consequences of having to do extra work, pay extra money or whatever else follows from their lack of assertion. Second, they have the inner negative consequences of devaluing themselves because of their weakness.

- *Pleasant activities skills.* Lewinsohn and his colleagues (1986, p. 73) state: 'If you feel depressed, it is very likely that you are not involved in many pleasant activities.' Depressed clients can develop skills of identifying activities they find rewarding. Then they can develop and implement plans to participate more in them. As the old adage says, 'A little of what you fancy does you good.'

Managing anxiety

Anxiety is a normal survival mechanism. However, many, if not most, clients suffer from excessive or debilitating anxieties that interfere with happiness and fulfilment. Beck and Weishaar (1995, p. 240) observe: 'The anxious person's perception of danger is either excessive or based on false assumptions, while the normal response is based on a more accurate assessment of risk and the magnitude of danger. In addition, normal individuals can correct their misperceptions using logic and evidence.' Offer anxious clients a good counselling relationship. Many anxious clients are threatened by meeting new people, including counsellors. Clients can become anxious when talking about their anxieties. Assisting clients to develop skills of managing anxiety invariably involves focusing on how they think.

Sometimes anxious clients have good action skills, but let their anxieties get in the way of using them. For instance, some students perform well when examinations do not count, but poorly when they count. Some otherwise good to passing students have genuinely poor examination skills. Here it can be important to focus on action skills as well as on thinking skills. Table 17.3 shows some common thinking skills for managing anxiety. The requisite action skills are less easy to list, since they vary with clients'

Table 17.3 *Illustrative thinking and action skills for managing anxiety*

Thinking skills	Action skills
Using coping self-talk, e.g. calming, coaching, affirming	Skills required for specific situations (verbal, voice, body messages)
Choosing realistic personal rules, e.g. avoiding perfectionism	Relaxation skills
Perceiving accurately, e.g. perceiving danger accurately	
Predicting realistically, e.g. avoiding catastrophizing	
Setting realistic goals, e.g. not too high	
Using visualizing skills, e.g. calming, rehearsing	

problems. For example, clients require different action skills for attending job interviews and for developing intimacy.

THINKING SKILLS

- *Using coping self-talk.* Anxious clients engage in much anxious self-talk (Beck *et al.*, 1988a; Kendall and Hollon, 1989). Their anxiety symptoms are signals for telling themselves that they cannot cope or do anything right. In social situations, their self-talk may be about making fools of themselves. Often clients with panic disorders tell themselves that a vital system (for instance, cardiovascular or nervous) may collapse (Beck and Weishaar, 1995).

- *Choosing realistic personal rules.* Anxious clients tend to have personal rules that engender both fear of failure and self-devaluation (Ellis, 1995). Making perfectionist demands on self and others is a central characteristic of such rules. Anxious clients can be far too self-conscious because they possess musturbatory rules about needing, as contrasted with preferring, approval.

- *Perceiving accurately.* Anxious clients overemphasize the degree of threat in situations. They selectively perceive what might go wrong and insufficiently perceive what might go right. They possess skills deficits in their ability to assess evidence for the reality or otherwise of their perceptions. In addition, anxious clients underestimate both their ability to cope and the supports available to them (Beck and Emery, 1985; Beck and Weishaar, 1995). Defensiveness, in which clients deny or distort aspects of themselves they find threatening, is another way that anxiety interferes with perception.

- *Predicting realistically.* The predictions of anxious clients exaggerate dangers and risks. Frequently anxious clients possess catastrophic thoughts and images about the future and their ability to cope with it. They are pessimists rather than optimists, either in general (pervasive anxiety) or in regard to the specific situations in which they become anxious (situational anxiety).

- *Setting realistic goals.* Some anxious clients set goals that are too low in order to protect themselves from failure. Many anxious clients set goals that are too high and become fearful about achieving them. The goals of other clients are realistically attainable, as long as they can manage their anxieties adequately.

- *Using visualizing skills.* Most anxious clients experience negative visual images prior to and concurrent with anxiety attacks (Beck *et al.*, 1974). Clients may have poor skills for using visualizing both to relax and also to rehearse action skills.

ACTION SKILLS

- *Skills required for specific situations.* Anxiety may be the cause of poor action skills, their consequence or a mixture of the two. Some clients may have good action skills, but experience difficulty implementing them under pressure. Other clients may need to develop specific skills: for instance, at public speaking, asking for a date, driving a car, managing a company, policing an angry crowd and so on. Their increased competence in these skills lowers anxiety.

- *Relaxation skills.* Many anxious clients have poor relaxation skills. They engage in insufficient pleasurable and relaxing activities. In addition, they may have poor muscular and mental relaxation skills.

Relaxation skills

Counsellors can train clients in muscular and mental relaxation skills (Bernstein and Borkovec, 1973; Jacobson, 1929, 1976; Wolpe, 1982; Wolpe and Wolpe, 1988). Impart these as self-helping rather than as counsellor-offered skills. Clients may use relaxation skills not only for managing anxiety, but for dealing with problems such as tension headaches, hypertension and insomnia. Relaxation skills may be used alone or as part of more complex skills: for instance, systematic desensitization (Deffenbacher and Suinn, 1988; Goldfried and Davison, 1976; Wolpe, 1982).

PROGRESSIVE MUSCULAR RELAXATION SKILLS Progressive muscular relaxation refers to the progressive cultivation of the relaxation response (Jacobson, 1929, 1976). Tell clients that the first step in physically relaxing themselves is to find a quiet space where they will be uninterrupted. They may use a bed, a recliner chair or a comfortable chair with a headrest. If possible, they should wear loose-fitting, comfortable clothing, and remove items such as glasses and shoes. Their arms should be either by their sides or on the arms of chairs. Their legs should be uncrossed and their eyes closed.

Progressive muscular relaxation involves clients in tensing and relaxing various muscle groups. You can demonstrate how clients should go through a five-step tension–relax cycle for each muscle group (Bernstein and Borkovec, 1973). These steps are: (1) *focus*, focus attention on a particular muscle group; (2) *tense*, tense the muscle group; (3) *hold*, maintain the tension for five to seven seconds; (4) *release*, release the tension in the muscle group; and (5) *relax*, spend 20 to 30 seconds focusing on letting go of tension and further relaxing the muscle groups.

Table 17.4, which you may give to clients as a handout, lists the various muscle groupings and self-instructions for tensing them. For take-away assignments, either provide clients with copies of existing relaxation cassettes or make them afresh.

Table 17.4 *Tensing self-instructions for progressive muscular relaxation*

Muscle group	Tensing self-instructions*
Right hand and forearm	Clench my right fist and tense the muscles in my lower arm.
Right biceps	Bend my right arm at the elbow and flex my biceps by tensing the muscles of my upper right arm.
Left hand and forearm	Clench my left fist and tense the muscles in my lower arm.
Left biceps	Bend my left arm at the elbow and flex my biceps by tensing the muscles of my upper left arm.
Forehead	Lift my eyebrows as high as possible.
Eyes, nose and upper cheeks	Squeeze my eyes tightly shut and wrinkle my nose.
Jaw and lower cheeks	Clench my teeth and pull the corners of my mouth firmly back.
Neck and throat	Pull my chin down hard towards my chest yet resist having it touch my chest.
Chest and shoulders	Pull my shoulder blades together and take a deep breath.
Stomach	Tighten the muscles in my stomach as though someone were about to hit me there.
Right thigh	Tense the muscles of my right upper leg by pressing the upper muscles down and the lower muscles up.
Right calf	Stretch my right leg and pull my toes towards my head.
Right foot	Point and curl the toes of my right foot and turn it inward.
Left thigh	Tense the muscles of my left upper leg by pressing the upper muscles down and the lower muscles up.
Left calf	Stretch my left leg and pull my toes towards my head.
Left foot	Point and curl the toes of my left foot and turn it inward.

* With left-handed people, tensing instructions for the left side of the body should come before those for the right.

However, later encourage clients to make their own self-instructional cassettes. Having said this, it remains uncertain how much home relaxation cassettes enhance treatment outcome (Hoelscher *et al.*, 1987).

Give relaxation instructions in a calm and soothing voice. In step 5 of the cycle, use repetition to enhance relaxation, for instance, 'Your forehead feels increasingly calm and relaxed ... calm and relaxed ... calm and relaxed.' When relaxing clients, observe their body posture and breathing as a check on how relaxed they are. Ask them how relaxed they feel and whether there are any muscle groupings requiring further attention. If so, spend extra time relaxing these muscles. You can end relaxation sessions by counting backwards from five to one and, when you get to one, asking clients to wake up feeling pleasantly relaxed.

Inform clients that progressive muscular relaxation requires practice to gain its full benefits. When learning, they should practise daily for at least 15 minutes. Ask clients whether they anticipate any obstacles to practice, such as finding a quiet place, and help them to devise strategies for dealing with them. Evidence exists that clients who monitor their relaxation practice are more likely to continue doing it (Tasto and Hinkle, 1973). Consequently, ask clients to keep logs monitoring between-session practice. Table 17.5 shows an entry in such a log.

Table 17.5 *Relaxation monitoring log*

Date	Time, place, length	Comments
3 Oct.	6 p.m., living room at home 15 to 20 minutes	Started off feeling tense after a day at work. Tensed and relaxed 16 muscle groups. At first thoughts about work interfered with relaxation. Ended feeling deeply relaxed.

BRIEF MUSCULAR RELAXATION SKILLS Brief muscular relaxation skills aim to induce deep relaxation with less time and effort. When clients are proficient in full progressive muscular relaxation, you can introduce such skills. Brief relaxation skills are useful both in counselling sessions and in daily life. Following are two examples.

Sequential brief relaxation Here you can first instruct clients and then get them to tell themselves the following instructions focused on tensing and relaxing in turn four composite muscle groupings.

'I'm going to count to ten in units of two. After each unit of two I will instruct you to tense and relax a muscle grouping. One, two ... focus on your leg and feet muscles ... tense and hold the tension in these muscles for five seconds ... release ... relax and enjoy the sensations of the tension flowing from your legs and feet. Three, four ... take a deep breath and focus on your chest, shoulder and stomach muscles ... tense and hold the tension in these muscles for five seconds ... release ... relax and enjoy the sensations of the tension flowing from your chest, shoulders and stomach. Five, six ... focus on your face, neck and head muscles ... tense and hold the tension in these muscles for five seconds ... release ... relax and enjoy the sensations of the tension flowing from your face, neck and head. Seven, eight ... focus on your arm and hand muscles ... tense and hold the tension in these muscles for five seconds ... release ... relax and enjoy the sensations of the tension flowing from your arms and hands. Nine, ten ... focus on all the muscles in your body ... tense all the muscles in your body together and hold for five seconds ... release ... relax and enjoy the sensations of the tension leaving your whole body as your relaxation gets deeper and deeper ... deeper and deeper ... deeper and deeper.'

Simultaneous brief relaxation. As at the end of the previous example, you can instruct clients to tense all muscle groupings simultaneously. You can say:

'When I give the signal, I would like you to close your eyes very tightly, take a deep breath and simultaneously tense your arm muscles, your face, neck and throat muscles, your chest, shoulder and stomach muscles, and your leg and foot muscles ... Now take a deep breath and tense all your muscles ... hold for five seconds ... now release and relax as quickly and deeply as you can.'

MENTAL RELAXATION SKILLS Often clients visualize restful scenes at the end of progressive muscular relaxation. Such a scene might be 'lying in a lush green meadow on a warm, sunny day, feeling a gentle breeze, watching the clouds'. Clients can visualize such scenes independent of muscular relaxation. In addition, clients can use 'counting to ten in groups of two' as a mental relaxation rather than as a muscular relaxation procedure. For example: 'One, two ... focus on your leg and feet muscles ... relax and enjoy the sensations of the tension flowing from your legs and feet.' As a mental relaxation procedure, clients edit out the tense, hold and release instructions.

Systematic desensitization

Progressive muscular relaxation forms an important part of systematic desensitization. Consider intervening with systematic desensitization when clients have specific anxieties and phobias, rather than general tension. The version of the originator of systematic desensitization, Joseph Wolpe, involves three elements: (1) training in deep muscular relaxation; (2) the construction around themes of hierarchies of anxiety-evoking situations; and (3) counsellors asking clients, when relaxed, to imagine items from the hierarchies (Wolpe, 1958, 1982; Wolpe and Wolpe, 1988). Wolpe's 'reciprocal inhibition' or counter-conditioning explanation is that the pairing of anxiety-evoking stimuli with the relaxation response brings about a lessening of the anxiety response, in effect weakening the bond between anxiety-evoking stimuli and anxiety responses. Other explanations exist for systematic desensitization's effectiveness. Increasingly counsellors present it as a self-control skill (Goldfried and Davison, 1976), thus emphasizing coping with anxiety rather than mastering it.

EXPLAIN SYSTEMATIC DESENSITIZATION Offer reasons for using systematic desensitization. Presumably, your client has some anxiety management skills deficits for which desensitization seems the preferred intervention. Briefly explain all three elements. Emphasize learning desensitization as a coping skill. Since I have already discussed muscular relaxation skills, I now turn to hierarchy construction skills.

CONSTRUCT HIERARCHIES Hierarchies are lists of stimuli centred on themes and ordered according to the amount of anxiety they evoke. Table 17.6 illustrates a hierarchy for a client with debilitating anxiety about maths examinations.

Following are hierarchy construction skills.

- *Identify suitable themes.* Give priority to themes or areas either most debilitating or of most immediate importance to clients.

- *Generate items around themes.* Assist clients to generate items around one or more themes. Items need to be described so that clients can imagine them. Sources for hierarchy items include information gathered during assessment, take-away assignments involving self-monitoring and suggestions from clients to you. You can ask clients to write items on index cards to make for ease of ordering.

- *Rank items to make hierarchies.* Ranking items involves clients rating those for each theme on a subjective anxiety scale and ordering them accordingly. A common way to check the anxiety-evoking potential of items is to say that 0

Table 17.6 *Hierarchy for client with maths exam anxiety*

Rank	Rating	Item
1	5	Thinking about a maths exam when revising at my desk one month before
2	10	Thinking about a maths exam when revising at my desk three weeks before
3	15	Thinking about a maths exam when revising at my desk two weeks before
4	20	Thinking about a maths exam when revising at my desk one week before
5	25	Thinking about a maths exam on the night before
6	30	Waking up on the morning of the maths exam
7	40	Driving my car on the way to the maths exam
8	50	Waiting outside the exam room
9	60	Going into the exam room
10	70	Sitting down at my desk in the exam room
11	80	Looking at the maths exam paper for the first time
12	90	Sitting in the exam room looking at everyone else working hard
13	100	Having a panic attack during the maths exam

represents no anxiety a..d 100 is the maximum anxiety possible for that theme. In general, avoid gaps of over ten units on the subjective anxiety scale. If necessary, generate intervening items. During treatment remain flexible: you and your clients may need to reorder, reword or generate further items.

- *Check clients' ability to imagine items.* A basic assumption of systematic desensitization is that clients are capable of imagining hierarchy items or scenes. Check your clients' ability to imagine items. Some clients imagine items better if describing them aloud. You can also describe the items more fully.

PRESENT HIERARCHY ITEMS A desensitization session starts with relaxing clients. When assured clients are deeply relaxed, present items along the lines of 'Now I want you to imagine you are sitting at your desk revising for a maths test one month before the test...' Start with the least anxiety-evoking item and ask clients to raise their index finger if experiencing anxiety. If they experience no anxiety, ask them to switch the item off and go back to feeling pleasantly relaxed. After 30 to 50 seconds you can ask clients to imagine the item again. If this causes no anxiety, withdraw the item, possibly spend further time relaxing clients and move on to the next item.

If clients indicate anxiety with items, you have two main choices. First, you can withdraw the item immediately, relax the client again and then present the item a second time. Second, and preferable for developing self-helping skills, you can instruct clients to continue imagining the item and encourage them to relax away their anxiety by calming and coaching self-talk and taking slow deep breaths (Goldfried, 1971; Goldfried and Davison, 1976; Meichenbaum, 1977). If clients repeatedly experience anxiety with an item, intersperse less threatening items.

Systematic desensitization assumes that once a low anxiety-evoking item, say ten units, ceases to stimulate anxiety, all other hierarchy items become less anxiety-evoking by ten units. Thus the 100 unit item becomes 90 units and so on. Consequently, you only present weak anxiety-evoking items to clients.

Record all item presentations and their outcomes. Wolpe's (1982) desensitization sessions last from 15 to 30 minutes. Initially, he may present a total of eight to ten items, possibly from different hierarchies. In later sessions, he may make as many as 30 to 50 presentations. Goldfried and Davison (1976) suggest covering from two to five items in each session. You can also cassette-record items, and get clients to work through them as take-away assignments.

Encourage clients, when preparing for or facing anxiety-evoking situations in daily life, to develop self-helping skills for relaxing away tensions, breathing slowly and deeply, and using coping self-talk. Where appropriate, give clients logs to monitor their use of self-helping skills.

IN VIVO DESENSITIZATION Two kinds of considerations may make *in vivo* or real-life, rather than visualized, desensitization the preferred intervention. First, clients may have difficulty imagining items. However, items for real-life desensitization need to be readily accessible. Second, where items are readily accessible, your intervention can be more powerful if you work with real rather than imaginary items. For instance, you may relax clients with public speaking anxiety at the start of each session, then over a number of sessions have them give short talks in front of increasing numbers of people. You can introduce answering questions into the hierarchy to make for increased difficulty and real-lifeness. Many visualized desensitization considerations – such as using relaxation, constructing hierarchies and the level of anxiety within which to present items – still apply to *in vivo* desensitization.

Use of medication

When assisting clients to manage feelings, many counsellors require familiarity with psychotropic drugs – drugs that act on the mind. You find difficulty assessing how clients feel unless you take into account the effects of any medication they are on. If medication seems advisable, you need to refer clients to physicians. Furthermore, if you are working with clients on medication, you may need to discuss appropriate dosage and side-effects with physicians or look it up in a reference source. In addition, clients themselves may wish to discuss their use of medication. Though you should not go out of your depth, your clients may feel reassured if you can conduct an informed discussion.

All psychotropic drugs have possible toxic or unwanted side-effects (Burns, 1980; Ponterotto, 1985). For instance, even minor tranquillizers can affect some clients with drowsiness, lessened muscular coordination, lowered sex urge and dependency. A drug like lithium carbonate, used for mania and depression, is highly toxic and requires close medical monitoring. The levels of dosage, both amounts and frequency, are considerations for physicians prescribing drugs and for counsellors working with clients on drugs. If you require information about drugs, you can ask physicians or look it up in the latest editions of regularly updated medical prescription reference sources, such as *MIMS* (latest edition) in Britain and Australia.

You may need to explore your and clients' attitudes towards using drugs. Some counsellors have prejudices against any use of drugs and, sometimes, also against the medical profession. Other counsellors, like some clients, may treat medication as a crutch. Clients' attitudes towards psychotropic drugs vary from viewing taking them as personal weakness to willing dependence on them. Though it is sometimes difficult to achieve, aim for clients to become psychologically self-reliant in managing feelings, including taking as little medication as possible. However, on occasion using medication may be appropriate: for instance, with seriously disturbed clients (American Psychiatric Association, 1994) or those requiring relief in crises. As counselling progresses, you may be able to wean clients off drugs, possibly by smaller and less frequent dosages. For quick-acting drugs, another option is to recommend that clients only use them in emergencies.

MANAGE YOUR OWN FEELINGS

Like clients, counsellors need to learn to acknowledge, accept, manage, appropriately express and not be overwhelmed by the strength of their feelings. On the principle that 'Many a true word is said in jest', I end this chapter with two jokes about sexuality and counselling.

The first one is about the notorious Californian psychiatrist, Dr Randolph Yavis. The good doctor was said to have acquired his surname because of his marked tendency to work only with female patients who were also Young, Attractive, Verbal, Intelligent and Sexy. No prizes for guessing Randolph's nickname! To what extent do you consider that your selection of which clients you counsel and for how long is influenced by their personal attractiveness for you?

The second joke is about a person-centred counsellor being seduced by a client.

> **Client:** I quite like you.
> **Counsellor:** You quite like me.
> **Client:** Yes, I think you're kinda cute.
> **Counsellor:** Yes, you think I'm kinda cute.
> **Client:** I find you attractive.
> **Counsellor:** You find me attractive.
> **Client:** I find you really attractive.
> **Counsellor:** You find me really attractive.
> **Client:** I find you so attractive that I would like to go to bed with you.
> **Counsellor:** You find me so attractive that you would like to go to bed with me.
> **Client:** Yes, why don't we go ahead and do it?
> **Counsellor:** I can't go to bed with you, I'm your counsellor.
> **Client:** Well, you're fired as my counsellor. Let's go to bed!

How you manage your sexual feelings constitutes an important area of professional ethics. I have personally known both a counselling student and a group leader who were unable to resist the temptation to turn counselling into sexual relationships. Managing sexuality is a fertile area for self-deception. Counsellor, beware!

CHAPTER HIGHLIGHTS

- *Counsellors are feelings educators who use relationship and training skills to assist clients to experience, express and manage feelings.*

- *Always assume that clients are responsible for their feelings and that counsellors are responsible for showing clients how to implement this responsibility.*

- *Counsellors can assist clients to experience feelings by explaining reasons for focusing on feelings, focusing on thinking skills, using rewarding listening, training clients in inner listening, using feelings and physical reactions questions, being authentic and appropriately self-disclosing, challenging inauthenticity, raising consciousness, teaching sensate focus, using role-play methods, using empty chair dialogue and encouraging action.*

- *Thinking skills for expressing feelings include using coping self-talk, perceiving others accurately and predicting realistically.*

- *Action skills for expressing feelings include proficiency in sending relevant verbal, voice, body, touch and action messages.*

- *Thinking skills for managing anger include owning responsibility for anger, using coping self-talk, choosing personal rules, perceiving accurately and using visualizing skills.*

- *Action skills for managing anger include those for assertion, handling aggressive criticism, relaxing, managing stress and helping one another.*

- *Thinking skills for managing depression centre on overcoming a negative outlook and include choosing realistic personal rules, perceiving accurately, explaining cause accurately and predicting realistically.*

- *Action skills for managing depression include relating skills, such as initiating contact and self-disclosing, assertion skills and pleasant activities skills.*

- *Thinking skills for managing anxiety centre on overcoming an excessive sense of danger and include using coping self-talk, choosing realistic personal rules, perceiving accurately, predicting realistically, setting realistic goals and using visualizing skills.*

- *Action skills for managing anxiety include relaxation and the skills required for competent performance in specific situations.*

- *Relaxation skills may be used on their own or as part of more complex interventions like systematic desensitization. Relaxation skills include progressive muscular relaxation, brief muscular relaxation and mental relaxation.*

- *Present systematic desensitization as a self-helping skill. In addition to training in progressive muscular relaxation, systematic desensitization includes constructing hierarchies around anxiety-evoking themes and getting clients to imagine hierarchy items when relaxed.*

- *Many counsellors require knowledge of psychotropic drugs – drugs that work on the mind. All such drugs have unwanted side-effects. Counsellors can explore their own and clients' attitudes towards using medication.*

EXERCISE 17.1   EXPLAINING REASONS FOR FOCUSING ON FEELINGS

As appropriate, complete parts of this exercise on your own, with a partner or in a group.

Part A   Developing explanatory statements
What might you say when you explain reasons for focusing on feelings to the following clients?

1.   A client with problems *experiencing* his or her feelings.
2.   A client with problems *expressing* a feeling (specify which).
3.   A client with problems *managing* a negative feeling (specify which).

Part B   Explaining reasons for focusing on feelings
Take turns in role-playing with a partner who acts as a client. Explain reasons to him or her for focusing on each of the following skills areas.

1.   Experiencing feelings.
2.   Expressing a specific feeling.
3.   Managing a specific negative feeling.
4.   Combinations of the above.

At the conclusion of each role-play hold a brief sharing and feedback session.

EXERCISE 17.2   EXPLORING THINKING SKILLS DEFICITS FOR EXPERIENCING FEELINGS

As appropriate, complete parts of this exercise on your own, with a partner or in a group.

Part A   Assessing how thinking skills deficits interfere with experiencing feelings
1.   How might each of the following thinking skills areas interfere with clients' abilities to experience feelings?

   (a) owning responsibility for choosing
   (b) using coping self-talk
   (c) choosing realistic personal rules
   (d) perceiving accurately
   (e) explaining cause accurately
   (f) predicting realistically
   (g) setting realistic goals

(h) using visualizing skills
(i) making decisions realistically
(j) preventing and managing problems

2. Discuss the advantages and disadvantages of focusing on how clients think to assist them in experiencing feelings.

Part B   Assisting a client with a thinking skills deficit that interferes with experiencing feelings
Counsel a partner who role-plays a client with difficulty experiencing a feeling (specify which) or feelings. Within the context of a good counselling relationship, identify and intervene with regard to at least one of your client's thinking skills deficits. Afterwards, hold a sharing and feedback session and then reverse roles. Playing back audio-cassettes or video-tapes of this exercise may help your learning.

EXERCISE 17.3   DEVELOPING CLIENTS' INNER LISTENING SKILLS

As appropriate, complete parts of this exercise on your own, with a partner or in a group.

Part A   Listening to yourself
1. Sit in a quiet place, close your eyes for three to five minutes and try to tune into your bodily sensations. Focus on the flow of what your body feels rather than on what you think. In other words, focus on physical sensations.

2. Sit in a quiet place with eyes closed and, for the next one to three minutes, focus on the sensations of your breathing.

3. Write down the bodily sensations attached to your experiencing the following feelings.

    (a) anger
    (b) sadness
    (c) fear
    (d) joy

Part B   Assisting a client to develop inner listening skills
Partner A attempts to train partner B, who acts as a client, in inner listening as a self-helping skill. Partner A goes through the following steps with partner B.

1. Explain reasons for focusing on inner listening.
2. Stress creating sufficient time and psychological space.
3. Present and demonstrate the skill.
4. Coach.

5. Negotiate a take-away assignment.

When you have finished hold a discussion and feedback session and, after an appropriate interval, reverse roles.

EXERCISE 17.4 USING ROLE-PLAY METHODS TO EXPERIENCE AND EXPRESS FEELINGS

As appropriate, complete parts of this exercise on your own, with a partner or in a group.

Part A   Using visualized role-play yourself
Visualize a recent encounter with another person in which you may have felt strongly, but did not experience and hence show the full extent of your feelings. Role-play in your imagination first how the encounter was and, then, how you would have felt and acted without your inhibitions. Concentrate on inner physical sensations as well as outer verbal, voice and body messages.

Part B   Using role-play to assist a client to experience and express feelings
Partner A encourages partner B, who acts as a client, to describe a two-person encounter in which he or she may have felt strongly, but did not experience and hence show the full extent of his or her feelings. Partner A and partner B then reenact the scene: (1) first as it was and, then, (2) with partner B being encouraged to experience what he or she inhibited and express with verbal, voice and body messages what he or she left unsaid. Then partner A uses active listening skills to process partner B's feelings and thoughts concerning the role-play. Afterwards, hold a sharing and feedback session, before reversing roles. Playing back video-tapes of role-plays may assist learning.

EXERCISE 17.5 ASSISTING CLIENTS TO EXPRESS FEELINGS

As appropriate, complete parts of this exercise on your own, with a partner or in a group.

Part A   Restating, stating goals and planning how to express a feeling
Think of a feeling you or the group experiences difficulty in expressing.

1. Restate your problem feeling in skills terms. In this, thinking skills deficits/goals to consider include owning responsibility for choosing, using coping self-talk, choosing realistic personal and relationship rules, perceiving accurately, explaining cause accurately, predicting realistically, setting realistic goals, using visualizing skills, realistic decision-making and preventing and managing problems. Focus on

action skills deficits/goals, namely in the verbal, voice and body messages with which you express the feeling and, where relevant, in your touch and action messages. Use the following two-column format for your restatement.

Thinking skills deficits/goals	Action skills deficits/goals

2. Alter your skills restatement into a statement of goals – you may use white-out to do this.

3. Develop a plan of self-helping interventions to attain your goals.

Part B   Assisting a client to express a feeling
Work with a partner, who role-plays a client with difficulty expressing a feeling (if possible, use real-life material). Restate the expressing a feeling problem in skills terms, state goals and develop a plan to attain them. When finished, hold a sharing and feedback session with your partner. Playing back either an audio-cassette recording or a video-tape recording of your session may assist learning. After an appropriate interval, reverse roles.

EXERCISE 17.6   ASSISTING CLIENTS TO MANAGE FEELINGS

As appropriate, complete parts of this exercise on your own, with a partner or in a group.

Part A   Restating, stating goals and planning how to manage a feeling
Think of an unwanted feeling you or the group experiences difficulty in managing.

1. Restate your unwanted feeling in skills terms. In doing so, thinking skills deficits/ goals to consider include owning responsibility for choosing, using coping self-talk, choosing realistic personal and relationship rules, perceiving accurately, explaining cause accurately, predicting realistically, setting realistic goals, using visualizing skills, realistic decision-making and preventing and managing problems. Focus on action skills deficits/goals: namely in the verbal, voice, and body messages with which you express the feeling and, where relevant, in your touch and action messages. Use the following two-column format for your restatement.

Thinking skills deficits/goals	Action skills deficits/goals

2.   Alter your skills restatement into a statement of goals – you may use white-out to do this.

3.   Develop a plan of self-helping interventions to attain your goals.

Part B   Assisting a client manage a feeling
Work with a partner who is a client with difficulty managing an unwanted feeling in a specific situation (if possible, use real-life material). Restate the managing an unwanted feeling problem in skills terms, state goals and develop a plan to attain them. When finished, hold a sharing and feedback session with your partner. Playing back either an audio-cassette recording or a video-tape recording of your session may assist learning. After an appropriate interval, reverse roles.

EXERCISE 17.7   PROGRESSIVE MUSCULAR RELAXATION

Complete Parts A and B of this exercise on your own and with a partner, respectively.

Part A   Making and using your own relaxation cassette
Progressive muscular relaxation entails finding a quiet and comfortable place and then, with eyes closed, going through a five-step tension–relax cycle for each muscle group. The five steps are: (1) *focus* – focus attention on a particular muscle group; (2) *tense* – tense the muscle group; (3) *hold* – maintain the tension for five to seven seconds; (4) *release* – release the tension in the muscle group; and (5) *relax* – spend 20 to 30 seconds focusing on letting go of tension and further relaxing the muscle group. Make up a progressive muscular relaxation cassette using the muscle groups and tensing self-instructions shown in Table 17.4. Record the five-step tension–relax cycle for each muscle group. Include a visualized relaxation instruction at the end.
    Practise relaxing yourself for 15 to 20 minutes a day for the next week and keep a log monitoring your relaxation homework.

Part B   Assisting a client by making a relaxation cassette
Part A makes up a progressive muscular relaxation cassette as he or she relaxes partner B, who acts as a client, using the five-step tension–relax cycle. Alter the Table 17.4 tensing self-instructions to tensing instructions by substituting 'your' for 'my' throughout. Present a visualized relaxation scene at the end. Afterwards, check how relaxed your client became and provide further relaxation instructions for any muscle group where he or she still feels tense. Then negotiate a progressive muscular relaxation take-away assignment with your client. After an appropriate interval, reverse roles.

EXERCISE 17.8   SYSTEMATIC DESENSITIZATION

Work with a partner, who is a client wanting help to manage a specific phobia (if possible real, otherwise role-played) and complete the following tasks.

1. *Explain systematic desensitization.* Explain systematic desensitization to your client and offer reasons for suggesting it as an intervention. Present systematic desensitization as a coping skill.

2. *Construct a hierarchy.* Table 17.6 is an example of a systematic desensitization hierarchy for a client with a maths exam anxiety. Work with your partner to construct a hierarchy around the theme of his or her phobia. On a scale from 0 to 100 units of anxiety, have no items further apart than ten units.

3. *Present hierarchy items.* Relax your partner with his or her eyes closed. When assured that he or she is deeply relaxed, present items along the lines of 'Now I want you to imagine you are sitting at your desk revising for a maths exam one month before the exam ... If you experience any anxiety, raise your index finger.' Let the client imagine the item for about ten seconds. If he or she experiences no anxiety, ask him or her to switch the item off and go back to feeling pleasantly relaxed. After about 30 seconds, you may present the item again. If your client experiences anxiety in either presentation, instruct him or her to continue imagining the item and encourage him or her to relax away the anxiety, take slow deep breaths and use coping self-talk. If the client repeatedly experiences anxiety with an item, intersperse a less threatening item. If possible, during this exercise, take your client through at least the first three items on his or her hierarchy.

End by encouraging your client, when preparing for or facing the phobic situation in daily life, to use self-helping skills of relaxing away tensions, taking slow deep breaths, and using coping self-talk.

Afterwards, hold a sharing and feedback session with your partner and then reverse roles.

PART SIX

Stage 5: Emphasize Take-away and End

Chapter 18 reviews some important skills so that clients can take away lifeskills developed during counselling for use after counselling. Chapter 19 examines how to end counselling contacts with clients and how to evaluate your effectiveness.

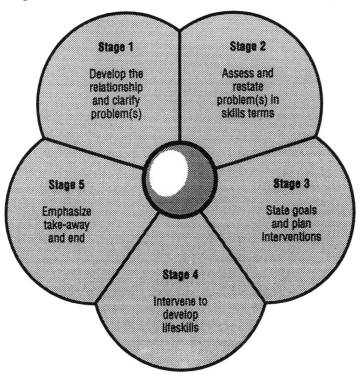

EIGHTEEN

Emphasize take-away of lifeskills

Care and diligence bring luck.
Thomas Fuller

CHAPTER QUESTIONS

- *Why is emphasizing take-away of lifeskills important?*

- *What are some important concepts in emphasizing take-away?*

- *How can counsellors focus on how clients think to enhance take-away?*

- *What are some of the main ways when planning to enhance take-away?*

- *What are some of the main ways when intervening to enhance take-away?*

INTRODUCTION

As well as overcoming clients' resistances to positive change, counsellors can develop clients' resistances to negative change and to losing rather than retaining targeted skills. Stage 5 of the lifeskills counselling model focuses on emphasizing take-away and on terminating contact with clients. I used to call this stage 'end and consolidate self-helping skills'. Now I call the stage 'emphasize take-away of lifeskills and end' because the term 'take-away' communicates more clearly than 'consolidate' that the purpose of counselling is to develop skills for use afterwards. Also, the term 'take-away' possesses meaning for clients from all social backgrounds. The term take-away can be used throughout counselling and not just when counselling terminates. Emphasize take-away in every session. Ensuring transfer of targeted skills to daily life is much too important to be left to the final session or sessions.

Why is emphasizing take-away of skills so important? The following are examples of counselling outcomes not lasting.

> Last year, after some sessions with his school coun-sellor, Col, 17, was able to cope much better with exam anxiety. Again, this year Col's work suffers because he gets anxious at the thought of exams.

> Simone, 39, is a single mother with two teenage boys. Two years ago, Simone received help to im-prove her managing conflict skills with regard to her oldest boy, James. Simone now experiences similar difficulties with her second son, Dave, who is three years younger than James.

> With his counsellor's assistance, Henry, a 51-year-old widower, started gaining confidence about going into social situations. A year after treatment, Henry is back to being an unhappy 'loner'.

A central assumption of the lifeskills counselling approach is that clients require skills not just for managing current problems but also for coping with future similar problems. Problems tend to repeat themselves if clients fail to correct underlying skills deficits. Systematically attend to developing clients' lifeskills for afterwards. Remember that the 'train and hope' approach to the maintenance and transfer of treatment gains is unreliable (Kazdin, 1994; Martin, 1990; Nemeroff and Karoly, 1991; Stokes and Osnes, 1989).

Defining take-away of lifeskills

Generalization, maintenance, transfer and development are four terms, albeit over-lapping, for understanding what I mean by emphasizing take-away skills (Kazdin, 1994; Nemeroff and Karoly, 1991).

- *Generalization.* Generalization signifies that targeted thinking skills and action skills carry over or generalize to conditions other than those included in counsel-ling. Clients apply targeted lifeskills flexibly in their daily lives in regard to other situations and stimuli.

- *Maintenance.* Maintenance, or resistance to extinction, refers to the extension and degree of permanence after counselling of skill development achieved during counselling. Maintenance is not always consistent. Clients can suffer lapses, but over time still maintain skills. The opposite to maintenance is going back to baseline or worse.

- *Transfer.* Transfer or transfer of training means that skills trained for and developed inside counselling become transferred so that clients use them outside of counselling and, it is hoped, maintain them once counselling terminates.

- *Development.* When counselling ends, some former clients not only maintain targeted skills, but develop them to higher levels. Such people assume responsibility for shifting the balance of strengths and deficits in one or more skills areas still further in the direction of strengths.

WORK WITH CLIENTS' THINKING SKILLS

Though it is insufficiently emphasized in the counselling literature (for example, Kazdin, 1994; Stokes and Osnes, 1989), assisting clients to take away trained skills as self-helping skills requires counsellors to pay close attention to how clients think. Even in brief counselling, you can make it easier for clients to retain skills by focusing on thinking. In longer-term counselling, you have considerably more scope. In addition, in longer-term counselling, you can spend more time specifically addressing issues of take-away: for instance, preventing relapses. Last, but not least, counsellors have more opportunity to impart the elegant goal of using the lifeskills counselling model as a way of life.

Make clear restatements in skills terms

If you make accurate and clear restatements of clients' problems in skills terms, you lay the foundation for clients to develop and take away targeted thinking and action skills for afterwards. The very notion of skills implies that clients need work not only to acquire but also to maintain them. Clear restatements in skills terms provide clients with insight and a way of remembering how they have contributed to their problems and can change. Together, counsellor and client can state goals and plan to how best to develop targeted skills. Then counsellors can use a range of interventions to develop these skills as take-away skills. Without a high degree of clarity and relevance in initially conceptualizing problems, counselling can become unfocused and woolly. Both counsellor and client may go either in the wrong direction or round in circles. Under such circumstances, clients experience great difficulty learning skills in the first place, let alone remembering and using them afterwards.

A big issue in counselling is helping clients to remember useful material. Counsellors' memories are fallible too. You can do a brilliant restatement in skills terms, yet afterwards you, your client or both of you can either forget or mistakenly remember significant parts of it. Therefore it is essential for developing take-away skills that each of you writes the restatement down – either before or, preferably, after you translate it into a statement of goals.

Following are some other thinking skills that can contribute to clients maintaining and developing lifeskills as take-away skills.

Owning responsibility for choosing

A basic assumption of lifeskills counselling is that clients are personally responsible for making choices conducive to their survival, happiness and fulfilment. Stress the importance for clients of choosing to maintain lifeskills. Unlike in certain medical conditions, there is no concept of cure. Rather clients face choices, sometimes daily, in which they can either use or fail to use targeted lifeskills.

Using coping self-talk

Take-away of lifeskills can be enhanced if counsellors ensure that clients understand the sequences of choices in targeted skills well enough to instruct and coach themselves. For example, when demonstrating assertion or interview skills, you can demonstrate self-instructions too. Furthermore, you can get clients to summarize self-instructions either during counselling sessions or as take-away assignments. I frequently make up cassettes for clients in which I guide them through self-instructions as they visualize themselves performing. Often clients need to work and practise to retain self-instructions, including listening to cassettes repeatedly.

Clients can rehearse and use coping self-talk before, during and after difficult situations, for example, speaking in public or job interviews. If necessary, they can make up cue cards to remind themselves of appropriate self-talk. Clients can also use coping self-talk to deal with 'hot' thinking connected with temptations such as food, alcohol, drugs or high-risk sex. Watson and Tharp advocate that as soon as clients become aware of high-risk situations they should say: 'Danger! This is risky. I could have a lapse here' and then give themselves specific instructions as to what to do (Watson and Tharp, 1989, p. 278). A similar approach to high-risk situations is for clients to say: 'Stop ... think ... calm down' and then instruct themselves what to do. Further instructions include telling themselves that cravings will pass, engaging in distracting activities or thoughts and reminding themselves of the benefits of resisting temptation and the costs of giving in.

Even during counselling, you can emphasize the notion of recovery skills or retrieval skills for dealing with lapses and difficulties. Developing, using and maintaining skills is never going to be smooth sailing always. When clients face difficulties, they can say to themselves: 'Now is the time for me to use my recovery skills' or 'Now is the time for me to use my retrieval skills.' For instance, Paul Fleming, the client mentioned earlier with golf swing anxiety, learned to replace his anxiety-engendering self-talk when his golf ball ended up in awkward situations by telling himself 'No upheaval, just retrieval.' You can also make cassettes for clients in which they face difficulties, instruct themselves to use their recovery skills, calm themselves down and then coach themselves in the skills of competent performance needed to retrieve lapses or difficulties. As with Paul Fleming, recovery or retrieval self-talk can empower clients to cope with rather than be overwhelmed by difficulties.

Choosing realistic personal rules

Clients may require assistance in restating unrealistic into more realistic rules about learning and maintaining lifeskills. The following are examples.

Unrealistic rule: Change must be easy.
Restatement: I have not only to develop new and better skills strengths, but also to unlearn previous deficits. Consequently, achieving my goals requires effort and practice.

Unrealistic rule: During and after counselling I must improve all the time.
Restatement: Developing any skill involves mistakes, uncertainty and setbacks. All I can do is to learn from mistakes and cope with setbacks as well as possible.

Unrealistic rule: Others must support and approve of my efforts to develop skills.
Restatement: Though I might prefer that others approve, what is important is that I keep my skills development goals in mind and work hard to attain them.

Above are just a few unrealistic rules that clients might possess about learning and maintaining lifeskills. You can identify, clarify, dispute and restate other unrealistic rules that either you or your clients possess.

Perceiving accurately

Assist clients to monitor and perceive skills strengths and deficits accurately. Clients discourage themselves if they pay disproportionate attention to setbacks rather than successes. Discouragement can also result when clients exaggerate how good they are and then fail to live up to expectations. If necessary, clients can challenge their own thinking by identifying possibly inaccurate perceptions, separating fact from inference, looking for alternative perceptions and choosing the 'best fit' perception.

Clients can also discourage themselves if they fail to distinguish between a temporary lapse and a more permanent relapse (Watson and Tharp, 1989). When lapses occur, train clients not to commit the perceiving error of overgeneralizing them into relapses: 'Since I have gone back to my old behaviour once, I have permanently relapsed and can do nothing about it.' Lapses should stimulate using retrieval or 'getting back on the track' skills rather than giving up. Clients should also beware of thinking about skills in black and white terms: 'Either I possess a skill or I don't.' In virtually all skills areas, clients possess both strengths and deficits. Clients can also discourage themselves if they misperceive others' reactions. For example, they may be unnecessarily self-conscious and excessively sensitive to signs of disapproval. Furthermore, clients may become defensive when given constructive feedback.

Explaining cause accurately

Clients require accuracy in explaining the causes of positive and negative events as they develop and implement skills. For instance, where justified, assist clients to ascribe the cause of their successes to factors such as effort, willingness to take reasonable risks and use of targeted skills. Especially assist clients to make connections between the process of using skills and positive outcomes resulting from this process. Following are examples of two responses that each focus on clients making connections between skills and outcomes. If anything, I prefer the second response since it challenges the client to articulate the skills that contributed to the more successful outcome.

> **Client statement:** My last interview went better.
> **Counsellor response 1:** What you seem to be saying is that you used your skills and as a consequence did better at your last interview.

> **Client statement:** My last interview went better.
> **Counsellor response 2:** I'm glad. What skills did you use in the interview that you may not have been using before?

Clients can also wrongly explain the causes of positive and negative events as they develop and implement skills. In such instances, counsellor and client need to review the evidence for the explanations of cause. For instance, a shy client who is learning to phone girls up for dates may have a specific setback, yet explain the cause of the setback as permanent and pervasive – 'I'll never be any good at relating with women or with anyone else either.' Both during counselling and afterwards, clients require skills of challenging their explanations of negative events as due to factors that are permanent and pervasive. Counsellors should assist clients to analyse setbacks realistically. In many instances, they are events that have moderately specific explanations. Clients who understand that they can use recovery or retrieval skills possess a useful insight for extracting themselves from permanent and pervasive explanatory errors.

Predicting realistically

Predicting realistically can assist clients to maintain skills in many ways. First, clients able to predict high-risk situations can develop strategies to deal with them. Watson and Tharp (1989, p. 273) observe: 'A high risk situation is one that presents a greater than usual temptation to lapse into the unwanted behaviour.' Characteristics of high-risk situations can include feeling emotionally distressed, feeling lonely, social pressure from others and losing control under the influence of alcohol. Second, clients who predict that they may have failures and lapses may feel less discouraged when they occur. Third, clients able to predict the consequences of their first post-counselling failure or lapse can develop strategies for getting back on track (Marx, 1982). Fourth, clients can strengthen their resolve to maintain skills if they are able to predict benefits of continuing to use them and costs of giving them up. Fifth, clients can maintain skills in specific situations where realistic risk-taking is desirable if they focus on the gains of action as well as on potential losses. For example, excessively anxious clients can develop and maintain skills of challenging and counterbalancing 'dangerous' predictions.

Setting realistic goals

Clients should always have the goal of at least maintaining end of counselling skills levels. In addition, clients may have goals to develop skills still further. Such skills development goals should be specific and realistic, and possess a time frame. Counsellors and clients can plan how to develop targeted skills after counselling. If so, remember the importance of stating sub-goals and sequencing graded tasks. Clients who set themselves unrealistic post-counselling goals may even end up losing gains made during counselling. Clients should always review goals in the light of experience and feedback. In addition, be sensitive to clients' commitment to attaining goals. If you sense that clients have insufficient commitment, you can share this observation and together explore the issue more fully.

Using visualizing skills

Clients can use visualizing skills both to develop skills strengths and to prevent skills deficits. For instance, clients can visually rehearse and practise desired skills, possibly with accompanying self-talk. As mentioned in the section on self-talk, I frequently make up cassettes in which I guide clients through the imagery of competent performance accompanied by appropriate self-talk. In addition, clients can visualize anticipated high-risk situations and develop strategies for coping with them. Clients can also visualize the negative consequences of engaging in or relapsing back to unwanted behaviours. Some clients may need to exaggerate the negative consequences to strengthen their will power (Cautela, 1967; Lazarus, 1984).

Using self-reward

Clients can use self-reward not only to acquire, but also to maintain, lifeskills. They can continue administering external rewards contingent on desired actions: for example, having a cup of coffee after 50 minutes of study. In addition, clients can encourage themselves with internal rewards like 'Well done', 'I hung in there and made it' and 'I'm happy that I'm maintaining my skills.' Sometimes clients can use self-reward to help them attain natural rewards. For instance, shy clients might encourage themselves as they continue working on skills that elicit the natural rewards of positive social interaction.

FURTHER SKILLS FOR EMPHASIZING TAKE-AWAY

In addition to focusing on clients' thinking skills, the following are counsellor skills for increasing the likelihood that clients will take away and use trained skills not only during counselling, but after it ends.

Emphasize take-away when planning

In Chapter 12, I distinguished between structured and open plans for developing targeted skills. Counsellors can both write maintenance considerations into structured plans and keep them in mind when adopting open plans. The following are some ways that counsellors can enhance take-away when planning.

MAINTAIN A SKILLS FOCUS Use skills language. Plans containing a clear skills focus assist clients to think in skills terms both during and after counselling.

ALLOW FOR OVERLEARNING Where possible, train clients very thoroughly in targeted skills. Remember that clients require skills for both now and later. Goldstein and Keller (1987, p. 116) state: 'Overlearning involves the training of a skill beyond what is necessary to produce changes in behavior.' Strategies for overlearning include: limited goals; repeated skills demonstrations; emphasizing coaching and learning by doing; and ensuring adequate time and supervision of homework and practice.

EMPHASIZE REAL-LIFENESS Emphasizing 'real-lifeness' means that counsellors focus on practical ways of ensuring that clients can use skills in real life as contrasted with artificial settings. Plan to tailor presentations and demonstrations to clients' real-life situations. Role-play rehearsals should resemble real interactions. Plan take-away assignments that enhance transfer of skills to home settings.

TRAIN DIVERSELY Stokes and Osnes (1989, p. 345) state: 'What has frequently been documented is the fact that focused training frequently has focused effects.' Beware of narrow training that does not help clients to respond flexibly to situations. For instance, if rehearsing a client in asking for a pay rise, ensure that you have trials in which the boss responds in different ways.

PLAN REWARD STRATEGIES Counsellors can plan reward strategies that enhance maintenance (Goldstein and Keller, 1987; Nemeroff and Karoly, 1991; Stokes and Osnes, 1989). For instance, you may reward clients frequently as they initially acquire skills and then reward them intermittently as they use them. Applying reward schedules in this way is called 'thinning'. Nemeroff and Karoly (1991, p. 146) observe: 'it is particularly helpful if one can ensure that the behavior being trained will come to elicit *natural* reinforcers in the real world – money, competence, approval, and so on.' In addition, prompts and reminders can be gradually withdrawn or 'faded'.

Emphasize take-away when intervening

A professional colleague of mine used to say that, instead of a memory, he had a forgetory. The same observation holds true for most clients and counsellors. When intervening, make a major effort to ensure that clients remember and can use targeted skills. Following are some counsellor skills that I use to emphasize take-away of lifeskills for outside and after counselling.

KEEP INTERVENTIONS SIMPLE Keep interventions as clear and simple as possible. Even with clients who are seemingly well educated and intelligent, this guideline applies. In order to enhance ease of memory and application, skilled lifeskills counsellors deliver interventions that are clearly structured. Put another way, the interventions have nice clean lines. They are not cluttered with unnecessary verbiage and features.

TRAIN THOROUGHLY In my experience, the interventions of most beginning counselling students leave much to be desired. The overriding reason for this is that the students have failed to grasp the necessity for developing good training skills and then delivering specific interventions thoroughly. Common errors include: not understanding the intervention properly; understanding it, yet presenting it in a confused way; either failing to or inadequately demonstrating the intervention; inadequately drawing the client into the training process; either failing to or insufficiently coaching and rehearsing the client in the targeted skill; and either failing to or insufficiently negotiating adequate take-away assignments. If you think that all or part of the cap fits, please refer back to Chapter 13, on delivering interventions skills.

USE VISUAL PRESENTATION Most frequently, when I deliver an intervention I incorporate some use of the whiteboard. I find that in counselling, just as in classroom teaching, visual presentation enhances verbal presentation. However, be careful not to lecture clients. Use the whiteboard as a shared space in which you can work together: for instance, when cooperating to challenge the unrealistic personal rule, 'I must be liked by everyone.' Though the counsellor may write up the suggestions, both counsellor and client generate and evaluate the challenges or disputations. Material written on whiteboards can be taken down for both client and counsellor records.

MAKE UP TAKE-AWAY CASSETTES Frequently, I make up tailor-made take-away cassettes to help clients to remember and use skills. Since many clients are anxious about situations in which they require targeted skills, often I include some mental relaxation instructions at the front. Here is an example of a self-help cassette made up for Louise Donovan to help her stay task-oriented and manage her anxieties when going for interviews for senior accountancy positions.

'I'm going to count to ten in units of two. After each unit of two I will instruct you to tense and relax a muscle grouping. One, two ... focus on your leg and feet muscles ... relax and enjoy the sensations of the tension flowing from your legs and feet. Three, four ... focus on your chest, shoulder and stomach muscles ... relax and enjoy the sensations of the tension flowing from your chest, shoulders and stomach. Five, six ... focus on your face, neck and head muscles ... relax and enjoy the sensations of the tension flowing from your face, neck and head. Seven, eight ... focus on your arm and hand muscles ... relax and enjoy the sensations of the tension flowing from your arms and hands. Nine, ten ... focus on all the muscles in your body ... relax and enjoy the sensations of the tension leaving your whole body as your relaxation gets deeper and deeper ... deeper and deeper ... deeper and deeper. Now focus on your breathing and take some slow deep breaths with a particular emphasis on exhaling ... in ... out ... out ... in ... out ... out ... in ... out ... out ... just breathe slowly and regularly on your own for about thirty seconds. Now I'd like you to imagine that you are lying on a beach on a nice sunny day enjoying the warmth of the sunshine on your body ... you hear the rhythmic sound of the sea in the background ... imagine the sounds, smells and textures of lying on the beach on a warm sunny day ... you enjoy the peace and calm ... peace and calm ... peace and calm ... you haven't a care in the world as you're lying on the beach on a warm sunny day ... hold that scene for about thirty seconds.

'Now I'd like you to imagine you're waiting outside the interview room about to be interviewed for a senior position ... you feel a little nervous, but as you experience your anxiety you tell yourself "Calm down, I can cope with this situation, my anxiety is a signal for me to use my coping skills, just let's review what skills I need to use when I go in the interview room ... I need to walk in calmly keeping my body facing the panel, smile and say 'hello' and sit down with a relaxed erect body posture and look at the chairperson to show I am ready for the first question." Now imagine yourself going in and sitting down looking competent and professional and using your skills. The chairperson asks the first question: "Now, Ms Donovan, why have you applied for this position?" Imagine yourself answering the question by repeating the crux of the question at the front of your answer: "I have applied for this position for three main reasons ... " You speak in a calm and relaxed person-to-person manner with a voice volume that is comfortable to listen to. You make good eye contact with the panel and appropriately emphasize your points with facial expressions and gestures. Now just imagine yourself answering the first question competently and using good interview skills. Then continue for as long as you think it valuable rehearsing in your mind how to perform competently at interview for a senior accountancy position.'

USE TAKE-AWAY SHEETS AND ENCOURAGE CLIENT RECORD-KEEPING The two main take-away sheets in lifeskills counselling are the assessment of deficits/statement of goals form and the take-away sheet. Counsellors may enhance take-away by encouraging clients to keep counselling records. Arguably it is more important for clients than for counsellors to keep records. What clients call their counselling records is up to them. The purpose of clients' counselling records is to store important information and learnings collected during and after counselling. Contents of client records can include: statements of deficits/goals; monitoring logs; take-away sheets of work conducted during counselling sessions; handouts describing skills; answers to take-away assignments; diary entries; and so on.

The counselling record enhances take-away of self-helping skills in many ways. First, by making the effort to keep the record, clients show a commitment to maintaining targeted skills. Second, clients can use the record for revising. Third, they can use the record for monitoring and evaluating progress. Fourth, after counselling ends, they can update the record as they keep working on targeted skills until they are firmly established in their repertoires. Fifth, if later on they experience difficulties, then they have a source of information for self-helping.

EMPHASIZE TAKE-AWAY ASSIGNMENTS Both counsellors and clients require a commitment to take-away assignments as a bridge between learning and maintaining skills. Take-away assignments should be a feature of virtually all between-session periods. Such assignments can give clients the opportunity to practise skills in diverse situations. In subsequent sessions, always review how clients performed and enquire about related thoughts and feelings. If appropriate, not only discuss difficulties and setbacks that clients experience, but also use role-plays and rehearsals to develop relevant skills.

CHAPTER HIGHLIGHTS

- *Counsellors need systematically to attend to developing clients' lifeskills after counselling.*

- *Generalization, maintenance, transfer and development are important considerations in assisting clients to take away self-helping skills from counselling.*

- *Counsellors need to work with clients' thinking skills to enhance take-away and maintenance of lifeskills. This includes clearly restating clients' deficits/goals in skills terms.*

- *Considerations in emphasizing take-away when planning include maintaining a skills focus, allowing for overlearning, emphasizing real-lifeness, training diversely and planning reward strategies.*

- *Considerations in emphasizing take-away when intervening include keeping interventions simple, training thoroughly, using visual presentation, making up take-away cassettes, using take-away sheets and encouraging client record-keeping, and emphasizing take-away assignments.*

EXERCISE 18.1 WORKING WITH CLIENTS' THINKING SKILLS

As appropriate, complete this exercise on your own, with a partner or in a group.

1. With regard to a client group with whom you either currently work or might work in future, indicate how you might use each of the following thinking skills to help clients to take away from counselling trained skills as self-helping skills for afterwards.

   (a) making clear restatements in skills terms
   (b) owning responsibility for choosing
   (c) using coping self-talk
   (d) choosing realistic personal rules
   (e) perceiving accurately

(f) explaining cause accurately
(g) predicting realistically
(h) setting realistic goals
(i) using visualizing skills
(j) using self-reward

2. Summarize the main ways in which you might work with clients' thinking skills to help clients to take away from counselling trained skills as self-helping skills for afterwards.

EXERCISE 18.2 EMPHASIZING TAKE-AWAY WHEN PLANNING AND INTERVENING

As appropriate, complete the parts of this exercise on your own, with a partner or in a group.

Part A Emphasizing take-away when planning
1. With regard to a client group with whom you either currently work or might work in future, indicate how you might use each of the following skills to assist clients to take away from counselling trained skills as self-helping for afterwards.

(a) maintaining a skills focus
(b) allowing for overlearning
(c) emphasizing real-lifeness
(d) training diversely
(e) planning reward strategies

2. Summarize the main ways in which, when planning, you might emphasize assisting clients to take away from counselling trained skills as self-helping skills for afterwards.

Part B Emphasizing take-away when intervening
1. With regard to a client group with whom you either currently work or might work in future, indicate how you might use each of the following skills to help clients to take away from counselling trained skills as self-helping for afterwards.

(a) keeping interventions simple
(b) training thoroughly
(c) using visual presentation
(d) making up take-away cassettes
(e) using take-away sheets and encouraging client record-keeping
(f) emphasizing take-away assignments

2. Summarize the main ways in which, when intervening, you might emphasize

assisting clients to take away from counselling trained skills as self-helping skills for afterwards.

NINETEEN
End and evaluate

If we do meet again, why, we shall smile.
If not, why then, this parting was well made.

William Shakespeare

CHAPTER QUESTIONS

- *When should counselling end?*

- *What are different formats for ending counselling?*

- *What tasks are entailed in ending counselling?*

- *What are some skills for ending counselling?*

- *How can counsellors evaluate their effectiveness?*

INTRODUCTION

The boundaries for ending counselling are imprecise. As implied in the chapter on emphasizing take-away skills, lifeskills counselling has its ending built into its beginning. In another sense, the ending of formal counselling is the beginning of independent self-helping. Despite advocating count-downs to ending in earlier sessions, here for the sake of simplicity, I define ending counselling as starting with the penultimate session and concluding when all scheduled contact between clients and counsellors finishes.

WHEN SHOULD COUNSELLING END?

Start counsellor–client termination discussions before final sessions and aim for convergence either then or by the final session. Throughout counselling, counsellors and clients collect information relevant to termination decisions. Following are sources of and kinds of relevant information.

CLIENT SELF-REPORT Clients may perceive themselves as better able to cope with problems. They may think they have attained their thinking and action skills goals. They may feel more confident and less prone to negative emotions. They perceive that they no longer require the support of counsellors and can maintain skills.

COUNSELLOR OBSERVATION Over a series of sessions, counsellors may notice improvements in how well clients use targeted thinking skills and action skills. These observations come from various sources: the counselling conversation, role-plays and other structured activities and probes about how well clients use skills outside counselling. You may observe clients feeling happier and more relaxed. They no longer have the symptoms that brought them to counselling: for instance, excessive anxiety. Problems that previously seemed insurmountable now seem manageable. Clients use better skills in responding to such problems. In addition, they seem to understand and use targeted skills well enough to maintain them.

FEEDBACK FROM SIGNIFICANT OTHERS Another set of reasons for considering ending helping is 'when significant others in clients' lives give clients feedback that they are different, or have changed, or make comments such as "you never used to do that before"' (Teyber, 1989, p. 190). Sometimes feedback may come direct to you: for instance, from counsellor's aides, spouses, bosses or parents.

ATTAINMENT OF MEASURABLE GOALS Clients can have easily measurable goals. For example, they may pass an examination or driving test. Other examples of measurable goals include losing a stipulated amount of weight and maintaining the loss over a given period, cutting down on smoking and maintaining the reduction, keeping off alcohol and only spending a certain amount of money each week. Clients' goals can be both objective and subjective: for instance, making a given number of friends in a set period of time. The given number and set period are objective, whereas the definition of friends is more subjective.

If you and your clients consistently obtain positive information from all four of the above sources, your decision about when to end is easy. However, if positive changes are recent, it may pay to 'wait and see' if clients maintain them. Inconsistent information, either from within or between different sources, merits further exploration.

FORMATS FOR ENDING COUNSELLING

The following are possible formats for ending counselling.

FIXED ENDING Counsellor and client may have a contract that they work for, say, ten sessions in one or more problem or problematic skills areas. Advantages of fixed endings include lessening the chance of dependency and motivating clients to use counselling to best effect. Potential disadvantages are restricting coverage of problems and thoroughness of attention to problematic skills. Sometimes external factors make for fixed endings: for instance, upcoming exams or ends of semesters.

OPEN ENDING WHEN GOALS ARE ATTAINED With open endings, counselling concludes when counsellors and clients agree that clients have obtained their goals. Such goals include managing a specific problem, developing skills to manage current and future problems and, sometimes, staying in counselling long enough to become thoroughly grounded in the lifeskills philosophy of life.

FADED ENDING Here the withdrawal of counselling assistance is gradual. For example, instead of meeting weekly, the final sessions could be at fortnightly or monthly intervals.

ENDING WITH BOOSTER SESSION(S) Booster sessions, say after three months, are not to teach new skills, but to check clients' progress in consolidating skills, to motivate them and to help them to work through difficulties in taking away and using trained skills into home environments.

ENDING WITH SCHEDULED FOLLOW-UP PHONE CALLS Counsellors can schedule follow-up phone calls with clients. Such phone calls perform the same functions as booster sessions. From both phone calls and booster sessions counsellors obtain feedback on how successful counselling was in assisting clients to maintain skills.

Premature ending

Clients sometimes leave counselling before counsellors think they are ready. However, what may seem premature to counsellors may seem different to clients. Beck and his colleagues cite, as reasons for premature termination, rapid relief of symptoms, negative reactions to the therapist and lack of sustained improvement or relapse during treatment (Beck et al., 1979). Premature ending may also take place where there is a mismatch between the kind of counselling relationship that counsellors offer and that clients expect (Lazarus, 1993). Counsellors who clumsily handle clients' doubts about and resistances to counselling increase the likelihood of premature termination. Further reasons why clients leave prematurely include pressure from significant others, laziness, defensiveness, lack of money, moving to another location and fear of being trapped by counsellors unwilling to 'let go'.

Counsellors may consider it premature if clients leave counselling feeling able to cope with immediate problems, but insufficiently having consolidated thinking and action skills for dealing with future problems. In such instances, counsellors and clients can still have done useful work together. Former clients may now possess insights about skills needed to cope with future problems and be more inclined to seek further assistance, if needed.

EMPHASIZING TAKE-AWAY WHEN ENDING COUNSELLING

The main task in ending counselling is 'the consolidation of what has been achieved in terms of some durable benefit for the interviewee' (Sullivan, 1954, p. 41). Many skills that you use in this stage build on skills you have used earlier. With clients who come for brief, focused counselling, you may compromise in what you can achieve in the ending stage. Following are some skills for enhancing consolidation of take-away skills when ending counselling.

Make transition statements

During counselling, you may make statements indicating its finiteness, for instance, comments about developing self-helping skills for after counselling. Such comments may encourage clients to make the most of sessions. You can introduce ending counselling with one or more transition statements.

> 'Our next session is the final session. I think we should discuss how we can use the time we have left to help you retain and build on the skills you've learned for managing your problem.'

> 'I think the agenda for this final session should mainly be how to help you use the skills you've learned here for afterwards. For instance, we can review how much you've changed, where you still need to change, how you might go about it, and how you can deal with high-risk situations.'

Summarize

Already I have stressed the need throughout counselling for counsellor and client summaries. When ending, continue to develop clients' monitoring and self-assessment skills. End of counselling summaries can review both important learning and perceptions of progress. Summarizing progress can be a take-away assignment prior to final sessions. You can also ask clients to cassette record their summaries as reminders. Another idea is for clients to keep cassette recordings of final sessions.

Rehearse coping with high-risk situations and with lapses

Rehearsing coping with high-risk situations and lapses should be part of structured activities during counselling, and not an afterthought left until the end. Counsellors and clients can rehearse thinking and action skills for implementing how they are going to maintain skills. For example, clients can role-play how to use appropriate thinking and action skills in specific high-risk situations. In addition, they can rehearse and write down appropriate self-talk for handling lapses, underachievement and failure.

Counsellors can re-emphasize clients' responsibility for their lives. When they are in difficulty, looking at the adequacy of their own thinking, acting and use of targeted skills is the best place to start. Clients can ask themselves questions like 'What are my goals and how is my behaviour blocking me from attaining them?', 'What are my characteristic thinking and action skills deficits in relation to this problem?' and 'How well am I using the skills I have learned and how can I improve?' Stress the importance of clients developing good retrieval skills and realizing that maintaining gains requires continuing effort.

Work with counsellor's aides

During the ending stage, counsellors can contact their aides to receive assessments of clients' progress outside counselling. Counsellors can also work with aides to identify ways in which they can continue supporting clients once counselling ends. Sometimes three-way meetings between counsellors, clients and aides are desirable. For example, at the end of a series of counselling sessions designed to help an elementary school child become more outgoing, teacher, child and school counsellor might together plan how the teacher could continue supporting the child.

Explore arrangements for continuing support

Self-support is the main way in which clients can receive continuing support. However, given the likelihood of some degree of lapse in using targeted skills, think through how clients might receive ongoing support. The following are some options.

- *Further contact with counsellor.* Possibilities for further contact with counsellors include scheduled booster sessions, follow-up sessions at clients' request and either scheduled or unscheduled phone calls. You can discuss with clients how you view further contact with them.

- *Referral for further individual counselling.* Though clients may have made considerable progress with the problems and problematic skills for which they came to counselling, they may still require further professional assistance. For many reasons you may decide to refer such clients to other counsellors: for instance, your time may be limited or another counsellor has special expertise in an emerging problem area.

- *Using outside supports.* In Chaper 16, I mentioned the counsellor skill of assisting clients to identify and use supports as they develop lifeskills. Many of the supports clients identify during counselling should be available afterwards. In addition, during and at the end of counselling, you can encourage clients to view identifying and using supports as a useful self-helping skill. Friendly constructive criticism from supportive third parties can help clients to build and maintain targeted skills.

One way of using others as supports is to encourage them to give honest feedback in non-threatening ways. Also, open acknowledgement by others of positive behaviour changes can motivate clients to keep working.

• *Group counselling.* Some clients might gain from joining groups in which they can practise and develop targeted skills. Peer self-help groups provide an alternative to professionally led groups. Counsellors can also discuss opportunities for participating in courses or workshops run by themselves or others.

• *Further reading and audiovisual material.* Some clients appreciate the support provided by further reading. Clients can also listen to and watch self-helping audio-cassettes and video-tapes. On your own initiative or by request, you can suggest appropriate books, training manuals, audio-cassettes and video-tapes.

FURTHER ENDING COUNSELLING TASKS AND SKILLS

In addition to the major task of consolidating self-helping skills, there are other tasks when you are ending counselling. How you handle them varies with length of counselling, nature of problem(s) and problematic skills, and the counsellor–client relationship.

Deal with feelings

Most lifeskills counselling contacts are focused and short to medium term. Furthermore, though the relationship is important, it is not the central feature of lifeskills counselling. Consequently, there is less likelihood of clients feeling angry, sad, anxious and abandoned than in longer-term relationship-oriented counselling. In addition, clients should feel better able to cope with problems and problematic skills as a result of counselling. Often, they achieve a sense of accomplishment and optimism.

Clients' feelings at the end of counselling fall into two main categories: feelings about how they are going to fare without counsellors and feelings towards counsellors and the counselling process. Many clients have feelings of ambivalence about how they will cope after counselling. On the one hand, they feel more competent; on the other hand, they still have doubts about their abilities to implement skills. Counsellors can facilitate open discussion of clients' feelings about the future. Looking at how best to maintain skills also addresses the issue of clients' lingering doubts. Other clients will feel that they can cope very well without you – possibly a sign that together you have done a good job!

Clients may also wish to share feelings about you and the counselling process. Since the counselling relationship is not the main agenda, do not get side-tracked into lengthy discussions of unfinished emotional business. Nevertheless, allow clients the opportunity to share feelings about their contact with you. You may obtain valuable feedback about how you come across. You may also share feelings with clients: for instance, 'I enjoyed working with you', 'I admire the courage with which you face your situation' or 'I'm delighted with your progress.'

Say goodbye

Saying goodbye or the formal leave-taking 'should be a clean-cut, respectful finish that does not confuse that which has been done' (Sullivan, 1954, p. 216). Last impressions as well as first impressions are important. Aim to say goodbye in a business-like, yet friendly, way, appropriate to professional rather than personal relationships. By ending counselling sloppily, you may undo some of your influence in helping clients to maintain skills.

End ethically

A number of important ethical issues surround ending counselling. For example, counsellors need to think through their responsibilities to clients after counselling. Too much support may engender dependency, too little may fail to carry out professional obligations. Each case must be judged on its merits. Another ethical issue is what to do when you think clients have other problems on which they need work. I suggest bringing your views tactfully to their attention.

A further set of ethical issues surrounds the boundaries between personal and professional relationships. Most professional associations have ethical codes covering issues in providing counselling services (for instance, Australian Psychological Society, 1986; British Association for Counselling, 1993; British Psychological Society, 1993, 1995). When ending counselling, allowing your personal and professional wires with clients to become quickly crossed is not only unethical, but can make it more difficult to counsel them if future need arises. If you are considering post-counselling personal relationships, be guided by ethical codes, conscience, advice of respected colleagues and, above all, clients' best interests.

Evaluate your counselling skills

When counselling terminates, counsellors have many sources of information for evaluating their counselling skills. These sources of information include attendance, client feedback, both intentional and unintentional, perceptions of client progress, session notes, possibly video-tape or audio-cassette feedback, feedback from third parties and compliance and success in carrying out take-away assignments. Effective counsellors, like good clients, evaluate their skills throughout counselling. You can make a final evaluation of your work with each client soon after counselling ends. Questions to ask yourself include 'To what extent did the client achieve the targeted goals?' and 'How well did I use the skills for each stage of the lifeskills counselling model?' If you leave such an evaluation too long, you risk forgetting valuable information. Beware of perceiving errors when evaluating your counselling skills – you may be too hard or too easy on yourself. What you seek is a balanced appraisal of strengths and deficits.

CHAPTER HIGHLIGHTS

- *Sources of information for when to end counselling include client self-report, counsellor observation, feedback from significant others and attainment of measurable goals.*

- *Formats for ending counselling include fixed ending, open ending when goals are attained, faded ending and ending with booster session(s) or scheduled follow-up phone calls.*

- *Reasons for clients leaving counselling prematurely include rapid relief of symptoms, negative reactions to counsellors and/or to counselling approaches, unfulfilled expectations and pressure from significant others.*

- *Counsellors should raise the issue of when to end before the final session.*

- *Skills for emphasizing take-away when ending counselling include making transition statements, summarizing, rehearsing coping with high-risk situations and with lapses, working with counsellor's aides and exploring arrangements for continuing support.*

- *Further ending counselling tasks include dealing with feelings, saying goodbye and ending ethically.*

- *When clients end counselling, counsellors can evaluate how well they used their skills with that client.*

EXERCISE 19.1   CONSIDERING ENDING COUNSELLING

As appropriate, answer the questions in this exercise on your own, with a partner or in a training group.

1. What is the relevance of each of the following considerations for when counselling should end?

   (a) client self-report
   (b) counsellor observation
   (c) feedback from significant others
   (d) attainment of measurable goals
   (e) other factors not mentioned above

2. Discuss the merits of different formats for ending counselling.

3. How can counsellors prevent clients ending counselling prematurely?

4. To what extent should and how might counsellors arrange for the continuing support of clients?

5. What are some of the main feelings attached to ending counselling and what skills do counsellors require to deal with them?

6. What are some of the main ethical issues attached to ending counselling?

EXERCISE 19.2 PREPARING CLIENTS FOR HIGH-RISK SITUATIONS AND LAPSES

Complete the parts of this exercise with one or more partners. If in a training group, two members can role-play the counsellor and client parts, while the remainder of the group act as observers and provide feedback.

Part A Preparing a client for a high-risk situation

Work with a partner, who role-plays a client with a specific high-risk situation where, when counselling ends, he or she is vulnerable to not using targeted skills. Assist your client to identify strategies and skills for coping with the high-risk situation. Then, using role-play, rehearse your client in relevant thinking and action skills.

Using the whiteboard, develop a reminder for your client of recommended strategies and skills. Then, both you and your client write this reminder down on a lifeskills counselling take-away sheet.

After your session, discuss and give feedback. Then reverse roles. Audio-cassette or video-tape playback of your role-plays may assist learning.

Part B Preparing a client for a post-counselling lapse

How former clients handle post-counselling setbacks can be very important for whether or not they maintain counselling gains. Counsellors need to assist clients to develop retrieval skills for getting back on track. Work with a partner, who role-plays a client. You are in the final session. Assist your client to identify the first post-counselling situation where he or she might fail to use his or her skills well or have a lapse. Then identify and rehearse appropriate skills, particularly thinking skills, for getting back on track.

Using the whiteboard, develop a reminder for your client of recommended strategies and skills. Then, both you and your client write this reminder down on a lifeskills counselling take-away sheet.

After your session, discuss and give feedback. Then reverse roles. Audio-cassette or video-tape playback of your role-plays may assist learning.

EXERCISE 19.3   CONDUCTING A FINAL SESSION

Complete this exercise with one or more partners. If in a training group, two members can role-play the counsellor and client parts, while the remainder of the group act as observers and provide feedback. Alternatively, the group can work in counsellor–client–observer threesomes.

Conduct a final session with a partner, who role-plays a client with whom, for at least four previous sessions, you have worked to develop one or more targeted lifeskills. In the final session, as appropriate, use the following skills:

- making transition statements

- summarizing and encouraging the client to summarize

- facilitating monitoring

- rehearsing coping with high-risk situations and with lapses

- reinforcing effective thinking skills

- working with counsellor's aides

- exploring arrangements for continuing support

- dealing with feelings

- saying goodbye

- ending ethically

At the end of the session, discuss and receive feedback. Playing back an audio-cassette or video-tape of the session may assist learning. Afterwards, reverse roles.

EXERCISE 7.5: CONDUCTING A FINAL SESSION

PART SEVEN

Looking Ahead

Chapter 20 looks ahead to how you can monitor, maintain and develop your counselling skills.

TWENTY

Develop your counselling skills

Courage is the self-affirmation of being in spite of the fact of nonbeing.

Paul Tillich

CHAPTER QUESTIONS

• *What is the current state of your counselling skills?*

• *How can you maintain your counselling skills?*

• *How can you develop your counselling skills still further?*

• *What is the challenge for counsellors and helpers?*

INTRODUCTION

This chapter focuses on how you can maintain and develop your counselling skills. For the remainder of your life you are faced with the possibility of making good or poor counselling skills choices: choices that help clients to achieve goals or choices that cause clients trouble. Maintaining your counselling skills requires effort and vigilance. In addition, for the sake of clients and yourself, you have an ethical duty to develop your skills still further.

Monitor your counselling skills

Exercise 20.1 at the end of this chapter asks you to reassess your counselling skills for each stage of the DASIE model in the light of reading this book. I hope that you have completed some, if not all, of the exercises. You will probably have tried to develop many of the skills by practising them in the opportunities you have to counsel. Take your time over the exercise. Accurate assessment is vital in pinpointing deficits. Once deficits are clearly identified, you have made considerable progress in doing something about them. You may wish to complete Exercise 20.1 periodically in future to monitor your skills.

MAINTAIN AND DEVELOP YOUR COUNSELLING SKILLS

Once you have acquired some counselling skills strengths, how can you keep them? There are numerous pressures on you not to maintain counselling skills. Some pressures are internal and come from yourself. For instance, when you have recently learned skills strengths, you may still feel the pull of long-established deficits. You may also lack confidence in your ability to practise recently learned skills on your own without a trainer. You may possess thinking skills deficits, like perfectionism, that undermine your motivation. You may give up too easily because you have insufficiently learned that maintaining counselling skills involves a deeply held value of commitment to competence.

Some pressures not to maintain your skills are external. You may have insufficient opportunity to work with clients. Clients themselves may reward deficits rather than strengths: for example, you may be more comfortable for clients if passively listening rather than if actively seeking to break down and restate how they sustain problems in skills terms. Feedback from supervisors and colleagues can be for good or ill. Be careful not to allow their counselling skills deficits to become yours too.

Whether the pressures are internal, external or both, it is easy to backslide and transfer counselling skills strengths into deficits. However, where possible, you can go in the other direction. Below are some suggestions for maintaining and developing your counselling skills.

Keep viewing counselling in skills terms

This book stresses the importance of viewing counselling in skills terms and emphasizes that counselling skills represent choices that can be well or poorly made. Because seeing counselling in skills terms is new to you, you may lose both this perspective and its benefits: namely, a set of skills 'handles' you can use to help clients. The lifeskills counselling approach assumes that counsellors are personally responsible for making specific choices conducive to their own professional competence and to clients' happiness and fulfilment. Consequently, the approach keeps counselling out of the realm of magic and firmly in the realm of practicality.

Clarify your values

What are the values by which you choose to lead your life? What ultimately is of worth to you? How can you develop and sustain the inner strength to be an effective counsellor? Some counsellors may need to clarify their values before they can gain a genuine commitment to counselling effectively. For example, instead of viewing counselling mainly in terms of either materialistic values – 'How much money is there in it for me?' – or needs for approval – 'How can I be really popular with my clients?' – some counsellors require access to more fundamental human values. Such values include: a concern for developing clients' full humanity; prizing the uniqueness of each client; being committed to working with clients for their sakes and not just for your own; and helping clients to make their own choices. Some counsellors find inner strength and guidance from religious beliefs. The more deeply centred clients are in fundamental human values, the more they strive to consolidate and improve their counselling skills. Similarly, committed clients are less likely to be side-tracked into superficial values and actions. Clarifying your values is partly a matter of self-help and of listening more deeply to yourself (Gendlin, 1981), and partly a matter of working with and learning from others.

Discipline your thinking

You need to discipline your thinking to keep growing as a counsellor. Thinking skills to work on include: owning responsibility for how you think, feel and act; getting in touch with your feelings about both your clients and yourself; using coping self-talk when faced with difficulties and setbacks; choosing realistic rules and avoiding 'musturbations' about perfectionism and approval; accurately perceiving feedback from clients and supervisors; explaining cause accurately for maintaining and developing counselling skills; predicting both clients' and your own future realistically; setting realistic goals for yourself and your clients; using visualizing to rehearse and enhance your counselling strengths and cope with setbacks; and using managing problems skills to think yourself through difficulties rather than react impulsively (Beck and Weishaar, 1995; Ellis, 1995; May and Yalom, 1995; Meichenbaum and Deffenbacher, 1988; Nelson-Jones, 1995). Like clarifying your values, disciplining your thinking is partly a matter of self-help and partly a matter of working with and learning from others.

Observe and listen to skilled counsellors

In this book, I emphasize learning by observing. One of the best ways to develop counselling skills is by observing and listening to the work of skilled counsellors. The counsellors you observe need not necessarily adopt the lifeskills counselling model. For example, you may learn much about active listening and developing counselling relationships by observing competent person-centred counsellors. The following are a number of ways to observe skilled counsellors.

BEING PRESENT You may be allowed to sit in the room while counselling is in progress. It may be easier for clients if you are unobtrusive. For instance, you sit out of sight and do not participate in discussions or activities.

OBSERVING THROUGH A ONE-WAY MIRROR Observers may watch counselling from behind one-way mirrors. A microphone and speaker system can provide sound. One-way mirror observation has the advantages of relative unobtrusiveness and of seeing proceedings both life-sized and as they happen.

VIEWING CLOSED CIRCUIT TV A video camera may be connected to a monitor in another room. Disadvantages of closed circuit TV include the possible obtrusiveness of a camera in counselling rooms and a lessening of visual detail through problems of camera angle and monitor size.

BEING A CLIENT Try to obtain the experience of being the client of a skilled lifeskills counsellor. This way, you receive first-hand experience of the application of each stage of the DASIE model. Being a client of skilled counsellors adopting other approaches can also provide you with valuable opportunities to learn from observing and experiencing. If you are in supervision, another approach to being a client is to have your supervisor demonstrate how to deliver an intervention, with you role-playing the real client.

LISTENING TO CASSETTES Cassettes of interviews conducted by leading counsellors and helpers are available in Australasia, Britain and North America. Generally, it is easier to get real clients to agree to cassette-record interviews than to video-record them, since the situation is more anonymous. Most often cassettes will contain some commentary concerning what the counsellor wants the listener to learn. Where such commentaries do not exist, one possibility is to listen to whole sessions and focus on the counsellor, the client and the process. Another possibility is to listen to smaller segments of interviews, say five minute segments, and target specific skills for observation. A good tip is to focus on the interactive patterns between counsellors and clients and not just on each in isolation.

Those readers wishing to take a more systematic approach to assessing the processes of counselling interviews can start by familiarizing themselves with the counselling research literature (for example, Heppner *et al.*, 1992; Hill *et al.*, 1994). However, this literature has gaps as well as strengths. For instance, two important gaps are studies about using voice messages and studies about using visual methods, such as whiteboards.

LOOKING AT VIDEO-TAPES AND FILMS Video-tapes and films have the added advantage over audio-cassettes of observing counsellor and client body messages and their interactions. Lifeskills counselling video-tapes can show how to work on the whiteboard. Films are expensive to produce and difficult to screen. Furthermore, films are less flexible than video-tapes for stopping and playing back.

There is a dearth of good counsellor training video-tapes and films. In Britain, films and video-tapes may be hired from the British Association for Counselling (1 Regent Place, Rugby, Warwickshire CV21 2PJ; tel. 01788 550899; fax 01788 562189). I have made a two video-tape package of how to use the lifeskills counselling model based on a real client who was role-played by a colleague: the first video covers Stages 1 to 3 of the model; the second video focuses on a number of different interventions during Stage 4 (Nelson-Jones, 1996c).

READING TRANSCRIPTS Though the disadvantage of written demonstration is that you lose the live quality of audio-cassettes and video-tapes, nevertheless you may learn something from them. Transcripts of interviews by leading counsellors are available. Such transcripts may be read in their entirety. Alternatively, you may wish to look either at smaller segments or for illustrations of particular skills. Another possibility is to go down the pages covering up the counsellor's responses, forming your own, then checking the counsellor's responses. You can do the same with audio-cassettes and video-tapes by pressing the pause button after the client speaks.

An important issue in observational learning is how many counselling sessions to watch or to listen to. Another issue is whether or not observers engage in discussion of what they have observed. Observing or listening to single counselling sessions can be very valuable. Nevertheless, added benefits accrue from observing or listening to a series of sessions. Observers may see or hear counsellors using the different skills applicable to each stage of the lifeskills model. Observers may also watch the development, or lack of development, of clients' skills. Where possible, observers should have the opportunity for during session or post-session discussion with peers, trainers and/or supervisors. These discussions are best held when material is still fresh in observer's minds.

Supervised practical experience

Supervised practical experience is an excellent way for you to develop your counselling skills. Some readers may already have access to suitable clients, whereas for others access to clients may be a major stumbling block to adequate supervision. Counsellor training courses of reasonable duration are remiss if they do not attempt to ensure that their students, when ready, have enough access to clients. Students require good support and supervision, especially when first assuming responsibility for clients. In settings where the focus is on less formal counselling (for example, nurses in hospitals), the more experienced can help the less experienced to develop their skills. However, for many reasons, even experienced counsellors and helpers may find it beneficial to receive some supervision. These reasons include: guarding against falling into bad habits; updating knowledge and skills; obtaining assistance with difficult clients; and, if necessary, receiving personal and/or professional support.

Much of the value of supervised practical experience depends on the quality of supervision. Of all methods of supervising students' practical work, I consider observing video-tapes – failing that, listening to audio-cassettes – to be by far the most effective. Clients will often grant permission for recording as long as they are assured that the material will be treated as confidential, erased in the near future and only used for training purposes. Without this recorded evidence, supervisors are unable to focus on how students respond to clients and on student–client interactive patterns. Consequently, the very important area of specific verbal, voice and body responding choices is largely lost to supervision.

Broadly speaking, there are two main approaches to viewing supervision video-tapes: supervisor-centred and supervisee-centred. In the supervisor-centred approach there is an expert–neophyte relationship. Supervisors control the sessions and stop the video playback to point out good and poor use of skills. The supervisee-centred approach is represented by Kagan's Interpersonal Process Recall method (Kagan, 1984). Here supervisees control the proceedings and stop the video playback when they want. The supervisor's role is to facilitate the supervisee's recall by making inquiries: for example 'What were you trying to do?', 'What were you feeling?' and 'Were there any risks for you?' Much supervision adopts a mixed model. A variation of the mixed model is to have supervisors with more control in early supervision sessions, with supervisees assuming more control as they become more skilled.

Whoever makes the decisions, an important issue is which parts of a video-tape to observe. A risk is that you spend so much time watching the first few minutes, so that later work in sessions never receives the attention it deserves. One way to counteract this potential imbalance is to agree in advance to sample a session's beginning, middle and end. Another approach is to ask supervisees to watch tapes before supervisions and note the times of events throughout the session to discuss in supervision.

Important elements in supervision include focusing on supervisees' ability to assess and restate problems in skills terms, state goals and plan, intervene, emphasize take-away and end counselling. In addition, supervision can address the supervisory relationship, theory, ethics and professional behaviour (Sweeney, 1995). Supervision can focus on supervisees' understanding of and effectiveness within institutional and agency contexts in which they work.

Opinions differ about whether supervision is best done with just one supervisee at a time, in twos, in threes or with even larger numbers. Reasons for keeping supervision on an individual basis include the time-consuming nature of watching video-tapes or listening to cassette-recordings; for instance, discussion of only part of a tape can take much of a supervision session. In addition, there is the possibility that supervisees explore themselves as counsellors and persons more deeply in individual supervision. Reasons for supervising in groups of two, three or more include making it possible for supervisees to comment on one another's work and to learn from each other. There are also obvious reasons of economy and of practicality if there is a shortage of good supervisors.

For practising counsellors and helpers, there is much to be said for peer supervision in which you facilitate, challenge and learn from one another. *Co-counselling* is one model for peer supervision. For instance, you may each occupy 45 minutes, reversing supervisor/supervisee roles at half time. Furthermore, you can negotiate the role you wish your supervisor to play – facilitator, trainer, personal support etc. – so that you 'control' your own supervision. *Peer supervision groups* are another model for peer supervision. The group can decide how best to use the talents and resources of its members. Again, individual members who present material can be given the opportunity of stating what kind of assistance they want from the group.

Attend conferences, training courses and workshops

There are no hard and fast distinctions between conferences, training courses and workshops. However, if anything, training courses are spread out over a longer period, say two months or more, whereas workshops are relatively intense experiences lasting

Table 20.1 *Checklist for assessing training courses and workshops*

1. What are the goals?
2. What methods will be employed?
3. What is the pertinent training and experience of the group leader?
4. What is the size of the training course or workshop? Is there a screening process prior to entry?
5. When does the course or workshop start? How long is each session? Over what period will the course or workshop continue? Where will it be held? Are the facilities adequate?
6. What is the fee for the course or workshop, if any? Will it involve additional expenses?

one or two days, a weekend or possibly a week. Training courses may be full-time, half-time, day-release or a few hours a day. Table 20.1 provides a checklist for assessing training courses and workshops.

It may be possible to obtain details of training courses and workshops in counselling, psychology and other relevant areas. For instance, the British Association for Counselling (BAC) regularly publishes and updates a list of training courses. Furthermore, details of short courses, workshops and conferences are provided in the BAC's quarterly journal *Counselling*, as well as in the British Psychological Society's monthly *The Psychologist*. In Australia, details of conferences and workshops can be found in the *Bulletin of the Australian Psychological Society* and in the newsletters of the society's state branches. Other sources of information are the journals and newsletters of the Australian Counselling and Guidance Association and the Australian Association of Social Workers. In New Zealand, information about conferences and workshops can be found in the journals and newsletters of the New Zealand Psychological Society and the New Zealand Counselling and Guidance Association.

If you are interested in developing your skills in a particular approach to counselling, enquire whether there is an agency to help to train people in the approach. For instance, training in rational emotive behaviour therapy has reached the stage where it is conducted on an international basis with local trainers. I hope that, in time, the same will hold true for lifeskills counselling. In the meantime, you can develop skills in the constituent parts of lifeskills counselling, which is an integrative approach. For instance, you can attend workshops and courses in cognitive-behavioural and existential-humanistic counselling approaches. In addition, if you are interested in developing your skills in a particular area of counselling – for example relationship or careers – again it is advisable to make specific enquiries.

Counselling skills reading

Leaving aside the theoretical literature that contributes to underpinning practice, there are two main sources of counselling skills reading: skills *books* and applied research and continuing education *journals*.

The bibliography section of this book cites numerous other counselling skills *books*. In addition, you may wish to follow up more specialized reading, both on the skills of particular approaches and on the application of skills to particular problems and populations.

Journals provide an excellent means of keeping abreast of counselling and helping skills developments. Journals specifically focused on counselling include the *Australian Journal of Guidance and Counselling*, the *British Journal of Guidance and Counselling*, the British Association for Counselling's *Counselling*, the American Association of Counseling and Development's *Journal of Counseling and Development* and *Counselor Education and Supervision*, the *New Zealand Counselling and Guidance Association Journal* and the *International Journal for the Advancement of Counselling*.

Psychological society journals include *The Australian Counselling Psychologist*, the journal of the Australian Psychological Society's College of Counselling Psychologists; *Counselling Psychology Review*, the journal of the British Psychological Society's Division of Counselling Psychology; and the American Psychological Association Division of Counseling Psychology's *The Counseling Psychologist*, geared to the continuing education of practitioners, and *Journal of Counseling Psychology*, which publishes research papers. *Cognitive Therapy and Research* and *Behavior Therapy* are two American applied research journals that I find useful.

Numerous other journals, without necessarily having counselling as their primary focus, have articles relevant to practical counselling and helping skills. Some of these are counselling and psychology journals, some are journals of other groups: for example, personnel managers, social workers, nurses and teachers.

Self-help

Self-help is a good way to address personal problems and issues that can interfere with your counselling work. In short, you become your own best counsellor and apply the lifeskills counselling model to yourself. For example, you can consciously try to become better at listening to your own feeling. Furthermore, your skills for focusing clients' thinking skills deficits can be transferred to exploring your own deficits and disciplining yourself to think more realistically. If you experience problems in acting effectively, you should possess some insight into ways of changing relevant verbal, voice and body messages.

The notion of self-help can be extended to knowing how to seek and utilize support, be it from friends, relatives, other counsellors or other helping professionals, on an *ad hoc* basis. Further suggestions for self-help include engaging in regular co-counselling with a suitable person and becoming a member of a self-help group. Counsellors who do not assume responsibility for looking after themselves and managing stresses in their work and personal lives tend to be excellent candidates for burnout, if not breakdown.

Personal counselling

In Chapter 4, I raised the issue of personal counselling for students learning how to counsel. The purpose of such counselling was to help students to lessen debilitating anxieties and also gain insight into skills they would be assisting clients to acquire. During your career, you may face personal problems and crises where you require the extra space and attention provided by skilled counselling. Quite independently of any pressing personal problems, you can seek out skilled counsellors who can help you to improve both your lifeskills and your counselling skills.

As with individual counselling, participation as a client in group counselling can assist both personal effectiveness and acquiring group counselling skills. Consider joining appropriate lifeskills training groups. Here, you have the dual agendas of learning the targeted skill and observing how to lead lifeskills training groups.

THE CHALLENGE FOR COUNSELLORS AND HELPERS

As counsellors and helpers, assuming responsibility for maintaining and developing your skills may seem so obvious that it scarcely merits mention. A basic assumption for clients of the lifeskills counselling approach is that maintaining lifeskills requires constant vigilance. The same holds true for counselling skills. A note of realism, if not pessimism, is in order. The obstacles to maintaining and developing your counselling skills are considerable and I have already mentioned some of them. Others include the following.

- The pressures and compromises in earning a living that impinge on your counselling work: for instance, the obvious and sometimes subtle pressures on either school counsellors or private practitioners.

- The pressures of heavy case loads and risks of burnout and breakdown.

- The dangers of institutionalization, for those working in institutions, and of isolation, for those working on their own.

- The blinkers given you by your trainers through their own possibly narrow allegiances.

- The tendency to associate in networks of like-minded counsellors, possibly sustaining allegiances to narrow positions.

- The restrictive influence of professional and voluntary agency hierarchies, with preferment sometimes being more a matter of allegiance to a particular hierarchy than recognition of ability.

- The fact that developing your counselling skills often has financial costs, for example, fees, purchase of books, income forgone.

- The heavy expenditure of time and effort required to keep abreast of the relevant counselling literature.

The challenge for counsellors and helpers is the same as the challenge for clients. It is to possess the courage to *affirm* your existence, despite the various inner and outer pressures than can diminish you. I sincerely hope that you have found reading and working with this book a rewarding experience. I wish you every success in living up to the challenge to make the choices that define you as effective counsellors and helpers. In short, I wish you GOOD LIFESKILLS AND COUNSELLING SKILLS.

CHAPTER HIGHLIGHTS

- *Counsellors have an ethical duty to maintain and develop their counselling skills.*

- *Counsellors can regularly monitor their skills for each stage of the DASIE lifeskills counselling model.*

- *Ways of maintaining and developing your counselling skills include keeping viewing counselling in skills terms, clarifying your values, disciplining your thinking, observing and listening to skilled counsellors, supervised practical experience, attending conferences, training courses and workshops, and counselling skills reading.*

- *Self-help and personal counselling are two ways in which counsellors can address personal problems that may interfere with their work.*

- *Counsellors face numerous inner and outer obstacles to maintaining and developing counselling skills.*

- *The challenge for counsellors and helpers is to possess the courage, despite difficulties, to affirm your existence.*

EXERCISE 20.1   MONITORING MY COUNSELLING SKILLS

First do this exercise on your own. Then, if appropriate, discuss with a partner or in a group.

By filling out the worksheet below, monitor your skills strengths and deficits in using the lifeskills counselling model. Focus on your thinking skills as well as on your action skills. For more information about specific skills areas, turn to the relevant chapters.

Skills area	My evaluation of strengths/deficits
Stage 1 *Developing the relationship* (a) My strengths (b) My deficits *Clarifying problems* (a) My strengths (b) My deficits	**Develop the relationship and clarify problem(s)**
Stage 2 *Assessing feelings and physical reactions* (a) My strengths (b) My deficits *Assessing thinking* (a) My strengths (b) My deficits *Assessing actions* (a) My strengths (b) My deficits *Restating problem(s) in skills terms* (a) My strengths (b) My deficits	**Assess and restate problem(s) in skills terms**
Stage 3 *Stating goals* (a) My strengths (b) My deficits *Planning interventions* (a) My strengths (b) My deficits	**Stage goals and plan interventions**

Stage 4   **Intervene to develop lifeskills**
Speaking skills
(a) My strengths
(b) My deficits
Demonstrating skills
(a) My strengths
(b) My deficits
Coaching skills
(a) My strengths
(b) My deficits
Negotiating take-away assignment skills
(a) My strengths
(b) My deficits
Possessing a repertoire of interventions
(a) My strengths
(b) My deficits

Stage 5   **Emphasize take-away and end**
Emphasizing take-away of skills
(a) My strengths
(b) My deficits
Ending counselling
(a) My strengths
(b) My deficits

Additional tasks:

1. Write a paragraph summarizing your main counselling skills strengths.

2. Write a paragraph summarizing your main counselling skills deficits.

3. Identify the counselling skills deficits on which you want to work. Refer back to the relevant chapter for suggestions and exercises on how to improve specific skills.

EXERCISE 20.2   MAINTAINING AND DEVELOPING MY COUNSELLING SKILLS

First do this exercise on your own. Then, if appropriate, discuss with your partner or in a group.

Below are listed a number of different methods whereby you can maintain and develop your relating skills. Using the worksheet below, assess whether and how you might use each method.

Method	My assessment of whether and how I can use each method
Monitoring my counselling skills	
Viewing counselling in skills terms	
Clarifying my values	
Disciplining my thinking	
Observing skilled counsellors	
Supervised practical experience	
Attending conferences, training courses and workshops	
Counselling skills reading	
Self-help	
Personal counselling	
Other methods not mentioned above	

Questions

1. What do you consider the most useful methods for you to maintain and develop your counselling skills?
2. Apart from doing exercises in this book, state goals and then make and implement a plan for maintaining and developing your counselling skills.

Bibliography

Abramson, L. Y., Seligman, M. E. P. and Teasdale, J. D. (1978) Learned helplessness in humans: critique and reformulation. *Journal of Abnormal Psychology*, **87**, 49–74.

Albee, G. W. (1984) A competency model must replace a defect model. In J. M. Joffe, G. W. Albee and L. D. Kelly (eds) *Readings in Primary Prevention of Psychopathology: Basic Concepts*. Hanover, NH: University Press of New England, pp. 228–46.

Alberti, R. E. and Emmons, M. L. (1990) *Your Perfect Right: A Guide to Assertive Living* (6th edn). San Luis Obispo, CA: Impact Publishers.

Allport, G. W. (1955) *Becoming: Basic Considerations for a Psychology of Personality*. New Haven, CT: Yale University Press.

Allport, G. W., Vernon, P. E. and Lindzey, G. (1951) *A Study of Values* (rev. edn). Boston: Houghton Mifflin.

Alpert, R. and Haber, R. N. (1960) Anxiety in academic achievement situations. *Journal of Abnormal and Social Psychology*, **61**, 204–15.

American Psychiatric Association (1994) *Diagnostic and Statistical Manual of Mental Disorders* (4th edn). Washington, DC: APA.

Argyle, M. (1983) *The Psychology of Interpersonal Behaviour* (4th edn). Harmondsworth: Penguin Books.

Argyle, M. (1984) Some new developments in social skills training. *Bulletin of the British Psychological Society*, **37**, 405–10.

Argyle, M. (1986) Rules for social relationships in four cultures. *Australian Journal of Psychology*, **38**, 309–18.

Argyle, M. (1992) *The Social Psychology of Everyday Life*. London: Routledge.

Argyle, M. and Henderson, M. (1985) *The Anatomy of Relationships*. Harmondsworth: Penguin Books.

Arlow, J. A. (1995) Psychoanalysis. In R. J. Corsini and D. Wedding (eds) *Current Psychotherapies* (5th edn). Itasca, IL: Peacock, pp. 15–50.

Arroba, T. (1977) Styles of decision making and their use: an empirical study. *British Journal of Guidance and Counselling*, **5**, 149–58.

Australian Bureau of Statistics (1995) *Australian Demographic Statistics: December Quarter 1994*. Canberra: Australian Bureau of Statistics.

Australian Psychological Society (1986) *Code of Professional Conduct*. Melbourne: APS.

Bacorn, C. N. and Dixon, D. N. (1984) The effects of touch on depressed and vocationally undecided clients. *Journal of Counseling Psychology*, **31**, 488–96.

Bandura, A. (1986) *Social Foundations of Thought and Action: A Social Cognitive Theory*. Englewood Cliffs, NJ: Prentice Hall.

Bandura, A. (1989) Human agency in social cognitive theory. *American Psychologist*, **44**, 1175–84.

Bandura, A., Grusec, J. E. and Menlove, F. L. (1966) Observational learning as a function of symbolization and incentive set. *Child Development*, **37**, 499–506.

Barrett-Lennard, G. T. (1962) Dimensions of therapeutic response as causal factors in therapeutic change. *Psychological Monographs*, **76**, whole no. 562.

Barrett-Lennard, G. T. (1981) The empathy cycle: refinement of a nuclear concept. *Journal of Counseling Psychology*, **28**, 91–100.

Batson, C. D. (1990) How social an animal? The human capacity for caring. *American Psychologist*, **45**, 336–46.

Beck, A. T. (1976) *Cognitive Therapy and the Emotional Disorders*. New York: New American Library.

Beck, A. T. (1978) *Depression Inventory*. Philadelphia: Centre for Cognitive Therapy.

Beck, A. T. (1988) *Love is Never Enough: How Couples Can Overcome Misunderstandings, Resolve Conflicts, and Solve Relationship Problems through Cognitive Therapy*. New York: Harper and Row.

Beck, A. T. (1991) Cognitive therapy: a 10-year retrospective. *American Psychologist*, **46**, 368–75.

Beck, A. T. and Emery, G. (1985) *Anxiety Disorders and Phobias: A Cognitive Perspective*. New York: Basic Books.

Beck, A. T., Epstein, N., Brown, G. and Steer, R. A. (1988a) An inventory for measuring clinical anxiety: psychometric properties. *Journal of Consulting and Clinical Psychology*, **56**, 893–7.

Beck, A. T., Laude, R. and Bohnert, M. (1974) Ideational components of anxiety neurosis. *Archives of General Psychiatry*, **31**, 319–25.

Beck, A. T., Riskind, J. H., Brown, G. and Steer, R. A. (1988b) Levels of hopelessness in DSM-111 disorders: a partial test of content specificity in depression. *Cognitive Therapy and Research*, **12**, 459–69.

Beck, A. T., Rush, A. J., Shaw, B. F. and Emery, G. (1979) *Cognitive Therapy of Depression*. New York: John Wiley.

Beck, A. T. and Weishaar, M. E. (1995) Cognitive therapy. In R. J. Corsini and D. Wedding (eds) *Current Psychotherapies* (5th edn). Itasca, IL: Peacock, pp. 229–61.

Bem, S. L. (1974) The measurement of psychological androgyny. *Journal of Consulting and Clinical Psychology*, **42**, 155-62.

Bem, S. L. (1981) Gender schema theory: a cognitive account of sex typing. *Psychological Review*, **88**, 354–64.

Bernstein, D. (1988) *Put It Together, Put It Across: The Craft of Business Presentation*. London: Cassell.

Bernstein, D. A. and Borkovec, T. D. (1973) *Progressive Relaxation Training: A Manual for the Helping Professions*. Champaign, IL: Research Press.

Beutler, L. E. and Sandowicz, M. (1994) The counseling relationship: what is it? *The Counseling Psychologist*, **22**, 98–103.

Blackwell, R. T., Galassi, J. P., Galassi, M. D. and Watson, T. E. (1985) Are cognitive assessment methods equal? A comparison of think aloud and thought listing. *Cognitive Therapy and Research*, **9**, 399–413.

Blatner, A. (1995) Psychodrama. In R. J. Corsini and D. Wedding (eds) *Current Psychotherapies* (5th edn). Itasca, IL: Peacock, pp. 399–408.

Bordin, E. S. (1979) The generalizability of the psychoanalytic concept of the working alliance. *Psychotherapy: Theory, Research and Practice*, **16**, 252–60.

Bowlby, J. (1979) *The Making and Breaking of Affectional Bonds*. London: Tavistock.

BPS Division of Clinical Psychology (1979) *Report of the Working Party on the Psychological Therapies*. Leicester: British Psychological Society.

British Association for Counselling (1993) *Code of Ethics and Practice for Counsellors*. Rugby: BAC.

British Psychological Society (1993) *Code of Conduct, Ethical Principles and Guidelines*. Leicester: BPS.

British Psychological Society (1995) Code of Conduct. *The Psychologist*, **8**, 452–3.

Bugental, J. F. T. (1981) *The Search for Authenticity*. New York: Irvington Publishers.

Burns, D. D. (1980) *Feeling Good: The New Mood Therapy*. New York: New American Library.

Buss, D. M. (1995) Psychological sex differences: origins through sexual selection. *American Psychologist*, **50**, 164–8.

Carkhuff, R. R. (1987) *The Art of Helping* (6th edn). Amherst, MA: Human Resource Development Press.

Castles, I. (1993) *Australia in Profile: Census of Population and Housing 6 August 1991*. Canberra: Australian Bureau of Statistics.

Cautela, J. (1967) Covert sensitization. *Psychological Reports*, **20**, 459–68.

Cautela, J. R. (1976) The present status of covert modeling. *Journal of Behavior Therapy and Experimental Psychiatry*, **6**, 323–6.

Charles-Edwardes, D. (1989) A personal view: counselling pearls and priorities. *British Journal of Guidance and Counselling*, **17**, 2–7.

Christensen, C. P. (1989) Cross-cultural awareness development: a conceptual model. *Counselor Education and Supervision*, **28**, 270–87.

Clark, A. J. (1991) The identification and modification of defense mechanisms in counseling. *Journal of Counseling and Development*, **69**, 231–6.

Corey, G. (1991) *Theory and Practice of Counseling and Psychotherapy* (4th edn). Pacific Grove, CA: Brooks/Cole.

Corey, M. S. and Corey, G. (1992) *Group Counselling: Process and Practice* (4th edn). Pacific Grove, CA: Brooks/Cole.

Corey, G., Corey, M. S. and Callanan, P. (1993) *Issues and Ethics in the Helping Professions* (4th edn). Pacific Grove, CA: Brooks/Cole.

Cormier, W. H. and Cormier, L. S. (1991) *Interviewing Strategies for Helpers: Fundamental Skills and Cognitive Behavioral Interventions* (3rd edn). Pacific Grove, CA: Brooks/Cole.

Corsini, R. J. (1995) Introduction. In R. J. Corsini and D. Wedding (eds) *Current Psychotherapies* (5th edn). Itasca, IL: Peacock, pp. 1–14.

Daley, M. F. (1969) The 'reinforcement menu': finding effective reinforcers. In J. D. Krumboltz and C. E. Thoresen (eds) *Behavioral Counseling: Cases and Techniques*. New York: Holt, Rinehart and Winston, pp. 42–5.

Davidson, F. (1988) *The Art of Executive Firing*. Melbourne: Information Australia.

Deffenbacher, J. L., Oetting, E. R., Huff, M. E. and Thwaites, G. A. (1995) Fifteen month follow-up of social skills and cognitive-relaxation approaches to general anger reduction. *Journal of Counseling Psychology*, **42**, 400–5.

Deffenbacher, J. L. and Suinn, R. M. (1988) Systematic desensitization and the reduction of anxiety. *The Counseling Psychologist*, **16**, 9–30.

DeVoe, D. (1990) Feminist and nonsexist counseling: implications for the male counselor. *Journal of Counseling and Development*, **69**, 33–6.

Dryden, W. (1991) *A Dialogue with Arnold Lazarus: 'It depends'*. Milton Keynes: Open University Press.

D'Zurilla, T. J. and Maydeu-Olivares, A. (1995) Conceptual and methodological issues in social problem-solving assessment. *Behavior Therapy*, **26**, 409–32.

Edwards, C. E. and Murdock, N. L. (1994) Characteristics of therapist self-disclosure in the counseling process. *Journal of Counseling and Development*, **72**, 384–9.

Egan, G. (1994) *The Skilled Helper: A Problem Management Approach to Helping* (5th edn). Pacific Grove, CA: Brooks/Cole.

Egan, G. and Cowan, M. (1979) *People in Systems: A Model for Development in the Human-service Professions and Education*. Pacific Grove, CA: Brooks/Cole.

Ekman, P., Friesen, W. V. and Ellsworth, P. (1972) *Emotions in the Human Face*. New York: Pergamon Press.

Elliott, R. (1985) Helpful and nonhelpful events in brief counseling interviews: an empirical taxonomy. *Journal of Counseling Psychology*, **32**, 307–22.

Ellis, A. (1962) *Reason and Emotion in Psychotherapy*. New York: Lyle Stuart.

Ellis, A. (1977) *Anger: How to Live with and Without It*. New York: Lyle Stuart.

Ellis, A. (1980) Overview of the clinical theory of rational-emotive therapy. In R. Grieger and J. Boyd (eds) *Rational-Emotive Therapy: A Skills Based Approach*. New York: Van Nostrand Reinhold, pp. 1–31.

Ellis, A. (1985) *Overcoming Resistance: Rational-Emotive Therapy with Difficult Clients*. New York: Springer.

Ellis, A. (1987) The impossibility of achieving consistently good mental health. *American Psychologist*, **42**, 364–75.

Ellis, A. (1991) The revised ABC's of rational-emotive therapy (RET). *Journal of Rational-Emotive and Cognitive-Behavior Therapy*, **9**, 139–72.

Ellis, A. (1995) Rational emotive behavior therapy. In R. J. Corsini and D. Wedding (eds) *Current Psychotherapies* (5th edn). Itasca, IL: Peacock, pp. 162–96.

Emery, G. (1982) *Own Your Own Life*. New York: New American Library.

Enns, C. Z. (1991) The 'new' relationship models of women's identity: a review and critique for counselors. *Journal of Counseling and Development*, **69**, 209–17.

Enns, C. Z. and Hackett, G. (1990) Comparison of feminist and nonfeminist women's reactions to variants of nonsexist and feminist counseling. *Journal of Counseling Psychology*, **37**, 33–40.

Epps, J. and Kendall, P. C. (1995) Hostile attributional bias in adults. *Cognitive Therapy and Research*, **19**, 159–78.

Erikson, E. H. (1963) *Childhood and Society* (2nd edn). New York: W. W. Norton.

Feifel, H. (1990) Psychology and death: meaningful rediscovery. *American Psychologist*, **45**, 537–43.

Fischer, R. L. (1972) *Speak to Communicate: An Introduction to Speech*. Encino, CA: Dickenson Publishing Company.

Frankl, V. E. (1959) *Man's Search for Meaning*. New York: Washington Square Press.

Frankl, V. E. (1967) *Psychotherapy and Existentialism*. Harmondsworth: Penguin Books.

Frankl, V. E. (1969) *The Doctor and the Soul*. Harmondsworth: Penguin Books.

Frankl, V. E. (1975) *The Unconscious God: Psychotherapy and Theology*. New York: Simon and Schuster.

Freud, S. (1936) *The Problem of Anxiety*. New York: W. W. Norton.

Freudenberger, H. J. (1980) *Burnout: The High Cost of High Achievement*. London: Arrow Books.

Fromm, E. (1956) *The Art of Loving*. New York: Bantam Books.

Gazda, G. M. (1989) *Group Counseling: A Developmental Approach* (4th edn). Boston: Allyn and Bacon.

Geldard, D. (1989) *Basic Personal Counselling: A Training Manual for Counsellors*. Sydney: Prentice Hall.

Gelso, C. J. and Carter, J. A. (1985) The relationship in counseling and psychotherapy: components, consequences and theoretical antecedents. *The Counseling Psychologist*, **13**, 155–244.

Gelso, C. J. and Carter, J. A. (1994) Components of the psychotherapy relationship: their interaction and unfolding during treatment. *Journal of Counseling Psychology*, **41**, 296–306.

Gendlin, E. T. (1962) *Experiencing and the Creation of Meaning.* New York: The Free Press of Glencoe.

Gendlin, E. T. (1981) *Focusing* (2nd edn). New York: Bantam Books.

Gilbert, T. F. (1978) *Human Competence: Engineering Worthy Performance.* New York: McGraw-Hill.

Glasser, W. (1965) *Reality Therapy: A New Approach to Psychiatry.* New York: Harper and Row.

Glasser, W. (1984) *Control Theory: A New Explanation of How We Control Our Lives.* New York: Harper and Row.

Glasser, W. and Wubbolding, R. (1995) Reality therapy. In R. J. Corsini and D. Wedding (eds) *Current Psychotherapies* (5th edn). Itasca, IL: Peacock, pp. 293–321.

Goddard, R. W. (1989) Use language effectively. *Personnel Journal*, **68**, 32–6.

Goldfried, M. R. (1971) Systematic desensitization as training in self-control. *Journal of Consulting and Clinical Psychology*, **37**, 228–34.

Goldfried, M. R. and Davison, G. C. (1976) *Clinical Behavior Therapy.* New York: Holt, Rinehart and Winston.

Goldstein, A. P. and Keller, H. (1987) *Aggressive Behavior: Assessment and Intervention.* New York: Pergamon.

Good, G. E., Dell, D. M. and Mintz, L. B. (1989) Male role and gender role conflict: relationships to help seeking in men. *Journal of Counseling Psychology*, **36**, 295–300.

Good, G. E., Gilbert, L. A. and Scher, M. (1990) Gender aware therapy: a synthesis of feminist therapy and knowledge about gender. *Journal of Counseling and Development*, **68**, 376–80.

Gordon, T. (1970) *Parent Effectiveness Training: The Tested New Way to Raise Responsible Children.* New York: Wyden.

Greenberg, L. S., Rice, L. N. and Elliott, R. (1993) *Facilitating Emotional Change: The Moment by Moment Process.* New York: Guildford Press.

Hall, E. T. (1966) *The Hidden Dimension.* New York: Doubleday.

Harrington, T. F. and O'Shea, A. J. (1993) *Manual: The Harrington–O'Shea Career Decision-making System, Revised.* Circle Pines, MN: American Guidance Service.

Havighurst, R. J. (1972) *Developmental Tasks and Education* (3rd edn). New York: David McKay.

Henley, N. M. (1977) *Body Politics: Power, Sex and Nonverbal Communication.* Englewood Cliffs, NJ: Prentice Hall.

Heppner, P. P. (1995) On gender role conflict in men – future directions and implications for counseling: comment on Good et al. (1995) and Cournoyer and Mahalik (1995). *Journal of Counseling Psychology*, **42**, 20–3.

Heppner, P. P., Kivlighan, D. M. and Wampold, B. (1992) *Research Design in Counseling*. Pacific Grove, CA: Brooks/Cole.

Heppner, P. P., Rogers, M. E. and Lee, L. (1984) Carl Rogers: reflections on his life. *Journal of Counseling and Development*, **63**, 14–20.

Hewitt, P. L. and Dyke, D. G. (1986) Perfectionism, stress, and vulnerability to depression. *Cognitive Therapy and Research*, **10**, 137–42.

Hill, C. E. (1994) What is the therapeutic relationship?: a reaction to Sexton and Whiston. *The Counseling Psychologist*, **22**, 90–7.

Hill, C. E., Nutt, E. A. and Jackson, S. (1994) Trends in psychotherapy process research: samples, measures, researchers and classic publications. *Journal of Counseling Psychology*, **41**, 364–77.

Ho, D. Y. F. (1985) Cultural values and professional issues in clinical psychology: implications from the Hong Kong experience. *American Psychologist*, **40**, 1212–18.

Ho, D. Y. F. (1995) Internalized culture, cultrocentrism, and transcendence. *The Counseling Psychology*, **23**, 4–24.

Hoelscher, T. J., Lichstein, K. L., Fischer, S. and Hegerty, T. B. (1987) Relaxation treatment of hypertension: do home relaxation tapes enhance treatment outcome? *Behavior Therapy*, **18**, 33–7.

Holland, J. L. (1973) *Making Vocational Choices: A Theory of Careers*. Englewood Cliffs, NJ: Prentice Hall.

Hopson, B. and Scally, M. (1981) *Lifeskills Teaching*. London: McGraw-Hill.

Hutchins, D. E. and Cole, C. G. (1992) *Helping Relationships and Strategies* (2nd edn). Pacific Grove: CA: Brooks/Cole.

Ivey, A. E. (1987) Cultural intentionality: the core of effective helping. *Counselor Education and Supervision*, **26**, 168–72.

Ivey, A. E. (1994) *Intentional Interviewing and Counseling: Facilitating Client Development in a Multicultural Society* (3rd edn). Pacific Grove, CA: Brooks/Cole.

Jacobson, E. (1929) *Progressive Relaxation*. Chicago: University of Chicago Press.

Jacobson, E. (1938) *Progressive Relaxation* (2nd edn). Chicago: University of Chicago Press.

Jacobson, E. (1976) *You Must Relax*. Boston: Unwin Paperbacks.

Jacobson, N. S. (1989) The maintenance of treatment gains following social learning-based marital therapy. *Behavior Therapy*, **20**, 325–36.

Jacobson, N. S. (1992) Behavioral couple therapy: a new beginning. *Behavior Therapy*, **23**, 493–506.

Jahoda, M. (1958) *Current Concepts of Positive Mental Health*. New York: Basic Books.

Janis, I. L. and Mann, L. (1977) *Decision Making: A Psychological Analysis of Conflict, Choice, and Commitment*. New York: The Free Press.

Johnson, D. (1993) *Reaching Out: Interpersonal Effectiveness and Self-actualization* (5th edn). Englewood Cliffs, NJ: Prentice-Hall.

Jones, J. M. (1990) Correspondence from Associate Professor J. M. Jones, Classics Department, University of Western Australia, dated 2 June.

Jourard, S. M. (1964) *The Transparent Self: Self-disclosure and Well-being*. Princeton, NJ: Van Nostrand.

Kagan, N. (1984) Interpersonal process recall: basic methods and recent research. In D. Larsen (ed.) *Teaching Psychological Skills*. Pacific Grove, CA: Brooks/Cole, pp. 261–9.

Kanfer, F. H. and Gaelick-Buys, L. (1991) Self-management methods. In F. H. Kanfer and A. P. Goldstein (eds) *Helping People Change: A Textbook of Methods* (4th edn). New York: Pergamon Press, pp. 305–60.

Kaplan, H. S. (1974) *The New Sex Therapy: Active Treatment of Sexual Dysfunctions*. Harmondsworth: Penguin Books.

Kaplan, H. S. (1987) *The Illustrated Manual of Sex Therapy* (2nd edn). New York: Brunner/Mazel.

Karoly, P. and Harris, A. (1986) Operant methods. In F. H. Kanfer and A. P. Goldstein (eds) *Helping People Change: A Textbook of Methods* (3rd edn). New York: Pergamon Press, pp. 283–345.

Kazdin, A. E. (1976) Developing assertive behaviors through covert modeling. In J. D. Krumboltz and C. E. Thoresen (eds) *Counseling Methods*. New York: Holt, Rinehart and Winston, pp. 475–86.

Kazdin, A. E. (1994) *Behavior Modification in Applied Settings* (5th edn). Pacific Grove, CA: Brooks/Cole.

Kelly, E. W. (1995) Counselor values: a national survey. *Journal of Counseling and Development*, **73**, 648– 53.

Kelly, G. A. (1955) *A Theory of Personality: The Psychology of Personal Constructs*. New York: W. W. Norton.

Kelly, J. A., Sikkema, K. J., Winett, R. A., Solomon, L. J., Roffman, R. A., Heckman, T. G., Stevenson, L. Y., Perry, M. J., Norman, A. D. and Desiderato, L. J. (1995) Factors predicting continued high-risk behavior among gay men in small cities: psychological, behavioral, and demographic characteristics related to unsafe sex. *Journal of Consulting and Clinical Psychology*, **63**, 101–7.

Kendall, P. C. and Hollon, S. D. (1989) Anxious self-talk: development of the anxious self-statements questionnaire (ASSQ). *Cognitive Therapy and Research*, **13**, 81–93.

Kendall, P. C., Hollon, S. D., Beck, A. T., Hammen, C. L. and Ingram, R. E. (1987) Issues and recommendations regarding use of the Beck Depression Inventory. *Cognitive Therapy and Research*, **11**, 289–99.

King, M. L. (1963) *Strength to Love*. Philadelphia, PA: Fortress Press.

Kinsey, A. C., Pomeroy, W. B. and Martin, C. E. (1948) *Sexual Behavior in the Human Male*. Philadelphia, PA: W. B. Saunders.

Kinsey, A. C., Pomeroy, W. B., Martin, C. E. and Gebhard, P. H. (1953) *Sexual Behavior in the Human Female*. Philadelphia, PA: W. B. Saunders.

Kohlberg, L. and Gilligan, C. (1971) The adolescent as philosopher: the discovery of the self in a postconventional world. *Daedalus*, **100**, 1051–86.

Kruger, A. H. (1970) *Effective Speaking: A Complete Course*. New York: Van Nostrand Reinhold.

LaFromboise, T. D. and Foster, S. L. (1992) Cross-cultural training: scientist-practitioner model and methods. *The Counseling Psychologist*, **20**, 472–89.

LaFromboise, T. D., Trimble, J. E. and Mohatt, G. V. (1990) Counseling intervention and American Indian tradition: an integrative approach. *The Counseling Psychologist*, **18**, 628–54.

Lazarus, A. A. (1984) *In the Mind's Eye*. New York: The Guilford Press.

Lazarus, A. A. (1992) Multimodal therapy: technical eclecticism with minimal integration. In J. C. Norcross and M. R. Goldfried (eds) *Handbook of Psychotherapy Integration*. New York: Basic Books, pp. 231–63.

Lazarus, A. A. (1993) Tailoring the therapeutic relationship, or being an authentic chameleon. *Psychotherapy*, **30**, 404–7.

Lazarus, A. A. (1995) Multimodal therapy. In R. J. Corsini and D. Wedding (eds) *Current Psychotherapies* (5th edn). Itasca, IL: Peacock, pp. 332–55.

Lazarus, A. A., Beutler, L. E. and Norcross, J. C. (1992) The future of technical eclecticism. *Psychotherapy*, **29**, 11–20.

Lazarus, A. A. and Lazarus, C. N. (1991) *Multimodal Life History Inventory*. Champaign, IL: Research Press.

Lebo, R. B., Harrington, T. F. and Tillman, R. (1995). Work values similarities among students from six countries. *The Career Development Quarterly*, **43**, 350–62.

Lee, D. Y. and Uhlemann, M. R. (1984) Comparison of verbal responses of Rogers, Shostrom and Lazarus. *Journal of Counseling Psychology*, **31**, 91–4.

Lenihan, G. and Kirk, W. G. (1990) Using student paraprofessionals in the treatment of eating disorders. *Journal of Counseling and Development*, **68**, 332–5.

Lewinsohn, P. M., Munoz, R. F., Youngren, M. A. and Zeiss, A. M. (1986) *Control Your Depression* (rev. edn). New York: Prentice-Hall.

Litvinoff, S. (1991) *The Relate Guide to Better Relationships: Practical Ways to Make Your Love Last from the Experts in Marriage Guidance*. London: Vermilion.

Lyddon, W. J. (1990) First- and second-order change: implications for rationalist and constructivist cognitive therapies. *Journal of Counseling and Development*, **69**, 122–7.

McCarthy, P. R. (1982) Differential effects of counselor self-referent responses and counselor status. *Journal of Counseling Psychology*, **29**, 125–31.

McNair, D. M., Lorr, M. and Droppleman, L. F. (1981) *EITS Manual for the Profile of Mood States*. San Diego, CA: Educational and Industrial Testing Service.

MacPhillamy, D. J. and Lewinsohn, P. M. (1982) The Pleasant Events Schedule: studies on reliability, validity and scale intercorrelation. *Journal of Consulting and Clinical Psychology*, **50**, 363–80.

Maracek, J. and Johnson, M. (1980) Gender and the process of therapy. In A. M.

Brodsky and R. Hare-Mustin (eds) *Women and Psychotherapy: An Assessment of Research and Practice*. New York: Guilford Press, pp. 67–93.

Martin, J. (1990) Confusion in psychological skills training. *Journal of Counseling and Development*, **68**, 402–7.

Marx, R. (1982) Relapse prevention for managerial training: a model for maintenance of behavior change. *Academy of Management Review*, **7**, 433–41.

Maslow, A. H. (1962) *Towards a Psychology of Being*. New York: Van Nostrand.

Maslow, A. H. (1970) *Motivation and Personality* (2nd edn). New York: Harper and Row.

Maslow, A. H. (1971) *The Farther Reaches of Human Nature*. Harmondsworth: Penguin Books.

Masterpasqua, F. (1989) A competence paradigm for psychological practice. *American Psychologist*, **44**, 1366–71.

Masters, W. H., Johnson, V. E. and Kolodny, R. C. (1986) *Masters and Johnson on Sex and Human Loving*. London: Pan Macmillan.

Mathews, A. M., Gelder, M. G. and Johnston, D. W. (1981) *Programmed Practice for Agoraphobia: Clients' Manual*. London and New York: Tavistock Publications.

May, R. (1958) Contributions of existential psychotherapy. In R. May, E. Angel and H. F. Ellenberger (eds) *Existence*. New York: Basic Books, pp. 37–91.

May, R. (1975) *The Courage to Create*. New York: Norton.

May, R. and Yalom, I. D. (1995) Existential psychotherapy. In R. J. Corsini and D. Wedding (eds) *Current Psychotherapies* (5th edn). Itasca, IL: Peacock, pp. 262–92.

Meichenbaum, D. H. (1977) *Cognitive-Behavior Modification: An Integrative Approach*. New York: Plenum.

Meichenbaum, D. H. (1983) *Coping with Stress*. London: Century Publishing.

Meichenbaum, D. H. (1985) *Stress Inoculation Training*. New York: Pergamon Press.

Meichenbaum, D. H. (1986) Cognitive-behavior modification. In F. H. Kanfer and A. P. Goldstein (eds) *Helping People Change: A Textbook of Methods* (3rd edn). New York: Pergamon Press, pp. 346–80.

Meichenbaum, D. H. and Deffenbacher, J. L. (1988) Stress inoculation training. *The Counseling Psychologist*, **16**, 69–90.

Meltzoff, J. and Kornreich, M. (1970) *Research in Psychotherapy*. New York: Atherton.

Mintz, L. B. and O'Neil, J. M. (1990) Gender roles, sex, and the process of psychotherapy: many questions and few answers. *Journal of Counseling and Development*, **68**, 381–7.

Moir, A. and Jessel, D. (1989) *Brain Sex*. London: Mandarin.

Moon, J. R. and Eisler, R. M. (1983) Anger control: an experimental comparison of three behavioral treatments. *Behavior Therapy*, **14**, 493–505.

Moreno, Z. T. (1959) A survey of psychodramatic techniques. *Group Psychotherapy*, **12**, 5–14.

Murgatroyd, S. (1985) *Counselling and Helping*. London: Methuen.

Murgatroyd, S. (1993) Counselling and the organisation: an introduction. *British Journal of Guidance and Counselling*, **21**, 121–3.

National Training Laboratory (1967) *Feedback and the Helping Relationship.* Washington, DC: NTL Institute for Applied Behavioral Sciences (mimeo).

Nelson-Jones, R. (1982) The counsellor as decision-maker: role, treatment and responding decisions. *British Journal of Guidance and Counselling*, **10**, 113–24.

Nelson-Jones, R. (1984) *Personal Responsibility Counselling and Therapy: An Integrative Approach.* London: Harper and Row.

Nelson-Jones, R. (1986) Toward a people centred language for counselling psychology. *The Australian Counselling Psychologist*, **2**, 18–23.

Nelson-Jones, R. (1988) The counselling psychologist as developmental educator. *The Australian Counselling Psychologist*, **4**, 55–66.

Nelson-Jones, R. (1989) *Effective Thinking Skills: Preventing and Managing Personal Problems.* London: Cassell.

Nelson-Jones, R. (1991) *Lifeskills: A Handbook.* London: Cassell.

Nelson-Jones, R. (1995) *Theory and Practice of Counselling* (2nd edn). London: Cassell.

Nelson-Jones, R. (1996a) *Relating Skills: A Practical Guide to Effective Personal Relationships.* London: Cassell.

Nelson-Jones, R. (1996b) The STCs of lifeskills counselling. *Counselling*, **7**, 46–9.

Nelson-Jones (1996c) *The Lifeskills Counselling Model* (Videotape 1. The initial interview – Stages 1–3; Videotape 2. Intervening – Stage 4).

Nelson-Jones, R. and Cosolo, W. (1994) How to assess cancer patients' thinking skills. *Palliative Medicine*, **8**, 115–21.

Nemeroff, C. J. and Karoly, P. (1991) Operant methods. In F. H. Kanfer and A. P. Goldstein (eds) *Helping People Change: A Textbook of Methods* (4th edn). New York: Pergamon, pp. 122–60.

Nicklaus, J. (1985) Learn from your follow-through. *Australian Golf*, January, 22–3.

Novaco, R. (1977) Stress inoculation: a cognitive therapy for anger and its application to a case of depression. *Journal of Consulting and Clinical Psychology*, **45**, 600–8.

Oakley, A. (1972) *Sex, Gender and Society.* London: Temple Smith.

Osipow, S. H., Walsh, W. B. and Tosi, D. J. (1984) *A Survey of Counseling Methods* (rev. edn). Homewood, IL: Dorsey Press.

Patterson, C. H. (1974) *Relationship Counseling and Psychotherapy.* New York: Harper and Row.

Patterson, C. H. (1986) *Theories of Counseling and Psychotherapy* (4th edn). New York: Harper and Row.

Pavio, S. C. and Greenberg, L. S. (1995) Resolving 'unfinished business': efficacy of experimental therapy using empty-chair dialogue. *Journal of Consulting and Clinical Psychology*, **63**, 419–25.

Pease, A. (1981) *Body Language: How to Read Others' Thoughts by Their Gestures.* Sydney: Camel.

Perls, F. S. (1973) *The Gestalt Approach and Eyewitness to Therapy.* New York: Bantam Books.

Perls, F. S., Hefferline, R. F. and Goodman, P. (1951) *Gestalt Therapy*. New York: Souvenir Press.

Perry, M. A. and Furukawa, M. J. (1986) Modeling methods. In F. H. Kanfer and A. P. Goldstein (eds) *Helping People Change: A Textbook of Methods* (3rd edn). New York: Pergamon, pp. 66–110.

Perry, W. G. (1970) *Forms of Intellectual Development in the College Years*. New York: Holt, Rinehart and Winston.

Petersen, C., Semmel, A., von Baeyer, C., Abramson, L. Y., Metalsky, G. L. and Seligman, M. E. P. (1982) The Attributional Style Questionnaire. *Cognitive Therapy and Research*, **6**, 287–99.

Petersen, C. and Villanova, P. (1988) An expanded attributional style questionnaire. *Journal of Abnormal Psychology*, **97**, 87–9.

Pfeiffer, J. W. and Jones, J. (1969–85) *Structured Exercises for Human Relations Training, Vols. 1–10*. San Diego, CA: University Associates.

Ponterotto, J. G. (1985) A counselor's guide to psychopharmacology. *Journal of Counseling and Development*, **64**, 109–15.

Poon, D., Nelson-Jones, R. and Caputi, P. (1993) Asian students' perceptions of culture-sensitive and culture-neutral counselling. *The Australian Counselling Psychologist*, **9**, 3–16.

Raskin, N. J. and Rogers, C. R. (1995) Person-centred therapy. In R. J. Corsini and D. Wedding (eds) *Current Psychotherapies* (5th edn). Itasca, IL: Peacock, pp. 128–61.

Rennie-Peyton, P. (1995) Bullying within organisations. *Counselling Psychology Review*, **10** (4), 10–11.

Rhoads, R. A. (1995) Learning from the coming out experiences of college males. *Journal of College Student Development*, **36**, 67–74.

Robertson, J. and Fitzgerald, L. F. (1990) The (mis)treatment of men: effects of client gender role and life-style on diagnosis and attribution of pathology. *Journal of Counseling Psychology*, **37**, 3–9.

Rogers, C. R. (1951) *Client-centered Therapy*. Boston: Houghton Mifflin.

Rogers, C. R. (1957) The necessary and sufficient conditions of therapeutic personality change. *Journal of Consulting Psychology*, **21**, 95–103.

Rogers, C. R. (1959) A theory of therapy, personality and interpersonal relationships as developed in the client-centered framework. In S. Koch (ed.) *Psychology: A Study of Science*. New York: McGraw-Hill, pp. 184–256.

Rogers, C. R. (1961) *On Becoming a Person: A Therapist's View of Psychotherapy*. Boston: Houghton Mifflin.

Rogers, C. R. (1962) The interpersonal relationship: the core of guidance. *Harvard Educational Review*, **32**, 416–29.

Rogers, C. R. (1975) Empathic: an unappreciated way of being. *The Counseling Psychologist*, **5** (2), 2–10.

Rogers, C. R. (1980) *A Way of Being*. Boston: Houghton Miflin.

Rogers, S. M. and Turner, C. F. (1991) Male–male sexual contact in the USA: findings from five sample surveys, 1970–1990. *Journal of Sex Research*, **28**, 491–519.

Rogoff, B. and Morelli, G. (1989) Perspectives on children's development from cultural psychology. *American Psychologist*, **44**, 343–8.

Rokeach, M. (1967) *Value Survey*. Palo Alto, CA: Consulting Psychologists Press.

Rokeach, M. and Ball-Rokeach, S. J. (1989) Stability and change in American value priorities, 1968–1981. *American Psychologist*, **44**, 775–84.

Rosenthal, T. L. and Steffek, B. D. (1991) Modeling methods. In F. H. Kanfer and A. P. Goldstein (eds) *Helping People Change: A Textbook of Methods* (4th edn). New York: Pergamon, pp. 70–121.

Sarason, I. G. (1976) Using modeling to strengthen the behavioral repertory of the juvenile delinquent. In J. D. Krumboltz and C. E. Thoresen (eds) *Counseling Methods*. New York: Holt, Rinehart and Winston, pp. 56–66.

Sartre, J. P. (1956) *Being and Nothingness*. New York: Philosophical Library.

Schier, M. F. and Carver, C. S. (1992) Effects of optimism on psychological and physical well-being: theoretical overview and empirical update. *Cognitive Therapy and Research*, **16**, 201–28.

Schreier, B. A. (1995) Moving beyond tolerance: a new paradigm for programming about homophobia/biphobia and heterosexism. *Journal of College Student Development*, **36**, 19–26.

Schulman, R., Seligman, M. E. P. and Amsterdam, D. (1987) The attributional style questionnaire is not transparent. *Behaviour Research and Therapy*, **25**, 391–5.

Schwartz, S. H. (1992) Universals in the content and structure of values: theoretical advances and empirical tests in 20 countries. In M. Zanna (ed.) *Advances in Experimental Social Psychology*, Vol. 25. New York: Academic Press, pp. 1–65.

Schwartz, S. H. and Bilsky, W. (1990) Toward a theory of the universal content and structure of human values: extensions and cross-cultural replications. *Journal of Personality and Social Psychology*, **53**, 550–62.

Seidner, M. L. and Kirschenbaum, D. S. (1980) Behavioral contracts: effects of pretreatment information and intention statements. *Behavior Therapy*, **11**, 689–98.

Seligman, M. E. P. (1991) *Learned Optimism*. Milsons Point, NSW: Random House Australia.

Seligman, M. E. P., Abramson, L. Y., Semmel, A. and von Baeyer, C. (1979) Depressive attributional style. *Journal of Abnormal Psychology*, **88**, 242–7.

Sharpley, C. F. and Sagris, A. (1995) When does counsellor forward lean influence client-perceived rapport? *British Journal of Guidance and Counselling*, **23**, 387–94.

Sichel, J. and Ellis, A. (1984) *RET Self-help Form*. New York: Institute for Rational-Emotive Therapy.

Skinner, B. F. (1953) *Science and Human Behavior*. New York: MacMillan.

Skinner, B. F. (1969) *Contingencies of Reinforcement*. New York: Appleton-Century-Crofts.

Skinner, B. F. (1971) *Beyond Freedom and Dignity*. Harmondsworth: Penguin Books.

Spielberger, C. D. (1983) *Manual for the State-Trait Anxiety Inventory (Form Y)*. Palo Alto, CA: Consulting Psychologists Press.

Spitzer, R. L. and Williams, J. B. W. (1984) *The Initial Interview: Evaluation Strategies for DSM 111 Diagnosis – Interviewer's Manual*. New York: BMA Audio Cassette Publications.

Steiner, C. M. (1974) *Scripts People Live*. New York: Bantam Books.

Stevens-Smith, P. (1995) Gender issues in counselor education: current status and challenges. *Counselor Education and Supervision*, **34**. 283–93.

Stock, J. and Cervone, D. (1990) Proximal goal-setting and self-regulatory process. *Cognitive Therapy and Research*, **14**, 483–98.

Stokes, T. F. and Osnes, P. G. (1989) An operant pursuit of generalization. *Behavior Therapy*, **20**, 337–55.

Strong, S. R. (1968) Counseling: an interpersonal influence process. *Journal of Counseling Psychology*, **15**, 215–24.

Strong, S. R. (1978) Social psychological approach to psychotherapy research. In S. L. Garfield and A. A. Bergin (eds) *Handbook of Psychotherapy and Behavior Change: An Empirical Analysis*. New York: Wiley, pp. 101–35.

Strong, S. R., Welsh, J. A., Cocoran, J. L. and Hoyt, W. T. (1992) Social psychology and counseling psychology: the history, products, and promise of an interface. *Journal of Counseling Psychology*, **39**, 139–57.

Strong, S. R., Yoder, B. and Cocoran, J. (1995) Counseling: a social process for constructing personal powers. *The Counseling Psychologist*, **23**, 374–84.

Stuart, R. B. (1980) *Helping Couples Change: A Social Learning Approach to Marital Therapy*. New York: Guilford Press.

Sue, D. W., Arredondo, P. and McDavis, R. J. (1992) Multicultural counselling competencies and standards: a call to the profession. *Journal of Counseling and Development*, **70**, 477–86.

Sue, S. and Zane, N. (1987) The role of culture and cultural techniques in psychotherapy. *American Psychologist*, **42**, 37–45.

Sugarman, L. (1986) *Life-span Development: Concepts, Theories and Interventions*. London: Methuen.

Sullivan, H. S. (1953) *The Interpersonal Theory of Psychiatry*. New York: W. W. Norton.

Sullivan, H. S. (1954) *The Psychiatric Interview*. New York: W. W. Norton.

Sweeney, C. (1995) An integrative model of supervision: an obvious choice for counselling psychologists. *Counseling Psychology Review*, **10**, 10–16.

Tasto, D. L. and Hinkle, J. E. (1973) Muscle relaxation for tension headaches. *Behaviour Research and Therapy*, **11**, 347–9.

Teague, A. (1993) Ethnic groups: first results from 1991 Census. *Population Trends*, **72**, 12–17.

Teyber, E. (1989) *Interpersonal Process in Psychotherapy: A Guide for Clinical Training*. Pacific Grove, CA: Brooks/Cole.

Thoresen, C. E. and Mahoney, M. J. (1974) *Behavioral Self-control*. New York: Holt, Rinehart and Winston.

Tillich, P. (1952) *The Courage to Be*. New Haven: Yale University Press.

Tyler, L. (1961) *The Work of the Counselor* (2nd edn). New York: Appleton-Century-Crofts.

Truax, C. B. and Carkhuff, R. R. (1967) *Toward Effective Counseling and Psychotherapy*. Chicago, IL: Aldine.

van Hesteren, F. and Ivey, A. E. (1990) Counseling and development: toward a new identity for a profession in transition. *Journal of Counseling and Development*, **68**, 524–33.

Watkins, C. E. (1990) The effects of counselor self-disclosure: a research review. *The Counseling Psychologist*, **18**, 477–500.

Watson, D. and Friend, R. (1969) Measurement of social-evaluative anxiety. *Journal of Consulting and Clinical Psychology*, **33**, 448–57.

Watson, D. L. and Tharp, R.G. (1989) *Self-directed Behavior: Self-modification for Personal Adjustment* (5th edn). Pacific Grove, CA: Brooks/Cole.

Webster-Stratton, C., Hollinsworth, T. and Kolpacoff, M. (1989) The long-term effectiveness and clinical significance of three cost-effective training programs for parents with conduct-problem children. *Journal of Consulting and Clinical Psychology*, **57**, 550–3.

Wehrenberg, S. B. (1988) Learning contracts. *Personnel Journal*, **62**, 100–2.

Weiner, B. and Kukla, A. (1970) An attributional analysis of achievement motivation. *Journal of Personality and Social Psychology*, **15**, 1–20.

Weinstein, N. D. (1980) Unrealistic optimism about future events. *Journal of Personality and Social Psychology*, **39**, 806–20.

Weinstein, N. D. (1984) Why it won't happen to me: perceptions of risk factors and susceptibility. *Health Psychology*, **3**, 431–57.

Wellings, K., Field, J., Johnson, A. M. and Wadsworth, J. (1994) *Sexual Behaviour in Britain: The National Survey of Sexual Attitudes and Lifestyles*. Harmondsworth: Penguin.

Whelan, J. P., Mahoney, M. J. and Meyers, A. W. (1991) Performance enhancement in sport: a cognitive behavioral domain. *Behavior Therapy*, **22**, 307–27.

Wilcox-Matthew, L. and Minor, C. W. (1989) The dual career couple: concerns, benefits and counseling implications. *Journal of Counseling and Development*, **68**, 194–8.

Wolpe, J. E. (1958) *Psychotherapy by Reciprocal Inhibition*. Stanford, CA: Stanford University Press.

Wolpe, J. E. (1973) *The Practice of Behavior Therapy* (2nd edn). New York: Pergamon Press.

Wolpe, J. E. (1982) *The Practice of Behavior Therapy* (3rd edn). New York: Pergamon Press.

Wolpe, J. and Wolpe, D. (1988) *Life without Fear: Anxiety and Its Cure*. Oakland, CA: New Harbinger Publications.

Woolfolk, R. L., Parish, M. W. and Murphy, S. M. (1985) The effects of positive and negative imagery on motor skill performance. *Cognitive Research and Therapy*, **9**, 335–41.

Yalom, I. D. (1980) *Existential Psychotherapy*. New York: Basic Books.

Yalom, I. D. (1985) *The Theory and Practice of Group Psychotherapy* (3rd edn). New York: Basic Books.

Yalom, I. D. (1989) *Love's Executioner: And Other Tales of Psychotherapy*. London: Bloomsbury.

Yeo, A. (1981) *A Helping Hand: Coping with Personal Problems*. Singapore: Times Books International.

Name Index

Perls, F. S. 432, 436
Perry, M. A. 322
Perry, M. J. 367
Perry, W. G. 8
Petersen, C. 230
Pfeiffer, J. W. 410
Pomeroy, W. B. 69
Ponterotto, J. G. 451
Poon, D. 139
Publilius Syrus 282

Raskin, N. J. 5, 19, 102, 106,
    125–6
Rennie-Peyton, P. 135
Rhoads, R. A. 63
Rice, L. N. 436
Riskind, J. H. 366
Robertson, J. 73
Roffman, R. A. 367
Rogers, C. R. 5, 6, 19, 24, 29, 61,
    63, 98, 102, 103, 106, 125–6,
    201, 311, 433
Rogers, M. E. 103, 492
Rogers, S. M. 69
Rogoff, B. 79
Rokeach, M. 73–4
Roosevelt, Eleanor 64
Rosenthal, T. L. 319
Rush, A. J. 224, 348, 363, 391,
    400, 442, 478
Russell, Bertrand 426

Sagris, A. 111
Sandowicz, M. 97
Sarason, I. G. 417
Sartre, J.-P. 20
Scally, M. 291, 324
Scher, M. 73, 136
Schier, M. F. 366
Schreier, B. A. 71
Schulman, R. 363
Schultz, C. 244
Schwartz, S. H. 74
Seidner, M. L. 302

Seligman, M. E. P. 227, 230, 363,
    366, 431, 442, 443
Semmel, A. 230, 363
Shakespeare, William 335, 476
Sharpley, C. F. 111
Shaw, B. F. 224, 348, 363, 391,
    400, 442, 478
Shaw, George Bernard 343
Sichel, J. 346–7
Sikkema, K. J. 367
Skinner, B. F. 25, 411
Spielberger, C. D. 207
Spitzer, R. L. 158–9
Steer, R. A. 366, 444
Steffek, B. D. 319
Steiner, C. M. 27
Stevens-Smith, P. 71
Stevenson, L. Y. 367
Stock, J. 403
Stokes, T. F. 464, 465, 470
Strong, S. R. 102, 245
Stuart, R. B. 391, 414
Sue, D. W. 79, 138, 245
Sue, S. 102
Sugarman, L. 8
Suinn, R. M. 373
Sullivan, H. S. 29, 65, 139, 159,
    181, 201, 339, 349, 479, 482
Sweeney, C. 494

Tasto, D. L. 447
Teague, A. 78, 80
Teasdale, J. D. 366, 443
Teyber, E. 202, 206, 477
Tharp, R. G. 271, 413, 466, 467,
    468
Thoresen, C. E. 396, 414
Thwaites, G. A. 373, 441
Tillich, P. 21, 59, 489
Tillman, R. 75
Tosi, D. J. 155, 324
Trimble, J. E. 79
Truax, C. B. 7
Turner, C. F. 69
Tyler, L. 7

Uhlemann, M. R. 126

van Hesteren, F. 6
Vernon, P. E. 74
Villanova, P. 230
von Baeyer, C. 230, 363

Wadsworth, J. 68, 69
Walsh, W. B. 155, 324
Watkins, C. E. 173
Watson, D. 230
Watson, D. L. 271, 413, 466, 467,
    468
Watson, T. E. 229
Webster-Stratton, C. 321
Wehrenberg, S. B. 327
Weiner, B. 364
Weinstein, N. D. 366
Weishaar, M. E. 20, 170, 181,
    223, 228, 348-9, 350, 400, 403,
    430, 431, 443, 444, 491
Wellings, K. 68, 69
Welsh, J. A. 102
Whelan, J. P. 403
Wilcox-Matthew, L. 73
Wilde, Oscar 375
Williams, J. B. W. 158–9
Winett, R. A. 367
Wolpe, D. 373, 445, 448
Wolpe, J. E. 207, 373, 445, 448,
    450
Woolfolk, R. L. 374
Wubbolding, R. 141, 228, 338,
    406-7

Yalom, I. D. 20, 21, 29, 60, 68–9,
    105, 140, 219, 228, 287, 338,
    339, 491
Yeo, A. 61
Yoder, B. 102, 245
Youngren, M. A. 413, 443

Zane, N. 102
Zeiss, A. M. 413, 443

Subject Index